ALL THE WORLD'S A STAGE

All The World's
A Stage

MODERN PLAYS FOR YOUNG PEOPLE

EDITED BY

Lowell Swortzell

PROFESSOR OF EDUCATIONAL THEATRE
NEW YORK UNIVERSITY

Decorations by HOWARD SIMON

DELACORTE PRESS / NEW YORK

Acknowledgments

AMAHL AND THE NIGHT VISITORS by Gian-carlo Menotti: copyright 1951, 1952 by G. Schirmer, Inc. International Copyright Secured. All rights of any kind with respect to this opera and any part thereof, including but not limited to stage, radio, television, motion picture, mechanical reproduction, translation, printing and selling, are strictly reserved. License to perform AMAHL AND THE NIGHT VISITORS in whole or in part must be secured in writing from the Publisher. Terms will be quoted upon request.

THE BILLY-CLUB PUPPETS by Federico García Lorca from FIVE PLAYS, translated by James Graham-Lujan and Richard L. O'Connell: copyright © 1963 by New Directions Publishing Corporation. Reprinted by permission of New Directions Publishing Corporation. CAUTION: All persons are hereby warned that these plays are published in translations authorized by the García Lorca Estate, being fully protected under the copyright laws of the United States of America, the Universal Copyright Convention, the Berne and Pan-American Copyright Conventions, and all countries of the world belonging to these conventions, are subject to royalty. All rights, including professional, amateur, motion picture, recitation, public reading, radio and television broadcasting, recording on tape or by any means, reprint or reproduction in any form including typescripts, are strictly reserved. All inquiries regarding amateur uses of these plays should be made to Samuel French, Inc., 25 West 45th Street, New York, N. Y. 10036; 7623 Sunset Boulevard, Hollywood, California; Samuel French Ltd. (Canada), 27 Grenville Street, Toronto, Conada.

All inquiries regarding professional, motion picture, broadcasting or other reproduction, reprint or other rights not mentioned, should be made to New Directions, 333 Sixth Avenue, New York, N. Y. 10014.

They are also warned that the original Spanish works from which they are translated are also copyrighted throughout the world.

Any inquiries about the translation of these plays, or any other works by Federico García Lorca, into any language whatever, should also be made to New Directions, New York, who act as agents for the García Lorca Estate.

THE CHIEF'S BRIDE by Desmond Dudwa Phiri: copyright © 1968 by Desmond Dudwa Phiri. Reprinted by permission of Evans Brothers Ltd., Montague House, Russell Square, London, W. C. 1, England, to whom all requests for permission to perform the play should be addressed.

CHILDHOOD by Thornton Wilder: copyright © 1960 by Grant N. Nickerson, Trustee. Reprinted by permission of Brandt & Brandt.

THE END OF THE BEGINNING by Sean O'Casey from THE COLLECTED PLAYS OF SEAN O'CASEY. This book is copyright in all countries which are signatories to the Berne Convention. Reprinted by permission of St. Martin's Press, Inc., Macmillan & Co. Ltd., and The Macmillan Company of Canada Limited.

THE GENIE OF SUTTON PLACE by Kenneth Heuer and George Selden: copyright © 1957 by Kenneth Heuer and George Selden. Reprinted by permission of the authors and the agent, James Brown Associates, Inc., 22 East 60th Street, New York, N. Y. 10022, to whom requests for permission to perform the play should be addressed.

HE WHO SAYS YES and HE WHO SAYS NO by Bertolt Brecht. Reprinted by permission of the translator, Dr. Gerhard Nellhaus, and The University of Illinois Foundation.

THE JAR by Luigi Pirandello from PIRANDELLO'S ONE-ACT PLAYS by Luigi Pirandello. Translation copyright © 1970 by William Murray. All Rights Reserved. Reprinted by permission of the publisher, Funk & Wagnalls, New York.

LITTLE RED RIDING HOOD by Eugene Schwartz, translated and adapted from the Russian by George Shail: copyright © 1972 by George Shail; copyright © 1969 DETSKAYA LITERATURA contained in EVGENY SHVARTS, SKAZI POVESTI, P'ESY (The Fairy Tales, Stories, and Plays of Evgeny Shvarts).

LOOK AND LONG by Gertrude Stein: copyright 1948 by Houghton Mifflin Company. Reprinted by permission of the Estate of Gertrude Stein, Daniel C. Joseph Administrator.

THE MAN WITH HIS HEART IN THE HIGHLANDS by William Saroyan: copyright © 1938 by William Saroyan. Reprinted by permission of the author.

Poem Plays: A BEAUTIFUL DAY, PLAY 1, PLAY 2 and PLAY 3 by Ruth Krauss from THE CANTILEVER RAINBOW: copyright © 1963, 1964, 1965 by Ruth Krauss. Reprinted by permission of Pantheon Books, A Division of Random House, Inc.

THE POST OFFICE by Rabindranath Tagore: copyright 1914 by The Macmillan Company, renewed 1942 by Rabindranath Tagore. © 1961 The Macmillan Company. Reprinted from A TAGORE READER, edited by Amiya Chakravarty, by permission of The Macmillan Company, The Macmillan Company of Canada, Macmillan & Company Ltd., and the Trustees of the Tagore Estate.

SOUL GONE HOME by Langston Hughes: copyright 1937 by Langston Hughes. Reprinted from FIVE PLAYS BY LANGSTON HUGHES by permission of Harold Ober Associates Incorporated.

SWANWHITE by August Strindberg from FIVE PLAYS OF STRINDBERG (Doubleday), translated by Elizabeth Sprigge: copyright © 1960 by Elizabeth Sprigge. Reprinted by permission of Collins-Knowlton-Wing, Inc. and Elizabeth Sprigge.

THE THWARTING OF BARON BOLLIGREW by Robert Bolt: copyright © 1966 by Robert Bolt. Reprinted by permission of Heinemann Educational Books Ltd and The Press, Kingswood, Tadworth, Surrey, England. This book may be obtained through Theatre Art Books, New York.

THE TINGALARY BIRD by Mary Melwood: copyright 1964 by Mary Melwood. Reprinted by permission of Caryl Jenner Productions Limited. American and Canadian requests for permission to perform the play should be made to New Plays for Children Inc. of New York, Box 2181, Grand Central Station, New York, N. Y. 10017. Inquiries of any other nature should be directed to Unicorn Play Department, Unicorn Theatre for Young People, Arts Theatre, Great Newport Street, London, W. C. 2, England.

YOUR OWN THING by Hal Hester, Danny Apolinar and Donald Driver from YOUR OWN THING AND TWELFTH NIGHT, TWELFTH NIGHT by William Shakespeare and YOUR OWN THING by Hal Hester and Danny Apolinar, book by Donald Driver, music and lyrics by Hal Hester and Danny Apolinar: copyright © 1970 by Dell Publishing Co., Inc., Copyright © 1968 by Donald Lee Driver, music and lyrics Copyright © 1968 by S & S Music Company, Copyright © 1968 by National General Music Publishing Co., Inc. and S & S Music Company. Reprinted by permission of Dell Publishing Co., Inc.

FOR NANCY

Contents

Introduction

WE MAY safely assume that children and young people have been a component of theatre as long as there has been theatre. Certainly, as Plato tells us, they were in the audiences in Ancient Greece, and perhaps on the stage playing the child characters that appear in *Medea, The Trojan Women, Alcestis* and *Oedipus the King.* A Greek boy could not be too familiar with the heritage of the *Iliad* and *Odyssey:* In school he learned passages from tragedies based on these beloved epics; in the theatre he saw them come to life and was moved and enlightened by their meaning, power and beauty. Teachers further encouraged pupils to participate in activities we regard as theatrical: oral reading, music, rhetoric, recitation of poetry, singing and gymnastics. In Rome, Plautus facetiously objected to noisy children and crying babies in attendance at his comedies and asked nurses to keep their charges quiet or to take them home. In the Middle Ages, children proved essential to the performance of morality, mystery and miracle plays. A child might play a speaking role in *The Brome Abraham and Isaac,* or appear as a supernumerary in a mystery play (Satan traditionally surrounded himself with a host of tiny devils emanating from a smoking hell-mouth), or assist his elders in the preparation of plays associated with Christmas, Easter and other religious holidays. Nativity plays, then as now, introduced countless children to drama both as spectators and participants; youngsters also took part in dramatizations of the Noah legend, the Slaughter of the Innocents, and of other Biblical stories performed in cycles that portrayed scenes from both Old and New Testaments. The boy actors of Elizabethan England became so popular that they threatened the livelihood of the adult performers and drew from Shakespeare the disdainful appellation of "little eyases," suggesting that they cried out in the manner of unfledged birds. Yet Shakespeare himself created a number of vivid child characters and wrote plays that appealed to young Elizabethans of every walk of life.

The continuum can be traced up to the first decades of the present century, with numerous instances of great plays enthralling young people: works by Molière and Beaumarchais in France, Goldoni in Italy, Sheridan and Goldsmith in England, Schiller in Germany and so on. The nineteenth century witnessed great players rather than plays, but, once again, theatregoing was a family affair as generations cherished favorite actors in such long-lived plays as *Uncle Tom's Cabin, Our American Cousin, Rip Van Winkle,* and in countless stagings of stories by Charles Dickens. Musical entertainments such as *Evangeline, A Trip to Chinatown, Babes in Toyland* and *The Wizard of Oz* delighted young and old alike in New York City and on tours throughout the country.

Until the present century, few plays were written specifically for children. Even the exceptions represent works that pleased audiences of all ages. The first play in English designated for the young did not exclude others, for *A New Interlude for Children to Play Named Jack Juggler, both Witty and Very Pleasant,* composed sometime between 1553 and 1558, mixed classic and native elements in a Plautine plot of mistaken identity that was as widely appreciated then as it had been when presented to Roman audiences and as it continues to be in modern manifestations, such as *The Boys from Syracuse* and *A Funny Thing Happened on the Way to the Forum.* It was a plot for all seasons, cultures and ages.

When Mme de Maintenon commissioned Jean Racine to write tragedies for performance by young girls attending her school at Saint-Cyr, it was with the thought that these plays would be seen by the French court. And indeed Louis XIV and courtiers recognized in the title characterization of *Esther* a flattering portrait of Mme de Maintenon herself. Nevertheless, Racine's *Esther* and *Athalie* transcended both the school and the court for which they were intended to become distinguished examples of neoclassic tragedy, plays that by refusing to speak to one age level speak to several.

One might expect that when dramatists began writing explicitly for young people's pleasure and edification, as they have in recent decades, children's theatre would be the better for their efforts. But the majority of children's plays of this century prove this not to be the case. In fact, the dramas most loved by youngsters have come from the adult theatre: *Peter Pan, The Blue Bird, Make-Believe, Toad of Toad Hall, Mrs. McThing* and Paul Sills' *Story Theatre,* a Broadway "hit" in the early 1970s. Sir James Barrie, among other authors of these plays, did not regard himself as a dramatist for children. If young people claim his plays as their own, it is because they enjoy them, just as they have claimed a number of novels not originally categorized as "children's literature": *Robinson Crusoe, Gulliver's Travels, Pride and Prejudice, The Yearling, Catcher in the Rye, Lord of the Flies,* and *The Hobbit.* But because so few plays are available for young people to read, no similar widespread adoption has taken place and the canon of child drama remains alarmingly limited.

The question thus arises of whether the polarization of "adult's" and "children's" theatres may have performed a cultural disservice to the youth of this century. By giving them a theatre of their own, one composed heavily of hackneyed dramatizations and stereotyped musicals. we deprive children of the best drama of their time. They are left with a few volumes of plays (the list of Recommended Readings at the end of this book reveals how few), most of which were written twenty, thirty and forty years ago by dramatists of little distinction. It should come as no surprise, then, to learn that seventeen of the plays offered here were written by playwrights established in the adult theatre; with the possible exception of the plays from Russia and Africa, all can be enjoyed by children *and* adults, together in the same theatre or when read aloud in the living room.

Even though children's theatre has rooted itself throughout this country since World War II with the assistance of such groups as The Children's Theatre Conference and its parent organization, The American Educational Theatre Association, it stands today largely as a regional effort with no professional identity and few major spokesmen, dramatists and directors. Some original work has been achieved, most notably in the innovative concepts of the Paper Bag Players, a New York City troupe dedicated to a form of theatre based on mime and dance, which has won international favor. Aurand Harris, a professional playwright, has demonstrated talent in a number of works, as have several other dramatists. But too often the gifts of the playwright are channeled into dramatizations of already familiar stories or into standard costume plays. Decade after decade goes by without a good script concerned with contemporary people and problems. Playwrights are not blind to the present, but they know that such efforts will be ignored by the majority of producers, who traditionally offer tried-and-true titles, plays that retread past theatrical bestsellers, running the nonadventuresome gamut from *The Wizard of Oz* to *The Wizard of Oz.*

In the early 1950s Mary Chase, Pulitzer Prize winner for her still popular *Harvey,* emerged as a candidate for the title of America's foremost dramatist of the young when in *Mrs. McThing* she mixed a Barrie-like whimsey with fantasy and comedy of manners. Helen Hayes, with a supporting cast including Ernest Borgnine, Brandon de Wilde, Irwin Corey, Fred Gwynne, Jules Munshin and Enid Markey, turned this play into a Broadway success to which children could take their parents without regret. *Mrs. McThing* enjoyed a substantial run and a popular tour. But in subsequent comedies, it became clear that Mrs. Chase's special insights into young people had waned and that she would not create the basis for a continuous children's repertory.

In later years hopes were pinned to musicals such as *West Side Story, The Sound of Music, Carnival!* and *Oliver!,* but, here again, in spite of producers eager to sell four and five tickets instead of two, the "family musical" failed to materialize as a lasting enterprise of the American stage. At present, New York City parents take their offspring to matinees at Lincoln Center where the New York State Ballet and Opera Companies present *The Magic Flute, Cinderella, The Love of Three Oranges, Harlequinade, A Midsummer Night's Dream* and *The Nutcracker* in productions that rank as the best this country has to offer young people. During the 1960s Lincoln Center has become for thousands of youths the focal cultural attraction of the Eastern seaboard, but one which has yet to produce a single play for young people.

In other cities vigorous groups present numerous plays; Nashville, Evanston and Seattle are well known among many worthwhile sponsors of children's theatre. However, play selection in regional theatres almost exclusively relies upon traditional titles rather than upon experiments with new or unusual scripts of merit. Nor have attempts to encourage dramatists by holding frequent playwriting contests markedly altered the quality of children's drama. Not one of this country's several hundred producing theatres has developed a playwright of national interest.

New York's Off-Broadway provides the major area of so-called "professional" children's theatre in the United States. Here weekend and holiday performances are presented by companies at the YM-YWHA, Town Hall, and in various small playhouses throughout Manhattan. On occasion these offerings prove to be original, but more often they are impaired by budgetary restrictions, small casts,

mediocre actors, utilitarian settings, and the lack of permanent theatres in which to build sound repertories. To keep in business,
producers frequently fall back on customary productions of *Pi-
nocchio, Alice in Wonderland* and *The Wizard of Oz.* When they do
acknowledge the present, it is often in the capricious manner of rock
musicals bearing titles such as *Mother Goose à Go-Go* or *Mother Goose
on the Loose,* in which the beat is the only relevant ingredient.

Children's theatre in New York City aptly has been labeled "the
jelly bean circuit" and all too often the confection handed out to the
departing audience is of better quality than the performance that
preceded it. Realizing that they are being bribed into thinking they
had a good time by a few gum drops or caramels, children (not to
mention parents) compare the cost of the candy with the price of
theatre tickets and spend their money accordingly. Company after
company appears for a few seasons and then disappears forever, not
having been able to build or to keep an audience even with productions of the supposed ever-popular favorite stories. Off-Broadway's
contribution to children's theatre grows more insecure as it grows
more routine.

European directors and producers, unlike their American counterparts, often offer repertories that include plays by Brecht, Lorca, even
Samuel Beckett, whose *Waiting for Godot* is among the first productions mounted by England's new theatre, The Young Vic, an auxil-
iary company of the famous National Theatre. European playwrights
sometimes tend to be experimental, as may be observed in this volume
in Robert Bolt's tongue-in-cheek comedy, *The Thwarting of Baron
Bolligrew,* and in Mary Melwood's unorthodox "theatre piece," *The
Tingalary Bird.* Both plays were commissioned by professional theatres, the first by The Royal Shakespeare Company and the second by
London's Unicorn Theatre, and both with aid from the British Arts
Council. So far, American art councils and foundations have not
recognized children's theatre by awarding ample grants to producers
and playwrights willing to test new forms, ideas and styles of theatre.

Given the dismal circumstances of children's theatre in America,
we may well wonder if good plays for young people exist. Yes, of
course, they do, even if infrequently seen or read by our young people. By merely bringing the plays and their audience together we may
accomplish the first step in creating a modern theatre for children.
The contemporary repertory need not depend upon dramatizations

written decades ago by Charlotte Chorpenning and her imitators; these plays kept community threatres operating for many years and on occasion when carefully produced can still be entertaining. But today they accomplish little more, especially now that sophisticated levels of fiction and substantive nonfiction lead children to expect more, when the banality of television drama makes them require more, and when the paucity of appropriate motion pictures makes them want more of living theatre. Where, then, can we find the plays to satisfy this audience?

Dramas of the past constitute one place to locate worthwhile texts. The pertinency of the classics, discovered anew almost every season in adult theatre, should be revealed regularly in our children's theatres. Britain's Young Vic in addition to presenting *Waiting for Godot* offers in its repertory Sophocles' *Oedipus* in the translation of William Butler Yeats and Molière's *The Adventures of Scapin*. This impressive assembly could give producers everywhere the long-needed impetus to re-examine their play lists in the light of present-day audiences. Each major period of dramatic literature abounds in plays of interest to young people, yet they remain on library shelves where children cannot find them unless they look in anthologies published for adults. Here they may be discouraged by scholarly apparatus and tiny print. A few high school drama directors, disillusioned by traditional senior-class plays drawn from the catalogue of *Junior Miss, A Date with Judy* and *Time Out for Ginger*, have turned boldly to the classics, winning acclamation from students and parents alike. The Upper Darby Senior High School, in Upper Darby, Pennsylvania, for example, has produced *The Miser, The Would-Be Gentleman, The Imaginary Invalid, Fashion, The Importance of Being Earnest, Charley's Aunt, The Admirable Crichton, Pygmalion, The Devil's Disciple* and *Androcles and the Lion,* a selection of plays that would honor any theatre, as it undoubtedly does the students performing and witnessing them. Many other schools include each year at least one classic in full production.

All the World's a Stage reflects the conviction that dramas of this century also must be recruited for the children's theatre repertory. Already high schools have introduced young people to outstanding works, such as *Death of a Salesman, Liliom, The Skin of Our Teeth, Our Town, Ah, Wilderness!, Harvey, The Madwoman of Chaillot, J.B.* and the *Antigone* of Anouilh, all of which have been mounted by the school mentioned above. Other schools, in addition to producing a wide selection of musical comedies from the Broadway theatre, stage plays as various and difficult as *The Crucible, The Miracle Worker, The Teahouse of the August Moon, Under Milkwood, The Lark, Noah* and the one-act plays of Ionesco, Pinter and Albee.

A repertory that runs the gamut from Euripides to Albee, which at the same time gives proportionate attention to fairy-tale and adventure plays (there is need for *The Wizard of Oz* and its counterparts, of course), and which serves children over ten years old with as much concern as those under, will result in a theatre that is more than entertaining, one which is also stimulating and rewarding because it is alive with action and inspiration. Any play that excites and expands a young person's intellect and emotional experience can be included in this repertory whether or not that play was written specifically for children. While we wait for an American version of The Young Vic to come about (and that may be like waiting for Godot himself), the community theatres, universities and high schools must bring these plays into the lives of young people in ever-increasing numbers. Youngsters who have no such forward-looking teachers and theatres in their town may read the plays that follow as samples of the diversity of form and idea existing in modern drama.

Some readers, adults more likely than the young for whom the volume is intended, may question the number of serious plays that appear here, including several that are outright tragedies. Themes of death pervade *The Post Office* and *Childhood*, while *He Who Says Yes* is stark in its nihilism. Young people have responded with enthusiasm to these works, even performing them with complete understanding and appreciation. Now that serious subjects no longer are taboo in children's literature (*Charlotte's Web*, a modern classic, for instance, openly confronts death), there is no reason why they should be barred from drama. Even Tagore was not ahead of his time when in 1912 he wrote *The Post Office*, for already Maurice Maeterlinck's monumental dramatic tombstone, *The Blue Bird*, had been seen by thousands of children who instead of being scared out of their wits by its constant parade of ghosts were moved by its poetry, mysticism and immense theatricality, proving that young people long have been able to digest serious and unusual themes in good health.

Even so, care has been expended to balance the serious with the comic, and here, too, subjects and characters appear that may be considered unconventional. Homosexuality is mentioned in *Your Own Thing;* the old and odd couple in *The Tingalary Bird* often act as if they were in a play by Edward Albee; *Soul Gone Home* presents a prostitute without apology. The characters in *Look and Long* sound as if they belong in a play by Gertrude Stein, as they do, and this in itself may frighten readers unwilling to be daring. But as long as young readers dare, there is hope for older ones.

A Note On Reading Plays

INTEREST in a play on stage is focused and directed by a variety of theatrical devices. A spotlight emphasizes one character more than another. The director arranges his performers into pictures and compositions intended to attract the eye. Sound effects and music hold the ear. Actors capture audience attention by the way they speak, or move, or by the way they just seem to be themselves—natural and unaffected. Designers of settings, costumes, and lighting employ color, mood, and atmosphere to communicate in their variously vivid ways what the play is all about. The playhouse is constructed to provide every spectator with an unobstructed view of the stage or area where the drama is enacted. Today theatre even incorporates film, slides, and moving projections as a means of evoking and controlling concentration (*Your Own Thing* illustrates one notable use of mixed media in the theatre).

We have none of these aids when we read a play; we have only ourselves. Without stage trappings and an auditorium to block out the rest of the world, a play just as print on paper could prove to be an incomplete form of entertainment. Fortunately, it isn't because when read it can receive the most ideal production possible—our very own. We are not required to hire actors, directors, and designers, to rent an auditorium, or even to buy tickets and to be in our seats at a certain time. Instead, we visualize a performance in our imagination where words, not actors, create the characters, emit the theme, and fabricate the plot. Words translated into images also paint scenery and splash color and light across our inner eye. And we discover that we don't need the help of anyone else. Professor Kenneth Rowe in the title of one of his books declared that there is a theatre in your head; and it is true that everyone possesses a personal playhouse whether or not performances have been held there. All that we require to open its doors and to ring up its curtain is a good play, some curiosity, an imagination healthy from exercise, and sufficient time to think about what we behold.

[xix]

When we are not accustomed to reading plays, it is helpful and fun to read them aloud. Even though we speak all the words, the characters begin to emerge with individual voices and personalities that find divers ways of expression by which to distinguish themselves. We may be surprised to discover how many different voices they produce, enough for the family of five in *Childhood* or even for the entire town in *The Billy-Club Puppets*. The plays with songs can have readers singing with a variety of voices as well. When reading aloud with family and friends, it is a good idea for one person to read the stage directions, which never should be skipped or slighted inasmuch as they describe the physical action of the play and provide essential information about location and mood. Certain plays contain almost no directions on purpose (*The Post Office* and *Look and Long,* for example) because the dramatist wishes to produce an effect that comes directly from the dialogue; if he were to state anything else for the reader, the poetry of the play could be damaged, perhaps destroyed. But stage directions in most plays clarify the action and define the scene, as may be observed in Strindberg's long description of the setting in *Swanwhite* or in the careful detail of *The Tingalary Bird*.

We read a play simply by asking and answering basic questions as we move moment by moment, scene by scene, and act by act. Because without action there can be no drama, the fundamental question at every point is "what is happening?" Next we attempt to discover the significance of the events and ask, "Why does the action take place and what does it mean?" Why, for instance, does the Mother in *Amahl and the Night Visitors* steal gold from the coffers of the three kings? Does this act indicate that she is wicked? When we answer these questions, we know that just the opposite is true for hers is a deed of goodness motivated by love of Amahl and a desire to have money to care for him. Drama exists in the suspense of the moment because we ask ourselves what will happen if she gets caught? What will the Kings do? What will Amahl do? Reading on, we participate in the action, we even experience Amahl's experience as he rushes forward to protect and defend his mother. Here the dramatist makes the moment live not only for his characters on stage and page but also for his spectators and readers because he makes them go together through an idea, an emotion, an event, and face together the consequences.

What we experience in a play is the key to our enjoyment of a play.

But we must also ask ourselves in what ways the experience was worthwhile. This is the key to appreciating, as well as to criticizing, the play. Many answers may exist and no two people may agree to any one, but this will matter little as long as each reader is satisfied with his own response.

We also ask questions about the characters. What are their goals in life, what do they want for themselves and from each other? What stands in their way of obtaining these wishes? Can they overcome these obstacles or will they be defeated by them? The same sort of questions pertain to what is said, for we always want to know why a character speaks as he does, what it means as far as the scene is concerned and what it means as far as the entire play is concerned.

By asking and answering these and other questions that will arise as we proceed, we can give the plays that follow a long and prosperous engagement in the reader's private playhouse. Moreover, when a play proves to be exciting through its theme, story, characters, poetry, and color, and when the experience it affords proves to be genuine, we discover that there is a theatre not only in the head but also in the heart.

All the world's a stage,
And all the men and women merely players:
They have their exits and their entrances;
And one man in his time plays many parts,
His acts being seven ages. At first the infant,
Mewling and puking in the nurse's arms.
And then the whining school-boy, with his satchel
And shining morning face, creeping like snail
Unwillingly to school. And then the lover,
Sighing like furnace, with a woeful ballad
Made to his mistress' eyebrow. Then a soldier,
Full of strange oaths and bearded like the pard,
Jealous in honour, sudden and quick in quarrel,
Seeking the bubble reputation
Even in the cannon's mouth. And then the justice,
In fair round belly with good capon lined,
With eyes severe and beard of formal cut,
Full of wise saws and modern instances;
And so he plays his part. The sixth age shifts
Into the lean and slipper'd pantaloon,
With spectacles on nose and pouch on side,
His youthful hose, well saved, a world too wide
For his shrunk shank; and his big manly voice,
Turning again toward childish treble, pipes
And whistles in his sound. Last scene of all,
That ends this strange eventual history,
Is second childishness and mere oblivion,
Sans teeth, sans eyes, sans taste, sans everything.

WILLIAM SHAKESPEARE
Act II, Scene vii
As You Like It

Swanwhite

BY

AUGUST STRINDBERG

in a translation by Elizabeth Sprigge

PLAYWRIGHTS as diverse as George Bernard Shaw, Eugene O'Neill, Sean O'Casey and Thornton Wilder have acknowledged their debt, as well as that of modern drama in general, to August Strindberg, author of more than 60 plays that have influenced and stretched the scope and form of world theatre in this century. Not only does his power live on in the works of other playwrights—especially to be noted in contemporary dramatists such as Edward Albee, Harold Pinter and Tennessee Williams—but also in his own plays, which continue to be read and produced with new understanding and appreciation of their strange and special genius.

As the fourth son of 11 children of a former Stockholm barmaid, Strindberg (1849–1912) suffered a childhood marked by unhappiness and a sense of shame regarding his ignoble origin (his penniless father married his mother only shortly before he was born). Poverty punctuated his education; death surrounded his household, taking, among others, his mother when he was thirteen years old; strife, internal and external, lacerated his life as he developed into a rebellious adolescent, brilliant as he was sensitive. He resented his stepmother, who had been the family housekeeper before his mother died and who made life unpleasant for him; he defied formal academic learning and made enemies of his instructors. In and out of the universities of Uppsala and Stockholm, he interspersed his studies with jobs as a teacher, journalist, doctor's assistant, librarian, photographer, painter, would-be actor and amateur chemist. His early plays won royal patronage that enabled him to further a literary career, the first success of which was a realistic novel, *The Red Room,* written in 1879.

Artistic recognition did not bring with it happiness, however, for Strindberg's marriage to the former wife of a baron turned into a turbulent pattern of love and hate, exploding in the bitterest of domestic conflicts and ending in divorce. But, as was so often the case, his writing seemed to profit from his own personal misery and he created a formidable study of antifeminism, *The Father* (1887), followed a year later by a milestone in the development of psychological character portrayal, *Miss Julie*. This play, too, continued the theme of the sexual duel between men and women which Strindberg was to examine in a number of works, including the grotesque tragedy *The Dance of Death* (1901), written the same year as the diametrically opposite fairy-tale play, *Swanwhite*. Even though he lived abroad a great deal of his life, his native country became a familiar dramatic theme in a series of some 20 history plays that chronicle an illustrious gallery of Swedish monarchs, great and weak, kind and cruel.

Falling into depression following the end of his second marriage and a calamitous stay in Paris, during which he turned to science, mysticism and self-torment that included a long period of hospitalization, he triumphed once more with another outpour of dramatic works. Always interested in fresh forms, he experimented in a variety of dramatic styles including realism, naturalism, expressionism and symbolism, which together display a virtuosity perhaps unmatched in modern drama. In *A Dream Play* (1902) he attempted to produce a theatre piece in the shape of a dream, exploring the realms of unconscious existence in a timeless and spaceless universe of hallucination. Writing these plays out of his own fear, agony and peculiar vision of life and death, he continued to investigate original techniques of allegory, morality and spiritual symbolism until shortly before he died of cancer in 1912.

Swanwhite, which Strindberg called his "fairy play," has remained in relative obscurity because it was long overshadowed by another symbolistic fantasy, *The Blue Bird,* even though Maurice Maeterlinck wrote his play eight years afterwards. Yet, for today's audiences, *Swanwhite* undoubtedly holds greater appeal than the Belgian's faded masterpiece, which was evident when it was produced effectively in an hour-long television version recently seen in England and the United States.

Strindberg wrote the play, a paean to pure love, as his wedding gift to the young actress Harriet Bosse, who became his third wife (this marriage, too, after a few years ended in divorce). At the time of composition, he was deeply in love and hoped that his wife would create the role of Swanwhite, but when the play was staged successfully some years later, it was with another actress. A number of productions followed in Scandinavia, Germany and Hungary, often employing the incidental music which Sibelius wrote for it in 1907.

In *Swanwhite* Strindberg dramatizes the spirituality of a love that transcends tests, tricks, evil spells and, finally, even death itself. The stage is laden with magical effects, an ominous peacock, three mysterious closets, apparitions, ghosts, flowers that bloom and die on cue, flights of swans and a host of theatrical enchantments for eye and ear. In this romantic world Strindberg achieved a state of happiness rare in his work and in his life.

Elizabeth Sprigge, the translator of *Swanwhite* and of all of Strindberg's major plays, has written *The Strange Life of August Strindberg* (1949), a biography recommended to readers who want to know more about his Promethean career. Another of her books, *The Life of Gertrude Stein* (1957), also will be of interest to readers of this volume.

Swanwhite

CHARACTERS

SWANWHITE
THE YOUNG KING
THE DUKE
THE STEPMOTHER
THE PRINCE
SIGNE ⎫
ELSA ⎬ *maids*
TOVA ⎭
THE GARDENER
SWANWHITE'S MOTHER
THE PRINCE'S MOTHER
THE EXECUTIONER
THE EQUERRY
THE STEWARD
THE HERB GARDENER
THE FIRST KNIGHT
THE SECOND KNIGHT
THE FISHERMAN
Etc.

SCENE FOR THE WHOLE PLAY

An Apartment in a medieval stone castle. The walls and cross-vaulted ceiling are completely white. At the back, three arches open on to a stone balcony. There are rich curtains with which they can be closed. Below the balcony is a garden, and the tops of rose trees can be seen bearing pink and white blooms. In the distance is a glimpse of a white sandy beach and blue sea.

Right of the triple-arched doorway is a small door which, when open, shows a vista of three Closets, opening one into the other. The first is the Pewter Closet, in which are pewter vessels arranged on shelves. The second is the Clothing Closet, in which can be seen gorgeous raiment, and the third is the Fruit Closet, which reveals a store of apples, pears, pumpkins, and melons.

The whole floor is inlaid with black and red squares. In the center of the apartment stands a gilded dining-table covered with a cloth; on it are a clock, a dish of fruit, and a single rose in a vase. Over the table hangs a branch of mistletoe, and beside it stand two ornate gilded stools. On the floor in the foreground a lionskin is spread. Over the small doorway can be seen two swallows' nests. In the foreground on the left is a white bed with a rose-colored canopy supported at the head by two posts; at the foot are no posts. The bed coverings are white except for one coverlet of palest blue silk.[1]

Behind the bed is a vast wall cupboard. Beside the bed are a small romanesque gilded table (round on a single column) and a lamp-stand bearing a Roman lamp of gold. Right is a beautifully carved chimney-piece, on which stands a white lily in a vase. Front right is a gilded treasure-chest.

In the left arch of the main doorway a peacock is asleep on a perch with its back to the audience. In the right arch is a great golden cage containing two sleeping white doves.

[1] Strindberg indicates a filmy white nightdress lying on the bed. I have omitted this, as it disagrees with the text. The only white garment should be the one brought Swanwhite by her mother. E.S.

ACT I

As the curtain rises, the three MAIDS *are seen, half-hidden by the doorways of each Closet.* SIGNE, *the false maid, is in the Pewter Closet,* ELSA, *who is tiny and pretty, is in the Clothing Closet,* TOVA, *the ugly faithful maid, is in the Fruit Closet.*
THE DUKE *enters by the main doorway, followed by* THE STEPMOTHER *with a steel whip in her hand.*
The stage is dim as they enter. Outside a horn is blown.

THE STEPMOTHER (*Gazing round her*): Is Swanwhite not here?

THE DUKE: You can see. . . .

THE STEPMOTHER: I can see, but I cannot see *her.* (*Calls.*) You maids! Signe! [2] Elsa! Tova! [2] (THE MAIDS *come in, one after the other, and stand in front of* THE STEPMOTHER.) Where is the Lady Swanwhite? (SIGNE *crosses her arms over her breast and is silent.*) You do not know? (*Shakes the whip.*) Then . . . do you know what I have in my hand? . . . Quick, answer me! (*Pause.*) Quick! (*Swings the whip so that it whistles.*) Listen to the whistle of the Falcon. It has claws and a beak of steel. And what is it?

SIGNE: It is the steel whip.

THE STEPMOTHER: Yes, the steel whip. Now—where is the Lady Swanwhite?

SIGNE: I cannot tell what I do not know.

THE STEPMOTHER: Ignorance is a failing, but heedlessness is a crime. Are you not here to keep watch over your young mistress? Take off your kerchief. (*Despairingly,* SIGNE *obeys.*) Get down on your knees! (THE DUKE *turns his back in horror at the scene.*) Hold out your neck! Now I shall put such a necklace on it that no young suitor

---

[2] Pronounced "Seenya" and "Toova."

will ever put his lips to it again. . . . Stretch out your neck!
Further!

SIGNE: For Christ's sake, have mercy!

THE STEPMOTHER: It is mercy enough that you keep your life.

(THE DUKE *draws his sword and tests it first on one of his nails,
then, on his long beard.*)

THE DUKE (*Ironically*): Her head should be cut off, put in a sack . . .
hung from a tree . . .

THE STEPMOTHER: So it should indeed.

THE DUKE: We are of one mind, you see.

THE STEPMOTHER: We were not so yesterday.

THE DUKE: And perhaps we shall not be tomorrow.

(SIGNE, *still on her knees, is stealthily crawling away.*)

THE STEPMOTHER: What are you doing? Stay where you are. (*She
raises the whip and strikes.* SIGNE *turns, so that the lash merely cuts
the air.* SWANWHITE *comes from behind the bed and falls on her
knees. She is simply dressed and has dirty bare feet.*)

SWANWHITE: Here I am, Stepmother. I am the guilty one. Signe is
innocent.

THE STEPMOTHER: Say "Mother." Say "Mother."

SWANWHITE: I cannot. No human being has more than one mother.

THE STEPMOTHER: Your father's wife is your mother.

SWANWHITE: My father's second wife is my stepmother.

THE STEPMOTHER: You are a stubborn daughter, but this steel is pliant
and makes others pliant. (*She lifts the whip to strike* SWANWHITE.)

THE DUKE (*Raising his sword*): Beware! Your head is in danger.

THE STEPMOTHER: Whose head?

THE DUKE: Your own.

(THE STEPMOTHER *recoils in rage, but controls herself and remains silent. Long pause. Then, seeing herself beaten, she
changes her tone.*)

THE STEPMOTHER: Very well. Now perhaps you will inform your
daughter what is in store for her.

THE DUKE (*Sheathing his sword*): My beloved child, come and find refuge in my arms.

SWANWHITE (*Springing into his arms*): Oh Father, you are like a royal oak tree, and my arms are not long enough to embrace you! But beneath your foliage I can hide from threatening storms . . . (*She hides her face in his great beard.*) . . . and I will swing on your branches like a bird. Lift me up so that I may climb to the very top. (*He lifts her on to his shoulder.*) Now I have the earth beneath me and the air above. Now I can see out across the rose garden to the white sands and the blue sea, and to all the seven kingdoms. . . .

THE DUKE: Then you can see the Young King, to whom you are betrothed.

SWANWHITE: No, I cannot see. Him I have never seen. Is he handsome?

THE DUKE: It will depend on your own eyes, dear heart, how he appears to you.

SWANWHITE (*Rubbing her eyes*): On my own eyes? . . . All that they see is beautiful.

THE DUKE (*Kissing her foot*): Black little foot, foot of my little blackamoor.

(*During this scene* THE STEPMOTHER *has signed to* THE MAIDS *to resume their places in the doorways of the Closets. With the stealthy movement of a panther,* THE STEPMOTHER *goes out through the middle arch.* SWANWHITE *jumps down.* THE DUKE *seats her on the table and sits on a stool beside her.* SWANWHITE *watches* THE STEPMOTHER *disappear and expresses her relief.*)

SWANWHITE: Has the sun risen? Has the wind changed to the south? Has spring come back again?

THE DUKE (*Putting his hand over her mouth*): Little chatterbox. Joy of my old age—my evening star. Open your rosy ears and shut the little red shell of your mouth. Listen to me. Obey me and all will go well with you.

SWANWHITE (*Putting her fingers in her ears*): I hear with my eyes, I see with my ears. Now I cannot see at all. I can only hear.

THE DUKE: Child . . . while you were still in the cradle you were betrothed to the young King of Rigalid.[3] You have never seen him,

---

[3] Pronounced "Reegaleed."

for such is Court etiquette. Now the day is drawing near when the sacred knot must be tied, but in order to teach you the ways of the Court and the duties of a Queen, the King has sent hither a young Prince, with whom you are to study books, learn to play chess, to dance a measure, and play upon the harp.

SWANWHITE: What is this Prince's name?

THE DUKE: My child, that is something you must never ask, neither of him nor of any other, for it is prophesied that whosoever calls him by his name must love him.

SWANWHITE: Is he handsome?

THE DUKE: Yes—since your eyes see nothing but beauty.

SWANWHITE: But is he not beautiful?

THE DUKE: Yes, he is beautiful. So, set a guard on your young heart, which belongs to the King, and never forget that in the cradle you were made a Queen. . . . And now, my beloved child, I am going to leave you, for I must go to war. Be humble and obedient to your stepmother. She is a hard woman, but your father loved her once, and a sweet nature may melt a heart of stone. (*From under his cloak he takes a horn of carved ivory.*) If, against her sworn word, her malice should exceed all bounds, then blow upon this horn— and help will come. But do not blow it unless you are in peril, great peril. . . . Do you understand?

SWANWHITE: But what am I to do?

THE DUKE: My child, the Prince is below in the Ladies' Chamber. Do you wish to receive him now?

SWANWHITE (*excited*): Do I wish . . . ?

THE DUKE: Shall I not first bid you farewell?

SWANWHITE: Is the Prince here already?

THE DUKE: He is here already and I am already there—there, far away, where the heron of forgetfulness puts its head under its wing.

SWANWHITE (*Throwing herself into* THE DUKE's *arms and burying her face in his beard*): Don't say such things. Don't say them. You cover me with shame.

THE DUKE (*Tenderly*): You should be beaten for forgetting your old father so quickly at the thought of a young Prince. . . . (*A horn sounds in the distance. He rises hastily, picks* SWANWHITE *up in his arms, throws her up, and catches her again.*) Fly, little bird, fly! High above the dusty earth with the clear air beneath your wings. . . . (*He puts her down.*) There. Down once more to earth. . . . I am called by war and glory—you by love and youth. (*Girds on his sword.*) And now hide your magic horn that no evil eyes may see it.

SWANWHITE: Where shall I hide it? Where?

THE DUKE: Inside your bed.

SWANWHITE (*Hiding the horn in the bedclothes*): Sleep there. Sleep well, my little herald. When the time comes, I'll waken you. Do not forget to say your prayers.

THE DUKE: And you, child, do not forget my last behest: obey your stepmother.

SWANWHITE: In everything?

THE DUKE: In everything.

SWANWHITE: Not in what is unclean. My mother gave me two changes of linen every week. *She* gives me only one. My mother gave me water and soap—these my stepmother denies me. You have seen my poor little feet.

THE DUKE: Keep pure within, my daughter, and you shall be pure without. You know that holy men who renounce ablutions for a penance grow white as swans, while the wicked turn black as ravens.

SWANWHITE: Then I will grow so white, so white.

THE DUKE: Come to my arms once more—and then farewell! (*They embrace.*)

SWANWHITE: Farewell, great warrior—my glorious father. May good fortune follow in your train and make you rich in years and friends and victories.

THE DUKE: Amen. May your gentle prayers protect me. (*He closes the visor of his golden helmet.*)

SWANWHITE (*Kissing his visor*): The golden gates are shut, but through the bars I see your kind and watchful eyes. (*She knocks at the visor.*) Open, open, for Little Red Ridinghood! . . . No one is in. "Come in and see," said the wolf, who was lying in the bed.

THE DUKE: Sweet flower of mine, grow fair and fragrant. If I return— so be it, I return. If not, my eyes will watch over you from the starry vault and never again will you be lost to my sight. For there we mortals shall be all-seeing as our Lord Creator.

(*He goes out firmly, with a gesture forbidding her to follow.* SWANWHITE *falls on her knees and prays. A wind sighs. All the rose trees sway. The peacock moves its wings and tail.* SWANWHITE *rises, goes to the peacock, and strokes its back and tail.*)

SWANWHITE: Pavo, dear Pavo, what do you see? What do you hear? Is someone coming? Who is coming? Is it a young Prince? Is he handsome—and kind? Surely you can see with so many, many blue eyes. (*She lifts one of the bird's tail feathers and gazes intently at its eye, then continues in a changed voice.*) Oh, are you going to keep your eye on us, you horrid Argus? Do you mean to watch in case the hearts of two young people beat too fast? You stupid creature! I shall draw the curtain, see! (*She draws a curtain so that it hides the peacock, but not the landscape. Then she goes over to the doves.*) My white doves—oh so white, white, white! You shall see the whitest thing of all. . . . Hush wind, hush roses, hush doves—my Prince is coming!

(*For a moment she looks out through the arches, then withdraws to the Pewter Closet. She puts on stockings* [4] *while she peeps out at* THE PRINCE, *who does not see her.* THE PRINCE *enters through the middle arch. He is in black with steel armor. Having carefully observed everything in the room, he sits down by the table, takes off his helmet, and studies it. His back is turned to the door where* SWANWHITE *is hiding.*)

THE PRINCE: If anyone is here, let him answer. (*Pause.*) Someone is here, for I can feel the warmth of a young body wafted to me like a breeze from the south. I can hear breathing—it has the fragrance of roses—and gentle as it is, it stirs the plume on my helmet. (*He puts the helmet to his ear.*) My helmet murmurs like a great seashell. It it murmuring of the thoughts in my head, swarming like bees in a hive. "Bzz, bzz," they go . . . just like bees. They are buzzing round their Queen—the little queen of my thoughts and my dreams. (*He puts the helmet on the table in front of him and gazes at it.*) Dark and arched it is, like the night sky—but starless, for ever since my mother died, the black plume has spread darkness everywhere. . . . (*He turns the helmet round and stares at it again.*) Yet there, deep in the darkness inside it . . . I see beyond, a shaft of light. Is it a rift in the heavens? And there in the rift I see—no, not a star, for that would be a diamond—but a blue sapphire, queen of jewels, blue as the summer sky, set in a milk-white cloud, shaped like the egg of a dove. What is it? Not my ring? Now

---

[4] Added stage direction, to correspond with the text. E.S.

another feathery cloud, black as velvet, passes by. . . . (SWAN-WHITE *smiles.*) The sapphire is smiling—so sapphires can smile. Now a flash of lightning, mild and without thunder. (*She flashes a startled glance at him.*) What are you? Who are you? (*He looks at the back of the helmet.*) Not there. Not here. Nowhere at all. (*He puts his face close to the helmet.*) As I draw nearer, you go further away. (SWANWHITE *steals toward him on tiptoe.*) Now there are two . . . two eyes! Young human eyes . . . I kiss you. (*He kisses the helmet.* SWANWHITE *goes to the table and slowly seats herself opposite* THE PRINCE. *He rises, bows with his hand on his heart, and gazes at her.*)

SWANWHITE: Are you the Prince?

THE PRINCE: The Young King's faithful servant, and your own.

SWANWHITE: What message has the Young King sent his bride?

THE PRINCE: He sends the Lady Swanwhite a thousand tender greet-ings. He would have her know that the thought of the sweet joys to come will shorten this long torment of his waiting.

SWANWHITE (*Looking searchingly at* THE PRINCE): Will you not be seated, Prince?

THE PRINCE: If I were to sit while you were sitting, when you stood up I should have to kneel.

SWANWHITE: Tell me about the King. What is he like?

THE PRINCE: What is he like? . . . (*Puts his hand up to his eyes*). How strange! I can no longer see him.

SWANWHITE: How do you mean?

THE PRINCE: He has gone away. He is invisible.

SWANWHITE: Is he tall?

THE PRINCE (*Studying* SWANWHITE): Wait—now I can see him. Taller than you are.

SWANWHITE: And beautiful?

THE PRINCE: He is no match for you.

SWANWHITE: Speak of the King, not of me.

THE PRINCE: I am speaking of the King.

SWANWHITE: Is he fair or dark?

THE PRINCE: If he were dark, seeing you he would at once become fair.

SWANWHITE: There is more flattery than sense in that. Are his eyes blue?

THE PRINCE (*Glancing at his helmet*): I had better look.

SWANWHITE (*Holding her hand up between them*): Oh you, you!

THE PRINCE: Y-o-u—you. Y-o-u-t-h—youth.

SWANWHITE: Are you to teach me spelling?

THE PRINCE: The Young King is tall and fair, with blue eyes, broad shoulders, and hair like a young forest. . . .

SWANWHITE: Why do you wear a black plume?

THE PRINCE: His lips are red as berries, his skin is white, and his teeth would not shame a young lion.

SWANWHITE: Why does your forehead glisten?

THE PRINCE: His mind knows no fear, and his heart is free from guilt.

SWANWHITE: Why is your hand trembling?

THE PRINCE: We were to speak of the Young King, not of me.

SWANWHITE: Is it for you to lecture me?

THE PRINCE: That is my duty—to teach you to love the Young King, whose throne you are to share.

SWANWHITE: How did you cross the sea?

THE PRINCE: By bark and sail.

SWANWHITE: With the wind so high?

THE PRINCE: Without wind one cannot sail.

SWANWHITE: How wise you are, boy . . . will you play with me?

THE PRINCE: I shall do whatever is required of me.

SWANWHITE: Now you shall see what I have in my chest. (*She kneels beside the chest and takes out a doll, a rattle, and a toy horse. She brings the doll to* THE PRINCE.) Here is my doll. It is my child, my child of sorrow who can never keep her face clean. I have carried her down to the laundry myself, and scoured her with silver sand . . . but she only grew dirtier. I have beaten her, but that did not help either. Now I have thought of the worst punishment of all for her.

THE PRINCE: And what is that?

SWANWHITE (*Glancing round*): She shall have a stepmother.

THE PRINCE: But how can that be? She must have a mother first.

SWANWHITE: I am her mother, and if I marry again, I shall be her stepmother.

THE PRINCE: Oh no, that is not the way of it!

SWANWHITE: And you will be her stepfather.

THE PRINCE: No, no.

SWANWHITE: But you must be kind to her even if she cannot wash her face. Take her. Let me see if you know how to hold a child. (THE PRINCE *unwillingly takes the doll.*) You do not know yet, but you will learn. Now take this rattle and rattle it for her. (*Gives him the rattle.*) I see you do not know how to do that at all. (*Takes back the doll and the rattle and throws them into the chest. She brings him the horse.*) Here is my steed. It has a saddle of gold and shoes of silver and it can cover forty miles in an hour. On its back I have ridden through the forest, over the great moor, across the King's bridge, along the highway, through the Valley of Fear to the Lake of Tears. Once it dropped a golden shoe.[5] It fell into the lake, but up came a fish and along came a fisherman, and so I got back the golden shoe. That's the end of that story. (*She throws the horse back into the chest and brings out a chessboard with red and white squares and chessmen of silver and gold.*) If you would like to play with me, come and sit down on the lionskin. (*She seats herself and begins to put up the pieces.*) Sit down—the Maids can't see us here. (THE PRINCE *sits shyly down beside her. She runs her hand through the lion's mane.*) It is like sitting on the grass, not the green grass of a meadow, but desert grass which has been burned by the sun. Now you must tell me about myself. Do you like me a little?

THE PRINCE: Shall we play?

SWANWHITE: Play? What do I care about that? (*Sighs.*) Oh, you should teach me something!

THE PRINCE: Alas, what can I teach you other than how to saddle a horse and carry arms? Such things would be of small service to you.

SWANWHITE: Are you sad?

THE PRINCE: My mother is dead.

SWANWHITE: Poor Prince . . . My mother is in heaven too—with God. She is an angel now. Sometimes in the night I see her. Do you see your mother?

THE PRINCE (*Hesitating*): No.

SWANWHITE: And have you a stepmother?

THE PRINCE: Not yet. It is so short a time since my mother died.

SWANWHITE: You must not be so sad. Everything passes in time. (*Pause. She fetches a banner from her chest.*) I will give you a banner to gladden your heart. Oh! It is true, I made this one for the Young King—but I will make another one for you. This is the King's with seven flaming fires—you shall have one with seven red roses. First you must hold this skein of yarn for me. (*She takes a skein of rose-colored yarn from the chest and arranges it over* THE PRINCE's *hands.*) One, two, three. Now I will begin, but you must not let your hands tremble. Perhaps you would like one of my hairs woven into the banner. Pull one out.

[5] Strindberg has this discrepancy—"shoes of silver"—"golden shoe." E.S.

THE PRINCE: No, no, I cannot.

SWANWHITE: Then I will do it. (*She pulls out one of her hairs and winds it into a ball of yarn.*) What is your name?

THE PRINCE: You must not ask that.

SWANWHITE: Why not?

THE PRINCE: Did not the Duke tell you?

SWANWHITE: No. What would happen if I said your name? Something terrible?

THE PRINCE: Surely the Duke told you?

SWANWHITE: I have never heard of such a thing. A person not able to tell his own name!

(*The curtain behind which the peacock is hidden moves, and a faint sound is heard as of castanets.*)

THE PRINCE: What was that?

SWANWHITE (*Uneasily*): It is Pavo—the peacock. Do you think he understands what we are saying?

THE PRINCE: You never know.

(*Pause.*)

SWANWHITE: Tell me your name.

(*The same sound is repeated.*)

THE PRINCE: This frightens me. You must not ask me that again.

SWANWHITE: He is snapping his beak, that's all. Keep your hands still. Have you ever heard the story of a Princess who was not allowed to say the Prince's name, for fear something terrible should happen? Do you know what . . . ?

(*The curtain hiding the peacock is drawn aside. The peacock has turned round and spread his tail. All the "eyes" seem to be gazing at* SWANWHITE *and* THE PRINCE.)

THE PRINCE: Who drew that curtain? Who told that bird to spy on us with its hundred eyes? You must not ask me that again.

SWANWHITE: Maybe not. Go back and keep quiet, Pavo. (*The curtain is drawn again.*) There.

THE PRINCE: Is this place haunted?

SWANWHITE: You mean because things like that happen? Yes, many things happen here, but I am used to it. In fact . . . (*She lowers her voice.*) . . . they say that my stepmother is a witch. There, now I have pricked my finger.

THE PRINCE: How did you prick it?

SWANWHITE: There was a splinter in the yarn. When the sheep have been kept in the barns all the winter, that does sometimes happen. Can you take the splinter out?

THE PRINCE: Yes, but we must sit at the table so that I can see.

(*They seat themselves at the table.*)

SWANWHITE (*Holding out her little finger*): Can you see anything?

THE PRINCE (*Rather bolder than hitherto*): What do I see? (*He holds her hand up to the light.*) The inside of your hand is pink, and through it I see the world and all life in a rosy light.

SWANWHITE: Pull out the splinter. It is hurting me.

THE PRINCE: But I shall have to hurt you. Forgive me first.

SWANWHITE: Yes, yes, but do it now.

(THE PRINCE *takes the splinter out of her little finger*).

THE PRINCE: Here is the wretched thing which dared to hurt you. (*He throws the splinter on the floor and stamps on it.*)

SWANWHITE: Now you must suck the blood to keep the wound from festering.

(*He puts his lips to her finger.*)

THE PRINCE: Now I have drunk your blood, so I am your foster-brother.

SWANWHITE: My foster-brother. Yes, but you were already that, or how could I have talked to you as I did?

THE PRINCE: Or I to you.

SWANWHITE: Now I have a brother—and that is you. Dear brother, take my hand.

THE PRINCE (*Taking her hand*): Dear sister. (*He feels the pulse in her finger.*) What is it that keeps ticking in there? . . . One, two, three, four . . . (*Continues to count soundlessly while looking at the clock.*)

SWANWHITE: Yes, what is it that ticks? Tick, tick, tick—so steadily. My heart cannot be in my finger, for it is beneath my breast. . . . Put your hand here and you will feel it. (*The doves begin to stir and coo.*) What is the matter with my little white creatures?

THE PRINCE (*Who has gone on counting*): . . . sixty. Now I know what it is that ticks. It is time. Your little finger is the second-hand. It ticks sixty times for every minute that passes. (*Looking at the clock on the table.*) Do you think there is a heart inside that clock?

SWANWHITE (*Touching the clock*): A clock's works are as secret as a heart's. Feel my heart beating.

(SIGNE *enters from the Pewter Closet, carrying the steel whip, which she lays on the table.*)

SIGNE: The Duchess commands the Prince and Princess to sit at oppo-site ends of the table.

(*They sit as directed.* SIGNE *returns to the Pewter Closet.* THE PRINCE *and* SWANWHITE *gaze at each other for a while in silence.*)

SWANWHITE: We are far apart, yet nearer even than before.

THE PRINCE: People are never so close as when they are parted.

SWANWHITE: How do you know that?

THE PRINCE: I have just learned it.

SWANWHITE: Now you are beginning to teach me.

THE PRINCE: It is you who are teaching me.

SWANWHITE (*Pointing to the dish of fruit*): Will you have some fruit?

THE PRINCE: No, eating is ugly.

SWANWHITE: Yes, it is ugly.

THE PRINCE: Three maids are standing there—one in the Pewter Closet, one in the Clothing Closet, and one in the Fruit Closet. Why are they there?

SWANWHITE: To watch us—lest we do what is forbidden.

THE PRINCE: May we not go into the rose garden?

SWANWHITE: I can only go into the garden in the morning, for my stepmother's bloodhounds are let loose there. And I am never al-lowed to go down to the sea . . . and so I can never bathe.

THE PRINCE: Have you never seen the sands? Never heard the song of the waves on the beach?

SWANWHITE: No. Only the roaring of the breakers in a storm reaches me here.

THE PRINCE: Have you never heard the murmuring of the winds as they sweep over the water?

SWANWHITE: That cannot reach me here.

THE PRINCE (*Pushing his helmet across the table to* SWANWHITE): Hold this to your ear and you will hear it.

SWANWHITE (*Holding the helmet to her ear*): What is it I hear?

THE PRINCE: The sea singing and the winds whispering.

SWANWHITE: No, I hear human voices. Hush! It is my stepmother. She is talking to the Steward. She is speaking of me—and of the Young King. She is saying evil things. She is swearing that I shall never be a Queen—and she is vowing . . . that you . . . that you shall marry her daughter . . . that ugly, wicked Lena.

THE PRINCE: Can you hear all that in my helmet?

SWANWHITE: Yes, yes, I can.

THE PRINCE: I did not know it had such power. Yet the helmet was a christening present from my godmother.

SWANWHITE: Will you give me a feather from the plume?

THE PRINCE: With all my heart.

SWANWHITE: Shape it into a quill, so that I may write with it.

THE PRINCE: You know how to write?

SWANWHITE: That my father taught me.

> (*Meanwhile she has pushed the helmet back to* THE PRINCE *and he has pulled a black feather from the plume. He takes a silver knife from his belt and shapes the quill.* SWANWHITE *brings out an inkhorn and parchment from the drawer of the table.*)

THE PRINCE: Who is this Lady Lena? (*He gives* SWANWHITE *the quill.*)

SWANWHITE (*Writing*): Who is she? Do you want her?

THE PRINCE: There is evil brewing in this house.

SWANWHITE: Have no fear. My father left me a gift which will bring help in time of need.

THE PRINCE: What was this gift?

SWANWHITE: The magic horn Standby.

THE PRINCE: Where is it?

SWANWHITE: That you must read in my eyes. I dare not speak, for fear of the Maids.

THE PRINCE (*Looking into her eyes*): I have seen.

SWANWHITE (*Pushing writing materials across to* THE PRINCE): Write it down. (*He writes and hands her the parchment.*) Yes, that is the hiding place. (*She writes.*)

THE PRINCE: What are you writing?

SWANWHITE: Names. All the beautiful names a Prince may have.

THE PRINCE: All but my own.

SWANWHITE: Yours too.

THE PRINCE: No, no, not that.

SWANWHITE: Now I have twenty names—all that I know—so yours must be among them. (*She pushes the parchment across to him.*) Read! (*He reads. She claps her hands.*) Oh, I read it in your eyes!

THE PRINCE: Do not say it. For pity's sake, do not say it.

SWANWHITE: I read it in your eyes.

THE PRINCE: But do not say it. Do not say it.

SWANWHITE: But why? What would happen? . . . Is Lena to say it? Your bride, your love.

THE PRINCE: Hush! Oh hush, hush!

SWANWHITE (*Rising and beginning to dance*): I know his name. The most beautiful name in all the land. (THE PRINCE *rises, catches hold of her, and holds his hand over her mouth.*) Now I am biting your hand, now I am drinking your blood, now we are brethren twice over. Do you understand?

THE PRINCE: We are of one blood.

SWANWHITE (*Throwing back her head*): O-o-o-h! Look, there is a hole in the roof, and I can see the sky, a tiny piece of heaven, a window-pane, and behind the window is a face. Is it an angel's face? . . . Look, look . . . it is your face.

THE PRINCE: The angels are young girls, not boys.

SWANWHITE: But it is you.

THE PRINCE (*Gazing up*): It is a mirror.

SWANWHITE: Woe to us then! It is my stepmother's magic mirror. She has seen everything.

THE PRINCE: I can see the hearth in the mirror. There is a pumpkin hanging in it.

SWANWHITE (*Taking from the hearth a queerly shaped mottled pumpkin*): What can this be? It has the look of an ear. So the witch has heard us too. Alas, alas! (*She throws the pumpkin into the fire and runs toward the bed. Suddenly she stops and raises one foot.*) Oh, she has strewn the floor with needles. (*She sits down and rubs her foot.* THE PRINCE *kneels to help her.*) No, you must not touch my foot, you must not.

THE PRINCE: Dear heart, you must take off your stocking if I am to help you.

SWANWHITE (*Sobbing*): You must not, you must not see my foot.

THE PRINCE: But why, why?

SWANWHITE (*Drawing her foot under her*): I cannot tell you, I cannot. Go away. Leave me. I will tell you tomorrow, but today I cannot.

THE PRINCE: But your poor foot is hurting. I must take out the needle.

SWANWHITE: Go away, oh go away! No, no, you must not touch it. Were my mother alive this would never have happened. Mother, Mother, Mother!

THE PRINCE: I do not understand. Are you afraid of me?

SWANWHITE: Do not ask. Only go away. Oh!

THE PRINCE (*Rising, sadly*): What have I done?

(*Pause.*)

SWANWHITE: No, do not leave me. I did not mean to grieve you—but I cannot tell you. Oh, if only I might reach the shore, the white sand of the beach. . . .

THE PRINCE: What then?

SWANWHITE: I cannot say, I cannot tell you. (*She hides her face in her hands. Once more the peacock snaps his beak and the doves stir. The three* MAIDS *enter one after the other. A gust of wind is heard and the tops of the rose trees sway. The golden clouds that have hung over the sea disappear and the blue sea darkens.* SWANWHITE *watches this transformation and then speaks.*) Is this the judgment of heaven on us? There is ill luck in the house. Oh, that my sorrow could bring back my mother from her dark grave!

THE PRINCE (*With his hand on his sword*): My life for yours.

SWANWHITE: Alas, she can even turn the edge of your sword. . . . Oh, that my sorrow could bring back my mother from her grave! (*The swallows in the nest twitter.*) What was that?

THE PRINCE (*Looking at the nest*): A swallows' nest! I had not noticed it.

SWANWHITE: Neither had I. How did it get there—and when? Surely
it is a good omen. . . . Yet the sweat of fear is on my brow . . .
and I can scarcely breathe. Look, even the rose is withering as that
evil woman draws near—for it is she who is coming.

(*The rose on the table begins to close and drops a petal.*)

THE PRINCE: But the swallows, where did they come from?
SWANWHITE: Not from that evil woman—for swallows are good. . . .
Here she is!

(THE STEPMOTHER *enters through the main arch with her
panther-like step. The rose droops.*)

THE STEPMOTHER: Signe! Take the horn out of the bed. (SIGNE *obeys.*
THE PRINCE *moves toward the door.*) Where are you going, Prince?
THE PRINCE: The day is almost over, madam. The sun is setting and
my bark must set sail for home.
THE STEPMOTHER: The day *is* over. The gates are closed and the
hounds let loose. Do you know my bloodhounds?
THE PRINCE: Yes, I know them. But do you know my sword?
THE STEPMOTHER: What is there to know?
THE PRINCE: Sometimes there is blood upon it.
THE STEPMOTHER: Ah, but surely never the blood of women. Will
you sleep in the Blue Room, Prince?
THE PRINCE: No, by heaven, I will sleep at home in my own bed.
THE STEPMOTHER: Have you many to aid you?
THE PRINCE: Many?
THE STEPMOTHER: How many? As many as these? One, two, three . . .

(*As she counts, the members of the household begin to pass across
the balcony in single file. All appear grim. Some are armed. None
looks into the room. Among them are* THE STEWARD, THE BAILIFF,
THE GUARD, THE CHEF, THE EXECUTIONER, THE EQUERRY, *and* THE
GROOM.)

THE PRINCE (*Crushed*): I will sleep in the Blue Room.
THE STEPMOTHER: I thought you would. And so I bid you a thousand
times good night—and so too does Swanwhite.

(There is music as of the flight of swans. A swan flies across the garden. A poppy drops from the ceiling on to THE STEPMOTHER. *She and* THE MAIDS *fall asleep on their feet.)*

SWANWHITE (*Going up to* THE PRINCE): Good night, Prince.

THE PRINCE (*Taking her hand and speaking in a low voice*): Good night. I am to sleep under the same roof as my Princess. My dreams shall enfold your dreams, and tomorrow we shall awake to play together and . . .

SWANWHITE (*Low*): Now you are the only one I have on earth. You are my father, for she has robbed me of his great strength. Look, she is asleep.

THE PRINCE: Did you see the swan?

SWANWHITE: No, but I heard it. It was my mother.

THE PRINCE: Come, fly with me!

SWANWHITE: That we may not do. Be patient. We shall meet in our dreams, shall we not? But to do this, you must love me more than all the world. Oh, love me, love me! . . .

THE PRINCE: My King, my loyalty.

SWANWHITE: Your Queen, your heart—this is what I am.

THE PRINCE: I am a knight.

SWANWHITE: But I am not. And so, and so, I take you, Prince . . . (*She puts her hand to his mouth and whispers his name.*)

THE PRINCE: Alas, what have you done?

SWANWHITE: I have given myself to you through your own name. With me on your wings you have found yourself again. You . . . (*Whispers his name again.*)

THE PRINCE (*With a movement of his hand, as if catching the word in the air*): Was that a rose you threw me? (*He throws a kiss to her.*) Swanwhite!

SWANWHITE (*Catching it and looking in her hand*): You have given me a violet. It is you. It is your soul. (*She puts her hand to her mouth.*) Now I drink you in, now I have you in my breast, in my heart.

THE PRINCE: And you are mine. Who then is the owner?

SWANWHITE: We two.

THE PRINCE: We. You and I. My rose.

SWANWHITE: My violet.

THE PRINCE: Rose.

SWANWHITE: Violet.

THE PRINCE: I love you.

SWANWHITE: You love me.

THE PRINCE: You love me.

SWANWHITE: I love you. (*The stage grows light again. The rose on the table lifts its head and opens. The faces of* THE STEPMOTHER *and* THE MAIDS *are lighted and appear beautiful, kind, and happy.* THE STEPMOTHER *lifts her drowsy head and, with her eyes still closed, appears to be watching the joy of the young people with a sweet smile.*) Look, look! The cruel one is smiling as at a memory of youth. See how false Signe is transformed by truth and hope. How ugly Tova has become beautiful, and little Elsa has grown tall.

THE PRINCE: This is the power of our love.

SWANWHITE: Can love do this? Praise be to God, mighty God the Creator! (*She falls on her knees and weeps.*)

THE PRINCE: Are you weeping?

SWANWHITE: Yes, for I am so full of joy.

THE PRINCE: Come to my arms, and smile.

SWANWHITE: In your arms I shall die.

THE PRINCE: Smile then and die.

SWANWHITE (*Rising*): If I might die . . .

(THE PRINCE *takes her in his arms.* THE STEPMOTHER *awakens. On seeing the young people embracing, she strikes the table with the whip.*)

THE STEPMOTHER: I must have fallen asleep. Ah, so this was your trick! Did I say the Blue Room? It was the Blue Tower I meant. That is where you shall sleep, Prince—with the Iron Maiden. Signe! Elsa! (*The three* MAIDS *awaken.*) Show the Prince the nearest way to the Blue Tower, and if in spite of your help he should lose his way, call the Guard, the Executioner, the Equerry, and the Groom.

THE PRINCE: There will be no need for them. Wheresoever I go, through fire or water, beneath the earth or above the clouds, there I shall meet my Swanwhite. She will be with me always, and so now I go to meet her—in the Blue Tower. How is that for witchcraft, Witch? Can you surpass it? I think not—for in you there is no love. (*He and* SWANWHITE *gaze long at one another. Then he goes out, followed by* THE MAIDS. SWANWHITE *approaches* THE STEP-MOTHER *with a pleading gesture*.)

THE STEPMOTHER: What is it? Do not waste words, but tell me briefly what you wish.

SWANWHITE: Most of all I want pure water in which to bathe my feet.

THE STEPMOTHER: Is the water to be cold or warm?

SWANWHITE: If I may choose, I should like it to be warm.

THE STEPMOTHER: What else do you desire?

SWANWHITE: A comb to take the tangles from my hair.

THE STEPMOTHER: A golden comb or one of silver?

SWANWHITE: Are you—oh, are you being kind to me?

THE STEPMOTHER: Is it to be gold or silver?

SWANWHITE: Wood or horn would do well enough for me.

THE STEPMOTHER: What else do you wish?

SWANWHITE: A clean shift.

THE STEPMOTHER: Of silk or linen?

SWANWHITE: Of linen.

THE STEPMOTHER: Ha! Now I have heard your wishes, listen to mine. You are to have no water, neither cold nor warm. You are to have no comb, neither of wood nor of horn, still less of gold or of silver. This is my kindness. You are to have no clean shift, but to get you into the closet and cover your body with a coarse black smock. These are my orders. If you were to leave this apartment, which in any case you cannot do, you would be trapped to your death. And if you escaped that, I would mark your pretty face with the steel whip, so that neither Prince nor King would ever look at you again. Now, get yourself to bed! (THE STEPMOTHER *strikes the table with the whip and goes out through the center archway. She closes the doorway with a golden grille, which squeaks and rattles as she locks it.*)

ACT II

SCENE: *As before. The golden grille is still closed. The peacock and the doves are sleeping. Clouds, landscape and sea are dark.* SWANWHITE *is asleep on the bed in a garment of black homespun.* THE PRINCE'S *helmet still lies on the table.*

In the doorways of the Closets stand the three MAIDS, *their eyes closed and lighted Roman lamps in their hands.*

A swan flies over the garden. Music of swans' flight as in Act I.

THE MOTHER OF SWANWHITE *appears outside the grille, clothed in white. Over one shoulder is the plumage of a swan and she carries a small golden harp. As she touches the grille, it opens of its own accord. She enters and it closes behind her. She takes off the plumage and puts the harp on the table. She looks round the room and, as she sees* SWANWHITE, *the harp begins to play.* THE MAIDS' *lamps go out one after another, beginning with that furthest away. Then the three Closet doors close one after another, the innermost first.*

Slowly the clouds grow golden. THE MOTHER *lights the lamp beside the bed and kneels down. The harp continues to play during the following scene.*

THE MOTHER, *still kneeling, takes off* SWANWHITE's *stockings. She bends over her daughter's feet as if bathing them with her tears, then wipes them with a white cloth and kisses them. She puts sandals on* SWANWHITE's *feet, which now appear shining white. She takes a comb of gold and smooths* SWANWHITE's *hair, then lays a garment of white linen beside her on the bed. She kisses her daughter on the forehead and prepares to leave. A white swan flies past and the swan music is repeated.* THE PRINCE'S MOTHER *appears. She too is clothed in white and enters the grille in the same way as* SWANWHITE's MOTHER, *taking off her swan plumage.*

SWANWHITE'S MOTHER: Well met, my sister. How long before cock crow?

THE PRINCE'S MOTHER: Not long, I fear. The dew is rising from the roses, the corn-crake calls, and the breath of dawn is wafted from the sea.

SWANWHITE'S MOTHER: We must make haste with what we have to do.

THE PRINCE'S MOTHER: You called me here for our dear children's sake.

SWANWHITE'S MOTHER: Yes. I remembered how, as I walked in the green fields of the land that knows no sorrow, I met you—whom I had always known, but never seen before. You were lamenting the fate of your poor child, left alone down here in the vale of sorrow. You opened your heart to me and stirred my own thoughts, which shunned the earth they hated. Then my mind turned once more to earth and sought out my poor deserted daughter. I found

her destined to marry the Young King, who is a cruel man and
evil.

THE PRINCE'S MOTHER: And so I said to you: "Like unto like. May
Love, the all-powerful, prevail and join these two lonely hearts
so that they may find comfort in each other."

SWANWHITE'S MOTHER: And now their hearts are joined, and the soul
of each enfolds the other. May sorrow turn to joy and the earth
rejoice at their young happiness!

THE PRINCE'S MOTHER: If this is granted by the Powers on high.

SWANWHITE'S MOTHER: Their love will be tested in the fire of suffering.

(THE PRINCE'S MOTHER *takes* THE PRINCE'S *helmet in her hand
and changes the black feathers for white and red ones.*)

THE PRINCE'S MOTHER: May sorrow turn to joy this very day when
he has mourned his mother for a year!

SWANWHITE'S MOTHER: Give me your hand my sister, and let the test
begin.

THE PRINCE'S MOTHER: Here is my hand and with it goes the hand of
my son. Now we have pledged them.

SWANWHITE'S MOTHER: In chastity and honor.

THE PRINCE'S MOTHER: I go to open the Blue Tower, that the young
lovers may fly to each other's arms.

SWANWHITE'S MOTHER: In chastity and honor.

THE PRINCE'S MOTHER: And you and I shall meet again in the green
meadows that know no sorrow.

SWANWHITE'S MOTHER (*With a gesture toward* SWANWHITE): Listen,
she is dreaming of him. . . . Oh, foolish cruel woman who believes that lovers can be parted! . . . They are holding one another
by the hand as they walk in the Land of Dreams under whispering
pines and singing limes. They are laughing and playing. . . .

THE PRINCE'S MOTHER: Hush! The dawn is breaking. I hear the robins
calling and the stars are fading from the sky. Farewell, my sister.

SWANWHITE'S MOTHER: Farewell.

(THE PRINCE'S MOTHER *goes out, drawing her swan's plumage
about her.* SWANWHITE'S MOTHER *passes her hand over* SWAN-
WHITE *in blessing, takes her plumage and leaves. The grille*

*opens and closes as before. The clock on the table strikes three.
The harp is silent for a moment, then begins to play a new
melody, sweeter even than before.*

(SWANWHITE *awakes, gazes round her, and listens to the harp.
She rises, runs her fingers through her hair, and looks with joy
at her white feet. She sees the white garment on the bed. She
sits at the table where she sat before, and seems to see someone
sitting opposite her in* THE PRINCE'S *place. She looks into his eyes
and smiles and holds out her hands. Her lips move as if she is
speaking, and then she seems to be listening to a reply. She
points meaningly at the red and white plume on the helmet and
bends forward as if whispering. Then she leans her head back
and breathes deeply as if inhaling some fragrance. She catches
something in the air, kisses her hand, and blows the kiss back.
She picks up the quill and caresses it as if it were a bird, then
writes and pushes the parchment across the table. She appears
to be watching him as he writes an answer; then she takes back
the parchment, reads it, and hides it in her dress. She strokes her
black dress as if commenting on the sad change in her appearance, then she smiles as if at an answer and finally bursts into
ringing laughter. She indicates in mime that her hair has been
combed. She rises and goes a little way away from the table,
shyly holding out one of her white feet. She stays for a moment
like this, awaiting an answer; when she hears it, she is puzzled
and hastily hides her foot. She goes to the chest and takes out
the chessboard and men. She places them on the lionskin with a
gesture of invitation, then lies down, puts up the men, and begins
to play with an invisible partner.*

(*The harp is silent for a moment, then starts a new melody.
The game of chess ends and* SWANWHITE *seems again to be talking
to her invisible companion. Suddenly she draws away as if he is
coming too close. With a warning gesture, she springs lightly to
her feet. She gazes long and reproachfully at him, then takes the
white garment and hides behind the bed.*

(THE PRINCE *appears outside the grille. His hair has grown
gray, his cheeks are pale. He tries in vain to open the grille. He
raises his eyes to heaven with an expression of despair.*)

SWANWHITE (*Coming forward*): Who comes with the rising of the
sun?

THE PRINCE: Your love, your Prince, your heart's desire.

SWANWHITE: Whence comes my love?

THE PRINCE: From the Land of Dreams, from the flush of dawn behind the rose-tipped hills, from the whispering pines and singing limes.

SWANWHITE: What did my love in the Land of Dreams behind the rose-tipped hills?

THE PRINCE: He laughed and played. He wrote her name. He sat on the lionskin at a game of chess.

SWANWHITE: With whom did he laugh? With whom did he play?

THE PRINCE: With Swanwhite.

SWANWHITE: Then you are he. Welcome to my castle, to my table, to my arms.

THE PRINCE: Who will open the golden grille?

SWANWHITE: Give me your hand. . . . It is as cold as your heart is warm.

THE PRINCE: My body slept in the Blue Tower, while my soul escaped to the Land of Dreams. In the Tower it was cold and dark.

SWANWHITE: I will warm your hand against my breast. I will warm you with my gaze and with my kisses.

THE PRINCE: Lighten my darkness with the radiance of your eyes.

SWANWHITE: Are you in darkness?

THE PRINCE: In the Blue Tower there is neither sun nor moon.

SWANWHITE: Rise, sun! Blow warmly, wind! Rock gently, waves! Oh, golden grille, you believe you can hold apart two hearts, two hands, two pairs of lips—but nothing can divide them!

THE PRINCE: Nothing.

(*Two doors slide in front of the grille and close, so that* SWANWHITE *and* THE PRINCE *can no longer see one another.*)

SWANWHITE: Alas, what word has fallen? Who heard? Who punishes?

THE PRINCE: I am not parted from you, dear love, for the sound of my voice still reaches you. It goes through copper, steel and stone to touch your ear in sweet caress. In my thoughts you are in my arms; in my dreams I kiss you, and nothing on this earth can part us—nothing.

SWANWHITE: Nothing.

THE PRINCE: I see you, although I cannot see you with my eyes. I taste you, for you fill my mouth with roses.

SWANWHITE: Oh, that I could hold you in my arms!

THE PRINCE: I am in your arms.

SWANWHITE: Alas, I ache to feel the beat of your heart against my own! I yearn to fall asleep within your arms. Oh, grant us each other, dear God, grant us each other! (*The swallows chirp. A small white feather falls to the ground.* SWANWHITE *picks it up and finds that it is a key. She opens the gates of the grille.* THE PRINCE *enters.* SWANWHITE *springs into his arms and they kiss.*) Why do you not kiss me?

THE PRINCE (*Kissing her again*): I kiss you, I kiss you.

SWANWHITE: I cannot feel your kisses.

THE PRINCE: Then you do not love me.

SWANWHITE: Hold me close. I cannot feel your arms.

THE PRINCE: I shall crush the life out of you.

SWANWHITE: I am still breathing.

THE PRINCE: Give me your soul.

SWANWHITE: I have given it to you. So give me yours.

THE PRINCE: Here is my soul. Now I have yours, and you have mine.

SWANWHITE (*Breaking away*): I want my soul again.

THE PRINCE (*Uneasily*): And I want mine.

SWANWHITE: Search for it.

THE PRINCE: Each of us is lost. You are me and I am you.

SWANWHITE: We are one.

THE PRINCE: God, who is merciful, has heard our prayer. We have each other.

SWANWHITE: We have each other, yet you are no longer mine. I cannot feel the touch of your hand or the caress of your lips. I cannot see your eyes, or hear your voice. You have gone from me.

THE PRINCE: But I am here.

SWANWHITE: You are here on earth. I must meet you in the Land of Dreams.

THE PRINCE: Then let us fly upon the wings of sleep.

SWANWHITE: With my hand in yours.

THE PRINCE: In my embrace.

SWANWHITE: Within your arms.

THE PRINCE: For this is bliss.

SWANWHITE: Eternal bliss without flaw or end.

THE PRINCE: Can any part us now?

THE PRINCE: Are you my bride?

SWANWHITE: Are you my bridegroom?

THE PRINCE: Bridegroom and bride are we in the Land of Dreams—
but here we are not.

SWANWHITE: Here? Where are we then?

THE PRINCE: We are below, down below on earth.

SWANWHITE: Where the clouds gather and the ocean rages, where
each night the earth sheds its tears upon the grass, waiting for the
sun to rise. Where the hawk destroys the dove and the swallow
kills the fly, where leaves fall and turn to dust, where hair grows
white and cheeks grow hollow, where eyes lose their luster and
hands lose their strength. Down here on earth below.

THE PRINCE: Let us fly.

SWANWHITE: Yes, let us fly.

(THE GARDENER *suddenly appears behind the table. He wears
cap, apron, and breeches, one side entirely green, the other
entirely blue, and has shears and a knife in his belt. He carries
a small sack, from which he scatters seed around.*)

THE PRINCE: Who are you?

THE GARDENER: I sow, I sow.

THE PRINCE: What do you sow?

THE GARDENER: Seeds, seeds, seeds.

THE PRINCE: What kind of seeds?

THE GARDENER: Onefold and twofold. One pulls this way, the other
pulls that way. When the bridal dress is on, unity has gone. In
discord I shall sow, and in concord you shall reap. One and one
make one, but one and one also make three. One and one make
two, but two make three. Do you understand?

THE PRINCE: Earthworm, moldwarp. You who live with your nose to
the ground and turn your back on heaven—what can you teach me?

THE GARDENER: That you are a mole and an earthworm. And that
since you turn your back on the earth, the earth will turn its back
on you. Good day to you. (THE GARDENER *disappears behind the
table.*)

SWANWHITE: What was that? Who was he?

THE PRINCE: It was the Green Gardener.

SWANWHITE: Green? Surely he was blue.

THE PRINCE: He was green, my love.

SWANWHITE: Why do you say what is not true?

THE PRINCE: Beloved, I said only what is true.

SWANWHITE: Alas, he does not speak the truth!

THE PRINCE: Whose voice is this? Not my Swanwhite's.

SWANWHITE: Who is this my eyes behold? Not my Prince, whose name alone once charmed me like the spell of the water sprite, like the song of a mermaid in green deeps. . . . Who are you, you stranger with evil eyes—and hair grown gray?

THE PRINCE: You see it only now—my hair that turned gray in the Tower, in a single night mourning the loss of Swanwhite, who is no more.

SWANWHITE: But here is Swanwhite.

THE PRINCE: No. I see before me a black-clad maiden whose face too is dark.

SWANWHITE: Did you not see before that I was clad in black? Then you do not love me.

THE PRINCE: Love her who stands there hard and cruel? No.

SWANWHITE: Your vows were false.

THE PRINCE: When I made my vows, another one stood there. Now— now you are filling up my mouth with nettles.

SWANWHITE: Your violets smell of stinkweed—faugh!

THE PRINCE: Now I am punished for betraying my Young King.

SWANWHITE: Would I had awaited the Young King!

THE PRINCE: Wait. He will come.

SWANWHITE: I shall not wait. I shall go and meet him.

THE PRINCE: I will not stop you.

SWANWHITE (*Moving toward the doorway*): And this was love.

THE PRINCE (*Distraught*): Where is Swanwhite? Where, where is she? The loveliest, the kindest, the most fair.

SWANWHITE: Seek her!

THE PRINCE: Alas, she is not here!

SWANWHITE: Seek her then elsewhere. (*She goes sadly out.*)

(*Left alone,* THE PRINCE *seats himself at the table, covers his face with his hands, and weeps. A gust of wind sets the draperies and curtains fluttering, and a sigh is heard from the strings of the harp.* THE PRINCE *rises and goes over to the bed. He looks at the impression of* SWANWHITE'S *head on a pillow, then picks it up and kisses it. A clamor is heard outside. He hastily seats himself at the table again. The doors of the Closets fly open. The three* MAIDS *are seen with darkened faces.* THE STEPMOTHER *comes through the arch; her face too is dark.*)

THE STEPMOTHER (*Sweetly*): Greeting, dear Prince. Did you enjoy a good night's sleep?

THE PRINCE: Where is Swanwhite?

THE STEPMOTHER: She has gone to marry the Young King. (*Pause.*) Is there no such thought, Prince, in your own mind?

THE PRINCE: In my mind is but one thought.

THE STEPMOTHER: Of young Swanwhite?

THE PRINCE: Is she too young for me?

THE STEPMOTHER: Gray hairs should keep company with good sense. I have a daughter of good sense.

THE PRINCE: And I, gray hairs?

THE STEPMOTHER: He does not know. He does not believe it. Maids! Signe, Elsa, Tova, come look at the young suitor with his gray hairs!

(THE MAIDS *laugh and* THE STEPMOTHER *joins in.*)

THE PRINCE: Where is Swanwhite?

THE STEPMOTHER: Follow the clues. Here is one. (*She hands him a parchment.*)

THE PRINCE (*Reading*): Did she write this?

THE STEPMOTHER: You know the hand—it is hers. What has she written?

THE PRINCE: That she hates me and loves another—that she was only playing with me—that she will spew out my kisses and throw my heart to the swine. My only desire now is to die—for I am dead.

THE STEPMOTHER: A knight does not die because a wench makes a fool of him. He shows his mettle and takes another.

THE PRINCE: Another? When there is only one?

THE STEPMOTHER: There are two at least, and my Magdalena has seven casks of gold.

THE PRINCE: Seven?

THE STEPMOTHER: And more beside.

(*Pause.*)

THE PRINCE: Where is Swanwhite?

THE STEPMOTHER: Magdalena is skilled in many crafts.

THE PRINCE: In witchcraft too?

THE STEPMOTHER: She could bewitch a young Prince.

THE PRINCE (*Gazing at the parchment*): Did Swanwhite write this?

THE STEPMOTHER: Magdalena would not write in such a way.

THE PRINCE: Is Magdalena kind?

THE STEPMOTHER: Kindness itself. She does not play with sacred feelings, or seek revenge for little slights. She would be true to the
one she . . . (*Hesitates, cannot say the word "loves."*) . . . cares
for.

THE PRINCE: Then she is fair.

THE STEPMOTHER: She is not fair.

THE PRINCE: Then she cannot be kind. Tell me more of her.

THE STEPMOTHER: See her for yourself.

THE PRINCE: Where?

THE STEPMOTHER: She shall come here.

THE PRINCE (*Looking at the parchment*): But did Swanwhite write
this?

THE STEPMOTHER: Magdalena would have written tenderly.

THE PRINCE: What would she have written?

THE STEPMOTHER: That . . . (*Hesitates.*)

THE PRINCE: Say the word. Say the word "love" if you are able to.
(THE STEPMOTHER *stammers and cannot say it.*) You cannot say that
word. (*She tries again.*) No, no, you cannot say it.

THE STEPMOTHER: Magdalena can say it. Shall she come to you?

THE PRINCE: Let her come.

THE STEPMOTHER (*Rising and speaking to* THE MAIDS): Blindfold the
Prince, then he will find in his embrace a Princess who has no peer
within the seven kingdoms. (SIGNE *comes forward and binds* THE
PRINCE'S *eyes.* THE STEPMOTHER *claps her hands. Pause.*) Why does
she not come? (*The peacock snaps his beak, the doves coo.*) Has my
art deserted me? What has happened? Where is the bride?

> (*Four* YOUNG GIRLS *come through the arches, carrying baskets of
> pink and white roses. Music is heard from above.* THE GIRLS *strew
> the bed with roses. Two* KNIGHTS *enter with closed visors. Be-
> tween them is* THE BRIDE, *deeply veiled.*[6] *With gestures* THE STEP-
> MOTHER *bids all depart except the bridal pair. She herself leaves
> last of all, closing the curtains and locking the grille.*)

THE PRINCE: Is my bride here?

THE BRIDE: Who is your bride?

[6] Stage direction slightly altered to agree with Act III. E.S.

THE PRINCE: I have forgotten her name. Who is your bridegroom?

THE BRIDE: He whose name may not be spoken.

THE PRINCE: Speak it if you can.

THE BRIDE: I can, but I will not.

THE PRINCE: Speak it if you can.

THE BRIDE: Speak my name first.

THE PRINCE: Seven casks of gold. Hunchback, Harelip, Hatred. What is my name? Say it if you can.

THE BRIDE: Prince Grayhair.

THE PRINCE: You are right.

(THE BRIDE *throws off her veil, and* SWANWHITE *is revealed, dressed in white with a wreath of roses on her hair.*)

SWANWHITE: Now who am I?

THE PRINCE: You are a rose.

SWANWHITE: You are a violet.

THE PRINCE (*Taking the scarf off his eyes*): You are Swanwhite.

SWANWHITE: And you . . . you are . . .

THE PRINCE: Hush!

SWANWHITE: You are mine.

THE PRINCE: But you went away. You fled from my kisses.

SWANWHITE: I have come back—because I love you.

THE PRINCE: You wrote cruel words.

SWANWHITE (*Tearing up the parchment*): I have destroyed them—because I love you.

THE PRINCE: You called me false.

SWANWHITE: What does that matter since you are true?—And I love you.

THE PRINCE: You wished to go to the Young King.

SWANWHITE: But came instead to you—because you are my love.

THE PRINCE: Now tell me how I have offended.

SWANWHITE: I have forgotten—because you are my love.

THE PRINCE: If I am your love, are you my bride?

SWANWHITE: I am your bride.

THE PRINCE: May heaven bless our union.

SWANWHITE: In the Land of Dreams.

THE PRINCE: In my arms. (THE PRINCE *leads* SWANWHITE *to the bed, on which he places his sword. She lies down on one side of the sword and he on the other. The clouds become rose-colored, the treetops murmur, the harp plays softly and sweetly.*) Good night, my Queen.

SWANWHITE: Good morning, oh my soul's beloved! I hear the beating
of your heart. I hear it beating like the waves of the sea, like the
hoofs of a steed, like the wings of an eagle. Give me your hand.

THE PRINCE: Here is my hand. Now we will take wing.

(*Pause. Music.* THE STEPMOTHER *enters with the three* MAIDS,
carrying torches. All four have become gray-haired.)

THE STEPMOTHER: Now I shall see my work accomplished before the
Duke returns. Magdalena, my daughter, is plighted to the Prince,
and Swanwhite is shut up in the Tower. (*Approaches the bed.*)
They are asleep in one another's arms. Bear witness to this, Maids!
(*They approach.*) What is this I see? The hair of all three of you is
gray.

SIGNE: Your hair too is gray, madam.

THE STEPMOTHER: Mine? Let me see. (ELSA *holds up a mirror.*) This is
the work of evil powers—then perhaps the Prince's hair is no longer
gray. . . . (THE MAIDS *hold their torches so that they light up the
bed.*) Great heaven, that is so! Look! How beautiful they are! But
the sword? Who placed the sword between them to sever a plighted
troth? (*She tries to remove the sword, but, without waking,* THE
PRINCE *clings to it.*)

SIGNE: Here is some devilry, madam.

THE STEPMOTHER: How so?

SIGNE: This is not the Lady Magdalena.

THE STEPMOTHER: Who is it? Give my eyes some help.

SIGNE: See—it is the Lady Swanwhite.

THE STEPMOTHER: Swanwhite? Is this some devilish apparition, or
have I done what I least wished? (THE PRINCE, *still sleeping, turns
his head so that his lips touch* SWANWHITE'S. THE STEPMOTHER *is
suddenly moved by the beauty of the sight.*) Never have I seen a
sight more fair. Two roses blown together by the wind, two stars
falling from heaven and joining as they fall. This is beauty itself.
Youth, beauty, innocence, love . . . What memories this awakens,
what sweet memories of the days when I lived in my father's house
and was loved by *him.* (*Breaks off in astonishment.*) What did I
say?

SIGNE: You said, madam, that you were loved. . . .

THE STEPMOTHER: Then I did speak that word of power. Beloved. So he called me once, when he was setting forth for war—Beloved. *(She is lost in thought.)* He went away . . . and they married me to another, whom I could not love. . . . Now my life is drawing to its close, and I must watch joy and happiness I have never had myself. I must find joy in others' happiness, some kind of joy at least— in others' love . . . some kind of love at least. . . . But my Magdalena, what joy is there for her? O love omnipotent, O eternal God the Creator, how you have softened my heart, my tiger's heart! Where is my power? Where is my hatred, where my vengeance? *(She sits on the bed and looks long at the sleeping pair.)* I remember a song, a love song which *he* sang when I was young—which he sang on that last evening. . . . *(Suddenly she rises as if waking from a dream and flies into a rage. Shouts:)* Here, men of the Castle —Guards, Bailiff, Executioner—all of you, come here! *(She tears the sword from the bed and throws it behind her.)* Come, all of you, come here! *(Clamor. The members of the household enter as before.)* Behold! The Prince, the Young King's vassal, has defiled his master's bride. Bear witness to the shameful deed. Let the traitor be taken in chains and irons to his lord—and into the spiked cask with the hussy. *(THE PRINCE and SWANWHITE awaken.)* Grooms and Executioner, seize the Prince!

(*They take hold of him.*)

THE PRINCE *(Struggling)*: Where is my sword? Not against evil, but for innocence I fight.
THE STEPMOTHER: Whose innocence?
THE PRINCE: My bride's.
THE STEPMOTHER: The hussy's innocence! Prove it.
SWANWHITE: O Mother, Mother!

(*The white swan flies past.*)

THE STEPMOTHER: Bring scissors, Maids! I will cut off the harlot's hair. (SIGNE *brings scissors.*) Now I will cut off your beauty and your love. (THE STEPMOTHER *catches hold of a lock of* SWANWHITE's *hair and tries to cut it, but the blades of the scissors will not close. She is suddenly seized with panic, which spreads to the men and* THE MAIDS.) Is the enemy upon us? Why are you trembling?

SIGNE: Madam, the dogs are barking and the horses neigh. Strangers are approaching.

THE STEPMOTHER: Quick, to the drawbridge, one and all! Man the ramparts! Fire, water, sword, and axe!

(Amid great turmoil the curtain falls.)

ACT III

The three MAIDS *are standing in the Closets at their work:* SIGNE *in the Pewter Closet,* ELSA *in the Clothing Closet,* TOVA *in the Fruit Closet.* THE GARDENER *enters and beckons to* SIGNE, *who comes out to meet him.*

THE GARDENER: Signe, my daughter, I need your help.

SIGNE: First tell me who it was that came with so much din and clamor? Was it the Duke, our master, returning from the war?

THE GARDENER: No, it was not the Duke. It was an Envoy from the Young King, Lady Swanwhite's bridegroom, and with him a great armed retinue. Misfortune is upon us. There will be war—and this domain will blaze with fire.

SIGNE: Your seed has grown, your seed of discord. This is the harvest of your sowing.

THE GARDENER: False Signe, it was you who betrayed us, when you obeyed the Duchess and seized the guardian horn Standby.

SIGNE: A faithful servant must be false to her mistress's enemies.

THE GARDENER: But now, if the Duke does not come, the castle will be razed to the ground. How will he get here in time?

SIGNE: Time brings its own solution. However, now there is to be a banquet. I am polishing the pewter, Elsa is arranging the robes, and Tova is preparing the fruit. Are you sure the Young King has not come himself?

THE GARDENER: Only the Envoy and his retinue.

SIGNE: Where then is the Young King?

THE GARDENER: Who knows? Disguised perhaps among the retinue.

SIGNE: And the Prince?

THE GARDENER: In the Tower. Why do you hate him?

SIGNE: Hate him? I do not hate him. Oh no, no!

THE GARDENER: Perhaps you . . . ?

SIGNE: Do not say it.

THE GARDENER: Can one hate the man one loves?

SIGNE: Yes, when one cannot have him.

THE GARDENER: When one cannot have him? But the Lady Swanwhite cannot have her Prince, yet she loves him unto death and beyond death.

SIGNE: Is the Prince to die?

THE GARDENER: You know that.

SIGNE: No. O God in heaven, he must not die! Save him, save him!

THE GARDENER: How can I?

SIGNE: By the secret passage—you know the way. Here is the entrance to it, here in the floor.

THE GARDENER: The Duchess has already had the secret passage flooded.

SIGNE: You must find a way through. Oh, save him, save him, before it is too late! Get him to a boat and out to sea.

THE GARDENER: I go to mend what I have broken. If I do not come again, you will know I have atoned.

SIGNE: May God protect you on your journey!

(SWANWHITE *enters by the archway.*)

SWANWHITE: You evil man, why are you here?

THE GARDENER (*Falling on his knees*): I am here to right the wrong I did. (*He rises and sows seed.*)

SWANWHITE: How can you do that? You sowed the seed of discord. What are you sowing now?

THE GARDENER: I sow Concord, Heartsease, Peace, Good to all and ill to none. Do not condemn me, Lady, for your dispute was not my fault.

SWANWHITE: Dispute? You mean as to whether you were green or blue?

THE GARDENER: Even so. Look at me now, Lady, with both your lovely eyes.

SWANWHITE: I am looking.

THE GARDENER (*Spinning round*): Then see, I am green on one side, and blue upon the other.

SWANWHITE: So you are both colors. Old simpleton, you have taught me wisdom, and I thank you for it. (*He goes to the trapdoor.*) But where are you going now?

THE GARDENER: To rescue the Prince.

SWANWHITE: You? Can evil turn to good?

THE GARDENER: Not always. . . . Now I shall take the secret passage—and return with him, or not return at all.

SWANWHITE: The blessing of God go with you and protect you on this journey. (THE GARDENER *goes out through the trapdoor in the floor.* THE EXECUTIONER *rolls the spiked cask onto the terrace and stands beside it, half hidden.*[7] SWANWHITE *watches, then turns to* SIGNE.) Have you betrayed your father?

SIGNE: No, not my father.

SWANWHITE: The Prince then?

SIGNE: No, not the Prince.

SWANWHITE: Then me? (SIGNE *is silent.*) Then me?

SIGNE: My young mistress, disaster is upon us all. One alone can save us now—the Duke, your father.

SWANWHITE: Yes, the Duke, my mighty father. But he does not hear us in our need, because you betrayed me and gave the horn into the hands of the Duchess.

SIGNE: Do you know where she has hidden it?

SWANWHITE: Let me think. (*She thinks.*)

SIGNE: Where?

SWANWHITE: Hush! (*Pause.*) Now I can see it. . . . It is behind the mirror . . . in . . . in her silver closet.

SIGNE: Then I will fetch it.

SWANWHITE: You will do this—for my sake?

SIGNE: Do not thank me. Disaster is upon us. No, do not thank me.

SWANWHITE: You will not betray us?

SIGNE: Us? Neither all, nor one, nor any if I know it. He whom one loves, one hates—though not always. But he whom one hates, one does not love—ever. I am quite confused. We shall see Standby. . . . I shall stand by and be perhaps a bystander. (*She goes out.*)

SWANWHITE: She speaks in riddles. Elsa, Tova, come in here! (*They obey.*) Here, stand close to me, for someone is listening to us. My pretty Elsa, my faithful Tova, stay by my side. I fear something which I cannot explain. Something is coming which I do not know. I hear with the ears of my heart, I see with the eyes of my breast—danger. I feel a breath as cold as ice. A brutal hand clutches at my

---

[7] Added stage direction. E.S.

breast like a bird of prey swooping on a dove. Woe is me, nettles
and goatsbeard, foul flesh and all that reeks! . . . He has come,
the Young King.

(THE YOUNG KING *enters, full of lust and drink.* ELSA *and* TOVA
stand close together, with SWANWHITE *behind them.* THE KING
comes up to them insolently.)

THE YOUNG KING: Ha, three of you! Do you know who I am?
ELSA: Knight of the wine barrel.
THE YOUNG KING: Impertinent chit. Give me a kiss, for you are little
   and bad, but pretty. (*To* TOVA.) You are good, I know, but plain.
   Tell me where the Princess Swanwhite is.
ELSA: Can you not guess?
THE YOUNG KING: Are you she? . . . Aha! But your hands are red—
   you are no Princess. Do you know my name?
ELSA: Lord Goat.
THE YOUNG KING: I like impudent girls. You little scamp, come to my
   arms!
ELSA: Here? Now?

(*They flirt.*)

THE YOUNG KING: Think if the Princess were to hear us.
TOVA: She does not hear such things. She has ears only for the song of
   the nightingales, for the whisper of leaves, for the murmur of the
   wind and the waves.
THE YOUNG KING: Don't be so long-winded, ugly one. You talk too
   much at a time. Remember your manners, chits, and tell me where
   the Princess is. Or else, by Satan and all his devils, the Stepmother's
   steel whip shall rain down fire upon your backs. Where is the
   Princess Swanwhite?
SWANWHITE (*Coming forward*): She is here.
THE YOUNG KING (*Gazing at her*): She? (*Pause.*) Impossible. I saw her
   portrait, and it was beautiful—but that was painted by the wily
   Prince so as to deceive me. You have no nose, my girl. You are
   cross-eyed and your lips are too thick. . . . I ask you—is this Swan-
   white?
SWANWHITE: I am she.
THE YOUNG KING (*Sitting down*): So it is true, well, well . . . Can you

dance, play, paint, sing? (*Pause.*) You can do nothing. And for this nothing, I am about to storm the castle, burn, sack . . . (*Pause.*) Can't you at least speak? Can you while away a long evening in conversation? (*Pause.*) Not that either.

SWANWHITE (*Whispering*): I can speak, but not to you.

THE YOUNG KING: Your voice is toneless as a feather brush. Perhaps you are deaf?

SWANWHITE: Certain voices do not reach my ears.

THE YOUNG KING: And blind, and lame as well. (*Pause.*) This is too great a venture for too small a gain. Go in peace—or rather let me go. Prince Faithless may pluck his goose with the plaintiff. And with me.

(*He strides out.* SWANWHITE, ELSA, *and* TOVA *lift their hands in joy. A melody sounds from the harp.* THE PRINCE *comes up through the trapdoor.* SWANWHITE *springs into his arms. The harp continues to play.* ELSA *and* TOVA *go out through the arch.* THE PRINCE *and* SWANWHITE *try to speak to each other, but cannot find words.* THE YOUNG KING *is seen stealing into the Clothing Closet, where he stands hidden, spying and listening.*)

SWANWHITE: Is this farewell?

THE PRINCE: Do not say that word.

SWANWHITE: He is here—he has been here, the King, your King.

THE PRINCE: Then it is farewell—for ever.

SWANWHITE: No. He did not see me. He did not hear me. He did not like me.

THE PRINCE: But he seeks my life.

SWANWHITE: All of them seek your life. . . . Where will you go?

THE PRINCE: Down to the shore.

SWANWHITE: Out on the sea in the storm of winds and waves? You who are my love, my heart's delight.

THE PRINCE: In the waves I shall drink our marriage cup.

SWANWHITE: Then I shall die.

THE PRINCE: And we shall meet never to part, never, never more to part.

SWANWHITE: Never more. But if I did not die, my sorrow would bring you back from the grave.

(*The stage begins to darken.*)

THE PRINCE: For each tear that is shed from your bright eyes, there is a drop of blood in my coffin. Each hour you walk on earth in happiness fills it with petals of roses.

SWANWHITE: It is growing dark.

THE PRINCE: I walk in light, in your light, because I love you.

SWANWHITE: Take my soul, take my life!

THE PRINCE: I have yours. Take mine, take mine! Now my body must depart, but my soul stays here.

SWANWHITE: My body must stay here, but my soul departs—with you.

(*As before,* THE PRINCE *and* SWANWHITE *try to speak, but their lips move soundlessly.* THE PRINCE *goes down through the trapdoor.* THE YOUNG KING *has witnessed the scene with growing emotion. He sees* SWANWHITE *as she really is. He is first ashamed, then enraptured. When* THE PRINCE *has gone,* THE YOUNG KING *hastens out and falls on his knees.*)

THE YOUNG KING: Swanwhite, fairest work of God's hand, do not fear me, for now I have seen you in all your perfection, and heard your voice as of silver strings. But it was with *his* eyes that I saw and with *his* ears that I heard. Alone, I had no powers, for I have not your love. . . . Your stony gaze tells me that you do not see me, that you do not hear my words, that you exist for him alone—that if I took you, it would be a corpse that I held in my arms. Forgive what I have destroyed. Forget that I ever was. Believe that I would never dare defile you by one impure thought, though the memory of you will pursue me and be my punishment. One thing alone I ask. Give me your voice in farewell, that I may carry its echo within my heart. One word to remember, one only.

(*Pause.*)

SWANWHITE (*Harshly*): Go!

THE YOUNG KING (*Springing up*): Raven! Now hear my answer: Blood! (*He draws his sword.*) None shall possess you, save only me. I will have the raven. I love the strong, the fierce, the cruel. The dove is not the bird for me.

SWANWHITE (*Retreating behind the table*): Help me, my father! Standby, come to me, come, come!

THE YOUNG KING (*Falling back*): There it comes. The silver voice. The sound of the Angelus on some saint's day. My strength is gone from me.

SWANWHITE (*Half singing*): Come, come, come!

THE YOUNG KING: Your voice is so lovely that my sword weeps for shame. Go in and hide yourself. No sword then, but fire. Fire to the castle, death to the traitor. (TOVA *steals in with the horn.*) Who is there?

TOVA: Here it is. Take it, take it!

SWANWHITE (*Taking it*): You have brought it, not Signe?

TOVA: I took it from Signe. She was faithless still.

(SWANWHITE *blows the horn. Another horn answers in the distance.* THE YOUNG KING, *panic-stricken, shouts to his unseen men.*)

THE YOUNG KING: To horse! Let loose the reins, press in the spurs, ride for dear life! (*He rushes out.*)

(SWANWHITE *blows the horn again, and the other horn answers.*)

TOVA: He is coming, the glorious hero. He is coming.

(*After a pause* SWANWHITE *blows again and* THE DUKE *enters.* TOVA *goes out.*)

THE DUKE: Sweet treasure of my heart, what is at stake?

SWANWHITE: Your child's life is at stake, Father. Look at the spiked barrel there.

THE DUKE: What has my child done to deserve such a fate?

SWANWHITE: I learned the Prince's name in the way that only those who love can learn. I spoke it and lost my heart to him.

THE DUKE: This does not merit death. What more?

SWANWHITE: I slept beside him—with the sword between.

THE DUKE: Nor does this merit death, although it was not wise. What more?

SWANWHITE: That is all.

THE DUKE (*To* THE EXECUTIONER): Away with the spiked barrel! (*He obeys.*) And now, my child, where is the Prince?

SWANWHITE: Sailing for home in his coracle.

THE DUKE: Now in this raging storm? Alone?

SWANWHITE: Alone. Oh, what will befall him?

THE DUKE: That is in the hand of God.

SWANWHITE: Is he in danger?

THE DUKE: Fortune sometimes favors the brave.

SWANWHITE: Oh, he deserves it!

THE DUKE: If he is innocent.

SWANWHITE: He is, he is, more innocent than I.

(THE STEPMOTHER *enters.*)

THE STEPMOTHER (*To* THE DUKE): How did you come here?

THE DUKE: By the shortest way. Would I had been here sooner.

THE STEPMOTHER: Had you come sooner, your daughter would have escaped this injury.

THE DUKE: What injury?

THE STEPMOTHER: The one for which there is no remedy.

THE DUKE: Have you proof?

THE STEPMOTHER: I have eyewitnesses.

THE DUKE: Call the Steward.

THE STEPMOTHER: He knows nothing of this.

THE DUKE (*Grasping the hilt of his sword*): Call the Steward! (THE STEPMOTHER *shudders. She claps her hands four times.* THE STEWARD *enters.*) Have a pie prepared without delay—a pie of beasts' entrails, seasoned with fennel, roots, rank herbs, and fungus. (THE STEWARD *glances at* THE STEPMOTHER.) Why this glance? Obey me instantly. (THE STEWARD *goes out. To* THE STEPMOTHER.) Now call the Herb Gardener.

THE STEPMOTHER: He is ignorant.

THE DUKE: And shall remain so. But come he must. Summon him. (THE STEPMOTHER *claps her hands six times.* THE HERB GARDENER *enters.*) Bring me three lilies—one white, one red, one blue. (THE HERB GARDENER *glances at* THE STEPMOTHER. THE DUKE *touches his sword.*) Have a care of your head. (THE HERB GARDENER *goes out.* THE DUKE *turns back to* THE STEPMOTHER.) Now call the witnesses. (THE STEPMOTHER *claps her hands once.* SIGNE *enters.*) What did you see? Give evidence. But choose your words with care.

SIGNE: I saw the Lady Swanwhite and the Prince together in one bed.

THE DUKE: With the sword between?

SIGNE: There was no sword.

SWANWHITE: Signe, Signe, you are bearing false witness against me—I who saved you from the steel whip! You do me such wrong, such wrong. (*Pause.*) You betrayed me that night—you know it. Why did you do this to me?

SIGNE: I did not know what it was I did. I did what I had no will to do. I did the will of another. Now I no longer wish to live. Forgive me for our Savior's sake.

SWANWHITE: I forgive you. Do you also forgive yourself, for you are without guilt since an evil will possessed you.

SIGNE: Punish me, punish me!

SWANWHITE: Is not your repentance punishment enough?

THE DUKE: I do not think so. . . . Are there more witnesses? (*The two* KNIGHTS *enter.*) Were you the Bride's escort? Give your evidence.

THE FIRST KNIGHT: I escorted the Lady Magdalena to her bridal couch.

THE SECOND KNIGHT: I escorted the Lady Magdalena to her bridal couch.

THE DUKE: What is this? A snare that shall entrap the snarer. The next witness. (*Enter* ELSA.) Give your evidence.

ELSA: I swear, by God the Just, I saw the Lady Swanwhite and the Prince, fully clothed and with the sword between them.

THE DUKE: One for and one against . . . and two not relevant. I leave it to God to judge. (TOVA *enters.*) The flowers shall testify.

TOVA (*Coming forward*): My gracious master, noble Lord . . .

THE DUKE: What have you to tell me?

TOVA: That my sweet Lady is innocent.

THE DUKE: Oh child, child, do you know this? Then let us know it too.

TOVA: I have said what is true.

THE DUKE: And no one believes you. Yet when Signe says what is not true, she is believed. And what does Swanwhite say herself? Does not her pure brow, do not her candid eyes and innocent mouth declare that she is slandered? Do not my own eyes, the eyes of a father, tell me this too? Now Almighty God shall judge, so that all men may believe. (THE HERB GARDENER *enters, carrying the three lilies in narrow vases of glass.* THE DUKE *places them in a semicircle on the table.* THE STEWARD *enters with a huge platter on which is a steaming pie.* THE DUKE *places the platter within the semicircle of flowers.*) For whom does the white lily stand?

ALL (*Except* SWANWHITE *and* THE STEPMOTHER): For Swanwhite.

THE DUKE: And the red lily?

ALL (*Except* SWANWHITE *and* THE STEPMOTHER): For the Prince.

THE DUKE: And the blue?

ALL (*Except* SWANWHITE *and* THE STEPMOTHER): For the Young King.

THE DUKE: So be it. Tova, my child, you who believe in innocence because you are innocent yourself, interpret God's judgment for us. Tell us the subtle secrets of these flowers. What do you see?

TOVA: What is evil I cannot speak.

THE DUKE: I shall do that—you speak the good. In the reek of the burning wild beasts' blood, in the vapors of those sensual herbs, what do you see?

(TOVA *gazes at the three lilies, which behave as she describes.*)

TOVA: The white lily closes its petals against defilement. This flower is Swanwhite's.

ALL (*As before*): Swanwhite is innocent.

TOVA: The red flower, the Prince's lily, closes too. But the blue, the Young King's flower, opens wide to breathe the sensual fumes.

THE DUKE: Well read. What do you see now?

TOVA: The red lily bows its head in reverent love before the white. But the blue flower writhes with envious rage.

THE DUKE: Well read. Who then shall have Swanwhite?

TOVA: The Prince. His desire is purer and therefore stronger.

ALL (*As before*): The Prince shall have Swanwhite.

(SWANWHITE *throws herself into* THE DUKE'S *arms.*)

SWANWHITE: Father, Father!

THE DUKE: Call back the Prince! Let every horn and trumpet call him. Let every bark on shore set sail. . . . But one thing more—for whom is the spiked barrel? (*All are silent.*) Then I will tell you. It is for the Duchess, the arch-liar, the destroyer. Now, evil woman, you have seen that for all the power of your spells, they cannot conquer love. Go, and go quickly! (THE STEPMOTHER *makes a movement with her hands, which for a moment seems to stun* THE DUKE. *Then he lifts* SWANWHITE *on to his shoulder, draws his sword, and points it at* THE STEPMOTHER). Out upon you, evil one! My sword will pierce your spells. (THE STEPMOTHER *goes slowly out to the balcony backwards, with the dragging step of a panther.*) Now for the Prince. (THE STEPMOTHER *stops on the balcony as if turned to stone, and opens her mouth as if pouring out venom. The peacock and the doves fall down dead. Then* THE STEPMOTHER *begins to swell. Her clothes become inflated until they hide her head and shoulders; then they seem to be on fire, flaming in a pattern of snakes and branches. The sun begins to rise. The ceiling sinks slowly into the room. Smoke and flame pour from the hearth.* THE DUKE *raises the cross-shaped hilt of his sword toward* THE STEP-MOTHER). Pray, people, pray to Christ our Savior!

ALL: Christ have mercy upon us!

(*The ceiling returns to its place, the smoke and the fire cease. The sound of many voices is heard outside.*)

THE DUKE: What is this? What has happened now?

SWANWHITE: I know. . . . I see. I hear the water dripping from his hair, I hear the silence of his heart. I hear that he no longer breathes. . . . I see that he is dead.

THE DUKE: Where do you see this? And who . . . ?

SWANWHITE: Where? . . . I see it.

THE DUKE: I see nothing.

SWANWHITE: Let them come quickly, since they must come.

(*Four young* MAIDS-OF-HONOR *enter with baskets, from which they strew the floor with branches of yew and white lilies. Next come four* PAGES, *ringing silver bells of different tones. Then a* PRIEST, *bearing a crucifix, and finally the* PALLBEARERS, *carrying a bier, on which* THE PRINCE *lies under a white shroud strewn with pink and white roses. His hair is dark again and his face youthful, rosy, and radiantly beautiful. His eyes are closed, but he is smiling. The harp begins to play. The sun rises fully. The bewitched shape of* THE STEPMOTHER *bursts and she resumes her own form. She steps away. The bier is set down in the rays of the sun.* SWANWHITE *throws herself on her knees beside it and kisses* THE PRINCE. *All present hide their faces in their hands and weep.* THE FISHERMAN, *who has been standing in the doorway, comes in.*)

THE DUKE: Tell us the brief tale, Fisherman.

THE FISHERMAN: Does it not tell itself, my noble Lord? The young Prince had scarcely crossed the Sound when he was seized by such longing for his love—that he must return. Since his bark had lost its rudder, he plunged into the water and swam against spring tide and wave and wind. I saw his young head top the billows, I heard his voice call out her name. . . . Then his dead body dropped gently on the white sand at my feet. His hair had turned gray that night in the Tower, his cheeks had grown hollow with sorrow and care, his lips had lost their power to smile. . . . Now in death he was young again and beautiful. His dark locks framed his rosy cheeks . . . he smiled, and see, he is smiling still. The people gathered on the shore, awed by this sad sweet sight, and one whispered to another: "See, this is Love!"

SWANWHITE: He is dead. His heart no longer sings, his eyes no longer light my life, his breath no longer sheds its dew on me. He smiles, but not at me—it is at heaven that he smiles. I will join him on his journey. (*She kisses him and prepares to lie down beside him.*)

THE DUKE: Do not kiss a dead man's lips, for they bear poison.

SWANWHITE: Sweet poison if it brings me death, that death which for me is life.

THE DUKE: They say, my child, that the dead do not meet again at will, and that what a man has prized in life has little worth beyond it.

SWANWHITE: But love? Can love not reach to the other side of death?

THE DUKE: Our wise men have denied it.

SWANWHITE: Then he must come back to earth again. O God, dear God, send him back from Your heaven!

THE DUKE: A vain prayer, I fear.

SWANWHITE: I cannot pray. Alas, an evil eye still rules this place.

THE DUKE: You mean the witch whom the sunlight pierced. Let her then be taken to the stake and burned alive.

SWANWHITE: Burned alive? No, no. Let her go in peace.

THE DUKE: She shall be burned alive. You men, build the pyre close to the shore, that her ashes may be strewn to the winds.

(SWANWHITE *falls on her knees before* THE DUKE.)

SWANWHITE: No, no. I pray for her, my executioner. Have mercy on her, mercy!

(THE STEPMOTHER *enters, changed. She is freed from the evil powers that have held her under their spell.*)

THE STEPMOTHER: Mercy? Who spoke that sacred word? Who prayed a prayer from the heart for me?

SWANWHITE: I prayed for you. . . . I, your daughter . . . Mother.

THE STEPMOTHER: O God in heaven, she calls me Mother! At whose bidding is this?

SWANWHITE: At the bidding of love.

THE STEPMOTHER: Blessed be love that works such miracles. Ah child, it has the power too to call back the dead from death's dark realm! I cannot do this, for love has been denied me. But you, you can do it.

SWANWHITE (*Humbly*): I, what can I do?

THE STEPMOTHER: You can love, you can forgive, and so, mighty child, you can do everything. Learn this from me, who may not use my powers. Go to him. Call the name of your beloved and lay your hand upon his heart. Then with the help of Almighty God—but only with His help—your love will hear your voice—if you can believe.

SWANWHITE: I believe. I will. I pray. (*She goes to the bier and lays one hand on* THE PRINCE's *heart and raises the other to heaven.*) With my mind. (*She bends down and whispers something in his ear.*) With my heart. (*She whispers again.*) With my soul. (*She whispers a third time.*[8])

(THE PRINCE *awakens. He rises and takes* SWANWHITE *in his arms. All kneel in praise and thanksgiving. The music swells to a climax*).

---

[8] Strindberg puts only that Swanwhite whispers three times in the Prince's ear. "With my mind," "with my heart," and "with my soul" have been added to express what is implied: three stages of will. E.S.

The Post Office

BY

RABINDRANATH TAGORE

ALBERT SCHWEITZER called him "the Goethe of India"; Albert Einstein said he was an ideal seer of his people; and Jawaharlal Nehru claimed that his art symbolized "the full-blooded emblem of India's awakened spirit." These tributes were paid to Rabindranath Tagore (1861–1941), poet, playwright, musician and philosopher, who won the Nobel prize for literature in 1913. His canon of nearly 50 plays brought about a Hindu theatre renaissance in the early years of this century and continues to be the cornerstone of modern Bengali drama. He explained India's mysticism and aesthetics to the rest of the world without distorting the civilization he deeply loved and prized, and with such lyricism that he made his fellow citizens love and prize it all the more.

Tagore traveled throughout much of his life, always transporting India with him and leaving a better knowledge of its life and customs in the minds of the people he met. His lectures took him to Europe, the United States, China and Japan; everywhere he made a striking appearance as a handsome man more than six feet tall, dressed in robes of ancient design, with long hair and white beard, the embodiment of an Indian philosopher and artist.

As a young man, he journeyed to England in 1877 to study law, but soon returned to India to oversee his father's vast landholdings with their more than 100,000 tenants. His poems of this period, revealing a dedicated nationalistic interest, became popular, as did many of his plays, with the uneducated and poor laborers. Even when away from India for long periods as a citizen of the world (Britain knighted him in 1915), he never lost concern for the plight of these people.

Tagore's association with theatre dated from his youth, when he performed in a play written by his brother. His own first play was produced when he was twenty. In addition to acting and writing, he also directed many plays, some of which were performed at his family estate near Calcutta. Although his concepts of drama changed throughout his career, his plays often incorporated dance, song, mime, poetry, symbolism and allegory. *The King of the Dark Chamber* (1924) well represents this combination of theatrical elements as it tells the story of a monarch who moves invisibly among his people. This musical spectacle was produced successfully off-Broadway a few seasons ago.

Other of his plays, including *The Post Office*, place little or no emphasis upon elaborate production, but upon feeling—the feeling the audience derives from character, atmosphere and meaning. In these plays action has been replaced by lyricism and symbolism, much in the manner prescribed by Maurice Maeterlinck in his theory of "static drama," which advocated that the inner purpose of a play was to discover the forces of life beneath the surface of reality.

Tagore's later plays were mostly dance-dramas based on indigenous forms of Bengali and Hindu tradition in a language metaphorical and mystical, of which *The Kingdom of Cards* is a noteworthy example. Tagore wrote in his native Bengali but often translated his plays into English himself or closely supervised the translations of others.

The Post Office, written in 1912, represents Tagore in a typically philosophic and symbolic mood. The play was first performed in London in 1914 by The Irish Theatre; its gentleness and sense of peace earned high praise from the great Irish poet William Butler Yeats. Productions followed in Paris (where it was translated by André Gide) and in Berlin, as well as in India. Tagore conceived the play in a period of personal restlessness during which he yearned to explore the world, particularly the West, and felt confined and stifled by the life around him. When the constriction became intolerable, he sat down and in three or four days wrote this tragic portrait of a child pining for freedom.

A detailed introduction to the theatre of Tagore may be found in Edward Thompson's helpful study, *Rabindranath Tagore, Poet and Dramatist*. Other plays, as well as samples of his poetry, philosophy, criticism, fables, letters, short stories, autobiography and conversations, appear in *A Tagore Reader*, edited by Amiya Chakravarty.

The Post Office

CHARACTERS

MADHAV, *a well-meaning old man*
THE PHYSICIAN
GAFFER, *Madhav's friend*
AMAL, *a delicate young boy*
THE DAIRYMAN
THE WATCHMAN
THE HEADMAN
SUDHA, *the young daughter
    of the flowerseller*
A TROOP OF BOYS
THE KING'S HERALD
THE STATE PHYSICIAN

SCENE

*Amal's bedroom in the house of Madhav; a plain room with one
small window through which can be glimpsed a rural village in India.*

ACT I

MADHAV's *house.*

MADHAV: What a state I am in! Before he came, nothing mattered; I felt so free. But now that he has come, goodness knows from where, my heart is filled with his dear self, and my home will be no home to me when he leaves. Doctor, do you think he—

PHYSICIAN: If there's life in his fate, then he will live long. But what the medical scriptures say, it seems—

MADHAV: Great heavens, what?

PHYSICIAN: The scriptures have it: "Bile or palsy, cold or gout spring all alike."

MADHAV: Oh, get along, don't fling your scriptures at me; you only make me more anxious; tell me what I can do.

PHYSICIAN (*Taking snuff*): The patient needs the most scrupulous care.

MADHAV: That's true; but tell me how.

PHYSICIAN: I have already mentioned, on no account must he be let out of doors.

MADHAV: Poor child, it is very hard to keep him indoors all day long.

PHYSICIAN: What else can you do? The autumn sun and the damp are both very bad for the little fellow—for the scriptures have it:
      "In wheezing, swooning, or in nervous fret,
      In jaundice or leaden eyes—"

MADHAV: Never mind the scriptures, please. Eh, then we must shut the poor thing up. Is there no other method?

PHYSICIAN: None at all: for "In the wind and in the sun—"

MADHAV: What will your "in this and in that" do for me now? Why don't you let them alone and come straight to the point? What's to be done, then? Your system is very, very hard for the poor boy; and he is so quiet too with all his pain and sickness. It tears my heart to see him wince, as he takes your medicine.

PHYSICIAN: The more he winces, the surer is the effect. That's why the sage Chyabana observes: "In medicine as in good advice, the least palatable is the truest." Ah, well! I must be trotting now. (*Exits.*)

(GAFFER *enters.*)

MADHAV: Well, I'm jiggered, there's Gaffer now.

GAFFER: Why, why, I won't bite you.

MADHAV: No, but you are a devil to send children off their heads.

GAFFER: But you aren't a child, and you've no child in the house; why worry then?

MADHAV: Oh, but I have brought a child into the house.

GAFFER: Indeed, how so?

MADHAV: You remember how my wife was dying to adopt a child?

GAFFER: Yes, but that's an old story; you didn't like the idea.

MADHAV: You know, brother, how hard all this getting money has been. That somebody else's child would sail in and waste all this money earned with so much trouble—Oh, I hated the idea. But this boy clings to my heart in such a queer sort of way—

GAFFER: So that's the trouble! and your money goes all for him and feels jolly lucky it does go at all.

MADHAV: Formerly, earning was a sort of passion with me; I simply couldn't help working for money. Now, I make money, and as I know it is all for this dear boy, earning becomes a joy to me.

GAFFER: Ah, well, and where did you pick him up?

MADHAV: He is the son of a man who was a brother to my wife by village ties. He has had no mother since infancy; and now the other day he lost his father as well.

GAFFER: Poor thing: and so he needs me all the more.

MADHAV: The doctor says all the organs of his little body are at loggerheads with each other, and there isn't much hope for his life. There is only one way to save him and that is to keep him out of this autumn wind and sun. But you are such a terror! What with this game of yours at your age, too, to get children out of doors!

GAFFER: God bless my soul! So I'm already as bad as autumn wind and sun, eh! But, friend, I know something, too, of the game of keeping them indoors. When my day's work is over I am coming in to make friends with this child of yours. (*Exits.*)

(AMAL *enters.*)

AMAL: Uncle, I say, Uncle!

MADHAV: Hullo! Is that you, Amal?

AMAL: Mayn't I be out of the courtyard at all?

MADHAV: No, my dear, no.

AMAL: See there, where Auntie grinds lentils in the quern [hand mill], the squirrel is sitting with his tail up and with his wee hands he's picking up the broken grains of lentils and crunching them. Can't I run up there?

MADHAV: No, my darling, no.

AMAL: Wish I were a squirrel!—it would be lovely. Uncle, why won't you let me go about?

MADHAV: The doctor says it's bad for you to be out.

AMAL: How can the doctor know?

MADHAV: What a thing to say! The doctor can't know and he reads such huge books!

AMAL: Does his book learning tell him everything?

MADHAV: Of course, don't you know!

AMAL (*With a sigh*): Ah, I am so stupid! I don't read books.

MADHAV: Now, think of it; very, very learned people are all like you; they are never out of doors.

AMAL: Aren't they really?

MADHAV: No, how can they? Early and late they toil and moil at their books, and they've eyes for nothing else. Now, my little man, you are going to be learned when you grow up; and then you will stay at home and read such big books, and people will notice you and say, "He's a wonder."

AMAL: No, no Uncle; I beg of you, by your dear feet—I don't want to be learned; I won't.

MADHAV: Dear, dear; it would have been my saving if I could have been learned.

AMAL: No, I would rather go about and see everything that there is.

MADHAV: Listen to that! See! What will you see, what is there so much to see?

AMAL: See that far-away hill from our window—I often long to go beyond those hills and right away.

MADHAV: Oh, you silly! As if there's nothing more to be done but just get up to the top of that hill and away! Eh! You don't talk sense, my boy. Now listen, since that hill stands there upright as a barrier, it means you can't get beyond it. Else, what was the use in heaping up so many large stones to make such a big affair of it, eh!

AMAL: Uncle, do you think it is meant to prevent us crossing over? It seems to me because the earth can't speak it raises its hands into the sky and beckons. And those who live far off and sit alone by their windows can see the signal. But I suppose the learned people—

MADHAV: No, they don't have time for that sort of nonsense. They are not crazy like you.

AMAL: Do you know, yesterday I met someone quite as crazy as I am.

MADHAV: Gracious me, really, how so?

AMAL: He had a bamboo staff on his shoulder with a small bundle at the top, and a brass pot in his left hand, and an old pair of shoes on; he was making for those hills straight across that meadow there. I called out to him and asked, "Where are you going?" He answered, "I don't know; anywhere!" I asked again, "Why are you going?" He said, "I'm going out to seek work." Say, Uncle, have you to seek work?

MADHAV: Of course I have to. There are many about looking for jobs.

AMAL: How lovely! I'll go about like them too, finding things to do.

MADHAV: Suppose you seek and don't find. Then—

AMAL: Wouldn't that be jolly? Then I should go farther! I watched that man slowly walking on with his pair of worn-out shoes. And when he got to where the water flows under the fig tree, he stopped and washed his feet in the stream. Then he took out from his bundle some gram flour, moistened it with water and began to eat. Then he tied up his bundle and shouldered it again; tucked up his cloth above his knees and crossed the stream. I've asked Auntie to let me go up to the stream, and eat my gram flour just like him.

MADHAV: And what did your Auntie say to that?

AMAL: Auntie said, "Get well and then I'll take you over there." Please, Uncle, when shall I get well?

MADHAV: It won't be long, dear.

AMAL: Really, but then I shall go right away the moment I'm well again.

MADHAV: And where will you go?

AMAL: Oh, I will walk on, crossing so many streams, wading through water. Everybody will be asleep with their doors shut in the heat of the day and I will tramp on and on seeking work far, very far.

MADHAV: I see! I think you had better be getting well first; then—

AMAL: But then you won't want me to be learned, will you, Uncle?

MADHAV: What would you rather be, then?

AMAL: I can't think of anything just now; but I'll tell you later on.

MADHAV: Very well. But mind you, you aren't to call out and talk to strangers again.

AMAL: But I love to talk to strangers!

MADHAV: Suppose they had kidnaped you?

AMAL: That would have been splendid! But no one ever takes me away. They all want me to stay in here.

MADHAV: I am off to work—but, darling, you won't go out, will you?

AMAL: No, I won't. But, Uncle, you'll let me be in this room by the roadside.

(MADHAV *exits*.)

DAIRYMAN: Curds, curds, good nice curds.

AMAL: Curdseller, I say, Curdseller.

DAIRYMAN: Why do you call me? Will you buy some curds?

AMAL: How can I buy? I have no money.

DAIRYMAN: What a boy! Why call out then? Ugh! What a waste of time!

AMAL: I would go with you if I could.

DAIRYMAN: With me?

AMAL: Yes, I seem to feel homesick when I hear you call from far down the road.

DAIRYMAN (*Lowering his yoke pole*): Whatever are you doing here, my child?

AMAL: The doctor says I'm not to be out, so I sit here all day long.

DAIRYMAN: My poor child, whatever has happened to you?

AMAL: I can't tell. You see, I am not learned, so I don't know what's the matter with me. Say, Dairyman, where do you come from?

DAIRYMAN: From our village.

AMAL: Your village? Is it very far?

DAIRYMAN: Our village lies on the river Shamli at the foot of the Panch-mura hills.

AMAL: Panch-mura hills! Shamli river! I wonder. I may have seen your village. I can't think when, though!

DAIRYMAN: Have you seen it? Been to the foot of those hills?

AMAL: Never. But I seem to remember having seen it. Your village is under some very old big trees, just by the side of the road—isn't that so?

DAIRYMAN: That's right, child.

AMAL: And on the slope of the hill cattle grazing.

DAIRYMAN: How wonderful! Cattle grazing in our village! Indeed there are!

AMAL: And your women with red saris fill their pitchers from the river and carry them on their heads.

DAIRYMAN: Good, that's right! Women from our dairy village do come and draw their water from the river; but then it isn't everyone who has a red sari to put on. But, my dear child, surely you must have been there for a walk some time.

AMAL: Really, Dairyman, never been there at all. But the first day the doctor lets me go out, you are going to take me to your village.

DAIRYMAN: I will, my child, with pleasure.

AMAL: And you'll teach me to cry curds and shoulder the yoke like you and walk the long, long road?

DAIRYMAN: Dear, dear, did you ever? Why should you sell curds? No, you will read big books and be learned.

AMAL: No, I never want to be learned—I'll be like you and take my curds from the village by the red road near the old banyan tree, and I will hawk it from cottage to cottage. Oh, how do you cry— "Curds, curds, fine curds"? Teach me the tune, will you?

DAIRYMAN: Dear, dear, teach you the tune; what a notion!

AMAL: Please do. I love to hear it. I can't tell you how queer I feel when I hear you cry out from the bend of that road, through the line of those trees! Do you know I feel like that when I hear the shrill cry of kites from almost the end of the sky?

DAIRYMAN: Dear child, will you have some curds? Yes, do.

AMAL: But I have no money.

DAIRYMAN: No, no, no, don't talk of money! You'll make me so happy if you take some curds from me.

AMAL: Say, have I kept you too long?

DAIRYMAN: Not a bit; it has been no loss to me at all; you have taught me how to be happy selling curds. (*Exits.*)

AMAL (*Intoning*): Curds, curds, fine curds—from the dairy village—from the country of the Panch-mura hills by the Shamli bank. Curds, good curds; in the early morning the women make the cows stand in a row under the trees and milk them, and in the evening they turn the milk into curds. Curds, good curds. Hello, there's the watchman on his rounds. Watchman, I say, come and have a word with me.

WATCHMAN: What's all this row about? Aren't you afraid of the likes of me?

AMAL: No, why should I be?

WATCHMAN: Suppose I march you off, then?

AMAL: Where will you take me to? Is it very far, right beyond the hills?

WATCHMAN: Suppose I march you straight to the King?

AMAL: To the King! Do, will you? But the doctor won't let me go out. No one can ever take me away. I've got to stay here all day long.

WATCHMAN: The doctor won't let you, poor fellow! So I see! Your face is pale and there are dark rings round your eyes. Your veins stick out from your poor thin hands.

AMAL: Won't you sound the gong, Watchman?

WATCHMAN: The time has not yet come.

AMAL: How curious! Some say the time has not yet come, and some say the time has gone by! But surely your time will come the moment you strike the gong!

WATCHMAN: That's not possible; I strike up the gong only when it is time.

AMAL: Yes, I love to hear your gong. When it is midday and our meal is over, Uncle goes off to his work and Auntie falls asleep reading her Ramayana, and in the courtyard under the shadow of the wall our doggie sleeps with his nose in his curled-up tail; then your gong strikes out, "Dong, dong, dong!" Tell me, why does your gong sound?

WATCHMAN: My gong sounds to tell the people, "Time waits for none, but goes on for ever."

AMAL: Where, to what land?

WATCHMAN: That none knows.

AMAL: Then I suppose no one has ever been there! Oh, I do wish to fly with the time to that land of which no one knows anything.

WATCHMAN: All of us have to get there one day, my child.

AMAL: Have I too?

WATCHMAN: Yes, you too!

AMAL: But the doctor won't let me out.

WATCHMAN: One day the doctor himself may take you there by the hand.

AMAL: He won't; you don't know him. He only keeps me in.

WATCHMAN: One greater than he comes and lets us free.

AMAL: When will this great doctor come for me? I can't stick in here any more.

WATCHMAN: Shouldn't talk like that, my child.

AMAL: No. I am here where they have left me—I never move a bit. But, when your gong goes off, dong, dong, dong, it goes to my heart. Say, Watchman?

WATCHMAN: Yes, my dear.

AMAL: Say, what's going on there in that big house on the other side, where there is a flag flying high up and the people are always going in and out?

WATCHMAN: Oh, there? That's our new Post Office.

AMAL: Post Office? Whose?

WATCHMAN: Whose? Why, the King's, surely!

AMAL: Do letters come from the King to his office here?

WATCHMAN: Of course. One fine day there may be a letter for you in there.

AMAL: A letter for me? But I am only a little boy.

WATCHMAN: The King sends tiny notes to little boys.

AMAL: Oh, how splendid! When shall I have my letter? How do you know he'll write to me?

WATCHMAN: Otherwise why should he set his Post Office here right in front of your open window, with the golden flag flying?

AMAL: But who will fetch me my King's letter when it comes?

WATCHMAN: The King has many postmen. Don't you see them run about with round gilt badges on their chests?

AMAL: Well, where do they go?

WATCHMAN: Oh, from door to door, all through the country.

AMAL: I'll be the King's postman when I grow up.

WATCHMAN: Ha! ha! Postman, indeed! Rain or shine, rich or poor, from house to house delivering letters—that's very great work!

AMAL: That's what I'd like best. What makes you smile so? Oh, yes, your work is great too. When it is silent everywhere in the heat of the noonday, your gong sounds, Dong, dong, dong,—and sometimes when I wake up at night all of a sudden and find our lamp blown out, I can hear through the darkness your gong slowly sounding, Dong, dong, dong!

WATCHMAN: There's the village headman! I must be off. If he catches me gossiping there'll be a great to-do.

AMAL: The headman? Whereabouts is he?

WATCHMAN: Right down the road there; see that huge palm-leaf umbrella hopping along? That's him!

AMAL: I suppose the King's made him our headman here?

WATCHMAN: Made him? Oh, no! A fussy busybody! He knows so many ways of making himself unpleasant that everybody is afraid of him. It's just a game for the likes of him; making trouble for everybody. I must be off now! Mustn't keep work waiting, you know! I'll drop in again tomorrow morning and tell you all the news of the town. (*Exits.*)

AMAL: It would be splendid to have a letter from the King every day. I'll read them at the window. But, oh! I can't read writing. Who'll read them out to me, I wonder! Auntie reads her Ramayana; she may know the King's writing. If no one will, then I must keep them carefully and read them when I'm grown up. But if the postman can't find me? Headman, Mr. Headman, may I have a word with you?

HEADMAN: Who is yelling after me on the highway? Oh, it's you, is it, you wretched monkey?

AMAL: You're the headman. Everybody minds you.

HEADMAN (*Looking pleased*): Yes, oh yes, they do! They must!

AMAL: Do the King's postmen listen to you?

HEADMAN: They've got to. By Jove, I'd like to see—

AMAL: Will you tell the postman it's Amal who sits by the window here?

HEADMAN: What's the good of that?

AMAL: In case there's a letter for me.

HEADMAN: A letter for you! Whoever's going to write you?

AMAL: If the King does.

HEADMAN: Ha! ha! what an uncommon little fellow you are! Ha! ha! the King, indeed; aren't you his bosom friend, eh! You haven't met for a long while and the King is pining for you, I am sure. Wait till tomorrow and you'll have your letter.

AMAL: Say, Headman, why do you speak to me in that tone of voice? Are you cross?

HEADMAN: Upon my word! Cross, indeed! You write to the King! Madhav is a devilish swell nowadays. He's made a little pile; and so kings and padishahs [rulers] are everyday talk with his people. Let me find him once and I'll make him dance. Oh, you—you snipper-snapper! I'll get the King's letter sent to your house—indeed I will!

AMAL: No, no, please don't trouble yourself about it.

HEADMAN: And why not, pray! I'll tell the King about you and he won't be long. One of his footmen will come presently for news of you. Madhav's impudence staggers me. If the King hears of this, that'll take some of his nonsense out of him. (*Exits.*)

AMAL: Who are you walking there? How your anklets tinkle! Do stop a while, won't you?

(*A* GIRL *enters.*)

GIRL: I haven't a moment to spare; it is already late!

AMAL: I see, you don't wish to stop; I don't care to stay on here either.

GIRL: You make me think of some late star of the morning! Whatever's the matter with you?

AMAL: I don't know; the doctor won't let me out.

GIRL: Ah me! Don't go, then! Should listen to the doctor. People will be cross with you if you're naughty. I know, always looking out and watching must make you feel tired. Let me close the window a bit for you.

AMAL: No, don't, only this one's open! All the others are shut. But will you tell me who you are? I don't seem to know you.

GIRL: I am Sudha.

AMAL: What Sudha?

SUDHA: Don't you know? Daughter of the flowerseller here.

AMAL: What do *you* do?

SUDHA: I gather flowers in my basket.

AMAL: Oh, flower-gathering! That is why your feet seem so glad and your anklets jingle so merrily as you walk. Wish I could be out too.

Then I would pick some flowers for you from the very topmost branches right out of sight.

SUDHA: Would you really? Do you know as much about flowers as I?

AMAL: Yes, I *do*, quite as much. I know all about Champa of the fairy tale and his six brothers. If only they let me, I'll go right into the dense forest where you can't find your way. And where the honey-sipping hummingbird rocks himself on the end of the thinnest branch, I will blossom into a *champa*. Would you be my sister *parul*?

SUDHA: You are silly! How can I be sister *parul* when I am Sudha and my mother is Sasi, the flowerseller? I have to weave so many garlands a day. It would be jolly if I could lounge here like you!

AMAL: What would you do then, all the day long?

SUDHA: I could have great times with my doll Benay the bride, and Meni the pussycat, and—but I say, it is getting late and I mustn't stop, or I won't find a single flower.

AMAL: Oh, wait a little longer; I do like it so!

SUDHA: Ah, well—now don't be naughty. Be good and sit still, and on my way back home with the flowers I'll come and talk with you.

AMAL: And you'll let me have a flower, then?

SUDHA: No, how can I? It has to be paid for.

AMAL: I'll pay when I grow up—before I leave to look for work on the other side of that stream.

SUDHA: Very well, then.

AMAL: And you'll come back when you have your flowers?

SUDHA: I will.

AMAL: You will, really?

SUDHA: Yes, I will.

AMAL: You won't forget me? I am Amal, remember that.

SUDHA: I won't forget you, you'll see. (*Exits.*)

(*A* TROOP OF BOYS *enter.*)

AMAL: Say, brothers, where are you all off to? Stop here a little.

A BOY: We're off to play.

AMAL: What will you play at, brothers?

A BOY: We'll play at being plowmen.

ANOTHER BOY (*Showing a stick*): This is our plowshare.

ANOTHER BOY: We two are the pair of oxen.

AMAL: And you're going to play the whole day?

A BOY: Yes, all day long.

AMAL: And you will come home in the evening by the road along the riverbank?

A BOY: Yes.

AMAL: Do you pass our house on your way home?

A BOY: Come out and play with us; yes, do.

AMAL: The doctor won't let me out.

A BOY: The doctor! Do you mean to say you mind what the doctor says? Let's be off; it is getting late.

AMAL: Don't go. Play on the road near this window. I could watch you, then.

A BOY: What can we play at here?

AMAL: With all these toys of mine that are lying about. Here you are; have them. I can't play alone. They are getting dirty and are of no use to me.

BOYS: How jolly! What fine toys! Look, here's a ship. There's old mother Jatai. Isn't this a gorgeous *sepoy?* [1] And you'll let us have them all? You don't really mind?

AMAL: No, not a bit; have them by all means.

A BOY: You don't want them back?

AMAL: Oh, no, I shan't want them.

A BOY: Say, won't you get a scolding for this?

AMAL: No one will scold me. But will you play with them in front of our door for a while every morning? I'll get you new ones when these are old.

A BOY: Oh, yes, we will. I say, put these *sepoys* into a line. We'll play at war; where can we get a musket? Oh, look here, this bit of reed will do nicely. Say, but you're off to sleep already.

AMAL: I'm afraid I'm sleepy. I don't know, I feel like it at times. I have been sitting a long while and I'm tired; my back aches.

A BOY: It's hardly midday now. How is it you're sleepy? Listen! The gong's sounding the first watch.

AMAL: Yes, Dong, dong, dong; it tolls me to sleep.

A BOY: We had better go, then. We'll come in again tomorrow morning.

AMAL: I want to ask you something before you go. You are always out—do you know of the King's postmen?

BOYS: Yes, quite well.

---

[1] A horseman; Amal has given them his toy soldiers. Ed.

AMAL: Who are they? Tell me their names.

A BOY: One's Badal.

ANOTHER BOY: Another's Sarat.

ANOTHER BOY: There's so many of them.

AMAL: Do you think they will know me if there's a letter for me?

A BOY: Surely, if your name's on the letter they will find you out.

AMAL: When you call in tomorrow morning, will you bring one of them along so that he'll know me?

A BOY: Yes, if you like.

ACT II

AMAL *in bed.*

AMAL: Can't I go near the window today, Uncle? Would the doctor mind that too?

MADHAV: Yes, darling; you see you've made yourself worse squatting there day after day.

AMAL: Oh, no. I don't know if it's made me more ill, but I always feel well when I'm there.

MADHAV: No, you don't; you squat there and make friends with the whole lot of people round here, old and young, as if they are holding a fair right under my eaves—flesh and blood won't stand that strain. Just see—your face is quite pale.

AMAL: Uncle, I fear my fakir will pass and not see me by the window.

MADHAV: Your fakir; whoever's that?

AMAL: He comes and chats to me of the many lands where he's been. I love to hear him.

MADHAV: How's that? I don't know of any fakirs.

AMAL: This is about the time he comes in. I beg of you, by your dear feet, ask him in for a moment to talk to me here.

(GAFFER *enters in a fakir's guise.*)

AMAL: There you are. Come here, Fakir, by my bedside.

MADHAV: Upon my word, but this is—

GAFFER (*Winking hard*): I am the Fakir.

MADHAV: It beats my reckoning what you're not.

AMAL: Where have you been this time, Fakir?

GAFFER: To the Isle of Parrots. I am just back.

MADHAV: The Parrots' Isle!

GAFFER: Is it so very astonishing? I am not like you. A journey doesn't cost a thing. I tramp just where I like.

AMAL (*Clapping*): How jolly for you! Remember your promise to take me with you as your follower when I'm well.

GAFFER: Of course, and I'll teach you so many travelers' secrets that nothing in sea or forest or mountain can bar your way.

MADHAV: What's all this rigmarole?

GAFFER: Amal, my dear, I bow to nothing in sea or mountain; but if the doctor joins in with this uncle of yours, then I with all my magic must own myself beaten.

AMAL: No. Uncle won't tell the doctor. And I promise to lie quiet; but the day I am well, off I go with the Fakir, and nothing in sea or mountain or torrent shall stand in my way.

MADHAV: Fie, dear child, don't keep on harping upon going! It makes me so sad to hear you talk so.

AMAL: Tell me, Fakir, what the Parrots' Isle is like.

GAFFER: It's a land of wonders; it's a haunt of birds. No men are there; and they neither speak nor walk, they simply sing and they fly.

AMAL: How glorious! And it's by some sea?

GAFFER: Of course. It's on the sea.

AMAL: And green hills are there?

GAFFER: Indeed, they live among the green hills; and in the time of the sunset when there is a red glow on the hillside, all the birds with their green wings go flocking to their nests.

AMAL: And there are waterfalls!

GAFFER: Dear me, of course; you don't have a hill without its waterfalls. Oh, it's like molten diamonds; and, my dear, what dances they have! Don't they make the pebbles sing as they rush over them to the sea! No devil of a doctor can stop them for a moment. The birds looked upon me as nothing but a man, merely a trifling creature without wings—and they would have nothing to do with me. Were it not so I would build a small cabin for myself among their crowd of nests and pass my days counting the sea waves.

AMAL: How I wish I were a bird! Then—

GAFFER: But that would have been a bit of a job; I hear you've fixed up with the dairyman to be a hawker of curds when you grow up;

I'm afraid such business won't flourish among birds; you might land yourself into serious loss.

MADHAV: Really this is too much. Between you two I shall turn crazy. Now, I'm off.

AMAL: Has the dairyman been, Uncle?

MADHAV: And why shouldn't he? He won't bother his head running errands for your pet fakir, in and out among the nests in his Parrots' Isle. But he has left a jar of curds for you saying that he is busy with his niece's wedding in the village, and has to order a band at Kamlipara.

AMAL: But he is going to marry me to his little niece.

GAFFER: Dear me, we are in a fix now.

AMAL: He said she would be my lovely little bride with a pair of pearl drops in her ears and dressed in a lovely red sari and in the morning she would milk with her own hands the black cow and feed me with warm milk with foam on it from a brand-new earthen cruse; and in the evenings she would carry the lamp round the cow house, and then come and sit by me to tell me tales of Champa and his six brothers.

GAFFER: How charming! It would even tempt me, a hermit! But never mind, dear, about this wedding. Let it be. I tell you that when you marry there'll be no lack of nieces in his household.

MADHAV: Shut up! This is more than I can stand. (*Exits.*)

AMAL: Fakir, now that Uncle's off, just tell me, has the King sent me a letter to the Post Office?

GAFFER: I gather that his letter has already started; it is on the way here.

AMAL: On the way? Where is it? Is it on that road winding through the trees which you can follow to the end of the forest when the sky is quite clear after rain?

GAFFER: That is where it is. You know all about it already.

AMAL: I do, everything.

GAFFER: So I see, but how?

AMAL: I can't say; but it's quite clear to me. I fancy I've seen it often in days long gone by. How long ago I can't tell. Do you know when? I can see it all: there, the King's postman coming down the hillside alone, a lantern in his left hand and on his back a bag of letters; climbing down for ever so long, for days and nights, and where at the foot of the mountain the waterfall becomes a stream he takes to the footpath on the bank and walks on through the rye;

then comes the sugar-cane field and he disappears into the narrow lane cutting through the tall stems of sugar canes; then he reaches the open meadow where the cricket chirps and where there is not a single man to be seen, only the snipe wagging their tails and poking at the mud with their bills. I can feel him coming nearer and nearer and my heart becomes glad.

GAFFER: My eyes are not young; but you make me see all the same.

AMAL: Say, Fakir, do you know the King who has this Post Office?

GAFFER: I do; I go to him for my alms every day.

AMAL: Good! When I get well I must have my alms too from him, mayn't I?

GAFFER: You won't need to ask, my dear; he'll give it to you of his own accord.

AMAL: No, I will go to his gate and cry, "Victory to thee, O King!" and dancing to the tabor's sound, ask for alms. Won't it be nice?

GAFFER: It will be splendid, and if you're with me I shall have my full share. But what will you ask?

AMAL: I shall say, "Make me your postman, that I may go about, lantern in hand, delivering your letters from door to door. Don't let me stay at home all day!"

GAFFER: What is there to be sad for, my child, even were you to stay at home?

AMAL: It isn't sad. When they shut me in here first I felt the day was so long. Since the King's Post Office was put there I like more and more being indoors, and as I think I shall get a letter one day, I feel quite happy and then I don't mind being quiet and alone. I wonder if I shall make out what'll be in the King's letter?

GAFFER: Even if you didn't, wouldn't it be enough if it just bore your name?

(MADHAV *enters.*)

MADHAV: Have you any idea of the trouble you've got me into, between you two?

GAFFER: What's the matter?

MADHAV: I hear you've let it get rumored about that the King has planted his office here to send messages to both of you.

GAFFER: Well, what about it?

MADHAV: Our headman Panchanan has had it told to the King anonymously.

GAFFER: Aren't we aware that everything reaches the King's ears?

MADHAV: Then why don't you look out? Why take the King's name in vain? You'll bring me to ruin if you do.

AMAL: Say, Fakir, will the King be cross?

GAFFER: Cross, nonsense! And with a child like you and a fakir such as I am? Let's see if the King be angry, and then won't I give him a piece of my mind!

AMAL: Say, Fakir, I've been feeling a sort of darkness coming over my eyes since the morning. Everything seems like a dream. I long to be quiet. I don't feel like talking at all. Won't the King's letter come? Suppose this room melts away all on a sudden, suppose—

GAFFER (*Fanning* AMAL): The letter's sure to come today, my boy.

(DOCTOR *enters.*)

DOCTOR: And how do you feel today?

AMAL: Feel awfully well today, Doctor. All pain seems to have left me.

DOCTOR (*Aside to* MADHAV): Don't quite like the look of that smile. Bad sign, his feeling well! Chakradhan has observed—

MADHAV: For goodness' sake, Doctor, leave Chakradhan alone. Tell me what's going to happen?

DOCTOR: Can't hold him in much longer, I fear! I warned you before —this looks like a fresh exposure.

MADHAV: No, I've used the utmost care, never let him out of doors; and the windows have been shut almost all the time.

DOCTOR: There's a peculiar quality in the air today. As I came in I found a fearful draft through your front door. That's most hurtful. Better lock it at once. Would it matter if this kept your visitors off for two or three days? If someone happens to call unexpectedly— there's the back door. You had better shut this window as well, it's letting in the sunset rays only to keep the patient awake.

MADHAV: Amal has shut his eyes. I expect he is sleeping. His face tells me—Oh, Doctor, I bring in a child who is a stranger and love him as my own, and now I suppose I must lose him!

DOCTOR: What's that? There's your headman sailing in!—What a bother! I must be going, brother. You had better stir about and see to the doors being properly fastened. I will send on a strong dose directly I get home. Try it on him—it may save him at last, if he can be saved at all. (MADHAV *and* DOCTOR *exit.*)

(*The* HEADMAN *enters.*)

HEADMAN: Hello, urchin!—

GAFFER (*Rising hastily*): Sh, be quiet.

AMAL: No, Fakir, did you think I was asleep? I wasn't. I can hear everything; yes, and voices far away. I feel that Mother and Father are sitting by my pillow and speaking to me.

(MADHAV *enters.*)

HEADMAN: I say, Madhav, I hear you hobnob with bigwigs nowadays.

MADHAV: Spare me your jokes, Headman; we are but common people.

HEADMAN: But your child here is expecting a letter from the King.

MADHAV: Don't you take any notice of him, a mere foolish boy!

HEADMAN: Indeed, why not! I'll beat the King hard to find a better family! Don't you see why the King plants his new Post Office right before your window? Why, there's a letter for you from the King, urchin.

AMAL (*Starting up*): Indeed, really!

HEADMAN: How can it be false? You're the King's chum. Here's your letter (*showing a blank slip of paper*). Ha, ha, ha! This is the letter.

AMAL: Please don't mock me. Say, Fakir, is it so?

GAFFER: Yes, my dear. I as Fakir tell you it is his letter.

AMAL: How is it I can't see? It all looks so blank to me. What is there in the letter, Mr. Headman?

HEADMAN: The King says, "I am calling on you shortly; you had better have puffed rice for me.—Palace fare is quite tasteless to me now." Ha! ha! ha!

MADHAV (*With folded palms*): I beseech you, Headman, don't you joke about these things—

GAFFER: Joking indeed! He would not dare.

MADHAV: Are you out of your mind too, Gaffer?

GAFFER: Out of my mind; well then, I am; I can read plainly that the King writes he will come himself to see Amal, with the State Physician.

AMAL: Fakir, Fakir, shh, his trumpet! Can't you hear?

HEADMAN: Ha! ha! ha! I fear he won't until he's a bit more off his head.

AMAL: Mr. Headman, I thought you were cross with me and didn't love me. I never could have believed you would fetch me the King's letter. Let me wipe the dust off your feet.

HEADMAN: This little child does have an instinct of reverence. Though a little silly, he has a good heart.

AMAL: It's hard on the fourth watch now, I suppose. Hark, the gong, "Dong, dong, ding—Dong, dong, ding." Is the evening star up? How is it I can't see—

GAFFER: Oh, the windows are all shut; I'll open them.

(*A knocking outside.*)

MADHAV: What's that?—Who is it?—What a bother!

VOICE (*From outside*): Open the door.

MADHAV: Headman—I hope they're not robbers.

HEADMAN: Who's there?—It is Panchanan, the headman, who calls.— Aren't you afraid to make that noise? Fancy! The noise has ceased! Panchanan's voice carries far.—Yes, show me the biggest robbers!—

MADHAV (*Peering out of the window*): No wonder the noise has ceased. They've smashed the outer door.

(*The King's* HERALD *enters.*)

HERALD: Our Sovereign King comes tonight!

HEADMAN: My God!

AMAL: At what hour of the night, Herald?

HERALD: On the second watch.

AMAL: When my friend the watchman will strike his gong from the city gates, "Ding dong ding, ding dong ding"—then?

HERALD: Yes, then. The King sends his greatest physician to attend on his young friend.

(STATE PHYSICIAN *enters.*)

STATE PHYSICIAN: What's this? How close it is here! Open wide all the doors and windows. (*Feeling* AMAL's *body.*) How do you feel, my child?

AMAL: I feel very well, Doctor, very well. All pain is gone. How fresh and open! I can see all the stars now twinkling from the other side of the dark.

PHYSICIAN: Will you feel well enough to leave your bed when the King comes in the middle watches of the night?

AMAL: Of course, I'm dying to be about for ever so long. I'll ask the King to find me the polar star.—I must have seen it often, but I don't know exactly which it is.

PHYSICIAN: He will tell you everything. (*To* MADHAV.) Arrange flowers through the room for the King's visit. (*Indicating the* HEADMAN.) We can't have that person in here.

AMAL: No, let him be, Doctor. He is a friend. It was he who brought me the King's letter.

PHYSICIAN: Very well, my child. He may remain if he is a friend of yours.

MADHAV (*Whispering into* AMAL's *ear*): My child, the King loves you. He is coming himself. Beg for a gift from him. You know our humble circumstances.

AMAL: Don't you worry, Uncle.—I've made up my mind about it.

MADHAV: What is it, my child?

AMAL: I shall ask him to make me one of his postmen that I may wander far and wide, delivering his message from door to door.

MADHAV (*Slapping his forehead*): Alas, is that all?

AMAL: What'll be our offerings to the King, Uncle, when he comes?

HERALD: He has commanded puffed rice.

AMAL: Puffed rice. Say, Headman, you're right. You said so. You knew all we didn't.

HEADMAN: If you would send word to my house I could manage for the King's advent really nice—

PHYSICIAN: No need at all. Now be quiet, all of you. Sleep is coming over him. I'll sit by his pillow; he's dropping asleep. Blow out the oil lamp. Only let the starlight stream in. Hush, he sleeps.

MADHAV (*Addressing* GAFFER): What are you standing there for like a statue, folding your palms?—I am nervous.—Say, are there good omens? Why are they darkening the room? How will starlight help?

GAFFER: Silence, unbeliever!

(SUDHA *enters.*)

SUDHA: Amal!

PHYSICIAN: He's asleep.

SUDHA: I have some flowers for him. Mayn't I give them into his own hand?

PHYSICIAN: Yes, you may.

SUDHA: When will he be awake?

PHYSICIAN: Directly the King comes and calls him.

SUDHA: Will you whisper a word for me in his ear?

PHYSICIAN: What shall I say?

SUDHA: Tell him Sudha has not forgotten him.

The Jar

BY

LUIGI PIRANDELLO
in a translation by William Murray

*L*UIGI PIRANDELLO in an essay attempting to revitalize the Italian stage boasted that his country possessed the first and foremost theatre of the world, greater even than that of Lope de Vega, Shakespeare and Molière. While he did not succeed in making an entirely convincing case in his chauvinistic argument, there can be no doubt that Pirandello himself is Italy's first and foremost playwright of the twentieth century as well as one of the world's finest. He was recognized with the Nobel prize in 1934, and his highly individualistic theatre continues to advance in significance as his plays maintain a major position on the stages of Europe and the United States.

Born on a country estate in southern Sicily, the son of a wealthy sulfur-mine owner, Pirandello (1867–1936) never forgot the customs he observed in a region where violence was commonplace among a primitive people as poor as they were volatile. Many of his short plays dramatize aspects of Sicilian life, and some even were written in the dialect of Sicily. *The Jar,* one of the best of his folk plays, glorifies the comic exuberance of these peasants, but Pirandello knew and understood their darker and more savage side equally well.

Pirandello was educated at home, later at the universities of Palermo, Rome and Bonn, from which he graduated with a doctorate in philosophy in 1891. He returned to Rome prepared to become a professional writer (while still a student he had published two volumes of verse) and in 1893 completed his first novel. His future seemed assured, for even though it was not possible to live by writing alone in Italy at this time, his father was willing to support his literary ambitions, and his early work gained favorable critical attention. At the request of his family, he married a Sicilian girl he did not know, the daughter of another mine owner, and in the next few years they had three children.

Suddenly Pirandello's fortunes turned, as intensely and dramatically as the events in a play. His wife, at first jealous and given to causing embarrassing scenes, became increasingly deranged. When she heard the news that floods had destroyed both family mines and liquidated their income, she suffered a paralysis of the legs that prevented her from moving for six months. Her mental condition worsened steadily, but Pirandello would not allow his wife to be institutionalized and for the next 15 years kept her at home, where he lived an existence not unlike that to be seen in several of his dramas, as he moved in and out of the worlds of reality and insanity. Although he disliked teaching, he was forced to lecture on Italian literature at a girls' school in Rome, but he also continued to write even more feverishly than before—in one year completing as many as nine plays. Signora Pirandello remained in a hospital for the mentally disturbed from 1919 until her death in 1959.

The playwright's reputation spread rapidly outside Italy after the appearance of three of his major plays: *Right You Are* (1917); *Six Characters in Search of an Author* (1921); and *Enrico IV* (1922). To explain further his ideas and to foster interest in his plays, Pirandello traveled to Paris, Berlin, London and New York City. For several years during the 1920s he participated in his own theatre group in Rome, the Teatro D'Arte, which was an artistic success but financial failure.

Fame, however, allowed Pirandello the privilege of retiring from public view in order to pursue a lifelong literary obsession that resulted in volumes of poems, critical essays, short stories, novels, scenarios and 43 plays. In addition to Sicilian folk plays, he wrote symbolic and philosophic dramas often of a nihilistic nature expressing his disillusioned but sympathetic view of mankind's suffering. Perhaps in part the result of his wife's sickness, but also in part his own cerebral questioning, he delved into the modern mind, and just as Strindberg had brought the shape and form of dreams to the stage, so Pirandello brought the image and abstraction of psychosis and schizophrenia. Particularly interested in examining the difference between the appearance of reality and reality itself, he concluded that appearance is reality and that man is foolish to think otherwise. In Pirandello's plays illusion, dreams and fantasy all penetrate the surface of reality by becoming the surface of reality. Yet his theatre is always more than an intellectual playground because his characters are human, passionate and touching; their endurance of life is ironic and immediate, and frequently dressed in a

comic mask that momentarily conceals the tragedy existing underneath.

Pirandello wrote *The Jar* as a short story before dramatizing it as a
folk comedy that was first presented in the Sicilian dialect in Rome in
1917. The color of the countryside is evoked on every page of this
knockabout farce in which a community of olive growers confronts
the problem of mending an expensive but imperfect jar. Pirandello
creates two levels of reality here as he contrasts the everyday life outside the jar with the special world inside, which Uncle Dima at one
point refers to as paradise. However, it is not necessary to view the
jar as a symbol; you will laugh robustly at this delightful bit of buf-
foonery if you merely think of the jar as what it is—the jar.

The Jar

THE CAST

DON LOLÒ ZIRAFA
UNCLE DIMA LICASI, *a tinker*
SCIMÈ, *a lawyer*
FRIEND PÈ, *a farmhand*
TARARÀ
FILLICÒ } *olive shakers*
TANA
TRISUZZA } *olive pickers*
CARMINELLA
A MULE DRIVER
NOCIARELLO, *an eleven-year-old peasant boy*

A Sicilian countryside.

A grassy yard in front of the farmhouse of DON LOLÒ ZIRAFA, *on the crest of a slope. At the left, the front of the rustic one-story house. The door, a slightly faded red, is in the middle and a small balcony hangs directly over it. There are windows above and below, those at ground level with gratings. At right, an ancient olive tree whose gnarled and twisted trunk is encircled by a stone seat. Beyond the tree, the yard is entered by a dirt road. At rear, the tops of other olive trees slope away down the hill. It is October.*

At curtain, FRIEND PÈ *is standing on the stone seat and gazing down the road up which the* WOMEN *come, carrying baskets of olives on their heads or in their arms, and singing a working song of the fields.*

PÈ (*shouting*): Hey, watch what you're doing! You there, snotnose! Take it easy, goddamn it to hell—you're spilling them all over the road!

(*The* WOMEN *and* NOCIARELLO *stop singing and enter up the road.*)

TRISUZZA: So what's eating you, Friend Pè?

TANA: Saints preserve us, where did you learn to swear like that?

CARMINELLA: It won't be long before the trees begin to swear in this place.

PÈ: You expect me to sit here quietly and watch you spill the olives all over the road?

TRISUZZA: What do you mean? I haven't spilled one, not one.

PÈ: If Don Lolò, God help us, had been watching you from the balcony . . .

TANA: So let him watch! Night and day, if he wants to! You do your job right, there's nothing to worry about.

[85]

PÈ: Sure, singing with your nose up in the air like that.

CARMINELLA: What is this? We can't even sing now?

TANA: No, but it's all right to swear. They're having a contest, him and his boss, to see whose mouth is dirtier.

TRISUZZA: Why the good Lord hasn't struck down the place and every tree in it I just don't know!

PÈ: All right, that'll do! Damned cacklers! Go and unload, and stop your bellyaching!

CARMINELLA: You want us to go on picking?

PÈ: What do you think this is, a half-holiday? You still have time for two more trips. Come on, quick now, get going! (*He shoos the* WOMEN *and* NOCIARELLO *around the corner of the house. On their way out, one of them, out of spite, starts to sing again.* PÈ *looks up at the balcony. Calling.*) Don Lolò!

DON LOLÒ (*from within*): What is it?

PÈ: The mules with the manure are here!

(DON LOLÒ *comes storming out of the house. He's a big, angry-looking man of about forty, with the eyes of a suspicious wolf. He has two small gold bands in his ears and wears an old, battered white hat with a broad brim. He is coatless and his coarse checkered shirt is open to reveal a hairy chest; the sleeves are rolled up to the elbow.*)

DON LOLÒ: The mules? At this hour? Where are they? Where'd you send them?

PÈ: They're over there, take it easy. The driver wants to know where to unload them.

DON LOLÒ: Oh, is that so? Unload them before I get a chance to see what he's brought me? Well, I can't right now. I'm talking to my lawyer.

PÈ: Ah, about the jar?

DON LOLÒ: Listen, so who promoted you?

PÈ: I only said—

DON LOLÒ: You just say nothing! Obey and shut up! And where'd you get the idea I was talking to my lawyer about the jar?

PÈ: Because I'm worried—I mean, I'm scared sick—at the idea of leaving the new jar back there in the millhouse. (*Pointing off left.*) Get it out of there, for God's sake!

DON LOLÒ: No! I've told you a hundred times! I want it there and no one's to touch it!

PÈ: It's right by the door, and with all these women and boys coming and going—

DON LOLÒ: By the blood of all the—what are you trying to do, drive me crazy?

PÈ: Just as long as nothing happens to that jar.

DON LOLÒ: I don't want to be bothered until I've finished talking to my lawyer. Where do you want me to put this jar? We can't put it in the storeroom until we take the old barrel out of there, and I haven't time now.

(*The* MULE DRIVER *enters at right.*)

DRIVER: All right now, where do you want me to dump this manure? It'll be dark any moment.

DON LOLÒ: Another one! Sweet Jesus, I hope you break your fool neck, you and all your damn mules! At this hour you show up?

DRIVER: I couldn't come before.

DON LOLÒ: No? Well, I'm not buying any pig in a poke. I want you to pile it up around the fields where and when I tell you to. And now it's too late.

DRIVER: You know what, Don Lolò? I'm going to dump it right where they're standing, behind the wall over there, and then I'm going to clear out of here.

DON LOLÒ: Try it! I'd like to see you try it!

DRIVER: Just watch me! (*He starts out in a rage.*)

PÈ (*holding him back*): Hey now, what a temper!

DON LOLÒ: Let him go, let him go!

DRIVER: He's not the only one around here who can get mad! It's impossible to deal with him! This happens every time!

DON LOLÒ: You want to mess around with me, huh? All right, look! See this? (*He produces a little red book from his pocket.*) Know what that is? Looks like a prayer book, doesn't it? It's the Civil Code, that's what it is! My lawyer gave it to me, the one who's here with me now. And I've learned how to read it. I know what it says in this little book and no one messes around with me any more, not even God the Father! It's all provided for in here, case by case. And besides, I pay my lawyer a nice fat yearly fee!

PÈ: Here he comes now.

(SCIMÈ, *the lawyer, emerges from the house. He wears an old straw hat and holds an open newspaper.*)

SCIMÈ: What's up, Don Lolò?

DON LOLÒ: This clown here shows up with his mules and his load of manure for my fields when it's getting dark, and instead of apologizing—

DRIVER (*interrupting, to the lawyer*): I told him I couldn't come earlier—

DON LOLÒ:—he threatens—

DRIVER: What? I did not!

DON LOLÒ: You did, too! He threatens to dump his load behind my wall—

DRIVER:—because you—

DON LOLÒ: I what? I want you to dump it where I need it, where you're supposed to, in regular piles all the same size.

DRIVER: Go on! Why doesn't he come and tell me, then? There's still two hours of daylight left. It's because he wants to count it and measure it himself, turd by turd. I know him!

DON LOLÒ: Never mind the lawyer! He's here to advise me, not you! Pay no attention to him, Scimè. Take your regular walk down the road over there, sit down under your mulberry tree, and read your paper in peace. We'll finish our discussion about the jar later. (*To the* DRIVER.) Let's go, let's go now. How many mules have you got? (*Starts off with the* DRIVER *at right.*)

DRIVER (*following him*): Didn't you say twelve? So I've got twelve. (*They both disappear behind the house.*)

SCIMÈ (*raising his hands and waving them about in despair*): Out, out, out! First thing in the morning, out of here and home! He's making my head spin like a top!

PÈ: Not a moment's peace for anyone. And that's a fine present you gave him, let me tell you, with that little red book! First, when something happened, he used to shout, "Saddle up the mule!"

SCIMÈ: Yes, so he could gallop into town to see me and fill my head full of hot air like a balloon. That's the reason I gave him that little book, my friend. He digs it out of his pocket, looks it up himself, and leaves me in peace. Still, it must have been the devil himself who inspired me to come and spend a week here! But what could I do? When he found out my doctor told me to spend a few days in the country, he nailed me up on a cross and kept pestering me to accept his hospitality. I told him I'd come only if he promised not to talk to me about anything. For five days now he's been gassing steadily about some jar—I don't know what kind of jar—

PÈ: Yes, sir, the big jar for the olive oil. It arrived only a few days ago from Santo Stefano di Camastra, where they make them. It's a beauty, big around like this and as high as my shoulder—a Mother Superior of a jar! What's up? He wants to sue the maker?

SCIMÈ: That's right. Because, for the price he paid, he says it should have been bigger.

PÈ (astounded): Bigger?

SCIMÈ: That's all he's been talking about for five days. (He starts off down the road at right.) Ah, but tomorrow, good-by, so long, out! (He exits. From somewhere in the distance, beyond the olive grove, the singsong cry of DIMA LICASI can now be heard.)

DIMA (off stage): Cups to mend, plates to mend . . .

(TARARÀ and FILLICÒ enter from the road at right, carrying ladders and poles.)

PÈ (seeing them): Hey, what are you doing? You've stopped already?

FILLICÒ: The boss told us to. He came by with the mules.

PÈ: And he told you to go home?

TARARÀ: Oh, no, not him! He said we should wait around to do some kind of job in the storeroom.

PÈ: To take out the old barrel?

FILLICÒ: That's right. And make room for the new jar.

PÈ: Good! I'm glad he listened to me at least once. Come on, come with me. (They start off at left, but the WOMEN reappear from behind the house, carrying their empty baskets.)

TANA (seeing the two olive shakers): What? Finished shaking them down already?

PÈ: Finished for today, that's all.

TRISUZZA: And what about us? What are we supposed to do?

PÈ: Wait till the boss comes back. He'll tell you.

CARMINELLA: And till then we stand around here and count our fingers?

PÈ: What do you want me to tell you? Go and start sorting out.

TANA: Oh, no, not unless he says so. I'm not taking any chances.

PÈ: Then one of you go and ask him.

(*The* MEN *exit.*)

CARMINELLA: You go, Nociarello.

TANA: Tell him this: the men have stopped shaking the trees and the women want to know what they're supposed to do.

TRISUZZA: Ask him if he wants us to start sorting. Ask him that.

NOCIARELLO: All right.

CARMINELLA: Hurry up, run!

(NOCIARELLO *runs out down the road.* FILLICÒ, TARARÀ, *and* FRIEND PÈ *reappear, one after the other, in a state of alarm, waving their arms about.*)

FILLICÒ: Holy Mother of God, what'll we do now?

TARARÀ: He'll kill us, he'll kill us!

PÈ: God help us, God help us!

WOMEN (*crowding around and all talking at once*): What happened? What is it? What's wrong?

PÈ: The jar! The new jar!

TARARÀ: Broken!

WOMEN (*all together*): The jar? Really? Oh, Holy Mother!

FILLICÒ: Split in half! Like you would with a knife: zing!

TANA: How's that possible?

TRISUZZA: No one touched it!

CARMINELLA: No one! But wait till you hear what Don Lolò has to say!

TRISUZZA: He'll go right off his rocker!

FILLICÒ: I'm not going to stick around to find out!

TARARÀ: What do you mean? You're running away? Stupid! Then he'll never believe we didn't do it! Everyone stay right here! (*Turning to* PÈ.) And you go and call him. No, no, better call him from here. Give a shout.

PÈ (*climbing on the stone seat around the olive tree*): All right, like this, from here. (*Cups his hands around his mouth and calls out several times.*) Don Lolò! Hey, Don Lolò-o-o! He can't hear us. He's shouting like a madman behind those mules. Don Lolò-o-o! It's no good. I'd better run and get him.

TARARÀ: But for God's sake don't give him the idea—

PÈ: Don't worry. How could I blame you? (*He exits on the run down the road.*)

TARARÀ: Now remember, we're all agreed and we all stick together: the jar broke by itself!

TANA: It's happened before—

TRISUZZA: Right! New jars are liable to do that!

FILLICÒ: Because very often—you know how it is—when they bake them in the oven, a spark gets caught and forms a little bubble, then suddenly—wham!—it blows up on you.

CARMINELLA: That's right. Just like a gunshot. (*The voices of* DON LOLÒ *and* FRIEND PÈ *are heard approaching at right.*) God help us now! (*She makes the sign of the Cross.*)

DON LOLÒ (*off stage*): By Christ, I want to know who did it!

PÈ (*off stage*): No one, I swear it!

TRISUZZA: Here he comes!

TANA: God help us!

(DON LOLÒ, *pale with fury, enters, followed by* FRIEND PÈ *and* NOCIARELLO.)

DON LOLÒ (*rushing first at* TARARÀ, *then at* FILLICÒ, *grabbing each of them by the shirt front and shaking them*): Was it you? Who did it? You or you, one of the two of you must have done it and by God you'll pay for it!

TARARÀ *and* FILLICÒ (*simultaneously freeing themselves*): Me? You're crazy! Let go of me! Take your hands off me or I swear to God I'll—

(*During the above exchange, all the others crowd around, shouting in chorus.*)

OTHERS: It broke by itself! It's nobody's fault! We found it broken! I told you over and over!

DON LOLÒ (*still in a fury, addressing first one, then the other of them*): So I'm crazy, eh? Oh, sure, you're all innocent! It broke by itself! I'll make you pay for it, all of you! Now go and get it and bring it here! (*The* MEN *rush out to fetch the jar.*) In the light we'll see if there are any marks on it. And if someone kicked it or pushed it over, I'll eat him alive! You'll pay for it, every damn one of you!

WOMEN (*in chorus*): What? Us? You're out of your mind! Make us pay for it, too? When we haven't even so much as seen it?

DON LOLÒ: You were going in and out of there, all of you!

TRISUZZA: Oh, sure, we broke the jar for you by brushing it like this, with our skirts! (*She takes her skirt in one hand and contemptuously flicks it against his leg. Meanwhile,* FRIEND PÈ, TARARÀ, *and* FILLICÒ *return, carrying the broken jar.*)

TANA: Oh, too bad! Look at that!

DON LOLÒ (*wailing*): My new jar! After what I paid! And where will I store the oil? Oh, my beautiful new jar! The envy, the meanness of it! All that money thrown away! And this such a good year for the olives! Oh, God, what a disaster! What'll I do now?

TARARÀ: No, look—

FILLICÒ: It can be fixed—

PÈ: It's just one piece—

TARARÀ: Just one—

FILLICÒ: A clean break—

TARARÀ: There must have been a crack in it.

DON LOLÒ: What do you mean, there must have been a crack in it? It rang like a bell!

PÈ: He's right. I checked it myself.

FILLICÒ: It'll be as good as new, take my word for it, if you send for a good tinker. You won't even see the mark.

TARARÀ: Call Uncle Dima, Uncle Dima Licasi! He's around here somewhere. I heard him.

TANA: He's the best. He has a marvelous cement. Not even a hammer can dent it, once it takes hold. Hurry, Nociarello, he's around here somewhere! Try Mosca's place.

(NOCIARELLO *exits on the run.*)

DON LOLÒ (*shouting*): Shut up, all of you! I can't hear myself think! I don't believe in miracles! For me, the jar is gone!

PÈ: Ah, I told you, didn't I?

DON LOLÒ (*in a fury again*): What did you tell me, you horse's ass? What did you tell me, if it's true the jar broke by itself, without anyone touching it? Even if we'd stored it in church, it would have broken just the same, if it broke all by itself!

TARARÀ: He's right. Don't waste your breath.

DON LOLÒ: Damn me, what an imbecile!

FILLICÒ: Just a few lire and it'll be all fixed, you'll see. And you know what they say: a broken jug lasts longer than a sound one.

DON LOLÒ: Goddamn it to hell, I've still got the mules on my hands back there! (*To* FRIEND PÈ.) What are you standing around for with your mouth open? Go and keep an eye on them at least! (FRIEND PÈ *exits down the road.*) My head, my head's spinning! To hell with this Uncle Dima! It's the lawyer I have to see! If it broke by itself, it means there was something wrong with it. But it rang, it rang like a bell when it got here! And I was sure it was all right. I even signed for it. All that money thrown away. I can kiss it good-by.

(UNCLE DIMA LICASI, *a hunchback, enters at left, followed by* NOCIARELLO.)

FILLICÒ: Ah, here's Uncle Dima!

TARARÀ (*softly to* DON LOLÒ): Listen, he doesn't say much.

TANA (*almost mysteriously*): A man of very few words.

DON LOLÒ: Is that so? (*To* UNCLE DIMA.) Don't you even say good evening? Where are your manners?

DIMA: You want my manners or my help? Don't waste my time. Tell me what to do and I'll do it.

DON LOLÒ: If words are so precious to you, why don't you save others the trouble, too? Can't you see what you have to do? (*Indicates the jar.*)

FILLICÒ: Mend this big jar, Uncle Dima, with that cement of yours.

DON LOLÒ: They say it works miracles. Make it yourself? (UNCLE DIMA *looks at him sullenly and doesn't answer.*) Hey, answer when I talk to you! And let's have a look at it!

TARARÀ (*softly to* DON LOLÒ): If you approach him like that, you won't get anything out of him.

TANA: He won't let anyone see it.

DON LOLÒ: What the hell is it? (*To* DIMA.) Just tell me if you think you can fix it.

DIMA (*putting his toolbox down and taking out a small bundle wrapped in an old blue handkerchief*): Just like that? Have to look at it first. Need time. (*He sits down on the ground and slowly, very cautiously opens the bundle. Everyone looks at him curiously and attentively.*)

TANA (*softly to* DON LOLÒ): It must be the cement.

DON LOLÒ (*indicating his stomach*): It gets me right here.

(UNCLE DIMA *finally produces from the bundle an old pair of broken eyeglasses held together by bits of string.*)

ALL (*laughing*): Oh, his eyeglasses! God knows what we thought it was! We thought it was the cement! Looks like he sat on them!

(UNCLE DIMA *polishes the lenses very deliberately with a corner of the handkerchief, then sets the glasses on the end of his nose and examines the jar.*)

DIMA: It can be fixed.

DON LOLÒ: Boom! The court has handed down its sentence! But I'm telling you now, I don't trust this marvelous cement of yours. I want rivets. (UNCLE DIMA *turns to look at him; then, without a word, he drops his handkerchief and his glasses angrily into the toolbox, picks it up, and starts out.*) Hey! What are you doing?

DIMA: I'm going.

DON LOLÒ: In a pig's—you're what?

FILLICÒ (*detaining him*): Come on, Uncle Dima, take it easy!

TARARÀ: Do what he says, Uncle Dima!

DON LOLÒ: Who does he think he is, Garibaldi? Miserable damned jackass, I'll tell the world! I have to put oil in it and it'll soak through! Split a mile long and he wants to fix it with cement alone! It needs rivets! Cement *and* rivets! I'm the boss here!

DIMA: All the same! All the same! Ignoramuses! A jug, a bowl, a cup, a plate—rivets! Like an old woman's teeth gnashing at the world, saying: "Look, I'm busted and they fixed me up!" I offer you something good and no one wants it. And I'm never allowed to do a job the way it ought to be done! (*Going up to* DON LOLÒ.) You listen to me. If this jar doesn't ring like a bell with the cement alone—

DON LOLÒ: I said no! And that's all there is to it! (*To* TARARÀ.) And you said he didn't talk! (*To* UNCLE DIMA.) It's no good preaching! Save your breath! If everyone wants rivets, it's because rivets are called for. Their judgment against yours!

DIMA: What judgment? Sheer ignorance!

TANA: It may be ignorance, but it looks to me like you do need rivets, Uncle Dima.

TRISUZZA: Sure, they hold better.

DIMA: But they make holes. Can't you understand? Every stitch is two holes; twenty stitches, forty holes. With the cement alone—

DON LOLÒ: Christ, what a head! Worse than a mule! They make holes, but I want them! I'm the boss here! (*Turning to the* WOMEN.) Come on, come on, let's go. You start sorting. (*To the* MEN.) And the rest of you, come with me. Let's get the barrel out of there. Let's go! (*Shoos them off toward the house.*)

DIMA: Hey, wait a minute!

DON LOLÒ: We'll settle up when you're done. I haven't any time to waste on you.

DIMA: You're leaving me all alone here? I need somebody to help me hold the broken piece in place. It's a big jar.

DON LOLÒ: Oh, well then—(*To* TARARÀ.)—you stay here. (*To* FILLICÒ.) And you come with me. (*He exits with* FILLICÒ. *The* WOMEN *and* NOCIARELLO *have already gone.* UNCLE DIMA *immediately sets to work with bad grace. He takes out his tools and begins to punch holes in the jar and along the edge of the broken fragment.*)

TARARÀ (*chattily*): Thank God he took it as easy as he did! I can't believe it. I thought the world was going to come to an end to-night! Don't take it so hard, Uncle Dima. He wants rivets? Give him rivets. Twenty, thirty of them—(DIMA *looks up at him.*) More? Thirty-five? (DIMA *continues to stare at him.*) How many, then?

DIMA: You see this bit? Every time I use it—ping, ping, ping!—it punches a little hole, right here in my heart!

TARARÀ: Tell me, is it true the formula for your cement came to you in a dream?

DIMA (*working*): In a dream, yes.

TARARÀ: And who appeared to you in the dream?

DIMA: My father.

TARARÀ: Ah, your father! He came to you in the dream and told you how to make it?

DIMA: Blockhead!

TARARÀ: Me? Why?

DIMA: You know who my father is?

TARARÀ: No, who?

DIMA: The devil, and he's going to get you!

TARARÀ: Oh, so you're the son of the devil?

DIMA: And what I've got in there is the pitch you're all going to boil in.

TARARÀ: So it's black, is it?

DIMA: White. It was my father who taught me to make it white. You'll find out how strong it is when you're boiling in it. But down there it's black. Stick it on your fingers and you'll never get them apart again. And if I glue your lip to your nose, you'll look like a Ubangi for the rest of your life.

TARARÀ: Then how come you can touch it and nothing happens?

DIMA: Idiot! Does a dog bite its own master? (*Drops his tools and gets up.*) Come here now. (*Makes him hold the broken piece.*) Hold this. (*From his box he takes out a smaller one of tin, opens it, scoops out some of the cement on his fingers and displays it.*) See? Looks like any other cement, eh? Watch. (*He spreads the cement first along the broken edge of the jar, then along the detached fragment itself.*) Three or four good smears like this—just enough. . . . Hold it in place. Now I'll get inside.

TARARÀ: Inside the jar?

DIMA: Of course, jackass. If I have to use rivets, I have to stitch them from the inside. Wait. (*Rummages in his box.*) Wire and pliers. (*Takes what he needs and climbs inside the jar.*) Now you—wait till I get set in here—set the piece carefully in place, so it fits just right—easy—good—like that. (TARARÀ *carries out* DIMA's *orders and so encloses him in the jar. Shortly after,* DIMA's *head emerges from the mouth of the jar.*) Now pull, pull! No rivets yet. Pull as hard as you can. See? You can't pull it away, can you? Ten pairs of oxen couldn't pull it away now. Go, go tell your boss!

TARARÀ: Excuse me, Uncle Dima, but are you sure you can get out of there now?

DIMA: Why not? I always have out of all the other jars.

TARARÀ: But this one—I don't know—the neck looks a little narrow for you. Try it.

(FRIEND PÈ *returns up the road.*)

PÈ: What's the matter? Can't he get out?

TARARÀ (*To* DIMA, *inside the jar*): Easy now. Wait. That side.

PÈ: Your arm, get one arm out first.

TARARÀ: His arm? What do you mean?

DIMA: Now what the hell! I'm stuck in here?

PÈ: So big around in the middle and so narrow up top.

TARARÀ: What a laugh, if he can't get out now that he's fixed it! (*Laughs.*)

DIMA: What's so funny? Goddamn it, give me a hand! (*Bouncing furiously up and down in the jar.*)

PÈ: Wait! Don't do that! Let's see if by tilting it—

DIMA: No, that's worse! Stop it! It's too tight in the shoulders.

TARARÀ: Of course. You've got a little hump on one of them.

DIMA: Me? You said yourself the jar was too small!

PÈ: Well, now what?

TARARÀ: If this isn't something to write home about! (*Laughs and runs toward the house, calling.*) Fillicò! Tana! Trisuzza! Carminella! Come here, come here! Uncle Dima's stuck in the jar!

(FILLICÒ, TANA, TRISUZZA, CARMINELLA, *and* NOCIARELLO *enter at right.*)

ALL (*in chorus, laughing, skipping, clapping their hands*): Stuck in the jar? Great! How'd it happen? Can't he get out?

DIMA (*simultaneously, snarling like an animal*): Get me out! Give me my hammer! It's in the box!

PÈ: Your hammer? You're crazy! I have to tell the boss first!

FILLICÒ: Here he comes, here he comes!

(DON LOLÒ *enters on the run.*)

WOMEN (*running to meet him*): He's walled himself up in the jar! By himself! He can't get out!

DON LOLÒ: In the jar?

DIMA (*simultaneously*): Help! Help!

DON LOLÒ: How can I help you, you old imbecile, if you forgot to measure your hump before getting in?

(*All laugh.*)

TANA: Look what happens to him, poor old Uncle Dima!

FILLICÒ: Funniest damn thing I ever saw!

DON LOLÒ: Wait. Easy now. Try to get one arm out.

PÈ: It's no good. We tried everything.

DIMA (*who has with difficulty managed to get one arm out*): Ouch! Easy! You're dislocating it!

DON LOLÒ: Patience! Try to—

DIMA: No! Let go of me!

DON LOLÒ: What do you want us to do then?

DIMA: Take my hammer and break the jar!

DON LOLÒ: What? Now that it's fixed?

DIMA: You don't think you're going to keep me in here, do you?

DON LOLÒ: First we have to see what can be done.

DIMA: What's there to see? I want to get out! I want to get out, damn it!

WOMEN (*in chorus*): He's right! You can't keep him in there! If there's no other way!

DON LOLÒ: My head! My head! Shut up, all of you! This is something new! Nothing like this has ever happened before! (*To* NOCIARELLO.) Come here, boy. No, you, Fillicò. (*Points down the road.*) The lawyer's down there, under his tree. Tell him to come here right away. . . . (*As* FILLICÒ *leaves, turning to* UNCLE DIMA, *who is bouncing about in the jar.*) Stand still, you! (*To the others.*) Hold him still! That's no jar! It's the devil himself! (*To* DIMA *again, who continues to writhe about.*) Hold still, I said!

DIMA: Either you break it or I'll smash it up against a tree! I want to get out! I want to get out of here!

DON LOLÒ: Wait till the lawyer comes. He'll solve the case. Meanwhile I'm going to protect my jar and begin by doing my duty. (*Takes a big, old leather wallet out of his pocket and produces a ten-lire note.*) You're all witnesses! Ten lire for the work done on the jar!

DIMA: Keep your money! I don't want it! I want to get out!

DON LOLÒ: You'll get out when the lawyer says you can. Meanwhile I'm paying you. (*He drops the money into the jar.* SCIMÈ, *laughing, enters, followed by* FILLICÒ.)

DON LOLÒ (*seeing him*): What's so funny? It's no skin off your nose! The jar is mine!

SCIMÈ (*unable to stop laughing any more than the rest of them*): What do you think—think you're do—doing? Keep—keep him— him in there? Keep him in there so you—ah ha ha!—so you won't lose the jar?

DON LOLÒ: So you think it's up to me to pay, huh?

SCIMÈ: You know what this is? Kidnapping, that's what!

DON LOLÒ: Kidnapping? Who kidnapped him? He did it himself! Is that my fault? (*To* UNCLE DIMA.) Who's keeping you in there? Get out!

DIMA: You get me out, if you think you can!

DON LOLÒ: Why should I? I didn't put you in! You did it all by yourself! Now come out of there!

SCIMÈ: Ladies and gentlemen, please! May I say something?

TARARÀ: Speak up! Let the lawyer speak! Quiet!

SCIMÈ: There are two aspects to this case. I want you to listen carefully and come to an agreement. (*Turning first to* DON LOLÒ.) On the one hand, you, Don Lolò, must immediately set Uncle Dima free.

DON LOLÒ (*quickly*): How? By breaking the jar?

SCIMÈ: Wait. Then there's the other aspect. Let me finish. But you must realize you can't hold him. That's kidnapping. (*Turning now to* UNCLE DIMA.) On the other hand, you, Uncle Dima, have to answer for the damage you've caused by getting into the jar without first making sure you could get out of it.

DIMA: I didn't make sure, Mr. Scimè, because during all the years I've been at this job I've fixed hundreds of jars, and every one of them from the inside, to put the rivets in the way you're supposed to. Not once have I ever been unable to get out. So it's up to him to go and see the man who made this jar with such a narrow damn neck! It's not *my* fault.

DON LOLÒ: And what about your hump? I suppose the man who made the jar stuck it there so you wouldn't be able to get out! If we try and sue, Scimè, and he shows up in court with that hump of his, the judge will laugh himself sick! I'll have to pay all the expenses and that's that!

DIMA: No, that's not true! Because hump or no hump, I never had any trouble getting in and out of all those other jars! Just like walking in and out of my own house it was!

SCIMÈ: I'm sorry, Uncle Dima, but that's not good enough. It was up to you to make sure you could get out before going in.

DON LOLÒ: So he has to pay for the jar, right?

DIMA: What?

SCIMÈ: Easy, easy. Pay the price of the jar as new?

DON LOLÒ: Certainly. Why not?

SCIMÈ: Because it was already broken, for God's sake!

DIMA: And I fixed it for him!

DON LOLÒ: You fixed it? So then it's as good as new. Not broken. Now if I break it so you can get out, I won't be able to have it fixed again and I'll have lost the jar for good. Right, Scimè?

SCIMÈ: That's why I said Uncle Dima would have to pay his share! Now let me handle this!

DON LOLÒ: Go on, go on.

SCIMÈ: My dear Uncle Dima, one of two things: either your cement is good for something or it isn't.

DON LOLÒ (*in ecstasy, to the others*): Listen, now you're going to hear something! The trap is closing! When he starts off like this . . .

SCIMÈ: If your cement is no good, then you're just an ordinary crook. If it is good, then the jar, just as it is, has to be worth something. What is it worth? You tell me. Give us an estimate.

DIMA: With me in it?

(*All laugh.*)

SCIMÈ: No jokes now! Just as it is.

DIMA: I'll tell you. If Don Lolò had let me fix the jar with cement only, as I wanted to do, then I wouldn't be in here in the first place, because I would have been able to fix it from the outside. So then the jar would have been as good as new and worth just as much as before, no more, no less. Patched up as it is now and full of holes like a sieve, what can it be worth? Maybe a third of what he paid for it.

DON LOLÒ: A third?

SCIMÈ (*quickly to* DON LOLÒ, *signaling him to be silent*): A third! Quiet! A third—meaning?

DON LOLÒ: I paid four big bills for it, so that makes one and a third.

DIMA: Maybe less, certainly not more,

SCIMÈ: I'll take your word for it. Pay it to Don Lolò.

DIMA: Who? Me? Pay him?

SCIMÈ: So he'll break the jar and let you out. You'll pay him exactly what you yourself estimated it was worth.

DON LOLÒ: In cash.

DIMA: Me pay him? You're crazy! I'll let the worms eat me first. Hey, Tararà, get my pipe, from the box over there.

TARARÀ (*doing so*): This one?

DIMA: Thanks. Give me a light. (TARARÀ *strikes a match and lights*

DIMA's *pipe.*) Thanks. And I kiss your hands, all of you. (*Puffing on his pipe, he disappears into the jar, amid general laughter.*)

DON LOLÒ (*dumbfounded*): Now what do we do? Suppose he won't come out?

SCIMÈ (*scratching his head and smiling*): Well, that's true. As long as he wanted to come out, we could deal. But if he doesn't . . .

DON LOLÒ (*going up to the jar and addressing* UNCLE DIMA): Hey, what are you going to do? Live in there?

DIMA (*sticking his head out*): I like it in here. It's nice and cool. Paradise, in fact. (*He disappears again. Puffs of pipe smoke drift up out of the jar.*)

DON LOLÒ (*furiously, as all laugh*): Stop laughing, by God! And you're all witnesses that he won't come out now, so he won't have to pay me what he owes me, while for my part I'm ready to break the jar! (*To the lawyer.*) Couldn't I sue him for squatting on my property?

SCIMÈ (*laughing*): Sure, why not? Get yourself an eviction notice.

DON LOLÒ: But he's keeping me from using the jar.

DIMA (*sticking his head out again*): You're wrong. I'm not here because I want to be. Let me out and I'll go, dancing and singing. But as for making me pay, forget it. I'll stay here forever.

DON LOLÒ (*grabbing the jar and shaking it furiously*): Oh, you will, will you! You will, eh!

DIMA: What a cement! No rivets in there, you know.

DON LOLÒ: Crook! Swindler! Villain! Who's responsible for this, you or me? And you expect me to pay for it?

SCIMÈ (*pulling him away*): Don't do that. You only make it worse. Let him spend the night in there and tomorrow morning, you'll see, he'll beg to be let out. (*To DIMA.*) All right, you—pay up or else! (*To DON LOLÒ.*) Let's go now. Forget about him. (*He and DON LOLÒ start toward the house.*)

DIMA: Hey, Don Lolò!

SCIMÈ (*To DON LOLÒ as they walk away*): Pay no attention. Come on.

DIMA (*before they exit into the house*): Good night, Mr. Scimè. I've got my ten lire right here! (*As soon as they've gone, turning to the others.*) Now we'll have a party, all of us! My housewarming party! Tararà, run to Mosca's and buy wine, bread, fried fish, and salted peppers! We're going to celebrate!

ALL (*clapping their hands as* TARARÀ *runs off*): Hurray for Uncle Dima! Hurray for Uncle Dima! A party!

FILLICÒ: And a full moon to boot! Look! There it is! (*Points off left.*)
   Like daylight!

DIMA: I want to see! I want to see! Carry me over there, but take it
   easy. (*They all help roll the jar slowly toward the road.*) That's it
   —easy—like that. Ah, what a beauty! I see it, I see it! Like the sun?
   Who'll sing us a song?

TANA: You, Trisuzza!

TRISUZZA: Not me! Carminella!

DIMA: We'll all sing! Fillicò, play your harmonica, and the rest of
   you, a song. All together now, a nice song, while you dance around
   the jar!

   (FILLICÒ *produces his harmonica and begins to play. The others,
   singing and shouting, hold hands and dance wildly around the
   jar, egged on by* UNCLE DIMA. *After a few moments, the door of
   the house is flung open and* DON LOLÒ *rushes out, screaming.*)

DON LOLÒ: Goddamn it to hell, where do you think you are, in a
   tavern? Here, you old devil, go and break your fool neck! (*He
   delivers a tremendous kick on the jar, which topples over and rolls
   away down the slope. Screams, shouts. Then the noise of the jar
   smashing into a tree.*)

TANA (*with a scream*): Ah, he's killed him!

FILLICÒ: No! There he is! He's out! He's getting up! He's all right!

   (*The* WOMEN *all clap their hands gaily.*)

ALL: Hurray for Uncle Dima! Hurray for Uncle Dima! (*They lift him
   to their shoulders and carry him off across the stage in triumph.*)

DIMA (*waving his arms*): I win! I win!

He Who Says Yes

AND

He Who Says No

BY

BERTOLT BRECHT

in a new translation by Gerhard Nellhaus

THE PLAYS of Bertolt Brecht deal with social conflicts of modern man, many of which he experienced himself in his tormented quest to create a new theatre for a new society. His was a life dominated by war, revolution, exile, protest, anger and despair, all of which coalesced to make his writing a propelling force that succeeds in its aim to unsettle and challenge the minds of viewers. Perhaps more than any other dramatist of this century, Brecht was able to create a theatre that in style and content was his own, stamped with an unmistakable trademark among the most contemporary in modern drama.

Born in 1898 in Augsburg, Germany, where his father managed a paper factory, Brecht early developed a talent for writing nationalistic poems and when sixteen years old wrote his first play. Intending to become a doctor, he studied medicine at the University of Munich until he was inducted into the army in 1918 as a medical orderly. This experience, dealing with the sick and wounded in the final days of the war, strengthened his strong pacifist views and provided nightmare impressions that were to reappear in subsequent plays and poems. After the war, he participated in the unsuccessful political upheaval in his native Bavaria and wrote his first important plays, *Baal* and *Drums in the Night,* both of which reflect a disgust for a war and a revolution that did nothing to improve or even change society. His early plays gained recognition in Munich, but he settled in Berlin in 1924 and married the actress Helene Weigel, who was to create a number of leading roles in his plays. The success of *The Threepenny Opera,* which he had written with Kurt Weill, brought Brecht fame and the security to develop his theories of "epic theatre." His plays of the late 1920s often mirrored a growing Marxist persuasion although he could not join the Communist party at this time inasmuch as *avant-garde* artists were held in disfavor. Nor was Hitler's Germany the place to be for so outspoken a social and political critic, and the day after the Reichstag was burned in 1933, Brecht fled to

Denmark. During the next fifteen years, the Brecht family moved precariously about the world, first through Scandinavia, always just ahead of the Nazi invaders, then on through Russia, and finally to the United States in the early 1940s, when they settled uneasily in California. These years of flight enabled Brecht to write his major plays, most of which went unproduced for many years. *The Private Life of the Master Race, Mother Courage and Her Children, Galileo, The Good Woman of Setzuan* and *The Caucasian Chalk Circle* all date from this period. The playwright arranged for only one production of a play while he was in the United States and that was a failure. After being examined in Washington, D.C. by the Committee on Un-American Activities in 1946, he left for Europe where the government of East Berlin provided him with a theatre in which his troupe founded one of the outstanding acting companies of this century, the famous Berliner Ensemble. Hereafter, he was able to show the world how he intended his own plays to be performed. Firmly established in a Communist stronghold, Brecht nevertheless appeared politically discontent and was often the center of controversy among party leaders. However, after his death in 1956, Walter Ulbricht allowed his widow to continue operating the Berliner Ensemble, which in recent years has held no exclusive claim to Brecht's repertory as theatres throughout the West have produced his major plays and many of his minor pieces. Broadway, so long unwilling to accept Brecht, saw a number of his plays in the 1960s, and several more have been produced off-Broadway with considerable success.

The concept of "epic theatre" developed by Brecht called for a series of episodes or scenes, each of which was to make a statement or to contribute a point of view to the total presentation. Throughout the play the spectator was to be reminded that he was just that— a spectator experiencing theatrical subterfuge of every variety. This might take the form of printed signs spelling out the dramatist's message, a ballad sung directly to the audience, loud noises, bright white lights (sometimes aimed directly into the eyes of the audience), or mirrors angled to reveal the audience watching themselves. Because Brecht wanted his dramas to teach as well as to entertain, he felt a play should not allow the audience empathetic involvement with characters but instead should make them concerned with themes, messages, yes, even lessons. He called his didactic techniques the "alienation effect." By this he meant a kind of intellectual distancing that outlawed emotional attachment and substituted strong theatrical bombardment to reinforce the ideas of the play. To Brecht "ideology" was the play's most significant component.

Yet, in spite of the author's purpose to move the mind of the beholder and not the heart, his plays often do both, and, no matter how many alienation effects are employed, the characters win the affection or admiration of the audience. Certainly this is true of the boy hero of the following plays; the audience cannot help but be touched by his loyalty in the first text and by his determination in the second.

When Brecht and Kurt Weill collaborated on *He Who Says Yes* in 1930, they already had produced their famous *The Threepenny Opera* (1928) and *The Rise and Fall of the City of Mahagonny* (also 1930). Now they wished to create what they called a "school opera," a work of genuine musical stature that could be sung by students who were expected to design costumes and scenery in addition to playing all the instruments in the orchestra. Weill believed that the performance of opera could be an educational undertaking that also would provide training for future singers and develop tastes for new forms of musical theatre. The experiment succeeded brilliantly and *He Who Says Yes* was performed by professionals as well as by students throughout Germany until it was suppressed by the Nazis, who feared that its fable contained critical political implications. But the genre of school opera and opera for children has been carried forward by other notable examples such as Paul Hindemith's *We Build a City* (1930), Benjamin Britten's *Let's Make an Opera* (1949), and Gian-carlo Menotti's *Amahl and the Night Visitors* (1951), the text of which is included in this volume.

He Who Says Yes relates the story of a boy who joins his teacher on a long journey over high mountains in order to secure medicine for his dying mother and other victims of an epidemic. When he falls ill along the way, his classmates remember an age-old custom that allows travelers to abandon anyone who slows their progress. The boy consents to tradition but asks that, rather than to be left to die alone, he be thrown into the abyss. As this powerful work ends, the students hurl the boy into the valley and proceed on their way toward the needed medicine. Kurt Weill's music, which may be heard on the Heliodor recording, supports the tragic tension and builds steadily to the stark and haunting conclusion.

Boys producing the opera at the Karl Marx School in Berlin saw no reason why the hero had to consent to his death. Why, they asked Brecht and Weill, could not a new custom replace the old one which would permit the boy to live? Brecht agreed to write the opposite point of view but, in so doing, made several significant changes. In *He Who Says No* the epidemic has been removed and the mother no longer is desperately ill; here the expedition is merely a research trip. Under these circumstances, as the translator Gerhard Nellhaus has pointed out, there is no "necessity" for the boy's death, and he can say "no." His answer contains the idea governing these parables when he cries out for society to discard its exhausted traditions: "I need a great new custom, one we must introduce here and now: the custom to give each new situation new thought." The urgency and strength of this impassioned lesson scarcely can be more pertinent than to the youth of our times.

Brecht retained the theatrical form of *Taniko,* the Japanese Noh play, on which the operas are closely patterned. The chorus is seated on either side of the stage, where they observe and comment upon the action taking place on central platforms and levels that represent the two rooms mentioned in the text, as well as the mountain road and abyss. The staging is highly symbolic, not realistic. The death of the boy is best enacted in simple pantomime and dance, without melodramatics.

Dr. Nellhaus has prepared new translations of both plays, which are printed here for the first time. Readers seeking information about the playwright and this theatre should examine *Brecht: The Man and His Work* by Martin Esslin.

He Who Says Yes

AND

He Who Says No

CHARACTERS

THE TEACHER
THE BOY
THE MOTHER
THE THREE STUDENTS
THE GREAT CHORUS

SCENE

Japan—many years ago.
(See the preceding headnote for a description
of the setting and style required for the
presentation of these plays.)

He Who Says Yes

I

GREAT CHORUS:

    Above all learn when to say Yes.[1]
    Many say Yes without understanding.
    Many are not asked, and many
    Say Yes to falsehoods.[2] Therefore:
    Above all learn when to say Yes.[1]

(*The* TEACHER *is now in Room 1, the* MOTHER *and* BOY *in Room 2.*)

TEACHER: I am the teacher. I teach school in the city and I have a student whose father is dead. He has only his mother to take care of him. I've come to say goodbye to them now because I am about to start on a trip over the mountains. An epidemic has broken out among us, and in the city beyond the mountains live some famous doctors. (*He knocks at the door.*) May I come in?

BOY (*Stepping from Room 2 into Room 1*): Who is it? Oh, the teacher; teacher's come to visit us!

TEACHER: Why haven't you been to school for so long?

BOY: I couldn't come because Mother was sick.

TEACHER: I didn't know that your mother, too, was ill. Please tell her I'm here.

BOY (*Calling into Room 2*): Mother, Teacher is here.

MOTHER (*Sitting in Room 2*): Ask him to come in, please.

BOY: Please come in.

(*They enter Room 2.*)

[1] Or: Above all, seek understanding. G.N.
[2] Or: Many reach an understanding with falsehoods. G.N.

TEACHER: I haven't been here for a long time. Your son tells me that you, too, have caught the sickness. Are you feeling any better now?

MOTHER: No, unfortunately I'm not getting any better; nobody here knows how to treat this disease.

TEACHER: A way must be found. That's why I came to say goodbye: tomorrow I'm starting out on a trip over the mountains to get medicine and advice. For in the city beyond the mountains live the famous doctors.

MOTHER: A relief expedition over the mountains! Yes, indeed, I've heard that the famous doctors live there, but I've also heard that the trip is dangerous. Were you thinking of taking my boy with you?

TEACHER: That's no trip for a child!

MOTHER: I agree. I hope you will return safely.

TEACHER: I have to go now. Goodbye. Get well. (TEACHER *goes to Room 1*.)

BOY (*Follows the* TEACHER *into Room 1*): I want to say something.

(MOTHER *listens at the door*.)

TEACHER: What do you want to say?

BOY: I want to go over the mountains with you.

TEACHER:

>As I've already told your mother
>The trip is hard and dangerous.
>You won't be able to come along. Besides:
>How can you want to leave your mother
>When she is so ill?
>Stay here. It's really impossible
>For you to come along.

BOY:

>Just because Mother is sick, I want
>To come with you.
>I must get her
>Medicine and advice
>From the famous doctors in the city beyond the mountains.

TEACHER: I must talk this over with your mother. (*He returns to Room 2.* BOY *listens at the door*.) As you see, I've come back. Your son has asked to come with us. I told him he couldn't leave you

while you are ill; and also that it is a hard and dangerous trip. It
was out of the question for him to come along, I said. But he said
he had to come with us to the city beyond the mountains to get
medicine and advice for you.

MOTHER: I heard what he said. I know the boy means well and would
like to make the dangerous trip with you. Come in, Son. (*The* BOY
enters Room 2.)

> Ever since
> Your father left us
> I've had no one
> But you at my side.
> You were never longer
> Out of my mind and out of my sight
> Than it took
> To prepare your meals
> To fix your clothes and
> To earn a living.

BOY: What you say is true. But still you can't get me to change my
mind.

BOY, MOTHER, TEACHER:

> I am (he is) going to make the dangerous trip
> To get for your (my, her) illness
> Medicine and advice
> In the city beyond the mountains.

GREAT CHORUS:

> You saw that no argument
> Could move him.
> Then the teacher and the mother said
> In one voice:

TEACHER *and* MOTHER:

> Many say Yes to falsehoods [3]
> But he says Yes not to illness
> But that illness be healed.

GREAT CHORUS: Now the Mother said:

MOTHER:

> I have no more strength.
> If it has to be

---

[3] Or: Many reach an understanding with falsehoods. G.N.

Go with the teacher.
But hurry, hurry,
Return to me soon.

II

GREAT CHORUS:

The people have started
On the trip over the mountains
Among them the teacher
And the boy.
The boy was not equal to the strain:
He overworked his heart
In their hurry to return.
At dawn at the foot of the mountains
He could hardly
Drag himself on.

(*Into Room 1 enters the* TEACHER, *the* THREE STUDENTS *and finally the* BOY *with a jug.*)

TEACHER: We climbed rapidly. There is the first hut. Let's rest there a while.
THREE STUDENTS: We'll do that.

(*They step on the raised platform in Room 2. The* BOY *holds the* TEACHER *back.*)

BOY: I want to say something.
TEACHER: What do you want to say?
BOY: I don't feel well.
TEACHER: Not another word. Whoever undertakes a trip such as this must not say such things. Perhaps you're just tired, not being used to climbing. Stop and rest a while. (*He steps on the platform.*)
THREE STUDENTS: It seems that the boy is tired from climbing. Let's ask the teacher.
GREAT CHORUS: Yes, do.
THREE STUDENTS (*To the* TEACHER): We hear that the boy is tired from

climbing. What's the matter with him? Are you worried about him?

TEACHER: He said he didn't feel well, but he really is all right. He is tired from climbing.

THREE STUDENTS: Then you aren't worried about him? (*Long pause, then the* STUDENTS *among one another.*)

Do you hear? The teacher said
The boy is only tired from climbing.
But doesn't he look strange?
Right after the hut comes the narrow pass.
Only clutching the cliff
With both hands
Can you pass.
Let's hope he's not sick.
For if he cannot go on, we must
Leave him here.

(*They call down to Room 1, forming a megaphone with their hands*): Are you sick?—He doesn't answer.—Let's ask the teacher again. (*To the* TEACHER.) When we asked you before about the boy you said he was only tired from climbing, but now he looks so strange. He even sat down.

TEACHER: I see that he has fallen ill. Try to carry him over the narrow pass.

THREE STUDENTS: We'll try. (*The* THREE STUDENTS *try to carry the boy over the narrow pass. This must be constructed so that the* THREE STUDENTS *can pass, one by one, but not carrying the* BOY.) We can't carry him over and we can't stay with him. In any event, we must move on, for a whole city is waiting for the medicine we are to bring back. We say it with dread but if he cannot go on we will have to leave him here in the mountains.

TEACHER: Yes, maybe you'll have to. How can I oppose you? But I think it only right that we should ask the sick boy if we should turn around for his sake. I feel a deep sorrow for this human being. I'll go and break his fate to him gently.

THREE STUDENTS: Please do. (*They face each other.*)

THREE STUDENTS *and* GREAT CHORUS:

We'll ask him (They asked him) whether he demands (demanded)
That we (they) turn around now for his sake.
But even if he demands (demanded) it,

We will (they would) not turn back,
But leave him here and go on.

TEACHER (*Has gone to the* BOY *in Room 1*): Listen closely. Since you are sick and cannot go on we must leave you here. But it is only right to ask the one who is sick if we should turn around for his sake. But custom demands also that the sick person answer: You shall not turn back.

BOY: I understand.

TEACHER: Do you demand that we turn back for your sake?

BOY: No, you shall not turn back!

TEACHER: Then you agree to stay behind?

BOY: I must think this over. (*Pause of reflection.*) Yes, I agree.

TEACHER (*Calls from Room 1 into Room 2*): He answered as necessity demanded.

GREAT CHORUS *and* THREE STUDENTS (*The latter are going down to Room 1*): He said yes. Go on! (THREE STUDENTS *stand still.*)

TEACHER:

> Go on now, don't stop.
> For you've decided to move on.

(*The* THREE STUDENTS *stand still.*)

BOY: I want to say something: I ask you not to let me lie here but to throw me into the valley, for I'm afraid to die alone.

THREE STUDENTS: We cannot do that.

BOY: Why not? I demand it.

TEACHER:

> You have decided to move on and to leave him here.
> It is easy to decide his fate
> But hard to carry it out.
> Are you ready to throw him into the valley?

THREE STUDENTS: Yes. (*The* THREE STUDENTS *carry the* BOY *to the platform in Room 2.*)

> Lean your head on our arms.
> Don't strain yourself
> We'll carry you carefully.

(*The* THREE STUDENTS *stand in front of the* BOY, *hiding him, on the furthest edge of the platform.*)

BOY (*Not visible*):

> I knew that on this trip
> I might lose my life.
> The thought of my mother
> Tempted me to go.
> Take my jug
> Fill it with the medicine
> And on your return
> Give it to my mother.

GREAT CHORUS:

> Then the friends took the jug
> And bewailed the hard ways of the world
> And its bitter necessities,
> And threw the boy down.
> Shoulder on shoulder they pressed together
> At the edge of the abyss
> And closing their eyes they hurled him down,
> No one guiltier than his neighbor.
> And they threw clumps of earth
> And flat stones
> After him.

He Who Says No

I

GREAT CHORUS:

> Above all learn when to say Yes [1]
> Many say Yes without understanding.
> Many are not asked, and many
> Say Yes to falsehoods.[2] Therefore:
> Above all learn when to say Yes.[1]

(*The* TEACHER *is now in Room 1, the* MOTHER *and the* BOY *in Room 2.*)

TEACHER: I am the teacher. I teach school in the city and I have a student whose father is dead. He has only his mother to take care of him. I've come to say goodbye to them now, because I'm about to start a trip over the mountains. (*He knocks at the door.*) May I come in?

BOY (*Stepping from Room 2 into Room 1*): Who is it? Oh, the teacher; the teacher's come to visit us!

TEACHER: Why haven't you been to school for so long?

BOY: I couldn't come because Mother was sick.

TEACHER: I didn't know that. Please tell her I am here.

BOY (*Calling into Room 2*): Mother, Teacher is here.

MOTHER (*Sitting in Room 2*): Ask him to come in please.

BOY: Please come in.

(*They enter Room 2.*)

TEACHER: I haven't been here for a long time. Your son tells me you've been sick. Are you feeling any better now?

MOTHER: No need to worry about my illness. It left no bad effects.

[1] Or: Above all, seek understanding. G.N.
[2] Or: Many reach an understanding with falsehoods. G.N.

[117]

TEACHER: Glad to hear it. I came to say goodbye to you because I'm going on a research trip over the mountains soon. For in the city beyond the mountains live the famous teachers.

MOTHER: A research trip over the mountains! Yes, indeed, I've heard that the famous teachers live there, but I've also heard that the trip is dangerous. Were you thinking of taking my boy with you?

TEACHER: That's no trip for a child!

MOTHER: I agree. I hope you will return safely.

TEACHER: I have to go now. Goodbye. Get well. (TEACHER *goes to Room 1*.)

BOY (*Follows the* TEACHER *into Room 1*): I want to say something.

(MOTHER *listens at the door*.)

TEACHER: What do you want to say?

BOY: I want to go over the mountains with you.

TEACHER:

> As I've already told your mother
> The trip is hard and dangerous.
> You won't be able to come along. Besides:
> How can you want to leave your mother
> When she is ill?
> Stay here. It's really impossible
> For you to come along.

BOY:

> Just because Mother is sick, I want
> To come with you;
> I must get her
> Medicine and advice
> From the famous doctors in the city beyond the mountains.

TEACHER: But would you agree to everything that might happen to you on the trip?

BOY: Yes.

TEACHER: I must talk this over with your mother. (*He returns to Room 2.* BOY *listens at the door*.) As you see, I've come back. Your son has asked to come with us. I told him he couldn't leave you while you are still ill; and also that it is a hard and dangerous trip. It was out of the question for him to come along, I said. But he said he had to come with us to the city beyond the mountains to get medicine and advice for you.

MOTHER: I heard what he said. I know the boy means well and would
like to make the dangerous trip. Come in, Son. (*The* BOY *enters
Room 2.*)

> Ever since
> Your father left us
> I've had no one
> But you at my side.
> You were never longer
> Out of my mind and out of my sight
> Than it took
> To prepare your meals,
> To fix your clothes and
> To earn a living.

BOY: What you say is true. But still you can't get me to change my
mind.

BOY, MOTHER, TEACHER:

> I am going (He is going) to make the dangerous trip
> To get for your (my, her) illness
> Medicine and advice
> In the city beyond the mountains.

GREAT CHORUS:

> You saw that no argument
> Could move him.
> Then the teacher and the mother said
> In one voice:

TEACHER *and* MOTHER:

> Many say Yes to falsehoods [3]
> But he says Yes not to illness
> But that illness be healed.

GREAT CHORUS: Now the mother said:

MOTHER:

> I have no more strength.
> If it has to be
> Go with the teacher.
> But hurry, hurry
> Return to me soon.

[3] Or: Many reach an understanding with falsehood. G.N.

II

GREAT CHORUS:
> The people have started
> On the trip over the mountains
> Among them the teacher
> And the boy.
> The boy was not equal to the strain:
> He overworked his heart
> In their hurry to return.
> At dawn at the foot of the mountains
> He could hardly
> Drag himself on.

(*Into Room 1 enter the* TEACHER, THREE STUDENTS, *and finally the* BOY *with a jug.*)

TEACHER: We climbed rapidly. There is the first hut. Let's rest there a while.
THREE STUDENTS: We'll do that.

(*They step on the raised platform in Room 2. The* BOY *holds the* TEACHER *back.*)

BOY: I want to say something.
TEACHER: What do you want to say?
BOY: I don't feel well.
TEACHER: Not another word. Whoever undertakes a trip such as this must not say such things. Perhaps you're just tired, not being used to climbing. Stop and rest a while. (*He steps on the platform.*)
THREE STUDENTS: It seems that the boy is tired from climbing. Let's ask the teacher.
GREAT CHORUS: Yes, do.
THREE STUDENTS (*To the* TEACHER): We hear that the boy is tired from climbing. What's the matter with him? Are you worried about him?
TEACHER: He said he didn't feel well, but he really is all right. He is tired from climbing.
THREE STUDENTS: Then you aren't worried about him? (*Long pause,* then the STUDENTS *among one another.*)

Do you hear? The teacher said
The boy is only tired from climbing.
But doesn't he look strange?
Right after the hut comes the narrow pass.
Only clutching the cliff
With both hands
Can you pass.
We can't carry anyone.
Should we follow the great custom
And hurl him into the valley?

(*They call down to Room 1, forming a megaphone with their hands*):
Are you sick from climbing?
BOY:

No!
See, I'm still standing up.
Wouldn't I sit down
If I were sick? (*Pause. The* BOY *sits down.*)
THREE STUDENTS: We'll tell the teacher. Sir, when we asked you before
about the boy you said he was only tired from climbing, but now
he looks so strange. He even sat down. We say it with dread, but
since ancient times a great custom has ruled here: He who can go
no further is hurled into the valley!
TEACHER: What? You want to throw this child into the valley?
THREE STUDENTS: Yes!
TEACHER: As you say. This is a great custom existing since ancient
times. How can I oppose it? But doesn't the great custom also demand that we should ask the sick one if we should turn around for
his sake? I feel a deep sorrow for this human being. I'll go and
gently tell him of the great custom.
THREE STUDENTS: Please do. (*They face each other.*)
THREE STUDENTS *and* GREAT CHORUS:

We'll ask him (They asked him) whether he demands (demanded)
That we turn around now for his sake.
But even if he demands (demanded) it,
We will (they would) not turn back
But hurl him into the valley.
TEACHER (*Has gone down to the* BOY *in Room 1*): Listen closely. Since
ancient times a law has ruled that he who falls ill on such a trip
must be hurled into the valley. Death is instant. But the custom

also demands that we should ask the sick one if we should turn back for his sake. And the custom demands that the sick person answer: You shall not turn back. If I could take your place, how gladly I would die.

BOY: I understand.

TEACHER: Do you ask that we turn back for your sake? Or do you agree that we throw you into the valley as the great custom demands?

BOY: No! I do not agree.

TEACHER (*Calling from Room 1 and Room 2*): Come down here! He did not answer as the custom demands. He who says A, must also say B. When you were asked before whether you would agree to everything that might happen to you on this trip, you said yes.

BOY: The answer that I gave was false. But your question was even falser. He who says A, does not have to say B. He can also realize that A was false. I wanted to get medicine for my mother. But now that I am sick myself, it's no longer possible. And I want to turn back immediately now that things have changed. So I ask you to turn back and to bring me home. Surely, your research can wait. If there's something to learn over there, as I hope there is, then it can only be that in a situation such as ours now, we should turn around. And as for the great ancient custom, I see no sense to it. Rather, I need a great new custom, one we must introduce here and now: the custom to give each new situation new thought.

THREE STUDENTS (*To the* TEACHER): What are we to do? What the boy says is sensible, even if it's not heroic.

TEACHER: I leave it up to you to decide what to do now. But I must tell you: People will hurl laughter and disgrace at you if you turn back.

THREE STUDENTS: Isn't it a disgrace that he speaks for himself?

TEACHER: No, I see no disgrace in that.

THREE STUDENTS: Then we'll turn back and no laughter and no abuse shall keep us from doing the sensible thing; and no ancient custom shall keep us from agreeing to a valid thought.

> Lean your head on our arms.
> Don't strain yourself
> We'll carry you carefully.

GREAT CHORUS:

> So the friends took the friend
> And established a new custom

And a new law
And they brought the boy back.
Side by side they walked pressed together
Against the abuse,
Against the laughter, with open eyes,
No one more cowardly than his neighbor.

The Billy-Club
Puppets

BY

FEDERICO GARCÍA LORCA

*in a translation by James Graham-Lujan
and Richard L. O'Connell*

F EDERICO GARCÍA LORCA (1898–1936), a child of children's theatre if ever there was one, grew up in his Granada home surrounded by puppets, toy theatres and a miniature stage where productions took place of plays he either wrote or improvised himself, which were performed under his direction by servants wearing costumes that he had designed. This complete little man of the theatre also acted, sang, painted scenery and made masks; make-believe charmed the boy, who, according to his brother, "even then . . . had begun to transform the world of fiction into a reality and to identify all of reality with a fantastic dream." Family theatricals were supplemented by trips to real theatres and by a house filled with music, poetry and literature, all of which he consumed avidly. These pursuits resulted in part from enlightened parents but also from illness which long affected the boy, whose doting family encouraged his artistic expression and indulged his unmistakable talents. The creative enthusiasm of a happy childhood lingers on in much of his adult poetry, puppet plays, vaudevilles, farces and fantastic comedies, of which *The Billy-Club Puppets* is an outstanding example.

While studying law at the University of Granada his attention turned so greatly to the arts that he accepted the advice of his teachers who encouraged him to go to Madrid, the cultural capital of Spain, and there to develop his abilities as an artist, composer, pianist and author. Madrid indeed inspired the youth, still not twenty years of age but who already had had a volume of verse published and a play produced in a professional theatre. He immediately developed influential friendships among the city's leading artists, including the surrealistic painter Salvador Dali; the film maker Luis Buñuel; and the composer Don Manuel de Falla, who was later to create music for a number of Lorca's plays.

The United States made an indelible impression upon the young poet when he spent the year 1929–30 in New York City, ostensibly to study at Columbia University but in reality to absorb the life of the city in general and of Harlem in particular. His impressions of this new world culminated in the poems that comprise *Poet in New York,* a work that brought him fame in Spain. After a period of troubled introspection, part of which was spent in Cuba, he returned to Spain to undertake the golden years of productivity, which lasted from 1930 until he was brutally and stupidly assassinated in 1936.

Poetry is the essence of Lorca's dramatic expression whether he is being farcical or serious, whether his characters are servants or aristocrats, whether they are human beings or puppets or the Moon or the cockroaches, butterflies, mosquitoes, sprites, beetles and fireflies that abound in his plays. A lyricism prevails in even his most realistic works. His is a poetry shot through with laughter and tears, and it was these extremes that excited him as a view of life, which, his brother relates, he actually saw as a "great world stage." He found within him an astonishing number of voices to communicate the riches and realities of Spanish existence. His folk ballads, for which he wrote words and music, were songs of the peasants. His poems celebrated the Andalusian gypsies among whom he moved and lived. His lyrics often recognized the Moorish and Roman contributions of the past, as well as Spain's illustrious accomplishments in periods of glory. His folk plays examined traditions that had once given strength to his people but which he thought now made them weak, frustrated and often defeated in a social order grown antiquated. Deeply in love with his country, he nonetheless was acutely aware of its problems and the needs of its people.

It was of his countrymen he was thinking when in 1931 he organized and directed a traveling state-supported troupe, La Barraca, dedicated to taking theatre throughout the country, particularly to areas that had never known drama. For this company he wrote his three most famous plays: the poetic tragedy *Blood Wedding* (1933); the passionate tragedy *Yerma* (1934); and the realistic tragedy *The House of Bernarda Alba* (1936). Recognized today as outstanding examples of poetry fused with drama, these works are considered by many to be lyric masterpieces of modern theatre. Each play is noted, too, for its searching insights into Spanish women, who are seen confronting their own desires in conflict with a society that suppresses and suffocates them. The popularity of La Barraca throughout Spain took Lorca to Buenos Aires and other Latin-American cities, where again his own plays were well received.

Spain in the mid-1930s was a divided country, caught in the strife of political upheaval, revolts and counterrevolts. Lorca had been asked to bring his plays to Mexico but, before leaving the country, decided to return to Granada for a farewell visit with family and friends. While he was there, the civil war began and soldiers, sweeping through the countryside, seized the playwright, who was shot before a firing squad in an open field and buried in an unmarked grave. While still a young man this great poetic voice was stilled, but gradually his plays and poems have been translated and now are known throughout the world.

The Billy-Club Puppets, written between 1922 and 1925 (although parts of it may have been tried out long before by Lorca in his puppet theatre), was produced in Madrid in 1935. It is a favorite play for young people in Spanish-speaking countries and has been performed in Spanish in New York City by The New York Shakespeare Festival Theatre, as has another Lorca fantasy, The Butterfly's Evil Spell. From the moment Mosquito quiets the audience at the outset, Lorca makes us know we are in the theatre and thereafter keeps reminding us with a variety of imaginative delights: tinkling bells, the appearance of an Hour dressed in yellow who steps suddenly out of the wall clock, changing colors, passing sunbeams and moonbeams, the arrival of Don Cristobita in a carriage drawn by cardboard horses, a palm tree that fills with little silver lights, a flute that finishes Figaro's speeches, a slapstick wedding and a mock funeral. The characters further add to the abundant theatricality, for they are all larger than life, cartoon figures possessing human hearts. They shift from tear-shedding heartbreak to delirious happiness, often within seconds and with full force, well illustrating Lorca's love of extremities when depicting emotions. Traces of Italian commedia dell'arte and Punch-and-Judy traditions further add to their histrionic energy and stylization. The question that they create for the reader—are they puppets acting like people or people acting like puppets?—is left unanswered by Lorca on purpose, and we must decide for ourselves. Just when we think it is one way, a character will prove to us it is the other, and the ambiguity cheerfully persists. In stage performances, of course, the director has little choice but to make them human beings impersonating puppets. Bombastic, then soft, swaggering, then still, cruel, then kind, this fantasy, which Lorca called a tragicomedy, is also sweet, then bitter, for beneath its tinsel world of painted faces and fireworks is a poetic one of dreams fulfilled and unfulfilled. Remember as you read The Billy-Club Puppets that Lorca viewed life not only as a great world stage but also as a fantastic dream.

The Billy-Club Puppets

CHARACTERS

(In order of their appearance)
MOSQUITO
ROSITA
FATHER
COCOLICHE
COACHMAN
DON CRISTOBITA
SERVANT
AN HOUR
YOUNG MEN
SMUGGLERS
QUAKEBOOTS, *the tavern keeper*
CURRITO *from the harbor*
WEARISOME, *the cobbler*
FIGARO, *a barber*
AN URCHIN
A YOUNG LADY IN YELLOW
A BLIND BEGGAR
A BELLE WITH BEAUTY MARKS
AN ACOLYTE
GUESTS WITH TORCHES
FUNERAL PRIESTS
CORTEGE

ANNOUNCEMENT

Two trumpets and a drum sound. MOSQUITO *enters from wherever you wish.* MOSQUITO *is a mysterious personage, part ghost, part leprechaun, part insect. He represents the joy of a free life and the wit and poetry of the Andalusian people. He carries a little trumpet of the kind sold at village fairs.*

MOSQUITO: Men and women, attention! Son, shut your little mouth, and you, little girl, sit down, by all that's unholy. Now hush so the silence can grow as clear as if it were in its own spring. Hush so the dregs of the last whispers can settle down. (*A drum sounds.*) My company and I have just come from the theatre of the bourgeoisie, the theatre of the counts and the marquises, a gold and crystal theatre where the men go to fall asleep and the women to fall asleep too. My company and I were prisoners there! You can't imagine how unhappy we were. But one day, through the keyhole, I saw a star twinkling like a little fresh violet of light all aglow. I opened my eye as wide as I could (the wind kept trying to close it with its finger for me), and there, under the star, and furrowed by slow ships, a wide river smiled. Then I, ha! ha! ha!, told my friends about it, and we ran away over the fields, looking for the plain people, to show them the things, the little things, and the littlest little things of this world, under the green mountain moon and the rosy seashore moon. We're just as much at home at the midday's daylight as at the midnight's night light. Now the moon is rising and the fireflies slip slowly away to their little grottoes, and the great performance entitled "Tragicomedy of Don Cristóbal and Miss Rosita" is about to begin. Be ready to put up with the mean temper of that little fist shaker Cristóbal, and to weep over the sad lot of Miss Rosita, who, more than she is a woman, is a cold little bird on the pond, a delicate she-bird of the snows. Let's begin! (*Exits, but returns running.*) And now, wind! Fan all these astonished faces, carry every sigh high above the mountaintops and dry those fresh tears in the eyes of the young ladies who have no sweethearts. (*Music.*)

> Four little leaves were growing
> on my small tree,
> and the wind set them blowing.

SCENE 1

A downstairs room in DOÑA ROSITA'S *house. Upstage, a large window with a wrought-iron grating, and a door. Through the window, a little orange grove is seen.* ROSITA *wears a rose-colored dress with a bustle, trimmed with ribbons and laces. When the curtain rises, she is sitting at a large frame, embroidering.*

ROSITA (*Counting the stitches*): One, two, three, four. (*She pricks herself.*) Ouch! (*She puts her finger to her mouth.*) Four times I've pricked myself on the final *r* of "To My Adored Father." It's certainly true that needlepoint embroidery is hard work. One, two . . . (*She leaves the needle sticking in the canvas.*) Oh, how I'd like to get married! I'd dress up with a yellow flower right on my topknot and a veil trailing through the whole street. (*She rises.*) And when the barber's daughter looked out her window, I'd tell her, "I'm going to get married, and before you do, long before you do, and with bracelets and everything." (*Outside, someone whistles.*) Oh-ho-ho! It's my boy! (*She runs to the window.*)

FATHER (*Offstage*): Rosita-a-a-a!

ROSITA (*Frightened*): Wha-a-at?

(*A louder whistle. She runs and sits at the frame, but blows kisses toward the window.*)

FATHER (*Entering*): I just thought I'd come see if you were doing your embroidery. . . . Work on, my daughter, work on, for that's how we make our living! Oh, how we need the money! Of the five bags full of money we inherited from your uncle, the archpriest, there's not this much left!

ROSITA: What a beard my uncle, the archpriest, had! What an old darling he was! (*Whistle outside.*) And oh, how he could whistle! How he could whistle!

FATHER: But daughter, what's that you're saying? Have you gone crazy?

ROSITA (*Confused*): No, no . . . I made a mistake.

FATHER: Oh, Rosita, how deep in debt we are! What will become of us? (*He takes out his handkerchief and weeps.*)

ROSITA (*Weeping*): Well . . . if . . . you . . . I . . .

FATHER: If you'd at least consider getting married, a new day might dawn for us, but I suppose, just now. . .

ROSITA: Why, that's just what I have been considering.

FATHER: Really?

ROSITA: But, hadn't you noticed? How unperspicacious you men are!

FATHER: Well, that suits me to a *T*, to a *T!*

ROSITA: Why, just the thought of an upsweep hairdo and rouge on my cheeks . . .

FATHER: So, you agree, then.

ROSITA (*Demure as a nun*): Yes, Father.

FATHER: And you won't change your mind?

ROSITA: No, Father.

FATHER: And you'll always do as I say?

ROSITA: Yes, Father.

FATHER: Well, that's all I wanted to hear. (*He starts to leave.*) I'm saved from ruin. Saved! (*Exits.*)

ROSITA: What does he mean, "I'm saved from ruin, saved"? Because my sweetheart, Cocoliche, has even less money than we do. Much less! His grandmother left him three coins, a jar of quince preserves, and . . . that's all! Oh, but I love, love, love and double love him! (*This is spoken very rapidly.*) Dirty old money? That's for the rest of the world. I'll take love. (*She runs to the window and waves a large rose-colored 'kerchief through the bars.*)

COCOLICHE'S VOICE (*Singing, accompanied by a guitar*):

> Flying on the breeze
> go the sighs my love is sighing,
> flying on the breeze,
> and on the breezes flying.

ROSITA (*singing*):

> Flying on the breeze
> go the sighs my love is sighing,

flying on the breeze,
and on the breezes flying.

COCOLICHE (*Appearing at the grating*): Halt, who goes there?

ROSITA (*Hiding her face with a large fan and disguising her voice*):
A friend.

COCOLICHE: Does perchance a certain Rosita reside in this house?

ROSITA: She's taking the baths.

COCOLICHE (*Pretending to leave*): Well, may they do her good.

ROSITA (*Uncovering her face*): And would you have had the heart to
go?

COCOLICHE: No, I couldn't have. (*Sweetly.*) At your side my feet become like lead.

ROSITA: You want to know something?

COCOLICHE: What?

ROSITA: Oh, I don't dare!

COCOLICHE: Go on.

ROSITA (*Very seriously*): Look, I don't want to be one of those shame-
less hussies.

COCOLICHE: Well, it seems a very good idea to me.

ROSITA: Look here, it so happens that . . .

COCOLICHE: Say it!

ROSITA: Let me hide behind my fan.

COCOLICHE (*Desperate*): Oh, please!

ROSITA (*Her face covered*): I'm going to marry you.

COCOLICHE: What? What did you say?

ROSITA: Just what you heard.

COCOLICHE: Oh, Rosita!

ROSITA: And right away . . .

COCOLICHE: Right away I'm going to write to Paris for a baby . . .

ROSITA: Listen, not to Paris. I don't want it to talk like those French-
men with their *oui, oui, oui.*

COCOLICHE: Then . . .

ROSITA: We'll write to Madrid.

COCOLICHE: But does your father know of this?

ROSITA: And he's given his permission! (*She lowers the fan.*)

COCOLICHE: Oh, my Rosita! Come here, come. Nearer!

ROSITA: Now, don't get nervous.

COCOLICHE: I feel as if someone were tickling the soles of my feet.
Come closer.

ROSITA: No, no; I'll throw you a kiss from here. (*They kiss, at a dis-*

tance. Little bells tinkle.) It always happens! Somebody's coming. Goodbye till tonight.

(*Little bells are heard, and a carriage, drawn by small cardboard horses wearing plumed crests, appears outside the large window grating and stops.*)

CRISTOBITA (*From the carriage*): No doubt about it, she's the best-looking girl in town.

ROSITA (*Spreading out her skirts in a curtsy*): Thank you very much.

CRISTOBITA: I'll take her, definitely. She looks about three feet high. A woman should be just that tall, no more, no less. But what a figure, and what poise! She has almost, almost caught my fancy. Giddap, driver!

(*Carriage exits slowly.*)

ROSITA (*Mockingly*): Oh, is that so? "I'll take her." What an ugly-looking and bad-mannered gentleman! He must be one of those flirts that come here from other countries. (*A pearl necklace flies in through the window.*) Oh! What's this? My heavens, what a lovely pearl necklace! (*She puts it on and looks at herself in a little hand mirror.*) Genevieve of Brabant must have had one just like this when she'd go to the tower of her castle to wait for her husband. And it looks so well on me! But who could have sent it?

FATHER (*Entering*): Oh my daughter, joy's complete! Your wedding's all arranged!

ROSITA: How grateful I am to you, and Cocoliche will be so grateful too! Right now . . .

FATHER: Cocoliche? Cocoliche in a pig's eye! What do you mean? I've just given your hand to Don Cristobita, he of the billy-club, who just now came by here in his carriage.

ROSITA: Well, I won't have him, I won't, I won't! And as for my hand, you can't take it away from me. I already have a sweetheart. . . . And I'll throw this necklace away!

FATHER: Well, there's nothing more to be said. This man is very rich, he suits me, and I've made the arrangements because otherwise tomorrow we'd have found ourselves out begging.

ROSITA: I'd rather we begged.

FATHER: I give the orders here because I'm the father. What's done is done and the fat's in the fire. There's no more to be said.

ROSITA: But I . . .

FATHER: Quiet!

ROSITA: As far as I'm . . .

FATHER: Shut up! (*Exits.*)

ROSITA: Oh, oh! So he can dispose of my hand, just like that, and I have to put up with it because the law is on his side. (*She weeps.*) Why didn't the law stay home where it belongs? If I could only sell my soul to the devil! (*Shouting.*) Devil, come out; Devil, come out! I refuse to marry that Cristóbal!

FATHER (*Entering*): What's all this shouting? Be quiet and get on with your needlework! What's the world coming to? Are children going to tell parents what to do? You're going to obey my every command just as I obeyed my father when he married me to your mother, who, by the bye, had such a moon face that, well . . .

ROSITA: All right then. I'll be quiet!

FATHER (*Leaving*): Did you ever see the like?

ROSITA: All right. Between the priest and the papa we girls can only be completely disgusted. (*She sits down to embroider.*) Every afternoon—three, four—the priest tells us: you are going to Hell yet, you will die from overheat, worse than the dogs. . . . But I say the dogs marry whomever they wish and they fare very well with it. How I would like to be a dog! Because if I pay attention to my father—four, five—I will be in Hell, and if not, I will end up at the other Hell above for not following him. . . . The priests too should shut up and not talk so much . . . because . . . (*She dries her tears.*) If I don't marry Cocoliche, it will be the fault of the priest . . . yes, of the priest . . . to whom, after all, none of this is of the slightest concern. Ay, ay, ay, ay . . . !

CRISTOBITA (*At the window, with his* SERVANT): She's a nice bit. Do you like her?

SERVANT (*Trembling*): Yes, sir.

CRISTOBITA: Mouth a trifle too large, but oh, what a tasty dish of a body. . . . I haven't settled the deal yet. . . . I'd like to have a talk with her, but I don't want her to get too familiar. Familiarity is the mother of all vices. Don't you dare contradict me!

SERVANT (*Trembling*): But sire!

CRISTOBITA: There are only two ways to deal with people: either never get to know them, or get rid of them!

SERVANT: Merciful heaven!

CRISTOBITA: Listen, you like her!

SERVANT: The best is none too good for Your Grace.

CRISTOBITA: She's a juicy little piece, and she's mine! Mine alone!

(*Exeunt.*)

ROSITA: That's all I needed to know. Oh, I'm desperate now. Right away I'll poison myself with potions or with corrosive sublimate.

(*The wall clock opens and an* HOUR, *dressed in a yellow dress with a bustle, appears.*)

HOUR (*With her voice and with the bell*): Bong! Rosita, be patient. What can you do? How do you know how things are going to turn out? While it's sunshiny here, it's rainy somewhere else. How do you know what winds will whirl the weather vane on your roof tomorrow? I, since I'm here every day, will remind you of this when you're old and have almost forgotten this moment. Let the water run and the stars go on shining. Rosita, be patient! Bong! One o'clock.

(*The clock closes.*)

ROSITA: One o'clock . . . but I'll be damned if I feel like eating!

VOICE (*Offstage*):
                    Flying on the breeze
                    go the sighs my love is sighing.

ROSITA: Yes, I see them coming, my lover's sighs. (*The wall clock opens once more to reveal the* HOUR, *taking a nap. The bell alone sounds. Weepily.*) The sighs my love is sighing.

SCENE 2

The little stage represents the plaza of an Andalusian town. To the right, Miss ROSITA'S *house. There should be an enormous palm tree and a bench.* COCOLICHE *comes on from the left, haunting Rosita's neighborhood. He is carrying a guitar, and he wears a little green cloak with black facings. He is dressed in the popular costume of the early nineteenth century. He wears, with an air, a high-brimmed Calaña hat.*

COCOLICHE: Not a sign of Rosita. She's afraid of the moon. Moon-light is terribly hard on those who must love in secret. (*He whistles.*) My whistle has tapped like a little musical pebble against her windowpane. Yesterday she was wearing a black bow in her hair. She said to me: "A black ribbon in my hair is like the blight on a piece of fruit. If you ever see me like this, be sad, for soon the black will go down all the way to my feet." There's something gone wrong with her.

(*Her balcony, with its row of flower pots, begins to glow with a soft radiance.*)

ROSITA (*Offstage*):
　　　　　Oh this vito, vito thrills me,
　　　　　and I'll dance it till it kills me.[1]
COCOLICHE (*Going up closer*): Why wouldn't you come out?
ROSITA (*At the balcony, very affectedly and very poetically*): Ah, little lad of mine! This day the Moorish breeze sets all of Anda-lusia's weather vanes to whirling. One hundred years from now, they'll still be awhirl, and in a similar fashion.
COCOLICHE: What is it you're trying to say?
ROSITA: That you must learn to look on both sides of Time, right and left, and so teach your heart to be resigned.
COCOLICHE: I don't understand you.
ROSITA: It's the next part that's going to be a shock. That's what I'm trying to prepare you for. (*Pause, during which* ROSITA, *gasping for breath, sobs comically.*) I can't marry you!
COCOLICHE: Rosita!
ROSITA: You're the apple of my eye, but I can't marry you! (*She sobs.*)
COCOLICHE: Are you going to act as balky as a nun now? Have I done anything wrong? Oh, oh, oh! (*His weeping is halfway between childish and comic.*)
ROSITA: You'll find out all about it later. But now, goodbye.
COCOLICHE (*Shouting and stamping his feet*): Oh, no, no, no, no!
ROSITA: Goodbye. Father's calling me.

(*The balcony shutters close.*)

---

[1] The "vito" is a traditional Andalusian folk song and dance, collected by Federico García Lorca and repopularized by him.

COCOLICHE (*To himself*): My ears ring as if I were on top of a mountain. I feel like a paper doll, burning in the flames of my own heart. But I won't have it; no, no, no and no. (*Stamping his feet.*) What does she mean, she won't marry me? When I brought her that locket from the Mairena fair, she ran her hand over my face. When I gave her the shawl with the roses on it, she looked at me in such a way that . . . and when I brought her the mother-of-pearl fan, the one with Pedro Romero opening his bullfighter's cape on it, she gave me as many kisses as the fan had ribs. Yes, sir! That many kisses! Better if a bolt of lightning had split me in half instead! (*He weeps in excellent rhythm.*)

(*From the left, various* YOUNG MEN *dressed in Andalusian costume enter. One of them carries a guitar, another a tambourine. They sing.*)

> In the River Guadalquivir
> bathes the one whom I would wed.
> My love embroiders 'kerchiefs
> made of silk and colored red.

FIRST LAD: Why, there's Cocoliche.
SECOND LAD: What are you crying about? Get up and don't worry if a bird in the grove hops from one tree to another.
COCOLICHE: Leave me alone!
THIRD LAD: We can't do that. Come on, the wind across the fields will blow your sadness all away.
FIRST LAD: Come on, come on.

(*They take him with them. Voices, and music. The stage is left empty. The moon shines on the broad plaza. The door of Doña* ROSITA'S *house opens and her* FATHER *appears, dressed in gray, with a pink wig and pink face to match. Don* CRISTOBITA *enters, dressed in green; he has an enormous belly and a slight hump. He wears a necklace, a bracelet made of little bells, and carries a billy-club that serves him as a walking cane.*)

CRISTOBITA: So the deal is settled. Agreed?
FATHER: Yes, sir . . . but . . .
CRISTOBITA: But me no buts! The deal is closed. I give you the hun-

dred gold pieces so you can get out of debt and you give me your daughter Rosita . . . and you should be pleased because she's, well, a little . . . overripe.

FATHER: She's sixteen years old.

CRISTOBITA: I said overripe and overripe she is!

FATHER: Yes . . . sir, she is.

CRISTOBITA: But nevertheless, she's a charming girl. What the devil. *Un bocatto di cardinali!*

FATHER (*Very seriously*): Does Your Grace speak Italian?

CRISTOBITA: No; as a child I lived in France and Italy, serving a certain Monsieur Pantaloon. . . . But that's none of your affair!

FATHER: No . . . no, sir. . . . Not at all, sir.

CRISTOBITA: So, by tomorrow afternoon I want the blessings all said.

FATHER (*Terrified*): But that can't be done, Don Cristobita.

CRISTOBITA: Who's that just said no to me? I don't know why I don't send him to the cliff where I've pushed off so many others. This club you see here has killed a lot of men—French, Italian, Hungarian. . . . I have the list at home. Obey me!—or you'll be dancing to the same tune as the rest of them! It's a long time since this club had something to do and it's ready to jump out of my hands. Be careful!

FATHER: Yes . . . sir.

CRISTOBITA: Now, take the money. Mighty dear she's costing me. Mighty dear! But then, what's done is done. I'm a man who never goes back on his word.

FATHER: (Dear Lord, what kind of a man am I turning my child over to?)

CRISTOBITA: What's that? . . . Come, we'll tell the priest.

FATHER (*Trembling*): Very well.

ROSITA (*Offstage*):

> Oh this vito, vito thrills me,
> and I'll dance it till it kills me;
> for each moment deep desire
> sets me more and more on fire.

CRISTOBITA: What was that?

FATHER: My little girl singing . . . It's a lovely song!

CRISTOBITA: Bah! I'll give her something to make her voice hoarse —it's more natural!—and to sing that song that goes

> The frog goes croak, croak,
> croak, croak, cr-r-r-oak.

SCENE 3

A village tavern. At back, wine barrels and, on the white walls, blue pitchers. An old bullfight poster and three oil lamps. Nighttime. The tavernkeeper is behind the counter. He is a man in his shirt-sleeves, with bristly hair and a snub nose. His name is QUAKEBOOTS. *At right, a group of classic* SMUGGLERS, *dressed in velvet, bearded, and carrying blunderbusses. They play cards and sing.*

FIRST SMUGGLER:

> From Cádiz to Gibraltar,
> what a lovely lane!
> The sea knows by my sighing
> I passed that way again.
> Oh, my darling, my darling, oh,
> all those boats in the harbor,
> in the harbor of Málaga!
> From Cádiz to Sevilla,
> so many lemon trees!
> The lemon grove must know me;
> my sighs have stirred the breeze.
> Oh, my darling, my darling, oh,
> all those boats in the harbor of Málaga!

SECOND SMUGGLER: You there! Quakeboots! This blessèd little song makes me thirsty. Bring some Málaga wine!

QUAKEBOOTS (*Lazily*): Right away.

(*Through the center door appears a* YOUNG MAN *dressed in a full blue cape. He wears a little straight-brimmed hat. Suspense. He goes on and sits at a table at left, still without showing his face.*)

QUAKEBOOTS: Would Your Grace like something to drink?

YOUNG MAN: Ah, me! No!

QUAKEBOOTS: Have you been around here for some time?

YOUNG MAN: Ah, me! No!

QUAKEBOOTS: It sounds as if you sighed.

YOUNG MAN: Alas! Alas!

FIRST SMUGGLER: Who is he?

QUAKEBOOTS: I can't place him.

SECOND SMUGGLER: You don't suppose he's a . . .

FIRST SMUGGLER: Maybe we'd better be going.

SECOND SMUGGLER: The night is very bright.

FIRST SMUGGLER: And the stars almost touch the rooftops.

SECOND SMUGGLER: At daybreak we'll be in sight of the sea. (*Exeunt.*)

(*The* YOUNG MAN *is left alone on the stage. His little head can barely be seen. All the stage is illuminated with a penetrating blue light.*)

YOUNG MAN: I find the town whiter, much whiter. When I glimpsed it from the mountains, its light went clear through my eyes and right on down to my feet. One day we Andalusians will be whitewashing even our bodies. But on the inside I'm trembling just a little. Oh, Lord! I shouldn't have come.

QUAKEBOOTS: What a state he's in—worse off than Tancred was, but I . . . (*Guitars and merry voices sound in the streets. As* QUAKEBOOTS *is leaving.*) What's that?

(*Enter the group of* YOUNG MEN *with* COCOLICHE *leading them.*)

COCOLICHE (*Drunk*): Quakeboots, give us wine till it comes out of our eyes. Oh, but that will make our tears beautiful; topaz tears, ruby tears . . . Oh, lads, lads!

FIRST LAD: You're so young! We can't let you be sad!

ALL: That's right.

COCOLICHE: She used to say such delicate things to me! She'd say, "Your lips are like two strawberries, not yet quite ripe. . . ."

FIRST LAD (*Interrupting him*): She's a very romantic woman, that's all. For that very reason you shouldn't worry. Don Cristobita is fat, drunken, and a sleepyhead who before very long . . .

ALL: Bravo!

SECOND LAD: Who, before very long . . .

(*Guffaws.*)

QUAKEBOOTS: Gentlemen, gentlemen.

SECOND LAD: And now for a toast.

FIRST LAD: I drink to what I drink because of drinking is all I think. Cocoliche: at midnight you'll find the door wide open and everything else.

ALL: Olé! (*They play the guitars.*)

SECOND LAD: I drink to Doña Rosita.

YOUNG MAN (*Rising*): To Doña Rosita!

SECOND LAD: And may her future husband burst like a balloon!

(*Laughter.*)

YOUNG MAN (*Going up to them but still concealing his face*): One moment, gentlemen! I'm a stranger here and I'd like to know who this Doña Rosita is to whom you drink so merrily.

COCOLICHE: A stranger and yet so interested?

YOUNG MAN: It could be!

COCOLICHE: Quakeboots, shut the door; even though it's the month of May, this gentleman seems to be very cold.

SECOND LAD: Especially about the face.

YOUNG MAN: I ask you a civil question and you answer with something that's neither here nor there. I think jokes are uncalled for.

COCOLICHE: And just what is it to you who the lady is?

YOUNG MAN: More than you think.

COCOLICHE: Very well, then, the lady is Doña Rosita, who lives there on the plaza, the best singer in Andalusia and my . . . yes! my sweetheart!

SECOND LAD (*Coming forward*): And since she's marrying Don Cristobita today, this lad is . . . well, you can imagine!

ALL: Olé! Olé!

(*Laughter.*)

YOUNG MAN (*Very sadly*): I beg your pardon. I got interested in your talk because I once had a sweetheart who was called Rosita too . . .

SECOND LAD: And now she isn't your sweetheart any more?

YOUNG MAN: No, girls seem to prefer popinjays nowadays. Good night. (*He starts to go.*)

SECOND LAD: Sir, before you leave, I'd like you to drink a glass of wine with us. (*He holds out a glass to him.*)

YOUNG MAN (*At the door, nervously*): Thank you, but I'm not drinking! Good night, gentlemen. (*Aside, as he goes.*) I don't know how I've been able to hold on to myself.

QUAKEBOOTS: But who the devil was that man, and what did he come here for?

SECOND LAD: Just what I was about to ask you. Who was he, all muffled up in his cape? Why the disguise?

FIRST LAD: You're a poor tavernkeeper.

COCOLICHE: It has me worried, worried. . . . That man!

(*All are uneasy and speak among themselves in low voices.*)

SECOND LAD (*From the door*): Gentlemen, Don Cristobita is on his way here to the tavern!

COCOLICHE: Now's a good time to knock his face in.

QUAKEBOOTS: I don't want rows in my tavern, so you can just be on your way now.

FIRST LAD: Don't go looking for trouble, Cocoliche! Don't go looking for trouble!

(*Two* LADS *take* COCOLICHE *out while the others hide behind the tuns. The stage falls silent.*)

CRISTOBITA (*At the door*): Hr-r-r-rmph!

QUAKEBOOTS (*Terrified*): Good evening.

CRISTOBITA: You've plenty of wine, haven't you?

QUAKEBOOTS: Any kind you might want.

CRISTOBITA: I want them all, all!

FIRST LAD (*From a corner and in a squeaky voice*): Cristobita.

CRISTOBITA: Eh? Who's that?

QUAKEBOOTS: Some puppy, out in the garden.

CRISTOBITA (*Takes his stick and recites*):
> Hide your tail if you're a fox,
> for this club knows where it knocks.

QUAKEBOOTS (*Upset*): There's sweet wine . . . white wine . . . sour wine . . . winey wine. . . .

CRISTOBITA: And cheap, eh? You're all a bunch of thieves! Say it, "a bunch of thieves."

QUAKEBOOTS (*Trembling*): A bunch of thieves.

CRISTOBITA: Tomorrow I get married to Miss Rosita and I want a lot of wine so I can . . . drink it all myself.

FIRST LAD (*From a barrel*): Cristobita, who drinks and falls asleep!

SECOND LAD (*From another barrel*): Who drinks and falls asleep.

CRISTOBITA: Br-r-r-r. Br, Br, Br! Do your vats talk, or are you trying to joke with me?

QUAKEBOOTS: Who, me?

CRISTOBITA: Smell the club! What does it smell like?

QUAKEBOOTS: Why, it smells . . . like . . .

CRISTOBITA: Say it!

QUAKEBOOTS: Why, like brains!

CRISTOBITA: What did you think? (*Furiously.*) And about that drinking and sleeping, we'll see who drinks or sleeps, you or me.

QUAKEBOOTS: But Don Cristóbal, but Don Cristóbal.

SECOND LAD (*From a vat*):

Cristobelly,
old pot belly!

FIRST LAD: Potbelly!

CRISTOBITA (*With his club*): Your hour has come, rascal, rascal, scoundrel!

QUAKEBOOTS: Oh, Don Cristobita, my friend so dear!

SECOND LAD: Potbelly!

CRISTOBITA: Make fun of me, will you? We'll see about that. Take that, belly; take that, belly! (*Exeunt, Don* CRISTOBITA *whacking him with the club and* QUAKEBOOTS *screeching like a rat. The* LADS *roar with laughter from the vats. Music.*)

SCENE 4

The same plaza as before but with the moon shining not nearly so brightly. The yellow palm tree stands out against a blue, starless sky. Two LADS *enter, Left, tipsy, bringing* COCOLICHE, *drunk also.*

FIRST LAD: That blessed Don Cristobita has a nasty temper.

SECOND LAD: What a beating he gave that poor tavernkeeper.

FIRST LAD: Say, what're we going to do with this one?

SECOND LAD: Leave him here, and don't worry; he'll wake up when the dew hits his face. (*Exeunt.*)

(*A flute is heard, coming nearer rapidly, and* MOSQUITO *appears. The light grows brighter. Seeing the sleeping* COCOLICHE, *he*

goes up near to him and blows his little trumpet in one ear.
COCOLICHE *slaps at it and* MOSQUITO *backs away.)*

MOSQUITO: He doesn't know what's happening—of course!—he's only
a child. But the situation is that Miss Rosita's heart, a heart this
tiny, is about to be lost by him. (*He laughs.*) Miss Rosita's soul is
like those little mother-of-pearl boats they sell at fairs, little boats
from Valencia fitted out with a pair of scissors and a thimble. Now
he'll write "Souvenir" on its stiff sail and go on trudging, trudging.
. . . (*Exits, playing his little trumpet, and the stage is dark once
more.*)

(*Enter, the cloaked* YOUNG MAN *and a village* LAD.)

YOUNG MAN: I'm glad, now, that I came, but I'm so angry I can hardly
speak. You say she's getting married?
LAD: Tomorrow, to a certain Don Cristobita, a rich, lazy old man,
such a brute that even his shadow breaks things. But I think she's
forgotten you by now.
YOUNG MAN: Impossible; she loved me so much, and that was
only . . .
LAD: Five years ago.
YOUNG MAN: You're right.
LAD: Why did you leave her?
YOUNG MAN: I don't know. I used to get so tired here. Going down
to the harbor, coming back from the harbor. . . . You know! I
used to think that the world was a place where bells were always
ringing, and that white inns stood along the roads with blonde
serving maids in them, wearing their sleeves rolled up to their
elbows. But there's nothing like that! It's so dull!
LAD: So what do you plan to do?
YOUNG MAN: I want to see her.
LAD: That's impossible. You don't know Don Cristobita.
YOUNG MAN: Well, I want to see her, cost what it may.

(*Enter, Right,* WEARISOME.)

LAD: Ah! Here's someone who can help us; it's Wearisome, the cobbler. (*Calling.*) Wearisome!

WEARISOME: What . . . what . . . what?

LAD: Look, you're going to be very helpful to this gentleman.

WEARISOME: To who . . . to . . . who?

YOUNG MAN (*Uncovering his face*): Look at me!

WEARISOME: Currito!

CURRITO: Yes, Currito from the harbor.

WEARISOME (*Whacking him on the belly with his hand*): Why, you little scoundrel, how fat you've got.

LAD: Isn't it true that tomorrow you're going to Miss Rosita's to try her bridal shoes on her?

WEARISOME: Yes, . . . yes, . . . yes.

LAD: Then you'll have to let this man go in your place.

WEARISOME: No, no; I don't want to get into any trouble.

CURRITO: But if you knew how well I'd pay you. Come on, now, for your children's sake, I ask you to let me go.

LAD: What's more, he *will* pay you well. He's got money.

CURRITO: Remember, Wearisome, (*Pretending to cry.*), how much my father loved you.

WEARISOME: Hush! What can I do? I'll let you go! I'll stay home. And it's true . . . (*He brings out a large hempen handkerchief.*) your father really did love me, very, very much.

CURRITO (*Embracing him*): Thank you, many thanks!

WEARISOME: Are you going back to peddling oranges? You used to call out your wares in such a fine way: "O-ranges! O-ranges!" (*They go out.*)

(*Moonlight begins to flood the stage and the music of guitars runs through it.*)

COCOLICHE (*Talking in his sleep*): Cristobita will beat you, my love. Cristobita has a green belly and a green hump. At night he won't let you sleep with his snorting. And I would have given you so many kisses! How sad, when I saw you with the black ribbon in your hair. . . . "The black will go down to my toes."

(*The melody of the vito fills the stage. Left, an apparition from* COCOLICHE's *dream appears. It is Doña* ROSITA, *dressed in dark blue, with a wreath of spikenards on her hair and a silver dagger in her hand.*)

VISION OF ROSITA (*Singing*):

>With this vito, vito, vito,
>with this vito that I hum you . . .
>Every hour, oh, my darling,
>I go farther, farther from you.

(*The yellow palm tree fills with little silver lights and every-thing takes on a theatrical blue tinge.*)

COCOLICHE: Holy Virgin! (*He jumps up, but in that moment every-thing vanishes.*) I'm awake; there's no doubt about it, I'm awake. It was she . . . dressed in mourning. I can still almost see her before my eyes . . . and that music . . .

(*Now, from the balcony,* ROSITA'S *voice can really be heard; she is singing, unable to sleep.*)

ROSITA:

>Oh this vito, vito thrills me,
>and I'll dance it till it kills me . . .
>for each moment deep desire
>sets me more and more on fire.

COCOLICHE: This is the first time I've really wept! I swear it. The first time!

SCENE 5

An Andalusian street with whitewashed houses. The first house is a cobbler's, the second, a barber's with his armchair and mirror out in the street. Farther down; a great doorway with this sign: "Inn of All the Disillusioned Lovers of the World." Drawn on its door is a huge heart pierced by seven daggers. Morning. WEARISOME, *in his cobbler's shop, is seated at his bench, sewing on a riding boot. Waiting at his chair is* FIGARO, *dressed in green, wearing a black hairnet and curls at his temples, and sharpening a razor on a long strop.*

FIGARO: Today's the day I'm expecting the great visit.
WEARISOME: Who's co . . . ? Who's com . . . ?

(A flute backstage finishes out the words.)

FIGARO: Don Cristobita's coming; Don Cristobita, the one with the club.
WEARISOME: Don't you thi . . . ? Don't you thi . . . ?

(A little flute finishes out the phrase.)

FIGARO: Yes, yes! Of course! *(He laughs.)*
AN URCHIN:
> Shoemaker-aker, thread your thread
> thread it through the needle's head!

FIGARO: Ah! You great rascal! You rascal! *(He runs out in pursuit.)*

(Enter, CURRITO from the harbor, from the opposite side. He is, as usual, muffled in his cloak. At the center of the stage, he bumps into FIGARO, who has turned around rapidly and is coming back.)

CURRITO: If you stick me with that razor, I'll gouge your eyes out.
FIGARO: Pardon, M'sieu; are you in need of a shave? My barber shop . . . *(A piccolo goes on while FIGARO eulogizes his own talents in pantomime.)*
CURRITO: Go to the devil!
FIGARO *(Mimicking CURRITO's call)*: O-ranges! O-ranges! *(He whistles.)*
CURRITO *(Arriving at the cobbler's)*: Wearisome, give me the little boots and the box.
WEARISOME: But . . . but . . . but . . . *(He trembles.)*
CURRITO *(Furiously)*: Give them to me, I said!
WEARISOME: Take them . . . take them. . . .
FIGARO *(Capering)*:
> A-pushing and pulling
> my thimble was gone. . . .
> A-pushing and pulling
> I put it back on.

CURRITO *(Caressing a pair of rose-colored boots)*:
> Oh, little boots
> of Doña Rosita!
> To have the legs in them
> would be much sweeter!

WEARISOME: Now leave me alone! Oh, get away from me! (*He goes on plying his awl.*)

CURRITO (*Full of excitement over his boots*): They're like two little wineglasses, two nuns' pincushions, two little sighs.

FIGARO: Something's going on! Without a doubt something's going on! The town reeks of news. Ah, news! but it'll come to my barber shop.

CURRITO (*Leaving, with the boots in hand*): Can it be you're no longer mine, Rosita? (*He kisses the boots.*) They're like two tears of an early evening's moon, like two little towers in elfland . . . like two . . . (*A big kiss.*) like two . . . (*Exits.*)

FIGARO: I'll find out what's going on. News can't reach the world till it's first been classified at the barber's. Barber shops are the clearing houses for news. This razor you see here helps break the shell on any secret. We barbers have a scent keener than that of a bulldog; we have a nose for dark words and mysterious gestures. And why not? We're the Lords Mayor of the pate, and, by dint of combing little roads through the forests of hair, we find out what thoughts are going on inside. What tales I could tell about the Sleepers Ugly of the barber's chair!

CRISTOBITA (*Entering*): I want a shave right now, yes, sir, right now because I'm going to get married! And I'm not inviting any of you because you're all of you a band of thieves.

(WEARISOME *closes his shop and shows his head through the little window.*)

FIGARO: They are!

CRISTOBITA (*Grabbing up his club*): You are!

FIGARO: They are . . . (*Very affirmatively.*) pointing to ten o'clock. (*He puts away his watch.*)

CRISTOBITA: Ten or eleven, I want a shave this minute.

WEARISOME: What a little villain he is!

CRISTOBITA (*Hitting* WEARISOME *on the head with his club*): Slam, bam, slam!

(WEARISOME, *squeaking like a rat, pulls his head back in.*)

CRISTOBITA: Let's go! (*He sits down.*)

FIGARO: What a very beautiful head you have! But really magnificent!
A very model of heads.

CRISTOBITA: Start shaving!

FIGARO (*Lathering*): Trala, la, la!

CRISTOBITA: If you nick me, I'll split you in two. I said in two, and
in two it'll be!

FIGARO: Admirable, Excellency! I'm charmed, Tra, lala, lala!

(*The door of the inn opens and a* YOUNG LADY *appears; she is
dressed in yellow with a scarlet rose in her hair. An old beggar
with an accordion takes a seat at the inn's door.*)

YOUNG LADY (*Singing and playing the castanets*):
>Oh, I have set my eyes
>on a boy of talent,
>tall, dark and slim of waist;
>he's a likely gallant.
>With the rose,
>and the pretty rose,
>and the olive's green shade . . .
>Combing her sunlit hair,
>sits the pretty maid.

ALL:
>With the rose,
>and the pretty rose,
>and the olive's green shade . . .
>and a-combing her sunlit hair
>sits the little maid.

YOUNG LADY:
>There in the olive groves,
>maiden, wait and be mine;
>I'll bring you homemade bread
>and a jug of wine.
>With the rose,
>and the pretty rose,
>and the olive's green shade . . .
>and a-combing her sunlit hair
>sits the little maid.

ALL:

> With the rose,
> and the pretty rose,
> and the olive's green shade . . .
> and a-combing her sunlit hair
> sits the little maid.

FIGARO (*Looking at the girl*): With the rose, what a pretty rose! Ha, ha, ha! Wearisome, come out here quickly!

(*The* GIRL *stands looking at the sleeping* CRISTOBITA *in great surprise.*)

CRISTOBITA (*Snoring*): Bz-z-z-z, bz-z-z-z . . .

WEARISOME (*Frightened*): No, I don't want to come out. (*He is sticking his head out the little window.*)

FIGARO: This is amazing! Just what I suspected. Really, how stupendous! Don Cristobita has a wooden head. Poplarwood! Ha, ha, ha! (*The* GIRL *goes up nearer.*) And look, look, what a lot of paint . . . what a lot of paint! Ha, ha, ha!

WEARISOME (*Coming out*): You'll wake him up!

FIGARO: He has two knots on his forehead. He probably sweats out the rosin there. This was the news! The great news!

CRISTOBITA (*Moving*): Hurry up, br-r-r-r, hurry up.

FIGARO: Excellency! Yes, yes . . .

YOUNG LADY:

> Oh, I have set my eyes
> on a boy of talent,
> tall, dark and slim of waist;
> he's a likely gallant.
> With the rose,
> and the pretty rose,
> and the olive's green shade,
> and a-combing her sunlit hair
> sits the little maid.

ALL (*Around the sleeping* CRISTOBITA, *but pianissimo so he won't hear them, but making fun of him*):

> With the rose,
> and the pretty rose,
> and the olive's green shade,

and a-combing her sunlit hair
sits the little maid.

(*A* BELLE *with beauty patches on her face looks out the window
of the inn. She opens and closes a fan.*)

SCENE 6

Doña ROSITA'S *house. Facing the audience, two large wardrobes with
shutters at the tops of the doors. An oil-burning lamp hangs from the
ceiling. The walls are lightly brushed in a pink sugar tone. Over the
door, a painting of Saint Rose of Lima under an arch of lemons. Doña*
ROSITA *wears a rose-colored dress—a bridal gown full of flounces and
most complicated bands. On her throat, a jet necklace.*

ROSITA: All is lost! All! I go to the scaffold just like Marianita Pineda.
She wore an iron necklace for her marriage to death and I'll wear
a necklace . . . yes, a necklace of Don Cristobita's (*She weeps
while she sings.*)
    The speckledy bird was a-sitting,
    sitting on the green lemon tree. . . .

(*She chokes.*)

   With her beak and her tail she stirred the leaves
   and blossoms so anxiously.
    When? Oh, when
   my love shall I see?

(*Outside a song is heard.*)

VOICE:
    Rosita, Rosita, to look at your toe,
    if this were allowed me,
    how far would I go?
ROSITA: Oh, Santa Rosa mine! Whose voice is that?
CURRITO (*Wrapped in his cloak, he appears suddenly at the door*):
May one come in?

ROSITA (*Frightened*): Who are you?

CURRITO: A man among men.

ROSITA: But, you have a face?

CURRITO: Very well known to those eyes.

ROSITA: That voice . . . !

CURRITO (*Throwing open his cape*): Look at me!

ROSITA (*Terrified*): Currito!

CURRITO: Yes, Currito—he who went out into the world but returns now to claim you in marriage.

ROSITA: No, no! Oh, good Lord, go away! I'm engaged now, and besides I don't love you; you left me once. I love Cristobita now. Go away, go away!

CURRITO: I won't go! What do you think I'm here for?

ROSITA: Oh! How unhappy I am! I have a little watch and a mirror of silver but even so, how unhappy I am!

CURRITO: Come away with me. I look at you and I go mad with jealousy.

ROSITA: You're trying to ruin me, you villain!

CURRITO (*Trying to embrace her*): My Rosita!

ROSITA: People are coming! Go away, you criminal! Right now!

FATHER (*Entering*): What's the matter?

CURRITO: I came to try on Miss Rosita's wedding shoes, because Wearisome couldn't come. They're precious. Worthy of the princesses at the palace.

FATHER: Try them on her!

(*Doña* ROSITA *sits on a chair.* CURRITO *kneels at her feet, and the* FATHER *reads a newspaper.*)

CURRITO: Oh, lilylike leg!

ROSITA (*In a low voice*): Villain!

CURRITO (*Loudly*): Raise your skirts a little.

ROSITA: There.

(CURRITO *puts one of the boots on her foot.*)

CURRITO: Let's see—a little bit higher?

ROSITA: That's enough, shoemaker.

CURRITO: A little bit higher!

FATHER (*From his chair*): Do as he says, child; a little higher.

ROSITA: Oh!

CURRITO: A little bit higher. (*He stares at* ROSITA's *leg.*) A little bit higher!

FATHER: I'm going now. The boots are lovely. . . . And on the way I'll close this door. It's a little chilly. (*As he tries to close the center door.*) Certainly hard to close. Must be the dampness.

CURRITO:

> Oh what lovely toes
> Your Grace has wherever she goes!
> Oh what lovely,
> what lovely toes!

ROSITA (*Rising*): Evil man! dog!

CURRITO: Rose. Little Rose of the Maytime.

ROSITA (*Screeching pianissimo*): Oh, oh, oh! (*She runs about the stage.*) Don Cristobita is coming! Run out this way! (*They find the door locked.*) Oh, did Father lock this door?

CURRITO (*Trembling*): The truth of the matter is that . . .

ROSITA: I can hear his footsteps on the stairs! Oh, Saint Rose inspire me! (*Meanwhile* CURRITO *is trying to open the door.*) Ah! . . . Come here! (*She opens the right corner wardrobe and hides him there.*) That's it! Oh, I thought I'd die.

CRISTOBITA (*Offstage*): Br-r-r-r-r!

ROSITA (*Singing and half crying*):

> The speckledy bird was a-sitting,
> sitting on the green lemon tree. . . .
> When? Oh, when
> my love shall I see? (*She chokes.*)

CRISTOBITA (*At the door*):

> I smell a human
> on which to sup.
> If I can't have him,
> I'll eat *you* up.

ROSITA: What won't you think up next, Cristobita!

CRISTOBITA: I don't want you talking with anybody. Anybody! I've warned you! (Oh, how tasty she is! What a pair of little hams she has!)

ROSITA: I, Cristobita . . .

CRISTOBITA: We're getting married right away. . . . And listen! You've never seen me kill anybody with the stick? No? Well, you will. I go, wham! wham! wham! . . . and over the cliff.

ROSITA: Yes, that's very nice.

ACOLYTE (*Through the window*): The Holy Father wants me to tell you you can come whenever you're ready now.

CRISTOBITA: We're coming! Olé, olé, we're coming! (*He picks up a bottle and dances while he drinks.*)

ROSITA: Well, then . . . I'll go put on my veil.

CRISTOBITA: I'm going too: I'll put on a huge hat and tie ribbons on my club. I'll be right back. (*He goes off dancing.*)

CURRITO (*Looking out through the wardrobe shutters*): Open the door.

(ROSITA *starts toward the wardrobe but just at that moment* COCO-LICHE *enters through the window with a great leap.*)

ROSITA: Oh! (*She runs to him and throws herself in his arms.*) Nobody! In all the world I don't love anybody but you.

(COCOLICHE *takes her in his arms.*)

COCOLICHE: Darling!

CURRITO (*From the wardrobe*): I suspected as much! You're a fallen woman.

COCOLICHE: What does this mean?

ROSITA: I'm going crazy!

COCOLICHE: What are you doing in that rat hole? Come out in the open like a man! (*He beats on the wardrobe.*)

ROSITA: Have pity on me!

COCOLICHE: Pity on you? Oh, despicable strumpet!

CURRITO: I'd like to strangle both of you.

COCOLICHE: Come out of there! Break the doors down! Coward!

ROSITA: Cristobita is coming! Have pity, Cristobita is coming!

CURRITO: O-o-o-pen!

COCOLICHE: Let him come! Then he'll see how his fiancée makes arrangements with her lover.

ROSITA: I'll explain to you later, my love. Run!

CRISTOBITA (*Offstage*): Rosita . . . little one!

ROSITA: It's too late. Here! (*She opens the other wardrobe and hides* COCOLICHE; *then she throws a pink veil over her head.*) I'm dying! (*She tries to pretend to sing.*)

CRISTOBITA (*Entering*): What was that noise?

ROSITA: It was . . . the guests, waiting at the door.

CRISTOBITA: I don't want any guests!

ROSITA: Well . . . they're here!

CRISTOBITA: Well, if they're here, let them go away. Let them go away! (*Aside.*) And I mean to find out about that noise. (*Aloud.*) Come, Rosita. Eh? Oh, how tasty she is!

(*The center door opens and the wedding* GUESTS *are seen. They carry large hoops decorated with colored paper roses under which* ROSITA *and Don* CRISTOBITA *pass.*)

FIRST GUEST: Long live the bride and groom!

ALL: Long may they live!

(*Music. The heads of* CURRITO *and* COCOLICHE *peek out through the shutters.*)

CURRITO: I'm going to explode!

COCOLICHE: So you're the lover of that creature? I'll meet you face to face later!

CURRITO: Whenever you say, stupid!

COCOLICHE: If this wardrobe weren't made of iron . . .

CURRITO: Ha!

COCOLICHE: I'd gladly take your nose off with a single bite! (*Outside may be heard a "Long live the bride and groom! Long may they live!"*) The ceremony is about to start . . . she's forgetting me forever! (*He weeps.*)

CURRITO (*Theatrically*): I returned to this town to learn how to forget.

COCOLICHE: Never again will she call me "Little Fruit Face" . . . nor I call her "Little Almond Face." . . .

CURRITO: I shall depart forever, forever!

COCOLICHE: Boo, hoo, hoo!

CURRITO: Ingrate, ingrate, ingrate!

(*Outside, church bells, fireworks and music can be heard.*)

COCOLICHE: I won't be able to go on living!

CURRITO: I'll never be able to look at another woman! (*The two puppets weep.*)

MOSQUITO (*Entering, Left*): There's no need to weep, little friends, there's no need. The earth is full of little white roads, smooth little roads, foolish little roads. . . . Ah, but lads, why spill away such pearls? You aren't princes. After all . . . the moon is not so much on the wane, and the breezes neither come nor go. . . . (*He sounds his little trumpet and goes.*) They neither come nor go. Neither come nor go . . .

(COCOLICHE *and* CURRITO *heave a deep sigh and stand staring at each other. The central door opens suddenly and the wedding* CORTEGE *appears. Don* CRISTOBITA *and Miss* ROSITA *bid them goodbye at the door and close it. There are music and the tolling of bells in the distance.*)

CRISTOBITA: Oh, Rosita of my heart! Oh, Rosita!

ROSITA: He'll probably kill me now with the club.

CRISTOBITA: Are you sick? I thought you sighed! But that's because I please you so. I'm old and I understand things. Look what a suit I'm wearing! And what boot! Trala-la-la! Ah, bring sweets and wine, lots of wine! (*Enter, a* SERVANT *with some bottles.* CRISTOBITA *takes one and begins to drink.*) Ah, pretty Rosita! Tiny thing! Little almond! Isn't it true that I'm very beautiful? I'll give you a kiss! Here! Here! (*He kisses her. At this moment* COCOLICHE *and* CURRITO *look out of the shutters and let out a scream of rage.*) What's that? Could it be that this house is haunted? (*He takes up the club.*)

ROSITA: No, no, Cristóbal! It's the termites! It's the children out in the street! . . .

CRISTOBITA (*Putting down the club*): They make a lot of noise, *caramba!* They make a lot of noise!

ROSITA (*Hiding her terror*): When are you going to tell me the stories you promised me?

CRISTOBITA: Ha, ha, ha! They're very pretty, pretty as that poppy-face of yours. (*He drinks.*) The story of Don Tancredo, mounted on his pedestal. You know it? Ho-o-o-o! And the story of Don Juan Tenorio, Don Tancredo's cousin, and my cousin too. Yes sir! My cousin! You say it. "My cousin!"

ROSITA: Your cousin!

CRISTOBITA: Rosa! Rosa! Tell me something!

ROSITA: I love you, Cristobita.

CRISTOBITA: Olé, olé! (*He kisses her. There is another scream that*

issues from the wardrobes.) I'll put a stop to this, a stop and a definite end! Br-r-r-r-r!

ROSITA: Oh! No, don't get angry.

CRISTOBITA (*With the stick*): Whoever is in there, come out!

ROSITA: Look, don't be angry. A bird just flew past the window, with
wings . . . this big!

CRISTOBITA (*Imitating her*): This big! This big! You think I'm blind?

ROSITA: You don't love me! . . . (*She weeps.*)

CRISTOBITA (*Softened*): Shall I believe you . . . or shall I not believe
you? (*He sets his club down.*)

ROSITA (*Affectedly poetic*): What a clear little night dwells now upon
the rooftops. At this hour, children count the stars and old men
fall asleep in the saddle.

(CRISTOBITA *sits down, places his feet on the table and starts to
drink.*)

CRISTOBITA: I'd like to be made all of wine and drink myself up.
Ho-o-o-o! And my belly to be a cake, a great curly cake with sugar
plums and sweet potatoes . . . . (COCOLICHE *and* CURRITO *look out
from the wardrobes and sigh.*) Who's that sighing?

ROSITA: I . . . It was I, thinking of when I was a litle girl.

CRISTOBITA: When I was a boy they gave me a cake bigger than the
moon and I ate it all by myself. Ho-o-o! All by myself.

ROSITA (*Romantically*): The mountains of Córdoba have shadows
under their olive groves, trampled shadows, dead shadows, that
never move. Oh, to be under their roots. The mountains of Granada have their feet of light and snowy headdresses. Oh, to be
under their springs! Seville has no mountains.

CRISTOBITA: It has no mountains, no . . .

ROSITA: Long roads, colored orange. Oh, to lose one's self along them!

(CRISTOBITA, *listening to her, much as a person listening to a
violinist, has fallen asleep with a bottle in his hand.*)

CURRITO (*very softly*): Open the door!

COCOLICHE: Don't open mine! I want to die here.

ROSITA: Be still, for heaven's sake!

(*Enter,* MOSQUITO, *who begins to blow his trumpet around* CRIS-TOBITA. *The latter slaps at him.*)

CURRITO: I'll go where you'll never see me again.
ROSITA: I never loved you. You're a wanderer.
COCOLICHE: What's this I hear?
ROSITA: You're the only one I love, my love!
COCOLICHE: Ah, but you're already married!
CRISTOBITA: Br-r-r-r . . . Pesky mosquitoes! Pesky mosquitoes!
ROSITA: Santa Rosa, don't let him wake up! (*She goes toward one wardrobe and very carefully opens it. All of this scene should be played very quickly, but in low voices.*)
CURRITO (*Coming out of the wardrobe*): Farewell forever, O ingrate! My one regret is that I'll never forget you.

(*At this moment* MOSQUITO *strikes* CRISTOBITA *a sharp blow on the head with the trumpet and wakes him up.*)

CRISTOBITA: Ah! What? What? This is unbearable! Br-r-r-r!
CURRITO (*Bringing out a dagger*): Patience, my dear sir, patience!
CRISTOBITA: I'll kill you, I'll run you through a grinder, I'll pulverize your bones! You'll pay for this. Miss Rosita, fallen woman! And you cost me a hundred coins! Br-r-r-r! Smash, bing, bang! I'm choking with rage! Bing! Bang! What are you doing there?
CURRITO (*Trembling*): What . . . whatever I please.
CRISTOBITA: Ahr-r-r-r! Whatever you please? Well, man! Take this, whatever! Take this, please! (CURRITO *stabs at* CRISTOBITA *with his dagger but it sticks in the sleepyhead's chest in a strange way. During all this,* ROSITA *has been trying to open the center door and at this moment has succeeded in throwing it wide.* CURRITO *flies through it, pursued by* CRISTOBITA *who is saying*): Take this, whatever! Take this, please!

(ROSITA *has been giving vent to piercing screams or laughing hysterically. During this while, the characters should be supported by various flutes from a little orchestra.*)

COCOLICHE: Let me out of here; I'll kill him when he comes back!
ROSITA: Let you out? (*She goes to open.*) No. I won't! Oh!
COCOLICHE: Rosita, let me strangle him.

ROSITA: Shall I? (*She goes to open.*) No, I won't! He's coming now and he'll kill us.

COCOLICHE: That way we'll die together!

ROSITA: Shall I? Oh, yes . . . I'll let you out! (*She opens the wardrobe.*) My little heart! Little tree out of my garden!

COCOLICHE (*Embracing her*): My hothouse carnation! Little handful of cinnamon!

(*An idyll, like an opera duet, begins.*)

ROSITA: Go back to your house; I'll stay here and die.

COCOLICHE: Never, little rose among flowers. There on that little star I'll make you a swing and a silvery balcony. From there we'll watch how the world shimmers, dressed in moonlight.

ROSITA (*Forgetful of everything and in great happiness*): How romantic you are, my darling! I believe I must be a flower, dropping my petals in your hands.

COCOLICHE: Every day you look rosier to me; every day you seem to strip off another veil and surge forth naked.

ROSITA (*Placing her little head upon her sweetheart's breast*): Inside your breast a thousand birds have taken wing; my love, when I look at you, I seem to stand before a little fountain. (*Offstage, CRISTOBITA's voice is heard, and ROSITA comes out of her ecstasy.*) Run!

CRISTOBITA (*Appearing at the doorway and standing thunderstruck*): Ahr-r-r-r! You have lovers by the pair! Get ready for the cliff! Bing! Bang! Br-r-r-r! (COCOLICHE *and* ROSITA *kiss desperately in front of* CRISTOBITA.) Unbearable! I'm the one who killed three hundred Englishmen, three hundred Constantinopolitans! I'll give you something to remember me by! Oh! Oouch! (*The club falls from his hand and a great grinding of springs is heard.*) Oh, my little belly! Oh, my little belly! It's your fault I've burst, I've died! Oh, I'm dying! Oh, tell them to call the priest! Oh!

ROSITA (*Screeching piercingly and running about the stage dragging her long train*): Papa-a-a! Papa-a-a!

CRISTOBITA: Ahr-r-r-r! Bang! I'm done for! (*He staggers backward with his arms on high and then falls across the footlights.*)

ROSITA: He's dead! Oh, good heavens, what a compromising situation!

COCOLICHE (*Going up to him fearfully*): Say, he doesn't have any blood!

ROSITA: No blood?

COCOLICHE: Look! Look at what's coming out of his belly button! Sawdust!

ROSITA: I'm frightened!

COCOLICHE: You know something?

ROSITA: What?

COCOLICHE (*Emphatically*): Cristobita wasn't a real person!

ROSITA: What? Oh, don't even tell me! How disgusting! Wasn't he really a person?

FATHER (*Entering*): What is it? What is it?

(*Enter, various* PUPPETS.)

COCOLICHE: Look!

FATHER: He's burst!

(*The center door opens and other* PUPPETS *appear, carrying torches. They wear red capes and little black hats.* MOSQUITO *goes in front, carrying a white banner and playing his trumpet. They bear an enormous coffin on which peppers and radishes are painted, instead of stars.* PRIESTS *come chanting. A funeral march is played on the flutes.*)

PRIEST:

Uri memento.
A man is dead.

ALL:

Dead and gone, dead and gone
Cristobalón.

A PRIEST:

Whether we sing or don't
We earn our five pesetas.

(*When they pick up* CRISTOBITA, *he resounds in an amusing manner, like a bassoon. They all step back, and Doña* ROSITA *weeps. They come back for him again and he doesn't sound quite as loudly as before, till finally his sighs are those of a piccolo, whereupon they throw him in the coffin. The cortege marches about the stage to the laments of the music.*)

COCOLICHE: Now I feel as if my chest were full of jingle bells, full of lots of little hearts. I'm just like a field of flowers.

ROSITA: My tears, my little kisses will all be for you; you're my carnation.

MOSQUITO (*As he leads off the assembly*):

> We're going to bury
> the great bread sack,
> Cristobita, the drunkard,
> who won't come back.
> Ran,
> rataplan,
> rataplan,
> rataplan.
> Rataplan!

(COCOLICHE *and* ROSITA *are left, embracing. Symphony.*)

The End of the Beginning

BY

SEAN O'CASEY

*P*ROBABLY no other country so small as Ireland has produced in the last three centuries a galaxy of playwrights the equal of Richard Brinsley Sheridan, Oliver Goldsmith, Dion Boucicault, Oscar Wilde, George Bernard Shaw, William Butler Yeats and John Millington Synge. Many nations would be proud to boast even the less well-known (but no less loved) Irish playwrights such as George Farquhar, Richard Steele, Lady Augusta Gregory, Padraic Colum, Lennox Robinson, Lord Dunsany, Paul Vincent Carroll, Brendan Behan and the contemporary dramatist Brian Friel, whose one-act play *Winners,* one of two plays comprising the Broadway success *Lovers,* is particularly recommended to teenaged readers of this volume. When one adds to this roster the illustrious expatriates James Joyce, Samuel Beckett and Sean O'Casey, Ireland's eminence in twentieth-century literature and theatre is spectacularly secured.

Of this impressive list, O'Casey (1880–1964) knew Irish slum existence as well as anyone could, being himself a product of the streets and tenements. The last of 13 children, he was born of impoverished Protestant parents in predominantly Catholic Dublin, and was one of only five who survived infancy. His father died when he was three and John Casey, as he then was named, confronted a life of hunger, squalor and rebelliousness. While still a boy, he attempted a series of jobs for which he was ill suited that brought him more personal discontent than monetary welfare. He successively sold newspapers, worked on the docks, broke stone, built roads, carried hod and performed hard labor for as many as 12 hours a day. Frequently he was fired, often because of his outspoken sense of independence and once because he would not remove his hat when he stepped before the paymaster to receive his wages.

A sickness that verged upon blindness kept him from attending school regularly and even from learning to read and write until he taught himself with the aid of his sister when he was thirteen years old. He claimed that he educated himself chiefly by reading the

Bible and Shakespeare. Along with another brother, he furthered his interests in drama by acting in amateur productions, often performing roles in plays by Shakespeare and Dion Boucicault, both of whom influenced his dramaturgy, the first by extolling great examples of language and character, the second by demonstrating a concern for present-day subject matter and Irish life. He attended performances of the Abbey Theatre, Dublin's foremost acting company, whenever he could afford admission, and saw there the great plays and players of the prospering Irish dramatic movement in the early years of this century.

As a youth, O'Casey became concerned with Ireland's struggle for freedom by joining the Irish Republican Brotherhood, a subversive group dedicated to the reestablishment of all things Irish, including the Gaelic language and the traditional music of the bagpipes. At this time he changed the spelling of his name and taught Gaelic to workers in the slums; he also participated in the labor movement, at one point becoming the secretary of the Irish Citizen Army, a union for unskilled laborers. Throughout the turbulent strikes, the blood bath of the Easter Rebellion in 1916, the years of machine-gunned patrol in Dublin, the street warfare fought between the Irish Republican Army and British forces, O'Casey observed the poor people, the wounded and the dying, and recorded his impressions in his first plays. Nowhere can one better experience Dublin's tumultuous and painful troubles than in O'Casey's *The Shadow of a Gunman* (1923) and *The Plough and the Stars* (1926). Life in the tenements during the civil war of 1922 forms the substance of *Juno and the Paycock* (1924), a realistic masterpiece in which dwell several of the playwright's most luminous characters: the bragging-coward paycock, "Captain" Jack Boyle; his patient but harassed wife, Juno; their children, who become victims of both the times and their parents' blindness; and Joxer Daly, a comic crony who helps lead the Captain to his inevitable tragic downfall.

Disillusioned when nationalism failed to improve the lot of the laborer and disappointed by a loss of ideals in the organizations he had zealously supported, O'Casey became alienated from the Dubliners he knew so well. After the riots that accompanied the opening night of *The Plough and the Stars* at the Abbey Theatre, during which he watched his fellow citizens rail against his play, he decided to leave Ireland to find a place where he could write in peace. This decision was reinforced when the directors of the Abbey rejected his next play, *The Silver Tassie* in 1928; with his departure, the theatre fell into an artistic decline from which it has never recovered.

In England O'Casey continued to write plays, outstanding among which are *Within the Gates* (1933), *Purple Dust* (1940), *Red Roses for Me* (1943), and *Cock-a-Doodle Dandy* (1943). Although the Abbey eventually returned to his works, twice producing *The Silver Tassie*, he remained a dramatist without a theatre. In order for O'Casey to earn a living it became necessary to undertake nondramatic writing, and in 1939 he published the first of six volumes of autobiography, which in lyrical prose recount his love-hate relationship with Ireland, which lasted until his death in his eighty-fourth year. Even when O'Casey was being proclaimed the greatest living playwright, professional productions of his plays were few in London and New York and, except at the Abbey, are seldom seen today. It is difficult for any save Irish actors to convey the full measure of his rich and rhythmic idiom, which may be enjoyed, however, in the reading of his plays. And in printed texts O'Casey's theatre flourishes today.

The End of the Beginning, in which Darry Berrill attempts to keep house as women do, with the assistance of his inept friend Barry Derrill, contains the germ of O'Casey's antiheroic themes, which recur in most of his plays dealing with Irish workaday life. In making total fools of themselves, the two "heroes" destroy their simple surroundings but remain true to their own kind to the final curtain. O'Casey here gives women every reason to be liberated from such men. Even though the playwright sees them for what they are—bunglers—he enjoys their refusal to admit their limitations and allows them to demonstrate, as Captain Jack and Joxer Daly had before them, that the whole world is in a terrible state of "chassis" (chaos); of this there is no doubt in this frantic farce, first produced at the Abbey Theatre on February 8, 1937.

The End of the Beginning

CHARACTERS

DARRY BERRILL, *about fifty-five; stocky, obstinate, with a pretty big belly. He is completely bald, except for a tuft of gray hair just above his forehead.*

BARRY DERRILL, *Darry's neighbor. Same age as Darry. Thin, easygoing, big moustache, and is very nearsighted.*

LIZZIE BERRILL, *Darry's wife. About forty-five. A good woman about the house, but that's about all.*

A big, comfortable kitchen. Steep stairs, almost like a ladder, leading to upper room, top right. Huge fireplace, right. Some chairs, one heavy, with rubbered castors. Small settee, and table. Chest of drawers, left, on top of which stands a gramophone. Door back, and to left of door a window. To right of door, a dresser, on which is, as well as delf (earthenware), a large clock of the alarm type. To right of dresser, on a nail, hangs a whip; to the left of dresser hangs a mandolin. On table, a quantity of unwashed delf. To right of fireplace, a lumber room. The room, at night, is lighted by an electric bulb, hanging from center of ceiling. It is a fine early autumn evening, with the sun low in the heavens. On wall, back, a large red card on which "Do It Now" is written in white letters. A sink under the window.

DARRY (*At door of room below. He is shaving, and his chin is covered with lather*): This shaving water's dead cold, woman. D'ye hear me? This shaving water's dead cold.

LIZZIE (*Busy about the room—quietly*): Come down and heat it, then.

DARRY (*Scornfully*): Too much to do, I suppose. I'd do all that has to be done here, three times over, 'n' when all was finished, I'd be sighing for something to do.

LIZZIE: If you had half of what I have to do here, at the end of the evening you'd be picked up dead out of the debris.

DARRY: I would?

LIZZIE: You would.

DARRY: Sure?

LIZZIE: Certain.

DARRY: If I only had half to do?

LIZZIE: Or less.

DARRY: I'd be picked up out of the debris?

LIZZIE: Out of the middle of it.

DARRY: Dead?

LIZZIE: As a mackerel.

DARRY (*Fiercely*): I'm always challenging you to change places for a few hours, but you won't do it. I'd show you what a sinecure of a job you had here, while I'm sweating out in the fields.

LIZZIE: Go out 'n' finish the mowing of the meadow. It'll take you only half an hour or so, 'n' there's plenty of light in the sky still.

DARRY (*Who has been shaving himself during this argument*): The meadow 'll do to be done tomorrow. Why don't you let me do what's to be done in the house, an' you go 'n' mow the meadow? Why don't you do that? 'don't you do that? 'you do that? Agony to look at you; agony to listen to you; agony, agony to be anywhere near you.

LIZZIE: I'd just like to see you doing what's to be done about the house—I'd just like to see you.

DARRY: What is there to be done about the house—will you tell us that?

LIZZIE: There's the pig 'n' the heifer 'n' the hens to be fed 'n' tended. There's ironing, cooking, washing, 'n' sewing to be done.

DARRY: Sewing! An' only a button back 'n' front of me so that it's next thing to a miracle that my trousers are kept from starting the neighbors talking.

LIZZIE: If you say much more, I'll go 'n' mow the meadow, 'n' leave you to see what you can make of the housework.

DARRY (*Angrily*): Buzz off, buzz off, then, and I'll show you how the work of a house is done. Done quietly; done with speed, 'n' without a whisper of fuss in its doing. Buzz off, if you want to, 'n' I'll show you 'n' all your sex how the work of a house is done!

(LIZZIE *violently pulls off a jazz-colored overall she is wearing, and flings it on the floor.*)

LIZZIE (*Furiously*): Put that on you, 'n' do what remains to be done about the house, while I go an' mow the meadow. Get into it, 'n' show the world an' your poor wife the wonders you can do when you're under a woman's overall.

DARRY (*A little frightened*): Oh, I'll manage all right.

LIZZIE: An' don't you let that Alice Lanigan in here while I'm away either, d'ye hear?

DARRY: What Alice Lanigan?

LIZZIE (*In a temper*): What Alice Lanigan! The Alice Lanigan I caught you chattering to yesterday, when you should have been mowing the meadow. The Alice Lanigan that's setting you on to nag at me about the little I have to do in the house. The Alice Lanigan that's goading you into the idea that if you were a little slimmer round the belly, you'd be a sheavaleer, an's getting you to do physical jerks. The Alice Lanigan that's on the margin of fifty, 'n' assembles herself together as if she was a girl in her teens, jutting out her bust when she's coming in, 'n' jutting out her behind when she's going out, like the Lady of Shalott, to catch the men—that's the Alice Lanigan I mean.

DARRY: I don't be thinking of Alice Lanigan.

LIZZIE: I've seen you, when you thought I slumbered 'n' slept, naked, with nothing at all on you, doing your physical jerks in front of the looking glass, 'n' that, too, when the lessons of a Mission were still hot in your heart—an' all for Alice Lanigan. Maybe you don't know that she has a kid who has never had a pat on the head from a father.

DARRY: You buzz off now, 'n' I'll show how the work of a house is done.

LIZZIE (*While she is putting a broad-brimmed hat on her head, pulling a pair of old gloves over her hands, and taking down a whip hanging from a nail in the wall*): I'm telling you it's a dangerous thing to shake hands with Alice Lanigan, even with a priest giving the introduction. The day'll come soon when you'll know she's making mechanical toys of you 'n' that other old fool, Barry Derrill, who's so nearsighted that he can't see the sky, unless the moon's shining in it!

DARRY: Cheerio.

LIZZIE (*At the door*): I'm going now, 'n' we'll see how you do the work of the house.

DARRY: Hail 'n' farewell to you. An' mind you, this'll be only the beginning of things.

LIZZIE: God grant that it won't be the end, an' that when I come back, I'll at least find the four walls standing. (*She goes out. DARRY strolls to the door, and watches her going down the road.*)

DARRY (*Scornfully to himself*): Mow the meadow! Well, let her see her folly out. (*As he shuts the door, the clock in the distant Town Hall strikes eight. DARRY returns, glances at the clock on the dresser, notices that it has stopped, takes it up, puts his ear against it, shakes it, begins to wind it, finds it difficult to turn, puts added strength into the turning, and a whirring rattle, like a strong spring break-*

ing, comes from the inside of the clock. He hastily replaces the clock on the dresser. After a few seconds' thought, he takes it up again, removes the back, and part of a big, broken spring darts out, which he hurriedly crams in again, and puts the clock back on the dresser.) Lizzie again! *(He catches sight of the gramophone, looks at it, thinks for a second, goes over to the chest of drawers, takes some records from behind it, and fixes one on the disc of the gramophone. He takes off his waistcoat, loosens his braces, stands stiff, strokes his thighs, pats his belly, and tries to push it back a little. He starts the gramophone going, runs to the center of the room, and lies down on the broad of his back. The gramophone begins to give directions for physical exercises, to which* DARRY *listens and, awkwardly, clumsily, and puffingly, tries to follow the movements detailed in the words spoken by the gramophone when the music commences.)*

GRAMOPHONE: Lie on back; hands behind the head; feet together—are you ready? Bend the right knee; draw it into the waistline, toward the chest—commence!

> *(*DARRY *is too slow, or the gramophone is too quick, for he can't keep up with the time of the music. When he finds that he is behind the time of the music,* DARRY *increases his speed by partial performance of the movements, and so gets into touch with the time, but presently, blowing and panting, he is out of time again by a beat or two. He climbs stiffly on to his feet, goes over to gramophone, and puts the indicator to "Slow.")*

DARRY: Phuh. Too quick, too damn quick altogether. *(He starts the gramophone going, runs to the center of the room, and again lies down on the broad of his back. When the music begins he goes through the movements as before; but the music is playing so slowly now that he finds it impossible to go slowly enough to keep to the time of the tune. When he finds himself in front of a beat, he stops and puffs and waits for the beat to catch up with him before he recommences. As he is going through these movements, the door opens, and* BARRY DERRILL *comes into the room. He has a mandolin under his arm, and is wearing wide-rimmed, thick-lensed spectacles.)*

BARRY *(Briskly)*: Come 'n' kiss me, sweet 'n' twenty—what the hell are you trying to do?

DARRY: Can't you see what I'm trying to do? Take off your spectacles 'n' get a closer look. Keeping meself fit 'n' flexible—that's what I'm trying to do.

BARRY: The rhythm's too slow, man; tense your muscles; you're not tun'd into the movements properly, man.

DARRY: The indicator must have shifted. Slip over 'n' put it to the point marked "Medium," 'n' then get down here 'n' give us a hand.

BARRY: What about the prologue of playing the song we're to sing at the Town Hall concert?

DARRY: Get down 'n' have five minutes of this, first; we'll both sing the better for it.

BARRY (*Dubiously*): Never done it to music, 'n' I wouldn't be able to keep in touch with the—with the measure.

DARRY: The music makes it easier, man. Keep your eye on me, 'n' move when I move. (BARRY *reluctantly takes off his coat and waistcoat, goes over to the gramophone, puts his nose against the instrument, and puts the indicator to "Fast."*) To do this thing properly you'd want to be wearing shorts. Right; now keep in touch with the rhythm, or you'll mar everything. Start her off, and stretch yourself down.

(BARRY *starts the gramophone, runs over and lies down opposite to* DARRY, *so that the soles of their feet are only a few inches apart.*)

GRAMOPHONE (*Very rapidly*): Lie on back; hands behind the head; feet together—are you ready? Bend the right knee; draw it into the waistline toward the chest; breathe out—commence!

(*The tempo of the tune forces them to do the exercises in a frantic way, till it dawns on* DARRY, *who is nearly exhausted, that there's something wrong. He stops while* BARRY *goes on manfully.*)

DARRY (*Scornfully*): Eh, eh, there, wait a minute, wait a minute, man. Don't you see anything wrong?

BARRY (*Stopping*): No; what's wrong?

DARRY (*Testily*): Aw, what's wrong! We're congestin' ourselves with speed; that's what's wrong. You must have jammed the indicator hard to "Fast." (*He gets up, goes to the gramophone, and puts it right.*) We're entertainin' ourselves, an' not tryin' to say the Rosary. (*He comes back and stretches himself again on the floor. The music begins and the two men commence the exercises. After a few moments,* DARRY *slows down a little, misses several beats, and tries to blame* BARRY. (*Excitedly keeping up the movements, but out of time, as he talks.*) Try to keep the proper rhythm up, man. (*He hums the tune of "Coming thro' the Rye."*) Dad th' didee dah th' diddy dah th' diddy dee—that way, man. Dah th' diddy dah th' diddy (*Rapidly*). Keep your eye on me. Dah th' diddy dee. (*After a few moments* DARRY *is out of time and breathless; he stops and sits up to complain, but he really wants to get a rest. With aggravated patience.*) Barry, you're spoiling the whole thing by getting out of time. Don't let your arms and legs go limber, tense your muscles. Three beats to the bar, see? Now! (*They start again;* DARRY *is soon behind time, blowing and puffing out of him.* BARRY *keeps to the beat of the tune splendidly. Angrily.*) You're going too damn quick altogether, now, man!

BARRY: No, I'm not—I'm there to the tick every time.

DARRY (*Violently*): There to the tick—how is it you're not in the line with me, then, if you're there to the tick? I don't know whether you're in front of me or behind me. Are you too stiff or what?

BARRY: I'm there to the second every time. It's you that's missin' a beat in the bar.

DARRY (*Indignantly, stopping to talk, while* BARRY *goes on*): I'm missin' it because I'm trying to foster you into the right balance 'n' rhythm of the movements. That's why I'm missin' it. (*Loudly.*) An' I'm wastin' me time!

BARRY (*Sharply*): I'm doing me best, amn't I?

DARRY (*More sharply still*): Your best's a hell of a way behind what's wanted. It's pitiful 'n' painful to be watchin' you, man. (*He stands up and looks at* BARRY, *who keeps going.*) Eh, eh, you'll do yourself an injury, Barry. Get up 'n' we'll do the song. (*As* BARRY *goes on.*) Oh, get up 'n' we'll do the song.

(BARRY *gets up reluctantly, and* DARRY *goes over and stops the gramophone.*)

BARRY: I was doin' it well enough, if you'd let me alone.

DARRY (*Scornfully*): Yes; like the Londonderry Air play'd in march time. (*They get their mandolins and stand side by side at the back.*)

Now we walk in a semicircle down to the front, 'n' bow, you remember? Ready?

BARRY: Yep.

DARRY: Go!

(*They both step off to the right, take a few steps, and then they
halt.*)

BARRY: Something wrong; we don't go round the same way, do we?

DARRY (*Testily*): Of course there's something wrong; of course we
don't go round the same way. Can't you try to remember, Barry?
You're to go to the left, to the left.

BARRY: I remember distinctly I was to go to the right.

DARRY (*Irritably*): Oh, don't be such an egotist, Barry. Now think
for a minute. (*A pause.*) Now make up your mind—d'ye want to
go to the left or the right?

BARRY (*Testily*): Oh, left, right—any way.

DARRY: Left, then. Go. (*They march round, one to the right, the
other to the left, meet in the front, and bow.*) You start, Barry,
my boy.

BARRY (*Singing*):

One summer eve a handsome man met a handsome maiden strolling,

DARRY:

Down where the bees were hummin' an' the wild flowers gaily growing;

BARRY:

Said she, We'll sit down here a while, all selfish thoughts controlling,

DARRY:

Down where the bees are hummin' an' the wild flowers gaily growing:

BARRY:

Said she, We'll meditate on things, things high 'n' edifying,

How all things live 'n' have their day 'n' end their day by dying.

He put his hand on her white breast an' murmur'd, Life is trying,

DARRY:

Down where the bees are hummin' an' the wild flowers gaily growing.

BARRY:

The moon glanc'd down 'n' wonder'd what the pair of them were
doing,

DARRY:

Down where the bees were hummin' an' the wild flowers gaily growing;

BARRY:

Then th' moon murmur'd, I feel hot, 'n' fear a storm is brewing,

DARRY:

Down where the bees were hummin' an' the wild flowers gaily growing.

BARRY:

She talk'd so well of things so high, he started to reward her,
The moon ran in behind a cloud, for there was none to guard her.
I'll take that off, she said, you'd ruin the lace that's round the border,

DARRY:

Down where the bees were hummin' an' the wild flowers gaily growing.

BARRY:

White-featur'd 'n' thin goodie-goodies rush around excited,

DARRY:

Down where the bees were hummin' an' the wild flowers gaily growing;

BARRY:

Proclaiming that the dignity of living has been blighted,

DARRY:

Down where the bees are hummin' an' the wild flowers gaily growing.

BARRY:

But when the light is soft 'n' dim, discovery disarming,
The modest moon behind the clouds, young maidens, coy 'n' charm-
ing,
Still cuddle men who cuddle them, 'n' carry on alarming,

DARRY:

Down where the bees are hummin' an' the wild flowers gaily growing.

(*When the song has ended,* DARRY *cocks his ear and listens.*)

BARRY: Shall we try it once more?
DARRY: Shush, shut up, can't you? (DARRY *goes over to the door, opens
it, and listens intently. There is heard the rattling whirr caused by
the steady and regular movement of a mowing machine. The dis-*

tant Town Hall clock strikes nine. Hastily putting the mandolin away.) I forgot. I'll have to get going.

BARRY: Get going at what?

DARRY: Housework. (*He begins to get into the overall left off by* LIZZIE.) I dared her, an' she left me to do the work of the house while she was mowing the meadow. If it isn't done when she comes back, then sweet goodbye to the status I had in the home. (*He finds it difficult to get the overall on.*) Dih dih dih, where's the back 'n' where's the front, 'n' which is which is the bottom 'n' which is the top?

BARRY: Take it quietly, take it quietly, Darry.

DARRY (*Resentfully*): Take it quietly? An' the time galloping by? I can't stand up on a chair 'n' say to the sun, Stand thou still there, over the meadow th' missus is mowing, can I?

BARRY: I know damn well you can't, but you're not going to expedite matters by rushing around in a hurry.

DARRY (*He has struggled into the overall*): Expedite matters! It doesn't seem to strike you that when you do things quickly, things are quickly done. Expedite matters! I suppose loitering to look at you lying on the broad of your back, jiggling your legs about, was one way of expediting matters; an' listening to you plucking curious sounds out of a mandolin, an' singing a questionable song, was another way of expediting matters?

BARRY: You pioneered me into doing two of them yourself.

DARRY (*Busy with the pot on the fire*): I pioneered you into doing them! Barry Derrill, there's such a thing in the world as a libel. You came strutting in with a mandolin under your arm, didn't you?

BARRY: I did, but—

DARRY: An' you sang your song.

BARRY: Yes, but—

DARRY: When you waltz'd in, I was doing calisthenics, wasn't I?

BARRY: I know you were; but all the same—

DARRY: An' you flung yourself down on the floor, and got yourself into a tangle trying to do them too, didn't you?

BARRY: Hold on a second—

DARRY: Now, I can't carry the conversation into a debate, for I have to get going. So if you can't give a hand, go, 'n' let me do the things that have to be done, in an orderly 'n' quiet way.

BARRY: 'Course I'll give a hand—only waiting to be asked.

DARRY (*Looking at the clock, suddenly*): Is the clock stopped?

BARRY (*Taking up clock and putting it close to his ear*): There's no ticking, 'n' it's hours slow.

DARRY: Lizzie again! Forgot to wind it. Give the key a few turns, Barry, an' put the hands on to half-past nine. (BARRY *starts to wind the clock.* DARRY *goes over to table, gets a basin of water, begins to wash the delf, humming to himself the air of the song, "Down where the bees are humming."* BARRY *winds and winds away, but no sign is given of a tightening of the spring inside. He looks puzzled, winds again, and is about to silently put the clock back where he found it, when* DARRY *turns and looks at him questioningly.*) You've broken the damn thing, have you?

BARRY: I didn't touch it.

DARRY: Didn't touch it? Amn't I after looking at you twisting an' tearing at it for nearly an hour? (*He comes over to* BARRY.) Show me that. (*He takes the clock from* BARRY *and opens the back, and the spring darts out.*) Didn't touch it. Oh, for God's sake be more careful when you're handling things in this house! Dih dih dih. (*He pushes the spring back, and slaps the clock down on the dresser.*) You must have the hands of a gorilla, man. Here, come over 'n wipe while I wash. (*A slight pause while the two of them work at the delf.* DARRY *anxiously watches* BARRY, *who, being very nearsighted, holds everything he wipes close up to his spectacles. Suddenly.*) Look out, look out, there—you're not leaving that jug on the table at all; you're depositing it in the air, man!

BARRY (*Peering down at the table*): Am I? Don't be afraid, I won't let anything drop.

DARRY (*Humming the song*): Dum dah de de dum da dee dee dum dah dee dee dee dah ah dum.

BARRY (*Swinging his arm to the tune*): Down where the bees are hummin' an' the wild flowers gaily growing.

DARRY: Fine swing, you know. Dum dah dee dee dum dah dee dee dum dah dee dee dee dah ah dum.

BARRY (*Swinging his arm*): Down where the bees are hummin'— (BARRY's *arm sends the jug flying off the table on to the floor.*)

DARRY (*Yelling*): You snaky-arm'd candle-power-ey'd elephant, look at what you're after doing!

BARRY (*Heatedly*): It's only a tiny jug, anyhow, 'n you can hardly see the pieces on the floor!

DARRY (*Just as heatedly*): An' if I let you do much more, they would soon be big enough to bury us! Sit down, sit down in the corner there; do nothing, say nothing, an', if I could, I'd put a safety curtain round you. For God's sake, touch nothing while I run out an' give the spuds to the pig. (DARRY *dashes over to the fire, whips the pot off, and runs out. He leaves the door open, and again the rattling whirr of a mowing machine can be heard.* BARRY *sits dejectedly in a corner. After a few moments a bump is heard outside, followed by a yell from* DARRY, *who, a second later, comes rushing madly in, a bloody handkerchief pressed to his nose. He flings himself flat on the floor on his back, elevating his nose as much as possible.*) Get me something cold to put down the back of my neck, quick!

BARRY (*Frightened*): What the hell did you do to yourself?

DARRY: I didn't bend low enough when I was going in, 'n' I gave myself such a—oh, such a bang on my nose on the concrete. Get something cold, man, to shove down the back of my neck 'n' stop the bleeding!

BARRY: Keep the nose sticking up in the air as high as you can. I don't know where to get something cold to shove down the back of your neck. I knew this rushing round wouldn't expedite matters.

DARRY (*With a moan of resentment as he hears "expedite matters"*): Oh, pull yourself together, man, 'n' remember we're in the middle of an emergency.

BARRY: A little block of ice, now, would come in handy.

DARRY: A little—oh, a little block of ice! An' will you tell us where you're going to get a little block of ice? An', even if we had one, how could you fasten it down the back of my neck? Eh? Can't you answer—where are you going to get a block of ice?

BARRY: How the hell do I know where I'm going to get it?

DARRY: D'ye expect me to keep lying here till the winter comes? (*During this dialogue* BARRY *is moving round the room aimlessly, peering into drawers, rattling the delf on the dresser with his nose as he looks along the shelves. As he hears the crockery rattling:*) Mind, mind, or you'll break something. I must be losing a lot of blood, Barry, an' I won't be able to keep my nose sticking up in the air much longer. Can't you find anything?

BARRY: I can see nothing.

DARRY: Run upstairs 'n' get the key of the big shed that's hanging on the wall, somewhere over the mantelpiece at the far end of the room. Go quick, man! (BARRY *runs upstairs, goes into room, comes out again, and looks down at* DARRY. *Up to him*:) Did you get it?

BARRY: Where's the switch? It's dark as pitch in there.

(DARRY, *with a moan of exasperation, sits up, but immediately plunges down on his back again.*)

DARRY: Starts pumping out again the minute I sit up. (*To* BARRY.) There's no switch in that room. We can't have a switch in every corner of the room just to suit you! You've only got to move down the center of the room till you come to the fireplace; then brush your hand over the mantelpiece, along the wall, till you feel the key hanging there. (BARRY *goes back into the room. After a few seconds' silence, there is a crash of falling crockery.* DARRY, *after a second of silent consternation, sits up with a jerk, but immediately plunges down on his back again. Sinking supine on the floor.*) What has he done now; oh, what has he done now? (*Shouting up to* BARRY.) Eh, you up there—what have you done now?

BARRY (*Sticking his head out of door above*): Nothing much—the washhand-stand fell over.

DARRY (*Angrily*): Nothing much. It sounded a hell of a lot, then. You're the kind of man if you're not chained up, 'll pull everything in the house asundher! Come down, come down, 'n' stop down, or that delicate little hand of yours 'll smash everything in the house!

BARRY: My eyes are used to the darkness, now, 'n' I can see. I'll get the key for you. (*He goes back into the room, leaving* DARRY *speechless. After a few seconds, he comes out of the room in a sweat of fright and anger, one hand tightly clasped over the other. He rushes down the stairs, and begins to pull the things out of the chest of drawers, every other moment leaving off to clasp one hand over the other. Frantically.*) Get your own key, get your own key. Half slaughtering myself for your sake! Why don't you keep your razor blades in a safe place, an' not leave them scattered about in heaps all over the mantelpiece? Where is there a bit of old rag till I bind up my wounds? Get your own key yourself, I'm tellin' you.

DARRY: Amn't I nicely handicapped, wanting help an' having only the help of a half-blind man?

BARRY: D'ye know I'm nearly after mowing my fingers off with your blasted razor blades? (*Coming near to* DARRY, *with a handkerchief in his hand, and showing the injured fingers to him.*) Look at them, uh, look at them—one looks as if only a thin thread of flesh was keeping it on. How am I going to play the mandolin now?

DARRY: You'd play it better if all your fingers were off.

BARRY (*Keeping the wounded hand in the air, and holding out the handkerchief to* DARRY *with the other*): Here, get a grip of this 'n' help me to bind up me wounds. (BARRY *kneels down beside the prostrate* DARRY, *who takes the handkerchief and proceeds to tie it round* BARRY's *wounded fingers.*)

DARRY (*Keeping his nose well up in the air*): You give that an unexpected honor, if you call that a wound! (DARRY *ties the handkerchief round* BARRY's *hand, who stands looking at it.*)

BARRY (*Reflectively*): Won't be able to do much for you with it now.

DARRY: It'll limit your capacity for breakin' things. (*A pause.*) Slip out, Barry, old son, 'n' see if the heifer's safe on the bank beside the house.

(BARRY *goes outside the door and stands looking up toward the top of the house. The light has been fading, and it is getting dark. Again can be heard the whirr of the mowing machine, and the Town Hall clock strikes ten.*)

BARRY: I think I can hear her croppin' the grass all right, but it doesn't seem wise to leave her there 'n' the dusk fallin'.

DARRY (*Testily*): I can't do anything till this bleeding stops, can I?

BARRY: The spuds are all scattered about here where you let them fall when you were runnin' in.

DARRY (*Moaning*): 'N' can't you get the broom 'n' sweep them up into a corner, 'n' not be trampling them into the ground; you see the state I'm in! (BARRY *gets the broom and starts to sweep outside the door. In to* DARRY.) How's it now?

DARRY (*Cautiously sitting up*): It's nearly stopped now, but I'll have to go cautious.

(BARRY, *sweeping with one hand, manages to bring the broom handle into contact with the window, and breaks a pane. A silent pause.*)

BARRY (*As if he didn't know*): What's that, what's that?

DARRY (*In an agony of anger*): What's that, what's that! Can't you
see, man, that you're after thrustin' the handle of the broom
through one of the windows?

BARRY (*Peering down at the hole in the window*): That's curious,
now, for I never felt the handle touchin' the window; but there's
a hole in it, right enough.

DARRY (*With angry mockery*): No, you wouldn't feel it touchin' it,
either. A hole in it—of course there's a hole in it! My God Almighty, I've a destroyin' angel in the house!

BARRY: Well, not much use of lookin' at it now.

DARRY (*Vehemently*): Oh, come in, come in, come in, man. Didn't
you hear the clock strikin' ten? I'll have to get goin' now. (*He
gets up gingerly, feeling his nose, and still keeping it at a high
angle.*)

BARRY (*Introducing another subject*): Hadn't you better stable the
heifer before you do anything?

DARRY (*Violently*): Haven't I to clean out the cowhouse first before
I stable her, man? With your exercisin', 'n' your singin', 'n' your
great 'n' godly gift of expeditin' matters, I haven't made a bit of
headway! I hadn't a chance to give her the graze she needs, so
let her get all she can on the bank at the back of the house.

BARRY: Supposing she wanders to the edge of the bank 'n' tumbles
off?

DARRY: I don't know what to do about that.

BARRY: Couldn't you tie her to something?

DARRY (*Angrily*): There's nothing to tie her to, man.

BARRY: What about putting a rope down the chimney 'n' tying it to
something in the room?

DARRY (*After a few seconds' thought*): That's a good idea, Barry.
There's a rope outside, an' I'll sling one end round her neck, let
the other end down the chimney, an' tie it to a chair. Wait here
a second 'n' get it when it comes down.

(*DARRY rushes out. After a few moments his voice is heard
faintly from above calling "Hello, hello!"* BARRY, *who has his
head a little up the chimney, the smoke making him cough,
answers, "Righto, let her come."* The rope comes down; BARRY
catches the end and pulls it into the room.* DARRY *returns, and
they tie the rope to a chair.*)

BARRY: Put the chair at the far end of the room, an' if the heifer wanders too far, we'll see the chair moving across the room.

DARRY (*With enthusiasm*): Now you're beginnin' to use your brains at last, Barry, me boy. (*He shifts the chair to the far end of the room.*) Now we can get goin' 'n' get everything shipshape before the missus toddles back. Let's put on the light and see what we're doin'. (*He snaps down the switch, but no light comes into the bulb. Annoyed*): Dih dih dih—must be the meter again. (*He hurries into the lumber room, stepping over the rope.*)

BARRY (*Speaking in to* DARRY): I wouldn't do much tamperin' with that.

DARRY (*Inside room—emphatically*): Oh, I know what I'm doin'. (DARRY *rushes out again, snaps down the switch, but no light comes. Irritably.*) Must be the blasted bulb. (*He rushes to a drawer.*) There's a bulb here, somewhere, we've had for a long time, 'n' never used. (*He takes one from the drawer.*) Here we are. (*He pulls a chair to the center of the room, stands on it, takes off the old bulb, and gives it to* BARRY.) See if you can see anything wrong with it.

BARRY (*Holding it to his nose*): Can't see anything.

DARRY: Leave it down, leave it down.

BARRY: Sure the one you're fixing's the right voltage?

DARRY (*Stopping to look at* BARRY): 'Course it's the right voltage. Why wouldn't it be the right voltage?

BARRY: If it wasn't, it might fuse.

DARRY: Fuse? No fear of it fusing. (*He starts to work again. The chair to which the rope is tied begins to move across the floor.*)

BARRY (*Startled*): Look out, look out—the heifer's moving!

DARRY: Catch hold of it, catch hold of it, before she disappears up the chimney! (BARRY *catches the chair, but the strain is too much, and he is pulled along.* DARRY *jumps down off the chair, leaves the bulb on the table, catches hold of the rope, and helps* BARRY *to tug the chair back to the far end of the room.*) You sit on the chair, 'n' then she can't move without our knowledge.

(BARRY *sits on the chair;* DARRY *mounts the chair again, and starts to fix the bulb. The chair begins to move with* BARRY *sitting on it.*)

BARRY (*Excitedly*): Eh, quick again, get down, the heifer's movin'!

(DARRY *jumps down again, and the two of them pull the chair back to its place.*)

DARRY: The missus'll be back 'n' nothin' done but damage. (*He gets up again and fixes the bulb; there is a flash, and the room is darker than ever.*)

BARRY (*Like a prophet*): I warned you, Darry; I saw it comin'.

DARRY (*Forcibly*):What are you blatherin' about? We're no worse off than we were before we fixed it. There's a drum of oil in the lumber room, 'n' if there's any left in it we can light the lamps. You light the one hangin' on the wall, while I see how we stand. (*He runs into the lumber room.* BARRY *takes the lamp from the wall, removes the chimney, and tries to light the wick, but he can't see it, and holds the match anywhere but near the wick.* DARRY *comes out of cellar. Jubilantly.*) Plenty of oil in it. Aw, you're not holding the match within a mile of the wick, man. Show it to me, show it to me. (*He takes the match from* BARRY, *and lights the lamp.*) Out with you now, 'n' get one of the old lamps you'll find on one of the shelves to the right in the shed at the back of the yard.

BARRY: How'll I see?

DARRY: Strike a match 'n' look. You'll see them staring at you. I'll take a canful of oil from the drum to put in it when you bring it back, 'n' then we'll have lashin's of light.

BARRY (*Going out by door*): I know I won't be able to see.

(DARRY, *with a can that has a long snout on it, runs back into the lumber room.* BARRY *has left the door open, and the rattling whirr of the mowing machine can be heard again. There is a slight pause. Suddenly* DARRY *rushes out of the lumber room over to the open door.*)

DARRY (*Shouting madly*): Barry, Barry, come here quick, man! I turned the key of the tap too much, 'n' it slipped out of me hand into a heap of rubbish 'n' I can't turn off the cock, 'n' I can't find the key in the dark. Come quick, man, or there won't be a drop of oil left in the drum! (*He rushes wildly back into the lumber room. Another slight pause. He rushes out again, with the drum in his arms, his thumb pressed to the tap outlet, and runs over to the door. Calling madly.*) Eh, Barry, Barry, d'ye hear me callin' you, man? I won't be able to keep this oil in much longer. Have you fallen asleep or what? (*There is heard outside a rattle, followed by a crash of falling pots, tins, and tools; then a dead silence for a moment. Staggering against the wall.*) Aw, Mother o' God, what's he after doin' now!

BARRY (*Outside, in a loud voice of great distress*): Darry, oh, Darry, I'm after nearly destroyin' meself! Where's the doorway?—I can't see!

DARRY (*Going over and standing in the doorway*): Here, here, man; no, to the left. (*As* BARRY *staggers in, dusty and frightened.*) What ruin are you after causin' now?

BARRY (*Moaningly*): I'm after gettin' an awful shock!

DARRY (*Appealingly*): Pull yourself together, for God's sake, can, 'n' tell us what's happened.

BARRY (*As he sinks down on a chair*): The blasted lamps were on top of the top shelf; there was nothing to stand on; I had to climb upon the shelves, and climbing up, the shelves 'n' all that was on them came down on top of me!

(DARRY *goes over and rests the drum in the sink, his hand still pressed over the outlet of the tap.*)

DARRY: 'N' why did you climb the shelves? What did you want to do that for? Couldn't you see, you sap, that they weren't fixed well in the wall? Why did you insist on climbing the shelves?

BARRY: I was just tryin' to expedite matters.

DARRY (*With a wail*): Tryin' to expedite matters. Oh, there'll be a nice panorama of ruin in front of Lizzie when she comes back!

BARRY: 'N' me spectacles were sent flyin' when the shelves fell.

DARRY: 'N' why didn't you grab them before they fell to the ground?

BARRY (*Hotly*): How could I grab them 'n' they fallin', when I was fallin' too!

DARRY (*Impatiently*): Well, get the lamp then, 'n' look for the lost key in the lumber room.

BARRY: 'N' maybe let it fall, 'n' set the house on fire?

DARRY (*Woefully*): Oh, amn't I in a nice predic—The chair, the chair—the heifer's movin'!

(*The chair to which the rope is tied begins to move across the floor.* BARRY *catches it, tugs manfully, but he is carried on toward the fireplace.*)

BARRY (*Anxiously*): Give us a hand, give us a hand, or I'll be up the chimney!

(DARRY, *leaving the drum, runs over to* BARRY'S *side, grips the rope in front of* BARRY, *and, to get a safer hold, takes the rope off the chair and puts it round him under his arms. With great pulling, they get the rope a little back. The oil flows from the drum into the sink unnoticed.*)

DARRY (*Panting*): Keep a strain, or we'll be up the chimney!

BARRY: How'm I goin' to get home tonight without me spectacles?

DARRY (*Loudly*): Keep a strain on her, man, keep a strain on her; we have to get this straightened out first, before we can brood over your spectacles!

BARRY (*Suddenly noticing the oil drum*): The oil, the oil! (*He lets go of the rope, and runs over to the oil drum.* DARRY *disappears up the chimney. Lifting the drum and shaking it.*) Not a drop left in it, not a single drop! What're we goin' to do n—(*He turns and sees that* DARRY *has disappeared.*)

LIZZIE (*Speaking outside in a voice of horror*): The heifer, the heifer!

DARRY (*Calling out*): Lizzie, Lizzie!

(LIZZIE *rushes in as* DARRY *falls down the chimney. He crawls out from the fireplace on his hands and knees, and halts there, exhausted and sooty.*)

LIZZIE (*Horrified*): What in the Name of God has happened?

DARRY (*To* LIZZIE): Now you see the result of havin' your own way! Why the hell didn't you hold on to the rope when you took it off the heifer, so that I wouldn't come down with a bump?

LIZZIE: How'd I know you were hangin' on the other end?

DARRY (*Indignantly*): You didn't know—my God, woman, can you do nothin' right!

MUSIC FOR SONG IN
"THE END OF THE BEGINNING"
Down Where The Bees Are Humming

One sum-mer eve a hand-some man met a hand-some maid-en

stroll - ing,   Down where the bees were hum-ming and the

wild flowers gai-ly   grow - ing; Said she, We'll sit down here a

while, all   self-ish thoughts con - troll - ing,   Down where the

bees are hum-ming and the   wild flowers gai - ly grow-ing: Said

she, We'll med-i-tate on things, things high and ed-i-fy - ing, How

all things live and have their day and end their day by dy - ing. He

put his hand on her white breast and mur-mured, Life is try - ing,

Down where the bees are hum-ming and the   wild flowers gai - ly grow - ing.

The Man With
the Heart
in the Highlands

BY

WILLIAM SAROYAN

"*L*IKE MYSELF, he's a genius," Johnny's father says in the play that follows in a voice that could be that of the playwright, for so William Saroyan has advertised himself. At various times during his career as novelist, short-story teller and playwright, he has appeared to be correct. Born of Armenian immigrant parents in Fresno, California, in 1908, Saroyan has continued to honor his family and town in much that he writes, always demonstrating pride that he is both Armenian and American. His father died when he was two years old and for five years he lived in an orphanage, until his mother found work and was able to support the family. Saroyan disliked the schools he attended and decided he would educate himself; so, between various jobs as a Western Union messenger boy and working in the vineyards, he read what he liked and sneaked into every kind of show he could find. He particularly delighted in popular entertainments such as circuses, county fairs and vaudeville shows, the theatricality of which influenced his own buoyantly undisciplined style of writing.

By the time he was seventeen, he felt he had exhausted Fresno's public library, as well as many of its odd jobs, and was ready to see the world. Declaring himself to be a writer, he set out to prove it in a series of sketches and short stories; with the publication of *The Daring Young Man on the Flying Trapeze* in 1934, he began to convince others that his indeed was an original, playful and important talent. The life that exudes even from his titles suggests the nimbleness of his works: *Razzle Dazzle; Sweeney in the Trees; Subway Circus; Jim Dandy; Hello, Out There; The Cave Dwellers;* and *Sam—The Highest Jumper of Them All.* Dexterously he juggles characters as if they were tenpins on fire; consequently, we remember his 1939 Pulitzer prizewinning play *The Time of Your Life,* written in six days, not for its story but for its iridescent cross section of humanity. The vividness of these miscellaneous characters was praised anew when the play was revived by Lincoln Center in New York City in 1969.

But in spite of early success, particularly during the first years of World War II, Saroyan has not contributed steadily to the commercial theatre. He remains truly independent, choosing as playwright and director to go his own way with an ever increasing number of new plays that remain unproduced. And, too, his excessive optimism and sentimentality have lost some of their appeal in a world that no doubt needs them more than ever but which also is less capable of accepting them. Undiminished in his recent work, however, is his swaggering spirit, still ready to perform theatrical high jinks, still ready after four decades to keep him aloft as the American theatre's most daring young man on the flying trapeze.

Saroyan has analyzed much of his early life, work and philosophy in his autobiography, *My Name Is Aram* (1940).

The Man With the Heart in the Highlands, written in the 1930s during the great economic depression that impoverished the nation, could be about poor people at any time in any place. Saroyan actually situates it many years earlier, August 1914, in Fresno, California, where the family of a six-year-old boy reside, without money or credit to buy bread for supper. (The playwright, by the way, was six years old that same summer and lived in Fresno.) But, to Saroyan, his characters possess something more important than food: a love of beauty and each other. The mutual understanding and admiration they share dramatize the author's theme that man does not live by bread alone. Moreover, the 18 neighbors who have food are just as hungry, for they crave the gratification that comes from music and poetry. Old MacGregor's bugle concert produces peace, good will and kindliness among these simple and beautiful people when two starving factions of society come together to share their wealth and talent.

At the play's end, Johnny and his poet father continue to face a hungry if happy future, destined someday to follow in MacGregor's footsteps, elderly and deranged, but with their hearts still in the highlands. Their childlike faith, together with their touch of the poet, will sustain them and make possible an everlasting quest of beauty and an enduring appreciation of the human race. These goals are prescribed by Saroyan again and again as the best way of life. It is significant that our youth today likewise often find more joy in song and self-expression than in what they have for supper.

This one-act version of the longer *My Heart's in the Highlands,* which was produced on Broadway by the Group Theatre in 1939, is filled with Saroyan's fanciful and highly personal strokes, such as Johnny's attempt in the opening pantomime to figure out "everything"; or the fact that Johnny and his father for four days have been living on popcorn, of all things. The playwright describes the old man's music, the epitome of artistic expression, as both beautiful and mournful. The poet's hope that money will be found on the street persists to the end, creating the kind of consummate optimism for which Saroyan is famous.

Note the superb spontaneity of the six short episodes that make up this play, illustrating the author's golden rule that no rules of playwriting would ever impair his swift and carefree techniques. However haphazardly constructed, the scenes are fused by the purity of the little boy and the gentleness of the old man, two of the most memorable characters in Saroyan's human comedy.

The Man With the Heart in the Highlands

CHARACTERS

JOHNNY, *age six*
JOHNNY'S FATHER
MACGREGOR
MR. KOSAK
JOHNNY'S GRANDMOTHER
RUFE APLEY
A YOUNG MAN
EIGHTEEN NEIGHBORS

SCENE

Fresno, California, August 1914.

SCENE 1

An old white broken-down frame house with a front porch on San Benito Avenue in Fresno, California. There are no other houses nearby, only a desolation of bleak land and red sky. It is late afternoon of a day in August 1914. The evening sun is going down.

JOHNNY, *aged six, but essentially ageless, is sitting, dynamic and acrobatic, on the steps of the porch, dead to the world and deep in thought of a high and holy order. Far away a train whistle cries mournfully. He listens eagerly, cocking his head on one side like a chicken, trying to understand the meaning of the cry and at the same time to figure out* everything. *He doesn't quite make it and when the cry ends he stops being eager. A fourteen-year-old boy on a bicycle, eating an ice-cream cone and carrying newspaper bags, goes by on the sidewalk in silence, oblivious of the weight on his shoulders and of the contraption on which he is seated because of the delight and glory of ice cream in the world. Johnny leaps to his feet and waves to the boy, smiling in a big humanitarian way, but is ignored. He sits down again and listens to a small overjoyed but angry bird. The bird flies away, after making a brief, forceful speech of no meaning.*

From inside the house is heard the somber voice of JOHNNY'S FATHER *reciting poetry of his own composition.*

JOHNNY'S FATHER: The long silent day journeys through the sore solemn heart, and—(*Bitter pause.*) And— (*Quickly.*) The long silent day journeys through the sore solemn heart, and—(*Pause.*) No. (*He roars and begins again.*) Crippled and weeping, time stumbles through the lone lorn heart.

(*A table or chair is pushed over in anger. A groan. Silence. The boy listens. He gets up and tries to stand on his head, fails, tries*

[197]

again, fails, tries again, and succeeds. While he is standing on
his head he hears the loveliest and most amazing music in the
world: a solo on a bugle. The music is so magnificent he doesn't
dare get to his feet or move a muscle. The song is "My Heart's
in the Highlands." The bugler, a very old man, finishes the solo
in front of the house. The boy leaps to his feet and runs up to
the old man, amazed, delighted and bewildered.)

JOHNNY: I sure would like to hear you play another song.

MACGREGOR: Young man, could you get a glass of water for an old
man whose heart is not here, but in the highlands?

JOHNNY: What highlands?

MACGREGOR: The Scotch Highlands. Could you?

JOHNNY: What's your heart doing in the Scotch Highlands?

MACGREGOR: My heart's grieving there. Could you get me a glass of
cool water?

JOHNNY: Where's your mother?

MACGREGOR: My mother's in Tulsa, Oklahoma, but her heart isn't.

JOHNNY: Where *is* her heart?

MACGREGOR: In the Scotch Highlands. I'm very thirsty, young man.

JOHNNY: How come the members of your family are always leaving
their hearts in the highlands?

MACGREGOR: That's the way we are. Here today and gone tomorrow.

JOHNNY (*Aside*): Here today and gone tomorrow? (*To* MACGREGOR.)
How do you figure?

MACGREGOR: Alive one minute and dead the next.

JOHNNY: Where's your mother's mother?

MACGREGOR: She's up in Vermont, in a little town called White River,
but her heart isn't.

JOHNNY: Is her poor old withered heart in the highlands, too?

MACGREGOR: Right smack in the highlands. Son, I'm dying of thirst.

(JOHNNY'S FATHER *comes out of the house in a fury, as if he has*
just broken out of a cage, and roars at the boy like a tiger that
has just awakened from evil dreams.)

JOHNNY'S FATHER: Johnny, get the hell away from that poor old man.
Get him a pitcher of water before he falls down and dies. Where
in hell are your manners?

JOHNNY: Can't a fellow try to find out something from a traveler once in a while?

JOHNNY'S FATHER: Get the old man some water, God damn it! Don't stand there like a dummy. Get him a drink before he falls down and dies.

JOHNNY: *You* get him a drink. You ain't doing nothing.

JOHNNY'S FATHER: Ain't doing nothing? Why, Johnny, you know I'm getting a new poem arranged in my mind.

JOHNNY: How do you figure I know?

JOHNNY'S FATHER (*Unable to find an answer*): Well, you ought to know. You're my son. If you shouldn't know, who should?

MACGREGOR: Good afternoon. Your son has been telling me how clear and cool the climate is in these parts.

JOHNNY (*Aside*): Jesus Christ, I didn't say anything about the climate. Where's he getting that stuff from?

JOHNNY'S FATHER: How do you do? Won't you come in for a little rest? We should be honored to have you at our table for a bite of supper.

MACGREGOR: Sir, I am starving. I shall come right in. (*He moves to enter the house.* JOHNNY *gets in his way, looking up at him.*)

JOHNNY: Can you play "Drink to Me Only with Thine Eyes"? I sure would like to hear you play that song on the bugle. That song is my favorite. I guess I like that song better than any song in the world.

MACGREGOR: Son, when you get to be my age you'll know songs aren't important, bread's the thing.

JOHNNY: Anyway, I sure would like to hear you play that song.

(MACGREGOR *goes up on the porch and shakes hands with* JOHNNY'S FATHER.)

MACGREGOR: My name is Jasper MacGregor. I am an actor.

JOHNNY'S FATHER: I'm mighty glad to make your acquaintance. Johnny, get Mr. MacGregor a pitcher of water.

(JOHNNY *runs around the house.*)

MACGREGOR: Charming boy.

JOHNNY'S FATHER: Like myself, he's a genius.

MACGREGOR: I suppose you're very fond of him?

JOHNNY'S FATHER: We are the same person—he is the heart of my youth. Have you noticed his eagerness?

MACGREGOR: I should say I have.

JOHNNY'S FATHER: I am the same way myself, though older and less brilliant.

> (JOHNNY, *running, returns with a pitcher of water, which he hands to the old man. The old man throws back his shoulders, lifts his head, his nostrils expand, he snorts, his eyes widen, he lifts the pitcher of water to his lips and drinks all the water in one long swig, while* JOHNNY *and his* FATHER *watch with amazement and admiration. The old man breathes deeply, looks around at the landscape and up at the sky and to the end of San Benito Avenue, where the evening sun is going down.*)

MACGREGOR: I reckon I'm three thousand miles from home. Do you think we could eat a little bread and cheese to keep my body and spirit together?

JOHNNY'S FATHER: Johnny, run down to the grocer's and get a loaf of French bread and a pound of cheese.

JOHNNY: Give me the money.

JOHNNY'S FATHER: You know I ain't got a penny, Johnny. Tell Mr. Kosak to give us credit.

JOHNNY: He won't do it. He's tired of giving us credit. He says we don't work and never pay our bills. We owe him forty cents.

JOHNNY'S FATHER: Go on down there and argue it out with him. You know that's your job.

JOHNNY: He says he doesn't know anything about anything, all he wants is the forty cents.

JOHNNY'S FATHER: Go on down there and make him give you a loaf of bread and a pound of cheese. You can do it, Johnny.

MACGREGOR: Go on down there and tell Mr. Kosak to give you a loaf of bread and a pound of cheese, son.

JOHNNY'S FATHER: Go ahead, Johnny. You haven't yet failed to leave that store with provender. You'll be back here in ten minutes with food fit for a king.

JOHNNY: I don't know. Mr. Kosak says we are trying to give him the merry run-around. He wants to know what kind of work you do.

JOHNNY'S FATHER (*Furiously*): Well, go ahead and tell him. I have nothing to conceal. I write poetry, night and day.

JOHNNY: Well, all right, but I don't think he'll be impressed. He says you never go out and look for work. He says you're lazy and no good.

JOHNNY'S FATHER (*Roaring*): You go on down there and tell him he's crazy, Johnny. You go on down there and tell that fellow your father is one of the greatest unknown poets living.

JOHNNY: He won't care, but I'll go. I'll do my best. Ain't we got nothing in the house?

JOHNNY'S FATHER: Only popcorn. We've been eating popcorn four days in a row now, Johnny. You got to get bread and cheese if you expect me to finish that long poem.

JOHNNY: I'll do my best.

MACGREGOR: Don't take too long, Johnny. I'm *five* thousand miles from home.

JOHNNY: I'll run all the way.

JOHNNY'S FATHER: If you find any money on the way, remember we go fifty-fifty.

JOHNNY: All right. (JOHNNY *runs down the street.*)

SCENE 2

The inside of MR. KOSAK'S *grocery store.* MR. KOSAK *is sleeping on his folded arms when* JOHNNY *runs into the store.* MR. KOSAK *lifts his head. He is a fine, gentle, serious man with a big blond old-fashioned mustache. He shakes his head, trying to waken.*

JOHNNY: Mr. Kosak, if you were in China and didn't have a friend in the world and no money, you'd expect some Christian over there to give you a pound of rice, wouldn't you?

MR. KOSAK: What do you want?

JOHNNY: I just want to talk a little. You'd expect some member of the Aryan race to help you out a little, wouldn't you, Mr. Kosak?

MR. KOSAK: How much money you got?

JOHNNY: It ain't a question of money, Mr. Kosak. I'm talking about being in China.

MR. KOSAK: I don't know nothing about nothing.

JOHNNY: How would you feel in China that way?

MR. KOSAK: I don't know. What would I be doing in China?

JOHNNY: Well, you'd be visiting there, and you'd be hungry and five thousand miles from home and not a friend in the world. You wouldn't expect a good Christian to turn you away without even a pound of rice, would you, Mr. Kosak?

MR. KOSAK: I guess not, but you ain't in China, Johnny, and neither is your Pa. You or your Pa's got to go out and work sometime in your lives, so you might as well start now. I ain't going to give you no more groceries on credit because I know you won't pay me.

JOHNNY: Mr. Kosak, you misunderstand me. I'm not talking about a few groceries. I'm talking about all them heathen people around you in China, and you hungry and dying.

MR. KOSAK: This ain't China. You got to go out and make your living in this country. Everybody's got to work in America.

JOHNNY: Mr. Kosak, suppose it was a loaf of bread and a pound of cheese you needed to keep you alive in the world, would you hesitate to ask a Christian missionary for those things?

MR. KOSAK: Yes, I would. I would be ashamed to ask.

JOHNNY: Even if you knew you would give him back *two* loaves of bread and *two* pounds of cheese instead of one loaf and one pound? Even then, Mr. Kosak?

MR. KOSAK: Even then.

JOHNNY: Don't be that way, Mr. Kosak. That's defeatist talk, and you know it. Why, the only thing that would happen to you would be death. You would die out there in China, Mr. Kosak.

MR. KOSAK: I wouldn't care if I would. You and your Pa have got to pay for bread and cheese. Why don't your Pa go out and get a job?

JOHNNY: Mr. Kosak, how are you anyway?

MR. KOSAK: I'm fine, Johnny. How are you?

JOHNNY: Couldn't be better, Mr. Kosak. How are the children?

MR. KOSAK: They're all fine, Johnny. Stepan is beginning to walk now.

JOHNNY: That's great. How's Angela?

MR. KOSAK: Angela's beginning to sing. How's your grandmother?

JOHNNY: She's fine. She's beginning to sing too. She says she'd rather be an opera singer than Queen of England. How's your wife, Martha, Mr. Kosak?

MR. KOSAK: Oh, swell.

JOHNNY: I can't tell you how glad I am to hear that everything is well at your house. I know Stepan is going to be a great man someday.

MR. KOSAK: I hope so. I'm going to send him to high school and see that he gets every chance I didn't get. I don't want him to open a grocery store.

JOHNNY: I have great faith in Stepan, Mr. Kosak.

MR. KOSAK: What do you want, Johnny, and how much money you got?

JOHNNY: Mr. Kosak, you know I didn't come here to buy anything. You know I enjoy a quiet philosophical chat with you every now and then. *(Quickly.)* Let me have a loaf of French bread and a pound of cheese.

MR. KOSAK: You got to pay cash, Johnny.

JOHNNY: And Esther? How is your beautiful daughter Esther?

MR. KOSAK: She's all right, Johnny, but you got to pay cash. You and your Pa are the worst citizens in this county.

JOHNNY: I'm glad Esther's all right, Mr. Kosak. Jasper MacGregor is visiting our house. He's a great actor.

MR. KOSAK: Never heard of him.

JOHNNY: And a bottle of beer for Mr. MacGregor.

MR. KOSAK: I can't give you a bottle of beer.

JOHNNY: Sure, you can.

MR. KOSAK: I can't. I'll let you have one loaf of French bread and a pound of cheese, but that's all. What kind of work does your Pa do when he works, Johnny?

JOHNNY: My father writes poetry, Mr. Kosak. That's the only work my father does. He's one of the greatest writers of poetry in the world.

MR. KOSAK: When does he get any money?

JOHNNY: He never gets any money. You can't have your cake and eat it too.

MR. KOSAK: I don't like that kind of work. Why doesn't your Pa work like everybody else, Johnny?

JOHNNY: He works harder than everybody else. My father works twice as hard as the average man.

(MR. KOSAK *hands* JOHNNY *a loaf of French bread and a pound of cheese.*)

MR. KOSAK: Well, that's fifty-five cents you owe me, Johnny. I'll let you have some stuff this time, but never again.

JOHNNY *(At the door)*: Tell Esther I love her.

MR. KOSAK: All right.

JOHNNY: Goodbye, Mr. Kosak.
MR. KOSAK: Goodbye, Johnny.

(JOHNNY *runs out of the store.* MR. KOSAK *swings at a fly, misses, swings again, misses, and, objecting to the world in this manner, he chases the fly all around the store, swinging with all his might.*)

SCENE 3

The same as Scene 1. JOHNNY'S FATHER *and the old man are looking down the street to see if* JOHNNY *is coming back with food. His* GRANDMOTHER *is standing on the porch, also eager to know if there is to be food.*

MACGREGOR: I think he's got some food with him.
JOHNNY'S FATHER (*With pride*): Of course he has. (*He waves at the old lady on the porch, who runs into the house to set the table.* JOHNNY *runs to his* FATHER *and* MACGREGOR.) I knew you'd do it.
MACGREGOR: So did I.
JOHNNY: He says we got to pay him fifty-five cents. He says he ain't going to give us no more stuff on credit.
JOHNNY'S FATHER: That's his opinion. What did you talk about?
JOHNNY: First I talked about being hungry and at death's door in China. Then I inquired about the family.
JOHNNY'S FATHER: How is everyone?
JOHNNY: Fine. I didn't find any money, though, not even a penny.
JOHNNY'S FATHER: That's all right.

(*They go into the house.*)

SCENE 4

The living room. They are all at the table after supper. MACGREGOR *finds crumbs here and there, which he places delicately in his mouth. He looks around the room to see if there is something more to eat.*

MACGREGOR: That green can up there, Johnny. What's in there?

JOHNNY: Marbles.

MACGREGOR: That cupboard. Anything edible in there, Johnny?

JOHNNY: Crickets.

MACGREGOR: That big jar in the corner there, Johnny. What's good in there?

JOHNNY: I got a gopher snake in that jar.

MACGREGOR: Well, I could go a bit of boiled gopher snake in a big way, Johnny.

JOHNNY: You can't have that snake.

MACGREGOR: Why not, Johnny? Why the hell not, son? I hear of fine Borneo natives eating snakes and grasshoppers. You ain't got a half dozen fat grasshoppers around, too, have you, Johnny?

JOHNNY: Only four.

MACGREGOR: Well, trot them out, son, and after we've had our fill, I'll play "Drink to Me Only with Thine Eyes" for you. I'm mighty hungry, Johnny.

JOHNNY: So am I, but I don't want anybody killing them poor things.

JOHNNY'S FATHER (*To* MACGREGOR): How about a little music? I think the boy would be delighted.

JOHNNY: I sure would, Mr. MacGregor.

MACGREGOR: All right, Johnny. (MACGREGOR *gets up and begins to blow into the bugle. He blows louder and more beautifully and mournfully than anybody ever blew into a bugle.* EIGHTEEN NEIGHBORS *gather in front of the house and cheer when he finishes the solo.*)

JOHNNY'S FATHER: I want you to meet your public.

(They go out on the porch.)

SCENE 5

The same as Scene 1. The crowd is looking up at JOHNNY'S FATHER, MACGREGOR, *and* JOHNNY.

JOHNNY'S FATHER: Good neighbors and friends, I want you to meet Jasper MacGregor, the greatest Shakespearean actor of our day.

MACGREGOR: I remember my first appearance in London in 1867 as if it was yesterday. I was a boy of fourteen from the slums of Glasgow. My first part was a courier in a play, the title of which I have unfortunately forgotten. I had no lines to speak but moved about a good deal, running from officer to officer, and from lover to his beloved, and back again, over and over again.

RUFE APLEY (*A carpenter*): How about another song, Mr. MacGregor?

MACGREGOR: Have you got an egg at your house?

RUFE APLEY: I sure have. I've got a dozen eggs at my house.

MACGREGOR: Would it be convenient for you to go and get one of them dozen eggs? When you return I'll play a song that will make your heart leap with joy and grief.

RUFE APLEY: I'm on my way already. (*He goes.*)

MACGREGOR (*To the crowd*): My friends, I should be delighted to play another song for you on this golden-throated bugle, but time and distance from home find me weary. If you will be so good as to go, each of you to his home, and return with some morsel of food, I shall be delighted to gather my spirit together and play a song I know will change the course of each of your lives, and change it, mind you, for the better. (*The people go.* MACGREGOR, JOHNNY'S FATHER, *and* JOHNNY *sit on the steps and remain in silence, and one by one the people return bringing food to* MACGREGOR: *an egg, a sausage, a dozen green onions, two kinds of cheese, butter, two kinds of bread, boiled potatoes, fresh tomatoes, a melon, tea, and many good things to eat.*) Thank you, my friends, thank you. (*He stands solemnly, waiting for absolute silence, straightens himself, looks about him furiously, lifts the bugle to his lips, and plays "My Heart's in the Highlands, My Heart Is Not Here." The people weep and go away.* MACGREGOR *turns to the father and son.*) Sir, if it is all the same to you I should like to dwell in your house for some time to come.

JOHNNY'S FATHER: Sir, my house is your house.

(*They go into the house.*)

SCENE 6

The same as Scene 4. Eighteen days later. MACGREGOR *is lying on the floor, face up, asleep.* JOHNNY *is walking about quietly in the room, looking at everybody. His* FATHER *is at the table writing poetry. His* GRANDMOTHER *is sitting in the rocking chair, rocking. There is a knock on the door. Everybody but* MACGREGOR *jumps up and runs to it.*

JOHNNY'S FATHER (*At the door*): Yes?

A YOUNG MAN: I am looking for Jasper MacGregor, the actor.

JOHNNY'S FATHER: What do you want?

JOHNNY: Well, ask him in anyway, Pa.

JOHNNY'S FATHER: Yes, of course. Excuse me. Won't you please come in?

(*The* YOUNG MAN *enters.*)

YOUNG MAN: My name is Philip Carmichael. I am from the Old People's Home. I have been sent to bring Mr. MacGregor home.

MACGREGOR (*Wakening and sitting up*): Home? Did someone mention home? I'm five thousand miles from home, always have been, and always will be. Who is this young man?

YOUNG MAN: Mr. MacGregor, I'm Philip Carmichael, from the Old People's Home. They've sent me to bring you back. We are putting on our annual show in two weeks and need you for the leading role.

MACGREGOR (*Getting up with the help of* JOHNNY'S FATHER *and* JOHNNY): What kind of a part is it? I can't be playing young adventurers any longer.

YOUNG MAN: The part is King Lear, Mr. MacGregor. It is perfect for you.

MACGREGOR (*To* JOHNNY'S FATHER, JOHNNY, *and the* GRANDMOTHER): Goodbye, my beloved friends. Goodbye. In all the hours of my life, in all the places I have visited, never and nowhere have I had the honor and pleasure to commune with souls loftier, purer, or more delightful than yours. Goodbye.

(*They say goodbye, and the old man and the young man leave the house. There is a long silence, full of melancholy and loneliness.*)

JOHNNY'S FATHER: Johnny, go on down to Mr. Kosak's store and get a little something to eat. I know you can do it, Johnny. Get *anything*.

JOHNNY: Mr. Kosak wants eighty-five cents. He won't give us anything more without money.

JOHNNY'S FATHER: Go on down there, Johnny. You know you can get that fine Slovak gentleman to give you a bit of something to eat.

JOHNNY (*With despair*): Aw, Pa.

JOHNNY'S FATHER (*Amazed*): What? You, my son, in a mood like that? Come on. I've fought the world this way before you were born, and after you were born we've fought it together, and we're going to keep on fighting it. The people love poetry but don't know it. Nothing is going to stop us, Johnny. Go on down there now and get something to eat. You didn't do so well last time. Remember? I can't write great poetry on the bird seed and maple syrup you brought back. Go on now.

JOHNNY: All right, Pa. I'll do my best. (*He runs to the door.*)

JOHNNY'S FATHER: Remember, if you find any money on the way, we go fifty-fifty.

Soul Gone Home

BY

LANGSTON HUGHES

POET, playwright, short-story writer, novelist, editor, folklorist, journalist, author of children's books, historian of the NAACP, translator of Black writers, librettist, and autobiographer, Langston Hughes (1902–1967) became one of the best-known literary figures of his time and a major spokesman of Black life in America.

Born in Joplin, Missouri, he moved about the continent as a result of his parents' separation, living for a time in Kansas, Ohio and Mexico. Because his mother constantly traveled in search of jobs, he was brought up by his grandmother and, after her death, by a kind and religious friend of the family, "Auntie" Reed. Keenly interested in sports and writing, he excelled at both while a student at Central High School in Cleveland, where he was a member of the track team and the editor of the yearbook. He claimed that he only became interested in writing when elected class poet in his grammar school and a poem was expected of him, but for the next five decades he never stopped writing.

In the splendid autobiography of his youth, *The Big Sea*, he recounts the summer of 1919 spent in Mexico with his father, a successful businessman, who abhorred poverty and all those who were poor. Langston found it difficult to understand this strange man who lived in self-imposed exile, isolated from his family and American roots, interested only in making money which he seldom spent, hating Blacks, and himself for being Black. His father urged him to leave the United States and to live on a ranch in Mexico when he finished high school. Having been close to pauperism most of his childhood, Langston Hughes knew that life in the United States was uncertain and problematical even for an educated black; his mother, who had attended the University of Kansas, had been reduced to menial tasks in order to survive. But he could not accept his father's offer or his attitude and, instead of pretending he was not black, forever after devoted himself to characterizing the American Negro, his reverses and advances, his heartsickness and jubilance, his ugliness and beauty.

Working his way through the world as a sailor and a waiter, Hughes traveled to Africa and throughout Europe before returning penniless to Washington, D.C., where he took a dreary job in a laundry. Sad, depressed, discouraged, he began to write poems to ease his pain; he discovered that periods of personal difficulty often resulted in his greatest creative productivity. While working at Washington's Wardman Park Hotel, he encountered the famous poet Vachel Lindsay, who read three of his poems which Hughes had placed beside his dinner plate. The next morning he was famous, for the newspapers proclaimed that Lindsay had discovered a Negro busboy poet. The publication of these and other works in *The Weary Blues* (1926) brought him to the attention of New York's literary circles, but in spite of praise and acceptance, he wanted more education before continuing this new career. He had spent one lonely year at Columbia University but disliked its bigness and quit; now, thanks to his poetic gifts, he received funds to return to school and selected the smaller Lincoln University in Pennsylvania, which he liked very much. Following his graduation in 1929, he began publishing regularly, including a book of poems for children, *The Dream Keeper*, in 1932. He continued to travel at the same time, working on a movie in Russia in 1933 and covering the Spanish Civil War in 1936 as a Madrid correspondent for *The Baltimore Afro-American* newspaper.

Always fascinated by theatre, he had as a child attended every show to which he could gain admittance; in New York City, no matter how short of funds, he fed his passion for plays and musicals, often standing with no supper in his stomach to see Florence Mills, Jeanne Eagels or Eleonora Duse. After participating in little-theatre groups, he began writing plays; his *Mulatto*, a tragic study of miscegenation produced on Broadway in 1935, had the longest run for a black playwright before Lorraine Hansberry's *A Raisin in the Sun* in 1959 (the title of her play was taken from Hughes' poem, "Montage of a Dream Deferred"). Thereafter followed many plays, musicals and operatic works, some of which were based on his own stories: *Don't You Want to Be Free?*, *Troubled Island*, *Simply Heavenly*, *Black Nativity*, *Tambourines to Glory* and *Jericho-Jim Crow*. He also contributed the book and lyrics to Kurt Weill's musical setting of *Street Scene*, first produced in 1947. The second volume of autobiography, *I Wonder as I Wander* (1956), outlines his adult life as a poet and playwright.

Soul Gone Home, although not written in verse, is clearly the work of a poet, for only a poet could extract so precisely the feelings of loneliness, hunger and sickness of a sixteen-year-old dead boy in the ghetto and make the reader know exactly what he suffered and how he came to die—all in four brief pages. The economy of the comedy (paradoxically, but on purpose, this tragedy emerges as a comedy), the importance of what is not said, and the incandescence of what is, further attest to the playwright's poetic powers. These graphically create the relationship of a resentful mother and a neglected son who through no fault of their own have made life impossible for each other. Hughes skillfully reinforces the black identity of the play by making the two city health employees white men wearing white coats who offer the mother no sympathy, no word of kindness, and move through the room as if they didn't see her. Through understatement and an ironic conclusion in which the woman whitens her face with powder, the poet strikes home his point.

It is to my students, black and white, that I owe a debt of gratitude, here acknowledged, for discovering, directing and performing this play in a number of separate productions, each presented with utter sincerity and comprehension, but with no loss of its comic values. High-school teenagers have enacted it with the same conviction, proving that Langston Hughes speaks to this generation with as much authority and artistry as ever.

Soul Gone Home

CHARACTERS

THE MOTHER
THE SON
TWO MEN

*Night. A tenement room, bare, ugly, dirty. An unshaded electric-
light bulb. In the middle of the room a cot on which the body of a*
NEGRO YOUTH *is lying. His hands are folded across his chest. There
are pennies on his eyes. He is a soul gone home. As the curtain rises,
his* MOTHER, *a large, middle-aged woman in a red sweater, kneels
weeping beside the cot, loudly simulating grief.*

MOTHER: Oh, Gawd! Oh, Lawd! Why did you take my son from me?
Oh, Gawd, why did you do it? He was all I had! Oh, Lawd, what
am I gonna do? (*Looking at the dead boy and stroking his head.*)
Oh, son! Oh, Ronnie! Oh, my boy, speak to me! Ronnie, say
something to me! Son, why don't you talk to your mother? Can't
you see she's bowed down in sorrow? Son, speak to me, just one
word! Come back from the spirit-world and speak to me! Ronnie,
come back from the dead and speak to your mother!

SON (*Lying there dead as a doornail. Speaking loudly*): I wish I
wasn't dead, so I *could* speak to you. You been a hell of a mama!

MOTHER (*Falling back from the cot in astonishment, but still on
her knees*): Ronnie! Ronnie! What's that you say? What you sayin'
to your mother? (*Wild-eyed.*) Is you done opened your mouth and
spoke to me?

SON: I said you a hell of a mama!

MOTHER (*Rising suddenly and backing away, screaming loudly*):
Awo-ooo-o! Ronnie, that ain't you talkin'!

SON: Yes, it is me talkin', too! I say you been a no-good mama.

MOTHER: What for you talkin' to me like that, Ronnie? You ain't
never said nothin' like that to me before.

SON: I know it, but I'm dead now—and I can say what I want to say.
(*Stirring.*) You done called on me to talk, ain't you? Lemme take
these pennies off my eyes so I can see. (*He takes the coins off his
eyes, throws them across the room, and sits up in bed. He is a very*

[215]

dark boy in a torn white shirt. He looks hard at his mother.) Mama, you know you ain't done me right.

MOTHER: What you mean, I ain't done you right? (*She is rooted in horror.*) What you mean, huh?

SON: You know what I mean.

MOTHER: No, I don't neither. (*Trembling violently.*) What you mean comin' back to haunt your poor old mother? Ronnie, what does you mean?

SON (*Leaning forward*): I'll tell you just what I mean! You been a bad mother to me.

MOTHER: Shame! Shame! Shame, talkin' to your mama that away. Damn it! Shame! I'll slap your face. (*She starts toward him, but he rolls his big white eyes at her, and she backs away.*) Me, what borned you! Me, what suffered the pains o' death to bring you into this world! Me, what raised you up, what washed your dirty didies. (*Sorrowfully.*) And now I'm left here mighty nigh prostrate 'cause you gone from me! Ronnie, what you mean talkin' to *me* like that— what brought you into this world?

SON: You never did feed me good, that's what I mean! Who wants to come into the world hongry, and go out the same way?

MOTHER: What you mean hongry? When I had money, ain't I fed you?

SON (*Sullenly*): Most of the time you ain't had no money.

MOTHER: 'Twarn't my fault then.

SON: 'Twarn't *my* fault neither.

MOTHER (*Defensively*): You always was so weak and sickly, you couldn't earn nothin' sellin' papers.

SON: I know it.

MOTHER: You never was no use to me.

SON: So you just lemme grow up in the street, and I ain't had no manners nor morals, neither.

MOTHER: Manners and morals? Ronnie, where'd you learn all them big words?

SON: I learnt 'em just now in the spirit-world.

MOTHER (*Coming nearer*): But you ain't been dead no more'n an hour.

SON: That's long enough to learn a lot.

MOTHER: Well, what else did you find out?

SON: I found out you was a hell of a mama puttin' me out in the cold to sell papers soon as I could even walk.

MOTHER: What? You little liar!

SON: If I'm lyin', I'm dyin'! And lettin' me grow up all bowlegged and stunted from undernourishment.

MOTHER: Under-nurse-mint?

SON: Undernourishment. You heard what the doctor said last week?

MOTHER: Naw, what'd he say?

SON: He said I was dyin' o' undernourishment, that's what he said. He said I had TB 'cause I didn't have enough to eat never when I were a child. And he said I couldn't get well, nohow eating nothin' but beans ever since I been sick. Said I needed milk and eggs. And you said you ain't got no money for milk and eggs, which I know you ain't. (*Gently.*) We never had no money, Mama, not even since you took up hustlin' on the streets.

MOTHER: Son, money ain't everything.

SON: Naw, but when you got TB you have to have milk and eggs.

MOTHER (*Advancing sentimentally*): Anyhow, I love you, Ronnie!

SON (*Rudely*): Sure you love me—but here I am dead.

MOTHER (*Angrily*): Well, damn your hide, you ain't even decent dead. If you was, you wouldn't be sittin' there jawin' at your mother when she's sheddin' every tear she's got for you tonight.

SON: First time you ever did cry for me, far as I know.

MOTHER: 'Tain't! You's a liar! I cried when I borned you—you was such a big child—ten pounds.

SON: Then *I* did the cryin' after that, I reckon.

MOTHER (*Proudly*): Sure, I could of let you die, but I didn't. Naw, I kept you with me—off and on. And I lost the chance to marry many a good man, too—if it weren't for you. No man wants to take care o' nobody else's child. (*Self-pityingly.*) You been a burden to me, Randolph.

SON (*Angrily*): What did you have me for then, in the first place?

MOTHER: How could I help havin' you, you little bastard? Your father ruint me—and you's the result. And I been worried with you for sixteen years. (*Disgustedly.*) Now, just when you get big enough to work and do me some good, you have to go and die.

SON: I sure am dead!

MOTHER: But you ain't decent dead! Here you come back to haunt your poor old mama, and spoil her cryin' spell, and spoil the mournin'. (*There is the noise of an ambulance gong outside. The* MOTHER *goes to the window and looks down into the street. Turns to* SON.) Ronnie, lay down quick! Here comes the city's ambulance to take you to the undertaker's. Don't let them white men see you dead, sitting up here quarrelin' with your mother. Lay down and fold your hands back like I had 'em.

SON (*Passing his hand across his head*): All right, but gimme that comb yonder and my stocking cap. I don't want to go out of here with my hair standin' straight up in front, even if I is dead. (*The* MOTHER *hands him a comb and his stocking cap. The* SON *combs his hair and puts the cap on. Noise of men coming up the stairs.*)

MOTHER: Hurry up, Ronnie, they'll be here in no time.

SON: Aw, they got another flight to come yet. Don't rush me, Ma!

MOTHER: Yes, but I got to put these pennies back on your eyes, boy! (*She searches in a corner for the coins as her* SON *lies down and folds his hands, stiff in death. She finds the coins and puts them nervously on his eyes, watching the door meanwhile. A knock.*) Come in.

(*Enter two* MEN *in the white coats of city health employees.*)

MAN: Somebody sent for us to get the body of Ronnie Bailey? Third floor, apartment five.

MOTHER: Yes, sir, here he is! (*Weeping loudly.*) He's my boy! Oh, Lawd, he's done left me! Oh, Lawdy, he's done gone home! His soul's gone home! Oh, what am I gonna do? Mister! Mister! Mister, the Lawd's done took him home! (*As the* MEN *unfold the stretchers, she continues to weep hysterically. They place the boy's thin body on the stretchers and cover it with a rubber cloth. Each man takes his end of the stretchers. Silently, they walk out the door as the* MOTHER *wails.*) Oh, my son! Oh, my boy! Come back, come back, come back! Ronnie, come back! (*One loud scream as the door closes.*) Awo-ooo-o! (*As the footsteps of the men die down on the stairs, the* MOTHER *becomes suddenly quiet. She goes to a broken mirror and begins to rouge and powder her face. In the street the ambulance gong sounds fainter and fainter in the distance. The* MOTHER *takes down an old fur coat from a nail and puts it on. Before she leaves, she smooths back the quilts on the cot from which the dead boy has been removed. She looks into the mirror again, and once more whitens her face with powder. She dons a red hat. From a handbag she takes a cigarette, lights it, and walks slowly out the door. At the door she switches off the light. The hallway is dimly illuminated. She turns before closing the door, looks back into the room, and speaks.*) Tomorrow, Ronnie, I'll buy you some flowers—if I can pick up a dollar tonight. You was a hell of a no-good son, I swear!

Look and Long

BY

GERTRUDE STEIN

T HE RESPONSE of some readers to *Look and Long* may be "Crazy!" or "Who does she think she's kidding?" or "Let's start again and see if we missed something." But others, some of whom the play has been tested upon, find in it a good deal that is not bewildering and much that is delightful. Divided reaction is just what Miss Stein received throughout her long career from critics and public alike for her short stories, poems, plays, operas, children's books, biographies and especially for her taste as a patron of the arts. She significantly encouraged Picasso, Matisse, Braque and a host of others well before they were critically or popularly recognized. Just as she was right in her praise of these artists, so it seems she was in her pursuit of her own work, notably in her theatre pieces (they are not plays in the conventional sense); and now, decades after they were originally written, several have been fashioned into the off-Broadway productions *In Circles* and *The Gertrude Stein First Reader*, which have pleased both critics and theatregoers in large numbers. This, the first American publication of *Look and Long*, one of several plays she wrote for children, no doubt will spark controversy, too, but in time also may prove that Miss Stein knew what she was doing.

Gertrude Stein (1874–1946) was born in Allegheny, Pennsylvania, but grew up in Oakland and San Francisco, California. As a student at Radcliffe College, she specialized in the study of psychology and was a favorite pupil of William James, perhaps the most famous American philosopher of his day. After four years of medical study at Johns Hopkins University, she left without a degree, having refused to take formal exams because they "bored" her. In 1903 she went to live permanently in Paris with a young San Francisco friend, Alice B. Toklas, her secretary and companion for the rest of her life. Supported by a private income, she began to purchase paintings by the young abstractionists whose theories fascinated her and who greatly influenced her own techniques of writing. Verbal abstraction was all-important to her. She stressed sounds of words rather than meanings; she discarded allegiance to syntax, grammar and punctuation for new and unorthodox forms; and she heightened the music within sentences to reemphasize their beauty. The language that resulted was barren of cliché and filled with interesting juxtapositions of isolated images, words and sentences, all unified by ebullient rhythms which Miss Stein controlled as strictly as a symphony conductor.

In turn, her style attracted and influenced a number of young writers who flocked to her house in Paris, which became a literary salon for the American expatriates she termed "the lost generation," members of which included Ernest Hemingway, Sherwood Anderson and F. Scott Fitzgerald. She remained in France even during the German occupation of World War II, living in the small village of Culoz, where in her last years she befriended American soldiers who gathered, as the artists and writers had before them, to hear her exciting conversation.

Among Miss Stein's plays, *Yes Is for a Very Young Man,* produced in 1947, remains well known, along with her libretti for the operas *Four Saints in Three Acts* (1934) and *The Mother of Us All* (1947), both with music composed by Virgil Thompson.

Look and Long particularly profits from reading aloud. But while special emphasis should be placed upon its unusual expression, we should not forget to take note of its plot (and there is one) or its character development (yes, they do, too), as well as to ponder over what it all means. If this is not immediately apparent, remember that there may be more than one reason why Miss Stein entitled this witty morality play *Look and Long.*

Look and Long

CHARACTERS

FOUR COUSINS
TWO BROTHERS: OLIVER, SILLY
TWO COUSINS: MURIEL, SUSIE
AN APPARITION

SCENE

In front of a house with trees.

ACT I

Enter OLIVER, *profoundly sad, he stops and looks about and folds his arms and looks up at the sky.*

OLIVER: I wonder, oh I wonder.

(Silence. From the other side enters MURIEL, *she too is profoundly sad and her eyes are cast down on the ground as she stands. Suddenly she sees a spider.)*

MURIEL: Araignée de matin, fait chagrin, and it is morning. *(She stops and crouches behind a chair in an agony of despair.)*

(In rush SUSIE *and* SILLY.*)*

SUSIE: Oh I have seen a goat a white goat and I milked him oh a lovely goat a lovely white goat.

SILLY: Silly Susie a goat is a she if she gives milk to three, beside it was not a goat, it was a chicken and it was an egg not milk even if it was white do you see.

*(*SILLY *and* SUSIE *dance around and suddenly they see* OLIVER *that is to say they bump against him.)*

SUSIE: Oh I thought he was a tree. When this you see remember me.

*(*OLIVER *pays no attention he continues to gloom looking up at the sky with folded arms.)*

[226]

SILLY: Oh look Susie look what is there, there behind that chair.

(SUSIE *and* SILLY *steal around quietly behind the chair and there is* MURIEL *her eyes fixed on the ground in despair.*)

MURIEL (*Murmurs*): The spider the spider oh the spider it is not there.

OLIVER (*Gives a start*): It was a cuckoo and (*with a bitter cry*) I have no money in my purse no money anywhere. Oh why did that cuckoo try to cry when I had no money no money, none.

MURIEL: No money.

SUSIE *and* SILLY: No money.

OLIVER: No money, none.

(*Just then there was a funny noise and in the middle of the four of them was a dancing* APPARITION.)

ALL TOGETHER: Oh (*and they watch her dance*).

SUSIE: Is it pretty.

OLIVER: Is it ugly.

MURIEL: Who is it.

SILLY: Where does it come from.

APPARITION (*Dancing*): I come from the moon, I come from the sun and I come to look at you one by one. (*And then suddenly stopping she points a finger at* OLIVER:) You you, one of these days you will split in two, you, you.

OLIVER (*Disdainfully*): I wonder.

APPARITION: You will wonder when it comes like thunder that you will split in two all through. (*And suddenly pointing her finger at* MURIEL:) And you.

MURIEL: Well what of it I have no share nor any care of any thing that happens to him.

APPARITION: No but you will get thin, get thin oh so thin, that you can slip through a ring and when you slip through a ring nobody can find you nobody can find where you have been nobody, nobody, nobody not even he and this is what the spider said and he was red the spider and this is what he said.

MURIEL: Oh (*And she began to sigh.*) Oh my.

APPARITION (*Pointing one finger at* SUSIE *and another at* SILLY): Silly
  will turn into Willy and Susie will turn into an egg and Willie
  will sit on the egg, and so they will wed Willie and the egg, although the egg was bad. Oh dear (*The* APPARITION *began to giggle
  and giggle.*) oh dear. (*And she faded away giggling.*)
OLIVER (*Gloomily*): I don't care for my share.
MURIEL (*With a gentle sigh*): I like to be thin, it is so interesting.

(SUSIE *and* SILLY *holding hands just laugh and laugh and the
curtain falls.*)

ACT II

OLIVER *comes in very gloomily and all tied up with string.*

OLIVER: I'll fool her, when I split in two if I do this string will hold
  me together whatever I do, so nobody can know not even she, and
  she is ugly, that I am not one but two, she'll see.

(MURIEL *coming in and in each hand a huge bottle of milk.*)

MURIEL: No I won't, yes I will, it would be a thrill to be thin and
  go through a ring, but I'll fool her yes I will, hullo Oliver are you
  in two, then I will be as thin as either one of you.
OLIVER (*Gloomily*): Go to bed.
MURIEL: Go to bed yourself, what do I care what happens to you.
OLIVER: You do too.

(MURIEL *begins to cry:* "Boohoo." *Just then* SUSIE *and* SILLY
come in giggling.)

SUSIE: I am an egg and I am cracked and Silly is Willy and he is so
  silly, see me crack, hear me crack.
SILLY: And the egg you are is addled at that.

(*And they giggle and giggle and the other two continue to be
gloomy.*)

SILLY: Hush I hear a noise, let us each get behind a tree so she cannot see and then we will know what she can do. Hush. (*And they
each get behind a tree.*)

(*The* APPARITION *comes in disguised as an* OLD WOMAN *picking
up sticks. As she picks them up she dances.*)

APPARITION: One stick is one two sticks are two three sticks are three
four sticks are four, four sticks are four, three sticks are three,
two sticks are two, one stick is one. Which one, which won (*and
she begins to giggle*). This one.

OLIVER: She is ugly but not the same, I don't know her name she
is ugly all the same, but she is not she, so I must not be scared
when she says this you see.

MURIEL: If I say one two three and she is she she will look at me.
(*She puts her head out and she calls out very loud.*) One two three
if you are she then look at me.

(*The* OLD WOMAN *pays no attention but goes on picking up and
throwing away sticks, always repeating.*) .

APPARITION: One stick is one, this one, two sticks are two for which
one, three sticks are three, suits me, four sticks are four, no more.
Four sticks are four, three sticks are three, two sticks are two, one
stick is one.

SUSIE: Oh Silly she scares me.

SILLY: Don't be silly but she scares me too.

SUSIE: Ouch.

SILLY: Ouch.

BOTH TOGETHER: We wish we were brave but we are not, not, not,
not.

(*Just then the* OLD WOMAN *says:*)

APPARITION: One stick is one (*and she suddenly hits* OLIVER *on the
back*).

APPARITION: One stick is one whack on the back.

OLIVER: Oh oh, I am in two oh in two in two. It is only the string
holds me together. Oh.

(*The* OLD WOMAN *then hits* MURIEL *on the back shouting:*)

APPARITION: Two sticks are two take that.

MURIEL (*Dropping both bottles of milk, which smash*): Oh I am getting thin it is most distressing, my milk, my milk, my ring oh I am getting so thin.

APPARITION (*Behind* SILLY): Three sticks are three (*and gives him a whack*).

SILLY: Oh I am not Silly I am only Willy and I do not want to be Willy I want to be Silly, oh.

(APPARITION *goes behind* SUSIE.)

APPARITION: Four sticks are four and there are no more whack on your back.

SUSIE: Oh I am an egg, a white egg, not even a brown egg, a dirty white egg and it is addled and never now can I wed with dear Silly who is only Willy.

(*And they all throw themselves on the ground lamenting and the* OLD WOMAN *dances away singing:*)

APPARITION: One stick is one two sticks are two three sticks are three four sticks are four, four sticks are four, three sticks are three two sticks are two one stick is one and now I am done.

OLIVER: I'll see to it that she never comes back.

MURIEL: Oh oh.

OLIVER (*Grimly*): I'll see to it that she never comes back, the ugly, I am in two but she will never get through to us again.

MURIEL: I am so thin, my ring my ring, I am so thin.

SUSIE *and* SILLY: Oh oh.

ACT III

Enter OLIVER *this time beside the string he has sticking plaster all down the front and the back of him holding him together and in his hand a large cardboard and wire and pincers.*

MURIEL *coming in with a doll's carriage filled with butter sugar milk and bread.* SUSIE *is a large white egg and* SILLY *is Willy. They come in slowly looking all around and sadly shaking their heads.*

OLIVER: I may be a twin but she will never get in.

MURIEL: Oh dear I am getting so thin, I eat milk and bread and sugar and butter and they say of butter, one pound of butter makes two pounds of girl and oh dear butter, butter, I get thinner and thinner and my ring oh dear I am so thin.

SUSIE: Oh I wish I was a fish and not an egg and then I could swim and not do anything.

SILLY: I wish I wish I was not Willie, I wish I wish I wish I was Silly so I could marry Susie oh dear.

OLIVER (*Darkly*): Well wait she cannot get in, see what I am doing. (*He commences to stop up the entrance between the trees with wire and in the middle of it he puts a large sign* NO TRESPASSING.) There what do I care if I am a twin, she never will get in never never.

MURIEL: Oh dear I am so thin, it is not interesting, oh dear I am so thin, oh dear where is my ring. I slip through my ring oh dear I am so thin.

SUSIE *and* SILLY: Oh dear oh dear.

(*Just then the* APPARITION *appears disguised as a* FRENCH POODLE. *She comes along barking and jumping.*)

OLIVER: Oh what a pretty dog. Dogs lick wounds and they heal perhaps he could lick me where I am in two and then I would be one, oh happy me not to be two but one. Which one. Oh happy day. Which one. One. One. One.

MURIEL: And perhaps he has a bone, bones make you fat oh it is that, I want to be fat, being thin is not interesting, being fat oh I want to be that.

SUSIE: Oh Willie sit on me quick it would be awful if he bit.

WILLY: If he bit he might make me Silly instead of Billy.

(*The* POODLE *comes in barking and rushing around and they all say:*)

ALL: And what a pretty dog. I would like a pretty dog like that.

(*The dog comes up to* OLIVER *barking and jumping.*)

APPARITION: Am I pretty am I witty and would you like to have a
dog like that.

OLIVER: You bet I would, I'd give my hat, I'd give my bat to have
a pretty dog like that.

APPARITION (*To* MURIEL): Am I pretty am I witty and would you
like to have a pretty dog like that.

MURIEL: Thin or fat I would oh I would like to have a pretty dog
like that and I would make him a pretty hat of roses and daisies
if I had a pretty dog like that.

APPARITION (*To* SUSIE *and* SILLY; WILLIE *is sitting on* SUSIE): Am I
pretty am I witty and would you like a pretty dog like that.

SUSIE *and* SILLY: We would that.

(APPARITION *barking and dancing licks* OLIVER *up and down
saying:*)

APPARITION: I lick you front and back do you feel that.

OLIVER: You bet I do and it tickles too but it is funny now I know
I am one and not two, thank you, thanks pretty doggie thanks for
that.

(APPARITION *kisses* MURIEL.)

MURIEL: Oh happy day oh little by little I am getting fat, a pound
today, not like yesterday, a pound every day oh I am getting fat.
Oh thank you witty pretty doggie thank you for that.

(APPARITION *jumps over* WILLIE *and* SUSIE *and they scream.*)

SUSIE *and* SILLY: Oh we are Susie and we are Silly and thanks pretty
dog for that.

(OLIVER *goes over to the wire and takes down the cardboard* NO
TRESPASSING *and gives it to the dog who begs and takes it and*

*dances with it tearing it up while the four cousins dance around
the dog singing:)*

ALL: The doggie is pretty the doggie is witty we all always want to
have a dog like that.

Little Red Riding Hood

BY

EUGENE SCHWARTZ

translated and adapted by George Shail

EUGENE SCHWARTZ (also spelled Evgeny Shvarts and Yevgeny Schwartz), who posthumously became one of Russia's best-known modern playwrights for his satirical comedies, enjoyed a long career closely associated with children's literature and children's theatre. Even his plays for adults, *The Shadow* and *The Dragon*, employ the fairy-tale form of Hans Christian Andersen to ridicule contemporary political and social life. Of course, his critical commentary did not go unnoticed by Soviet authorities and these plays which were written in the early 1940s were not allowed to hold the stages of Moscow and Leningrad until 20 years later when during the Stalin purge they became part of the modern repertory. *The Dragon* also has been favorably received by critics viewing productions in London and New York. Both plays are available in English and are recommended for their imaginative and witty attacks upon tyranny and totalitarianism.

Schwartz apparently never forgot the effects of despotism and brutality he experienced from the time of his childhood. Born in the city of Kazan in 1896 or 1897, he moved with his father, a physician with strong political persuasions, and his mother, an actress, to Dmitrov, where almost at once his father was arrested for activities in a socialist-democratic group to which he belonged. When Eugene and his mother visited the father in jail, a bearded guard suddenly spun upon the mother as she was kissing her husband goodbye, demanding that she hand over a note that he said the prisoner had smuggled to her. There was no note, but soon the room filled with policemen and the three-year-old boy began screaming as his father was led away. "I screamed so much that I grew hoarse and couldn't speak for an entire day," he recalled many years later.

Life was somewhat difficult for the Schwartz family after this. When the father was released, he was permitted to practice medicine only in certain provincial cities. Eugene, consequently, was educated in Maikop in the northern Caucasus but later enrolled in the law school at Moscow University, where his education was interrupted by financial needs (he had to support his family while his father served in the army in 1917) and by his increasing interest in an acting career.

The theatre was by no means new to him, for he had been taken to see his first play, *Hamlet*, at a very early age. Moreover, his mother and several aunts and uncles were provincial actors, and Eugene eagerly followed their example by joining an experimental theatre workshop composed of young hopefuls like himself. Their productions were good enough to gain them professional status, and after performances in several cities, the group was invited in 1921 to appear in Leningrad. But here the engagement was not successful and when the workshop disbanded, Eugene's acting career came to an end. He next turned to journalism, writing several years for a newspaper and a magazine, but his love of theatre remained undiminished.

Upon joining the State Children's Publishing House in Leningrad in 1925, he began a life devoted to children's literature, during which he prospered as an author, editor, storyteller and dramatist. In 1926 his first play was produced at the Leningrad Children's Theatre and the next 30 years saw a prolific dramatic outpouring. Even though few of his plays for children have been translated into English (*Little Red Riding Hood* is the first to be published), his reputation as a major Russian dramatist in this field is well known throughout Europe and America. His most famous plays for children include *The Two Maples, The Hidden Treasure, The Snow Queen* (a dramatization of Andersen, his favorite source of subject matter for plays), *The City of Puppets* and *A Distant Land,* a play about the evacuation of the children of Leningrad during World War II. He also wrote film scenarios and screenplays, the best known of which are those for *Cinderella* and the esteemed *Don Quixote.* He continued to write children's stories until his death in 1958, just two years before the productions of his adult plays gained him international attention. A substantial collection of his works for children, published in Leningrad in 1959, testifies to his abilities as a poet, playwright and creator of adventure stories, fables and fairy tales.

Although Schwartz employed famous fairy tales as the basis of his plays, he often altered them to suit his thematic purpose. The dragon in his play of that name turns out not to be a fire-spouting beast of whom everyone lives in dread but an ordinary man in an ordinary business suit who says that dragons have been among humans so long that they sometimes come to look like them. Yet he is a true dragon. Heroic Lancelot, prepared to slay the dragon, discovers that not everyone wishes to be freed from his domination nor saved from his villainy, for the townspeople have come to accept and depend upon the power of the brute. The shadow in the play of that name suddenly leaves the body of his owner for a life of his own but, unlike his fairy-tale counterpart, learns that he cannot live without his master. Yet the shadow, while independent, influences the court and impresses the Princess far more successfully than ever had its master, suggesting that Schwartz felt we sometimes honor outward appearances more than the true person within.

Readers of *Little Red Riding Hood* will note a number of changes from the original story that Schwartz has made for theatrical effect. Most conspicuous among them is the swallowing of the heroine and her grandmother by The Wolf and the scene that follows within its stomach. The author gives no indication of how this is to be accomplished on stage but witnesses of Russian performances say that the bed in which The Wolf rests is built very high in order to permit the two actors to play underneath in an area which gives the appearance that they indeed are enclosed in the stomach. The addition of Comrade Forester as a kind of guardian angel of the forest reflects that aspect of Soviet propaganda that is a part of Russian children's theatre, often far more so than in the present play. Likewise, the final song, in which the audience is admonished never to forget its enemies, may startle readers in the West as an inappropriate climax to a fairy-tale play.

But it is the character of Little Red Riding Hood herself that perhaps gives new meaning to the word "red" in the title. Schwartz here creates the ideal young pioneer, so totally brave, flawless and understanding that we are as surprised as she is when The Wolf actually swallows her. To be certain, this is but a temporary incarceration, during which the dauntless lass carefully plots a means of escape, which comes about through the assistance of the birds she dearly loves. Salvation through love is a favorite Schwartz theme, to be found in his plays for adults as well as for children. Red Riding Hood's need for "airborne reconnaissance" in what she terms her "war" with The Wolf also informs us that we are not dealing with the traditional little girl who innocently goes to her grandmother's house and encounters the big bad wolf, but with a child citizen steadfastly determined to make the forest a safe place for everyone to live.

The play has been in the mainstream of the Russian repertory since 1937, when it was first performed at the New Theatre for Young Spectators in Leningrad. A key to its success, much more so than its propaganda and possible satire, is the strong audience participation it elicits at every performance. According to report, Little Red Riding Hood receives the assistance of hundreds of children who cry out warnings that The Wolf is waiting for her or that The Fox is deceiving her; some children even attempt to join her animal friends in an effort to save her. The excitement and involvement the play engenders is reason enough for its long popularity among audiences in Russia's 45 theatres for children.

The English version printed here has been prepared by George Shail, a Teaching Fellow in the Program of Educational Theatre at New York University, whose speciality is children's theatre in the Soviet Union. He has translated a number of plays by Schwartz and other noted dramatists for the young.

Little Red Riding Hood

CHARACTERS

LITTLE RED RIDING HOOD
THE MOTHER *of Little Red Riding Hood*
THE GRANDMOTHER *of Little Red Riding Hood*
THE RABBIT BELOUKH, *a friend of Little Red Riding Hood*
A GRASS SNAKE, *another friend of Little Red Riding Hood*
THE BEAR MISHENKA, *also a friend of Little Red Riding Hood*
THE FOX, *a false friend of Little Red Riding Hood*
THE WOLF, *the enemy of Little Red Riding Hood*
THE MOTHER BIRD *and her* BABY BIRDS, *special friends of
Little Red Riding Hood*
COMRADE FORESTER, *who looks after everyone and
everything in the forest.*
RABBITS, *relatives of Beloukh*
BEES
A DOG, *the helper of Comrade Forester*

THE SCENES

*The entire play takes place in and about the great forest in which
dwell Little Red Riding Hood, her relatives, her animal friends,
and her enemy, The Wolf. Part of the action occurs in the stomach
of The Wolf.*

The time is today in Russia.

SCENE 1

The exterior of a tiny house in the forest. LITTLE RED RIDING HOOD *and her* MOTHER *emerge from the house.* LITTLE RED RIDING HOOD *is carrying a basket which contains a bottle of milk and a large piece of pie. Over her shoulder she wears a satchel.*

THE MOTHER: Well, goodbye, Daughter.

LITTLE RED RIDING HOOD: Goodbye, Mama.

THE MOTHER: Be careful, Daughter, when you go by the swamp. Don't stumble. Don't slip. Don't trip. Don't fall in the water.

LITTLE RED RIDING HOOD (*Speaking in the same manner as her* MOTHER): And you Mother, don't daydream. Don't stare into space. Don't worry about me while you're sewing, or you'll prick your finger.

THE MOTHER: And, Daughter, don't stop to talk with anyone except Comrade Forester.

LITTLE RED RIDING HOOD: All right. And, Mother, don't forget to put your scissors, needle, and thread in your pocket, or you'll lose them.

THE MOTHER: All right. Well, goodbye, Daughter.

LITTLE RED RIDING HOOD: Goodbye, Mama. (*Waves farewell.*)

THE MOTHER (*About to cry*): Oh dear, oh dear!

LITTLE RED RIDING HOOD: What's wrong, Mama?

THE MOTHER: I'll worry until you get back.

LITTLE RED RIDING HOOD: Mama, who will harm me in the forest? All the animals are my friends.

THE MOTHER: What about The Wolf?

LITTLE RED RIDING HOOD: He wouldn't dare to touch me. He knows my friends will protect me. . . . Well, goodbye, Mama. (*Kisses her.*)

THE MOTHER (*Sadly*): I know you have to go because Grandmother is sick. In your basket you have milk and pie for her. Goodbye, Daughter. It will be dull without you. Hurry back soon. (*Sighing deeply, she returns to the house.*)

(*As* LITTLE RED RIDING HOOD *departs, a* RABBIT *hops from behind the bushes and addresses her shyly.*)

THE RABBIT: Little Red Riding Hood.

LITTLE RED RIDING HOOD: Who's calling me?

THE RABBIT: It's Beloukh, the rabbit.

LITTLE RED RIDING HOOD: Hello, Beloukh.

THE RABBIT: Hello, dear, sweet, intelligent, kind Little Red Riding Hood. I have to talk with you about something very, very important.

LITTLE RED RIDING HOOD: Well, come here, please.

THE RABBIT (*Remaining in the bushes*): I'm afraid.

LITTLE RED RIDING HOOD: Still afraid?

THE RABBIT (*Agreeing*): Excuse me.

LITTLE RED RIDING HOOD: Didn't I give you courage?

THE RABBIT: Yes, you did.

LITTLE RED RIDING HOOD: Didn't I read books to you?

THE RABBIT: Yes, you did.

LITTLE RED RIDING HOOD: Didn't I teach all of the rabbits?

THE RABBIT: You taught us.

LITTLE RED RIDING HOOD: What did I teach you?

THE RABBIT: Bravery. And now we know The Wolf, The Fox and all the other horrible creatures. Because we're not afraid of them, we hide bravely. Aren't we wonderful?

LITTLE RED RIDING HOOD: And you're afraid to come to me?

THE RABBIT: Oh, excuse me, but your new boots squeak loudly. They frighten me. (*He trembles.*)

LITTLE RED RIDING HOOD: That means I've wasted my time teaching you.

THE RABBIT: No, we just haven't got past squeaky boots yet.

LITTLE RED RIDING HOOD: Farewell.

THE RABBIT: Oh, no, no, if you leave—excuse me—I'll fall over dead.

LITTLE RED RIDING HOOD: Well, Rabbit, come here then. Well! (THE RABBIT *keeps coming closer, then jumping back as he speaks. By the end of the following passage, he is next to* LITTLE RED RIDING

HOOD. *Firmly but kindly.*) Come here, take a good look. It is I, your friend. Would I scare you? Would I harm you? And if I scold you, I scold you from love. It is I, your friend. (THE RABBIT *extends his paw and shakes her hand.*) Good! Well, what did you want to tell me?

THE RABBIT: I implore you. Go back inside and lock all your doors.

LITTLE RED RIDING HOOD: Why?

THE RABBIT: (*Stuttering in fear*): The Wolf is looking for you.

LITTLE RED RIDING HOOD: Shhh! Mama might hear you.

THE RABBIT (*Whispering*): The Wolf has come for you from deep in the forest. He is lurking here and keeps threatening, "I'm going to eat Little Red Riding Hood. Just let her leave the house and I'll get her." Run back quickly. (LITTLE RED RIDING HOOD *smiles and puts down her basket.*) Why are you smiling?

LITTLE RED RIDING HOOD: I'm not afraid of him. He's not going to eat me. Goodbye, little Beloukh. And thank you. (*She shakes his paw once more, picks up her basket and starts to leave.*)

THE RABBIT (*Trying to hold her*): Oh!! You can't do it. I—excuse my roughness—won't let you go. . . . (*Tugs at her.*)

LITTLE RED RIDING HOOD (*Easily freeing herself from his hold*): Goodbye, little rabbit.

THE RABBIT: Oh dear, oh dear! I'll never see Little Red Riding Hood again. Poor girl. Poor us! (*Weeping, he exits into the bushes.*)

(A GRASS SNAKE *enters.*)

A GRASS SNAKE (*Hissing*): Ssss . . . Hello . . . sss . . . Little . . . sss . . . Red . . . sss . . . Riding . . . sss . . . Hood . . . sss. . . .

LITTLE RED RIDING HOOD: Hello, viper.

A GRASS SNAKE (*Annoyed*): I'm no viper . . . sss . . . I'm a grass . . . sss . . . sss . . . snake. I'm not dangerous . . . ssss . . . . (*He moves toward her.*)

LITTLE RED RIDING HOOD: I'm not afraid of you. (*She squeals:*) But don't touch me.

THE GRASS SNAKE: Ssssss . . . stop. I crawled here . . . sssss to tell you . . . sssss . . . something. Stay home today . . . sssss.

LITTLE RED RIDING HOOD: Why?

THE GRASS SNAKE: The Wolf is prowling about.

LITTLE RED RIDING HOOD: Shhh! Mama might hear you.

THE GRASS SNAKE: Excuse . . . ssss me. (*Lowering his voice*) Listen to me . . . ssss. I'm friends with the cows . . . sssss. I'm crazy about milk . . . ssss. The Wolf told a cow-friend of mine that he would . . . ssss . . . have eaten . . . ssss her, except that . . . ssss he had to leave . . . sssss . . . a place . . . sssss . . . in his . . . ssss . . . belly for Little Red Riding Hood! Do you hear me . . . sssssss?

LITTLE RED RIDING HOOD (*Absolutely calm*): I hear you, but I'm not afraid of The Wolf.

THE GRASS SNAKE: He'll eat you . . . sss. He'll eat you. . . . sssss. He'll eat you . . . sssss.

LITTLE RED RIDING HOOD: That will never happen. Goodbye. And thank you.

THE GRASS SNAKE: I wish you would lis . . . sss . . . ten. Lis . . . sss . . . ten. (THE GRASS SNAKE *disappears into the bushes;* THE BEAR *emerges and comes toward* LITTLE RED RIDING HOOD.)

THE BEAR: Hail, Little Red Riding Hood!

LITTLE RED RIDING HOOD: Hello, Mishenka. (*She starts to hurry into the forest.*)

THE BEAR: Stop! I have a couple of things to discuss with you.

LITTLE RED RIDING HOOD: All right, Mishenka, but I'm in a hurry.

THE BEAR (*Emphatically*): Two things. First, smear my face, please.

LITTLE RED RIDING HOOD: What?

THE BEAR: My nose is all swollen because some bees—impudent things —stung me. Smear me with iodine.

LITTLE RED RIDING HOOD: I'll take care of you. Sit down. (*She removes a bottle of medicine from her satchel and gently swabs the nose of* THE BEAR *with iodine. Immediately he lets out a scream and does cartwheels about the forest.*)

THE BEAR: Oh, it stings!!! It stings!

LITTLE RED RIDING HOOD: You'll feel better, friend Mishenka.

THE BEAR: Thank you. Now, let's get to the second thing. Namely, you should go home because . . .

LITTLE RED RIDING HOOD: Once again? Why?

THE BEAR: The Wolf . . .

LITTLE RED RIDING HOOD: Quiet, Mama might hear you.

THE BEAR: Run right home, I'm telling you . . .

LITTLE RED RIDING HOOD: I'm not afraid of The Wolf.

THE BEAR: But what can you do, my dear? With your short human nose, you won't be able to smell The Wolf from a distance. With your short human legs, you won't be able to run away. With your short human teeth, you won't be able to protect yourself. He'll eat you like a cookie. (*He sobs.*) Only this morning, The Wolf said to me, "I'll . . . ," he said, "eat," he said, "her," he said, "like a cookie," and, he said, "without fail." I would have struck him, but I'm forbidden to, or rather, I'm not supposed to because he's my first cousin.

LITTLE RED RIDING HOOD (*Undaunted*): I'm not afraid of anything. Thank you for the warning. Goodbye, Bear. (*She goes into the forest.*)

THE BEAR (*Sobbing*): Too bad, Red Riding Hood. "Like a cookie," he said.

A GRASS SNAKE (*Rising above the bushes*): He'll eat her ssurely . . . sss. . . .

THE RABBIT (*Leaning out from the trees*): I implore you. Please save her.

THE BEAR: Er . . . ah . . . But how?

THE RABBIT: I implore you. Let's run after her.

THE GRASS SNAKE: Yes, let'ssss.

THE RABBIT: And we'll protect her. I can't do it alone. I'm a coward. But if you're with me, it won't be so awful. You won't eat me, will you, Bear?

THE BEAR: Of course not. You're a friend of mine.

THE RABBIT: Thank you very much. Let's go after her quickly.

THE BEAR: I agree. Although The Wolf is my first cousin, I won't hand Little Red Riding Hood over to him.

THE RABBIT: No, let's go.

(*They hurry off. They have barely disappeared, when a* FOX *runs out from behind a tree.*)

THE FOX: Hee, hee, hee. (*To the audience.*) Look at those stupid, stupid animals. (*Imitating them.*) "Let's run, let's crawl, we'll protect her." I just stood behind a tree and laughed. Hee! Hee! Hee! I found out everything! (*Thinking.*) No, not quite everything. Little Red Riding Hood is a sly one. She's thought of something, or else she would be afraid of The Wolf. I'll run after her and find out. Then I'll tell everything to The Wolf. He'll eat the girl, and people will be angered with him and drive The Wolf away. And then the forest will be mine. No Wolf, no girl.

I'll be the Master here. I, The Fox. Hee, hee, hee. (*He runs out laughing.*)

SCENE 2

A forest glade. THE MOTHER BIRD *and her* BABY BIRDS *are talking back and forth in the treetops.* THE BABY BIRDS *are still in their nest. When* LITTLE RED RIDING HOOD *enters,* THE BIRDS *chirp joyfully.*

LITTLE RED RIDING HOOD: Hello, Birds.

THE BIRDS: Hello, Little Red Riding Hood! Hello, hello . . .

LITTLE RED RIDING HOOD: How are you feeling?

THE BIRDS: Very well, very well.

THE MOTHER BIRD: I have hatched some young.

THE BABY BIRDS (*In chorus*): We've been hatched, we've been hatched. We see you, do you see us?

THE MOTHER BIRD: Children, don't pester us. Little Red Riding Hood, aren't my fledglings smart? Only two weeks old and already they can talk.

THE BABY BIRDS: Aren't we smart? Aren't we smart?

LITTLE RED RIDING HOOD: Yes, very smart. (*She takes the satchel from her shoulder and puts it on the grass with the basket.*) Do you remember how the farmer's son was destroying your nests?

THE BIRDS: We remember, we remember. Of course, we remember.

LITTLE RED RIDING HOOD: Didn't I help you?

THE BIRDS: Yes, yes. You convinced him that he was wrong and now he is our friend. Thank you.

LITTLE RED RIDING HOOD: And now will you help me?

THE BIRDS: Help you? Who is wronging you?

LITTLE RED RIDING HOOD: The Wolf! (*Immediately* THE BIRDS *become silent.* THE FOX *looks out from behind a tree.*) Why are you all so silent?

THE MOTHER BIRD: We're terrified!

THE BABY BIRDS: Mother, climb higher in the tree. We're afraid, Mama!!

LITTLE RED RIDING HOOD: Don't be alarmed, Birds. I can foil The Wolf, if he doesn't attack me by surprise.

THE BIRDS: How? Tell us how?

THE FOX: Please tell them. Do! (*He strains to listen.*)

LITTLE RED RIDING HOOD: I've thought it all out. I have some pepper with me!

THE MOTHER BIRD: What for?

LITTLE RED RIDING HOOD: I'll throw it in his nose.

THE BABY BIRDS: And what will he do?

LITTLE RED RIDING HOOD: He'll sneeze.

THE BABY BIRDS: And what will you do?

LITTLE RED RIDING HOOD: I'll take a dry branch and light it.

THE BABY BIRDS: And what will he do?

LITTLE RED RIDING HOOD: He'll sneeze and come after me.

THE BABY BIRDS: And what will you do?

LITTLE RED RIDING HOOD: I'll wave the branch as I walk.

THE BABY BIRDS: And what will he do?

LITTLE RED RIDING HOOD: He'll run after me, but he won't dare to touch me, because he's afraid of fire. And that's how I'll catch him.

THE BABY BIRDS (*Not understanding*): How?

LITTLE RED RIDING HOOD: I'll lead him to the Old Oak Tree near the Wild Swamp. The hunters have placed a trap there. I'll step over the trap, and The Wolf will follow me. The trap will go "snap" and The Wolf will yell, "Ouch." And he'll be caught.

THE MOTHER BIRD: Very good, very good, very good!

THE BABY BIRDS: Mama, have her explain it again. We liked hearing it.

THE MOTHER BIRD: Quiet, children.

LITTLE RED RIDING HOOD: In a word, I'm going to war with The Wolf.

THE BIRDS: Very good, very good.

LITTLE RED RIDING HOOD: But what's a war without reconnaissance? This is where I need your help.

THE BIRDS (*Chirping*): We'll help, we'll help, we'll help!

THE BABY BIRDS: Mama, what's reconnaissance?

THE MOTHER BIRD: Quiet. I don't know myself. She'll explain it.

LITTLE RED RIDING HOOD: If The Wolf attacks me without warning, I won't be able to throw the pepper at him. But you can see everything from up high. And if you see The Wolf, shout, "Watch out!" Will you be my airborne reconnaissance?

THE BIRDS: Yes, oh, yes. Oh, yes.

LITTLE RED RIDING HOOD: Thank you. Well, look around carefully and report back to me.

THE BABY BIRDS: Mama, don't fly away. We're afraid.

THE MOTHER BIRD: Aren't you ashamed? You're already two weeks old.

LITTLE RED RIDING HOOD: Well, get flying, reconnaissance.

THE BABY BIRDS: What's reconnaissance, Mama?

THE MOTHER BIRD: Never mind, I'll look. You stay in the nest. (*She flies off.*)

(*As* LITTLE RED RIDING HOOD *waves goodbye,* THE FOX *steals out from behind the tree.*)

THE FOX (*To the audience*): Hee, hee, hee!! While they're looking up, I'll help my friend The Wolf. (*He sneaks up to the satchel and opens it.*)

LITTLE RED RIDING HOOD (*Calling off*): Do you see anything?

THE MOTHER BIRD (*Chirping from off*): Just a minute, just a minute, just a minute.

THE FOX: First, the pepper. (*He takes the pepper from the satchel.*) There we are. Quietly, on the sly. Now The Wolf won't do any sneezing. Hee, hee, hee! (*He throws the pepper in the bushes.*)

LITTLE RED RIDING HOOD (*Calling into the sky*): What do you see?

THE MOTHER BIRD (*Chirping*): Wait a minute, wait a minute, wait a minute.

THE FOX: And now the matches. Here they are. Now she won't have anything to light the branch with. Perfect. Hee, hee, hee! (*He slinks away.*)

(THE MOTHER BIRD *lands noisily on the branches.*)

THE MOTHER BIRD: I saw a wild cat, a badger, and a boar, but no Wolf.

LITTLE RED RIDING HOOD: No Wolf?

THE MOTHER BIRD: I saw a rabbit, a grass snake and a bear. They said they're coming after you . . . to protect you.

THE BABY BIRDS: Very good, very good, very good.

LITTLE RED RIDING HOOD: Do they think I'm a little child? Your help is all I need. (*She puts the satchel over her shoulder.*) Well, Birds, will you accompany me to Grandmother's house? Will you be my airborne reconnaissance?

THE BIRDS: Oh, yes, we will track The Wolf. We'll fly with you.

LITTLE RED RIDING HOOD: Thank you. (*They all go off.*)

(THE RABBIT, THE BEAR, *and* THE GRASS SNAKE *enter.*)

THE GRASS SNAKE: . . . Sssssstop. I'm tired . . . Let'ssssss . . . ssssit down.

THE BEAR: I agree. (*They sit.*)

THE RABBIT: I implore you. Let's go. She—excuse my rudeness—is all alone and needs our help.

THE BEAR: Stop it, brother. I haven't eaten in quite a while and you're beginning to smell delicious. You're a good rabbit, of course, but nevertheless you're eatable.

THE RABBIT: How can you think about food when Little Red Riding Hood is in danger?

THE BEAR: It doesn't matter.

THE RABBIT: How, excuse me, can you say it doesn't matter, when . . .

(*From the bushes we hear* THE FOX *calling, "Oh! Oh!"*)

THE BEAR: Who's moaning?

THE VOICE OF THE FOX: Oh! Oh!

THE BEAR: Who's moaning? Come out!

(THE FOX *crawls out of the bushes.*)

THE FOX: Oh, oh, oh! Hello, my dears. (*Pretending.*) I'm so sad, my friends. The sun is shining and the forest is in blossom, but I'm dying.

THE BEAR: There's nothing wrong with you. You're trying to trick me. I know you.

THE FOX: How can you say that, Mishenka. Why would I? Mishenka, he broke all my legs.

THE BEAR: Who did?

THE FOX: The Wolf. That horrid beast told me that he was going to eat Little Red Riding Hood.

THE BEAR: We'll see about that.

THE FOX: That's what I said to him. "We'll see about that." With these words, he jumped on me. "See about that," he cried, "See about that." And then he bit me.

THE RABBIT: Oh!! (*Shakes with fear.*)

THE FOX: I said exactly the same thing to him. "Oh," I said. And then he bit me again. So badly that I had to run home and get in bed. . . .

THE BEAR: That is quite a story. Ho, ho, ho!

THE FOX: I've been in bed for a week. But I'm still dying. Now, farewell, Mishenka. (*He pretends to be dying.*)

THE BEAR (*Still without sympathy*): Farewell, Fox.

THE FOX: So that you will remember me kindly, I want to make you happy. Do you know where the linden tree stands near the river?

THE BEAR: What about it?

THE FOX: In the hollow of this tree is a large amount of honey. And no bees.

THE BEAR (*Suddenly very interested*): No bees?

THE FOX: They've moved to another part of the forest.

THE BEAR: Ho, ho, ho. Nice.

THE FOX: Go there, Mishenka, and eat to your heart's content. But don't forget me. Hurry, or some other bear will get your honey.

THE BEAR (*Very excited*): Yes, that's true.

THE FOX: Farewell, Grass Snake.

THE GRASS SNAKE: Sssso long . . .

THE FOX (*Unctuously*): I want to make you happy, too. Do you know the bridge over the river? The farmer was taking his milk to market when a can fell off the wagon. He didn't hear it. A can of sweet fresh milk is lying by the bridge.

THE GRASS SNAKE: . . . sss . . . Sssssweet and fresh?

THE FOX: It's glistening in the sun.

THE GRASS SNAKE (*Distressed*): It will turn sssssssour. . . .

THE FOX: Not if you hurry. Oh, farewell, brothers. (*Melodramatically.*) Eat the honey, drink the milk, as I am dying. . . . (*Then forgets himself.*) Hee, hee, hee!

THE RABBIT: Why—excuse me—are you laughing?

THE FOX (*Trying to cover up*): I'm just coughing, my friend, just coughing. Farewell. . . . (*Forgetting again.*) Hee, hee, hee! (*He slinks away.*)

THE BEAR: Well, brothers, there's no sign of The Wolf and I would like some honey.

THE GRASS SNAKE: I would like some milk.

THE RABBIT: What are you doing? Do you believe him? Don't you realize he was deceiving you?

THE BEAR: Don't bother me. I'm hungry.

THE RABBIT: Then eat me, but don't abandon Little Red Riding Hood. Go ahead. Take me and swallow me!

THE BEAR: I prefer honey. Farewell.

THE GRASS SNAKE: I prefer milk. Sssssso long. (*They exit.*)

THE RABBIT: They've gone. They believed The Fox. . . . (*Calling off.*) Bear! Grass Snake! (*There is no answer.*) All is lost! And The Wolf will eat the little girl. But I won't desert her. After all, she taught me bravery. (*Gaining courage.*) I will face The Wolf, his big teeth, his long claws, his powerful jaws, his ravenous stomach, and crush him. (*Carried away with heroic eagerness.*) I won't spare myself for my friend. To battle, Beloukh, to battle! (*He dashes off.*)

SCENE 3

A swamp in the depths of the forest surrounded by a rock, a thicket, and a large trap intended to catch animals. This section of the forest is much more sinister than that we have seen before. There is a sense of danger hovering everywhere because this is the home of THE WOLF. *He is seen sharpening his teeth on a grinding stone which hisses as he speaks.*

THE WOLF: I'm sharpening my teeth . . . sssssssss, ssssssss. . . . How I hate little girls . . . ssssss, ssssssss. . . . I dislike their skinny legs and shrill voices . . . ssssss, ssssssss . . . I dislike their meddling in the forest . . . sssssss, ssssssss . . . How I hate little girls. . . . sssssss, ssssss. . . . I'm sharpening my teeth. . . .

(THE FOX *runs in.*)

THE FOX: My compatriot, my friend! Hide in the bushes quickly!

THE WOLF: What? H-o-w-l. (*He howls.*) To whom are you speaking?

THE FOX: To you, pal.

THE WOLF: Don't you call me that dog's name. I'm not your pal, I'm a wolf.

THE FOX: Hee, hee, hee. Whatever you wish. I've come to you out of friendship. . . .

THE WOLF: What? H-o-w-l. Out of friendship? Have you been studying with that girl? Out of friendship, indeed. . . . Because of friendship it's impossible to live in the forest. The rabbits are friends with the squirrels, the birds are friends with the rabbits. H-o-w-l! But I'm friends with no one. I'm for myself alone. H-o-w-l!

THE FOX: Hide in the bushes, I say.

THE WOLF: Don't tell me what to do. Why should I hide?

THE FOX: Because the birds are accompanying Little Red Riding Hood. They will notice you from above and tell her. It's smarter to attack the girl suddenly, before she sees you.

THE WOLF: I know that myself.

THE FOX: She wanted to throw pepper at you.

THE WOLF (*His anger rising*): H-o-w-l.

THE FOX: And she wanted to light a branch, and scare you with the fire.

THE WOLF (*Almost unable to contain himself*): Howl. H-O-W-L.

THE FOX: But I helped you by stealing the pepper and the matches.

THE WOLF: Don't say that word "help." Remember who I am and who you are. I don't need your help.

THE FOX: Get in the bushes, Little Wolf.

THE WOLF: Don't call me by another dog's name. I'm not Little Wolf, I'm *The* Wolf.

THE FOX: Oh, get going or you'll ruin everything.

THE WOLF (*He goes toward the bushes*): I'll go myself.

THE FOX: So, *do* it yourself.

THE WOLF: I myself know that it's smarter to attack her suddenly.

THE FOX: Yes, yes. Be quiet and listen.

THE WOLF: I know what I should listen to without your help.

THE FOX: Be silent!

THE WOLF: I myself know when I should be silent.

THE FOX (*Exasperated*): Oh, what a beast!

THE WOLF: Yes, you'll look a long time for another one like me. . . . Aha! Here she comes. Get out of the way. Give me room to charge. Here she comes. H-o-w-l!

(*We hear the chirping of* THE BIRDS *as* LITTLE RED RIDING HOOD *carefully looks out of the thicket.*)

LITTLE RED RIDING HOOD: This is a most dangerous place.

THE BIRDS: Why, why?

LITTLE RED RIDING HOOD: Here in the Wild Swamp the undergrowth is so thick that you can't see anything from above. Even so, I would like to meet The Wolf here.

THE BIRDS: Why, why?

LITTLE RED RIDING HOOD: Do you see the Old Oak Tree over there? Right under it is the trap into which I want to lure The Wolf.

(*From off stage we hear the desperate cry of the approaching* RABBIT.)

THE RABBIT: Stop, Little Red Riding Hood, stop!

THE BIRDS: The Rabbit is running this way, The Rabbit is running this way.

(THE RABBIT *hurries in.*)

THE RABBIT: Stop! Let me lead the way.

THE FOX (*To* THE WOLF): Forward, now!!

THE WOLF: I know that myself. (*He rushes toward* LITTLE RED RIDING HOOD.)

THE RABBIT (*Stepping in front of* THE WOLF, *bravely*): I—excuse me— will bite you.

(*Without saying a word,* THE WOLF *throws* THE RABBIT *aside with one sweep of his paw.* THE RABBIT *lands unconscious in the bushes.* LITTLE RED RIDING HOOD *takes a package from her satchel.* THE WOLF *springs, but* LITTLE RED RIDING HOOD *jumps aside.* THE BIRDS *cry out,* "Help, Help!" *The girl throws a pinch of pepper directly in the face of* THE WOLF.)

THE WOLF: What's this? Achoo-oo-oo. (*He sneezes.*)

LITTLE RED RIDING HOOD: It's pepper. Gesundheit!

THE WOLF: I'll eat you just the same. Achoo!

LITTLE RED RIDING HOOD: Gesundheit! No, you won't eat me.

THE WOLF: I'm stronger than you.

LITTLE RED RIDING HOOD (*Stepping toward the oak tree*): But I'm smarter.

THE FOX (*Jumping up*): Be careful! There's a trap there!

THE WOLF: I know that myself!

LITTLE RED RIDING HOOD: Oh dear, The Fox is here, too!

THE FOX: Yes, and I'm coming after you! It was I who yelled, "Be careful! There's a trap there!" Wait, little girl, I'm coming after you. (*He runs toward her.*)

LITTLE RED RIDING HOOD: Don't come near me, or I'll throw pepper at you, too.

THE FOX: Do you have that much of it?

LITTLE RED RIDING HOOD: Yes, I do. Even though someone took one package of it.

THE FOX: I didn't do it.

LITTLE RED RIDING HOOD: But I still have plenty of it. (*She throws some pepper at* THE FOX.)

THE FOX: Achoo!

THE WOLF: Achoo!

LITTLE RED RIDING HOOD: Gesundheit!

THE WOLF: Remember! Our battle is not over! H-o-w-l. (*With an evil howl, he slinks into the bushes.*)

THE FOX: Achoo! There's nothing we can do! She's won . . . clever girl. . . . Achoo! She's won . . . Achoo! (*He slinks into the bushes after* THE WOLF.)

THE BIRDS: Victory! Victory!

LITTLE RED RIDING HOOD: Nothing of the sort! He said that on purpose, in order to launch another underhanded attack!

THE BIRDS: The Wolf and The Fox have run away!

LITTLE RED RIDING HOOD: They'll be back. It's easy for you to rejoice up there, but for me down below it's terrifying.

THE BIRDS: But we're with you, we're with you!

LITTLE RED RIDING HOOD: I know that . . . and thank you . . . but . . . When I think about that Wolf, I want to run home and lock all the doors . . . (*Crying out.*) and windows!

THE BIRDS: She's crying! Oh! Little Red Riding Hood is crying.

LITTLE RED RIDING HOOD: Can't I cry?

THE BIRDS: Of course, of course!

LITTLE RED RIDING HOOD: I'm a little girl. I'm not made of stone.

THE BIRDS: No, no, you're not made of stone.

LITTLE RED RIDING HOOD: I've forgotten poor Beloukh! (*She rushes to the bushes.*) Little Rabbit! Rabbit!

THE BIRDS: He's sleeping! He fell asleep!

LITTLE RED RIDING HOOD: No, he's unconscious. I'll sprinkle a little water on his face! Rabbit! Oh, my little gray friend! Open your eyes! I overcame The Wolf as if he were a little cub! (*She fishes around in her satchel.*) Somewhere here there are some smelling salts. Here, Beloukh! Little bunny! Little rabbit! Wake up!

THE RABBIT (*Reviving and jumping up*): I'll bite them all. I won't let you be harmed! You're my one and only friend! I'm your friend.

LITTLE RED RIDING HOOD: Everything's all right! I overcame them all, Rabbit! Don't worry!

THE RABBIT: You won! Hurray! Oho!

LITTLE RED RIDING HOOD: Are you feeling better?

THE RABBIT: Am I feeling better? Now I'm strong like you. (*He staggers about.*) Only, my head is spinning and my tail is trembling something awful. (*He sits down.*)

LITTLE RED RIDING HOOD: Lie down, take a rest.

THE RABBIT: No! Who will accompany you?

LITTLE RED RIDING HOOD: Lie down, Bunny. Lie down, little Rabbit. Don't worry. The Wolf won't dare touch me.

THE RABBIT: He won't touch you?

LITTLE RED RIDING HOOD: Never! You go ahead and sleep, brave fellow!

THE RABBIT: I attacked The Wolf!

LITTLE RED RIDING HOOD: Yes, yes. But now I have to go, or Grandmother will be angry. Go to sleep. I feel happy. Everything's all right. (*She rises, picks up her satchel, and leaves.*)

THE RABBIT: No, I just can't sleep. Isn't it wonderful that I attacked The Wolf? Victory to Little Red Riding Hood! What's that noise? They're coming again! (*He rushes to the bushes.*) Hide me, bushes! Don't give me away. (*He hides.*)

(THE WOLF *and* THE FOX *stick their heads out of the thicket.*)

THE WOLF: She's gone. H-o-w-l. I'll go after her.

THE FOX (*Looking out from the other end of the thicket*): The birds will see you.

THE WOLF: Silence!!

THE FOX: From here on everything is open!

THE WOLF: I know that myself. Don't try to tell me anything.

THE FOX: Go over to that white rock there and roll around.

THE WOLF: You insolent fellow! Why should I do that?

THE FOX: That's chalk. Cover yourself with it and you'll look like a white dog. The little girl won't recognize you.

THE WOLF: Silence! (*He disappears behind the white rock.*) I'll do it myself.

THE FOX: So do it yourself.

THE WOLF: I myself know that I have to change color.

THE FOX: That's right.

THE WOLF (*As he smears himself*): How humiliating!

THE FOX: Why?

THE WOLF: For a wolf to look like a dog.

THE FOX (*Looking at him*): It's very becoming, pal.

THE WOLF (*Jumping into the open, all white*): I know that myself.

THE FOX: Good, comrade. Now run after the little girl.

THE WOLF: I know that myself. Wait! Someone's stirring in the bushes. Who's there? H-o-w-l!

THE RABBIT (*Emerging from the bushes,* THE RABBIT *heads for* THE WOLF): I . . . I'll . . . excuse me . . . bite you.

THE WOLF: What?

THE RABBIT (*Retreating*): I'll bite you! Don't growl! It's not my fault! I can't let the little girl fall into harm. I would run and tell her everything, but I'm so scared I can barely walk. But I have . . . (*He takes a step forward, and then steps back.*) . . . I have to fight with you. But don't growl, I really don't like fighting. (*He advances.*) You, excuse me, forced me to do it! You evil beast!

THE FOX: Lure him toward the oak tree, toward the oak tree.

THE WOLF: Don't tell me what to do!

THE RABBIT: What? What are you doing? Oh! (*He jumps forward.*) I don't understand what you're doing, you stupid beast. Come on and get me! (*There is a loud snap.* THE RABBIT *is caught in the trap.*)

THE RABBIT: What's this? Oh! Oh! Oh!

THE FOX: A trap! The trap in which Red Riding Hood wanted to catch The Wolf. Hee, hee, hee!

THE WOLF: Go away!

THE FOX: Come now, compatriot! What's the matter with you?

THE WOLF: Get out of here! I'm going to bite you!

THE FOX: Wait a minute, cousin. . . .

THE WOLF: I have no relatives. Out of here! Do you hear me? (*He rushes toward* THE FOX, *who runs into the thicket.*)

THE WOLF: There! (*To* THE RABBIT.) A rabbit has raised his paw to The Wolf. That's what things have come to. How did you dare to do it?

THE RABBIT: I'm a true friend of Little Red Riding Hood.

THE WOLF: Don't you dare to say that word! Let there be an end to friendship! Let there be an end to Little Red Riding Hood! One person alone will be master of the forest and that is I! H-o-w-l. (*He runs out.*)

THE RABBIT: What can I do? How can I save the girl now? Help! (*Crying loudly.*) Help! No one hears me. (*To the audience.*) Should I let her perish? No! I have to call out, to shout. Maybe someone in the forest will hear me. (*He yells louder.*) Help! I'm not afraid of anything anymore. Help!! (*Pause.*) No one. But I won't give up. I'll keep calling until all my brother rabbits come to my aid. We'll win yet. (*He starts drumming on the trap with his front paws and calls.*) Brother Rabbits! Brother Rabbits! Let's join together. Faithful rabbit hearts will endure to the last!

SCENE 4

A forest glade with flowers. THE WOLF *runs in and addresses the audience.*

THE WOLF: How clever I am! How smart I am! I got rid of The Fox. I know why he wanted to be on my side. He thought that people would kill me after I ate the little girl. Well, that won't happen. No one fools me. I'll find out where her grandmother lives. . . . H-o-w-l. . . . (*Looks off.*) Here she comes! (*We hear the chirping of* BIRDS.) If only I don't forget and howl in her presence. (LITTLE RED RIDING HOOD *appears in the glade. In a sweet and exaggerated voice*): Hello, dear Little Red Riding Hood.

LITTLE RED RIDING HOOD: Hello, white dog.

THE WOLF (*Forgetting and growling deeply*): I'm no dog. . . . (*Remembering.*) Yes, yes, I am a dog. . . . My name is Pal.

LITTLE RED RIDING HOOD: Pal? Hello, Pal. (*She goes to pet* THE WOLF, *but he jumps back.*) What's wrong with you, Pal?

THE WOLF: I got separated from a hunter. I don't know what to do without him.

LITTLE RED RIDING HOOD: How long have you been lost?

THE WOLF: Three days.

LITTLE RED RIDING HOOD: Poor dog! That means you must be hungry.

THE WOLF: No, thank you. I'm full. Your grandmother fed me.

LITTLE RED RIDING HOOD: My grandmother?

THE WOLF: Yes! She's the one who lives next to . . . (*He coughs.*) . . . next to . . . ?

LITTLE RED RIDING HOOD: Next to the old birch trees, beyond the millstream.

THE WOLF: Yes, that's right, that's right! She fed me.

LITTLE RED RIDING HOOD: How is she feeling?

THE WOLF: Not well. She's in bed.

LITTLE RED RIDING HOOD: I'd better go to her right away.

THE WOLF: Oh, no, no! She asked me to tell you that she would like to have a bouquet of flowers. (THE WOLF *stares at* LITTLE RED RIDING HOOD *and licks his lips.*)

LITTLE RED RIDING HOOD: Flowers? All right. Are you sure I couldn't give you something to eat? Why do you lick your lips when you look at me?

THE WOLF: It's just an old habit of mine.

LITTLE RED RIDING HOOD: Goodbye, Pal.

THE WOLF (*With his own voice*): I'm not Pal. . . . (*Remembering and changing his voice.*) Goodbye, little girl. Goodbye, my dear. (*He runs out.*)

LITTLE RED RIDING HOOD: Birds, why are you so quiet?

THE BIRDS: We didn't like that dog. He was wagging his tail as if he wasn't used to it. A very large dog! A strange dog! An evil dog!

LITTLE RED RIDING HOOD: You don't have to scare me. Why don't we pick flowers instead? (*She leads* THE BIRDS *off, picking flowers.*)

(THE FOX *slinks from behind the bushes.*)

THE FOX (*To the audience*): Hee, hee, hee! So that's what The Wolf had in mind. He'll run to Grandmother's house. First, he'll eat the grandmother, then he'll eat the girl. He thinks no one will see him. But watch what I do! Hee, hee, hee. (*Praising himself.*) Oh, you smart little thing. You dear little fox.

SCENE 5

The interior of GRANDMOTHER'S *house, with a fireplace, a rocking chair, a large bed with blankets, and a door and window through*

which we can see sky and forest. Above the fireplace hangs a gun.
GRANDMOTHER *is sitting by the window knitting.*

THE GRANDMOTHER: My neck is a little stiff, but I don't want to stay in bed. I'd rather burst than stay in bed. Already today I've run down to the river, picked mushrooms, dusted the house, and prepared tea. I even played a little on my balalaika. (*She hums a tune.*) But I won't tell Little Red Riding Hood anything about this. She'll scold me. She's very strict. (*From a distance we hear the cry of* "Help!" GRANDMOTHER *jumps up.*) What's that! Someone's calling for help. (*She looks out the window.*) Who's there?

(THE WOLF *runs in.*)

THE WOLF: Oh, help me, help me.
GRANDMOTHER: What's the matter? What's wrong?
THE WOLF: The Wolf is after me. . . .
GRANDMOTHER: That's nothing! I'll shoot him. . . . (*She takes down the gun.*)
THE WOLF: Oh, no, no! Do as you like, but I'm afraid! Hide me under the bed. I beg you.
GRANDMOTHER: What's wrong with you! Well, get under the bed.
THE WOLF (*Deeply*): Throw away the gun!
GRANDMOTHER: Why should I?
THE WOLF: Because! (*He knocks the gun from* GRANDMOTHER's *hand with his paw, opens his gigantic jaws and swallows her.*)
GRANDMOTHER (*From within* THE WOLF's *belly*): You didn't fool me. You're The Wolf, aren't you?
THE WOLF: What did you think? Ha, ha, ha! Where are your glasses? Here they are. Where's your cap? Here it is. Very good! Ha, ha, ha! (*He puts them on.*)
GRANDMOTHER: Don't you dare shake me.
THE WOLF: Now I look like the old lady.
GRANDMOTHER: I know what you're planning. You're planning to eat Little Red Riding Hood!
THE WOLF: Without fail.
GRANDMOTHER: Just you try it! I'll yell to her, "Go away! He wants to eat you!"
THE WOLF: But I'll cover myself with three blankets and she won't hear you.

GRANDMOTHER: Don't you dare! (THE WOLF *covers himself with two blankets.*) Don't you dare!

(THE WOLF *covers himself with still another blanket.* GRANDMOTHER *is no longer heard.*)

THE WOLF: Good. I can't hear her. But it's hot under three blankets. Someone's coming! Someone's coming! Howl! (*He gets into bed.*)

(LITTLE RED RIDING HOOD *enters with a bouquet of flowers in her hands. She talks to* THE BIRDS *outside.*)

LITTLE RED RIDING HOOD: Well, goodbye, dear Birds. Thanks for your help, my friends.

THE BIRDS (*From above the house*): We'll wait! We're afraid! It seems to us . . .

LITTLE RED RIDING HOOD: No, no, fly away!

THE BIRDS: Look in the windows. She's afraid! Let's wait! Let's see! Let's see! (BIRDS *look in window.*)

LITTLE RED RIDING HOOD: Grandmother, why are you so white?

THE WOLF: Because I have an upset stomach.

LITTLE RED RIDING HOOD: Grandmother, why is your voice so strange?

THE WOLF: Because I have a sore throat.

LITTLE RED RIDING HOOD: Grandmother, why do you have such big eyes today?

THE WOLF: The better to see you with.

LITTLE RED RIDING HOOD: Grandmother! Why do you have such big hands?

THE WOLF: The tighter to hug you with. Come here.

LITTLE RED RIDING HOOD: Grandmother! Why do you have such big teeth?

THE WOLF (*He growls*): In order to eat you! (*He swallows the little girl. Throwing off the blankets, he continues to lie in the bed.* THE BIRDS *cry out in desperation and surround the bed.*) Ah, ha, ha! At last! I did it! I swallowed her! I won!

LITTLE RED RIDING HOOD: And who else is there in The Wolf's belly?

GRANDMOTHER: Who else but Grandmother!

LITTLE RED RIDING HOOD: He ate you, too? Don't be afraid, Grandmother. We'll escape.

GRANDMOTHER (*Recognizing her*): Little Red Riding Hood!

LITTLE RED RIDING HOOD: Grandmother, I brought flowers and food. (*She begins to cry.*)

THE WOLF: Quiet, both of you! Don't disturb my sleep!

GRANDMOTHER (*To* LITTLE RED RIDING HOOD): Thank you, dear. Why are you crying?

LITTLE RED RIDING HOOD: I'm not crying because I'm afraid, Grandmother. I'm crying because he tricked me.

GRANDMOTHER: He's gained the upper hand over you for the moment, but you'll have your turn yet. Don't cry. Think of how we can save ourselves.

LITTLE RED RIDING HOOD: I know how. Birds, listen! Quickly!

THE BIRDS: Are you alive? Little girl? Are you alive?

LITTLE RED RIDING HOOD: Yes, Birds. Fly as fast as you can toward the east until you see Comrade Forester. Tell him everything. Fly away! Quickly!

THE BIRDS: Here we go. (*They fly out.*)

LITTLE RED RIDING HOOD: We'll soon be saved.

SCENE 6

A crossing of two roads in the forest. On a pine tree a sign is posted which reads "Observe all forest rules." One tree has a telephone concealed inside it. A FORESTER *is standing on duty; he addresses the audience.*

THE FORESTER: I stand guard, I watch over all the forest. I see all, I hear all, I look in all directions without hesitation or alarm. If you lose your way, I'll show you where to go. I am Comrade Forester. (*With* THE BEES *flying after him,* THE BEAR *runs in.* THE FORESTER *lets* THE BEAR *pass, but stops* THE BEES *with a hand signal.* THE BEAR *breathes a sigh of relief, laughs, and starts to run on, but* THE FORESTER *whistles.*) Halt! You've been after honey.

THE BEAR: The fact of the matter is . . . The Fox told me there were no Bees, but there were thousands of them.

THE FORESTER: To the police station.

THE BEAR: The fact of the matter is . . .

(*At* THE FORESTER'S *whistle,* A DOG *bounds from the bushes. He takes* THE BEAR *by the ear and leads him out. Now we hear the clanking of a metal can, which becomes closer and closer. Suddenly, a large milk can appears on the path.* THE FORESTER *raises his hand and orders the can to stop. It doesn't. But when he whistles, it stops immediately.*)

THE FORESTER: Who is in the milk can?

THE VOICE OF THE GRASS SNAKE: The Grass Snake.

THE FORESTER: And how did you get into it?

THE GRASS SNAKE: I crawled into the can to drink some milk, and The Fox slammed the lid shut on me. . . .

THE FORESTER: You crawled into the can? To the station!

THE GRASS SNAKE: The Fox . . . sssss.

THE FORESTER: He'll have his turn. (*He whistles and* THE DOG *appears.* THE FORESTER *gives him the order.*) To the station.

(THE DOG *starts rolling the can with his paws. He exits.* THE FOX *runs in.* THE FORESTER *stops him.*)

THE FOX: At your service, Comrade Policeman.

THE FORESTER: We'll see about that. It appears to me that you are chasing forest animals.

THE FOX: What are you saying? Hee, hee, hee! I'm hurrying because I have something important to tell you. The Wolf . . .

(THE BIRDS *fly in and go to* THE FORESTER.)

THE BIRDS: Don't believe him, oh, don't believe him. Listen to us.

THE FORESTER: What's the matter, Birds?

THE BIRDS: The Wolf has swallowed Little Red Riding Hood and her grandmother. The Fox was his accomplice. But they are both alive. She spoke to us from inside The Wolf's stomach.

THE FOX: What? She's alive? (*He takes a step backward.*)

THE FORESTER (*Grabbing him by the neck, he whistles. He gives the following order to* THE DOG, *who runs in at his whistle.*) To the station! (*He goes up to a tree and takes a telephone from the hollow of the tree. He speaks into the telephone.*) Send my relief. I have to leave on urgent business. (LITTLE RED RIDING HOOD'S MOTHER *appears on the path and listens.*) (*Into phone.*) Yes, it concerns Little Red Riding Hood. How do you know? The Grass Snake and The Bear told you? Aha! My relief has already left? Excellent. (*He hangs up.*)

THE MOTHER: Comrade Forester, what's wrong with my daughter? I've looked everywhere for her. Don't hide anything from me. Look, I'm not trembling. I won't cry. Please tell me.

THE FORESTER: Little. Red Riding Hood is in grave danger, but I am sure we can save her. (*To* THE BIRDS.) Show us the way. Forward! (*They all hurry out.*)

SCENE 7

GRANDMOTHER'S *house. As before,* THE WOLF *is sleeping in the bed. The door opens and* THE FORESTER *and* THE MOTHER *rush into the room.* THE FORESTER *goes to the dresser and looks for something in it.* THE MOTHER *takes a pair of scissors from her apron pocket and offers them to* THE FORESTER. *At this moment,* THE WOLF *awakens.* THE FORESTER *seizes his revolver from his holster and aims it at* THE WOLF. *With a howl* THE WOLF *lies down again.* THE MOTHER *ties* THE WOLF'S *paws with rope and cuts open his stomach. Alive and unharmed,* LITTLE RED RIDING HOOD *and her* GRANDMOTHER *emerge from the stomach of the beast. They embrace* THE MOTHER. *The music, which was getting louder and louder, breaks off.*)

LITTLE RED RIDING HOOD: Mama, are you angry with me because The Wolf ate me?

THE MOTHER: No, daughter, I'm not angry. But, see that it's the last time.

GRANDMOTHER (*Sternly, shaking her finger at* LITTLE RED RIDING HOOD'S MOTHER): Daughter, what should you say?

THE MOTHER: Oh, excuse me, Mama. (*Bowing to* THE FORESTER.) Thank you.

THE FORESTER: What are you talking about? It's I who should thank you, citizen. You helped me.

GRANDMOTHER (*To* THE FORESTER): Would you like to have some coffee or tea?

THE MOTHER: Would you like some cherry pie?

THE FORESTER: Nothing, thank you, citizen. But do you have a needle and some thick thread?

GRANDMOTHER: Have you lost a button? I'll sew it on.

THE FORESTER: No. We have to sew up The Wolf's stomach and bring him to the station.

GRANDMOTHER: Why sew it up? I'll darn it so that you won't even notice it. Where are my glasses? Where did my glasses go? Oh, that wretched Wolf is lying on my glasses. Here's my needle. Here's some gray thread. I'll darn his stomach in the twinkling of an eye. I'm fast.

(LITTLE RED RIDING HOOD, *her* MOTHER, *and* THE FORESTER *go to the window.*)

LITTLE RED RIDING HOOD: Well, goodbye, Birds.

THE BIRDS: Goodbye, little girl! Goodbye, Little Red Riding Hood.

THE FORESTER: Thank you for reporting to me so fast.

THE BIRDS: Think nothing of it, think nothing of it. We're so glad, we're so glad. (*They fly away.*)

GRANDMOTHER: Well, it's all done. I darned it so that he himself won't be able to find where he was cut open. Isn't that wonderful?

LITTLE RED RIDING HOOD (*Going to* GRANDMOTHER): Yes.

THE MOTHER: Everything is fine now.

GRANDMOTHER: The dreadful beast is tightly bound.

LITTLE RED RIDING HOOD: How well everything ended!

THE MOTHER: All our troubles are behind us!

LITTLE RED RIDING HOOD: Hello, Mama!

THE MOTHER: Hello, my daughter.

THE FORESTER: Excuse me for interrupting, but I must be going. Duty! Remember once and for all, little girl: a wolf of a different color is still a wolf! A wolf! A wolf! (THE FORESTER *turns toward the bed.* THE WOLF *is gone from the bed.*) The Wolf has escaped!

GRANDMOTHER: Help!!

THE FORESTER: We bound his paws, but we forgot about his jaws! He chewed through the rope with his teeth and went out the back door. (*He rushes in that direction.*)

LITTLE RED RIDING HOOD: We're with you.

THE FORESTER: He'll be caught anyway. (*They run out.*)

SCENE 8

The swamp where BELOUKH *sits in the trap. He is surrounded by several* RABBITS.

THE RABBIT: Be quiet now. So we can hear The Wolf coming!

THE RABBITS: We hear the oak tree rustling. We hear the swamp water lapping. But not The Wolf.

THE RABBIT: He moves very quietly, brothers. He might even be in the bushes now.

THE RABBITS (*Frightened*): Oh, Oh!

THE RABBIT: Nonsense! You swore not to be cowards. Hold your ears up, Rabbits. When The Wolf comes, attack him and drag him to the people for trial and punishment!

THE WOLF (*Coming out of the bushes, toward* THE RABBITS): Out of the way!

THE RABBIT: Don't move! Never! Hit him, brothers!

(*A hail of pine cones fly at* THE WOLF.)

THE WOLF: H-o-w-l! What's this! Remember who I am! I'll swallow all of you. Get out of the way! I'll count to three: one, two . . .

THE BEAR (*Coming out of the bushes*): Three! What's the matter, cousin, weren't you expecting me?

THE WOLF: I'm not your cousin! I have no cousins! I'm all for myself!

THE BEAR: Leave these Rabbits alone or I'll become angry!

THE WOLF: I'm not afraid of anyone today! I'll devour a lion. Howl. What's a clumsy bear?

THE BEAR: What? Ho, ho, ho! Well, I'll show you. . . . Out of the way, Rabbits. Give me room.

(THE RABBITS *hide.* THE WOLF *and* THE BEAR *start fighting.*)

THE GRASS SNAKE (*Rising from the bushes, he hisses*): Here . . . ssss. Here . . . sssss.

(THE FORESTER, GRANDMOTHER, THE MOTHER, *and* LITTLE RED RIDING HOOD *appear.*)

THE FORESTER (*He whistles*): Stop fighting!

THE WOLF (*Rushing at* THE FORESTER): Stay out of this! I'll kill you!

THE FORESTER (*Aiming his revolver at* THE WOLF): Paws up! (THE WOLF *falls and raises his paws.* THE MOTHER *ties his paws with a rope. To* THE BEAR *and* THE GRASS SNAKE.) And how did you get here?

THE BEAR: They . . . let us go.

THE FORESTER: Did they fine you?

THE BEAR: No.

(*While this conversation is going on,* LITTLE RED RIDING HOOD *frees* BELOUKH. *She leads him forward.*)

LITTLE RED RIDING HOOD: Well, Rabbit, it was almost the end of The Wolf this time.

THE WOLF: Howl! The little girl has outsmarted me!

THE BEAR: It doesn't matter.

THE MOTHER: Little Red Riding Hood, do you know what time it is?

LITTLE RED RIDING HOOD: Yes, Mama. It's time to go home! Goodbye, Rabbit!

BELOUKH: I'll accompany you!

LITTLE RED RIDING HOOD: Goodbye, Bear!

THE BEAR: I'll also go with you, sister.

LITTLE RED RIDING HOOD: Goodbye, Grass Snake!

THE GRASS SNAKE: I'll crawl along with you.

LITTLE RED RIDING HOOD: Goodbye, Comrade Forester!

THE FORESTER: Farewell, Little Red Riding Hood!

(*They march across the stage singing:*)
>We have finished with the war.
>One, two! one, two!
>The Wolf is caught, The Fox is caught!
>One, two! One, two!
>Victory is attained.
>One, two! one, two!
>Because we are friends,
>One, two! One, two!
>We rushed boldly into battle.
>One, two! One, two!
>And now we're going home!

One, two! One, two!
But keep your eyes open, friends.
One, two! One, two!
Endless is the evil of the Wolf.
One, two! One, two!
Never forget your enemy!
One, two! One, two!
Farewell, my friends.
One, two! One, two!

Amahl and
the Night Visitors

BY

GIAN-CARLO MENOTTI

AS A MEMBER of a musical family, Gian-carlo Menotti presented marionette shows with his nine brothers and sisters in their home in Cadegliano, Italy, where he was born in 1911. His mother encouraged his musical interests by taking him to La Scala in Milan to hear opera and by arranging for him to study the piano from the time he was six. His talent, so unmistakable that he was considered a prodigy, took him to Milan's Conservatory and there he studied with outstanding teachers who quickly developed his gifts. While still a teenaged student, he was called upon to give concerts in Milan, but his mother was not satisfied with his progress and brought her son to the United States, enrolling him in the Curtis Institute of Music in Philadelphia. Only a few years later he had composed *Amelia Goes to the Ball,* a satirical comic opera based on the society he had observed in Italy. When *Amelia* entered the repertoire of the Metropolitan Opera in 1938, Menotti was still in his twenties.

Whether serious or comic, his operas possess such dramatic strength that they frequently have proved successful in the legitimate theatre. Such was the case when *The Medium* and *The Telephone* opened at the Barrymore Theatre in 1947 and played to enthusiastic theatre-goers, many of whom had never before seen an opera. *The Consul* (1950), also produced originally on Broadway, garnered additional popular and critical acclaim that included a Pulitzer prize and the New York Drama Critics Circle Award. For this work, a tragedy about the futility of obtaining a visa in a country that has replaced freedom with bureaucratic red tape and total dehumanization, Menotti served as dramatist, composer and stage director. In 1954 the less successful but no less dramatic *The Saint of Bleecker Street* further developed his theories of opera as music drama, which he extended in a number of later works, notably *Maria Golovin* (1958) and *The Last Savage* (1964). Throughout his career Menotti has maintained a loyal interest in composing for young people as well as

[271]

about them. His *Death of the Bishop of Brindisi* (1963) is based on the Children's Crusade in 1212, when thousands of children made a vain attempt to reach the Holy Land. Suffering pain and hardship, they traveled from Germany across the Alps into Italy, where the Bishop, realizing the futility of their mission, attempted to send them home. But their determination could not be altered and they sailed off, with the Bishop's blessing, to become victims of sea storms and pirates who sold them into slavery. Menotti makes it clear to the tragic end that the children never wavered in their purpose, innocence or faith.

In a program note to *Help! Help! the Globolinks* (1969), Menotti stated he had composed the opera for children because they are a truly candid audience who come to the theatre with open minds, unprejudiced by musical trends and reputations. His joy in writing for these ideal listeners pervades this science-fiction story of an invasion of earth by strange creatures from outer space. A human being when touched by a Globolink loses his speech and within 24 hours turns into one of the wacky, tubular and tentacled beings who converse in ugly electric sounds. Music, the only effective weapon against these invaders, causes them to flee or dissolve altogether. Menotti in his satire of electronic music uses a child to represent the kind of heartfelt melodies he believes can save the human race. The opera, praised at its premiere in Santa Fe, New Mexico, also delighted New York City during the Christmas season of 1969, when it was paired with another of Menotti's tributes to childhood, *Amahl and the Night Visitors*.

Certainly, of all the titles in this volume, *Amahl* is the best known and the work most often seen in performance. Its many television showings, professional productions and nationwide school, church and community presentations have been viewed by millions since the first NBC performance on Christmas Eve of 1951. That an opera should reach so vast an audience and entrench itself so deeply in our culture is remarkable indeed; among American operas, only Gershwin's *Porgy and Bess* has achieved a similar distinction. The present publication of the libretto demonstrates one reason why this popularity persists by reminding us that *Amahl* is a good story and economically told. An analysis of the opera as drama discloses Menotti's skill in making it Biblical without being specifically religious, universal without being overly generalized and sweet without being confection. Menotti does little more than set forth the events of a few hours that change Amahl's life forever. But more than the events—and they are extraordinary, to be sure—it is the night itself the audience is made to experience, to see and to feel just as clearly as Amahl does in his lyric description: "All its lanterns are lit, all its torches are burning, and its dark floor is shining like crystal." These lines require no help from scenery nor even from music. Without Menotti's score, music is everywhere in the libretto: in the mystery and wonder of the sky, in the poignancy of the central character (who as a pipe-playing shepherd is himself a musician), in the powerful love of the mother, in the majesty of the kings, and in the inspiring confidence of the conclusion. But, most of all, there is music in the drama's simplicity, which Menotti derived from memories of his family's Christmas celebrations. He has stated that *Amahl* is an opera for children because it attempts to capture his own childhood, and particularly that night on which the Three Kings traditionally deliver gifts to Italian children. For him and his brother this was a time of great suspense and anticipation, as well as a test of endurance as they tried to stay awake to see the royal visitors. The boys always fell asleep just before they arrived (although one year Menotti thought he heard camel hooves crushing the snow outside). In *Amahl and the Night Visitors* he achieves his wish. When he actually sees Kaspar, Melchior and Balthazar, he shares with us the drama and music of that night and the gifts of dawn that follow.

Amahl and
the Night Visitors

CHARACTERS

AMAHL, *a crippled boy of about 12*
HIS MOTHER
KASPAR, *slightly deaf* ⎫
MELCHIOR   ⎬ *The Three Kings*
BALTHAZAR ⎭
THE PAGE
CHORUS OF SHEPHERDS AND VILLAGERS
DANCERS

The curtain rises. It is night. The crystal-clear winter sky is dotted with stars, the Eastern Star flaming amongst them. Outside the cottage, not far from its door, AMAHL, *wrapped in an oversized cloak, sits on a stone, playing his shepherd's pipe. His crudely-made crutch lies on the ground beside him. Within,* THE MOTHER *works at household chores. The room is lighted only by the dying fire and the low flame of a tiny oil lamp.*

THE MOTHER (*She pauses in her work to listen to the piping, then calls*): Amahl! Amahl!

AMAHL: Oh!

THE MOTHER: Time to go to bed!

AMAHL: Coming! (AMAHL *does not stir. After a moment he begins to play again.*)

THE MOTHER: Amahl!

AMAHL: Coming! (*With a shrug of his shoulders,* AMAHL *continues to play. Impatiently,* THE MOTHER *goes to the window, opens it sharply, and leans out.*)

THE MOTHER: How long must I shout to make you obey?

AMAHL: I'm sorry, Mother.

THE MOTHER:
    Hurry in! It's time to go to bed.

AMAHL:
    But Mother, let me stay a little longer!

THE MOTHER:
     The wind is cold.

AMAHL:
    But my cloak is warm,
    let me stay a little longer!

THE MOTHER:
     The night is dark.

AMAHL:
    But the sky is light,
    let me stay a little longer!

THE MOTHER:

The time is late.

AMAHL:

But the moon hasn't risen yet,
let me stay a little . . .

THE MOTHER (*Clapping her hands*):

There won't be any moon tonight.
But there will be a weeping child very soon,
if he doesn't hurry up and obey his mother.

(THE MOTHER *closes the window. with a sharp little bang.*)

AMAHL:

Oh, very well.

(*Reluctantly,* AMAHL *rises, takes up his crutch, and hobbles into the house. On the pegs to one side of the door he hangs his heavy cloak and shepherd's cap. His pipe he places carefully in the corner.* THE MOTHER *kneels at the fireplace, trying to coax a flame from the few remaining twigs.* AMAHL *returns to the open door and leans against it, looking up to the sky.*)

THE MOTHER:

What was keeping you outside?

AMAHL:

Oh, Mother, you should go out and see!
There's never been such a sky!
Damp clouds have shined it
and soft winds have swept it
as if to make it ready for a King's ball.
All its lanterns are lit,
all its torches are burning,
and its dark floor
is shining like crystal.
Hanging over our roof
there is a star as large as a window,
and the star has a tail,
and it moves across the sky
like a chariot on fire.

THE MOTHER (*Wearily*):

> Oh! Amahl, when will you stop telling lies?
> All day long you wander about in a dream.
> Here we are with nothing to eat,
> not a stick of wood on the fire,
> not a drop of oil in the jug,
> and all you do is to worry your mother
> with fairy tales.
> Oh! Amahl, have you forgotten your promise
> never, never to lie to your mother again?

AMAHL:

> Mother darling, I'm not lying.
> Please, do believe me. (*He tugs at her skirt.*)
> Come outside and let me show you.
> See for yourself . . . See for yourself . . .

THE MOTHER (*She brushes his hand aside*):

> Stop bothering me! Why should I believe you?
> You come with a new one every day!
> First it was a leopard with a woman's head.
> Then it was a tree branch that shrieked and bled.
> Then it was a fish as big as a boat,
> with whiskers like a cat and wings like a bat
> and horns like a goat.
> And now it is a star as large as a window . . .
> or was it a carriage . . .
> And if that weren't enough,
> the star has a tail and the tail is of fire!

AMAHL:

> But there is a star and it has a tail this long.

(AMAHL *measures the air as wide as his arms can reach. At her frown, he reduces the size by half.*)

> Well, maybe only . . . this long. But it's there!

THE MOTHER:

> Amahl!

AMAHL:

> Cross my heart and hope to die.

THE MOTHER (*Clasping* AMAHL *in her arms*):

> Poor Amahl!

Hunger has gone to your head.
Dear God, what is a poor widow to do,
when her cupboards and pockets are empty
and everything sold?

(*She moves disconsolately to the fireplace.*)

Unless we go begging
how shall we live through tomorrow?
My little son, a beggar!

(*She sinks, weeping, onto a little stool.* AMAHL *goes to her and embraces her tenderly, stroking her hair.*)

AMAHL:

Don't cry, Mother dear,
don't worry for me.
If we must go begging,
a good beggar I'll be.
I know sweet tunes to set people dancing.
We'll walk and walk from village to town,
you dressed as a gypsy and I as a clown.
At noon we shall eat roast goose and sweet almonds,
at night we shall sleep with the sheep and the stars.
I'll play my pipes, you'll sing and you'll shout.
The windows will open and people lean out.
The King will ride by and hear your loud voice
and throw us some gold to stop all the noise.
At noon we shall eat roast goose and sweet almonds,
at night we shall sleep with the sheep and the stars.

THE MOTHER:

My dreamer, good night!
You're wasting the light.
Kiss me good night.

AMAHL:

Good night.

(THE MOTHER *rises and bends to receive the good-night kiss.* AMAHL *goes to his pallet of straw at one side of the fireplace.* THE

MOTHER *secures the door, takes* AMAHL'S *cloak and spreads it over him, touches his head tenderly, then, having snuffed out the tiny oil lamp, she lies down on the bench. The lights die from the room except for a faint glow in the fireplace and the radiance of the sky through the window.*

(In the distance among the hills, we see a tiny winking light from a lantern, then the small figures of THE THREE KINGS *and* THE PAGE, *wending their way along the mountain road.* AMAHL *raises himself on one elbow and listens with astonishment to the distant singing. The figures disappear at a turn in the road.* AMAHL *throws back his cloak and, leaning on his crutch, hobbles over to the window. At the left, on the road, appear* THE THREE KINGS: *first* MELCHIOR, *bearing the coffer of gold, then* BALTHAZAR, *bearing the chalice of myrrh, and finally* KASPAR, *bearing the urn of incense. All are preceded by* THE PAGE, *who walks heavily, bent beneath the load of many bundles, among them a rich Oriental rug, a caged parrot, and an elaborate jeweled box. In one hand* THE PAGE *carries a heavy lantern to light the way.)*

KASPAR, MELCHIOR, BALTHAZAR:

> From far away we come and farther we must go.
> How far, how far, my crystal star?
> The shepherd dreams inside the fold.
> Cold are the sands by the silent sea.
> Frozen the incense in our frozen hands,
> heavy the gold.
> How far, how far, my crystal star?
> By silence-sunken lakes the antelope leaps.
> In paper-painted oasis the drunken gypsy weeps.
> The hungry lion wanders, the cobra sleeps.
> How far, how far, my crystal star?

(As the travelers approach the door of the cottage, THE PAGE *steps aside to let* KING MELCHIOR *knock upon the door.)*

THE MOTHER (*Without stirring from her bed*):

> Amahl, go and see who's knocking at the door.

AMAHL:

> Yes, Mother.

(AMAHL *goes to the door and opens it a crack. He quickly closes
the door and rushes to his* MOTHER.)

Mother, Mother, Mother, come with me.
I want to be sure that you see what I see.

THE MOTHER (*Raising herself on her elbow*):
What is the matter with you now?
What is all this fuss about?
Who is it then?

AMAHL (*Hesitatingly*):
Mother . . . outside the door there is . . .
there is a King with a crown.

THE MOTHER:
What shall I do with this boy,
what shall I do?
If you don't learn to tell the truth,
I'll have to spank you!

(*Knocks. After a pause she sinks back on the bed.*)

Go back and see who it is
and ask them what they want.

(AMAHL *hurries to the door, again opens it just a crack, and
stares. He closes it once more and returns to his* MOTHER.)

AMAHL:
Mother, Mother . . . Mother, come with me.
I want to be sure that you see what I see.

THE MOTHER:
What is the matter with you now,
what is all this fuss about?

AMAHL:
Mother . . . I didn't tell the truth before.

THE MOTHER:
That's a good boy.

AMAHL:
There is not a King outside.

THE MOTHER:
I should say not!

AMAHL:

There are two Kings!

THE MOTHER:

What shall I do with this boy,
what shall I do?
Hurry back and see who it is,
and don't you dare make up tales!

(AMAHL *repeats again the action to the door and back.*)

AMAHL:

Mother . . . Mother . . . Mother, come with me.
If I tell you the truth,
I know you won't believe me.

THE MOTHER:

Try it for a change!

AMAHL:

But you won't believe me.

THE MOTHER:

I'll believe you if you tell the truth.

AMAHL:

Sure enough, there are not two Kings outside.

THE MOTHER:

That is surprising.

AMAHL:

The Kings are three,
and one of them is black.

THE MOTHER:

Oh! What shall I do with this boy!
If you were stronger I'd like to whip you.

AMAHL:

I knew it!

THE MOTHER:

I'm going to the door myself,
and then, young man,
you'll have to reckon with me!

(THE MOTHER *rises wearily and moves determinedly to the door.*
AMAHL *follows, holding onto her skirt. As the door swings open,*

she beholds THE THREE KINGS. *In utter amazement, she bows to them.*)

KASPAR, MELCHIOR, BALTHAZAR:

Good evening!

AMAHL (*Whispering*):

What did I tell you?

THE MOTHER (*To* AMAHL):

Sh! (*To* THE KINGS.) Noble sires!

BALTHAZAR:

May we rest a while in your house
and warm ourselves by your fireplace?

THE MOTHER:

I am a poor widow.
A cold fireplace and a bed of straw
are all I have to offer you.
To these you are welcome.

KASPAR (*Cupping his ear*):

What did she say?

BALTHAZAR:

That we are welcome.

KASPAR (*Excitedly*):

Oh, thank you, thank you,
thank you!

(MELCHIOR *and* BALTHAZAR *tap* KASPAR's *shoulder to restrain him.*)

KASPAR, MELCHIOR, BALTHAZAR:

Oh, thank you!

THE MOTHER:

Come in, come in!

(*Still bowing,* THE MOTHER *makes way for* THE KING *to enter, pulling* AMAHL *with her.* THE PAGE *enters first, places his lantern on the stool beside the fireplace, and drops his bundles. Almost immediately,* KING KASPAR *proceeds at a stately march to take his place on the bench, stage right.* THE PAGE *hurries to hold* KING KASPAR's *train. Once* KASPAR *has placed himself,* BALTHAZAR *enters and proceeds to a place beside him.* MELCHIOR *is the last to take his place.* THE PAGE *runs back and forth to carry the trains of each. When* THE THREE KINGS *are together, they sit as one.* THE PAGE *spreads the rug before them and sets upon it the gifts* THE KINGS *bear for the Child.* AMAHL *watches the procession with growing wonder and excitement.*)

MELCHIOR:

It is nice here.

THE MOTHER:

I shall go and gather wood for the fire.
I've nothing in the house.

(THE MOTHER *takes her shawl from the peg and goes to the door.*)

MELCHIOR:

We can only stay a little while.
We must not lose sight of our star.

THE MOTHER:

Your star?

AMAHL (*Whispering to his* MOTHER):

What did I tell you?

THE MOTHER:

Sh!

MELCHIOR:

We still have a long way to go.

THE MOTHER:

I shall be right back . . . and Amahl
don't be a nuisance (*She goes quickly.*)

AMAHL:

No, Mother.

(*The moment his* MOTHER *is gone,* AMAHL *goes to* BALTHAZAR. KASPAR *goes to the corner of the fireplace where* THE PAGE *has placed the parrot and the jeweled box. During the following scene he feeds the parrot bits of food from his pocket.*)

Are you a real King?

BALTHAZAR:

Yes.

AMAHL:

Have you regal blood?

BALTHAZAR:

Yes.

AMAHL:

Can I see it?

BALTHAZAR:

It is just like yours.

AMAHL:

What's the use of having it, then?

BALTHAZAR:

No use.

AMAHL:

Where is your home?

BALTHAZAR:

I live in a black marble palace
full of black panthers and white doves.
And you, little boy,
what do you do?

AMAHL (*Sadly*):

I was a shepherd, I had a flock of sheep.
But my mother sold them.
Now there are no sheep left.
I had a black goat who gave me warm sweet milk.
But she died of old age.
Now there is no goat left.
But Mother says that now
we shall both go begging from door to door.
Won't it be fun?

BALTHAZAR:

It has its points.

(AMAHL *crosses to* KASPAR, *who continues to feed the parrot.*)

AMAHL:

Are you a real King, too?

KASPAR:

> Eh?

(AMAHL *looks wonderingly at* BALTHAZAR, *who indicates that* KASPAR *is deaf.* AMAHL *repeats the question, shouting.*)

AMAHL:

> ARE YOU A REAL KING, TOO?

KASPAR:

> Oh, truly, truly, yes.
> I am a real King . . . am I not?

(KASPAR *looks questioningly at* BALTHAZAR.)

BALTHAZAR:

> Yes, Kaspar.

AMAHL:

> What is that?

KASPAR:

> Eh?

AMAHL:

> WHAT IS THAT?

KASPAR:

> A parrot.

AMAHL:

> Does it talk?

KASPAR:

> Eh?

AMAHL:

> DOES IT TALK?

KASPAR (*Indicating his deaf ears*):

> How do I know?

AMAHL:

> Does it bite?

KASPAR:

> Eh?

AMAHL:

> DOES IT BITE?

(KASPAR *displays a heavily bandaged finger.*)

KASPAR:

Yes.

AMAHL (*Pointing at the jeweled box*):

And what is this?

(*With great excitement,* KASPAR *opens one drawer at a time, concealing its contents from* AMAHL *until he lifts the jewels, the beads, and finally the licorice before the boy's amazed eyes.*)

KASPAR:

This is my box, this is my box.
I never travel without my box.
In the first drawer I keep my magic stones.
One carnelian against all evil and envy.
One moonstone to make you sleep.
One red coral to heal your wounds.
One lapis lazuli against quartern fever.
One small jasper to help you find water.
One small topaz to soothe your eyes.
One red ruby to protect you from lightning.
This is my box, this is my box.
I never travel without my box.
In the second drawer I keep all my beads.
Oh, how I love to play with beads,
all kinds of beads.
This is my box, this is my box.
I never travel without my box.
In the third drawer . . .
Oh, little boy! Oh, little boy! . . .
In the third drawer I keep . . .
licorice . . . black, sweet licorice.
Have some.

(AMAHL *seizes the candy and gobbles it down as his* MOTHER *enters from the outside, bearing a few sticks.*)

THE MOTHER:

Amahl, I told you not to be a nuisance!

AMAHL:

But it isn't my fault!

(Going to his mother, AMAHL *whispers discreetly.)*

They kept asking me questions.

THE MOTHER:

I want you to go and call the other shepherds.
Tell them about our visitors,
and ask them to bring
whatever they have in the house,
as we have nothing to offer them.
Hurry on!

AMAHL:

Yes, Mother.

*(*AMAHL *grabs up his cloak, claps his hat on his head, and hurries out as fast as his crutch will carry him.* THE MOTHER *crosses to the fireplace to set down the wood she has gathered. Suddenly she sees the coffer of gold, and the rich chalices of incense and myrrh which sit before* THE KINGS. *Irresistibly drawn, she moves toward them.)*

THE MOTHER:

Oh, these beautiful things . . .
and all that gold!

MELCHIOR:

These are the gifts to the Child.

THE MOTHER *(With great excitement)*:

The child?
Which child?

MELCHIOR:

We don't know.
But the Star will guide us to Him.

THE MOTHER:

But perhaps I know him.
What does he look like?

BALTHAZAR:

Have you seen a Child
the color of wheat, the color of dawn?
His eyes are mild,
His hands are those of a King,

as King He was born.
Incense, myrrh, and gold
we bring to His side,
and the Eastern Star is our guide.

THE MOTHER (*As though to herself*):
Yes, I know a child
the color of wheat, the color of dawn.
His eyes are mild,
his hands are those of a King,
as King he was born.
But no one will bring him incense or gold,
though sick and poor and hungry and cold.
He's my child, my son,
my darling, my own.

MELCHIOR, BALTHAZAR:
Have you seen a Child
the color of earth, the color of thorn?
His eyes are sad,
His hands are those of the poor,
as poor He was born.
Incense, myrrh, and gold
we bring to His side,
and the Eastern Star is our guide.

THE MOTHER:
Yes, I know a child
the color of earth, the color of thorn.
His eyes are sad,
his hands are those of the poor,
as poor he was born.
But no one will bring him incense or gold,
though sick and poor and hungry and cold.
He's my child, my son,
my darling, my own.

MELCHIOR:
The Child we seek holds the seas
and the winds on His palm.

KASPAR:
The Child we seek has the moon
and the stars at His feet.

BALTHAZAR:

> Before Him the eagle is gentle,
> the lion is meek.

(*Absorbed in her own thoughts,* THE MOTHER *moves slowly downstage.*)

THE MOTHER:

> The child I know
> on his palm holds my heart.
> The child I know
> at his feet has my life.
> He's my child, my son,
> my darling, my own,
> and his name is Amahl.

KASPAR, MELCHIOR, BALTHAZAR:

> Choirs of angels hover over His roof
> and sing Him to sleep.
> He's warmed by breath,
> He's fed by Mother
> who is both Virgin and Queen.
> Incense, myrrh, and gold
> we bring to His side,
> and the Eastern Star is our guide.

(*The call of* THE SHEPHERDS *falls sharp and clear on the air, breaking the hushed silence of the room.*)

SHEPHERDS:

> Shepherds! Shepherdesses!
> Who's calling, who's calling?
> Oh! Oh!

(THE MOTHER *looks instinctively to see if her room is ready to receive her neighbors, then she goes to the door and opens it wide.*)

THE MOTHER:

> The shepherds are coming!

MELCHIOR (*He nudges the dozing* KASPAR):
Wake up, Kaspar!

(*First singly, then in twos and threes,* THE SHEPHERDS *begin to appear. They come from all directions. On the hills in the distance lantern lights pierce the darkness. Slowly they converge and move down the road toward the hut, led by a radiant* AMAHL.)

SHEPHERDS:
Emily, Emily,
Michael, Bartholomew,
how are your children and how are your sheep?
Dorothy, Dorothy,
Peter, Evangeline,
give me your hand, come along with me,
All the children have mumps.
All the flocks are asleep.
We are going with Amahl, bringing gifts to the Kings.
Benjamin, Benjamin,
Lucas, Elizabeth,
how are your children and how are your sheep?
Carolyn, Carolyn,
Matthew, Veronica,
give me your hand, come along with me.

(*Ragged and joyous,* THE SHEPHERDS *approach the hut, bearing their baskets of fruit and vegetables.*)

Brrr! How cold is the night!
Brrr! How icy the wind!
Hold me very, very, very tight.
Oh, how warm is your cloak!
Katherine, Katherine,
Christopher, Babila,
how are your children and how are your sheep?
Josephine, Josephine,
Angela, Jeremy,
come along with me.

Oh! look!
Oh! look!

(THE SHEPHERDS *crowd together in the frame of the door of the hut, struck dumb by the sight of* THE KINGS, *not daring to enter. AMAHL, however, slips through the crowd to take his place beside his* MOTHER.)

THE MOTHER:

Come in, come in!
What are you afraid of?

(*Shy and embarrassed, everyone tries to push his neighbor in ahead of him, until all of them are crowded into one corner of the room.*)

Don't be bashful, silly girl!
Don't be bashful, silly boy!
They won't eat you.
Show what you brought them.

(*At last one shepherd boldly marches forward and lays his gifts before* THE KINGS, *then, bowing shyly, he retreats to his place.*)

SHEPHERDS:

Go on, go on, go on!
No! You go on!
Olives and quinces, apples and raisins,
nutmeg and myrtle, medlars and chestnuts,
this is all we shepherds can offer you.

KASPAR, MELCHIOR, BALTHAZAR:

Thank you, thank you,
thank you kindly.
Thank you, thank you,
thank you kindly, too.

(*A second shepherd crosses to* THE KINGS, *presents his gifts, and returns, bowing, to his place.*)

SHEPHERDS:

Citrons and lemons, musk and pomegranates,

goat-cheese and walnuts, figs and cucumbers,
this is all we shepherds can offer you.

KASPAR, MELCHIOR, BALTHAZAR:

Thank you, thank you,
thank you kindly.
Thank you, thank you,
thank you kindly, too.

(*Taking courage from the others, a third shepherd presents his gifts and returns to his place.*)

SHEPHERDS:

Hazelnuts and camomile, mignonettes and laurel,
honeycombs and cinnamon, thyme, mint, and garlic,
this is all we shepherds can offer you.

KASPAR, MELCHIOR, BALTHAZAR:

Thank you, thank you,
thank you kindly.
Thank you, thank you,
thank you kindly, too.

SHEPHERDS:

Take them, eat them,
you are welcome. (*To* THE PAGE.)
Take them, eat them,
you are welcome, too.

THE MOTHER (*Beckoning to the young people*):

Now won't you dance for them?

(*One young girl tries to flee. The young men pull her back, and after much embarrassed nudging and pushing, she returns. Meanwhile,* AMAHL *fetches his shepherd's pipe and sits at the fireplace beside an old bearded shepherd who already holds his pipe. The two begin to play and the dance follows.*)

SHEPHERDS:

Don't be bashful, silly girl!
Don't be bashful, silly boy!
They won't eat you!

(*The dance of* THE SHEPHERDS, *which may include two or more dancers, should combine the qualities of primitive folk dancing and folk ritual. It is both an entertainment and a ceremony of welcome and hospitality. The dancers are at first shy and fearful at the realization that they are in the presence of three great* KINGS, *and their movements are at times faltering and hesitant. But later, the dance assumes the character of a tarantella, gaining in pace and sureness and ending in a joyous frenzy.* BALTHAZAR *rises to thank the dancers, then resumes his seat.*)

BALTHAZAR:

Thank you, good friends,
for your dances and your gifts.
But now we must bid you good night.
We have little time for sleep and a long journey ahead.

SHEPHERDS:

Good night, my good Kings, good night and farewell.
The pale stars foretell that dawn is in sight.
Good night, my good Kings, good night and farewell.
The night wind foretells the day will be bright.

(THE SHEPHERDS *pass before* THE KINGS, *bowing as they depart.* THE MOTHER *bids them good night at the door and for a moment watches them down the road. After all have gone their voices are still heard on the winter air.*)

ALL:

Good night.

(*Having closed the door,* AMAHL *and* THE MOTHER *bid* THE KINGS *good night. While* THE MOTHER *prepares for herself a pallet of sheepskins on the floor,* AMAHL *seizes his opportunity and speaks to* KING KASPAR.)

AMAHL:

Excuse me, sir, amongst your magic stones
is there . . . is there one that could cure a crippled boy?

KASPAR:

Eh?

(*Defeated by* KASPAR'S *deafness*, AMAHL *goes sadly to his pallet of straw*.)

AMAHL:

Never mind . . . good night.

SHEPHERDS (*From off-stage*):

Good night, good night.
The dawn is in sight.
Good night, farewell, good night.

(THE MOTHER *and* AMAHL *have lain down on their pallets*. THE KINGS, *still sitting on the rude bench, settle themselves to sleep, leaning against each other.* THE PAGE *curls himself up at their feet, his arms laid protectively over the rich gifts. His lantern has been placed on the floor by the fireplace, leaving only a dim glow in the room. The lights in the hut are lowered completely to denote the passage of time. On the last chords of the interlude the interior of the hut is slowly lighted by the first pale rays of the dawn from the hills*.)

THE MOTHER (*Still sitting on her pallet,* THE MOTHER *cannot take her eyes from the treasure guarded by* THE PAGE):

All that gold! All that gold!
I wonder if rich people know what to do with their gold!
Do they know how a child could be fed?
Do rich people know?
Do they know that a house can be kept warm all day with burning
   logs?
Do rich people know?
Do they know how to roast sweet corn on the fire?
Do they know?
Do they know how to fill a courtyard with doves?
Do they know?
Do they know how to milk a clover-fed goat?
Do they know how to spice hot wine on cold winter nights?
Do they know?
All that gold! All that gold!
Oh, what I could do for my child with that gold!
Why should it all go to a child they don't even know?
They are asleep. Do I dare?
If I take some they'll never miss it . . .

(Slowly she draws herself across the floor, dragging her body with her hands. Her words become a hushed whisper.)

For my child . . . for my child . . . for my child . . .

(As THE MOTHER touches the gold, THE PAGE is instantly aroused. He seizes her arm, crying to his masters. THE MOTHER pulls frantically to free herself, dragging THE PAGE into the center of the room. She still clutches the gold and jewels she has seized.)

THE PAGE:

Thief! Thief!

(THE KINGS awaken in confusion and rise.)

MELCHIOR, BALTHAZAR:

What is it? What is it?

THE PAGE:

I've seen her steal some of the gold.
She's a thief! Don't let her go!
She's stolen the gold!

KASPAR, MELCHIOR, BALTHAZAR:

Shame! Shame!

THE PAGE:

Give it back or I'll tear it out of you!

(AMAHL awakens, at first completely bewildered. When he sees his MOTHER in the hands of THE PAGE, he helps himself up with his crutch and awkwardly hurls himself upon THE PAGE, beating him hysterically and pulling his hair, in an effort to force the man to release THE MOTHER.)

KINGS, THE PAGE:

Give it back! Give it back!

AMAHL:

Don't you dare!
Don't you dare, ugly man, hurt my mother!
I'll smash in your face!
I'll knock out your teeth!

Don't you dare!
Don't you dare, ugly man, hurt my mother!

(*Rushing to* KING KASPAR *and tugging at his robe.*)

Oh, Mister King, don't let him hurt my mother!
My mother is good.
She cannot do anything wrong.
I'm the one who lies. I'm the one who steals.

(*Rushing back to attack* THE PAGE.)

Don't you dare!
Don't you dare, ugly man, hurt my mother!
I'll break all your bones!
I'll bash in your head!

(*At a sign from* KASPAR, THE PAGE *releases* THE MOTHER. *Still kneeling, she raises her arms toward her son. Choked by tears,* AMAHL *staggers toward her and, letting his crutch fall, collapses, sobbing, into his* MOTHER'S *arms.*)

MELCHIOR:
Oh, woman, you may keep the gold.
The Child we seek doesn't need our gold.
On love, on love alone
He will build His kingdom.
His pierced hand will hold no scepter.
His haloed head will wear no crown.
His might will not be built on your toil.
Swifter than lightning
He will soon walk among us.
He will bring us new life and receive our death,
and the keys to His city belong to the poor.

(*Turning to the other* KINGS.)

Let us leave, my friends.

(*Freeing herself from* AMAHL's *embrace,* THE MOTHER *throws herself on her knees before* THE KINGS, *spilling the gold she has taken from her hands onto the carpet. Meanwhile,* AMAHL *is on his feet, leaning on his crutch.*)

THE MOTHER:

> Oh, no, wait . . . take back your gold!
> For such a King I've waited all my life.
> And if I weren't so poor
> I would send a gift of my own to such a child.

AMAHL:

> But, Mother, let me send him my crutch.
> Who knows, he may need one,
> and this I made myself.

THE MOTHER:

> But that you can't, you can't!

(THE MOTHER *moves to stop him as he starts to raise the crutch.* AMAHL *lifts the crutch. There is a complete hush in the room. The boy takes one step toward* THE KINGS, *then realizes that he has moved without the help of his crutch.*)

AMAHL (*In a whisper*):

> I walk, Mother . . .
> I walk, Mother!

KASPAR:

> He walks . . .

MELCHIOR:

> He walks . . .

BALTHAZAR:

> He walks . . .

THE MOTHER:

> He walks . . .

(*Step by step,* AMAHL *very slowly makes his way toward* THE KINGS, *the crutch held before him in his outstretched hands.* THE MOTHER *rises and draws back, almost fearful of the miracle she beholds.*)

KASPAR, MELCHIOR, BALTHAZAR:

> It is a sign from the Holy Child.
> We must give praise to the newborn King.
> We must praise Him.
> This is a sign from God!

(*Having placed the crutch in the outstretched hands of* KING
KASPAR, AMAHL *moves uncertainly to the center of the room.
With growing confidence,* AMAHL *begins to jump and caper
about the room.*)

AMAHL:

> Look, Mother, I can dance,
> I can jump, I can run!

KASPAR, MELCHIOR, BALTHAZAR:

> Truly, he can dance,
> he can jump, he can run!

(THE MOTHER *and* THE KINGS *follow* AMAHL *breathlessly, fearing
that he may fall. At last, as he turns a clumsy pirouette,* AMAHL
does stumble and fall to the floor.)

THE MOTHER (*She goes quickly to* AMAHL *and lifts him from the floor*):

> Please, my darling, be careful now.
> You must take care not to hurt yourself.

KASPAR, MELCHIOR, BALTHAZAR:

> Oh, good woman, you must not be afraid.
> For he is loved by the Son of God.

KASPAR:

> Oh, blessed child, may I touch you?

MELCHIOR:

> Oh, blessed child, may I touch you?

BALTHAZAR:

> Oh, blessed child, may I touch you?

(*One at a time,* THE KINGS *pass before* AMAHL *and lay their hands
upon him. Then each goes across to take up his gift to the Child,
ready to begin the departure.* THE PAGE *comes last, prostrating
himself on the floor before* AMAHL.)

THE PAGE:

Oh, blessed child, may I touch you?

AMAHL (*Enjoying a first taste of self-importance*):

Well, I don't know if I'm going to let *you* touch me.

THE MOTHER (*In gentle reproof*):

Amahl!

AMAHL:

Oh, all right . . . but just once.
Look, Mother, I can fight,
I can work, I can play!
Oh, Mother, let me go with the Kings!
I want to take the crutch to the Child myself.

KASPAR, MELCHIOR, BALTHAZAR:

Yes, good woman, let him come with us!
We'll take good care of him,
we'll bring him back on a camel's back.

(AMAHL *and his* MOTHER *are together apart from the others, she kneeling before him.*)

THE MOTHER:

Do you really want to go?

AMAHL:

Yes, Mother.

THE MOTHER:

Are you sure, sure, sure?

AMAHL:

I'm sure!

THE MOTHER:

Yes, I think you should go,
and bring thanks to the Child yourself.

AMAHL (*Not quite believing his ears*):

Are you sure, sure, sure?

THE MOTHER:

Go on, get ready.

KASPAR:

What did she say?

BALTHAZAR:

She said he can come.

KASPAR:

Oh, lovely, lovely, lo . . .

(*Again* BALTHAZAR *restrains* KASPAR'S *exuberance.*)

BALTHAZAR:

Kaspar!

THE MOTHER:

What to do with your crutch?

AMAHL:

You can tie it to my back.

THE MOTHER:

Don't forget to wear your hat!

AMAHL:

I shall always wear my hat.

THE MOTHER:

So, my darling, goodbye!

AMAHL, MOTHER:

So, my darling, goodbye!
I shall miss you very much.

THE MOTHER:

Wash your ears!

AMAHL:

Yes, I promise.

THE MOTHER:

Don't tell lies!

AMAHL:

No, I promise.
Feed my bird!

THE MOTHER:

Yes, I promise.

AMAHL:

Watch the cat!

THE MOTHER:

Yes, I promise.

AMAHL:

I shall miss you very much.

SHEPHERDS (*From off-stage*):

Shepherds, arise!

MELCHIOR:

Are you ready?

AMAHL:

Yes, I'm ready.

MELCHIOR:

Let's go then.

(*Led by* THE PAGE, *who has taken up his burdens and the heavy lamp,* THE THREE KINGS *start their stately procession out of the cottage.*)

SHEPHERDS:

Come, oh shepherds, come outside.
All the stars have left the sky.
Oh, sweet dawn, oh, dawn of peace.

(AMAHL *rushes into his* MOTHER'S *arms, bidding her goodbye, then hurries to catch up with the departing* KINGS. *Having taken his place at the end of the procession,* AMAHL *begins to play his pipes as he goes. Outside, the soft colors of dawn are brightening the sky, and a few great flakes of snow have begun to fall upon the road.* THE MOTHER *stands alone in the doorway of the cottage. Then she goes outside to wave once more to* AMAHL, *as he turns to her, just before he disappears at the bend in the road. The curtain falls very slowly.*)

Poem-Plays

BY

RUTH KRAUSS

*B*ORN in Baltimore, Maryland, in 1901, Ruth Krauss as a young woman pursued her interests in the graphic arts and her talents at the piano and violin, with time out to study anthropology at Columbia University, before embarking upon a distinguished career as a writer of children's books. Her understanding and appreciation of children's humor have enabled her to write a long succession of stories, poems and, most recently, plays, several of which have become modern classics in the juvenile field. Two of her books have been illustrated by her husband, Crockett Johnson, while Maurice Sendak has been responsible for a number of others, including *A Hole Is to Dig* (1952), *A Very Special House* (1953), *I'll Be You and You Be Me* (1954) and *I Want to Paint My Bathroom Blue* (1956). Her gift is playing with language in a childlike way that is sometimes "cute" because it reminds us of expressions we have heard children say but which is also authentic for the same reason. In the end, preciousness is overcome by precision, for the art of Ruth Krauss is the accuracy of her expression and the honesty of her inspiration.

In one of her poem-plays Miss Krauss says that what a poet wants in the middle of his sentence is a lake. Immediately a lake appears. Even stranger and more wonderful things happen throughout her plays. She thinks nothing of giving a stage direction for the entire theatre to fall down, brick by brick (perhaps it's just as well we're reading her plays at present and not seeing them!); for hundreds of train passengers to begin kissing each other; for flying pineapples, lemons on fire, ashcans or a slice of pie all to appear on cue. Her characters, too, may seem a bizarre gathering, for often they say nothing or only a few lines at most and bear such unusual identities as the Chorus of Children of the Leper-Colony Kindergarten, a glacier, the 50,000 dogwood trees at Valley Forge, an iceberg, everyone on roller-skates in bed, a left leg, sliced-up language, a poet covered with peaches, ladders that leap, and Winnie-the-Pooh and William Shakespeare. Some may think it impossible for all this to be realized on stage, but not at all, as productions of the poem-plays have attested at New York City's off-Broadway experimental theatres, the famed Café la Mama, Café Cino and the Poets' Theatre of Judson Memorial Church. Also, they have been performed in acting classes at Actors Studio and New York University and have been published as a book for children, *The Cantilever Rainbow* (1965), in an anthology of unconventional plays, *Theatre Experiment* (1967), and as a book of theatre poems, *There's a Little Ambiguity Over There Among the Bluebells* (1968).

How they are to be staged is the fascinating challenge they present to play directors and actors, because Miss Krauss does not say, and there is no *one* way. Directors, in the last two books listed above, offer a variety of interpretations and styles of possible presentations for the one-line play, *A Beautiful Day,* which follows; one of them devised four entirely different forms it can take, all of which were staged. Seven directors staged the play that requires a lake, in seven individual ways. And when employed in creative dramatics classes (that is, in informal drama groups where plays, characters and movement are improvised according to sensory stimuli and artistic impetus), they have induced 15 youngsters to invent and perform 15 original definitions. These plays are the beginning, and only that, of what the performer, director, designer, musician and dancer want to make of them. They are presented here for the fun of "performing" them in any manner you like, as well as for the pleasure that comes from reading them, also in any manner you like.

A Beautiful Day

GIRL: What a beautiful day!

The Sun falls down onto the stage

Play 1

NARRATOR: in a poem you make your point with pineapples

(*Pineapples fly onto the stage from all directions*)

SPY: and it would be nice to have a spy going in and out

Play 2

NARRATOR: in a poem you make your point with lemons-on-fire

(Lemons-on-fire fly out overhead across the horizons over into onto the stage from all directions the people run out and bow lie down and roll in the grass on the rooftops in the sand)

ICEBERG: and it would be nice to have an iceberg going in and out

Play 3

NARRATOR:

in a poem
you make your point with—

NIGHT flies onto the stage
from all directions however
it is summer
and full of tree-toads
car-brakes
Mack-the-Knife
and dog howl

The Genie
of Sutton Place

BY

KENNETH HEUER

AND

GEORGE SELDEN

*R*EADING a television play instead of seeing one is an act rarely experienced by most people, but in the instance of *The Genie of Sutton Place* it must be because this very funny fantasy has not been witnessed since it was first televised on *Studio One* nearly 15 years ago. The play's whimsy seems to have increased ever since then (it is ever more difficult to keep a dog in a big city today, much less a genie!) and so has its timeliness (occult sciences, without which there would be no plot, are much more a topic of discussion now than they were then). An additional pleasure is derived from reading it because in print the interesting world of the television studio becomes apparent in directions for the camera "to fade in," "to fade out," "to cut to," "to dissolve to," "to follow Timothy and Sam out into the hall," or "to give an extreme close-up of Aunt Lucy's astonished face," which impart knowledge of the special technical considerations dramatists must give to TV scripts.

When the first camera shot tells us that a major character is a middle-aged dog, we know that this play can be intended only for television or the movies. Sam is real, not an actor in a dog suit; his basset-hound expressions need to be viewed at close hand in order to know his reactions to Aunt Lucy and to discern his affection for Timothy. The private jokes and secrets shared by the characters, from which this play derives much of its comic energy, can best be seen through intimate exchange of glances. Also essential to its success is a pictorial excursion of New York City, where the action skits back and forth from a Sutton Place living room, kitchen and bedroom to the public library (including a visit to the rare-book room), with a stop at The Metropolitan Museum of New York. This is an adventure story that must move. Confined to one or two rooms, as it would be if written for the stage, it could no longer exist; on television it can go anywhere a camera can take it.

Yet for all its freedom of presentation, *The Genie of Sutton Place* is a genuine play; its plot complications are constructed tightly into a definite beginning, middle and end; its characters are clearly and steadily motivated; its dialogue is sharpened into an individual style of humor; and its pace is kept spiraling upward until the very end. Furthermore, it successfully makes fantasy out of modern-day life, something very few contemporary plays have achieved (of course, to do this requires an age-old genie or two, plus a full catalogue of ancient magic spells). The story could never happen (our middle-aged dogs simply do not turn into middle-aged men who marry our middle-aged aunts, more's the pity); still it does happen here, because the reader is made to feel so much a part of it.

Kenneth Heuer, interested in astronomy from childhood, lectured for five years at New York City's Hayden Planetarium and also became a member of the Royal Astronomical Society in England. Much of his writing has been devoted to the stars and heavens, including scientific studies that have attracted international praise. Today he is an editor and writer in New York City. George Selden attended Yale University before going to Italy for what he terms "a great year" as a Fulbright Scholar, during which time he was able to indulge his favorite hobby of archaeology in Greece, Turkey, France and England. He has written 11 books for children, including *The Cricket in Times Square* and *Tucker's Countryside*. Heuer and Selden wrote the story of "genie" with the intention that it would become a book for young people, but sensing its dramatic values, adapted it into their first television play.

Originally presented on May 14, 1956, *The Genie of Sutton Place* was performed with a cast that included Harvey Grant as Timothy, Polly Rowles as Aunt Lucy, Henry Jones as Sam the Man, and a famous canine personality, Morgan, as Sam the Dog.

The Genie
of Sutton Place

CHARACTERS

TIMOTHY WHITE, *a boy about eight*
AUNT LUCY, *Timothy's aunt*
ROSE, *Aunt Lucy's maid*
ABDULLAH, *a genie, timeless, but looks thirty*
AKBAR, *a second genie, more sinister than Abdullah*
MR. DICKINSON, *chief of rare books at the library*
A LIBRARY GUARD, *thirty, say, but it doesn't matter*
SAM THE DOG ⎫
SAM THE MAN ⎭ *middle-aged in both manifestations*
A MOTHER
A LITTLE BOY
A MUSEUM GUARD

SETS

AUNT LUCY'S *apartment*
   Living room, and hall to the kitchen, with a flight of stairs
   The kitchen
   TIMOTHY'S *bedroom*
The Library (the one on Fifth Avenue at 42nd Street)
   A small section of the steps outside
   The rare-book room
   The Near Eastern room of the Metropolitan Museum of Art

ACT I

Fade in: On SAM THE DOG—*a raggedy, friendly mongrel of slightly more than average size curled up in an armchair with his paws and head dangling over the edge. He has a patient, good-natured, but slightly woebegone face. A woman's voice is heard while the camera is still on* SAM, *who watches the speaker intently.*

AUNT LUCY: But dear, you *know* how fond I am of you. I love you more than anyone else on earth. (SAM *wags his tail.*) And I've always wanted you to come and live with me. (*Cut to:* AUNT LUCY, *an attractive, middle-aged woman, essentially warmhearted, but preoccupied with creating a stylish impression. She's sitting on the couch in her fashionable, upper East Side apartment.*) It's just that Sam's a little out of place here. I know he was all right when you and your father were living together in Greenwich Village, but you've left that life behind now.

> (*Cut to:* TIMOTHY, *a small boy, about eight years old, sitting quite conspicuously alone in a stiff-backed chair. He is a serious, sometimes solemn little man, never pompous, always polite, but determined in an unobtrusive way. At no time is he cute or precious.*)

TIMOTHY: Oh, Sam likes Sutton Place as well as the Village, Aunt Lucy.

AUNT LUCY (*Assuming a somewhat patronizing adult attitude*): I'm sure that he does, dear. That isn't quite what I meant. (*Trying a new tack.*) Let me put it this way: do you think Sam fits in here?

> (*Cut to* SAM *looking uncertainly at* TIMOTHY. *Then cut to* TIMOTHY, *looking uncertainly at* SAM.)

[316]

TIMOTHY: Do *I* fit in here?

AUNT LUCY (*Shocked at the idea*): Of course you do, darling! You're my nephew.

TIMOTHY: Well, Sam fits in if I do.

AUNT LUCY (*Sighing, slightly exasperated by* TIMOTHY's *passive resistance, she rises and moves restlessly about the room*): Timothy, you're making this rather difficult for me.

TIMOTHY: I'm sorry, Aunt Lucy.

AUNT LUCY: I only allowed you to bring Sam with you in the first place because I knew— (*Pausing a little awkwardly at the delicate subject.*)—Well, I realized how you must feel after your father's death. But that was over two months ago. It's time you began to adjust to your new life. And I'm afraid that it's going to mean more than giving up Sam.

TIMOTHY (*Alarmed*): Giving him up—!

AUNT LUCY: Yes, dear, giving Sam up. (*She sits on the couch again.*) He's just a plain nuisance—always following me around; I'm constantly finding him on my bed; and he scratches at my door *all night long!*

TIMOTHY: That's because he loves you, Aunt Lucy.

(*Cut to* SAM. *He jumps down from his chair and pads over to her.*)

AUNT LUCY: I'm very flattered by Sam's attention, but I wish he'd bestow it on another dog. (SAM *jumps up beside her and lays his head in her lap.*) Now there: that's exactly what I mean. (*She picks his head up fastidiously in her fingertips and pushes it away from her.*) Go away, Sam—go on now.

TIMOTHY: What's the matter, Aunt Lucy? Does affection embarrass you?

AUNT LUCY (*Somewhat sternly*): Don't try to cloud the issue, Timmy. We're talking about Sam—and you. (*She pats the cushion between* SAM *and herself. Speaking more kindly.*) Come over and sit beside me, dear. As long as we're having this little chat, there are a few other things I want to say to you.

(*Reluctantly* TIMOTHY *joins his aunt. They are all three—* TIMOTHY, AUNT LUCY, *and* SAM—*lined up on the couch, with the boy's right arm resting on the dog.*)

AUNT LUCY: Your father and I were never terribly close, I'm afraid. I didn't understand him. He was a rather eccentric man—not at all like other people.

TIMOTHY: That's why I liked him.

AUNT LUCY (*Ignoring* TIMOTHY'S *remark*): He was forever talking about his "studies" and collecting those queer books. And I still don't know what his "studies" consisted of.

TIMOTHY: Folklore and the Occult Sciences, Aunt Lucy.

AUNT LUCY (*Flaring slightly*): Well, isn't that an inane way for a grown man to spend his life! Now don't think I disliked your father, because I loved him very much. He was my only brother. But I do believe he brought you up very poorly. It was wrong of him to keep you down there in Greenwich Village without any woman to take care of you. It's made you shy. You stay by yourself too much. From now on I want you to see more of children your own age.

TIMOTHY: But I have Sam—

AUNT LUCY: Sam isn't a human being, Timothy. You depend on him more than you should. That's the main reason I want you to let him go. (*Lowering her voice to a serious but kind level.*) Now, would you like me to . . . find a new home for him?

TIMOTHY (*Pulls* SAM *closer to him. Quietly*): No, thank you, Aunt Lucy.

AUNT LUCY: Do you think you can take care of it, dear?

TIMOTHY (*Very quietly*): Yes, Aunt Lucy.

AUNT LUCY (*Soberly, but still trying to be kind*): I'd like him out of the house in a week. (*She rises and speaks more cheerfully.*) And when he's gone, I'll have a surprise for you. There's a pet shop on Fifty-seventh Street that specializes in French poodles. Wouldn't you like to have a nice poodle—all clipped the way they are, with a pompom on his tail? He'd be much happier here than Sam.

TIMOTHY (*Hopefully*): Couldn't we clip Sam's tail in a pompom?

(*Camera focuses on* SAM, *whose tail is conspicuously unfit for pompoms.*)

AUNT LUCY: I don't think so, dear. (*Close up of* AUNT LUCY. *She's obviously upset by the scene and wants to escape.*) I have to go out for a few minutes, now, but I'll be back for supper. (*At the door she pauses and turns.*) Please don't think of me too harshly, darling.

I'm trying to do what's right . . . and I'm awfully glad you're
living with me now.

> (*She goes out.* TIMOTHY *remains on the couch, stroking* SAM'S
> *head. He is distressed, but not panic-stricken.*)

TIMOTHY: Sam, I've got to get rid of you. You heard what Aunt Lucy
said. Is there any place you want to live? She said she could find a
home for you, but that means the dog pound. So I have to put you
somewhere before she does. (*Meditating.*) Who is there I could
give you to? . . . Somebody not too far away. (*He suddenly
brightens.*) *There's* someone! Come on, Sam! I've got an idea. (*He
picks* SAM *up in his arms, a real armful for a boy his size—crosses
the living room into a short hall and pushes his way through a
swinging door into the kitchen.*)

> (*Cut to:* ROSE, AUNT LUCY'S *cook, working at the sink. She's a
> young, energetic woman with an instinctive understanding of
> and sympathy for human problems.* ROSE *turns to watch* TIMOTHY
> *enter carrying his dog. He proceeds to the kitchen table and
> pours* SAM *out on it.*)

TIMOTHY: Do you like Sam, Rose?
ROSE (*Lifting* SAM *to the floor*): Sure, honey, I like him. But I like
him just as much on the floor.
TIMOTHY: I'm glad, Rose, I like him awfully much myself—and I'm
giving him to you as a present.
ROSE (*Astonished*): You're *what?!*
TIMOTHY: He's yours now. Aunt Lucy said I have to give him away.
(*Casually.*) Also I thought I might come to your room now and
then to visit him.

> (*During the course of the following* ROSE *pours* TIMOTHY *a small
> glass of milk and gives him a few cookies on a plate. He eats
> reflectively, handing one or two cookies down to* SAM, *who
> munches with equal concentration.*)

ROSE: That's a dear present, Timmy! I'd love to have Sam for my
own. But you got the wrong notion what your aunt wants. She's
bound to get him out of the house. If I was sleeping out now, I

could keep him with me—but I live right here in the apartment. She'd mind just as much if he was in my room as yours.

TIMOTHY (*Crestfallen*): I guess so.

ROSE (*Sounding him out*): What are you going to do with him?

TIMOTHY: I don't know yet.

ROSE: Maybe I can find some friends to take him. You want me to ask around my acquaintances?

TIMOTHY: Thank you very much, Rose, but Sam and I have to work this out ourselves.

ROSE (*With emphatic finality*): She won't let you keep that dog here, boy.

TIMOTHY (*Getting up*): We'll think of something.

ROSE: Where you going now?

TIMOTHY: Just up to my room.

ROSE (*Close up of her. Her face shows concern*): Don't do anything bad now.

> (*The camera follows* TIMOTHY *and* SAM *out into the hall and up the narrow flight of stairs of the duplex apartment. Cut to: The interior of* TIMOTHY'S *bedroom, which the camera explores. It's a child's room obviously decorated by an adult with little understanding of what children really enjoy. There are "cute" curtains and wallpaper, and various items of "kiddies" furniture. In sharp contrast, the only article which looks as if it belongs to* TIMOTHY *is a broken-down suitcase sitting in one corner, a relic of his former life. Cut to: The door.* TIMOTHY *enters dejectedly followed by* SAM. *He sits on the bed, purposefully avoiding the other furniture, with* SAM, *of course, beside him.*)

TIMOTHY (*After a moment's thought*): Sam, there's only one thing I can see for us to do. (*He goes over, gets his suitcase and brings it back to the bed. There new uncertainty assails him.*) Gee but, Sam, I hate to have to run away. Aunt Lucy's been awfully nice to us. And you like her too, don't you? (SAM *wags his tail.*) I wish she liked you as much as she does me. Do you think she'll miss me? I guess she will. She may cry. (*With a little shrug of maturity.*) Oh, well, she'll probably get over it. (*There is a pause while more doubt takes hold of him.*) Maybe she won't though. She may sicken and die. (*The vision of* AUNT LUCY'S *death convinces him.*) Sam, we can't go. And you can't stay. What are we going to do? (*His eyes scan the room, searching vainly for a suggestion of help. They settle on a child's desk in one corner. An expression of mixed fear and enthusiasm comes over his face. Secretively.*) Do you suppose there's something in the Occult Sciences that could help us? (*Quickly he goes over to the desk and takes a large, musty notebook out of the bottom drawer, placing it carefully on the top. Then he goes back to the bed and carries* SAM *over, putting him beside the notebook on the desk. He kneels on a chair to raise himself higher above the desk top. Gravely, pointing to the book.*) Sam, this is the Occult Sciences. Daddy put down everything he knew in here. It's dangerous to use it, but there's nothing else we can do. (*He opens the book and begins to turn its pages awesomely.*) Here's a recipe for turning lead into gold. If Aunt Lucy wasn't so rich we could pay her to keep you. . . . (*Reading further.*) Look, Sam—(*Obviously reading off a chapter title.*) "Ancient Methods of Determining the Future from the Movements of the Celestial Bodies." (*He is becoming more and more enthusiastic.*) . . . Here's a section on Near Eastern Folklore. Oh, and a poem, Sam! Listen: "October 13, 1935. Today my good friend Madame Sosostris, the celebrated medium, loaned me her translation, the only extant copy, of Abdul Al Hazred's *Cabala,* a curious work containing much es-o-ter-ic information. Among other things I noted the following singular rhyme, a formula for conjuring genies. On trial, as might have been expected, it proved a complete failure! Perhaps spoken in the original Arabic its success might be greater." And here's the poem, Sam:

> Genie formed of earth and sky,
> Skin of night, with lunar eye,
> Bone of mountain, blood of the sea,
> Come hither thou and wait on me.

I like that poem . . . (*He reflects on it a moment. Gradually his face changes, revealing the occurrence of an idea and the emotional progress from mere entertainment to an enthusiastic acceptance of it.*) Do you think it would really work if I said it in the Arabic? Daddy said it might. A genie would be a big help. I bet it would, Sam! But how can I get it put in the Arabic? (*Weighing various possibilities.*) At the library they'd know how. They know everything there—with all those books. (*He jumps up and lifts* SAM *to the floor.*) Come on, Sam—we've got to go to the library. (*He picks up the notebook and heads toward the door as the camera fades out.*)

(*Fade in: On one of the stone lions outside the Forty-second Street library. The camera drops to a section of steps beside the lion's pedestal. A* MOTHER *comes by, dragging a* LITTLE BOY *dressed in coonskin cap and frontier jacket.*)

LITTLE BOY (*Vigorously*): But, Mama, I don't *want* to learn how to use the library!

(*To no avail. His* MOTHER *drags him up the steps.* TIMOTHY *approaches with* SAM *and sits him on one of the steps.*)

TIMOTHY: You have to wait here, Sam. They don't let dogs in the library. I'll be right back, so don't go away anywhere. (*He climbs a few steps out of the camera's range.*)

(*Cut to: The interior of the rare-book room inside the library. It's a cubical room with a metal staircase leading to a balcony and books on both levels. The books are all behind glass and there are also individual floor cases for the exhibition of especially precious volumes. The floor space is occupied by several large tables for readers and a single desk for the chief of the rare-book room,* MR. DICKINSON. *After taking in the room at large, the camera focuses on the chief, a dapper, fastidious scholar with neatly trimmed, discreet mustache and graying hair. A chime is heard and* MR. DICKINSON *goes to the doors, of which there are two: the inner is of heavy glass and wood, the outer is an iron grill. He unlocks and opens the first door. Camera focuses through the grill on an imposing, elaborately dressed* LIBRARY GUARD. TIMOTHY *is by his side.*)

GUARD (*With exaggerated sobriety*): This gentleman has a linguistic problem, Mr. Dickinson.

MR. DICKINSON (*Smiling delightedly at* TIMOTHY, *whose head only comes up to the* GUARD's *belt*): He does?

GUARD: Yes, sir. He wants something translated into Arabic.

MR. DICKINSON: Oh, my!—then he'd better come in. (*He unlocks the outside door and admits* TIMOTHY. *To* GUARD.) Thank you, Paul. (GUARD *smiles and leaves.* TIMOTHY, *awestruck, gazes around the room while* MR. DICKINSON *looks on in benign amusement.*) Have you ever been in the rare-book room before?

TIMOTHY (*In a deep, library whisper*): No. It's very beautiful, isn't it?

MR. DICKINSON: I think so.

TIMOTHY (*Still whispering*): They told me downstairs that you know the Arabic.

MR. DICKINSON: Yes, I do. You can speak a little louder if you like.

TIMOTHY: I thought you were supposed to whisper in libraries.

MR. DICKINSON: Well, ordinarily that's a good rule to follow, but there's no one else here now.

TIMOTHY (*Clearing his throat, formally*): My name is Timothy White and I have something I would like translated.

MR. DICKINSON: My name is Martin Dickinson. How do you do?

(*They shake hands.*)

TIMOTHY: Fine, thanks. I had a cold last week, but I got over it.

MR. DICKINSON: Oh, I'm glad to hear that.

TIMOTHY: Are all these books yours?

MR. DICKINSON: I like to think that they are: I take care of them all. (*Amicably.*) Tell me, Timothy, are you interested in Arabic?

TIMOTHY: Mhmm—but more so in magic: it's a spell for conjuring genies I want translated.

MR. DICKINSON: How fascinating! Where did you find it?

TIMOTHY: In the Occult Sciences. (*He puts his father's book on one of the tables and opens it to the passage in question.*)

MR. DICKINSON (*Studying the notebook*): What a remarkable manuscript!

TIMOTHY: It was my father's. He had a lot of books, too, but he's dead now. (*Pointing to a page in the book.*) See, here's the spell.

MR. DICKINSON: Ah, yes—(*He reads a moment, with surprise.*) Why, it's from the Arab Abdul Al Hazred's *Cabala*. I've read fragments of the work in Latin, but I wasn't aware that there was an English translation.

TIMOTHY: A medium made it. She was a friend of my father's.

MR. DICKINSON: Your father must have been an extraordinary person.

Did you know that the man who made up this spell was mad? In fact, some people believed he was the devil disguised as a human being.

TIMOTHY (*Alarmed*): Was he?

MR. DICKINSON (*Softly but suggestively, feeding* TIMOTHY's *fancy*): I don't know. Shall I translate it now?

TIMOTHY (*Nervously*): Maybe we shouldn't—if he was a bad man.

MR. DICKINSON: I will if you want me to.

TIMOTHY (*Hesitating*): All right—go ahead. (MR. DICKINSON *slowly begins to translate the verse aloud into Arabic. Suddenly a look of consternation comes over* TIMOTHY's *face*) Stop! Stop! We don't want the genie to come here. He may disturb the library.

MR. DICKINSON (*Very much amused at* TIMOTHY's *concern*): That hadn't occurred to me. How *shall* I translate it then?

TIMOTHY: Write the spell down and mix up the lines when you read it to me.

MR. DICKINSON: Very well. I'll write it in English that sounds like the Arabic. (*He begins to do so.*) Now this is the first line. (*He pronounces it in Arabic and* TIMOTHY *repeats it after him.*)

(*Fade out. Fade in: On* SAM *still sitting at the base of the lion statue, but now surrounded by a crowd of friendly dogs. The camera plays over them for a moment before* TIMOTHY, *in a state of great excitement, runs down the library steps.*)

TIMOTHY (*Surveying* SAM's *new friends*): Who are all these people, Sam? (*The dogs bark a greeting and a few jump up on him.*) I got the Arabic. We have to go now though. Come on. (*To the other dogs.*) Goodbye, goodbye. Sorry—we'll come back later. Come on, Sam. (*They go off. Camera focuses on the dogs, who sit disconsolate a minute and then disperse, several heading up the steps toward the library. Cut to: A metal doorstop in the shape of a dog in* TIMOTHY's *bedroom. The door opens and* TIMOTHY *comes in with* SAM. *He is extremely nervous and shows it in his actions and the rapidity of his speech.*) Hurry, Sam. (SAM *pads into the middle of the room and sits on the floor.*) We better lock the door, I guess—and pull down the shades. (*He does so, after depositing his father's notebook on the desk.*) I don't know exactly what's going to happen. The man in the library said this spell was made by a crazy

Arab. (*He picks* SAM *up and puts him on the bed, where he barricades him behind several pillows.*) And you stay here—I don't want you to get hurt if anything goes wrong. (*Goes to the desk for the notebook and opens it to the right page. Breathlessly.*) Gee, I'm kind of scared, Sam. I never conjured a genie before. But we've got to do it. I guess you have to start sometime.

(*Solemnly and in a trembling voice, he recites the Arabic incantation. The camera is in an extreme close-up of his face. [See end of act for a transliteration of the Arabic.] After the formula there is a moment of acute tension. Then, abruptly, darkness blankets the room: a single note on a flute is heard, there is a burst of supernatural light: the flute note trails into silence. [Puffs of smoke are to be avoided.]* TIMOTHY's *face, still in close-up, registers amazement followed by fear. Cut to:* ABDULLAH, *the genie, seen from* TIMOTHY's *point of view—that is, from a lower position upwards, so that a greater impression of immensity is obtained. And indeed he is huge: a colossal figure dressed in classical Arabian costume—a turban, earrings, a short, sleeveless jacket, billowing pantaloons, and pointed shoes. His arms are crossed on his chest, his features are animated by a smile which may portend either violence or benevolence, and his eyes shine with a light at the same time fearful and wonderful.* TIMOTHY *begins to back away apprehensively, but the* GENIE *unfolds his arms and performs an elaborate Oriental obeisance, ending on his knees with his forehead pressed against the floor at* TIMOTHY's *feet and his arms outstretched.*)

ABDULLA (*As he bows*): Sayidee, hadartu min baeed Ieeoonafeetha matooreed. (*Which is a transliteration of the Arabic for, "Master, I come from the halls of endless waiting to do your bidding." But it isn't important, the audience knows what he says.*)

TIMOTHY (*Tentatively*): Excuse me, please—do you speak English?

ABDULLAH (*Rising*): Master, I speak all the tongues of Earth, the Dark World and Glorious Paradise.

TIMOTHY: I only speak English myself—and a little Arabic. Is it all right if we talk in English?

ABDULLAH: Master, to satisfy your will was I created.

TIMOTHY (*With growing eagerness*): You mean you're going to do what I say?

ABDULLAH: Yes, Master—even if it were to steal the seven eggs of the giant Roc that nests on the summit of Jebel Aja.

TIMOTHY: And you won't hurt me?

ABDULLAH: I would plunge myself into the Fire that knows no quenching first, Master.

TIMOTHY (*Gleefully*): Sam, you can come out!! He's harmless! (*Camera cuts to the bed, where* SAM *jumps out from behind the pillow fortress and begins to caper around* ABDULLAH, *barking excitedly and jumping up on him. In contrast to his usual sober conduct* TIMOTHY *joins* SAM *in his antics, exclaiming in delight at his success.*) Oh boy, Sam—isn't he wonderful! A real, live genie! And he's going to help us! (ABDULLAH *stands quite still as the two dance around him, but his dazzling smile and the barest hint of humor in his eyes reveals his own pleasure. Quieting down.*) Do you have a name?

ABDULLAH: I do, Master. The great sorcerer Al Hazred who made me called me Abdullah.

TIMOTHY: That's the man who invented the spell. (*Wonder-struck.*) Did he really *make* you?

ABDULLAH: Yes, Master. (*Very powerfully and grandly.*) Over a thousand years ago he kneaded my flesh from the golden sand of the burning desert mixed with the darkness of night; from the running tides of the sea he drew my blood, and carved my bones from granite mountains; moonlight he filtered for my eyes; and he tore my voice from the throat of the roaring simoon. And when he had made me, he said to me—"Live!" And I lived. (*Lifting his arms.*) I stood up and I laughed—I *laughed*! (*He roars with great laughter, as at the moment of his creation.*)—because I was alive!

TIMOTHY (*Breathlessly, overawed*): Did you serve him a long time?

ABDULLAH: For over one hundred years, Master, until he died. His magic kept him not from death.

TIMOTHY: Who did you work for after him?

ABDULLAH: Those who knew the secret spell, Master: Harun al-Rashid, the Caliph of Baghdad, Sir Edward Grenville, a Knight of the Crusades, and then Brother Miguel, a Dominican monk— we did many good works together. My last master was the Grand Mogul, Shah Jahan, of India. (*Sadly.*) For nearly three hundred years since then I have been in the Halls of Endless Waiting with the other genies.

TIMOTHY: What do you do while you're there?

ABDULLAH: We wait to be summoned, Master. And we miss the world.

TIMOTHY (*Sympathetically*): Gee, I'm sorry, Abdullah. I would have summoned you sooner if I'd known how.

ABDULLAH: Thank you, Master. But to have been called at last is enough.

TIMOTHY: I guess you've never been in New York before.

ABDULLAH (*Puzzled*): New York, Master?

TIMOTHY: Yes. It's a city in America.

ABDULLAH (*Suddenly comprehending*): Ah, America—the new world in the West! Brother Miguel's cousin sailed with a man called Columbus. I gave him a fair wind and clear sky the day they embarked.

TIMOTHY (*Goes to the window and lifts a corner of the blind, motioning* ABDULLAH *to come over*): Look, this is New York.

ABDULLAH (*Peeping under the blind. Awestruck*): Oh, Master!—it's bigger even than Baghdad. (*Bowing.*) How may I serve you in this most magnificent of cities?

TIMOTHY (*Sitting on the bed. Very practically*): Well, my problem is this: I have this dog, Sam—this is Sam, by the way—and my Aunt Lucy says I have to get rid of him. She doesn't like him very much. But I want to keep him. I've known Sam longer than anybody.

ABDULLAH: Master, let me turn Aunt Lucy into a fly, and then command a toad from the Caliph's garden to appear and eat the fly.

TIMOTHY (*After a moment's consideration*): No, I don't think we ought to do that: she's my father's only sister.

ABDULLAH: Then I must not hurt Aunt Lucy?

TIMOTHY: I'd rather not. Can't you think of something else?

ABDULLAH (*Reflects a minute*): Master, I must observe the situation. Let me go now and return in a few days.

TIMOTHY: You won't let anyone see you, will you?

ABDULLAH: They will not know what they do see, Master.

TIMOTHY: All right—you leave now. It's almost suppertime anyway. Do I have to recite the spell for you to come back?

ABDULLAH: No, Master; with your permission I may come and go at will. Only one thing you must know. Never pronounce the name of the Supreme Being whom the Children of the Prophet Mohammed worship. For if that name is spoken in my presence, I must vanish. I was made by magic, and I cannot endure where He is invoked.

TIMOTHY: I'll remember, Abdullah.

ABDULLAH (*Salaaming*): Farewell, then, little Master, even the stars shall do your bidding.

TIMOTHY: Goodbye. Don't forget to come back. (*There is a flicker of darkness, and the* GENIE *is gone.* TIMOTHY *pets* SAM *a minute, compressing his happiness.*) Oh boy, Sam—oh boy, oh boy.
(*Fade out.*)
Arabic for the incantation:

Djeeneeyun, sunee 'a min ardin wa samaa

Jildoohoo meena el lailee wa ainoohoo meena el kamaree

El'zamoohoo meena el jabalee wa damoohoo meena el bharee

Ta'aila hoona wa istami'a lima akooloo.

(*Consonants are very important in Arabic. When a syllable is accented, the consonant that precedes it receives just as much stress as the vowel. For instance, the first word of the spell is not pronounced Djeen-EE-yun, but Djeen-Nee-yun, with a strong nasal intonation. Accented syllables are marked above.* a *is long,* ai *is pronounced like I. The apostrophe indicates an Arabic consonant for which there is no equivalent in English. It is a combination of a* y *sound and the* ng *of* ing.)

ACT II

Fade in: The kitchen. TIMOTHY *is seated at the table having breakfast, parts of which he smuggles under it to* SAM. ROSE *brings him a second waffle from the stove.*

ROSE: I ought to serve you a double breakfast the amount you give that dog.

TIMOTHY: Sam likes your cooking, Rose.

ROSE: I'm glad I please such a connoisseur.

TIMOTHY: Sam used to eat in the best restaurants in Greenwich Village.

ROSE: He's going to be eating in the streets if you don't find a place for him soon. Have you made any plans yet?

TIMOTHY (*Airily*): Oh yes, I've made plans. But I can't tell you what they are.

ROSE: What's the matter? Haven't they materialized?

TIMOTHY: Well, they materialized *once*.

(*Cut to:* AUNT LUCY *coming in the kitchen door, pulling on her gloves in preparation for going out.*)

AUNT LUCY (*Kissing* TIMOTHY): Good morning, Timothy—Rose.

ROSE: Good morning, Miss Lucy. Would you like your breakfast now?

AUNT LUCY: No, thank you, Rose, Irene Winters is picking me up for brunch at the Plaza. (*Noticing* SAM *under the table.*) Timmy, don't forget what we agreed on last week. About Sam, I mean. I'd like you to take care of it today. (*Seeing some hesitation on* TIMOTHY's *part.*) You promised, you know.

TIMOTHY: I've been sort of waiting—

AUNT LUCY (*Gently*): I don't want you to wait any longer, darling. (*Pats his head.*) I'll be back in a couple of hours—and I *will* be home for dinner, Rose. (*She turns to go out, but stops at the door.*) By the way, there's something else I had to tell you. Someone's coming—I was hoping he'd be here before I left. (*A buzzer is heard.*) Oh good, that's probably who it is.

(ROSE *goes to the servants' entrance, which opens into the kitchen. Close-up of* TIMOTHY, *drinking a glass of milk. His eyes, looking over the rim, widen in astonishment as he sees who it is. Cut to:* ABDULLAH, *in a glistening chauffeur's uniform, standing in the doorway.*)

ABDULLAH (*Removing his cap*): Miss Lucy White's residence?

AUNT LUCY (*Going to the door*): Yes. That's all right, Rose. Come in Mr. Ben-Moolah. Did you have any trouble finding the way?

ABDULLAH (*Exchanging a clandestine glance with* TIMOTHY): No, Mistress.

AUNT LUCY: Good. Rose, Timothy, I'd like you to meet Mr. Abdullah Ben-Moolah. He's going to be our new chauffeur. (*To* ABDULLAH.) This is my nephew Timothy.

ABDULLAH (*Bowing slightly and smiling, with a little smile in his voice, too*): Master . . .

TIMOTHY (*Shaking hands with him*): How do you do?

AUNT LUCY (*Trying to be diplomatic*): And this is Miss Rose Johnson, who helps us out cooking and doing things.

ABDULLAH (*Nodding*): Mistress . . .

ROSE (*Immediately taken with the handsome stranger*): Most charmed to make your acquaintance.

AUNT LUCY: Abdullah's such a strange name. Has it been in your family long?

ABDULLAH: For over a thousand years, Mistress.

AUNT LUCY: How interesting! But we can hardly refer to you as "Abdullah." No one would believe us. (*Thinking.*) I tell you what: we'll call you "Dooley." Is that all right with you?

ABDULLAH: Certainly, Mistress.

AUNT LUCY: Fine—that's settled then. We're happy to have you with us, Dooley. (*To the others.*) I can't understand what happened to Maurice though. It wasn't a bit like him to leave so abruptly, without even giving notice. You never can tell what mischief's going to get into people.

ABDULLAH (*Piously*): True, Mistress.

AUNT LUCY: I won't need you now, Dooley, but there's something I'd like you to help Timmy with. He'll tell you about it.

ABDULLAH: Very well, Mistress.

AUNT LUCY: Oh, and Dooley, one thing more; you don't need to call me "Mistress." "Miss White" will do. I've always been terribly liberal. (*Kissing* TIMOTHY *on the head.*) Bye, darling. Rose, make Dooley at home.

ROSE: I will, Miss Lucy. (AUNT LUCY *leaves.*) Have you had your breakfast, Mr. Moolah?

ABDULLAH: No, Mistress. I need very little food.

ROSE: Why, a big man like you should have three hearty meals a day! Sit right down here with Timmy. I'll get you some coffee. (ABDULLAH *sits at the table.*) You want a couple of waffles?

ABDULLAH (*Uncomprehending*): Waffles, Mistress?

ROSE: Sure, waffles. Don't you like them?

TIMOTHY: Would you rather have some candy, Dooley?

ROSE: Of course, he doesn't want candy for breakfast! (*She gives* ABDULLAH *a doughnut.*) Here, Mr. Moolah, try one of my doughnuts.

TIMOTHY (*Enthusiastically*): Rose's doughnuts are delicious! (ROSE *hands him one, too.*) Thank you, Rose.

ABDULLAH (*Examining the doughnut*): Wonderful! It is like the bracelets worn by the women in the Caliph's harem.

ROSE: It's what?

ABDULLAH (*He takes a bite of the doughnut: his smile broadens*): And it tastes of the warm wind that blows through a grove of southern spices.

ROSE (*Entranced*): I never *heard* a man talk like you!

TIMOTHY (*Getting a little nervous*): Um, Dooley, there's something I've got to talk over with you.

ABDULLAH: Yes, Master, I know.

TIMOTHY: Maybe we could go for a ride. Could we, Rose? It's a very nice day out. I'd like to go to the Metropolitan Museum.

ROSE: Well, I guess it's all right, Timmy—if Mr. Moolah doesn't mind. Don't forget what your aunt said though.

TIMOTHY (*Jumping up from the table*): I won't, Rose. Come on, Sam. (SAM *pads out from under the table.*) Sam can stay in the car. Will you come upstairs while I get my jacket, Dooley? I'll show you my room.

ABDULLAH: Yes, Master. (*Pushing open the door into the hall.*) After you.

> (*He goes out with* TIMOTHY *and* SAM. ROSE *begins to clear the table. Then she tiptoes to the door and peeks out. Cut to: The hall. As he is about to go up the stairs,* ABDULLAH *turns and sees* ROSE *looking at him. He smiles dryly but warmly at her: She quickly shuts the door. Cut back to: The kitchen.* ROSE, *now smiling herself, resumes clearing the table.*)

ROSE (*As the possibilities of the situation occur more and more strongly to her*): Well . . . *Well!*

> (*Dissolve to:* TIMOTHY'*s bedroom.* TIMOTHY *and* ABDULLAH *enter. During the following,* TIMOTHY *gets a jacket from the closet and puts it on.*)

TIMOTHY: I'm awfully glad you got back, Dooley. I was beginning to worry. Today's the day I have to get rid of Sam.

ABDULLAH: I promised I would return, Master.

TIMOTHY: Yes, but you might have gotten lost. Out-of-towners always do in New York. Have you got any ideas how I can keep Sam?

ABDULLAH: This is one of the subtlest tasks I have ever been given, Master. If it were only to move a mountain or build a palace, I could perform it as easily as the dove constructs her simple nest. But to deal with human beings is to be ensnared in an endless web. (*Pause.*) Master, how old is Rose Johnson?

TIMOTHY: Oh, she's very old, Dooley—at least twenty-seven. But what are we going to do about Sam?

ABDULLAH (*To allay his concern*): Fear not, little master. Sam sits in the lap of Immortal Power.

TIMOTHY: Well, I'm glad to hear that. Maybe we'll get an idea what to do in the museum. It's easier to think there.

(*Cut to: The Near Eastern room in the Metropolitan Museum of Art. It's a high-ceilinged, airy room containing a number of enormous Oriental rugs hanging against the walls and other art objects such as a bronze incense burner and ewer, and a Byzantine alabaster capital. In one corner there is a large storage jar, and in another part of the room a curtained sedan chair big enough for two people. The same MOTHER from the library steps of Act I enters dragging her LITTLE BOY behind her. He's still wearing his coonskin cap and frontier jacket.*)

LITTLE BOY: But, Mama, I don't *want* to see the Metropolitan Museum of Art!

MOTHER: Don't dawdle, Daniel. We have three more wings to get through. (*Reading a sign near the entrance.*) Now this room contains "art objects of the Near East."

LITTLE BOY: I *hate* art objects of the Near East!

MOTHER (*Hurrying on*): Well, maybe you'll like the Far East better. (*She drags him off.* ABDULLAH *and* TIMOTHY *enter through a different door.*)

TIMOTHY: Isn't it nice here, Dooley? I wish I could bring Sam into the museum. He likes peaceful places. Did you enjoy going into the Egyptian tomb on the first floor?

ABDULLAH: Yes, Master. It reminded me of the time I was sent on an errand to the Valley of the Kings in Egypt.

TIMOTHY: I thought you might like to come to this room. There are things from the Near East here.

ABDULLAH (*Gazing around the room*): Ah, I see!—These gorgeous carpets. (*Suddenly he starts in wonder.*) Master! That little rug with the tree woven in it—it is the prayer rug of the great Shah Jehan. (*They go over to examine the rug. The genie speaks solemnly.*) Often I saw him kneel on this rug and face the East—and now here it is hung up for the gaze of many. . . . Oh the sadness of time, Master, and the changes it works on mortal existence. (*He turns away from the prayer rug and goes to sit on a bench against the wall.*)

TIMOTHY (*Sympathetically, looking up into his face*): I'm sorry, Dooley.

ABDULLAH (*Brooding*): It is the way of history! One must learn to accept it. (*More cheerfully.*) Why is it your aunt wants you to get rid of Sam, Master?

TIMOTHY: Oh, she says I depend on him, and he isn't a human being, and I stay by myself too much.

ABDULLAH (*His face lightens*): Would she object so much if he wasn't a dog?

TIMOTHY: What do you mean?

ABDULLAH: I could turn him into a human being.

TIMOTHY (*Astonished*): Could you really, Dooley?

ABDULLAH (*Easily*): With a flicker of my fingertips. That would remove the dog but not Sam.

TIMOTHY (*Dubiously*): What sort of a person would he be, do you think?

ABDULLAH: He would be the kind of a man that Sam is a dog.

TIMOTHY: How long would he stay a man?

ABDULLAH: As long as I were present, Master, to continue my spell over him.

TIMOTHY: Would it hurt?

ABDULLAH: Master, there *is* pain in being human, but the transformation would cause him none.

TIMOTHY (*Softly*): He might not like me any more.

ABDULLAH (*Slowly*): I think he will love you, Master—though men are less faithful than dogs.

TIMOTHY: Well, we can't do it now anyway. Sam's in the car.

ABDULLAH: I can summon him, Master.

TIMOTHY: You mean make him appear here?

ABDULLAH: If you command me to. (*Pointing at the jar in the corner.*) Shall I call him into that storage jar?

TIMOTHY (*Close-up of him struggling over his decision*): All right then, do it. (ABDULLAH *makes certain occult passes at the jar, then goes to it, gently tips it over and pours out* SAM. *Amazed.*) How did you do that?

ABDULLAH (*Enigmatically, flashing his smile*): By magic, Master. (*He picks the* DOG *up.*) Come, Sam. Look your last on the realm of beasts. The Society of Men shall be yours.

TIMOTHY (*He kisses* SAM'S *head*): Goodbye, Sam.

(*He watches anxiously as* ABDULLAH *takes* SAM *into the sedan chair. The* GENIE *pulls the curtains around the chair and* TIMOTHY *is left pacing up and down outside. A sudden fit of barking is heard. Then silence. A museum* GUARD *enters the room and looks suspiciously around.*)

GUARD: Have you got a dog in here?

TIMOTHY (*Nervously, with exaggerated innocence*): Me? A dog? Oh no: What kind of a dog? How big a one?

GUARD (*With another look around*): I was sure I heard barking. (*He goes out.*)

(*A moment later* ABDULLAH *steps out of the chair and holds the door ceremoniously open for its occupant.*)

ABDULLAH: Mister Sam, Master.

(*And* SAM THE MAN *emerges. His clothes, a sport shirt and rumpled pants, correspond in color and general dishevelment to the* DOG'S *unkempt appearance. His hair is shaggy, his face unshaven, but his whole personality has a certain easygoing, masculine appeal that vaguely recalls* SAM'S *charm.*)

SAM (*Tenderly, but a little embarrassed*): Hello, Timmy.

TIMOTHY (*Same tone*): Hello, Sam. Are you all right?

SAM: I think so.

TIMOTHY (*Quietly, uneasily*): Are you mad at me for letting Dooley turn you into a human being?

SAM: No, Timmy. I always wondered what it would be like.

TIMOTHY: If you want to be a dog again, I'll make him change you back.

SAM: I think I'd like to try it out for a while. (*Flexing his legs.*) My, it does seem strange to stand on two feet . . . (*Puzzled.*)

TIMOTHY: Don't you remember anything, Sam?—my Aunt Lucy and how she felt?

SAM: Was she the lady who didn't like me?

TIMOTHY: Yes. That's why we did it. She said I had to get rid of you— (*Stammering.*) I mean, of my dog.

ABDULLAH: Master, I think we should return. Rose Johnson may be worried.

TIMOTHY: Do you want to come home with me, Sam?

SAM (*Uncertain*): Would your aunt let me in the house?

TIMOTHY: Oh sure she will . . . now. She's very sociable with human beings.

SAM: Who are you going to tell her I am?

TIMOTHY: Gee, Sam, I don't know. I didn't think about that. We better decide. (*They sit on the bench against the wall.*)

SAM: Why don't you say I'm an old acquaintance of your family? I *have* known you for a long time.

TIMOTHY: Yes, and Daddy liked you very much, too. You can be a friend of his I met by accident this morning.

SAM (*Nervously*): Do you think she'll like me? I remember she was such an elegant lady. Her bed used to smell so nice. . . . Do I look all right?

TIMOTHY (*Surveying him critically*): You look very good, Sam—only you better comb your hair. Aunt Lucy said it was always mussed up. (*He hands* SAM *his pocket comb.*)

SAM (*Combing his hair*): I'm afraid it was. Did I shed a lot on the furniture?

TIMOTHY: Quite a bit usually. I think you need a shave, too. Do you have a razor, Dooley?

ABDULLAH: No, Master. I was not made with a beard.

TIMOTHY: Well, we could go to Grand Central Station. There are barbers there—and showers in the cellar. (*Enthusiastically.*) Sam, you can get a bath too: Daddy and I always did when we lived in the cold-water flat. (*Carried away by the idea.*) Dooley, would you like to take a bath?

ABDULLAH: I haven't bathed in a thousand years, Master. Not since the Chamber of Steaming Delights in the Caliph's palace.

TIMOTHY: Let's all have a bath then. (*He laughs gleefully, and the two others, catching his merriment, begin to laugh with him. However,* SAM's *laughter sounds remarkably like a bark.* TIMOTHY *looks suspiciously at him.*) Do you feel okay, Sam?

SAM: Yes, Timmy. Why?

TIMOTHY (*Lightly*): Oh—I was just wondering.

> (*Fade out. Fade in: The living room of the apartment.* AUNT LUCY *is at one of the windows, looking out, and* ROSE *stands beside her.*)

AUNT LUCY (*Turning*): But don't you have any idea what they meant to do with him?

ROSE: No, Miss Lucy. They just took off without saying a word a few minutes after you did. I haven't seen hide nor hair of them since.

AUNT LUCY: But that's quite a while ago. What's keeping them, I wonder.

ROSE: I couldn't say—but he certainly does love that dog.

AUNT LUCY: You don't need to tell me, Rose.

> (*The front door bell is heard.*)

ROSE: Maybe that's them now. (*She goes into the hall to open the door.* TIMOTHY's *voice is heard saying,* "Hi, Rose." *He bounces into the living room ahead of* ABDULLAH *and* SAM.)

TIMOTHY (*In very high spirits*): Hi, Aunt Lucy.

AUNT LUCY (*Meeting his mood, but uncertain why he should be so jolly*): Hi, darling—

TIMOTHY: Did you have a nice brunch?

AUNT LUCY: Yes, lovely, dear. What have you been doing? I was worried about you.

TIMOTHY: I've been in Grand Central Station. We took showers.

AUNT LUCY: "Showers—" (*Looking around.*) Dooley, what on *earth*— (*She sees* SAM *for the first time. He's standing uneasily in the door to the living room.*) Oh . . .

TIMOTHY: This is a friend of Daddy's, Aunt Lucy. (*Improvising as he goes along.*) Um, we met him this morning in the station—uh—where we went to look at the trains and the people and everything.

AUNT LUCY: I'm not so sure that I like the idea of your wandering around there, Timmy.

TIMOTHY: Oh it was all right. Dooley was with me—weren't you, Dooley?

ABDULLAH: Yes, Master.

TIMOTHY: And it's much more interesting than the zoo. Well, Sa— (*Catching himself.*) Daddy's friend was there, and he needed a shave, so he had a shave, and then a bath, and Dooley and I had one, too.

AUNT LUCY: Well, *really*, Timothy.

TIMOTHY (*Continuing excitedly*): Yes, really, Aunt Lucy. So I asked him to come home for awhile.

AUNT LUCY: Now, Timmy, quiet down. Doesn't Daddy's friend have a name?

TIMOTHY (*Taken aback. They hadn't thought of this*): A name? (*He looks desperately at* SAM.)

SAM (*Steps forward; modestly*): Mr. Bassinger, ma'am.

AUNT LUCY (*Extending her hand and smiling*): How do you do? I'm Lucy White, Timothy's aunt.

SAM (*He raises his hand, a little floppily, as a dog shakes hands, and takes hers*): Yes, ma'am, I've known about you for a long time.

AUNT LUCY (*Flattered*): Is that so? (*Coquettishly.*) An admirer from afar?

TIMOTHY: Not too far, Aunt Lucy.

AUNT LUCY: You make me very curious. (*To* ABDULLAH.) Rose has some lunch for you in the kitchen, Dooley.

ABDULLAH (*With a slight bow*): Thank you, Miss White. (*He goes off.*)

AUNT LUCY (*She's becoming quite interested*): Won't you sit down, Mr. Bassinger? (*They all sit.*) I don't recall my brother's ever mentioning you. He usually kept his friends to himself. Not that I minded—in most cases. Have you just gotten into town?

SAM: In a manner of speaking. I've lived here before though.

AUNT LUCY: I know just how you feel. One's first day back in New York is so hectic. I hope you'll be with us a long time.

SAM: I may settle here for good.

AUNT LUCY: Oh, fine . . . Did you have lunch on the train?

SAM: Well, no, as a matter of fact—

AUNT LUCY: Then please do stay and have it with Timmy. I've eaten, but I'll join you for a cup of coffee.

SAM: I'd be glad to.

AUNT LUCY: Good. I'll tell Rose to set another place. (*She stops on her way to the door.*) Mr. Bassinger, you may think I'm terribly forward, but have you a place to stay?

SAM (*He nervously scratches the back of his neck with quick, doglike motions of his forearm*): Not yet, Miss White.

AUNT LUCY: In that case I *insist* you be our guest for a few days. Timmy would love to have you—wouldn't you, dear?

TIMOTHY: Oh yes, Aunt Lucy!

AUNT LUCY: There: it's all settled. I'll tell Dooley to get your bags. (ABDULLAH *enters carrying a shining new set of luggage.* AUNT LUCY *is startled.*) Here they are already! Dooley, you read my mind.

ABDULLAH (*With his smile*): Yes, Miss White.

AUNT LUCY: Oh incidentally, Timmy, were you able to find a nice home for your dog?

TIMOTHY: Yes, Aunt Lucy. He's being well provided for.

AUNT LUCY: I'm glad. Now you take Mr. Bassinger up to the guest room. (*She goes off to the kitchen.*)

TIMOTHY (*Whispering*): Where'd you get the suitcases, Dooley?

ABDULLAH: Out of thin air, Master. (*He opens one bag, revealing a treasure of men's clothes.*) Your wardrobe, Mr. Bassinger. (*Takes a bulging wallet from the suitcase and hands it to* SAM.) And your wallet.

(TIMOTHY *and* SAM *gasp in wonder at the latter's new riches.* AB-DULLAH *exits.*)

TIMOTHY (*When he has recovered, as* ABDULLAH *closes the bag*): By the way, Sam, why did you say your name was Bassinger?

SAM: It's all I could think of. My father was a basset hound, and my mother was a springer spaniel.

(*Fade out. Fade in: On* ROSE's *hands cutting up onions on a chop-ping board.*)

ROSE (*Wiping her eyes*): I do hate onions—worst job there is for a cook. Have you ever worked in a kitchen, Dooley?

(*Camera pulls back to reveal* ABDULLAH . . . *see above.*)

ABDULLAH: No, Mistress.

ROSE (*Resumes her onion cutting*): Where did you get this "mistress" from? That isn't a word you call somebody. My name is Rose—Rose Johnson.

ABDULLAH (*Echoing her reflectively*): Rose Johnson . . . The roses of Babylon's Hanging Gardens, that bloomed beside the Sacred River, could not have been more fair.

ROSE (*Giggling*): Man, you sure have a line.

ABDULLAH (*Puzzled*): A line?

ROSE: Yes—the gift of gab: You know what to say to please the ladies.

ABDULLAH: Do I please you, Rose?

ROSE (*Madly embarrassed, chopping furiously*): Oh come on now!—don't make me blush.

ABDULLAH (*Laughing, teasing her*): Blush, Rose. The rose blushes. Let me see you blush.

ROSE (*Squealing*): Now *stop* it! You are the *strangest* man. In nearly two weeks I don't have an idea of where you came from or who you are. What kind of employment did you have before being a chauffeur?

ABDULLAH: Different kinds, Rose. Once I razed the walls of Samarkand, that great city.

ROSE: You mean you were on a demolition outfit?

ABDULLAH (*Roaring with laughter*): Yes, Rose—a demolition outfit. Another time I moved a mountain and rerouted a river.

ROSE: Worked in construction too, eh. I thought so: you don't get a build like that sitting down. (*She puts her knife down.*) Well, that's done finally. (*She rinses her hands and goes to get a towel.*) I'll have time for that crossword puzzle before I tackle the soufflé. Do you like crossword puzzles, Dooley? (*While her back is turned,* ABDULLAH *quietly gets up, makes a few passes over the chopped onions and sits down again. When* ROSE *comes back, there are three whole onions on the board. Close-up of her astonished face.*) Well, what in heaven—!

(*Fade out. Fade in: The living room.* SAM, AUNT LUCY *and* TIMOTHY *are present,* SAM *now well groomed and dressed in a handsome new suit.*)

AUNT LUCY: Now, Mr. Bassinger, I won't hear another word about it. It's been *marvelous* having you here. Timothy and I would be utterly desolate if you should desert us.

TIMOTHY: We really would, Mr. Bassinger.

SAM (*Psychologically as well as physically he has become more human in the interval*): That's very generous of you—I appreciate it. But

I don't feel I can go on taking advantage of your hospitality. It's beginning to bother my conscience.

AUNT LUCY: But it isn't even two weeks yet! Have you always had such a scrupulous conscience?

SAM: No, ma'am. As a matter of fact, it's quite new. For years I just used to lie around loafing, letting people take care of me. But a man's got to do something—doesn't he? He's got to make something out of himself. Otherwise he's just a—well, house pet.

AUNT LUCY: Oh, Mr. Bassinger, I do so admire a man with ambition! But you surely can stay a few more days, at least until you get your business settled. Wasn't there some transaction you were about to complete?

SAM: Yes, ma'am, there is.

AUNT LUCY: Timmy and I would love to hear about it.

SAM: I'm planning to open a pet shop. (TIMOTHY *together with* AUNT LUCY.) A *pet shop*! Oh! A pet shop? Boy! How lovely!

TIMOTHY (*Excitedly*): With all kinds of animals?—birds and cats and dogs and everything?

SAM (*Smiling*): Birds, cats, dogs, and everything.

AUNT LUCY (*To* TIMOTHY): Won't that be exciting, dear?

TIMOTHY (*Ecstatically*): Yes!

SAM: I was going to look at a store this afternoon.

TIMOTHY (*Eagerly*): May I go?—may I go?

SAM: Sure, Timmy, if your aunt will let you.

AUNT LUCY: Of course you can. I'll have Dooley drive you both.

SAM: Let me give the real-estate agent a call. Perhaps we can go right over. (*He goes out of the room.*)

AUNT LUCY: You like Mr. Bassinger, don't you, Timmy?

TIMOTHY: Yes, Aunt Lucy. I always have.

AUNT LUCY: I like him too.

TIMOTHY: He thinks you're *awfully* nice.

AUNT LUCY (*Tentatively*): Timothy, how would you like to have an uncle?

TIMOTHY: An uncle?

AUNT LUCY: Yes, dear. Someone who could take care of you—I mean, the way a man would. A person you could have as a friend too. Would you like that?

TIMOTHY: It all depends on who he is.

AUNT LUCY: I suppose it does at that. . . . Would you call Dooley for me?

TIMOTHY (*Goes into the hall and hollers*): Dooley—Dooley. (*Coming back to his* AUNT.) Who did you have in mind, Aunt Lucy?

AUNT LUCY: Oh, no one in particular. It was just an idea. (DOOLEY *enters, chuckling to himself.*) What's so amusing, Dooley?

ABDULLAH: Chopped onions, Miss White.

AUNT LUCY (*With a puzzled look*): Yes, they *are* hilarious, aren't they? I want you to run Mr. Bassinger and Timmy downtown on an errand. He'll tell you where it is.

ABDULLAH: Yes, Miss White.

ROSE (*Appears from the hall with a folded newspaper and a pencil in her hand*): Does anyone here know the name of—(*Reading.*)—"The Supreme Mohammedan Being"—in five letters. I've almost got this puzzle licked.

(*Close-up of first* TIMOTHY'S, *then* ABDULLAH'S *terror-stricken faces. Cut to:* AUNT LUCY.)

AUNT LUCY: I know that. It's—

TIMOTHY: Aunt Lucy, no—!

AUNT LUCY: Allah.

(*Cut to: The space, now empty, where* ABDULLAH *was standing.*)

ROSE: A-L-L-A-H. That's it, Miss Lucy!

AUNT LUCY (*Looking around*): Where did Dooley disappear to?

(*Barking is heard from the second floor, followed by the patter of feet down the stairs.* SAM THE DOG *runs into the room.*)

TIMOTHY (*Horrified*): Sam—!

AUNT LUCY (*Furiously*): Timothy, you've been concealing that dog!

TIMOTHY: No, Aunt Lucy, I haven't really—

AUNT LUCY: Answer me one question: has or has not Sam been in this apartment at any time during the past two weeks?

TIMOTHY (*Bewildered*): Well, yes—I mean, in a way—

AUNT LUCY (*Sternly*): Then that's all there is to it. Unless he's out—in half an hour—he goes to the dog pound.

(*Fade out.*)

ACT III

Fade in: TIMOTHY's *bedroom. The door bursts open and* TIMOTHY *enters, greatly shaken, carrying* SAM. *He deposits* SAM *on the bed and closes the door behind him.*

TIMOTHY: Don't you worry, Mr. Bassinger. Everything'll turn out all right. Just make yourself comfortable. (*He dashes around the room pulling down the window shades.*) I'm going to recite the Arabic and get Dooley back. He'll make you into a man again. I know how you were enjoying it. (*At the desk, he takes out his father's notebook and opens it to the magic page.*) Here I go! (*He recites the formula in Arabic. Close-up of him. The same darkness, same flute note and burst of light occur as in Act I. A look of shock springs into his face. He speaks anxiously.*) Who are you?

(*The camera focuses on the new arrival,* AKBAR, *a second genie, dressed similarly to* ABDULLAH *in his first appearance except that his earrings are much larger and his clothes of a darker color. Physically, however, he is entirely different: round-shouldered, cadaverously thin, and as tall as a church steeple. A subtle atmosphere of malevolence surrounds him, and when he speaks, it's a voice from the sepulcher.*)

AKBAR (*Prostrating himself in a servile manner*): Akbar the Genie, Master—servant of Tamerlane, servant of Ivan the Terrible, servant of Genghis Khan. (*Ironically.*) May I content you as well as I did them?

TIMOTHY: Where is Abdullah?

AKBAR (*Mocking*): Abdullah the Clown, Abdullah the Simpleton, the child's prankster, who uses his magic for mere amusement—he sits in the Halls of Endless Waiting. Only minutes ago he came there and burst into tears; he will speak to no one.

TIMOTHY (*Sadly*): Poor Dooley. Why didn't he come instead of you?

AKBAR (*Haughtily*): Does Master find the attendant genius of Genghis Kahn unworthy to wait upon him?

TIMOTHY (*Mollifying him*): Please don't get angry at me. I'm sure you're very talented. But I only thought Abdullah might come because he was here before.

AKBAR: Al Hazred made many genies, master. He called us his children. But each one must go in his turn. Any task that the Clown was given I can accomplish as well.

TIMOTHY: You shouldn't call Abdullah a clown. He was a good friend of mine.

AKBAR (*Same servile tone as before*): Your pardon, Master. What wonder may I work for your pleasure?

TIMOTHY (*Suspiciously*): Well—can you turn Mr. Bassinger into a man again?

AKBAR (*Contemptuously*): This dog? Oh, Master, command me not to squander my might on magician's tricks.

TIMOTHY (*Angrily*): You just better do what I tell you!

AKBAR (*Salaaming*): It is mine to obey, Master.

TIMOTHY: Then change him into a man.

AKBAR (*With evil suggestiveness in his voice*): Shall it be into one of the beast men who dwell on the end of the world? Their bodies are human, but their heads are dogs' heads with one great eye in their brow, and they feast their children on human flesh. (*Whispering in* TIMOTHY's *ear.*) Shall he be one of those?

TIMOTHY (*Pulling away. Emphatically*): No! I want him just the way he was.

AKBAR (*Sulking*): At least let me make a warlord, Master: one who will set out to conquer the world.

TIMOTHY: Don't you dare! Make him Mr. Bassinger again.

AKBAR: I know no Bassinger, Master. Was he a little man like a pigmy, or a stately tall man like the Watusi who proudly walks in the African sun?

TIMOTHY: He wasn't either. You better forget the whole thing and go back where you came from.

AKBAR (*Terrified*): No, Master!—do not bid me return to the Empty Halls! I will change your dog (*He picks* SAM *up.*)

TIMOTHY (*Frightened and furious*): You give me back Mr. Bassinger! (*He grabs* SAM *out of the* GENIE's *arms and runs to the other side of his room, calling over his shoulder.*) Allah! Allah! (*Darkness. A sickening wail as* AKBAR *vanishes.* TIMOTHY *looks around. He puts* SAM *down and drops into a chair. Very relieved.*) That was awful! He's gone though, Mr. Bassinger. I'll never use that spell again! Somebody even worse might come. (*Anxiously pondering a moment.*) But I don't know what we're going to do now. Aunt Lucy's probably calling the dog catcher. . . . Maybe that man at the library could help. Do you think so? He knew all about Arabic. (*Getting up.*) Let's go and ask him. . . . (*Fade out. Fade in: The base of the lion statue outside the library. Some of* SAM's *canine friends from Act I are gathered, sunning themselves on the steps.* TIMOTHY, *carrying his father's notebook, arrives with* SAM. *A few of the dogs go over to sniff them.*) I'm sorry you can't come in the library, Mr. Bassinger, but they wouldn't understand. Would you mind waiting here with these people? (SAM *wags his tail.*) I'll be out as soon as I can.

(*He mounts the steps out of the camera's range. Fade to the rare-book room.* MR. DICKINSON *is at his desk busily comparing two huge, archaic manuscripts. The chime is heard.*)

MR. DICKINSON (*Without looking up*): Yes—who is it?

THE GUARD'S VOICE: That Arabian philologist is back, Mr. Dickinson.

MR. DICKINSON (*Looking around*): What Arabian philolo—(*Cut to the* GUARD *with* TIMOTHY *at the door. The inner door is open.* MR. DICKINSON *rises.*) Oh yes, it's my little friend. How are you today, Mr. White?

TIMOTHY: Well, I'm kind of in trouble, I guess.

MR. DICKINSON (*Unlocking the outer door*): That's too bad. Come in and tell me about it. (TIMOTHY *enters and the* GUARD *leaves.*) What sort of trouble might it be?

TIMOTHY: You remember that spell you translated.

MR. DICKINSON: Indeed I do!

TIMOTHY: It worked. (*In breathless haste.*) This genie came—his name was Abdullah—and he turned my dog into a man—Mr. Bassinger. But Rose was doing a crossword puzzle, and my Aunt Lucy said, "Allah," so Abdullah had to vanish and Mr. Bassinger went back into a dog. Well, I said the spell again and a *horrible* person named Akbar, who wanted to change Mr. Bassinger—that is, the dog who was Mr. Bassinger—into a dog-headed man with one eye, but I got rid of him. What I want to know is, can you help me?

MR. DICKINSON (*Not believing him of course, but charmed by his imagination*): Wonderful!—wonderful! I do so envy you your age.

TIMOTHY (*Upset by* MR. DICKINSON's *disbelief*): No, but really, it *happened!*

MR. DICKINSON (*Going along with him*): I'm sure it did. But what can I do?

TIMOTHY: I thought you might know some way to get the first genie back.

MR. DICKINSON: Let's have a look at that spell of yours.

TIMOTHY (*Opening the book*): But we can't use it. Akbar said there were lots of genies waiting to get into the world. I want Abdullah.

MR. DICKINSON (*Gayly, enjoying this game*): Well, why not ask for him by name? Instead of saying "Genie formed of earth and sky," say "Abdullah formed of earth and sky."

TIMOTHY (*Jumping at the idea*): That might work! Would you mind if I conjured him here? I can't take my dog home again.

MR. DICKINSON (*Loving this*): I should be delighted!

TIMOTHY: Now don't be frightened when it gets dark and you hear the flute. If a bad genie comes, I'll say, "Allah," and he'll go away.

MR. DICKINSON: I'll do just what you want me to.

TIMOTHY: Okay. Are you ready?

MR. DICKINSON (*Sturdily*): Ready.

(*Timothy recites the spell. Same business as before.* ABDULLAH, *in his Arabian costume, does come. He's carrying a bundle wrapped in a gorgeous Oriental cloth.*)

TIMOTHY (*Rushing into* ABDULLAH'S *arms*): Dooley!

ABDULLAH (*Dropping down on his knees to* TIMOTHY'S *level*): Little Master Timothy. I thought never to see you again.

TIMOTHY (*Remembering* MR. DICKINSON, *who stands petrified*): Mr. Dickinson, I would like to introduce my friend Abdullah the genie. Dooley, this is the man who told me how to get you back.

ABDULLAH (*Bowing*): My everlasting gratitude for your great wisdom, say'idee.

MR. DICKINSON (*Flabbergasted*): You mean he's actually *real?*

TIMOTHY (*Nonchalantly*): Oh yes—aren't you, Dooley?

(ABDULLAH *smiles his smile and nods.*)

MR. DICKINSON (*His astonishment precipitating into the wildest delight*): How marvelous! A genie—and in the rare-book room!

(*The chime is heard again. Startled, they all look toward the door.*)

TIMOTHY (*Excitedly, when he sees who's on the other side of the glass door*): Dooley, look who it is!

MR. DICKINSON: Is that gentleman a friend of yours?

TIMOTHY: He's my dog. Can he come in too?

MR. DICKINSON (*A little hysterically*): Of course—why not? Everyone can come in. (*He admits* SAM THE MAN.)

TIMOTHY (*Going to* SAM): Hi, Mr. Bassinger! You're back again.

SAM (*In his joy he lifts* TIMOTHY *up above his head and then, instead of putting him down, he sits him on his shoulders*): I certainly am —and very glad to be here. I thought I was going to be Sam for good.

TIMOTHY (*Talking down from his shoulders*): I wouldn't have left you there. Did anyone see you when you got transformed?

SAM: No, I was out in the bushes beside the library when it happened. The guard in the lobby told me where you were.

TIMOTHY: This is Mr. Dickinson. He takes care of rare books.

SAM (*Shaking hands*): How do you do, sir? (*He lifts* TIMOTHY *to the floor.*)

MR. DICKINSON (*Dazed, as before*): Oh, I'm fine.

SAM: Dooley, why are you all dressed up?

ABDULLAH: This is genie's apparel. (*Smiling, he unwraps his bundle.*) But I brought my chauffeur's uniform, too.

TIMOTHY: You better put it on, Dooley. You can't go home like that.

MR. DICKINSON: Would you like to change in the stacks?

ABDULLAH: Thank you, *say'idee.* You are most kind. (*He retires behind one of the stacks of books.*)

MR. DICKINSON (*Twittering with pleasure*): He calls me "say'idee"!

TIMOTHY: Mr. Bassinger, we've got to do something to keep you from turning into a dog again. Suppose it happened in front of Aunt Lucy.

SAM: I'd be very embarrassed.

TIMOTHY: So would Aunt Lucy. She thinks you're a charming man. . . . There must be some way to make you stay human. Mr. Dickinson, do you know how we could?

MR. DICKINSON (*Removing and wiping his glasses. Professorially*): Well, as I understand it, your problem is to put Mr. Bassinger on a more or less permanent basis. Now, since he was changed by one of Al Hazred's genies, the logical place to look would be in Al Hazred's *Cabala.* And as I recall, one of the Latin fragments I read had to do with just such magical metamorphoses. Let me see if I can find it. (*He climbs up the metal staircase to the second level, where he opens one of the cases and takes out a volume.*) Yes, here it is. (*Reading aloud*) "*De magice creatorum natura.*" "On the Nature of Creatures Made by Magic." (*Reading to himself.*) Hm, hm, hm—listen to this! "Such creatures—meaning in this case transformed beings—may be rendered eternally human by gaining the love of mortal women, if they shall marry them."

TIMOTHY (*Interrupting him*): Hurray! That's it, Mr. Bassinger—

MR. DICKINSON: Wait—it goes on: "The same shall be true for Primary Created Magical Beings. They shall be of the condition of men till the Heavens are rolled away as a scroll."

TIMOTHY: What does that mean?

MR. DICKINSON: It means that your genie friend, who is a Primary Created Magical Being, can be human too.

TIMOTHY (*Showing excitedly over the stacks*): Did you hear that, Dooley? You can be a man if you marry somebody.

ABDULLAH (*Astonished, shouting back*): Can I indeed, Master? This information was withheld from us in the Halls of Waiting.

TIMOTHY: Thank you very much, Mr. Dickinson. You've been most helpful.

MR. DICKINSON (*Descending the staircase*): Not at all. Your friends just have to find someone to love them, and then get married.

TIMOTHY: Oh, they have them.

SAM (*This is news to him*): We do?

TIMOTHY: Of course. You can marry Aunt Lucy and Dooley gets Rose.

SAM: Do you think she would?

TIMOTHY (*Blithely*): Sure she will. Just this morning she asked me if I wanted an uncle. (ABDULLAH *comes out from behind the stacks in his chauffeur's uniform. He is carrying his genie's costume.*) Dooley, do you want to be human?

MR. DICKINSON: Think twice, Abdullah. Mr. Bassinger has nothing to lose but his fur, but you—you're an immortal being.

ABDULLAH (*Passionately*): I *do* wish it—I do. The life of a man lasts no longer than the scent of jasmine on the air, but truly, Master, it is sweet nonetheless.

TIMOTHY: Would you like to marry Rose?

ABDULLAH: Yes, Master. The thought of eternity apart from her overwhelmed me when I had to return to the Halls.

TIMOTHY: Okay then. Let's go and ask them.

MR. DICKINSON (*Hesitantly*): Abdullah, would you consider leaving your genie clothes to the library? (*To entice him.*) We have Walt Whitman's overcoat—and Doctor Johnson's smoking jacket.

ABDULLAH (*Handing him his costume*): Gladly, *say'idee.*

MR. DICKINSON: And do come back soon. There are hundreds of questions I want to ask you about Near Eastern mythology.

ABDULLAH (*Bowing*): I shall.

TIMOTHY: Goodbye, Mr. Dickinson—and thank you.

MR. DICKINSON: Goodbye, goodbye. It's been a glorious afternoon. (*Close-up of his enraptured face.*)

(*Fade out. Fade in: The kitchen of* AUNT LUCY'S *apartment.* ROSE *is alone, polishing silverware.* AUNT LUCY, *perplexed by the afternoon's events, comes in through the swinging door.*)

AUNT LUCY: Will someone please tell me what's going on in this apartment. Where's Mr. Bassinger? Where's Dooley? What's *happening!*

ROSE: I don't know, Miss Lucy. I heard Timmy run out about an hour ago. But he was alone, except for Sam.

AUNT LUCY: And *he's* not back either. Oh, I wish I'd never *seen* that dog! (*The front door bell rings.*) I'll get it. (*The camera follows her into the hall, where she opens the front door.*) Well—here you all are at last!

(TIMOTHY, SAM, *and* ABDULLAH *enter.*)

TIMOTHY: Mr. Bassinger has something very important to ask you, Aunt Lucy.

AUNT LUCY: Can't it even wait till we go into the living room?

TIMOTHY: It's about whether you might like to get married to him or not.

AUNT LUCY: *Timothy!*

TIMOTHY (*Casually*): Well, he just sort of thought you might.

AUNT LUCY (*Nonplussed*): Uh, Dooley, will you go into the kitchen and see if Rose needs your help.

TIMOTHY: You know what to do, Dooley.

ABDULLAH: Yes, master. (*He goes into the kitchen.*)

TIMOTHY: Wouldn't you like that, Aunt Lucy? I'd *love* to have him for an uncle.

AUNT LUCY: Perhaps Mr. Bassinger doesn't want to be your uncle. Don't you think he should speak for himself?

TIMOTHY: All right. Tell her, Mr. Bassinger.

SAM: Miss White, I—I—I—well, I mean—

TIMOTHY: There. Is that enough, Aunt Lucy?

AUNT LUCY: I'd hardly call it a proposal of marriage.

SAM: It's true what Timmy says, Miss White. Since I've been a man —(*Catching himself.*)—that is, in my adult life—you're the only woman I've ever become attached to and wanted to marry.

AUNT LUCY: Oh Mr. Bassinger, I'm sure a good-looking man like you has always been *hounded* by attractive females.

SAM: I've been hounded by a couple before, but they weren't the same. You couldn't exactly call them ladies—not like yourself anyway. You just seem to be what I've always dreamed of in a human being.

TIMOTHY: He feels at home around you too, Aunt Lucy.

AUNT LUCY (*Touched*): He does? That's very sweet.

TIMOTHY: Of course you'd have to love him also. Mr. Bassinger can't last without love.

AUNT LUCY (*To* SAM): I didn't realize you were such a romantic creature.

SAM: Oh I am, I am. You might say that love's the condition of my existence.

AUNT LUCY: It is of all human beings, I guess.

TIMOTHY: It's all settled then. You're going to get married to him.

AUNT LUCY: Timothy, I'm not sure. I haven't really thought—

TIMOTHY: Well think, Aunt Lucy. Tell us in half an hour.

AUNT LUCY (*Amused*): I may need a little longer, dear.

TIMOTHY: You can take as much time as you want—as long as you decide to do it.

AUNT LUCY (*Slipping her arm through* SAM'S): You know, I just may at that.

TIMOTHY: Good. Now don't go away. I'll be right back. (*The camera follows him into the kitchen, where* ABDULLAH *is standing tongue-tied before* ROSE.) Did you ask her yet, Dooley?

ABDULLAH: No, Master. It is difficult to speak as a man.

ROSE (*Polishing away*): He's just been standing there staring at me ever since he came in that door.

TIMOTHY: What he wants to tell you is, he loves you.

ROSE: *He does?* Well, why doesn't he say so?

TIMOTHY: You'll have to be patient, Rose, until he learns how—(*He pauses.*)

ROSE: Learns what?

TIMOTHY: How to be more like a natural man.

ROSE (*Her mouth watering*): And *I* get to teach him?

TIMOTHY: If you want to marry him.

ROSE (*Solemnly, as if she were at the altar already*): I *do!*

TIMOTHY: Come on into the living room. (*They join* AUNT LUCY *and* SAM.) Guess what! Dooley proposed to Rose. Isn't that nice? You can have a double wedding.

AUNT LUCY: Rose, I'm so happy for you.

ROSE (*Pointing at* SAM): You and him too?

AUNT LUCY: Timothy won't have it any other way. (*Looking from* TIMOTHY *to* SAM.) And I can't resist them. (*She sits in a chair and draws* TIMOTHY *to her.*) Darling, this is such a wonderful day—I can't bear for you not to be happy too. You can have Sam back. (*Expansively.*) We'll live here all together.

TIMOTHY (*Slyly*): No, Aunt Lucy. Let him stay where he is. Your happiness means more to me than my dog.

AUNT LUCY (*Kissing him*): You dear! (*To* SAM.) Isn't he, Mr.—Why, I don't even know your first name.

SAM (*Hesitantly*): It's—Sam, Lucy.

(*Close-up of* AUNT LUCY. *Her face is puzzled. For an instant she trembles on the brink of doubt, as if there were something she almost suspected. Then, abruptly, she begins to titter, then giggle, then laugh outright.*)

AUNT LUCY (*To* TIMOTHY): You see, Timmy: you lose one Sam and gain another. (*To* SAM.) Excuse us, please. It's just a little private joke that Timmy and I have between us.

(*But* TIMOTHY, SAM, *and* ABDULLAH *have their own little private joke, and are exchanging secret glances as the camera fades out.*)

The Thwarting of
Baron Bolligrew

BY

ROBERT BOLT

*R*OBERT BOLT has stated that of all his plays *The Thwart-ing of Baron Bolligrew* is the one that gives him the greatest pleasure. This is tribute indeed from the author of one of the outstanding dramas of the 1960s, *A Man for All Seasons,* as well as of the screen-plays for three of the most successful films, *Lawrence of Arabia, Doctor Zhivago* and *A Man for All Seasons.*

Born in 1924, Bolt is the son of a shopkeeper who sold furniture, glass and china in an English town near Manchester. Although he recalls no apparent reason for it to be the case, his childhood was unhappy; a poor student, he outwardly rebelled against school and inwardly dreaded the day when he would have to leave to cope in a world that horrified him. Because he always enjoyed English, at least creative expression if not grammar and spelling, he felt that no matter how much his teachers disliked him or how poor his grades, he was a highly intelligent person. Thus, with no other encouragement, he gained admission to the University of Man-chester, where he succeeded in his studies. At the age of eighteen he became a member of the Communist party but quickly realized that this was the serious mistake of a naïve and idealistic youth and left to read on his own the works of various philosophers. These men, Martin Buber, chief among them, influenced his life by im-parting to him an overwhelming appreciation of the importance of individuality in our society, a theme that dominates his plays and films and was especially apparent in his re-creation of Sir Thomas More in *A Man for All Seasons.*

As a teacher, he was called upon to produce the school Nativity play, an experience that so excited and pleased him that he deter-mined playwriting thereafter would be his main endeavor. Twelve radio plays, including several for children, followed. But it was not until the popular run of *Flowering Cherry* at London's Haymarket Theatre in 1957 that he stopped teaching to become a full-time dramatist. His new career was halted almost immediately when he went to prison for nuclear-disarmament activities as a result of his participation in Bertrand Russell's "Committee of a Hundred," which opposed the possession and production of atomic weapons. He regretted that he did not remain in jail for more than two weeks as a symbolic act for a cause he loyally supported.

The production of *A Man for All Seasons* in 1960 guaranteed his reputation as a major playwright of the modern theatre both on the stages of London and New York and in the subsequent award-winning film version. His other plays include *The Tiger and the Horse* (1960); *Gentle Jack* (1963); and the highly praised *Vivat! Vivat Regina!* (1970), a pageant-drama detailing the rivalry between Queen Elizabeth I and Mary, Queen of Scots. Bolt's ability to write great roles for actors is evidenced by the number of Britain's foremost performers who have played them: Sir Ralph Richardson, Paul Scofield, Sir Michael Redgrave, Vanessa Redgrave and Dame Edith Evans.

The Thwarting of Baron Bolligrew, produced by the Royal Shakespeare Company at the Aldwych Theatre in 1965 and repeated in 1966, was directed by Trevor Nunn, with Leo McKern as the Baron and the playwright appearing as the Dragon. It has been called one of the best plays ever written for children, and if their enjoyment in the playhouse were the only measure of its success, it indeed would rate the highest praise. As an entertainment, it contains ingredients certain to please a wide variety of age levels. Who can resist the Knights' presentation of tips of dragon tails in the opening scene? Or the arrival of an asbestos envelope, carried in a pair of tongs, which when opened emits smoke and contains a letter charred at the edges that states the Dragon is hungry? Sir Oblong Fitz Oblong, fat, in need of reassurance, unable to find his glasses when he wants to read, makes a refreshing nonheroic hero. The play's "Brechtian" techniques of antirealism often are inspired, as may be seen, in the effective sailing to the Bolligrew Islands by having the Captain carry "a mast and sail" across the stage, or in the miniature ruins of a church that the Storyteller puts in place in his capacity as stage manager. The play constantly reminds us that the adventure is taking place in a theatre. Audience participation, motivated here as dramatically as it is in *Peter Pan,* establishes essential rapport between the characters and their well-wishers. The spectacle of Professor Moloch's wizardry runs the full flamboyant gamut of stage magic.

—But when reviewed critically, certain reservations are inevitable. The plot is burdened by a superabundance of complications that can become tedious unless cleverly staged and performed. (When professionally presented in the United States, the play has been cut to good effect.) The use of the Storyteller to advance the action seems too easy a dramatic device (although, like the Common Man in *A Man for All Seasons,* he represents one of the very original and likable aspects of the play). Some scenes suffer from verbosity although the dialogue is constantly colorful, if sometimes too vernacular. Anachronisms vary in effect from the amusing arrival of Oblong's purple robes wrapped as a parcel-post package to the unfunny smoking of cigars by the villains, Bolligrew and Blackheart, and the obviousness of employing "The Colonel Bogey March" as the National Anthem of the Bolligrew Islands. Moloch at one point says that the watchword is "Let yourself go!"; frequently, it seems to be that of the play as well. The playwright has allowed himself too much of everything.

But when so few feasts exist among modern dramas for the young, we should be satisfied to find a comedy in which there is more than enough to enjoy. Here it is best to follow Moloch's advice by forgetting about excesses of plot, character and style and to set forth in these adventures to find all the fun that abounds. "Children are marvelous to write for," Bolt has said, and *Baron Bolligrew* shows why this form of theatre justifiably gives him pleasure.

The Thwarting of
Baron Bolligrew

PEOPLE IN THE PLAY

STORYTELLER, *should wear something unique, to set him apart.*

DUKE, *elderly, well-fed aristocrat, well meaning and indolent. Wears civilian garb, fairy-tale period.*

KNIGHTS, *wear armor, except for Juniper, who wears less magnificent civvies than Duke. Surcoats bearing the Royal Strawberry.*

SIR OBLONG FITZ OBLONG, *short, plump, pink innocent face topped by tonsure of white hair; pedantic and almost priggy, wears silver armor.*

CAPTAIN, *heavy proletarian; rough salt.*

JASPER, 15TH BARON BOLLIGREW, *small but burly; red face, black whiskers; choleric and selfish but with the fascination of childish greed. Anachronistically dressed in loud check jacket, bowler hat, breeches, gaiters, carries twelve-bore.*

SQUIRE BLACKHEART, *huge and stupid. Wears black armor topped by enormous black plumes.*

PEASANTS, *barefoot, dressed in ragged clothes of sacking.*

MEN-AT-ARMS, *conventional Medieval costume, surcoats bearing the golden toad of the Bolligrews.*

LORD MAYOR, *timid. Wears slightly less ragged peasant costume, with shoes, and topped by waistcoat and Chain of Office.*

MOLOCH, *snappish intellectual. Wears Academic gown.*

MAGPIE, *lifelike costume of pied feathers. Excitable and amoral.*
MAZEPPA, *identical with Magpie.*
DRAGON, *(voice only) languorous, upper-class, sinister.*

SCENERY, PROPS, MUSIC AND SOUND

No scenery, just drapes and cyclorama; but there should be good props and costumes. The Church is a model and commences with the "ruin," which consists of the foundations and the tower, mounted on runners so that it can be dragged about the stage and able to bear the weight of MAGPIE *in the nest which tops it. It is completed by four or five smaller segments constructed to fit into place.*

Music and sound from speakers in the auditorium are openly artificial and exaggerated.

ACT I

Curtain rises on a stage dark but for a single vertical spot in which stands the STORYTELLER.

STORYTELLER: A long time ago—in the days when dragons were still common—there lived a Duke. And whenever news was brought in of a dragon ravaging some part of the country the Duke sent one of his Knights away in shining armor to deal with it. After a few weeks the Knight would return with the tip of the dragon's tail to prove that he had killed it. Dragons are excessively vain, and when the tips of their tails are cut off they die, of mulligrubs. The return of the Knights would be announced like this: (*Fanfare. Lights up revealing* DUKE *and* KNIGHTS *at round table.*) Sir Digby Vayne-Trumpington!

(*Enter* TRUMPINGTON.)

DUKE: Ah, there you are, Trumpington. Glad to have you back. Got the tip of the dragon's tail? (TRUMPINGTON *places the bright blue tail-tip on table.* DUKE *inspects it.*) Not very big, is it?

TRUMPINGTON: It was not a large dragon, Your Grace, no; but singularly vicious.

1ST KNIGHT: They can be tricky, those little blue beggars.

(*Murmur of agreement.*)

DUKE: Not complaining, Trumpington. We can't all be St. Georges, can we?

(*While* TRUMPINGTON *sits, fanfare.*)

[358]

STORYTELLER: Sir Graceless Strongbody!

(Pause, all looking off expectantly.)

DUKE *(Indulgently)*: Likes to make an entrance, Strongbody . . .
(Pause continuing, less indulgently.) Call him again.

STORYTELLER: Sir Grace——!

(Enter STRONGBODY *dragging huge green tail. Murmur of appreciation and then polite clapping from* KNIGHTS.*)*

DUKE: I must *say*, Graceless! I think we'll have this stuffed, gentlemen. How d'you do it?

STRONGBODY *(Gruffly)*: Oh, usual methods, ye know.

DUKE: Aha—"Deeds not Words," the old Strongbody motto.

(Fanfare.)

STORYTELLER: Sir Percival Smoothely-Smoothe!

(Enter SMOOTHE.*)*

DUKE: Good show, Smoothe; back on time as usual. Find your
dragon? (SMOOTHE *puts down two red tail-tips.*) Good Lord, *two*
dragons!

SMOOTHE: No, Your Grace, one dragon with two tails.

DUKE: Well, I never saw such a thing in my life. Gave you a bit of
trouble I dare say?

SMOOTHE *(Sitting)*: Not really, Your Grace. It seemed to be confused.

DUKE: Ah, modest, modest. I like that, Smoothe, like it. Well now,
who's missing? *(The seat on his left is still vacant.)* Oh, Oblong.
Not like him to be late. Well, we'll just wait for Oblong, gentlemen, and then I have a little announcement to make, yes—

(Fanfare.)

STORYTELLER: Sir Oblong Fitz Oblong!

(Enter OBLONG, *sadly.)*

DUKE: There you are, Oblong, mission accomplished?

OBLONG: Yes, Your Grace.

DUKE: Got the tail?

OBLONG: Yes, Your Grace.

DUKE (*Kindly*): Well, perk up, man. Whatever's the matter?

OBLONG (*Producing tail*): It was a very small dragon, Your Grace. Small and, er pink. I don't think it can have been fully grown. It meant no harm I'm sure. (*Regards small pink tail on table, takes handkerchief from sleeve of armor and blows nose.*)

DUKE: Now, Oblong, we all know how you feel about animals, and I'm sure respect you for it. (*Looks round; murmur of confirmation from* KNIGHTS.) But—Duty First, eh?

OBLONG (*Bracing*): Yes, Your Grace.

DUKE: That's it. (*Patting* OBLONG'S *shoulder as he sits.*) Never knew an Oblong hold back in the face of duty. (*Briskly.*) Now, Juniper, my dear chap, read the next item on the agenda, will you?

JUNIPER: Er, Activities for the coming Season, Your Grace.

DUKE: Exactly! (*Rising.*) Gentlemen, a happy announcement: There *are* no activities for the coming season. These (*points to the tails on the table*) were the last dragons in the Dukedom. Thanks to your untiring efforts over the years our peasantry may now reap their harvests—and pay their taxes—without interference. Our townsfolk can make their profits—and pay their taxes—freely. And in short, there isn't a blessed thing for us to do.

(KNIGHTS *rise and congratulate one another noisily, shaking hands, patting backs, etc. Hubbub dies and all sit.*)

OBLONG: How perfectly splendid, Your Grace.

DUKE: Isn't it, isn't it?

OBLONG: Now we can move on somewhere else.

DUKE (*Faintly*): . . . Er, "move on," Oblong?

OBLONG: Yes, Your Grace.

DUKE: Whatever for?

OBLONG (*Mildly puzzled*): To succor the poor and needy, Your Grace. Up north, for instance—dragons, barons, goblins. Having a very thin time of it up north, the poor and needy.

DUKE: But my dear fellow—the climate!

OBLONG: Well, south, then, Your Grace.

SMOOTHE (*Gently*): May I say something, Your Grace?

DUKE: Smoothe! Yes! please, please.

SMOOTHE: Well, gentlemen, we've put this district into some sort of shape—and it's not been easy as you know. It seems to me we've earned a breather.

DUKE: Earned a breather. Well said, Smoothe. Late lie-in in the morning. Bit of jousting in the afternoon perhaps. Substantial supper; jolly good game of musical bumps and off to bed. (*Appealing all round.*) Where's the harm in that? (*Murmur of considered agreement.*) I'll put it to the vote. Democratic procedure—Can't say fairer than that, Oblong. All those in favor of the program just outlined, please say "Aye."

ALL BUT OBLONG: Aye!

DUKE: Thank you. All those in favor of moving on to wild, wet, baron and dragon infested areas, please say, "Aye."

OBLONG: Er, Aye.

DUKE (*Cheerfully*): Well, there it is, old man. You're outvoted.

OBLONG (*Diffident*): Under the terms of our Charter, Your Grace, I *think* a vote on this subject has to be unanimous. Nobody must disagree.

DUKE (*Weakly*): That right?

JUNIPER: I'm just looking. . . . Yes, here it is, Your Grace, Clause Seven . . . (*Passing Charter to* DUKE.)

DUKE: Well . . . (*Petulant.*) Very ill-judged clause, I would say. Now what?

JUNIPER: If we can't agree, Your Grace, we must refer the matter to the Royal Court.

STRONGBODY (*Gloomily*): And we know what they'll say. . . .

OBLONG: I'm sorry to be the fly in the ointment, gentlemen, but—to succor the poor and needy—dash it all, gentlemen, it's our Knightly Vow! (*At this, all look uncomfortably at the table. The small pink tail twitches slowly in the silence. All look.* OBLONG *distressed.*) Oh dear; Your Grace, would you mind—

DUKE (*Testy*): Yes, yes, take it away if it upsets you: take them *all* away.

OBLONG (*Muttering embarrassed*): 'Scuse me, gentlemen . . . I . . . (*Going, turns apologetic.*) . . . er . . . oh dear. . . . (*Exit* OBLONG *with tails, watched by all.*)

JUNIPER: Well there goes the late lie-in.

STRONGBODY: And the joustin'.

TRUMPINGTON: And the musical bumps.

JUNIPER: And the substantial suppers.

1ST KNIGHT (*Uneasy*): Got a point there, you know, about the Knightly Vow.

DUKE: Yes, yes; capital creature; heart of gold; but . . .

SMOOTHE: But inclined to be dogmatic, Your Grace.

DUKE: Exactly.

SMOOTHE: I think I see a possible solution. (*All raise heads, look to* SMOOTHE.) Supposing Oblong were to leave us. On a mission. A mission to—say—the Bolligrew Islands.

DUKE: The Bolligrew Islands!

1ST KNIGHT: I say, that's a bit steep.

TRUMPINGTON: D'you think he'd go?

JUNIPER: It's worth trying. Your Grace might have him appointed a Royal Knight Errant.

DUKE: And then when he'd gone we could put the matter to the vote again and—er—?

JUNIPER: And nobody would disagree!

DUKE: Unanimous vote, as required by our Charter!

SMOOTHE: Exactly, Your Grace.

DUKE (*Solemnly*): There's no doubt, gentlemen, the Bolligrew Islands *need* a Knight Errant.

JUNIPER: Unquestionably.

DUKE: And Oblong is the obvious choice.

1ST KNIGHT: That's true.

DUKE: I dare say he'll be very happy there. (SMOOTHE *coughs warningly and enter* OBLONG.) Oblong, my dear chap, what would you say to the idea of a mission to the Bolligrew Islands?

OBLONG: I should say it was a very *good* idea, Your Grace! When do we start?

DUKE: Well, we were thinking of a—more of a one-man mission, you know.

OBLONG: Oh . . . Me?

DUKE: Yes. Smoothe here suggested you.

OBLONG (*Sharply*): Very good of you, Smoothe. I'm not going.

DUKE: "Not," Oblong?

OBLONG: No! The Bolligrew Islands! That's where Baron Bolligrew lives—the one that pulled down the church!

DUKE (*Shocked*): Did he really? I didn't know that.

OBLONG: Well, he did. And there's that dragon in the Bolligrew Islands too.

SMOOTHE: A very *poor* specimen, I believe.

OBLONG: It isn't. It's one of those black ones with red eyes.

1ST KNIGHT (*Uncomfortably*): It's a bit steep, you know.

SMOOTHE: Quite right, quite right. We ought not to persuade Sir Oblong. (OBLONG *making for chair is arrested by*) It is a pity, though. I understand that Baron Bolligrew hunts.

OBLONG (*Sharply*): Hunts?

SMOOTHE (*Looking up in mock surprise*): Er, hunts, yes.

OBLONG (*Suspicious*): What does he hunt?

SMOOTHE: Pretty well anything, they say. . . . (*Looking to* DUKE.)

DUKE: Foxes.

SMOOTHE (*Nodding*): Foxes, bears . . .

TRUMPINGTON: Deer . . .

JUNIPER: Badgers . . .

OBLONG: Oh, the villain!

SMOOTHE (*Offhand*): Hares, of course—little, trembling hares . . .

OBLONG: It—really makes one's blood boil!

SMOOTHE: Your Grace, if Sir Oblong *were* going on this mission, I expect His Majesty would make him a Royal Knight Errant, don't you?

DUKE: Couldn't refuse. And then you could wear the purple robe, you know, with the Royal Coat of Arms and so on. I think Oblong would look well in purple, don't you, Juniper?

JUNIPER: I've always thought purple would be just the thing.

OBLONG (*Taken with it*): Really . . . ? I must say . . . Hares and badgers you say?

SMOOTHE: Oh anything.

OBLONG: The perfect brute! Your Grace, I'll go.

DUKE: Excellent conclusion to a good morning's work, gentlemen! How about a little refreshment?

STORYTELLER: Lemonade and ice cream on the South Terrace!

DUKE: Meeting adjourned!

(*Exit* DUKE *and* KNIGHTS, *rolling round table with them. Lights off but for single spot on* STORYTELLER.)

STORYTELLER: So Sir Oblong was appointed a Royal Knight Errant and at length—(*Brown paper parcel thrown on from wings, caught by* STORYTELLER.)—a parcel from the King's Court arrived at the Duke's Castle—(*Opens it.*)—containing Sir Oblong's purple robe. (OBLONG *enters spot, assisted into robe by* STORYTELLER.) Sir Oblong put it on and he found a berth on a ship—(*Enter* CAPTAIN, *carrying* "*mast and sail.*")—which was making the short but dangerous passage to the Bolligrew Islands.

(CAPTAIN *and* OBLONG *traverse the stage; lightning flash and thunderclap, in cover of which exit* STORYTELLER. *Lights up.*)

OBLONG: These are the Bolligrew Islands are they, Captain?

CAPTAIN: Yus. 'Orrible, aren't they? See that ruin up there? That's the church Baron Bolligrew pulled down some years back.

OBLONG: He's a difficult man to get on with, I believe.

CAPTAIN: 'Orrible. That's not the worst of it neither.

OBLONG: No?

CAPTAIN: No. See that 'illside; all black and smoky like?

OBLONG: Oh yes.

CAPTAIN: Dragon.

OBLONG: I beg your pardon?

CAPTAIN: Dragon done it. Breathin' fire like. 'Orrible.

OBLONG: Doesn't Baron Bolligrew do anything about it?

CAPTAIN: Not 'im. 'Untin's all 'e cares about. 'Untin' and grindin' the faces of the poor. Reg'lar terror. You thinkin' of settlin' 'ere?

OBLONG: Er, well, I was, yes . . .

CAPTAIN: Woudn't live 'ere for a million pounds myself. 'Ere we are, 'owever. If you'll just stand on one side, sir. Ava-a-a-ast! *Bel*-a-a-ay! (CAPTAIN *pulls cord, sail furls.*) There you are sir, now you can go ashore and—(*Crash of shotgun off.*) Look out! 'Ere 'e is.

(*Enter* BOLLIGREW *carrying shotgun. Walks deliberately to them. He is accompanied by* BLACKHEART, *who moons stolidly throughout interview, chewing moustache.*)

BOLLIGREW: Missed 'im. You Captain Asquith of the ship Winkle?

CAPTAIN: Yes, me lord.

BOLLIGREW: You brought me new whip?

CAPTAIN: Yes, me lord.

BOLLIGREW: New spurs?

CAPTAIN: Yes, me lord.

BOLLIGREW: New boots?

CAPTAIN: Boots, me lord?

BOLLIGREW: Yes, boots. Me new ridin' boots.

CAPTAIN: They didn't say nothin' about no boots, me lord.

BOLLIGREW: Ho, didn't they?

CAPTAIN: No, me lord.

BOLLIGREW: Well, you go back and get 'em.

CAPTAIN (*Glancing fearfully back at the "voyage" just made*): But, me lord—

BOLLIGREW: Don't argue with *me*, Asquith. Just turn your ship round and get me boots.

CAPTAIN: Yes, me lord. (CAPTAIN *hoists sail and exits to more thunder and lightning, watched by all.*)

BOLLIGREW: Insolent beggar. . . . Who might you be?

OBLONG: Oblong Fitz Oblong.

BOLLIGREW: Gentleman?

OBLONG: Yes?

BOLLIGREW: Me friend, Squire Blackheart.

BLACKHEART: 'D'you do?

OBLONG: How—

BOLLIGREW: Knight Errant, eh?

OBLONG: Yes. (*Modestly.*) A recent appointment.

BOLLIGREW: Knight Errant, Blackheart. (BLACKHEART *grunts, nods gloomily.*) D'you hunt?

OBLONG: Well, as a matter of—

BOLLIGREW: I do.

OBLONG: Yes, I hear you're a keen sportsman, Baron.

BOLLIGREW: Keen sportsman. Right. (*Lugging out enormous gold watch.*) See that? "Presented to the Master of the Bolligrew Hounds"—that's me, of course, "as a mark of admiration and gratitude, by the Chairman of the Hunt Committee." Handsome timepiece, eh?

OBLONG: Lovely. Who is the Chairman of the Hunt Committee?

BOLLIGREW: I am. Solid gold, that watch. Had to evict three or four entire families to pay for it, didn't we, Blackheart?

BLACKHEART: Mm.

BOLLIGREW: Blackheart does all the evictin' work round here. (*Replacing watch.*) Well. Give you a day tomorrow if you like.

OBLONG: Baron Bolligrew, I do not hunt!

(*Short silence.*)

BOLLIGREW: Doesn't hunt, Blackheart. (BLACKHEART *grunts, nods gloomily. To* OBLONG.) Afraid of horses, very likely.
OBLONG (*Stiffly*): Some of my best friends are horses. . . .
BOLLIGREW: Feller's potty, Blackheart.
BLACKHEART: Hey!
BOLLIGREW: What?
BLACKHEART: Magpie.

(BOLLIGREW *raises gun. All follow flight of unseen bird above, then* OBLONG *"accidentally" steps backwards onto* BOLLIGREW'S *foot.* BOLLIGREW *roars and gun roars.* BOLLIGREW *hops, furious, watched apprehensively by* OBLONG. BLACKHEART, *oblivious, continues to watch flight of bird, off.*)

BOLLIGREW (*Eyeing* OBLONG *narrowly*): Did you do that on purpose? He did that on purpose, Blackheart.
BLACKHEART (*Lowering his gaze to* BOLLIGREW): What?
BOLLIGREW: He trod on me toe. (*Still eyeing* OBLONG *narrowly.*) Now, look here, Oblong, if you don't 'unt, what've you come for?
OBLONG (*Searching armor for paper*): I have my instructions somewhere. . . . (*Putting on spectacles.*) . . . It's all pretty run-of-the-mill stuff. (*Clears throat.*) Item: Rebuild Bolligrew Island Church. Item: Restore justice to Bolligrew Island Magistrates Court. Item: Suppress Bolligrew Island Dragon.

(BOLLIGREW *listens with mounting indignation but now laughs.*)

BOLLIGREW: Suppress—? Feller's goin' to suppress the dragon, Blackheart! (BLACKHEART *grins, grin broadens, breaks into guffaws.*) And—and—restore justice to—to the Magistrates Court! (*They hold on to one another helpless. To* OBLONG, *wiping his eyes.*) HERE; here—you like to see the Court in session?
OBLONG: At the earliest opportunity, Baron.
BOLLIGREW: Nothing easier. (*He takes whistle from pocket and blows. Enter ragged* PEASANTRY, *also two* MEN-AT-ARMS *with bench which they put down.*) Ready, Blackheart old man?
BLACKHEART: Ready when you are, my dear feller. (*They sit.*) There you are, Oblong. Court's in session.

(OBLONG *sits.*)

BOLLIGREW: What the blazes do you think you're doing?

OBLONG: I am taking my seat on the Bench, Baron.

BOLLIGREW: And who the blazes gave you a seat on the Bench?

OBLONG: My Royal Commission gives me a seat on the Bench, Baron.

BOLLIGREW: Oh. (*Recovering.*) Well, that's all right. We don't mind, do we, Blackheart?

BLACKHEART: Don't we?

BOLLIGREW: No. Loyal subjects of His Majesty, Blackheart and me, Oblong—hope you'll notice that. Right—First Case!

(MEN-AT-ARMS *seize diminutive* PEASANT.)

MAN-AT-ARMS: *First* case!

PEASANT (*Fearfully*): Here, my lord.

2ND MAN-AT-ARMS: First case present, my lord!

BOLLIGREW: What's the charge?

MAN-AT-ARMS: On the last day of last month, my lord, at about tea time, prisoner was seen to prevent a horse from eating a double row of runner beans in 'is garden.

BOLLIGREW: Oh. But look here, why *should* he let horses eat his runner beans?

MAN-AT-ARMS (*Slightly shocked*): 'Twas your horse, my lord.

BOLLIGREW: Was it! Guilty!

OBLONG: *Not* guilty!

BOLLIGREW: Squire Blackheart, what do you think?

BLACKHEART: Guilty. Definitely.

BOLLIGREW: That's two to one. Seven days' bread and water and—let's see, prisoner, aren't you the one with the strawberry bed?

PEASANT: I 'ave got a few strawberry plants, my lord, yes—

BOLLIGREW: Good—and a fine of three baskets of strawberries. You can deliver them to the Castle—back door, mind—after you've served your sentence. Next case.

MAN-AT-ARMS: Here, my lord.

BOLLIGREW: You?

MAN-AT-ARMS: Yes, my lord.

BOLLIGREW: But that's one of your men, isn't it, Blackheart?

BLACKHEART (*Affixing monocle*): It is. It's my Second Huntsman.

BOLLIGREW: Who's had the blazin' impudence to charge this man?

LORD MAYOR (*Timidly determined*): Er, me, my lord.

BOLLIGREW: You, Lord Mayor? Well, I can only say that I'm surprised.

LORD MAYOR: My lord, if you feel that my bringing the case is in any way disrespectful, of course—

BOLLIGREW (*Holds up a solemn hand*): This is a Court of Law. Case is brought now, Lord Mayor, and must just go forward for an impartial hearing. So let's hear whatever cock-and-bull story you've cooked up.

LORD MAYOR: Well, yesterday morning, my lord, I was in my sweetshop when I saw this fellow coming along the High Street with a number of dogs.

BLACKHEART: Hounds, Lord Mayor. We call 'em hounds.

LORD MAYOR: Hounds. Thank you. (*Clears throat, continues to* BOLLIGREW.) He came into my shop, took down a jar of best quality humbugs and gave them to these hounds . . . !

BLACKHEART (*Brow clearing*): Oh, that's all right, Lord Mayor! Wouldn't do 'em any harm. Hounds like humbugs. Often noticed it myself.

LORD MAYOR (*Querulous*): Very well, Squire; if you can afford to give your hounds best quality humbugs at fourpence a quarter, very well. But my point is this—do you think your man paid for them? He did not. (*Shrill.*) He never does!

BOLLIGREW (*Weakly*): Blackheart, I don't think I can be followin'. Is he suggestin' that your man should *pay* for his humbugs.

BLACKHEART: That's your point, Lord Mayor?

LORD MAYOR: It is, Squire, yes.

BLACKHEART: Seems to be a deuced ugly spirit about, old man.

BOLLIGREW: Well, I—I'm dumbfounded, Blackheart. I leave it to you.

BLACKHEART: Case dismissed.

BOLLIGREW: Yes? Very well, then. Lord Mayor, I personally take the gravest possible view of this incident. But in the light of my colleague's recommendation to mercy and your hitherto excellent record, I will dismiss you with a caution. Next case!

OBLONG: But this is scandalous!

BOLLIGREW (*Nodding, humbly*): You're probably right, Oblong. I tell you frankly, I'm too softhearted to be a good Magistrate. (*Jovial.*) Ah—it's you, Bobblenob. Brought me money?

OBIDIAH: No, my lord . . . (*He kneels.*) Mercy . . .

OBLONG: Will somebody please tell me the circumstances of this case?

BOLLIGREW: Ah yes. The circumstances, my dear chap, are as follows: About ten months ago this man, Obidiah Bobblenob, wilfully and maliciously chucked half a brick through one of my greenhouses—

OBIDIAH: No, my lord! Beg pardon, my lord, but I didn't, really I didn't!

BOLLIGREW: You see the sort of chap he is, Oblong; thoroughly hardened character; refuses to admit it even now. Without the slightest provocation he pitches a brick through my greenhouse. And what did I do? I fined 'im a pound. One miserable pound. I think you'll agree I was lenient.

OBLONG: How do you make your living, Obidiah?

OBIDIAH: I'm an egg-painter by trade, sir. I sells 'ard-boiled eggs in the market, with designs and funny faces painted on them in different colors.

BOLLIGREW: And a very profitable line it is, as I expect you know!

OBLONG: Then did you pay your fine?

OBIDIAH: No sir, I couldn't!

OBLONG: Why not?

BOLLIGREW: It's a funny thing is that. It seems he had his eggs all ready for market, and the night before some hooligan broke into his cottage and smashed 'em up. That's right, isn't it, Bobblenob?

OBIDIAH (*Whispers*): Yes, my lord.

BOLLIGREW: Mm. So you see, Oblong, when the next Court came round he couldn't pay. However, I wasn't disposed to be hard on him—the Bobblenobs have lived on the estate for generations. Pretty little house Bobblenob lives in . . . got a pond in the garden, hasn't it, Bobblenob?

OBIDIAH: Yes, my lord.

BOLLIGREW: Yes . . . (*Briskly.*) So all I did was to add another pound to the fine, and leave it at that. (*He smiles complacently at* OBLONG, *as one expecting approval.*)

OBLONG: So then he owed you *two* pounds.

BOLLIGREW (*Calculating*): Er, one and one—two. Yes, exactly two pounds.

OBLONG: And then what?

BOLLIGREW: Well, Oblong, it's an extraordinary thing but the same thing happened again.

OBLONG: So he couldn't pay the fine again.

BOLLIGREW: Exactly—

OBLONG: So you added another pound—

BOLLIGREW: Making three.

OBLONG: And then it happened again.

BOLLIGREW: You're right, my dear chap; it did!

OBLONG: And it's gone on happening ever since.

BOLLIGREW: My dear Oblong, what a brain you must have!

OBLONG: And who is this mysterious "hooligan" who breaks in and smashes Obidiah's eggs every day before market day, so that he can't pay his fine on Court day?

BOLLIGREW: I've no idea. Have you Bobblenob?

OBIDIAH (*Fractional hesitation*): No, my Lord.

BOLLIGREW: Well now: It's nine so far so, today makes it ten. Nice round number. Ten pounds next Court, Bobblenob. Let's see, there's a market tomorrow morning, isn't there? We'll have a special Court for you that afternoon. And see what you can do at the market, there's a good chap.

OBIDIAH (*Whispers*): Yes, my lord.

BOLLIGREW: That's it. I'm relying on you, Bobblenob to save me from a painful duty. (*Digs* BLACKHEART *in the ribs and laughs.* BLACKHEART *stares at him woodenly.* BOLLIGREW *stops laughing, turns to* OBLONG, *sighs.*) I'm wasted on Black'eart, I really am. Well—Last Case?

MAN-AT-ARMS: *Last* case, my Lord!

BOLLIGREW: Court will rise—! (*He and* BLACKHEART *rise, then* OBLONG.) And you can all clear off. (*Exit hurriedly, all but* BLACKHEART, BOLLIGREW *and* OBLONG, MEN-AT-ARMS *taking bench.* BOLLIGREW *takes a cigar from pocket, lights it. Insolently.*) Got the picture?

OBLONG: I have indeed.

BOLLIGREW (*Nodding sympathetic*): There's nothing *you* can do here, Oblong. Go back where you came from, eh?

OBLONG: Baron, Squire—I wish you good-day. (*Going.*)

BOLLIGREW: Oblong! (OBLONG *turns.* BOLLIGREW *approaches, pointing at him, warningly.*) I've a short way with Knights Errant.

OBLONG: Well, I've a fairly short way with Barons. Good-day.

(*Exit* OBLONG. BOLLIGREW *looks after him thoughtfully. He turns and looks at* BLACKHEART. BLACKHEART *is mindlessly gazing over audience, sucking one end of his moustache.* BOLLIGREW *approaches him.*)

BOLLIGREW: Blackheart. Have a cigar.

BLACKHEART: Mm? Oh, thanks.

BOLLIGREW (*Lighting his cigar*): We shall have trouble with that feller, Blackheart.

BLACKHEART: Little fat feller just now?

BOLLIGREW: That's the one. He, er— (*Takes* BLACKHEART *by the elbow; they patrol front stage, smoking cigars.*) He fancies himself as a bit of a fighter for one thing.

BLACKHEART (*Interested*): Oh?

BOLLIGREW: Mm. Didn't you notice how he kept lookin' at you?

BLACKHEART: No?

BOLLIGREW: Oh.

BLACKHEART (*Anxious*): How was he lookin' at me?

BOLLIGREW: Well, you know, like he thought you were a big bag of wind.

BLACKHEART: What?

BOLLIGREW: Mm, you know—like he thought you were a big feller but not much good in a scrap.

BLACKHEART: He didn't!

BOLLIGREW: He did. I wondered how you could put up with it. "How does Blackheart put up with it?" that's what I kept wonderin'. I mean it's not the thing, is it, for a gentleman to put up with that?

BLACKHEART: I'll flatten 'im! (*Going.*)

BOLLIGREW: Er—Blackheart. (BLACKHEART *turns.* BOLLIGREW *beckons him back.*) There *is* a complication.

BLACKHEART: Oh?

BOLLIGREW: Mm. This feller's a Royal Knight Errant, ye see. Got the purple mantle.

BLACKHEART: *I'm* not afraid of—

BOLLIGREW: No, no, no—of course you're not. But—we could have trouble from the mainland you see. I mean, we don't want a Royal Commission, do we? I mean, we don't want the Islands *swarming* with Knights Errant, poking their long noses into every blazin' thing, do we?

BLACKHEART (*Sobered*): Goo' Lor' no. . . . Better leave 'im alone, eh?

BOLLIGREW: Mmm—don't know about that. You *are* a gentleman.

BLACKHEART (*Laughing*): Well, I should 'ope so!

BOLLIGREW: Yes. Well then, you're entitled to satisfaction. But, just make sure you do it in the proper form.

BLACKHEART: Right. (*Glances off, uneasy; draws close to* BOLLIGREW.)
What *is* the proper form?

BOLLIGREW: Oh. Well. First, you must throw down the gauntlet.

BLACKHEART (*Gazing at it*): Me gauntlet.

BOLLIGREW: That's it. Chuck it down. That's a challenge. Then if
he picks it up—

BLACKHEART: Yes?

BOLLIGREW: You can clobber him.

BLACKHEART: Right.

BOLLIGREW: If he *don't* pick it up—

BLACKHEART: Yes?

BOLLIGREW: Then insult him. And if he *still* won't fight—

BLACKHEART: Yes?

BOLLIGREW: Then you can't touch him.

BLACKHEART: Well, what's the good of that?

BOLLIGREW: Ah. You see, old man, you must do it in front of witnesses. This feller, ye see, has set himself up as the Champion of
the poor and needy. And if 'e won't fight after *that*—

BLACKHEART: Yes?

BOLLIGREW: Well then, his sweaty friends will see what sort of Champion they've got! Won't they?

BLACKHEART (*Grunts*): Yes, but look 'ere, where's me satisfaction?

BOLLIGREW: That, Blackheart, would satisfy any gentleman that ever
breathed.

BLACKHEART: Oh. Right. Let's have it again. That's gauntlet, insult,
sweaty . . . ?

BOLLIGREW (*Looks at him dubiously*): Tell you what. Come up to
the castle and I'll jot it down for you.

BLACKHEART: Oh. Right.

(*As they are going, enter* STORYTELLER, *struggling with Church
ruins.*)

BOLLIGREW: Evening.

STORYTELLER: Good evening, Baron.

BOLLIGREW: What you got there then?

STORYTELLER: The ruins of Bolligrew Church, Baron. We shall need
them for the next scene.

BOLLIGREW: Church ruins, Blackheart. Thought they looked familiar.

STORYTELLER (*Pausing, breathless*): I wonder if the Squire would—?

BLACKHEART: My good man, I'm not a laborer.

BOLLIGREW: Quite right. You got any heavin' and liftin' to do, find a peasant! (*Exit* BLACKHEART *and* BOLLIGREW. STORYTELLER *calls off.*)

STORYTELLER: Sir Oblong! (*Enter* OBLONG.) I wonder if you'd—

OBLONG: Of course. (*They lug the ruins into place.*) Church ruins, eh?

STORYTELLER: Yes, we need them for the next scene.

OBLONG: Mm, pretty. Must have been a pretty little place—I shall enjoy the first part of my mission. (*Anxious.*) However, I shall need assistance. . . .

STORYTELLER: The poor and needy?

OBLONG: Excellent.

STORYTELLER (*Addresses audience*): The poor and needy of the Island, when they heard that he had come to be their champion, flocked in upon the gallant Knight from every side!

(*Enter* PEASANTS, LORD MAYOR. OBLONG *addresses them.*)

OBLONG: Poor and needy, Lord Mayor. I have been sent here by the Duke to help you. Will you help me?

(*Dubious agreement from* PEASANTS.)

PEASANTS: Don't see why not—
         Give it a go—
         'Pends what kind of 'elp 'e wants.

OBLONG: In the first place I want information. Tell me something about Squire Blackheart. (*He notes down their replies.*)

1ST PEASANT: 'E's a 'ard case is the Squire, sir.

2ND PEASANT: You know that black armor of his, sir?

OBLONG: Yes?

2ND PEASANT: Never takes it off, sir.

3RD PEASANT: 'E sleeps in it.

OBLONG (*Noting it all down nodding gravely*): One of those, is he? . . . Now what about the Dragon?

(*On the word "Dragon"* PEASANTS *scatter. Stop. Return.*)

1ST PEASANT: 'Ere. Don't you go near Dragon, now.

2ND PEASANT: Gobble you up like a raspberry, 'e will.

3RD PEASANT: Baron 'isself is afeared of Dragon.

OBLONG: My understanding was that the Baron has some sort of arrangement with the Dragon.

4TH PEASANT: So 'e 'as, sir. Baron 'as this side of the Island for grindin' the faces of the poor, and Dragon 'as that side of the Island for ravagin'. That's the agreement. But I reckon the Baron be afeared of 'e all the same. . . .

OBLONG: Matters here are worse than I had realized. (*Flips shut his notebook.*) Now my first task is to rebuild this church. May I count on your assistance?

1ST PEASANT: Baron isn't goin' to like that, sir.

2ND PEASANT: 'E doan' 'old wi' churches, sir.

3RD PEASANT: I mean, 'e pulled it down; stands to reason 'e doan want it buildin' up again.

OBLONG: If we are to consult the likes and dislikes of the Baron at every turn, we shall accomplish very little. (*Awkward silence.*) Remember—you will be under the protection of the Duke!

5TH PEASANT: Meanin' no disrespect, sir, but Duke's a long way away. We ain't never seen Duke in the Islands, sir.

OBLONG: That is a just observation. . . . (*He considers, mounts ruin, addresses them, Crispin's Day fashion.*) There was a time when the peasants of this island were a byword for their fearlessness and sturdy independence! In time of Peace they followed the plow with straight backs and heads high! (PEASANTS *unconsciously straighten backs.*) In time of War—(PEASANTS *unconsciously fall into martial postures.*)—they pressed as though by instinct even to the thickest of the fray, hard after the great banner of the Bolligrew the Golden Toad, and were a terror to the very cream of foreign chivalry!

PEASANTS (*Carried away*): Hurrah!

OBLONG: These were your fathers! Are you their sons?

PEASANTS: Yes!

OBLONG: Then do we build the church?

PEASANTS: We do!

OBLONG: Then (*pointing dramatically*) building materials!

PEASANTS: Building materials! (PEASANTS *rush off stage enthusiastically.*)

LORD MAYOR: A wonderful gift for words you have.

OBLONG: Oh it's all part of our training, you know. Where do *you* stand in this business?

LORD MAYOR: You understand, Sir Oblong, I'm, er delicately situated.

OBLONG: I do see that.

LORD MAYOR: If there's anything I can do in proper form . . .

OBLONG: I understand.

LORD MAYOR: But I can hardly take part in, well, a popular uprising.

OBLONG: You're delicately situated.

LORD MAYOR: Thank you. Er (*He edges closer to* OBLONG.)—between ourselves, you've put your finger on the nub of the matter with this fellow Blackheart. Between ourselves (*glancing about*)—not really out of the top drawer.

OBLONG: No?

LORD MAYOR: No. For all his moustaches. His father (*glances around again*) his father was an under footman in the late Lord Bolligrew's time.

OBLONG: Really?

LORD MAYOR: I remember him. I went to school with Squire Black-heart so-called. An inveterate bully, Sir Oblong, and backward in his lessons, very backward. . . . (*He breaks off as noise of* PEASANTS *approaches. They enter bearing sections of church: one with wheelbarrow, one with stepladder.*)

1ST PEASANT (*Breathless*): There you are, sir!

2ND PEASANT: Building materials!

OBLONG: Splendid! (*Inspects contents of wheelbarrow.*) Mortar and trowel. Splendid, splendid. (*Takes handles of barrow.*) Now then. For your manhood and your ancient liberties. Forward! (*He steps out rhetorically with barrow, followed by* PEASANTS, *but stops, instantly as: enter* BLACKHEART. *Enter separately,* STORYTELLER, *who watches soberly.*) Good evening, Squire.

BLACKHEART: Tchah! (*He advances deliberately,* PEASANTS *shrinking back, and hurls down his gauntlet.*)

OBLONG: You've dropped your glove.

BLACKHEART: I've thrown down me gauntlet. Any gentleman'd know that.

OBLONG: You want me to fight a duel with you, Squire?

BLACKHEART: Right.

OBLONG: Well, I'm not going to.

BLACKHEART: Then—(an *effort of memory*)—I'm goin' to insult you!

OBLONG: Well, please be quick; I have a lot to do and the light's going.

BLACKHEART (*Studies a grubby scrap of paper*): Oblong, you're a—a, mm . . . (*He has difficulty in reading.* OBLONG *peers at the paper.*)

OBLONG: Varlet.

BLACKHEART: Right! A varlet! And a, mm . . .

OBLONG: Knave.

BLACKHEART: That's it! Knave and varlet! You—you're not a gentleman! Thought of that meself.

OBLONG: The subject seems to obsess you, Squire.

BLACKHEART (*Amazed*): Well, if you won't fight *now*—

OBLONG: No.

BLACKHEART (*Nonplussed, consults paper, brow clears*): Well then, your sweaty friends can see what kind of Champion they've *got!* (*To* 5TH PEASANT.) You.

5TH PEASANT (*Approaching, humbly*): Yes, Squire?

BLACKHEART: Pick up me glove.

5TH PEASANT: Yes, Squire. (*Does so.*)

(*Behind* OBLONG, PEASANTS *lay down sections of church.*)

BLACKHEART (*Going, to* OBLONG): And a very good evening to *you,* Fatty! (*Exit* BLACKHEART.)

OBLONG (*Watching him off*): What a deplorable exhibition! Well now—(*Turns to find* PEASANTS *going.*) What's the matter? Stop! (*Exit* PEASANTS, 5TH PEASANT *passing.*) My good friend—

5TH PEASANT: Sorry, sir. But if you'm afeared to tackle Squire, we'm afeared to 'elp you. And that's the top and bottom of it, sir. (*Exit* 5TH PEASANT.)

OBLONG (*To* LORD MAYOR): I'm not afraid of the Squire!

LORD MAYOR: No. No. Of course not.

OBLONG: But duelling is utterly against my principles.

LORD MAYOR: I agree with you, Sir Oblong, I agree with you. (*But he is backing toward the Exit.*)

OBLONG: Well, the two of us must just do what we can, eh? (*Attempts to lift large segment of church.*) Would you—?

LORD MAYOR: The fact is, sir, I ought to be getting back to the shop. I'm sorry, Sir Oblong, really I am. . . . (*Exit* LORD MAYOR.)

OBLONG: Dash it! (*Defiantly.*) Yes—I am not often intemperate in my language but *dash* it! . . . What shall I do now?

STORYTELLER: I'm afraid I can't tell you.

OBLONG: But you're the Storyteller aren't you?

STORYTELLER: I am the Storyteller, yes.

OBLONG: Well, what happens next in the story?

STORYTELLER: What happens next, Sir Oblong, is that you are left on your own. (*Exit* STORYTELLER.)

OBLONG: Well, that's very inconvenient—! (*Appeals to audience.*) What shall I do . . . ? Perhaps I ought to have fought that fellow Blackheart after all? What do you think? (*Continues ad lib till audience response strong.*) Might do him good to learn a lesson, eh? In my younger days I was national Broadsword Champion you know, and—and Area Champion three years running! (*Growing excited.*) After all, he challenged me, didn't he? Perhaps I ought to find the fellow now? Do a little challenging myself? Ha! (*Draws sword.*) Have at thee for a foul caitiff! Take that—and that—anthat-anthatanthat! (*When response maximum, pulls himself up.*) No. No. (*Sheathes sword.*) Certainly not. I have been sent here to set a good example. You ought to be ashamed of yourselves. Duelling is *wrong*. . . . I must manage somehow by myself. (*Attempts to lift segment of church.*) No . . . Now let's see . . . No . . . You know at this point in the story I do think they might send *some-body* to help me. (*Enter unseen by him* MAGPIE.) However . . . keep trying . . . No.

VOICE FROM AUDIENCE: Behind you!

OBLONG: What? Try a smaller piece? Right. Now, then . . . No . . . I really don't see how I'm going to manage, you know. . . . How about this bit . . . ? (*And so on, till audience response strong. Then turns, sees* MAGPIE.) Oh. Good evening.

MAGPIE: You talk.

OBLONG: Certainly.

MAGPIE: Most human beings only twitter.

OBLONG: Most human beings would say that most birds only twitter.

MAGPIE: Eh?

OBLONG: Mm. As a matter of fact, all human beings talk, among themselves.

MAGPIE: Don't believe it.

OBLONG: Well, that's rather narrow-minded of you. It takes all sorts to make a world, you know.

MAGPIE: My name's Mike Magpie. Your name's Oblong. You saved my life this morning.

OBLONG: Oh, was that you?

MAGPIE: Ark.

OBLONG: He might have missed, you know.

MAGPIE: Not 'im. You saved my life an' you can count on me.

OBLONG: For what?

MAGPIE: Anything! I'm a pretty smart character.

OBLONG: Are you now?

MAGPIE: Oh yes. Brilliant bird—always have been.

OBLONG: Well, the immediate task is to rebuild this church.

MAGPIE: Oh . . . Like, lugging stones about?

OBLONG: Yes?

MAGPIE: Like—work?

OBLONG: Yes, Michael, work.

MAGPIE: Well, look 'ere, Obby, work's not in my line. Anythin' in the thieving line now, or the telling lies line, or the leading up the garden path line—

OBLONG: Did you say "thieving"?

MAGPIE: Yes. You know—pinching things.

OBLONG (*Quietly*): What things?

MAGPIE: Shiny things. They're in my nest. 'D'you like to see?

OBLONG (*Mounting ladder*): Yes, Michael, I should.

MAGPIE: Hey! You're not going to take my shiny things, are you?

OBLONG: Yours, Michael? (*Peering into nest.*) Mm. I am on the whole relieved. Silver paper, bits of glass—but here is a silver tie-pin with a fox head on it which appears to be of some value.

MAGPIE: That's all right; that's Bolligrew's!

OBLONG (*Descending*): It makes not an atom of difference whose it is. Stealing is *wrong*.

MAGPIE: It's no good talking to me about right and wrong, Obby. It's not in my nature.

OBLONG: I know it's difficult for Magpies, Michael, but I want you to try. Imagine the impression it would make in the Islands if it were thought that I associated with a bird—I am sorry to say this —a bird of loose principles.

MAGPIE: Awk.

OBLONG: No more stealing then.

MAGPIE: Aw—(*Noise off.*) Awk! A person!

OBLONG: Hide. (MAGPIE *climbs to nest.* OBLONG *peers off, hand on sword. A light approaches.*) Who's that?

(*Enter* OBIDIAH.)

OBIDIAH: It's me, sir. Bobblenob the egg painter.

OBLONG: Ah, Obidiah. My poor friend, I'm sorry I wasn't able to help you in Court this morning.

OBIDIAH: You did your best, sir, and I thanks you for it. That's what I come to say, sir.

OBLONG: There's no chance of your having the ten pounds by next Court Day, I suppose?

OBIDIAH: How can a poor man like me come by ten pounds, sir?

OBLONG: If I had any money myself I'd give it to you, Obidiah, willingly. But I haven't. We're not allowed to, you know.

OBIDIAH: I know that, sir. I've sometimes thought if Knights Errant were provided with proper funds, sir, they might make more of an impression, sir.

OBLONG: It's not for us to question the regulation, Obidiah.

OBIDIAH: No, sir.

OBLONG: Can't you possibly make some eggs to sell at tomorrow's market?

OBIDIAH: I'd need a power of eggs to make ten pounds. And then again it's fiddlin' work, sir, is egg painting, and I couldn't get 'em finished by tomorrow, sir, if I 'ad 'em.

OBLONG: No, I suppose not.

OBIDIAH: And what if I did, sir, they'd only be smashed up again like the others.

OBLONG: Have you no idea who it is that breaks into your cottage and smashes up your eggs?

OBIDIAH: I *know* who it is, sir. It's Squire Blackheart.

OBLONG: Squire Blackheart! Obidiah, do you know what you are saying?

OBIDIAH: I seen 'im at it, sir, plain as I see you. But what can I do with a great strong gentleman like that? Well, sir, you yourself . . . I mean, you 'esitate don't you?

OBLONG: I hesitate no longer, Obidiah. (*He paces about restlessly.*) I find myself agitated. (*He stops.*) It's Baron Bolligrew who sends him, of course?

OBIDIAH: That's right, sir. 'Tisn't the money he wants, sir. 'Tis my cottage he's after. When he's raised the fine to fifteen pounds or thereabouts 'e'll take the cottage instead.

OBLONG: I see. Or rather, no, I don't see. What on earth does Baron Bolligrew want with a cottage?

OBIDIAH: Well, sir; this pond goes with the cottage—and there's trout in this pond, sir.

OBLONG: Aha!

OBIDIAH: Yes, sir. Baron an' Squire been keen fishermen many a year now. Mine be last trout in the Islands near enough. And finer, happier fish you never did see. I feeds 'em night and morning, sir, same as my father did before me. Friends of the family, they are, in a manner of speakin', sir.

OBLONG (*Looking at him sharply*): You converse with them, Obidiah?

OBIDIAH: Nothing I likes better of an evening, sir, than a quiet chat with the trout.

OBLONG: Then, Obidiah, I wish you to meet a friend of mine. (*Calls.*) Michael! Will you come here, please? A shrewd bird Bobblenob and knows the Island. Michael Magpie; Obidiah Bobblenob.

MAGPIE: Awk.

OBLONG: Michael, you have heard Obidiah's predicament?

MAGPIE: Awk.

OBLONG: What do you make of it?

MAGPIE: Tricky. How many eggs to make ten quid?

OBIDIAH: Two hundred seventy-seven.

OBLONG: And then we should have to paint designs on them, you see, before tomorrow morning's market.

MAGPIE: Oh, *that's* all right—I'm a dab hand with a paint brush.

OBLONG: Really? Mm—it is sad how often talent and deliquency go hand in hand.

MAGPIE: No, the real snag's getting the eggs in the first place. . . .

OBLONG: It is indeed. . . .

MAGPIE (*Suddenly to* OBIDIAH): Hen's eggs?

OBIDIAH: Well, how—?

MAGPIE: Not heron's eggs? Seagull's? Pheasant's? Peewit's?

OBIDIAH: Very tasty, when you can get 'em.

MAGPIE: I can get 'em.

OBIDIAH: Can you?

MAGPIE: Course, I can.

OBIDIAH: Two hundred seventy-seven?

MAGPIE: Easy. Couple each. Can't count, most of 'em.

OBLONG: Michael. There can be no question of *stealing* these eggs from your friends. No, Obidiah, not even for this.

MAGPIE: For this they'll give 'em, Obby.

OBLONG: Will they really?

MAGPIE: If I ask them.

OBLONG: Well, there we are then! Hope, Obidiah! Do you begin to hope?

OBIDIAH: I do, sir!

OBLONG: You fetch your materials; we will collect the eggs. (*To* MAGPIE.) When can we begin?

MAGPIE: As soon as the moon comes up.

OBLONG: Oh. (*Enter* STORYTELLER.) Ah. Would you bring the moon up? (*White moon ascends; bright moonlight.*) Thank you. Now my friends, to work!

(*Exit* OBIDIAH, *left.* OBLONG *and* MAGPIE *right.*)

STORYTELLER: For half that night they walked the island from one nest to another, and everywhere they met with success. Some birds gave their eggs because they knew Mike Magpie, many because they took a fancy to Sir Oblong, most because they detested Baron Bolligrew and wished to see him foiled. Some gave one, some gave two, some as many as half a dozen, and by one o'clock in the morning the collection totalled—

(*Enter* OBIDIAH *with implements,* OBLONG *and* MAGPIE *with basket of eggs.*)

OBLONG: Two hundred and seventy-seven! Michael my dear Magpie, I have no words to express my admiration for your resourcefulness and the high esteem in which you are evidently held by these excellent birds.

MAGPIE: Awk!

OBLONG: Now, Obidiah, we are in your hands. First I suppose we must boil them?

OBIDIAH: It's plain to see you don't know much about egg paintin', sir. First we paints 'em, then we boils 'em; thus preparing the egg itself for consumption and fixin' the colors used in the design. We don't speak of boilin' an egg in the trade, we speaks of fixin' an egg.

OBLONG: How interesting.

OBIDIAH: Yes. I have brought along one of my old books of sample designs.

OBLONG: Very sensible. (OBLONG *and* MAGPIE *look at book.*) Mm. These look rather ambitious, Obidiah.

OBIDIAH: These (*another book*) are simpler designs for the use of apprentices.

OBLONG: Ah. Ah, that's more like it.

MAGPIE: Pooh. (*Takes other book.*)

OBLONG: Well then, let's commence.

(*All in unison sit, take one egg, dip brush, work.*)

STORYTELLER: And so they commenced, each giving of his best according to his own ability. Obidiah Bobblenob produced his usual quota of highly professional eggs, Mike Magpie produced a small number of very ingenious eggs and Sir Oblong a large number of rather elementary eggs, some of which he painted bright blue all over. But when the moon went down and dawn came up, they had done.

(*Moon goes down; light changes, during which* SIR OBLONG *turns basket about, presenting painted side of eggs to audience.*)

OBLONG: Done!

OBIDIAH: And I thanks you all from the bottom of my heart.

MAGPIE: I'm tired.

BADGER: Me too.

OBLONG: I'm a bit fatigued myself. However. Now we must boil—er fix—them, I suppose?

OBIDIAH (*Settling himself comfortably*): One thing we never does in the trade, sir, is pass straight from the paintin' to the fixin'. The hand is unsteady and the brain excited. Many a panful of eggs I've seen split from top to bottom by some unchancy journeyman for lack of forty winks.

OBLONG (*Attracted*): Forty winks? Have we time?

(MAGPIE *already asleep.*)

OBIDIAH: Ample time, sir. Market don't open till ten o'clock. If we takes 'em down to my cottage at nine o'clock say, we take 'em straight from the fixin' to the market and—less chance of runnin' into Squire Blackheart, sir.

OBLONG: That's well thought of. (*Lying down.*) Though I'm bound to admit I shouldn't mind crossing swords with the fellow . . . upon a legitimate occasion. . . . Do you know his father was an under footman? (*But* OBIDIAH, *too, has fallen asleep.* OBLONG *sleeps, hands clasped on tummy.*)

STORYTELLER: Now Squire Blackheart, owing to his habit of sleeping in his armor, slept little and rose early. On this particular morning, disturbed by a loose rivet, he rose particularly early and went for an early morning walk—with his favorite hound.

(*Enter* BLACKHEART, *front stage, preceded by cut-out hound on wheels. Walk almost off, double-takes sharply, letting go of hound, which runs off into wings opposite.* BLACKHEART *tiptoes to the sleepers, inspects them. Sees eggs. Reacts. Looks furtively off, left and right, draws sword, raises it high in the air, flat side down, and is about to smash the eggs.*)

OBLONG (*Still recumbent, opening eye*): Good morning, Squire. (BLACKHEART *checks.* OBLONG *rises.*) What are you doing?

BLACKHEART: What d'you think I'm doin'?

OBLONG: I think you are about to destroy Obidiah's eggs.

BLACKHEART: Right.

OBLONG: Not, I think, for the first time.

BLACKHEART: Right. Out of me way, fatty—(*Pushing* OBLONG.)

OBLONG (*Resisting*): One moment. (*Clasps hand behind back.*) Yesterday, Squire, you permitted yourself to insult me. "Varlet and Knave" I think it was.

BLACKHEART: That's it; varlet and knave. I remember.

OBLONG: Blackheart, it is my considered opinion that you are a commonplace rogue and a disgrace to your profession.

BLACKHEART: *Eh?*

OBLONG: One moment. (*Puts his hand under* BLACKHEART's *nose, snaps finger and thumb.*)

BLACKHEART: A-aaah! (*Takes a terrific swipe, which* OBLONG *nimbly jumps over.*)

OBLONG: Not a bad stroke, Squire. Now—!

(OBLONG *draws sword. They fight.* BLACKHEART's *strokes are lethal but ponderous;* OBLONG *fights lightweight style, great dexterity but no knock-out punch.* STORYTELLER *enters and watches calmly. The whistle of* BLACKHEART'S *blade and the merry clatter of* OBLONG'S *short sword, their gasping breath, are taken up and exaggerated by Speaker.* OBLONG *is borne backwards off stage, followed by* OBIDIAH. MAGPIE *hides behind church with basket as* BLACKHEART *enters.*)

BLACKHEART: The eggs! Where are the blazin' eggs?

(*Enter* OBLONG, *limping but determined.*)

OBLONG: Come along, Squire, we haven't finished. (BLACKHEART *rushes at him. Enter* OBIDIAH *and* MAGPIE *emerges. Avoiding combatants they collide and* MAGPIE *falls.* BLACKHEART *kicks him.* MAGPIE *seizes* BLACKHEART'S *leg and nips ankle with beak.*) Michael, let go! One on to one! That's the rule! Let go immediately! (OBLONG *borne off again.* MAGPIE *and* OBIDIAH *exit, swiftly, tiptoes with basket. Noise of battle ceases on cry from* BLACKHEART. *Enter* OBLONG, *breathless.*) I'm getting, getting past it. . . . One does not realize.
STORYTELLER: Would perhaps (*nodding discreetly to exit opposite*) discretion be the better part of valor?
OBLONG: Run away? (*He seems tempted for a moment.*) No. There's life, life in the old dog yet.

(*Enter* BLACKHEART, *also limping.*)

BLACKHEART: Had enough, have you?
OBLONG: Certainly not. Lay on, and may the best man win!

(*They fight again. Despite their differing styles, they are well matched but it is* OBLONG *who is once again borne off, watched by* STORYTELLER. *Din of battle recedes.* STORYTELLER *walks slowly forward. The noise is now dwindling, goon-fashion, to infinity.*)

STORYTELLER: It is sad but true that when men fight, the fight goes not to the best man but to the best fighter.

(*Lights high. Enter* BOLLIGREW, *in tearing high spirits. Blows whistle.*)

BOLLIGREW: Court! Court's in session! Draw near! (*Enter* MEN-AT-ARMS, PEASANTS, LORD MAYOR, *as before.*) That's the spirit! Ah, there you are, Bobblenob! Good market this mornin'? Trade brisk? (OBIDIAH *smiles sadly.*) Ha ha! Just my little joke, you know. (*Sits.*) Well, now. (*Surprised.*) Where's me colleague?

MAN-AT-ARMS (*Looking off*): Coming now, my lord.

BOLLIGREW (*Calls, cheerfully*): Come on, Blackheart, I'm waitin'! (*Enter* OBLONG, *limping on stick adhesive plaster on forehead.*) Oh, it's you. (*Grins.*) Been in an accident, old man?

OBLONG: You might call it that. (*Sitting.*)

BOLLIGREW (*Sotto*): Challenged you, did he?

OBLONG (*Sotto*): He did challenge me, yes.

BOLLIGREW: Mm. Well, you may think you've had a hiding, but he's let you off pretty lightly—compared to some of the thumpings I've seen him hand out, eh, Corporal?

MAN-AT-ARMS: Yes, my lord; that gentleman 'e 'ad words with at the point-to-point.

BOLLIGREW: Blood all over the paddock. (BOLLIGREW *and* MEN-AT-ARMS *laugh reminiscently. Irritable.*) Wonder where he is?

MAN-AT-ARMS: 'Spect 'e's 'avin' forty winks, sir.

2ND MAN-AT-ARMS: Always likes forty winks after a scrimmage, does the Squire, sir. Makes him sleepy.

BOLLIGREW: Well, I'm not waitin'. Bobblenob, stand forward. Oh, it occurs to me, Oblong, that you and I might disagree on a verdict.

OBLONG: Quite likely.

BOLLIGREW: Well, we don't want poor old Bobblenob held up by the delays of Court, do we?

OBLONG: No.

BOLLIGREW: No. So I'll appoint another Magistrate. Corporal, you're a Magistrate. Siddown. I've been thinkin' about this case, Corporal, and I'm afraid I can't let it go on any longer. What do you think?

MAN-AT-ARMS: If 'e don't pay up today, my lord, I should put 'im inside.

BOLLIGREW: That would be *too* severe. But I'm afraid I shall have to take his cottage, you know.

MAN-AT-ARMS: If 'e don't pay up today, my lord, I should take 'is cottage.

BOLLIGREW: That's settled then. Cheer up, Oblong. Bobblenob's probably *got* the money today! Got the money, Bobblenob?

OBIDIAH: Yes, my lord.

BOLLIGREW: Well, now, look here, this can't go . . . *Eh?* You have?

OBIDIAH: Yes, my lord. Ten pounds; the proceeds of my painted-egg stall this morning.

OBLONG: You seem surprised, Baron?

BOLLIGREW: Surprised? Well, I—well—I—we—er—

OBLONG: We did have a little trouble getting the eggs.

BOLLIGREW (*Staring at him, hypnotized*): The eggs. Yes, you would.

OBLONG: And then of course the mysterious hooligan turned up.

BOLLIGREW: Oh. The 'ooligan . . .

OBLONG: Yes.

BOLLIGREW: You *beat* him?

OBLONG: With some difficulty, but yes, I think I may say I beat him.

BOLLIGREW (*Tears his eyes away from* OBLONG): Well, that's very satisfactory! Congratulations, Bobblenob. Glad your troubles are over. (*Taking the money.*) Court will rise—(BOLLIGREW *and* MAN-AT-ARMS *rise.*)

OBLONG: One moment, Baron!

BOLLIGREW (*Reluctantly*): Court sit. (BOLLIGREW *and* MAN-AT-ARMS *sit.*)

OBLONG: Baron, I think we can at last establish the identity of this hooligan.

BOLLIGREW (*Mopping forehead with handkerchief*): You do?

OBLONG: Yes. He left behind him a piece of tangible evidence. (*He produces the enormous black plume from* BLACKHEART's *helmet.*) Do you know who's it is?

BOLLIGREW (*Shaking head vigorously*): Never seen it before.

MAN-AT-ARMS: That's Squire Black'eart's, my lord.

BOLLIGREW: Idiot!

OBLONG: Well, I knew it was, of course, but I'm glad to have that confirmed by our colleague on the Bench here. People's exhibit One.

BOLLIGREW: Look here, Obby old man, what exactly are you goin' to do with that?

OBLONG: I thought of sending it to the Duke's High Court on the mainland.

BOLLIGREW: High Court, eh?

OBLONG: Yes. No doubt the Squire will explain to them *why* a gentleman in his position should persecute a humble egg painter. (*As one struck.*) Unless, of course . . .

BOLLIGREW: Yes?

OBLONG: Unless we were to deal with the case in our own little Court here.

BOLLIGREW: I knew you were the right sort, Obby! Just—just give me that thing and—you can rebuild the church!

OBLONG: I shall do that in any case. I was thinking now of the second part of my mission: the restoration of justice here.

BOLLIGREW: Anythin' you say old man.

OBLONG: Well, in the first place, I think Blackheart himself should resign from the Bench.

BOLLIGREW: He's resigned.

OBLONG: And then—(*confidential*)—is the Corporal really suitable? I mean, has he really the legal brain?

BOLLIGREW: Complete fool. He's resigned, too. You've resigned, you numbskull. Get off the Bench!

(MAN-AT-ARMS *does so.*)

OBLONG: And now, you see, there are just the two of us again.

BOLLIGREW: And very nice too, Obby. Couldn't be happier. Now let's have that, there's a good chap.

OBLONG: You see, there ought to be a third Magistrate in case, as you very shrewdly pointed out, you and I should disagree.

BOLLIGREW (*Licking his lips*): A third Magistrate?

OBLONG: What about the Lord Mayor? (*He offers the plume, but* BOLLIGREW's *hand checks.*)

BOLLIGREW: The—?

OBLONG: Lord Mayor. (*Withdrawing plume.*) Otherside, you see, I don't think we shall be competent to judge this case.

BOLLIGREW (*Sinister*): Lord Mayor . . . do you *want* to be a Magistrate?

LORD MAYOR (*Nervous giggle*): You see, Sir Oblong, I'm delicately situated.

OBLONG: Baron, persuade him.

BOLLIGREW (*Between his teeth*): Lord Mayor, I would take it as a personal favor if you would accept a seat on the Bench!

LORD MAYOR (*Another giggle*): Sir Oblong, may we take it that this morning you met Squire Blackheart in personal combat, and, er, defeated him?

OBLONG: Soundly, Lord Mayor.

LORD MAYOR: Then, Baron, I am happy to accept your invitation. (*He sits nervously at far end of Bench from* BOLLIGREW. OBLONG *offers plume,* BOLLIGREW *snatches it. Glowers.*)

BOLLIGREW: Court rise! (*He leaps to his feet;* LORD MAYOR *half rises.*)

OBLONG: The case, Baron.

BOLLIGREW: Eh?

OBLONG (*Indicating plume in* BOLLIGREW's *hands*): The case.

BOLLIGREW: Court sit. (BOLLIGREW *sits, heavily.*)

OBLONG: To my mind, gentlemen, those ten pounds belong to Obidiah Bobblenob.

BOLLIGREW (*Stares incredulously, then*): No!

OBLONG: Lord Mayor, what do you think?

BOLLIGREW (*Grimly*): Yes, Lord Mayor, what *do* you think?

(*All heads turn to* LORD MAYOR; PEASANTS *shuffle forward a step; suspense.* LORD MAYOR *licks his lips, grips his knees, avoids* BOLLIGREW's *glaring eye.*)

LORD MAYOR: . . . I agree with Sir Oblong!

OBLONG (*Beaming at him*): Well done, Lord Mayor! Very well done indeed! (*Takes money from* BOLLIGREW's *nerveless hand, gives it to* OBIDIAH.) Case dismissed?

LORD MAYOR (*Delighted with himself*): Case dismissed!

OBLONG: That's two to one, Baron.

BOLLIGREW (*Snarls*): Case dismissed!

(*Triumphal march music and cheering pours from Speaker;* OBLONG *and* LORD MAYOR *rise, cheering* PEASANTS *crowd round.*)

OBLONG: To the Church!

(*He leads the way, circuitously round the stage;* PEASANTS *fall in step behind him. In time to the march, the segments of Church are fitted into place. A bell is placed in tower, at which the cheerful pandemonium on Speaker is augmented by Church bells.* OBLONG *is carried shoulder high and all exit.* OBLONG *bow-*

ing and waving graciously to left and right. BOLLIGREW *is left slumped sullen and motionless on Bench. Off stage celebration dwindles to silence on Speaker. Enter* BLACKHEART, *cautiously; he looks nervously to left and right.* BOLLIGREW *turns head and watches him sourly. His plume is missing, bits of his armor have come loose and flap from him, his sword is broken short and sharply bent.*)

BLACKHEART: Has he gone?

BOLLIGREW: Ha! Me invincible Champion, battling Black'eart!

BLACKHEART: Now, don't take that tone, Bolligrew! (*Limps to Bench and sits with a clatter. Aggrieved.*) Feller's a professional. Don't fight like a gentleman. Jumps about like a grass'opper! Can't get a decent swipe at 'im. Look at me armor—me best suit!

BOLLIGREW (*Roars*): And 'oo paid for it, might I ask? 'Oo signed the whackin' great check for it? (*He rises and soliloquizes, trembling with self-pity.*) Here am I, doing no harm to anybody . . . ! Followin' the innocent pursuits of a retired country gentleman . . . ! Along comes this interferin' little barrel of a chap from the mainland and what do *you* do? You go swaggerin' off like you always do and come back lookin' like a half-opened sardine tin! (*He sits.*) Frankly, Black'eart, I'm disappointed.

BLACKHEART: All right, if you feel so inclined, *you* 'ave a go at 'im. An' I'll lay a five-pun'² note to one of your rotten cigars, you never even touch 'im!

BOLLIGREW: Now, now, Black'eart, it's no good carryin' on like that. We've got to think.

BLACKHEART (*Dubious*): Think?

BOLLIGREW: That's it; because I'll tell you what, Black'eart; this chap's some sort of disguised intellectual.

BLACKHEART: Oh Lor' . . .

BOLLIGREW: Yes, we're in trouble. Because it's no good pretendin' that you and me are brainy blokes, Blackheart. We're not. You especially. . . . (*He rises, he thinks.*) Got it! (*To* STORYTELLER.) You: fetch me Secretary.

STORYTELLER: My lord.

BOLLIGREW: We need help, Blackheart, and I think I know where we can get it. (*Enter* SECRETARY.) Secretary, take a letter. (SECRETARY

² I.e., five-pound.

mimes shorthand while BOLLIGREW *strolls about, dictating.*) To Doctor Beelzebub Moloch, Dean of the Faculty of Magic and Regius Professor of Wickedness, at the University, Oxford. "My dear Moloch, Finding myself in a difficulty, my thoughts turn to the most distinguished living practitioner of the Art of Magic." No, say "the Science of Magic." He'll like that. "The situation is one which I know will engage your disinterested attention, but I need hardly say that expense is no object." No, that's a bit crude. . . . "disinterested attention, but I shall of course expect to defray your expenses." Er, "Perhaps you could spare me a week or two of your valuable time during the next long vac., Yours etc. Bolligrew."

(*Enter* STORYTELLER, *looking grave.*)

STORYTELLER: Baron Bolligrew, there is a letter for *you.*
BOLLIGREW: Oh?
STORYTELLER: It's from the Dragon.

(*All flinch.*)

BLACKHEART (*Rising*): The *Dragon?*
SECRETARY: D-dragon!
BOLLIGREW: How d'you know it's from the Dragon?
STORYTELLER: I know the handwriting, my lord. And—it's in an asbestos envelope.
BOLLIGREW (*Licking his lips*): Well, bring it.

(*Exit* STORYTELLER.)

BLACKHEART (*Uneasy*): Look here, Bolligrew—
BOLLIGREW (*Excited though fearful*): No, wait a bit. This may be very handy. (*Enter* STORYTELLER. *He carries in a pair of tongs a large gray envelope, which smokes slightly.* BOLLIGREW *takes it, gingerly opens it. A magnesium flash and smoke rises from envelope.* BOLLIGREW *blows on his fingers, extracts paper, charred at the edges. The others watch as he reads.*) Ah—ha . . . ! Eh? . . . *What?* (*To* SECRETARY.) You get that letter off to Moloch.
BLACKHEART: What does he say?
BOLLIGREW: He says . . . he's hungry.

ACT II

Stage dark save for STORYTELLER'S *spot.*

STORYTELLER: When Doctor Moloch, the Professor of Magic, received the Baron's letter, he was at first reluctant to leave his luxurious rooms in the heart of an ancient University Town for so remote and uncultivated a spot as the Bolligrew Islands. But then he reflected that it would make a change from his usual routine and that the Baron, after all, was rich and could be made to pay.

(*Lights up. Enter* BOLLIGREW, MOLOCH, BLACKHEART.)

BOLLIGREW: Enjoy your meal, I hope, Doctor?

MOLOCH: Passable. Bolligrew, on the first of the month I must be back on the mainland. I am to address an important meeting of the Merlin Society. Let's get down to business.

BOLLIGREW: Right. Well, first there's this Royal Knight Errant, Oblong.

MOLOCH: Yes. You wish him made away with? Turned into a frog—something of that order?

BOLLIGREW: No! If he disappears altogether we shall have trouble from the mainland; Duke; King, maybe.

MOLOCH: Awkward. And then?

BOLLIGREW: Then there's the Dragon.

MOLOCH: Yes. This is an aspect of your matter which I don't much care for, Bolligrew. Tell me again?

BOLLIGREW: Well, as you know, we 'ave this agreement. I 'ave this side of the island for grindin' the faces of the poor, and Dragon 'as that side of the Island for ravagin'.

MOLOCH: And now he says?

BOLLIGREW: Now 'e says 'e's ravaged it! There's nothin' more to eat there, and he's hungry.

MOLOCH: Hungry. I like it less and less, you know. And in his letter he proposes—?

BOLLIGREW: He proposes that I should let him have half *my* half. Well, I can see as far through a brick wall as the next chap. Thin end of the wedge, that is.

MOLOCH: Mmm . . . You do realize, Bolligrew, that a spell against a Dragon would be expensive?

BOLLIGREW: Oh yes.

MOLOCH: I mean really very expensive.

BOLLIGREW: Bound to be. Not far short of ten quid, I was thinkin'.

MOLOCH (*Amused*): Ten pounds? Twenty-five. Guineas.

BOLLIGREW: . . . All right. Done. (*They shake hands.* MOLOCH *paces away considering.*)

BLACKHEART: Tricky situation, eh?

MOLOCH (*Patronizing smile*): I dare say we shall think of something, Squire. This Oblong—Unselfish? Gentle? High principles? Nice with the kiddies? Kind to animals? In short, a *good* man?

BLACKHEART: Sickenin'. He talks to animals.

MOLOCH: And they understand him?

BOLLIGREW: Seem to.

MOLOCH: Then he's very good. Unless like me he's very bad. Which isn't very likely. Excellent. Dragons like good men.

BLACKHEART: Do they?

MOLOCH: Yes, they have a flavor all of their own. . . . Gentlemen, if the Dragon were to eat Sir Oblong, this would dispose of Sir Oblong—pretty finally—and I don't think we need anticipate any very fevered reaction from the mainland. For a Knight Errant to be eaten is an occupational risk and common enough.

BLACKHEART: Right!

MOLOCH: If Sir Oblong had previously been treated with some reliable dragon poison . . . well, that would dispose of the Dragon, would it not?

BLACKHEART: I must say, Moloch, when you clever fellers put on your thinkin' caps—it's a treat to listen to yer.

MOLOCH: Thank you, Squire. It remains to effect a meeting between the Dragon and our victim.

BOLLIGREW: Yes, it does! 'Cause I tell you, Moloch, if once that beast sets foot in my half of the island—!

MOLOCH: No, no, the victim will go to him. Either you as my client, or I as your consultant, will say, "Oblong, at such an hour on such a day, be off to the Dragon's den," and off he will go.

BLACKHEART: Will he? Why?

MOLOCH: Because, my dear Squire, he will be under a spell; another rather expensive spell I'm afraid, Baron, the ingredients are very

costly, very rare—snake's feet, fish feathers, things of that sort—
shall we say another twenty-five?

BOLLIGREW: Another twent——! That's fifty quid!

MOLOCH: Guineas. Bolligrew, in mine as any other profession, cheap
is cheap—and your Dragon is no fool.

BLACKHEART: Somethin' in that, you know.

BOLLIGREW (*Venomous*): . . . All right. Agreed.

MOLOCH: Very wise. (*To* STORYTELLER.) I shall need a small basket of
apples.

STORYTELLER: I have them here, Doctor. (*Produces them from wings.*)

MOLOCH: These will do nicely. And now I need Sir Oblong.

STORYTELLER (*Gravely*): Yes, Doctor, I know. (*Going, turns.*) Doctor—

MOLOCH: Well?

STORYTELLER: Are you sure you want this?

MOLOCH: You are I think the Storyteller?

STORYTELLER: Yes.

MOLOCH: Then you know what's going to happen in the story?

STORYTELLER: Yes, that's why I—

MOLOCH (*Holds up hand*): You're certain you know what's going to
happen?

STORYTELLER: Quite certain.

MOLOCH: That must give you a pleasant feeling of superiority. However, if you're quite certain you know what will happen, whatever
it is will happen quite certainly.

STORYTELLER: Yes.

MOLOCH (*Shrill*): Then what is the good of asking me if I *want* it to
happen? . . . Like everyone else, so far as I'm able, I'll *do* what I
want.

STORYTELLER: Just so, Doctor.

MOLOCH: Then, Sir Oblong? (*Exit* STORYTELLER.) The path to Hell
is paved with good intentions. It must be very soggy underfoot.
(*Turns briskly and calls.*) Mazeppa!

(*Enter behind the others,* MAZEPPA, *a magpie, carrying box and
books.*)

BLACKHEART: Eh!

BOLLIGREW: Magpie! (*He raises gun. But* MOLOCH *stamps foot and
points an imperious finger; magnesium flash, gun flies from* BOLLI-

GREW's *hand, himself shaking as from electric shock.*) Wh-wh-wh-wa-wa-what the bl-up-lu-blazes—

MOLOCH (*Indifferently*): Mazeppa, my dear, prepare the ground for the mortification of apples while I look up the incantation. (MAZEPPA *takes chalk from box and draws complex cabalistic pattern on floor, while* MOLOCH *consults book.*) You have had a narrow escape, Bolligrew, Mazeppa is my familiar. The bird is priceless and took years to train. Had you shot him I should probably have lost my temper and done something irreversible to you. Yes, here we are. Is all ready, Mazeppa?

MAZEPPA: Ready, Master. (*Hands wand to* MOLOCH, *receiving from him the book from which he reads in a low, croaking monotone, circling round the pattern in which the apple is placed.*) Bumbly-wumbly, peejly-weejly. Weejly-peejly bumbly wumbly, etc. . . .

MOLOCH (*Over* MAZEPPA *and much clearer*):
> That Oblong with his own last breath
> May be the means of Dragon's death,
> Lord of Darkness, hear the plea
> Of Beezlebub Moloch, P.H.D.!

> Rosy apple, healthy fruit
> Of healthy tree with healthy root,
> I call down by magic art
> The unqualified canker of the heart.

> I summon up my utmost might
> And plant in you the invisible blight.
> That he who tastes may wish for more
> Taste sweet and sound, AND HAVE NO CORE!

(*Thin column of smoke rises from apple, as* MOLOCH *applies wand to it.*) Splendid. Clean up, Mazeppa, and make the usual entry in the journal. (*The others come cautiously forward and peer warily at the apple.*) It's quite safe, gentlemen; what you saw was merely the virtue leaving it. *But*—any person who eats so much as one bite of this apple, becomes instant Dragon poison.

BLACKHEART: Well I call that dashed ingenious.

(*Exit* MAZEPPA *with props.*)

MOLOCH: A simple process, Squire, but effective. Our next task is more difficult. In order to bring Oblong in our power, I need from him some dearly prized possession.

BLACKHEART: Oblong's got no prized possessions.

BOLLIGREW: Yes, 'e 'as. That purple mantle!

BLACKHEART (*Touched on the raw evidently*): Ah!

MOLOCK: He prizes it?

BLACKHEART (*Resentful*): 'E prizes it all right. Swaggerin' up an' down the 'Igh Street . . .

BOLLIGREW: Never takes it off!

MOLOCH: We must persuade him to.

BLACKHEART (*Looking off*): 'E's 'ere.

MOLOCH: I must have that mantle.

(*Enter* OBLONG.)

OBLONG: Good evening, Baron.

BOLLIGREW: 'Evening, Oblong! What brings you up here?

OBLONG: I have a serious complaint to make.

BOLLIGREW: Oh? (*Listens attentively to* OBLONG, *motioning* BLACK-HEART *to come behind and clumsily attempt to detach mantle.*)

OBLONG: Obidiah Bobblenob has been placed in the stocks on the village green.

BOLLIGREW: Has he?

OBLONG: He has. And your men-at-arms are pelting him with treacle pies. Hot treacle pies.

BOLLIGREW: Are they now?

OBLONG: They are, as I expect you know— (*Spins, draws sword.*) Blackheart, what are you about?

MOLOCH (*Hastily coming forward, benign, ecclesiastical*): Is it Oblong *Fitz* Oblong?

OBLONG: Er, well, yes.

MOLOCH: Let me take your hand, sir. In these degenerate days, a real Knight Errant of the good old school—a privilege. My name is Innocent, Doctor Innocent, Dean of Divinity and unworthy Professor of Goodness at the University.

OBLONG (*Respectfully*): Oh. A privilege to meet *you* sir.

MOLOCH: Er . . . (*Draws him aside.*) You're having a wonderful effect here, you know.

OBLONG: Things are a little better than they were I suppose.

MOLOCH: Wonderfully better, wonderfully. And you know (*very confidential*) you're beginning to have an effect on our friend here.

OBLONG: Bolligrew?

MOLOCH: I know. But I have been poor Jasper's spiritual adviser many years now—stony ground, Sir Oblong, stony ground—but there's good in the man, oh yes. And *you*, have set it in motion, where I failed.

OBLONG: Well, I should like to think so—

MOLOCH: My son—

BOLLIGREW: Er, yes, Father?

MOLOCH: I want you to go and release that poor fellow from the stocks.

BOLLIGREW: Oh. Er, very well, Father. (*Going.*)

MOLOCH: And humbly beg his pardon.

BOLLIGREW: Eh?

MOLOCH: As an act of repentance. You will feel the better for it, won't he, Sir Oblong? (*Behind* OBLONG's *back nodding vigorously at* BOLLIGREW.)

OBLONG: You will, Bolligrew, honestly.

BOLLIGREW: Oh. Well. If *you* say so, Oblong . . . (*To* BLACKHEART.) Comin' repentin' then? (*Exit with* BLACKHEART.)

OBLONG: I must say that's very gratifying.

MOLOCH: A great gift of yours, this, Sir Oblong. Mightier than the sword I do assure you.

OBLONG: Doctor, you make me ashamed.

MOLOCH: No, no. Yours is a noble calling. Ah, this is the famous purple mantle. A prized possession I imagine.

OBLONG: I must confess it is.

MOLOCH: And rightly so. Dear, dear, it's torn.

OBLONG: It's a hurly-burly sort of life, Doctor.

MOLOCH: Let me repair it. (*Trying to take it.*)

OBLONG: Oh no—(*alarmed*)—really—

MOLOCH (*Desists with a silvery chuckle*): The workman is worthy of his hire. I was at one time Abbot of St. Clare's and there our daily task was the repair and manufacture of—oh church vestments, altar cloths, exquisite work; I often regret those quiet days with the needle. (*Unfastens mantle.*) And you will give much pleasure to a foolish old man in the evening of his days.

OBLONG: But I never—(*falters under* MOLOCH's *gentle gaze*)—never take it off—really . . .

MOLOCH (*Wags a roguish finger*): Never take it off, Sir Oblong? Do I detect a little vanity at work? A last little flicker of worldly pride?

OBLONG (*Relinquishes it*): I shall value it more for your attention.

MOLOCH: Well . . . ! Oh—before I go, sir, let me press you to an apple. I always bring a basket for Jasper. I grow them myself in the college garden. Do tell me what you think. (*Hands* OBLONG *the enchanted apple.* OBLONG *bites.*)

MOLOCH: Good?

OBLONG: It's perfect!

MOLOCH: Well, you if anyone should know perfection—even in an apple.

OBLONG (*Delighted—deprecating*): Oh, Doctor—

MOLOCH: No false modesty I beg. (*Going, turns.*) Let Oblong put his faith in Oblong's goodness, and Oblong is invincible. (*Exit* MOL-OCH. *Enter* STORYTELLER.)

OBLONG: That excellent old man came just in time!

STORYTELLER: Indeed?

OBLONG: Indeed. I was in danger of adopting violent and even underhand methods on this mission.

STORYTELLER: And now?

OBLONG: Now I shall rely on simple goodness.

STORYTELLER: I see. Is that wise?

OBLONG: Wise? It's right! Oh, how much better to have reformed Bolligrew than merely to have conquered him.

STORYTELLER: Have you reformed Bolligrew?

OBLONG: I've made a start. (*Beaming, excited, complacent.*) It seems I have a gift for it.

STORYTELLER: And will you reform—the Dragon?

OBLONG: The Dragon . . . ! I say that *would* be something . . after all I reformed Michael Magpie.

STORYTELLER: Did you now?

OBLONG: Oh yes—he used to be a thief you know—

STORYTELLER: Used to be?

(*Enter* MAGPIE *running. Skids to a halt when he sees them. We see behind his back the twinkling* LORD MAYOR'S *Chain.*)

MAGPIE: Ark!

OBLONG (*Pleased*): Ah—Michael—we were just—(*Notices* MAGPIE'S *awkwardly innocent posture.*) Michael?

MAGPIE: Ark?

OBLONG: What have you got behind your back?

MAGPIE: Behind my back? (*Elaborately searches stage behind him, passing chain from hand to hand to keep it hidden as he turns.*)

OBLONG: Michael!

MAGPIE: Ark . . . (*Shows chain.*)

(STORYTELLER *coughs discreetly, looks dryly at* OBLONG.)

STORYTELLER: *Now*, what will you do? (*Adds quickly.*) Think, Sir Oblong.

OBLONG: Think? What is there to think about? Degenerate bird!

MAGPIE: I'm sorry, Obby. 'E left it in the garden you see, and the sun was shinin' and it twinkled . . .

OBLONG: That was the temptation. Did you resist? You did not. It twinkled, so you took it—and there we have you in a nutshell.

MAGPIE: Ark.

OBLONG: You may well say so. (*Takes chain.*) I am only thankful Dr. Innocent has not witnessed this.

MAGPIE: Ark; Well, if you ask me—there's something very fishy about that old geyser—

OBLONG: So! Not content with telling untruths, with breaking your word, with thieving—you would now plant in my mind contemptible suspicions against a fine old gentleman who was once the Abbot of St. Clare's! (STORYTELLER *makes gesture of helplessness and exits.*) Michael, it pains me to say this because there is something about you, a certain—gaiety . . . high spirits . . . which has won my affection.

MAGPIE (*Bending neck to* OBLONG's *caress. Softly*): Ark . . .

OBLONG (*Sharply removing hand*): But that is superficial! You are an unworthy instrument Michael, and until my mission is accomplished, I may not regard you as my friend. (*Exit* OBLONG.)

MAGPIE (*Stricken*): Ark! Obby—? I won't do it again . . . ! (*Silence. He sniffs.*) Well, *I* don't care. See if I do. (*Hops about stage, jaunty and forlorn, improvising.*)

> Hi diddledidee,
> A Magpie's life for me,
> I pinched the Lord Mayor's Chain . . .
> An I 'spect I'll do it again . . .

I'm happy and I'm free—
A Magpie's life . . . (*Voice tails, unhappily.*)

Oh dash it! Obby? (*He stumps off, saying tearful and aggrieved:*)
It *twinkled* . . . ! I *like* twinkly things . . . ! *I* can't help
it . . . !

(*Exit* MAGPIE. *Before his exit is complete, enter opposite* MA-
ZEPPA, MOLOCH, BLACKHEART, BOLLIGREW. *Lights dim. Their air
is tense, they keep their voices low. Stop. All look to* MOLOCH.)

MOLOCH: Twilight. I can now perform the spell to make one person
subject to another. The screen, Mazeppa.

(MAZEPPA *erects screen and carries box inside, while* MOLOCH
stands tense and listening.)

BOLLIGREW: Er, Moloch—
MOLOCH: Sh—!
BOLLIGREW: What?
MOLOCH: I want to hear an owl cry and a church clock strike the hour.
(*Instantly, distant bell chimes, and an owl shrieks nearby.*) Excel-
lent. Prized possession, Bolligrew. (*Goes toward screen.*)
BOLLIGREW: Moloch, I want to watch this.
MOLOCH: Watch? This is Grimbleboots, probably the most powerful
spell in the civilized world—it is certainly the most secret.
BOLLIGREW: I want to watch.
MOLOCH: Out of the question.
BOLLIGREW: In that case, Moloch, I'll ask you for a little demonstra-
tion?
MOLOCH: Demonstration?
BOLLIGREW: That's it. Pop this in with the other prized possession,
will you? (*Produces* BLACKHEART's *black plume from under jacket,
and gives it to* MOLOCH, *sweetly.*) Just to make sure I'm gettin' me
money's worth, you know.
MOLOCH: Bolligrew, I find you offensive.
BOLLIGREW: Aye, most chaps do.

(MOLOCH *behind screen;* BLACKHEART *turns.*)

BLACKHEART: 'Ave they started?

BOLLIGREW: Just goin' to. (*Together they regard the screen.*)

BLACKHEART (*Wistful*): I envy these brainy blokes, Bolligrew. Must make life deuced interestin'.

(BOLLIGREW *gives an unsympathetic grunt.*)

MOLOCH: *Quiet,* please gentlemen! (*Short pause. Then in the dispassionate manner of surgeons, airplane pilots or other practiced technicians.*) Retort?

MAZEPPA: Retort.

MOLOCH: Burner?

MAZEPPA: Burner.

MOLOCH: Essay. (*Thin column of illuminated pink smoke rises,* MOLOCH *and* MAZEPPA, *overlapping as before.*) Trim-spickle-tickle, trim-spickle-tickle, trim-spickle-tickle, trim-spickle-tickle, trim-spickly-wickly . . . Grimbleboots!

MAZEPPA:—Grimbleboots.

MOLOCH: Portent?

MAZEPPA: Portent.

MOLOCH: Presto!

(*A soft explosion and billowing cloud of blue smoke, brightly lit. Twangings and bashings of cymbals and harps on Speaker.*)

BLACKHEART: Fascinatin'.

BOLLIGREW: Yes. Needs to be, for fifty quid.

MOLOCH: Prognostication?

MAZEPPA: Possible.

MOLOCH: Proceed. (*Accompanied by more effects on Speaker, overlapping.*) Scrambled-shambles, pickled-winkles, frightening-lightning, eevil-weevil, Knight's a nuisance, Knight's a mess; what he has is his alone and won't be Bolligrew's *unless*—

MAZEPPA:—won't be *Bolligrew's unless*—

BLACKHEART (*Nudging* BOLLIGREW): Mentioned you then, old man.

BOLLIGREW: Shut up.

MOLOCH (*Rising excitement*): Shamble's scrambled—

MAZEPPA (*Rising excitement*): Winkle's pickled—

MOLOCH: Lightning frightens—

MAZEPPA: Weevil's evil—

BOTH: By powers of unhappiness!
MAZEPPA (*Cries out*): Misery!
MOLOCH (*Cries out*): Poverty!
MAZEPPA: Woe!
MOLOCH (*Screams*): Precipitation!

(*Frantic twangings and bashings on Speaker, a geyser of sparks, colored balls, magnesium streamers, cloud of smoke.* MOLOCH *emerges with mantle.*)

BLACKHEART: First-class show, Doctor. Never seen anythin' like it! Can I 'ave a squint be'ind the scenes?
MOLOCH: By all means, Squire.

(BLACKHEART *goes behind screen.* MOLOCH *hands mantle and plume to* BOLLIGREW.)

BOLLIGREW: Don't look any different to me, Moloch.
MOLOCH: I should hope not indeed. The prized possession must be returned to its owner. Only if he accepts it is he in your power.
BOLLIGREW: Oh. (*Calls.*) Blackheart!
BLACKHEART (*Emerging*): Terrible smell in there. Yes, old man? Me plume! Where d'you get it?
BOLLIGREW: Oh, feller picked it up somewhere. D'you want it?
BLACKHEART: I should say. (*Jamming it into socket of helmet.*) Felt 'alf naked without me plume.
MOLOCK: He is in our power. Squire—
BLACKHEART: Yes?

MOLOCH: Sit down!

(BLACKHEART *collapses instantly. Startled, then agreeably.*)

BLACKHEART: Like that?
MOLOCH: Get up. (BLACKHEART *levitates.*) Can you dance?
BLACKHEART: Dance? Lor' no—
MOLOCH: Try.

(*Minuet on Speaker;* BLACKHEART *dances.* BOLLIGREW *enchanted.*)

BOLLIGREW: 'Ere—'ere—let me 'ave a go—Black'eart!

(BLACKHEART *stops.*)

BLACKHEART: Yes, old man?

(BOLLIGREW *struggles with the wealth of possibility. A moment of inspiration.*)

BOLLIGREW: Be a teapot!

(BLACKHEART *stands on one leg, one arm cranked forward as the spout, the other crooked behind him as the handle.*)

MOLOCH: Enough, Baron?
BOLLIGREW (*Smile fades*): Not quite, Moloch. Blackheart. (*He points.*) Off to the Dragon's den.
BLACKHEART: Dragon's den, old man?
BOLLIGREW: That's right, old man.
BLACKHEART: Oh. All right. (*Goes clanking off stage, false exit.*)
BOLLIGREW: 'E's goin'!
MOLOCH: Yes, you'd better stop him.
BOLLIGREW: Blackheart!

(BLACKHEART *reenters.*)

BLACKHEART: Yes, old man?
BOLLIGREW: 'Ang on. (*To* MOLOCH, *delighted.*) 'E does it all quite willing, don't 'e?
MOLOCH: Oh, the victim does not know he is a victim. A small refinement of my own. Tell him to remove the prized possession.
BOLLIGREW: Take your plume off.

(BLACKHEART *takes off plume, shudders and "comes to." Magic effect on Speaker.*)

BLACKHEART: Well, if you ask me, Bolligrew, that was in dashed poor taste!

MOLOCH: Mazeppa, take the Squire's plume and burn it. And Mazeppa, kindly make your entry in the journal with more care. The one for this morning is barely legible.

MAZEPPA: Yes, Master. (*Exit* MAZEPPA *with props.*)

MOLOCH: Now let's see where we are: Oblong has eaten the apple—which makes him dragon poison. You have the prized possession—which gives you power to send him *to* the dragon. It remains to enquire of the Dragon when he would like to dine.

BOLLIGREW: Aye. Right.

BLACKHEART: Er. You goin' to the Dragon's den, old man?

BOLLIGREW: That's right, Black'eart, an' you're comin' with me.

BLACKHEART: Oh. When?

BOLLIGREW: Now. (*They turn backs to audience and freeze as lights dim further and* STORYTELLER *enters.*)

STORYTELLER: The Dragon lived in a black and silent valley which had once been green with pasture. His den looked like a railway tunnel without any signals or track. (*Black backdrop descends to cover church, with black archway in it.*) Those who had seen him, by moonlight, knew that he was bigger than four carthorses, and sleek, and black, and shiny. Like all black dragons he seldom came out except at night, because his eyes were weak. And in the day, these eyes were all that could be seen of him. (*Red eyes switched on in blackness of arch.*) And all that could be heard of him was an occasional roar—(DRAGON *roars on Speaker.*) And an occasional complaint; for the Dragon was always discontented, and talked to himself continually.

DRAGON (*On Speaker throughout*): "I'm bored. . . . There's no avoiding it; I'm thoroughly bored. . . ."

BLACKHEART: Look 'ere, Bolligrew. You see, I've just remembered a pressin' engagement.

BOLLIGREW: Well, forget it again. (*He draws the upstage toward the tunnel. Exit* STORYTELLER *simultaneously.*) Hello . . . ? Afternoon . . . ! Anyone at 'ome?

DRAGON: "Do I hear the voice of a human bean?"

(*On Speaker, noise between that of approaching train and cantering horse; eyes growing larger.*)

BOLLIGREW: It's me! Bolligrew!

(*Clatter of hooves, squeal of brakes. Hiss. Smoke curls from tunnel roof.*)

DRAGON: "Oh . . . Bolligrew. . . . Is that Moloch?"

BOLLIGREW: Dragon, we're a bit pressed for time. This proposal of yours for takin' over half of my half of the Island—

DRAGON: —"Yes?"

BOLLIGREW: Seems quite reasonable to me.

DRAGON: "It does? . . . That's odd. . . . Baron, there are no *strings* attached to this, are there?"

BOLLIGREW (*Reels out of* DRAGON's *sight, mopping brow with hand-kerchief. Shakily*): Strings, old chap? Don't know what you mean!

DRAGON: "Moloch. *You* haven't anything up your smelly old sleeve, have you?"

MOLOCH: A reasonable suspicion, Dragon, but the answer happens to be "no." There's something we want you to do.

DRAGON: "That's better. What?"

BOLLIGREW: Well, it's about this feller Oblong. I don't know if you've heard—

DRAGON: "I have heard, yes."

BOLLIGREW: Well, we were wonderin', if he 'appened to come wan-derin' over 'ere, if you might like to, er, well—nosh 'im!

DRAGON: "But, Baron, people *don't* wander over here."

MOLOCH: He will, Dragon, he will. We are using Grimblebook. He will come very quietly—if you wish it, *without* his sword.

DRAGON: "Understand. Is he a good man?"

MOLOCH: All the way through I think. I shall be interested to hear.

DRAGON: "Well. That's worth waiting for."

MOLOCH: Tomorrow then, at three o'clock?

DRAGON: "Tomorrow at three."

BOLLIGREW: There we are then! Goodbye, old chap!

DRAGON: "Goodbye, Baron, goodbye. . . ."

(*Eye lights off. Backcloth flies revealing Church.* MOLOCH, BOL-LIGREW, BLACKHEART *freeze until enter* OBLONG.)

MOLOCH: Ah, there you are, sir. We have been all over the Island looking for you. Here's your mended mantle.

OBLONG: Oh, thank you, Doctor.

MOLOCH: Turn around, sir, and I'll put it on.

(OBLONG *does so, but just before* MOLOCH *can clip it on his back, he moves away and turns.*)

OBLONG: I wonder if I should? You're right, you know—it's only vanity and worldly pride.

(*Consternation among the conspirators.* MOLOCH *recovers.*)

MOLOCH: Come, sir, don't be solemn. I spoke in jest!

OBLONG: Oh. (*An uneasy laugh. Returns, and* MOLOCH *tries again. Again* OBLONG *moves away.*) Many true words spoken in jest, Doctor.

MOLOCH (*Rather severe*): I shall begin to think so. Did Gallahad refuse his suit of snow-white armor?

BOLLIGREW: Yes.

MOLOCH: No. But Oblong will affect to be unworthy of his purple robe. Here's vanity indeed.

OBLONG: Oh. (*The same again. Moves away again.*) As a gesture of humility, you mean.

MOLOCH: Precisely.

(OBLONG *nods, is put into the mantle. Is struck by their sudden tension.*)

OBLONG: Gentlemen?

BOLLIGREW: 'Ow d'you feel?

OBLONG (*Puzzled*): Thank you, Baron, the best of health. . . .

MOLOCH (*Points*): Oblong, sit down.

(OBLONG *sits.*)

BLACKHEART: Stand up.

(OBLONG *obeys.*)

BOLLIGREW: On your knees.

(OBLONG *obeys. They loom over him.*)

BOLLIGREW: Well now, you are going to be my guest at the castle for a day.

OBLONG: Oh, thank you.

BOLLIGREW: Don't mention it. At three o'clock tomorrow you are going to the Dragon's Den.

OBLONG (*Pleasantly*): The Dragon's Den?

MOLOCH: Just a social call, you know.

BOLLIGREW: So leave your sword outside.

OBLONG: My sword? (*Seems to struggle for a moment, then:*) Whatever you say, Baron.

BOLLIGREW: That's it *exactly*—whatever I say. Stand up. Now cut down to the castle, introduce yourself to the butler, an' 'e'll show you straight to your dungeon.

OBLONG: Then I'll say *au revoir.*

BOLLIGREW: You say that.

OBLONG: *Au revoir.* (*Exit* OBLONG. BLACKHEART *and* BOLLIGREW *watch him, off, fascinated.*)

BLACKHEART: 'E 'asn't a clue, 'as 'e?

BOLLIGREW: Not a blazin' clue! (*Turns.*) An' will he go off, just like that, to the Dragon's Den?

MOLOCH: At three o'clock tomorrow, just like that; no power on earth can stop him!

(BOLLIGREW, MOLOCH, BLACKHEART, *exit. Enter* STORYTELLER.)

STORYTELLER: Now, while all this was happening on the Island, back on the mainland the Duke and his Knights in armor—(*Breaks off as enter* KNIGHTS *and* DUKE, *trundling Round Table, crossing others who push off Church. All sit and freeze.*)—The Knights in armor were finding that the program outlined by the Duke, and which they had so much looked forward to, was less enjoyable than they had thought.

DUKE (*Heavily*): Anything on the agenda, Juniper?

JUNIPER: The menu for Your Grace's birthday party; er, meringues, raspberry jelly, pickled shrimps, gingersnaps and lemonade. (*Murmur of boredom and discontent. Snappish.*) If any of you gentlemen can think of something better—!

DUKE: No. No. That will do as well as anything . . . I suppose. (*Looking round.*) Any other business?

TRUMPINGTON: There's a *rumor* going round that there's a dragon—

(*On "Dragon," stir of interest all round.*)—down Little Gidding way.

STRONGBODY: I've seen it, gentlemen. 'T's not a dragon. 'T's a big lizard.

(*All slump again.*)

SMOOTHE: Anyone know anything about this damsel in distress at East Coker?

(*Stir of interest again.*)

1ST KNIGHT: Went over yesterday, gentlemen. No more distressed than I am. (*All slump again.*) Deucedly plain girl she was, too. . . .

JUNIPER: Well (*sighs*) that seems to be all, then. (*Shuts minute book.*) Musical bumps?

DUKE: Might as well. (*Music on Speaker.* KNIGHTS *and* DUKE *tramp gloomily round stage in circle. Each time the music stops* KNIGHTS *careful to allow* DUKE *to seat himself first, then compete among themselves.* DUKE *calls out the losers.*) Trumpington . . . ! Dashwood . . . ! Graceless . . . ! (*Etc. until only* DUKE *and* SMOOTHE *left. Music stops,* SMOOTHE *assists* DUKE *to floor, where he remains, gloomily.*) You're out, Smoothe.

(SMOOTHE *returns to table. Flutter of halfhearted applause from* KNIGHTS.)

DUKE: What's the prize?

SMOOTHE (*Bringing it*): Chocolates, your Grace. (*Returns, sits.* DUKE, *still on floor.*)

DUKE: Don't know how it is, gentlemen. . . . Musical bumps—hasn't got the same excitement, somehow. . . . Nor chocolates.

1ST KNIGHT: Not like it was in Oblong's day.

STRONGBODY: Ah.

TRUMPINGTON: Always plenty goin' on then.

1ST KNIGHT: One thing after another.

JUNIPER: Best man we ever had.

1ST KNIGHT: First class.

SMOOTHE (*Uncomfortable*): Oh, capital.

DUKE (*From floor*): That was a dirty trick you played on Oblong, Smoothe.

SMOOTHE: Well, really!

DUKE: You thought of it.

1ST KNIGHT: Wonder how he's gettin' on there.

STRONGBODY (*Envious*): Up to his neck in it, I bet.

1ST KNIGHT: Deuced if I don't go and see!

TRUMPINGTON: Make a change.

SMOOTHE: —It would.

STRONGBODY: Hanged if I don't come with you!

SMOOTHE: So will I!

TRUMPINGTON:—Me too!

JONES:—And me!

(*Excited babble; all sitting forward.* DUKE *follows all this jealously and now rises.*)

DUKE: Gentlemen! (*Silence.*) An excellent suggestion, but there won't be cabin space for more than two—and *I* have had in mind for some time now to pay a State Visit to the Bolligrew Islands.

1ST KNIGHT (*Sotto*): Well, really . . . !

SMOOTHE (*Smoothly*): I remember Your Grace mentioned that to me the other day.

DUKE (*Surprised*): Did I? Yes, I believe I did. Smoothe, you can come with me.

SMOOTHE: Very civil of you, sir.

DUKE: I think that's all, gentlemen. Meeting adjourned.

1ST KNIGHT: Well, I'll be jiggered.

(*Exit* KNIGHTS *with Round Table.* DUKE *addresses* STORYTELLER.)

DUKE: Would you have my galleon got ready, please?

STORYTELLER: It's ready now, Your Grace.

(*Enter* CAPTAIN *as before, but now his sail is purple.*)

DUKE (*Nervously*): If you could arrange for the weather to be better than it usually is . . . ?

STORYTELLER: It's always the same for *that* voyage, Your Grace.

DUKE: No matter. It's not my way to be deflected from the path of duty by a little wind and rain.

STORYTELLER: No, Your Grace.

(DUKE *"boards" galleon, assisted by* SMOOTHE, *who enters with umbrella, which he opens as thunder and lightning crash and boat moves. Enter opposite,* BOLLIGREW *and* BLACKHEART.)

BOLLIGREW: Well, Black'eart, today's the day—at three o'clock this afternoon our troubles will be ov——(*Thunder and lightning.* DUKE *seasick upstage, presenting posterior,* SMOOTHE *solicitous.*) 'Ello? Must be someone comin'!

(BLACKHEART *scans* DUKE *through telescope.*)

BLACKHEART: Oh yes. Must be somebody important.

BOLLIGREW: Oh?

BLACKHEART: Purple sails.

BOLLIGREW: Purp——? (*Snatches telescope.*) Ber-lazes . . . ! It's the Duke!

BLACKHEART: 'Oo?

BOLLIGREW: The Duke! I'd know that face anywhere.

BLACKHEART: Ah. Duke, eh?

BOLLIGREW: Yes! 'E's comin' to see Oblong!

BLACKHEART (*Nodding sagely*): Very likely.

BOLLIGREW: So 'ow can we feed Oblong to the dragon?

BLACKHEART: Oh. We can't then.

BOLLIGREW: That's right, Blackheart, we can't. And what's Dragon goin' to do if we don't? I'll tell you what 'e's goin' to do, Black-heart—'e's goin' to ravage—indiscriminate! Whackin' great black dragon, ragin' up an' down the 'Igh Street like as not, roarin' for 'is nosh—as promised 'im, Blackheart, by you an' me—'an that's goin' to take a bit of explainin' too, isn't it?

BLACKHEART: Well, what are we goin' to do then?

BOLLIGREW: *I* don't know . . . ! (*Mumbles to himself.*) What are we goin' to do . . . ? (*Roars at audience.*) What are we—goin'—to— (*Breaks off as he sees* STORYTELLER.) 'Ere, you, what do we do?

STORYTELLER: You consult Dr. Moloch.

BOLLIGREW: Moloch!

BLACKHEART: Moloch!

BOLLIGREW (*calls*): Moloch!

(*Enter behind him* MOLOCH.)

MOLOCH: Yes?

BOLLIGREW: Look.

(MOLOCH *scans* DUKE, *as* DUKE, SMOOTHE, CAPTAIN *exit*.)

MOLOCH: Dear, dear. This is an unexpected complication.

BOLLIGREW: Unexpected com——? It's a blazin' disaster!

MOLOCH: On the contrary, a golden opportunity.

BOLLIGREW: You thought of somethin'?

MOLOCH: I have thought of a way whereby we can send Oblong to the Dragon, and send the Duke away well satisfied with matters here. I should not be surprised if he conferred a Knighthood on the Squire, and on yourself, the Order of the Golden Artichoke.

BOLLIGREW
BLACKHEART } (*Advancing, fascinated*): Eh? What? 'Ow?

MOLOCH: You wish a consultation?

BOLLIGREW: 'Ow much?

MOLOCH: My consultation fee is fifteen guineas.

BOLLIGREW: Make it quids.

MOLOCH: Guineas. The Duke will be here in half an hour.

BOLLIGREW: All right—guineas!

MOLOCH: Then listen to my plot. . . . (*They join him, put heads together, conspiratorial, backs to audience.*)

STORYTELLER: It was a very wicked plan which Dr. Moloch outlined— (*They all glance round baleful and suspicious at audience, then huddle again.*) As you shall shortly see.

(*They break up, guffawing.*)

MOLOCH: So, Baron, if I can handle Oblong, can you handle the Duke?

BOLLIGREW: Leave that to me—I know these bigwigs. Corporal!

(*Enter* CORPORAL *running.*)

CORPORAL: Me lord?

BOLLIGREW: Duke's comin'. Turn out the population. Everyone wearin' 'is best clothes, Corporal—don't want no ostentatious poverty, you understand.

CORPORAL: Yes, me lord.

BOLLIGREW: Issue 'em with shoes, an' everyone to 'ave one packet of paper streamers. Right gettit done. Lord Mayor!

(*Exit* CORPORAL, *enter* MAYOR *running.*)

MAYOR: Baron?

BOLLIGREW: Got those flags we 'ad for the Coronation?

MAYOR: Yes, Baron?

BOLLIGREW: Gettem up, Duke's comin'. Cook!

(*Exit* MAYOR, *enter* COOK *running.*)

COOK: My lord?

BOLLIGREW: Duke's comin'. Grade-one banquet, twelve o'clock sharp. Orchestra! (*Exit* COOK, *enter* DRUMMER *and* CYMBALIST *running. Thud and clash.*) Duke's comin'. We'll want the National Anthem an' somethin' jolly. Tune up.

(*Musicians tune noisily, Speaker augmenting, while enter* PEASANTS *carrying shoes, and* CORPORAL.)

CORPORAL: Lef-ri lef-ri lef-ri lef-riiii—'Alt! Siddown. Put yer shoes on. Other foot, stupid!

(*Enter* MAYOR, *backing, calling off.*)

MAYOR: Lower away then! Lower away! Thank you!

(*Strings of colored flags descend.*)

CORPORAL: On yer feet! (PEASANTS *rise,* CORPORAL *salutes.*) Ready me lord!

MOLOCH: Now then. (*Raises hand.*) Oblong, by the power of Grimble-boots, be here.

(*Enter* OBLONG, *followed unobtrusively by* OBIDIAH *and* MAGPIE.)

OBLONG: Good morning, Doctor, Baron. What's all this?

MOLOCH: The Duke has come to see you.

OBLONG: Oh, how kind of His Grace!

MOLOCH: Yes. Sir Oblong, when you *meet* the Duke, you are to . . .

OBLONG: I am to what?

MOLOCH: Disgrace yourself.

OBLONG: Disgrace myself? How?

MOLOCH: Well, there I thought that you might help me. . . .

BOLLIGREW: Pitch a brick through the Lord Mayor's window.

MOLOCH (*Hastily*): No, no. That's wildly out of character. If you did that His Grace might think that you had been bewitched!

OBLONG (*Deprecating chuckle*): Good heavens, that would never do!

MOLOCH: No. Have you ever in *fact* done anything disgraceful?

OBLONG: Oh, yes.

MOLOCH: What?

OBLONG: Er . . .

MOLOCH: You haven't, have you?

OBLONG: I do keep myself on a pretty tight rein, I suppose.

MOLOCH: Aha! I knew you'd have the answer! You have kept yourself on a tight rein now for—what? Fifty years?

OBLONG: Thereabouts.

MOLOCH: High time you let yourself go. Oblong, when you meet the Duke you will simply—let yourself go.

OBLONG: But what shall I do if I let myself go?

MOLOCH: You will do all those things which all those years you have wanted to do and have restrained yourself from doing.

OBLONG (*Roguish chuckle*): Oh dear . . .

MOLOCH: Yes. . . . Off you go then till you're wanted.

(OBLONG *going, checks.*)

OBLONG: Oh. At three o'clock I have an appointment with the Dragon, you know.

MOLOCH: There'll just be nice time. Off with you now. The watchword is: "Let yourself go."

BOLLIGREW ⎤
MOLOCH   ⎬ (*Softly in unison*): Let yourself go.
BLACKHEART ⎦

OBLONG: Well, we *are* going to have an eventful day. (*Exit* OBLONG, *enter* MAN-AT-ARMS.)

MAN-AT-ARMS: Duke's galleon comin' round the 'eadland now, me lord!

BOLLIGREW: Right! Duke's comin'! Everybody-y-y—SMILE!

(*Drum and cymbals strike up. Exit in march step led by* BOLLI-GREW, *all but* OBIDIAH *and* MAGPIE.)

OBIDIAH: What d'you think of that then?

MAGPIE: What do I think? I think—Witchcraft!

(*Boom of cannon and cheering on Speaker.*)

STORYTELLER: The cannon fired, the people cheered, and the Duke's private galleon sailed majestically into the harbor. And then for miles around the loyal people of the Island stood smartly to attention as the band struck up—the National Anthem!

(*"Colonel Bogey" on Speaker.* OBIDIAH *and* STORYTELLER *stand rigid.* MAGPIE *idly scratches himself until called to order by* OBIDIAH, *scandalized. More cheering, then, "The Lincolnshire Poacher" and grand entrance of* PEASANTS, MEN-AT-ARMS, DUKE, BOLLIGREW, BAND, SMOOTHE, BLACKHEART, MOLOCH *and* MAZEPPA. PEASANTS *prodded by* MEN-AT-ARMS, *cheering and throwing paper streamers over* DUKE, *who is enchanted.*)

DUKE: Thank you, good people! Thank you! Thank you! Well, I must say, Bolligrew, I hadn't expected anything like this!

BOLLIGREW: Their own idea, Your Grace. I told them Your Grace wouldn't expect any ceremony, but they would turn out. Of course Your Grace is very popular in the Islands.

DUKE: Well, that's very nice, very nice. I must say, Bolligrew, your people look well cared for.

BOLLIGREW: Now you couldn't 'ave said anythin' which would give me greater pleasure. That's always been my way: anythin' for the people. That's a leaf I took out of Your Grace's book, I don't mind admittin'.

DUKE: Well, I never. Bolligrew, I'm agreeably surprised. I'd been given to understand that you were a, well, rather a *bad* Baron?

BOLLIGREW (*Sadly*): Ah yes. I've 'eard the tales they tell about me on the mainland. That Church for instance, I dare say you've been told it was a ruin?

DUKE: I had, yes. . . .

BOLLIGREW: Well, there it is, there's no stoppin' idle tongues. Blackheart, I wonder where Oblong is?

DUKE: Yes. I take it somewhat amiss, Smoothe, that Oblong isn't here to meet me.

BOLLIGREW: Oh, I think we 'ave to make allowances, Your Grace. At 'is time of life we must expect a little neglect of duty. I know Blackheart here has quite a soft spot for the old reprobate, haven't you?

BLACKHEART: Er. Oh. Yes. Yes, rather. Very fond of 'im, I am in a way. Bit of a bully, of course, but—

DUKE: Oblong? A bully?

BOLLIGREW: Knocks the peasants about somethin' cruel sometimes.

LORD MAYOR (*Pushing forward, timidly desperate*): Your Grace!

BOLLIGREW: Yes, Lord Mayor? (*Two huge* MEN-AT-ARMS *close in on* LORD MAYOR.) Got somethin' to say?

LORD MAYOR: . . . No, my lord.

BOLLIGREW: Oh, sorry. Thought you 'ad, Lord Mayor. Your Grace, just recently appointed 'im a Magistrate. (*Rueful.*) Independent-minded little beggar. But I like the people to take part in their own government.

DUKE: Most commendable. But, Oblong—?

BOLLIGREW: He's been goin' to seed pretty rapid since he landed, I'm afraid. If it isn't wine-gums it's brandy-snaps. And it takes 'im very nasty.

DUKE: Smoothe! Do you hear this?

SMOOTHE: Yes, Your Grace. As Your Grace may remember, I always had my reservations about Oblong.

DUKE: You did, yes, you did.

BOLLIGREW: A good man in 'is day, I believe?

DUKE: The best I ever had!

BOLLIGREW (*Nodding*): My friend Dr. Innocent 'ere—'e's a very penetratin' observer of the 'uman scene—he tells me when you're like that, you know, keepin' yourself on a very tight rein, then you're likely to go downhill very rapid if once you *let yourself go.* (*Looks off as he says this phrase. Cheerful.*) And 'ere 'e is! (*Expression changes.*) Oh dear, oh dear . . .

(*Enter* OBLONG, *swaggering, carrying packet of sweets. All, flinch, amazed.*)

OBLONG: So! You finally got here! You backsliding old gormandizer.

(*Consternation among all.*)

BOLLIGREW: 'E's on the wine-gums again.
MAGPIE (*Amazed*): Ark!
OBLONG: Mike Magpie. How you doin', Mike? The only creature on these Islands I would care to call my friend. (*Takes sweet from the packet.*)
BOLLIGREW: The bird is a notorious thief, Your Grace.

(*Exclamation from* SMOOTHE.)

OBLONG: Mike, meet Smoothely-Smoothe. Slippery Smoothe we used to call him. Interesting man. Give you a sound opinion on anything under the sun and sell you his mother for threepence. (*Swaggers on to* DUKE.) Well, we've put it on a bit, haven't we? (*Chuckles, prodding* DUKE'S *stomach.*) How many chocolate éclairs have gone into that, I wonder? Whoops-a-daisy!

(*The* DUKE *is rocking, pop-eyed, on his heels as* OBLONG *prods. Total consternation among all.*)

SMOOTHE: But this is scandalous! (*Turns.*) The National Anthem! Play the National Anthem!

(*"Colonel Bogey" again. All rigidly to attention, eyes popping as* OBLONG *breaks gradually into a disgraceful can-can, presenting posterior to* DUKE, *etc. Anthem stops,* OBLONG, *very excited, breathless.*)

OBLONG: Ha! (*Snaps his fingers at* DUKE. *Gathers himself. Daring.*) Knickers!

(*All clap hands over ears.* OBLONG *laughs wildly. Exit* OBLONG. *All babble.* DUKE *falls fainting into arms of* SMOOTHE.)

SMOOTHE: His Grace! His Grace is unwell!

BOLLIGREW: Clear the field! Clear the field!

> (*Exit* PEASANTS *driven by* MEN-AT-ARMS. MAGPIE *and* OBIDIAH, *"hide," behind Church.* SMOOTHE *has lowered* DUKE *to ground.* MOLOCH *waving ginger-beer bottle under* DUKE'S *nose.*)

MOLOCH: His Grace revives.

DUKE (*Weakly*): Has he gone?

SMOOTHE: Yes, Your Grace.

DUKE (*Seizing* BOLLIGREW'S *wrist*): Oh, Bolligrew, this is the ruin of a noble spirit. Oblong! There never was one like him with a dragon!

BOLLIGREW: Alas, those days 'ave gone.

MOLOCH: Gone indeed. Oblong and our Dragon are on very friendly terms.

DUKE: Friendly—! Smoothe! Can I credit this?

SMOOTHE: It's my experience, Your Grace, that when a man fails in respect, then we may look to him to fail in anything.

DUKE: That's very sound, Smoothe. (*Scrambles up.*) And (*feeling his paunch*) failed in his respect he most emphatically has! But . . . *Oblong?*

BOLLIGREW: Goes over every afternoon to Dragon's den, Your Grace. See it for yourself if you wish.

DUKE: The Dragon's den? What for?

MOLOCH: A purely social call so far as one can see.

BOLLIGREW: I sometimes wonder if 'e 'asn't some arrangement with the brute.

MOLOCH: Oh no.

BOLLIGREW: What other explanation is there?

BLACKHEART: Always leaves 'is sword outside.

MOLOCH: That's true, that's true.

DUKE: Gentlemen! You can *show* me this?

BOLLIGREW: This very afternoon, Your Grace. I thought we'd 'ave a bite of lunch first: couple of roast oxen, three or four stuffed peacocks, nothin' elaborate.

DUKE: Chestnut stuffing?

BOLLIGREW: Yes, Your Grace.

DUKE: Then, gentlemen, to lunch and after that—Oh Oblong! Oblong!—To the Dragon's den! (*Exit* DUKE, *followed by* SMOOTHE,

BLACKHEART, BOLLIGREW. MOLOCH *cautiously watches them away,*
turns suddenly.)

MOLOCH: Now, Mazeppa, as you see, we approach the climax.

MAZEPPA: Yes, master.

MOLOCH: I'd be inclined to take a boat at once—

MAZEPPA: Master?

MOLOCH: But I haven't yet secured my fee from Bolligrew. Now
listen carefully, my dear; go straight down to the harbor, hire a
boat, and have it standing by. It's always possible that something
may miscarry.

MAZEPPA: Yes, master.

MOLOCH: Wait here. I'll bring our bags. (*Going.*) I packed them this
morning. (*Exit* MOLOCH, MAZEPPA *standing front stage, looking*
over audience in attitude of waiting. MAGPIE *and* OBIDIAH *emerge*
from behind Church.)

MAGPIE: What'd I tell you?

BADGER: Witchcraft?

OBIDIAH: Witchcraft.

(MAZEPPA *turns.* OBIDIAH *hides again.* MAZEPPA *and* MAGPIE *con-*
front one another. MAGPIE *has one hand behind back.*)

MAGPIE: Awk!

MAZEPPA: Awk.

MAGPIE: You're not from these parts, are you?

MAZEPPA: Me? From the Islands? (*Loftily.*) I'm from Oxford.

MAGPIE: Go on? You attached to the University, then?

MAZEPPA: Rather depends what you mean. I am personal assistant to
Dr. Moloch.

MAGPIE (*Admiring*): Moloch the Magician? You must 'ave quite a
head-piece on you.

MAZEPPA: I was chosen from a large number of applicants. Yes, I keep
our Journal.

MAGPIE: Journal?

MAZEPPA: Journal, yes. A record of all our spells. I often think I
could do better without Moloch than Moloch could without me.

MAGPIE: You keep a record of all your spells?

MAZEPPA: Yes.

MAGPIE: You keep it up to date, do you?

MAZEPPA: Oh, yes. Quite up to date.

MAGPIE: Is that Moloch coming now? (*Looking off.* MAZEPPA *looks to see.* MAGPIE *produces monstrous club from behind back, and deals* MAZEPPA *a great blow.*)

MAZEPPA: Awk! (*Falls into* MAGPIE'S *arms.* OBIDIAH *emerges from Church.*)

OBIDIAH: Eh, Mike, whatever are you doing—?

MAGPIE: No time now—help!

(*They drag* MAZEPPA *behind Church, just in time for* MAGPIE *to take up* MAZEPPA'S *stance as* MOLOCH *enters.*)

MOLOCH: There, my dear. That one has my clothes. (MAGPIE *takes case.*) This one our equipment. (MAGPIE *takes it, almost drops it from its weight.*) Careful!

MAGPIE: Blimey!

MOLOCH: Mazeppa, do you feel quite well?

MAGPIE: Dandy! Er—yes, master.

MOLOCH: Mazeppa, you're not going to have one of your nervous attacks, I hope?

MAGPIE: Awk. Er—no, master.

MOLOCH: Then off to the harbor to find a boat. Myself I'm going to get my fee from Bolligrew. At lunch I hope—if not—the Dragon's den. (*Exit* MOLOCH. OBIDIAH *emerges.* MAGPIE, *rummaging in case, produces heavy ledger.*)

OBIDIAH: My word—bit of quick thinkin' that was.

MAGPIE: What's this? (*The ledger.*)

OBIDIAH: Spells K to Z.

MAGPIE: This?

OBIDIAH: Spells A to K.

MAGPIE: Then this must be the Journal!

OBIDIAH: Right! (*Opens it.*) Here it is! "Sunday. Performed Spell Grimbleboots. Client: Bolligrew. Victim: Oblong. Purpose: Deliver same to Dragon . . ." The old devil . . . !

MAGPIE: Look up Grimbleboots!

OBIDIAH: What for?

MAGPIE: It'll give the antidote!

OBIDIAH: The antidote! (*Flipping pages.*) "Gattlefyg, Gollipog, Grimbleboots!" . . . "Ingredients, Method, Application, Antidote!" . . . (*A pause.*) "No antidote exists for this spell. . . ." (*He sits.*)

Baron's done some evil in 'is day. But this beats all. (*Silence.*) Pity
we can't put *'im* under a spell. . . .

MAGPIE: We can! Grimbleboots! If Grimbleboots gave Baron power
over Oblong, Grimbleboots will give us power over Baron.

OBIDIAH: Stands to reason that does! Mike Magpie—it's you that
should've been to that there University.

MAGPIE: Ha ha! Ingredients! What are the ingredients?

(OBIDIAH *reads while* MAGPIE *checks tins and bottles.*)

OBIDIAH: Snakes' feet.

MAGPIE: Snakes' feet.

OBIDIAH: Baking powder.

MAGPIE: Baking powder.

OBIDIAH: Fish feathers.

MAGPIE: Fish feathers.

OBIDIAH: Table salt.

MAGPIE: No table salt.

OBIDIAH: Got that at 'ome.

MAGPIE: What else?

OBIDIAH: Er—(*Face falls.*) Oh deary, deary me. . . . A prized possession of the victims. Prized possession of Bolligrew's, phew.

MAGPIE: Ark!

OBIDIAH: What?

MAGPIE: You won't tell Obby? (*Backing toward nest.*) It was twinklin',
you see. 'E left it on 'is dressin' table and the sun was shining, and
the window was open and it twinkled, so . . . (*He dangles the
huge gold watch.*) D'you think it'll do?

OBIDIAH: Do? Baron'll go ravin' mad when 'e misses that! That's 'is
presentation piece! Well, I never thought I'd live to thank a thiev-
ish Magpie! Right. Down to my cottage for the table salt. We'll
work the spell and then—(*Pause. They look at one another*)—the
Dragon's den.

(*Lights dim; backcloth descends as before. Enter* MOLOCH *and*
BOLLIGREW, *hastily.*)

BOLLIGREW: Well. (*Turning to* MOLOCH.) If those are the table manners of a Duke, commend me to the nearest cormorant. Never 'ave
I seen a man put back stuffed peacock the way 'e can.

MOLOCH: Bolligrew, I'm in a hurry.

BOLLIGREW: Aye! Right. (*Goes to den mouth.*) Hello? (*Eyes switch on.* BOLLIGREW *flinches.*) Oh, there you are.

DRAGON: "Here I am, where is Oblong?"

BOLLIGREW: Be comin' any minute.

DRAGON: "And you want me to eat him."

BOLLIGREW: Well, that's easy enough, isn't it?

DRAGON: "It is, Bolligrew, yes. That's what makes me, just a little, wonder . . ."

BOLLIGREW: Oh, you'll be doin' me a good turn, old man, don't you worry—All set then?

DRAGON: "All set, Bolligrew." (*Eyes switched off.*)

BOLLIGREW (*To* MOLOCH): Well. I'll go and bring up the Duke. Sorry you 'ave to go . . . (*Going.*)

MOLOCH: My fee. Sixty-five guineas.

BOLLIGREW (*Piteous*): Moloch—I'm a ruined man!

MOLOCH: Rubbish.

BOLLIGREW (*Pulls bag from pocket, can't part with it*): Knock off the shillings.

MOLOCH: No.

BOLLIGREW (*Enraged*): 'Ere you are then. (*Thrusts it at him.*) And bad luck to yer! (*Exits.*)

MOLOCH: Goodbye. (*He too is going, but pauses. Weighs money bag thoughtfully. Opens it. Takes out coin. Unwraps gilt foil. Puts coin in mouth, eats it carefully.*) I see. . . . Chocolate money. . . . Well, Bolligrew, this time, you've overreached yourself! (*Goes to den mouth.*) Dragon!

(*Eyes switch on.*)

DRAGON: "Yes, Moloch?"

MOLOCH: I have just found out that you are the object of a conspiracy!

DRAGON: "You amaze me, Moloch. Go on."

MOLOCH: Bolligrew has given Oblong mortified apples.

DRAGON: "Oh, yes?"

MOLOCH: Yes. I assume he got them from the mainland.

DRAGON: "*Must* have done, mustn't he? Any more?"

DRAGON: "Yes?"

MOLOCH: I'm afraid so. When you have eaten Oblong and have fallen dead.

DRAGON: "Yes?"

MOLOCH: Then Bolligrew and Blackheart with some show of gallantry will come in there and cut the tail off your corpse.

DRAGON: "Really. Now why would they do a thing like that?"

MOLOCH: The Duke is here.

DRAGON: "Understand. Ingenious scheme, Moloch."

MOLOCH: It has a certain squalid cunning, I suppose. Myself I will not be a party to it. In your place I should simply claw Oblong to death, and eat the gallant dragon slayers.

DRAGON: "Well, of course."

MOLOCH: Oh—Bolligrew is bringing up the Duke. I must go.

DRAGON: "Moloch."

MOLOCH: Yes.

DRAGON: "Very grateful for the information."

MOLOCH: Not at all.

DRAGON: "No, no, Moloch. Information must be paid for."

MOLOCH: Oh . . . (Hesitating.) Perhaps you'll send me a check.

DRAGON: "Cash, Moloch." (Noise of coins on Speaker.) "Come and get it."

MOLOCH (Licking lips, fascinated but frightened, hovers at mouth of den): Well I, er—

DRAGON: "Let's see; these seem to be ten guinea pieces. One (clink) two (clink) three (clink)—come in, Doctor, come in—" (MOLOCH, helplessly drawn into den, disappears from sight. His voice too comes on Speaker.) four (clink), five (clink)—"

MOLOCH: "It's very dark in here. . . ."

DRAGON: "Can you manage? I'm up here. Six (clink), seven (clink)—" (On Speaker, clatter and a little gasp from MOLOCH.) Mind the bones. That's it. Eight (clink), nine (clink)—and—" (Roar from DRAGON; shriek from MOLOCH.)

MOLOCH: "Put me down! Put me down!"

DRAGON: "Moloch, I don't believe that Bolligrew thought up that little scheme."

MOLOCH: "Help!"

DRAGON: "No. I think you did."

MOLOCH: "Help!"

DRAGON: "Anyway, I'm hungry."

MOLOCH: "Dragon—consider your stomach! I am the Regius Professor of Wickedness at—" (A shriek, cut short. Silence. Dreadful champing noise. Then:)

DRAGON: "Youugh . . . ! Disgusting."

(*Enter* DUKE, SMOOTHE, BOLLIGREW, BLACKHEART, MEN-AT-ARMS, PEASANTS, LORD MAYOR.)

BOLLIGREW: Shan't 'ave long to wait, Your Grace. Oblong's always 'ere 'bout teatime. Well, Sir Percy—ever seen a den as big as that?
SMOOTHE: It is very big . . .
BOLLIGREW (*To* DUKE): You see why, up till now, no one's cared to tackle 'im.
DUKE: Up till now?
BOLLIGREW: Yes, I think today may be the day. Blackheart's fair spoiling for it.
BLACKHEART: Just say the word, Bolligrew, an' I'll be in there an' 'ave 'is tail off in a jiffy.
BOLLIGREW: Courage of a lion, Your Grace. (*Indignant roar from* DRAGON. *All flinch. Then* BLACKHEART *shakes fist and roars back.*) Oh yes, he's workin' up to it. Today's the day all right.
DUKE: You mustn't let him, Bolligrew! That's not a one-man Dragon.
BOLLIGREW: One-man? Oh—I shall go in with 'im, naturally.
DUKE: Bolligrew!
BOLLIGREW: Matter of *noblesse oblige,* Your Grace. Er, if anything goes wrong, you'll not forget the poor and needy of these islands, will you?
DUKE (*Moved*): Good Heavens, Bolligrew. I'm overwhelmed. And all this while, Smoothe, Oblong—our official representative—is on familiar terms with the brute!
SMOOTHE (*Dry*): Yes, Your Grace. I can hardly believe it.
BOLLIGREW (*Pointing*): You'll believe your own eyes I hope?

(*All look off.*)

DUKE: It is. It's Oblong. Good Heavsns—he's *whistling!*

(*Enter behind them* MAGPIE *and* OBIDIAH, *who bears prominently watch.*)

OBIDIAH: Baron Bolligrew!

(*At his tone, all turn.*)

BOLLIGREW: Don't bother me n—— 'Ere! That's me presentation
   piece! (*Crosses; takes it.*) Where d'you get it?
MAGPIE: Ark . . .
BOLLIGREW (*Putting it on*): Oh you, was it?

(*Whistling—"Sir Eglamore"—approaches. All turn again, and as
whistling gets louder, shuffle back to prepare for* OBLONG'S *entrance. But:*)

OBIDIAH: Baron, cartwheel!

(BOLLIGREW *cartwheels. All turn to him.*)

MAGPIE: Another!
OBIDIAH: Another!
MAGPIE: Twirligig!

(BOLLIGREW *handsprings, crashes in sitting position, astounded.*)

DUKE: Bolligrew—?!

(*All spin again as enter* OBLONG, *whistling. Makes brisk semicircle. Sticks sword in stage frontstage. Pleasantly.*)

OBLONG: Bolligrew. Smoothe, People. (*And walks briskly toward den,
   drawing sweets from belt as he goes.*) Have a wine-gum, Tum-tum?
DUKE: Certainly not!
OBLONG: Suit yourself. (*Disappears into den.*)
BOLLIGREW: See! Just as I said!
OBIDIAH: Baron, call him back.
BOLLIGREW: Come back!
DUKE: Good Lord!

(OBLONG *reappears.*)

OBLONG (*Pleasantly*): Yes?
DUKE: Smoothe—Smoothe—what's going on?
OBIDIAH: Your Grace. The Baron 'as Sir Oblong in 'is power. And I
   'ave Baron in mine. Baron, tell 'im to remove 'is prized possession.
BOLLIGREW: Remove your prized possession.

OBLONG (*Plucks mantle from back. Comes to himself*): Good heavens
—Your Grace? Good Heavens—the Dragon's den—my sword—!
What's happening here? (*Finds sweet packet in belt, looks at it,
realizes what it is and throws it from him with horrified exclamation.*)

DUKE: Oblong is himself again. Old friend, I fear you have been
foully practiced on.

OBIDIAH: Tell 'Is Grace it is so.

BOLLIGREW: It is so.

DUKE: Oh infamous!

OBIDIAH: And tell His Grace that you, not Sir Oblong had an agreement with the Dragon.

BOLLIGREW: I, not Sir Oblong, had an agreement with the Dragon.

LORD MAYOR: And have had this many a year—!

BOLLIGREW: And have had this—you shurrup!

OBIDIAH: And tell His Grace you did it with the aid of Dr. Moloch,
calling himself Innocent.

BOLLIGREW: Did it with the aid of Dr. Moloch, calling 'imself Innocent, yes.

DUKE (*Amazed by his comfortably obedient tone*): And you confess
this freely?

BOLLIGREW: Do I blazes confess it freely! This man 'ere's bewitched
me somehow—'Ere . . . ! (*Fumbles to unfasten watch.*)

OBIDIAH: Baron. Hands off!

(BOLLIGREW's *hands fly out at arm's length.*)

BOLLIGREW: See! See? (*Turns for all to see him.*) An' if I'm not greatly
mistook, the 'ole of this is 'ighly illegal!

OBLONG: That's perfectly true. Evidence obtained by witchcraft is no
evidence whatever—and rightly so. Obidiah, I am deeply displeased.
Tell the Baron to remove his watch.

OBIDIAH ⎫ (*Together, overlapping*): But Sir—
MAGPIE   ⎭   Don't be daft—
                                       Eh, Obby—

OBLONG: Immediately, Obidiah.

OBIDIAH: Then, Baron, take it off.

(*He does.*)

DUKE: Now, Baron, repeat your story.

BOLLIGREW: I will do no such thing! Pack of lies from start to finish!

SMOOTHE: Oblong, my dear man, you've destroyed your own case.

OBLONG (*Quietly*): I can't help that, Smoothe. I cannot countenance the use of witchcraft.

BOLLIGREW: Well, I'm glad to see there's *one* honest man 'ere. Besides me! I tell you what, Obby—we've been practiced on you an' me! We'll 'ave the law on the lot of 'em. Uncover corruption in very 'igh places, I dare say. Black'eart saw it. 'E'll be witness!

OBLONG: Bolligrew, you are a transparent rogue and I have nothing to say to you. I hope His Grace will send some worthy gentlemen to take my mission to a successful conclusion. (*He sounds bitterly sad.*)

DUKE: Oblong, what's this?

OBLONG: Your Grace, I shall never forget how I misbehaved this morning.

DUKE: But you were made to.

OBLONG (*Quite sharply*): I was not. I was made to let myself go. I let myself go and misbehaved myself. (*He turns sadly, picks up the mantle.*) I fell prey to Dr. Moloch, by my vanity and pride.

DUKE: Oh, Oblong, really, that's ridiculous.

OBLONG: Not at all. (*Walks toward sword, thoughtfully, lovingly, folding and stroking it.*) I used to say I was not worthy. If truth were told, I thought I was too good. Here's my sword. Well, (*drapes mantle over sword*) I will never carry sword again.

BOLLIGREW: Eh, now look 'ere, Obby—

(*Immediately all join in, following and vociferously begging, cajoling, urging him to stay, according to their different natures. "Be a sport, Obby, don't take it like that." "Don't leave us, Sir Oblong, you're the first Knight Errant we ever 'ad and we don't wish for none better." "Oblong, my dear fellow, this is really very fine drawn stuff; I wish you'd reconsider." "Look man, every blessed person here is asking for you." "Ark! Obby! Don't go off to the mainland now and leave us 'ere to Bolligrew." "Come on, Obby, place won't be the same without you." "Sir Oblong, please —you are a familiar and well-loved figure in the Islands." "Remember 'ow we built the Church, sir—what's to become of that?"*)

OBLONG (*Repeats, but drowned so that we can only see his firmly up-held hand, his head shaking in refusal*): No, no, I thank you, but my mind is made up.

DRAGON: "My patience is exhausted!" (*Instant silence. All turn.*) "I can hear human beans. I can smell human beans. And—I'm—HUNGRY . . . !" (*On Speaker, noise of approaching* DRAGON, *eyes get larger.*)

ALL: The Dragon! The Dragon is at large! (*They scatter, leaving* OBLONG *isolated. A moment's hesitation, snatches mantle, wraps it round his arm, pulls sword from stage and rushes into den.*)

OBLONG: An Oblong! An Oblong!

DUKE (*Pointing*): Bolligrew! Redeem yourself!

(*Noise of conflict on Speaker.*)

BOLLIGREW: By Jove—! Tally-ho! (*Crams cartridges into shotgun and follows* OBLONG.)

DUKE: Smoothe—assist them! Smoothe! (SMOOTHE *follows rather reluctantly.*) Men-at-Arms! (*They cheer and follow.*) Poor and needy! (*They cheer and follow. Only* BLACKHEART *left. Indignant, rhetorical.*) Squire Blackheart! Are you a gentleman or are you not?

BLACKHEART: No, I blazin' well am not!

(*Climax on Speaker to din of shouts, roars, clashing swords, banging of shotgun. Sudden silence. Gush of smoke. Then* BOLLIGREW *and* OBLONG *emerge with huge black tail, followed by others all smoke-blackened.*)

DUKE: Oblong! Peerless Knight! You have surpassed yourself.

OBLONG: No, no, Your Grace. The principal credit belongs to the Baron.

DUKE: The Baron?

BOLLIGREW (*Shaking his shotgun, beaming excited*): Got 'im with both barrels. A left and a right! Pow! Pow! Didn't I, Obby?

OBLONG: He did. The beast was on the wing too. Beautiful shots, Baron!

BOLLIGREW: By Jove, that's what I call sport! You can keep yer pheasants. Eh—these Dragons—can you breed 'em, artificial?

OBLONG: I never heard of it. But there are lots of wild ones.

BOLLIGREW: Where?

OBLONG: Up north. Dragons, Goblins, Lord knows what. Very good sport up north, I believe.

BOLLIGREW: Black'eart, get ready to pack.

BLACKHEART: Now look 'ere, Bolligrew—

BOLLIGREW: You'll love it, Black'eart! (*Aiming gun at imaginary dragon.*) Pow! pow! Eh—what's the season?

OBLONG: All the year round.

BOLLIGREW: 'Ear that Black'eart—no closed season. Well, you needn't expect to see me back 'ere for some time, if at all. (*Stir of delight among all.*) No, no, I shall be missed, I know that, but me mind's made up.

(*Enter* STORYTELLER. *Rhymes commence.*)

STORYTELLER: Then who will rule your people when you've gone?

BOLLIGREW: Fat lot I care—pow! pow!—Anyone.

DUKE: That timorous gentleman over there?

LORD MAYOR (*Quailing under* BOLLIGREW's *appraisal*): I thank Your Grace, but I'll stay Lord Mayor.

DUKE: The barefooted fellow showed some resource.

OBIDIAH: I'll stick to my trade, sir—thanks of course.

STORYTELLER: Excuse me, Your Grace, but it is getting late.

BOLLIGREW (*Puts arm round* OBLONG): There's a perfectly obvious candidate!

STORYTELLER: And I ask you to name him with one voice.

ALL: Oblong Fitz Oblong!

STORYTELLER: The people's choice—Sir, I salute you in a world of smiles. First Baron Oblong of the Isles—and that of course concludes the play—

OBLONG: It certainly doesn't. I've something to say. (STORYTELLER *looks at him, struck by indignant tone.*) We've killed a Dragon, and mended a quarrel—

STORYTELLER: What of it—?

OBLONG:—What of it sir? The *moral!* (*As* OBLONG *steps forward.*)

STORYTELLER: I beg your pardon. But please keep it short.

OBLONG: It's simply this: My dears, do-what-you-ought. When there's something you want, and you can't do without it. There are various ways of going about it—

MAGPIE (*Righteous*): And a very good way is to—do-what-you-*should*.

OBLONG: Exactly.

MAGPIE: But a bit of what you fancy, does yer good!
OBLONG: Michael!
MAGPIE: Awk!

(*Music.*)

Childhood

BY

THORNTON WILDER

THORNTON WILDER, born in 1897 in Madison, Wisconsin, where his father was owner and editor of a newspaper, grew up in a family which emphasized religious and intellectual pursuits. As a result, he began writing stories and plays at a very young age. His education took an international turn when his father was appointed consul general in Shanghai and Hong Kong, and Thornton attended a missionary school until he was thirteen. Life in the Orient impressed him deeply and its theatre has been a lasting influence upon his unusual form of dramaturgy. After completing high school in California, he entered Oberlin College to study classics and completed his bachelor's degree at Yale in 1920. During his college years he continued writing short plays, a number of which were published in *The Angel That Troubled the Waters* (1928). At the American Academy in Rome he studied archaeology and later undertook graduate work at Princeton University. Thereafter he began to teach, first at the Lawrenceville Academy and later at the University of Chicago. He participated in both world wars, serving in the first in the Coast Artillery Corps, and in the second, although he was overage, as a member of the Air Force Intelligence, stationed in the United States, Africa and Europe. Throughout his life he has traveled a great deal, writing both at home and abroad.

Much too much has been made by teachers and anthologizers of the fact that Wilder's reputation as a titan among American playwrights rests on but three plays. There is no denying that *Our Town* (1938), *The Skin of Our Teeth* (1942) and *The Matchmaker* (1954) constitute the harvest of his full-length works except for a translation of Ibsen and adaptations of Obey and Sartre. (A fourth original play, *A Life in the Sun*, based on the *Alcestis* of Euripides, produced in England in 1955, has not yet appeared on the New York stage.) But to suggest that Wilder's long career has been anything but productive is to be misleading indeed, for concurrent with his dramatic output he has published a distinguished list of novels over a 40-year period:

The Cabala (1925); *The Bridge of San Luis Rey* (1927), which won his first of three Pulitzer prizes; *Heaven's My Destination* (1935); *The Ides of March* (1948); and *The Eighth Day* (1967). The three plays for which he is honored have proved to be especially durable theatre pieces. *Our Town,* when revived on Broadway in the autumn of 1969 with Henry Fonda as the Stage Manager, had theatregoers laughing and crying at its portrait of life and death in Grover's Corners, just as it had more than 30 years before. *The Skin of Our Teeth,* a comedy glorifying man's capacity to survive in spite of glaciers, wars and himself, remains audaciously alive in regional and university theatres. Although it failed when originally produced as *The Merchant of Yonkers, The Matchmaker* became a hit in London and New York with Ruth Gordon as Dolly Levi, and, of course, is the basis for the musical comedy *Hello, Dolly!,* which has achieved a record run on the American stage and has been made into a popular film.

In addition, Wilder's plethoric treasury of one-act plays ranks among the most innovative and original in American drama, contributing significantly to the rise of the short play as a major genre of modern theatre. Always an experimenter, Wilder began by composing brief character sketches, each lasting from three to five minutes, in which he depicted ordinary aspects of daily life in most extraordinary ways. In these and six plays published under the title *The Long Christmas Dinner and Other Plays* (1931), he rejected realism as a form of artistic expression and instead elected freely to explore time and space, life and death, and, most of all, the elements that make up theatre itself. Ninety years pass in 20 minutes, taking with them an entire family dynasty, in *The Long Christmas Dinner.* The Kirby family travels from Trenton to Camden, New Jersey, observing the cycle of life from birth to death, in the half hour it takes to perform *The Happy Journey from Trenton to Camden.* The solar system appears on stage as part of *Pullman Car Hiawatha,* in which time is personified by the entrance of the hours and space is represented by planets who hum above the action on a balcony. Even heavenly archangels materialize to complete the cosmic order, all in a play of 21 pages. The form of these plays, as well as of *Our Town,* aptly has been called "theatricalism."

In departing from the realistic style which he insists has thwarted the imaginative purpose of theatre, Wilder discards scenery and often requires no more than a group of chairs and stools or a stepladder. A stage manager sometimes appears to comment on the action (much in the manner of the chorus in classical drama), as well as to direct the movement and often to participate in it. Properties seldom are employed; actors in the plays just mentioned eat imaginary food, ride in an imaginary car and sleep on an imaginary train. Wilder's purpose is not to copy life (which is what would happen if he placed before his audiences real food, autos and trains), but to create the essence of life, at least his view of it, and this best can be accomplished by make-believe and what he calls the "multiplication of pretenses." The reality of existence, not of things, is the greater reality he strives to reveal by stripping his stage of clutter and by reducing his characters to their essential emotions and universal feelings. Unusual events seldom happen in his plays, because the routine of everyday life is made to be an event of great importance.

Both in form and idea *Childhood* shows Wilder at his best, for he is able to sweep through the conscious and unconscious lives of three children, revealing their most elemental attitudes and discovering in them a reality that is true of children everywhere. He can do this in just 18 pages, because once again neither his stage nor his characters are anchored in clinical detail; the children take an imaginary bus ride that symbolizes the journey through life merely by arranging several chairs on a bare stage. How effortlessly the play moves in and out of the dream. And, as in his earlier one-act plays, Wilder creates dramatic action (as well as symbolism) out of the simplest of endeavors, the playing of childhood games, for awake or dreaming the lives of his children are epitomized in games, which are the play's ultimate reality.

When Wilder wrote this play, one of three in *Plays for Bleecker Street,* produced by Circle in the Square in 1962, he was fascinated by arena staging. His directions indicate that *Childhood* is to be played in an arena with a few chairs to represent some bushes in a backyard, which later on become the imaginary bus. The audience may sit on three sides or encircle the action completely, as long as the aisles allow the actors access to the playing area. As presented on television with realistic settings—a large old-fashioned house surrounded by a yard filled with real trees—the play proved to be far less effective, suggesting that along with *Our Town* and *The Skin of Our Teeth* this play properly belongs in the living theatre it was intended to serve.

Wilder has stated that a play visibly represents "pure existing," and he makes this come true in the case of Caroline, Dodie and Billee in *Childhood*. Theirs is a somewhat painful existence, honest and uncompromising. Wilder gives no solution to the predicament of these children or of any children. Even though they move toward an understanding of their Mother and Father in the dream sequence, they know, as Caroline says in her final speech, that grown-ups can't be trusted. They may have a new sense of their need for parents, but they will remain as far apart as before. Moreover, the ending demonstrates that the parents are without any better knowledge of their children. As it should, the play upsets adults because there is no happy reconciliation; the great void is not bridged and, appropriately, the Father's last call to his children is not answered.

During the preparation of this volume, Thornton Wilder said that he had not written *Childhood* for children. Yet this play even when difficult to obtain (for almost ten years it remained unpublished except for an appearance in *The Atlantic Monthly* in 1960) was known to high-school students who read, acted and understood it. Their appreciation of a work that speaks to them as do few other serious dramas of recent years testifies to its importance and justifies its inclusion here.

Childhood

CHARACTERS

CAROLINE, *age twelve*
DODIE, *age ten*
BILLEE, *age eight*
MOTHER
FATHER

Some low chairs at the edges of the arena. These at first represent some bushes in the yard of the children's home. At the back, the door to the house; the aisle through the audience serves as a path to the street. Enter from the house CAROLINE, *twelve;* DODIE, *ten; and, with a rush,* BILLEE, *eight.*

DODIE: Sh! Sh! Don't let Mama hear you! Car'line, Car'line, play the game. Let's play the game.
CAROLINE: There's no time, silly. It takes time to play the game.
BILLEE: Play Goin' to China.
CAROLINE: Don't talk so loud; we don't want Mama to hear us. Papa'll be here soon, and we can't play the game when Papa's here.
DODIE: Well, let's play a little. We can play Going to a Hotel.
BILLEE (*Clamorously*): I want to be Room Service. I want to be Room Service.
CAROLINE: You know Going to a Hotel takes *hours*. It's awful when you have to stop for something.
DODIE (*Quickly*): Car'line, listen, I heard Mama telephoning Papa and the car's got to be fixed and Papa's got to come home by a bus, and maybe he'll never get here and we can play for a long time.
CAROLINE: Did she say that? Well, come behind the bushes and think.

(*They squat on their haunches behind the bushes.*)

BILLEE: Let's play Hospital and take everything out of Dodie.
CAROLINE: Let me think a minute.
MOTHER (*At the door*): Caroline! Dodie! (*Silence.*) Dodie, how often do I have to tell you to hang your coat up properly? Do you know what happened? It fell and got caught under the cupboard door and was dragged back and forth. I hope it's warm Sunday, because you can't wear that coat. Billee, stand out for a moment where I can see you. Are you ready for your father when he comes home?

Come out of the bushes. Billee, come out. (BILLEE, *a stoic already, comes to the Center of the Stage and stands for inspection.* MOTHER *shakes her head in silence; then:*) I simply despair. Look at you! What are you children doing anyway? Now, Caroline, you're not playing one of those games of yours? I absolutely forbid you to play that the house is on fire. You have nightmares all night long. Or those awful games about hospitals. Really, Caroline, why can't you play Shopping or Going to School? (*Silence.*) I declare. I give up. I really do. (*False exit.*) Now remember, it's Friday night, the end of the week, and you give your father a good big kiss when he comes home. (*She goes out.* BILLEE *rejoins his sisters.*)

DODIE (*Dramatic whisper*): Car'line, let's play Funeral! (*Climax.*) Car'line, let's play ORPHANS!

CAROLINE: We haven't time—*that* takes all day. Besides, I haven't got the black gloves.

   (BILLEE *sees his* FATHER *coming through the audience. Utter and final dismay.*)

BILLEE: Look't! Look!

DODIE: What?

ALL THREE: It's Papa! It's Papa!

   (*They fly into the house like frightened pigeons.* FATHER *enters jauntily through the audience. It's warm, and he carries his coat over his shoulder. Arriving at the Center of the Stage, he places his coat on the ground, whistles a signal call to his wife, and swinging an imaginary golf club, executes a mighty and very successful shot.*)

FATHER: Two hundred and fifty yards!

MOTHER (*Enters, kisses him and picks up the coat*): Why, you're early, after all.

FATHER: Jerry drove me to the corner. Picked up a little flask for the weekend.

MOTHER: Well, I wish you wouldn't open your little flask when the children are around.

FATHER (*Preparing a difficult shot*): Eleventh hole. . . . Where *are* the children?

MOTHER: They were here a minute ago. They're out playing some-where. . . . Your coat on the ground! Really, you're as bad as Dodie.

FATHER: Well, you should teach the children—little trouble with the dandelions here—that it's their first duty . . . when their father comes home on Friday nights . . . (*Shouts.*) Fore, you bastards! . . . to rush toward their father . . . to grovel . . . abject thanks to him who gave them life.

MOTHER (*Amused exasperation*): Oh, stop that nonsense!

FATHER: On Friday nights . . . after a week of toil at the office . . . a man wants to see . . . (*He swings.*) his wives and children cling-ing to his knees, tears pouring down their cheeks. (*He stands up very straight, holding an enormous silver cup.*) Gentlemen, I ac-cept this championship cup, but I wish also to give credit to my wife and children, who drove me out of the house every Sunday morning. . . . Where *are* the children? Caroline! Dodie!

MOTHER: Oh, they're hiding somewhere.

FATHER: Hiding? Hiding from their father?

MOTHER: They're playing one of those awful games of theirs. Listen to me, Fred: those games are morbid; they're dangerous.

FATHER: How do you mean, dangerous?

MOTHER: Really! No one told me when I was a bride that children are half crazy. I only hear fragments of the games, naturally, but do you realize that they like nothing better than to imagine us—away?

FATHER: Away?

MOTHER: Yes—dead?

FATHER (*His eye on the shot*): One . . . two . . . *three!* Well, you know what *you* said.

MOTHER: What did I say?

FATHER: *Your* dream.

MOTHER: Pshaw!

FATHER (*Softly, with lowest insinuation*): Your dream that . . . you and I . . . on a Mediterranean cruise . . .

MOTHER: It was Hawaii.

FATHER: And that we were—ahem!—somehow . . . *alone.*

MOTHER: Well, I didn't imagine them *dead!* I imagined them with Mother . . . or Paul . . . or their Aunt Henrietta.

FATHER (*Piously*): I hope so.

MOTHER: You're a brute, and everybody knows it. . . . It's Caroline.

She's the one who starts it all. And afterwards she has those night-mares. Come in. You'll see the children at supper.

FATHER (*Looking upward*): What has the weatherman predicted for tomorrow?

MOTHER (*Starting for the house*): Floods. Torrents. You're going to stay home from the golf club and take care of the children. And I'm going to the Rocky Mountains . . . and to China.

FATHER: You'll be back by noon. What does Caroline say in her nightmares?

MOTHER: Oh! When she's awake, too. You and I are—away. Do you realize that that girl is mad about black gloves?

FATHER: Nonsense.

MOTHER: Caroline would be in constant mourning if she could man-age it. Come in, come in. You'll see them at supper. (*She goes out.*)

FATHER (*He strolls to the end of the Stage farthest from the house and calls*): Caroline! (*Pause.*) Dodie! (*Pause.*) Bill-eeee! (*Silence. He broods aloud, his eyes on the distance.*) No instrument has yet been discovered that can read what goes on in another's mind, asleep or awake. And I hope there never will be. But once in a while, it would help a lot. Is it wrong of me to wish that . . . just once . . . I could be an invisible witness to one of my children's dreams, to one of their games? (*He calls again.*) Caroline!

(*We are in the game which is a dream. The* CHILDREN *enter as he calls them, but he does not see them and they do not see him. They come in and stand shoulder to shoulder as though they were about to sing a song before an audience.* CAROLINE *carries a child's suitcase and one of her mother's handbags; she is wear-ing black gloves.* DODIE *also has a suitcase and handbag, and no gloves.*)

CAROLINE: Dodie! Hurry before they see us.

FATHER: Dodie!

DODIE: Where's Billee gone?

FATHER (*Being bumped into by* BILLEE *as he joins his sisters*): Billee!

(*FATHER enters the house. MOTHER glides out of the house and takes her place at the further end of the Stage and turns and faces the* CHILDREN. *She is wearing a black hat, deep-black veil, and black gloves. Her air is one of mute acquiescent grief.* CARO-

LINE *glances frequently at her* MOTHER *as though for prompting. A slight formal pause.*)

CAROLINE: I guess, first, we have to say how sorry we are. (*To* MOTHER.) Shall we begin? (MOTHER *lowers her head slightly.*) This first part is in church. Well, in a kind of church. And there's been a perfectly terrible accydent, an airplane accydent.

DODIE (*Quickly*): No, it was an automobile accydent.

CAROLINE (*Ditto*): It was an airplane.

DODIE (*Ditto*): I don't want it to be an airplane.

BILLEE (*Fiercely*): It was on a ship. It was a *big* shipwreck.

CAROLINE: Now, I'm not going to play this game unless you be quiet. It was an airplane accydent. And . . . they were on it, and they're not here any more.

BILLEE: They got *dead*.

CAROLINE (*Glaring at him*): Don't say that *word*. You promised you wouldn't say that word. (*Uncomfortable pause.*) And we're very sad. And . . .

DODIE (*Brightly*): We didn't see it, though.

CAROLINE: And we'd have put on black dresses, only we haven't got any. But we want to thank Miss Wilkerson for coming today and for wearing black like she's wearing. (MOTHER *again lowers her head.*) Miss Wilkerson is the best teacher in Benjamin Franklin School, and she's the grown-up we like best.

BILLEE (*Suddenly getting excited*): That's not Miss Wilkerson. That's —I mean—*look!*

CAROLINE: I can't hear a word you're saying, and anyway, don't talk now!

BILLEE (*Too young to enter the dream; pulling at his* SISTERS' *sleeves urgently*): That's not Miss Wilkerson. That's *Mama!*

DODIE: What's the matter with your eyes?

CAROLINE: Mama's not here any more. She went away.

BILLEE (*Staring at* MOTHER, *and beginning to doubt*): It's . . . Mrs. Fenwick!

CAROLINE (*Low but strongly*): No-o-o-o! (*Resuming the ceremony.*) It wasn't so sad about Grandma, because she was more'n a hundred anyway.

DODIE: And she used to say all the time, "I won't be with you always," and things like that, and how she'd give Mama her pearl pin.

BILLEE: I guess she's glad she isn't any more.

CAROLINE (*Uncertainly*): So . . .

DODIE (*To* MOTHER, *with happy excitement*): Are we orphans now— real orphans? (MOTHER, *always with lowered eyes, nods slightly.*) And we don't have to do *things* any more?

CAROLINE (*Severely*): Dodie! Don't *say* everything. (*She consults her* MOTHER.) What do I say now?

MOTHER (*Almost inaudibly*): About your father . . .

CAROLINE: Yes. Papa was a very fine man. And . . .

DODIE (*Quickly*): He used to swear bad words.

BILLEE (*Excitedly*): All the *time!* He'd swear swear-words.

CAROLINE: Well, maybe a little.

DODIE: He *did.* I used to want to *die.*

CAROLINE: Well, nobody's perfeck. (*Slower.*) He was all right, some-times.

DODIE: He used to laugh too loud in front of people. And he didn't give Mama enough money to buy clothes. She had to go to town in rags, in terrible old rags.

BILLEE (*Always excited*): Papa'd go like this (*Pumping his arms up and down in desperation*), "I haven't got it! I haven't got it! You can't squeeze blood out of a stone."

DODIE: Yes, he did.

BILLEE: And Mama'd say: "I'm ashamed to go out in the street." It was awful. And then he'd say, "I'll have to mortgage, that's what I'll have to do."

CAROLINE: Billee! How can you say such an awful word? Don't you ever say that again. Papa wasn't perfeck, but he would never have done a mortgage.

BILLEE: Well, that's what he said.

CAROLINE (*Emphatically*): Most times Papa did his best. Everybody makes some mistakes.

DODIE (*Demurely*): He used to drink some, too.

BILLEE (*Beside himself again*): He used to drink *oceans.* And Mama'd say, "Don't you think you've had enough?" and he'd say, "Down the hatch!"

DODIE: Yes, he did. And, "Just a hair of the dog that bit him." And Mama'd say, "Well, if you want to kill yourself before our eyes!" I used to want to die.

CAROLINE: Billee, don't get so excited; and you too, Dodie. Papa was a very fine man, and he *tried.* Only . . . only . . . (*Reluctantly*) he didn't ever say anything very inneresting.

DODIE: He was inneresting when he told about the automobile accydent he'd seen and all the blood.

BILLEE: Yes, he was. But he stopped in the middle when Mama said, "Not before the children."

DODIE: Yes, he stopped then.

CAROLINE: Anyway, we're very sad. And . . . (*She looks to her* MOTHER *for prompting.*)

MOTHER (*Almost inaudibly*): Your mother . . .

CAROLINE: Yes. About Mama.

BILLEE (*Hot indignation*): Mama's almost never home. She's always shopping and having her hair made. And one time she was away *years,* to see Grandma in Boston.

DODIE: It was only five days, and Grandma was very sick.

BILLEE: No, it wasn't. It was years and years.

DODIE: Well, when she was away she didn't have to say Don't—Don't —Don't all the time, all day and night, Don't—Don't—Don't.

BILLEE (*Tentatively defending her*): Sometimes she makes good things to eat.

DODIE: Beans and mash potatoes, and I just hate them. "Now, you eat every mouthful, or you don't leave the table." Ugh!

CAROLINE (*Recalling them to the ceremony*): It wasn't her fault! Only she didn't unnerstand children. I guess there's not one in a hundred hundred that unnerstands children. (*To* MOTHER.) Is that enough, Miss Wilkerson? I can't think of anything else to say. And we've got to hurry, or Uncle Paul will come to get us, or Aunt Henrietta, or somebody even worse. So can we go now?

MOTHER (*A whisper*): I think it would be nice, you know, if you said how you loved them, and how they loved you.

CAROLINE: Yes—uh . . .

DODIE: It was awful when they got huggy and kissy. And when we got back an hour late, from Mary Louise's picnic, and Mama said, "I was frantic! I was frantic! I didn't know what had become of you."

CAROLINE (*Slowly*): She liked us best when we were sick and when I broke my arm.

DODIE: Yes. (*Exhausted pause.*) Miss Wilkerson, orphans don't have to be sad *all* the time, do they?

(MOTHER *shakes her head slightly.*)

BILLEE: Do we get any money for being orphans?

CAROLINE: We won't need it. Papa used to keep an envelope behind the clock with money in it, for accydents and times like that. I have it here. (*She goes to* MOTHER, *like a hostess getting rid of a guest.*) Thank you for coming, Miss Wilkerson. We have to go now. And thank you for wearing black.

DODIE (*Also shaking hands; conventionally*): Thank you very much.

(MOTHER, *with bowed head, glides into the house.*)

CAROLINE: Now be quiet, and I'll tell you what we're going to do. We've got to hurry, so don't interrup me. We're orphans and we don't have anybody around us or near us and we're going to take a bus. (*Sensation.*) All over the world. We're going to be different persons and we're going to change our names. (*Gravely she opens her suitcase. She takes out and puts on a hat and fur neckpiece of her mother's. She looks adorable.*) I'm Mrs. Arizona. Miss Wilson, please get ready for the trip.

DODIE: Wha-a-t?

CAROLINE: *Miss Wilson!* Will you put your hat on, please.

DODIE: Oh! (*She puts on a hat from her suitcase.*) I want to be married, too. I want to be Mrs. Wilson.

CAROLINE: You're too young. People would laugh at you. We'll be gone for years and years, and by and by, in China or somewhere, you can gradually be Mrs. Wilson.

BILLEE: I want to be somebody, too.

CAROLINE: You're only *eight!* If you don't cry all the time and say awful things, I'll give you a real name. Now we can start.

BILLEE: But aren't Papa and Mama coming? (*The* GIRLS *turn and glare at him.*) Oh! they're *dead.* (*More glaring.*)

CAROLINE: All right. S-s-stay at home and go to s-s-school, if you want to. Papa and Mama are *happy.* Papa's playing golf and Mama's shopping. Are you ready, Miss Wilson?

DODIE: Yes, Mrs. Arizona, thank you.

CAROLINE: Don't run, but if we hurry we can each get a seat by the window.

(FATHER *enters, wearing a bus conductor's cap and big dark glasses. He casually arranges the chairs so as to indicate some of*

the seats of a long bus pointing toward the exit through the
audience. The CHILDREN *form a line at the door of the bus,*
tickets in hand.)

FATHER: Take your places in line, please. The first stop, ladies and
gentlemen, will be Ashagorra-Kallapalla, where there will be
twenty minutes for lunch. That's the place where you get to eat
the famous heaven-fruit sandwich. (*He starts punching the tickets
of some imaginary passengers who precede the children.*) That cat
won't be happy, madam. That's our experience. (*Severely, palping
a passenger.*) You haven't got mumps, have you? Well, I'd appreciate it if you sat at a distance from the other passengers.
BILLEE (*Staggered*): But that's Papa!
DODIE: Don't be silly, Papa's *away.*
BILLEE: But it looks like Papa . . . and . . . (*Losing assurance*) it
looks like Dr. Summers, too.
CAROLINE: Billy, I don't know what's the matter with you. Papa
wouldn't be working as a bus conductor. Papa's a man that's got
more money than that.
FATHER (*To* CAROLINE): Your ticket, please, madam.
CAROLINE: We want to go to all the places you're going to, please.
FATHER: But you mean this to be a round-trip ticket, don't you?
You're coming back, aren't you?
CAROLINE (*None too sure; her eyes avoiding his*): Well, maybe I
won't.
FATHER (*Lowering his voice, confidentially*): I'll punch it on the side
here. That'll mean you can use it, whenever you want, to come
back here. (CAROLINE *takes her place on the bus.* MOTHER *glides
in and takes her place in the line behind* BILLEE. *She is now wear-
ing a brown hat and a deep-brown veil.* FATHER *punches* DODIE'S
ticket.) Why, I think I've seen your face before, madam. Weren't
you in that terrible automobile accident—blood all over the road
and everything?
DODIE (*Embarrassed; low*): No, no, I wasn't.
FATHER: Well, I'm glad to hear that. (DODIE *takes her seat behind*
CAROLINE. *To* BILLEE, *punching his ticket.*) And what's your name,
sir, if I may ask?
BILLEE: Billee.
CAROLINE (*Officiously*): His name is Mr. Wentworth.
FATHER: Mr. Wentworth. Good morning. (*Man to man, with a*

touch of severity.) No smoking in the first six rows, watch that, and . . . (*Significant whisper*) there'll be no liquor drinking on this bus. I hope that's understood. (BILLEE, *considerably intimidated, takes his place behind* DODIE. *During the following he sees* MOTHER *and stares at her in amazement.* FATHER *punches* MOTHER'S *ticket, saying in sad condolence:*) I hope you have a good trip, ma'am. I hope you have a good trip.

MOTHER (*A whisper*): Thank you. (*She takes a place in the last row.*)

CAROLINE (*Rummaging in her handbag*): Would you like a candy bar, Miss Wilson . . . and Mr. Wentworth?

DODIE: Thank you, Mrs. Arizona, I would.

BILLEE: Look! LOOK! That's Mama!

DODIE: Stop poking me. It's not. It's *not*.

FATHER: Well, now, all aboard that's going to go. (*He climbs on the bus, takes his seat, tries his gears, then rises and addresses the passengers weightily.*) Before we start, there are some things I want to say about this trip. *Bus travel is not easy.* I think you'll know what I mean, Mrs. Arizona, when I say that it's like family life: we're all stuck in this vehicle together. We go through some pretty dangerous country, and I want you all to keep your heads. Like when we go through the Black Snake Indian territory, for instance. I've just heard they're getting a little—restless. And along the Kappi-kappi River, where all those lions and tigers are, and other things. Now, I'm a pretty good driver, but nobody's perfect and everybody can make a mistake once in a while. But I don't want any complaints afterward that you weren't warned. If anybody wants to get off this bus and go home, this is the moment to do it, and I'll give you your money back. (*Indicating* MOTHER.) There's one passenger here I know can be counted on. She's made the trip before and she's a regular crackerjack. Excuse me praising you to your face, ma'am, but I mean every word of it. Now, how many of you have been trained in first aid—will you hold up your hands? (BILLEE *and* MOTHER *raise their hands promptly.* CAROLINE *and* DODIE *look at one another uncertainly but do not raise their hands.*) Well, we may have to hold some classes later—go to school, so to speak. Accidents are always likely to happen when we get to the tops of the mountains. So! I guess we're ready to start. When we start, we often have a word of prayer if there's a minister of the gospel on board. (*To* BILLEE.) May I ask if you're a minister of the gospel, Mr. Wentworth?

BILLEE: N-no.

FATHER: Then we'll just have to *think* it. (*Lowering his voice, to* BILLEE.) And, may I add, I hope that there won't be any bad language used on this bus. There are ladies present—and some very fine ladies, too, if I may say so. Well, here we go! Forward march.

CAROLINE (*To* DODIE, *confidentially*): If it's going to be so dangerous, I think we'd better move up a little nearer *him*.

(*They slip across the aisle and slide, side by side, into the second row behind* FATHER. BILLEE *has gone to the back of the car and stands staring at* MOTHER.)

BILLEE (*Indicating the veil*): Do you ever take that off?

MOTHER (*Softly, lowered eyes*): Sometimes I do.

CAROLINE: Billee! Don't disturb the lady. Come and sit by us.

MOTHER: Oh, he's not disturbing me at all.

(*Soon he takes the seat beside her, and she puts her arm around him.*)

FATHER (*As he drives, talking to the* GIRLS *over his shoulder*): It's hard work driving a bus, ladies. Did you ever think of that?

CAROLINE: Oh, yes. It must be hard.

FATHER: Sometimes I wonder why I do it. Mornings . . . leave my house and family and get on the bus. And it's no fun, believe me. (*Jerk.*) See that? Almost ran over that soldier. And—would you believe it—I don't get much money for it.

CAROLINE (*Breathless interest*): Don't they pay you a *lot?*

FATHER: Mrs. Arizona, I'm telling you the truth: sometimes I wonder if we're going to have enough to eat.

DODIE: Why, I think that's terrible!

FATHER: And if I can get enough clothes to wear. I see that's a nice furpiece you have on, Mrs. Arizona.

CAROLINE: Oh, this is *old*.

DODIE (*Very earnestly*): But at your house you do have breakfast and lunch and supper, don't you?

FATHER: Miss Wilson, you're awfully kind to ask. So far we have. Sometimes it's just, you know, beans and things like that. Life's not easy, Mrs. Arizona. You must have noticed that.

BILLEE (*Big alarm*): Mr. Bus Conductor, look't. Look over there!

FATHER (*Galvanized;* ALL *stare toward the Left*): Ladies and gentlemen, there are those goldarn Indians again! I want you to put
your heads right down on the floor! Right down! (ALL *except*
FATHER *crouch on the floor.*) I don't want any of them arrows to
come in the windows and hit you. (FATHER *fires masterfully from
the hip.*) They'll be sorry for this. BANG! BANG! That'll teach
them. BANG! (BILLEE *rises and whirls, shooting splendidly in all
directions.*) There! The danger's over, ladies and gentlemen. You
can get in your seats now. I'll report that to the Man Up There
in Washington, D.C., you see if I don't. (*To* MOTHER.) May I ask
if you're all right back there?

MOTHER: Yes, thank you, Mr. Bus Conductor. I want to say that Mr.
Wentworth behaved splendidly. I don't think that I'd be here
except for him.

FATHER: Good! Minute I saw him I knew he had the old stuff in him!
Ladies, I think you did A-number-one, too.

CAROLINE: Does that happen often, Mr. Bus Conductor?

FATHER: Well, you know what a man's life is like, Mrs. Arizona.
Fight. Struggle. Survive. Struggle. Survive. Always was.

DODIE: What if—what if you *didn't* come back?

FATHER: Do you mean, if I died? We don't think of that, Miss Wilson. But when we come home Friday nights we like to see the look
on the faces of our wives and children. Another week, and we're
still there. And do you know what I do on my free days, Miss
Wilson, after sitting cooped up behind this wheel?

DODIE (*Sudden inspiration*): Play golf.

FATHER: You're bright, Miss Wilson, bright as a penny.

CAROLINE (*Who has been glancing at* MOTHER): Mr. Bus Conductor,
can I ask you why that lady—why she's so sad?

FATHER: You don't know?

CAROLINE: No.

FATHER (*Lowering his voice*): She just got some bad news. Her children left the house.

CAROLINE: Did they?

FATHER: Don't mention it to her, will you?

CAROLINE (*Insecurely*): Why did they do that?

FATHER: Well, children are funny. Funny. Now I come to think of
it, it'd be nice if, a little later, you went back and sort of com-
forted her. Like Mr. Wentworth's doing.

DODIE: Wasn't she good to them?

FATHER: What's that?

DODIE: Wasn't she a *good* mother?

FATHER: Well, let me ask *you* a question: is there any such thing as a good mother or a good father? Look at me: I do the best I can for my family—things to eat, you know, and dresses and shoes. I see you've got some real pretty shoes on, ladies. But, well, *children don't understand,* and that's all you can say about it. Do you know what one of my daughters said to me last week? She said she wished she was an orphan. Hard. Very hard.

CAROLINE (*Struggling*): Lots of times parents don't understand children, either.

FATHER (*Abruptly breaking the mood*): But now, ladies and gentlemen, I have a treat for you. (*Stops the bus and points dramatically to the front Right.* ALL *gaze in awe.*) Isn't that a sight! The Mississippi River! Isn't that a lot of water!

MOTHER (*After a moment's gaze, with increasing concern*): But—but —Mr. Bus Conductor.

FATHER (*Looking back at her and sharing her anxiety*): Madam, I think I know what you're thinking, and it troubles me too. (MOTHER *has come halfway down the aisle, her eyes on the river.*) Ladies and gentlemen, the river's in flood. I don't think I've ever seen it so high. The question is: would it be safe to cross it today? Look yourselves—would that bridge hold?

MOTHER (*Returning to her seat*): Mr. Bus Conductor, may I make a suggestion?

FATHER: You certainly may.

MOTHER: I suggest that you ask the passengers to raise their hands if they think it's best that we don't cross the Mississippi today.

FATHER: *Very* good idea! That'll mean we turn around and go back to where we came from. Now think it over, ladies and gentlemen. All who are ready to do that raise their hands. (MOTHER *and* BILLEE *raise their hands at once. Then* DODIE. *Finally, unhappily,* CAROLINE. FATHER *earnestly counts the twenty hands in the bus.*) All right! Everybody wants to go back. So, here we go. (*He starts the bus.*) Now, I'm going to go pretty fast, so sit square in your seats. (*After a pause, confidentially over his shoulder to* CAROLINE.) I hope you really meant it when you put your hand up, Mrs. Arizona.

CAROLINE: Well . . .

FATHER: You *do* have some folks waiting for you at home, don't you?

DODIE (*Quickly*): Yes, we do.

CAROLINE (*Slowly, near to tears*): But we didn't get to China or to that river where the lions and tigers are. It's too soon to go back to where I come from, where everybody says silly things they don't mean one bit, and where nobody treats you like a real person. And we didn't get to eat the famous heaven-fruit sandwich at that place.

DODIE (*Embarrassed*): Car'line, you can do it another time.

(CAROLINE's *lowered head shows that she doesn't believe this.*)

FATHER (*Confidentially*): Mrs. Arizona, I'll honor that ticket *at any time,* and I'll be looking for you.

CAROLINE (*Raises her eyes to him gravely; after a minute she says, also, in a low voice*): Mr. Bus Conductor—

FATHER: Yes, Mrs. Arizona.

CAROLINE: Do you get paid just the same, even if you didn't go the whole way?

FATHER: I? Oh, don't you think of that, ma'am. We can tighten our belts. There's always something.

CAROLINE (*Groping feverishly in her handbag, with a quick sob*): No! I haven't got a *lot* of money, but—here! Here's more'n two dollars, and you can buy a lot of things to eat with that.

FATHER (*Quietly and slowly, his eyes on the road*): That's real thoughtful of you, Mrs. Arizona, and I thank you. But you put that away and keep it. I feel sure that this is going to be my good year. (*After a pause.*) Excuse me, may I put my hand on your hand a minute to show you know I appreciate what you did?

CAROLINE (*Shy*): Yes, you may.

(*He does so, very respectfully; then returns to his wheel.*)

DODIE: Car'line, what're you crying about?

CAROLINE: When . . . you try to *do* something for somebody . . . and . . .

FATHER (*Very cheerful and loud*): Gee whillikers! My wife will be surprised to see me back home so soon. Poor old thing, she doesn't have many pleasures. Just a little shopping now and then. (*He tosses off a snatch of song.*) "The son of a, son of a, son of a gambolier . . ." I think this would be a good time to go back and say a nice word to that lady who's had a little disappointment in her home, don't you?

CAROLINE: Well, uh . . . Come, Dodie. (CAROLINE *goes back and sits in front of* MOTHER, *talking to her over the back of the seat;* DODIE *stands beside her.*) The bus conductor says that everybody isn't in your house any more.

MOTHER (*Lowered eyes*): Did he? That's true.

CAROLINE: They'll come back. I know they will.

MOTHER: Oh, do you think so?

CAROLINE: Children don't like being treated as children *all the time.* And I think it isn't worthwhile being born into the world if you have to do the same things every day.

DODIE: The reason I don't like grown-ups is that they don't ever think any inneresting thoughts. I guess they're so old that they just get tired of expecting anything to be different or exciting. So they just do the same old golfing and shopping.

CAROLINE (*Suddenly seeing a landmark through the window*): Mr. Bus Conductor! Mr. Bus Conductor! Please, will you please stop at the next corner? This is where we have to get off. (*Under her voice, commandingly.*) Come, Dodie, Billee. Come quick!

(*They start up the aisle toward the bus exit, then turn back to* MOTHER. *Their farewells are their best party manners.*)

THE CHILDREN (*Shaking hands with both* PARENTS): I'm very glad to have met you. Thank you very much. I'm very glad to have met you.

FATHER (*As* MOTHER *joins him at the bus exit*): But you'll come on my bus again? We'll see you again?

CAROLINE (*To* DODIE *and* BILLEE, *low*): Now, run! (*They run into the house like rabbits. She stands at the bus door, with lowered eyes.*) Well . . . you see . . . you're just people in our game. You're not *really* alive. That's why we could talk to you. (*A quick glance at her* FATHER, *then she looks down again.*) Besides, we've found that it's best not to make friends with grown-ups, because . . . in the end . . . they don't act fair to you. . . . But thank you; I'm very glad to have met you.

(*She goes into the house.* FATHER *takes off his cap and glasses;*

MOTHER *her hat and veil. They place them on chairs.* FATHER *prepares to make a difficult golf stroke.*)

FATHER: Where *are* the children?

MOTHER: Oh, they're hiding somewhere, as usual.

FATHER: Hiding! Hiding from their father!

MOTHER: Or they're playing one of those awful games of theirs. Come in, come in. You'll see them at supper. (*She goes into the house.*)

FATHER (*He stands at the end of the Stage farthest from the house and calls*): Caroline! Dodie! Billee-ee-ee! (*Silence, of course. He goes into the house.*)

The Chief's
Bride

BY

DESMOND DUDWA PHIRI

THE CHIEF'S BRIDE will be of interest to American young people for the information it contains about contemporary life in East and Central Africa. A didactic play, sometimes devoid of humor, it nevertheless dramatizes vividly the changes that are taking place there, many of which have parallels within our own country. The liberation of women, for instance, is a topic of constant concern to Tamara, the heroine of the title, just as it is today in the United States. The generation gap also appears to be a problem of similar regard. The young Africans seen here question the traditions that govern their lives just as do many American youths, and they find some of the same difficulties in making understood their opposition to the past by those who disagree with them. Although the contrasts between village and city life in Africa and America are quite distinct, the challenges they present in this play have much in common. The cry for independence, equality and progress that is heard throughout *The Chief's Bride* is the genuine voice of Africa's young people and perhaps of young people everywhere.

Yet there are dissimilarities, too, in the life depicted. Tamara is promised as a bride to the chief when she is only thirteen years old. The absolute authority of the chief holds no counterpart in America. And the everyday life, which resplendently colors the drama, is quite contrary with its ceremonies, feasts, manners, customs and native dress. This is a play of Africa written for African students to perform and read.

Desmond Dudwa Phiri was born in 1931 in the Mzimba district of Northern Malawi in East Central Africa, where he was also educated until he left for England to attend the London School of Economics. While a student there, he visited Drury Lane Theatre and saw a performance of *My Fair Lady*, which instantly kindled his interest in theatre. Returning to Africa, he was employed in various government positions before he joined the diplomatic service and represented his country in Bonn, Germany, and later as a member of the Malawi delegation to the General Assembly of the United Nations. He now lives in Malawi with his wife and five children, and in addition to plays he is also at work on a novel. When not writing in English, he publishes fiction in his own Malawian dialect, called Tumbuka.

A group of students in Dar es Salaam wished to produce a play in 1963 and called upon Mr. Phiri for an appropriate script. He had just completed the first draft of a short story called "The Chief's Bride," which he immediately worked into a play that was read to the students. Their enthusiasm led to its production under the direction of Mrs. Chris Rosenfeld, with a cast that the author calls "quite international"; its members represented such various sections of Africa as Zambia, Kenya, Tanzania, Malawi, Rhodesia and Uganda.

The Chief's Bride

CHARACTERS

GWAZA, *the village headman*
ZINYANGA, *his wife*
TAMARA, *their daughter*
NYÉMBEZI, *her aunt*
LANGA, *friend of Gwaza*
YAMANYA, *his wife*
KHETIWE, *their daughter*
VILLAGERS, *men, women and children*
BIZINGO, *the Chief's drummer or herald*
CHIEF GAMA
SIMBA, *the village witch doctor*
YOUNG MAN, *from the town*
SMALL BOY, *from the village*
SENIOR COUNSELLOR, *adviser to the Chief*
VILLAGE HUSBAND
VILLAGE WIFE
MESSENGER

The action of the play takes place in and around the village where Gwaza is the headman in the land of Abanturika.

Act I

Scene 1: *Late aftenoon on the day of the Feast of the Harvest.*

Scene 2: *Some months later by a stream on the outskirts of the village. Afternoon.*

Scene 3: *On the roadside near the village the same evening.*

Act II

Scene 1: *Late afternoon on the day of the Feast of the Harvest the following year.*

Scene 2: *Interior of a hut used by the Chief. Nighttime, after the wedding.*

Scene 3: *The same, three days later. Afternoon.*

ACT I

The action of the play takes place in and around the village where GWAZA *is the headman. It is the dry season in the land of Abanturika. Harvesting has been completed and the people are about to celebrate it with the usual feast. There is much excitement because* CHIEF GAMA *is using the opportunity to visit the village in state. It is late in the afternoon. The villagers are assembled, led by* GWAZA, *who stands just in front of the others, to greet the* CHIEF. *There is a lively buzz of conversation and above it is the noise of the approaching procession with drums beating and people cheering.* (Note: *When the actors speak the background noises must recede, otherwise the audience will not hear what is said.*)

GWAZA: Everybody quiet now. I can see the Chief approaching. Let us all remember our good manners.

LANGA: Yes. We don't want to give the impression we are a lot of ignorant people who don't know how to behave.

(BIZINGO, *the Chief's drummer, enters heading a procession of men and women followed by* CHIEF GAMA *himself, regally dressed. The men jump and dance while the women lilt and clap hands in unison as they all sing. The* CHIEF *is led to a big chair on which is spread a lion's skin. When he is seated everybody bows and all stand, silent and respectful.*)

GWAZA: Welcome, oh Chief, to our village. This is my trusted friend Langa. He is our best basket-maker. (LANGA, *standing beside and slightly behind* GWAZA, *bows low.*)

[459]

CHIEF (*Nodding his head and leaning slightly forward*): I am pleased to meet you, Langa. Can I see some samples of your work?

GWAZA (*To his daughter* TAMARA): Lift up those baskets for the Chief to see. (TAMARA *holds up two baskets of different kinds: one small, one large.*) These two baskets were made by him, Chief.

CHIEF (*Examining the baskets*): This is indeed good craftsmanship, Langa. You have skilful hands.

LANGA (*Bows low*): Thank you, Chief, for your kind words. Great is the Chief.

(*The* VILLAGERS *and* ATTENDANTS *all shout,* "Great is the Chief," *and the* CHIEF *bows in acknowledgment.*)

GWAZA (*Continuing the introductions*): And this man crouching on the floor is old man Simba. He is our greatest witch doctor in this part of your chiefdom. At one time, whenever someone was ill we would have to travel many miles for a medicine man. These days, with Simba in our midst, we don't have to go for help. He cures any disease, even those which originate from evildoing.

CHIEF (*Appreciatively*): May the Great Spirit make you wiser in your profession and help you to protect my people from evildoers.

SIMBA (*Kneeling before the Chief*): How can I sing the praise of the Great Chief? I cannot stand straight any more. I am old and my feet tremble. Great is the Chief! (*Backs away and sits.*)

ALL: Great is the Chief!

(*A young man thrusts his way forward. He seems an impudent fellow and is dressed as though he comes from the town. He is certainly no villager.*)

GWAZA: I don't know who this young man is. He has pushed himself forward and says he knows you. He boasts of being educated and, as you see, doesn't mind keeping his hands in his pockets even in front of you. He shows little respect for anyone.

CHIEF: Young man, you should show some respect before your betters. Take your hands out of your pockets.

YOUNG MAN: What sort of introduction is this? Gwaza is biased against me. I don't mean to be offensive. I just like to keep my hands in my pockets.

LANGA: Be quiet, you have no respect for anyone.

YOUNG MAN: You are all wrong.

SIMBA: Take your hands out of your pockets in the Chief's presence!

YOUNG MAN (*Insolently to* CHIEF): You should be concerned with more important things.

CHIEF (*Angry*): Take your hands out! I command you.

YOUNG MAN: Since it will please you I will take them out. (*Does so.*)

CHIEF: That is better. Now, what do you want?

YOUNG MAN: We have met before. Do you not remember?

CHIEF: No. I don't think so. I don't associate with young men like you.

YOUNG MAN: That is the trouble. I've come here to say that it is in your own interest to include young fellows like me among your advisers.

(*The* VILLAGERS *murmur in anger and amazement.*)

LANGA: Hush! Hold your tongue, impudence!

CHIEF (*Angry but calm*): Thank you, Langa, for defending me, but there is no need. My father ruled with old men, some of whom are still with me. I, too, will rule with their advice. Young men are hotheads and full of seditious politics.

YOUNG MAN: You are wrong. To be popular with your people you need the advice of younger men who understand the law and appreciate democracy.

CHIEF: All your ideas have nothing to do with my prerogatives as a chief. You're nothing but a cheap politician.

YOUNG MAN: No, Chief. I am a progressive young man, that's all. But you will have to change your views about yourself as a chief.

CHIEF: The way my father ruled is good enough for me. It is my birthright.

YOUNG MAN: Think modern, old chap, or you'll not survive much longer.

(*Again the* VILLAGERS *murmur in anger and amazement.*)

GWAZA: Come, come! That is enough!

CHIEF: Don't you dare to talk to me like that or I shall have to punish you.

GWAZA: Chief, to continue to bandy words with this swollen head is not dignified. Let us banish him from our village.

LANGA: He is right, Chief. This boy has only a little learning, which is a dangerous thing.

YOUNG MAN: I warn you all! Things are changing. Every man demands a vote. Every woman shall have the right to speak for herself.

CHIEF: Stuff and nonsense! Take him away.

(*The* VILLAGERS *start to hustle the* YOUNG MAN *away.*)

YOUNG MAN: I warned you, Chief. You'll not last much longer.

LANGA: Command us to do something to this boy.

CHIEF: Where is my Drummer? Hah! Drummer! Take that young man behind Gwaza's hut and give him twelve strokes. Now!

DRUMMER (*With relish*): Yes, Chief. Right away.

LANGA: Why not twenty-four, Chief? He deserves it.

CHIEF: No. Twelve will do for now. Take him away. (*The* DRUMMER *produces a hippo-hide whip and lashes out at the* YOUNG MAN, *who hurriedly runs off pursued by the* DRUMMER *and angry* VILLAGERS. *There is a "crack" and a "yelp" and some cheering. Changing the subject.*) Well, we've got rid of him at last. What now?

GWAZA: Here comes my wife, Zinyanga, with a special calabash of beer for the Chief. Langa, you have a strong arm. Hold the calabash for the Chief so he can taste the "water."

LANGA: Holding calabashes for chiefs has always been my speciality. Will the mother of Tamara first taste the beer to prove its purity?

GWAZA: Zinyanga, taste it at once. I forgot to remind you.

(ZINYANGA *does so and then hands the calabash to* LANGA, *who holds it up to* CHIEF, *who drinks, first a sip, then deeply.*)

CHIEF: The woman who made this beer has perfect hands.

GWAZA (*Proudly*): It is the same woman, my wife Zinyanga.

CHIEF (*Very pleased*): Let the calabash be passed round. All drink!

ALL (*As they drink and pass it round*): Great is the Chief!

CHIEF: What next does the Chief see?

GWAZA: The dance of the girls, my Chief. (*Turns to the village girls.*) Dancers, dancers. Assemble. Get ready.

(*The girls form a circle.* TAMARA *sings first and the rest sing after her. The* CHIEF *watches with great attention.*)

CHIEF (*Pointing to* TAMARA): That girl dances beautifully. What is her name?

GWAZA: Tamara is her name, Chief.

CHIEF: The woman who bore her is a perfect woman. Whose daughter is she?

GWAZA: The same woman who brewed the beer you have just enjoyed.

CHIEF: So you are the father of Tamara.

GWAZA (*Pleased*): Should I reject that which is mine, Chief?

CHIEF: Your daughter is a wonderful dancer, Gwaza. I have never seen anyone dance so well.

GWAZA (*Bowing low*): I am happy to know she has pleased the Chief.

CHIEF: All of you, silence! Let me listen to her song. (*They all listen as* TAMARA *sings and her colleagues dance at fever pitch. At last they stop.*) That song goes right into my heart.

GWAZA: It is a sweet song indeed. She has many other songs, some sweeter than this.

CHIEF: Call her here.

GWAZA (*Beckoning*): Tamara, Tamara.

KHETIWE: Silence, ho! Tamara, you are being called.

GWAZA: Tamara, Tamara.

TAMARA: Yes, Father.

GWAZA: Come here, my beloved daughter. (*She arrives.*) Kneel down before the Chief. You have pleased him with your dancing.

CHIEF (*Looking at Tamara lovingly*): You are the best dancing girl I have ever seen. Your voice is like that of an angel. How long have you been dancing?

TAMARA (*Shyly*): I can't remember. I think it is a long time.

CHIEF: I understand you have many other good songs. Will you sing one for me?

(TAMARA *is embarrassed and covers her face with her hands.*)

GWAZA (*Encouragingly*): Come along, my daughter. Sing again and confirm that you are the best singer in the district.

TAMARA: I am shy, Chief. I—I can't sing again.

CHIEF (*Softly*): Don't be afraid. I want to hear your sweet voice again.

GWAZA (*Encouragingly*): Sing, sing, my daughter. You have the gift.

TAMARA (*Timidly*): What song should I sing?

CHIEF (*Promptly*): Choose your best. (TAMARA *sings, choosing a short, sad song which greatly affects the* CHIEF. *Looking at the girl as she finishes.*) Who else can sing like that? Come nearer, child, and receive your reward. (*He produces a gift from his garments.*) This necklace is a very valuable one but it is not as beautiful as your voice.

(TAMARA *receives the necklace, half bending her knees and then rises to leave.*)

GWAZA: Don't depart like that. Ask the people to help you in thanking the Chief.

TAMARA (*Obediently returns, closing her eyes briefly, ashamed of her ignorance*): Fathers, mothers, sisters, all—lend me your tongues. (*Turning toward the* CHIEF.) Great is the Chief.

ALL: Great is the Chief.

CHIEF (*Nods appreciatively and continues to look at her as she disappears into the crowd*): Your daughter, Gwaza, should be the wife of a chief. Don't you think so?

GWAZA (*Humbly, realizing the implication*): I'm sure I don't know that, Chief.

CHIEF: Your daughter deserves to be my wife.

GWAZA (*Bowing low*): That is a very difficult request, my Chief.

CHIEF: A difficult request, how?

LANGA (*Interrupting*): Chief, let me help you. (*Turning to* GWAZA.) What do you say, Gwaza? Do you mean to deny your daughter the privilege of being the Chief's wife? Have some sense, man. If Tamara marries the Chief, what will she be in need of? Even you will be well off. How then can you hesitate to give your daughter to the Chief? Everyone will think you are stupid if you don't agree.

GWAZA (*Smiling*): Ah, shut up.

LANGA: Do you think I am joking? Ignore my advice and you forfeit good fortune.

GWAZA: Oh Chief! I am honored and I am not opposed to the proposal, but my wife and sister insist that I consult them on anything that affects Tamara. That is the reason for my hesitation.

CHIEF: Aye, then consult them. The matter must be settled here and now.

LANGA: Shall I go and summon them here?

GWAZA: Please.

(LANGA *goes to find* ZINYANGA *and* NYEMBEZI, *who are only in the crowd, listening.*)

LANGA (*Leading them forward*): Here they are. I have brought them back.

GWAZA (*Loudly*): Zinyanga my wife, the Chief says he would like you to be his mother-in-law.

ZINYANGA (*Pretending surprise*): Oh, Chief, what a surprise and honor this is to our poor family.

CHIEF: Ah, you speak well, mother of beautiful Tamara. All the beer and all the meat you have made available are wonderful indeed. But how shall I thank you for these things unless you let Tamara be my bride?

ZINYANGA: Tamara is still only a child, Chief. She must grow a bit older before we can discuss her marriage.

CHIEF (*Keenly*): How old is she, then?

ZINYANGA: Thirteen years only.

CHIEF: Hmm. She is not quite a child. She will soon become a woman, so I am prepared to wait.

NYEMBEZI: Ah, good, Chief. I and my brother are glad to hear you say that. In that case we agree that it would be excellent if Tamara were married to our great Chief. Once my brother and myself agree about Tamara, that's enough. Nobody else matters.

ZINYANGA (*Sarcastically*): Nobody else matters!

NYEMBEZI (*Harshly*): I and my brother are the owners of Tamara.

ZINYANGA: Oh! And what about the woman who carried the baby Tamara on her back? Surely I am entitled to be consulted.

NYEMBEZI: Chief, I repeat, Tamara is yours if you are really interested in her.

CHIEF: Mother of Tamara, I respect your feelings and I hope you will agree. Aunt Nyembezi, you have spoken well. (*Turning toward* GWAZA.) By the way, why do we all call her aunt though only Tamara should do so?

GWAZA: Everyone has grown used to calling her Aunt Nyembezi, Chief, because she is the wisest of all our women here. She is wise in all matters concerning the bringing up of daughters and gives the best guidance to all who seek it.

CHIEF: I see. Anyway, Aunt Nyembezi has spoken well. But, Mother

Zinyanga, you seem to have reservations. Maybe you think I would not make a good son-in-law?

ZINYANGA (*Humbly*): That's not the reason, Chief. I am simply worried.

CHIEF (*Grandly*): It is the duty of the Chief to solve everybody's problems. Speak, then, Mother Zinyanga, what is worrying you?

ZINYANGA: I and my husband are a humble couple. How can we be the Chief's parents-in-law? I don't think we can ever fulfil the customary obligations.

CHIEF: Oh, I see, so that's your problem. A chief is a chief. (*Facing the people.*) Listen to me, all you elders. I have been very much impressed by the way village headman Gwaza has been conducting the affairs of this village and I now appoint him a subchief. His salary will be treble what he is earning now. Does anybody oppose me?

ALL: Nobody.

YOUNG MAN (*Coming forward*): I do oppose you, Chief, and most vigorously. It is corrupt for a chief to use his official position to influence a humble couple to surrender its daughter to him. Let there be an election to see if Gwaza deserves to be a subchief.

GWAZA: When did this pompous boy come back?

ALL: Hands on him.

YOUNG MAN: These are democratic days, these are democratic days! Down with traditionalism! (*Runs off, shouting.*)

LANGA (*Vehemently*): Chief, may I follow him and sew his lips together so that he may no longer utter nonsense?

CHIEF (*Laughing*): It's all right, leave him. Cowardly enemies cause no fear. If he comes, which I don't think he will, then punch him on the nose.

LANGA (*Aside*): He will certainly come back, this meddler.

ZINYANGA: Between us matters are settled. May I now go and ask Tamara what she feels about the proposal?

NYEMBEZI: Not you, I will do that. (*Aside, as she goes off*) Who knows what she will ask her? (*She returns with* TAMARA, *still whispering to her.*)

GWAZA: It's good you have come back again, my daughter. It is I and your mother who have called you. Have you heard anything from your aunt?

TAMARA: She says it is a good thing for me to marry the Chief.

NYEMBEZI: It is a very good thing for you to marry the Chief. What I and your father choose for you can never be wrong. Say "Yes, I'll marry the Chief."

TAMARA (*Obediently*): Yes, I'll marry the Chief.

NYEMBEZI: Now there you are, Chief. She has accepted your proposal fervently. Your people must now come forward with a financial offer and should approach us according to custom.

CHIEF: How splendid things have turned out. You have been most helpful, Aunt Nyembezi. (*Turning toward* GWAZA.) Tell the people to be quiet, I want to speak.

GWAZA: Everybody, silence ho! The Chief wants to speak. Quiet everyone!

CHIEF: My people! This has indeed been a happy day for me. It marks the beginning of our resting from the drudgery of the hoe. Our ancestors' spirits have blessed us with a good harvest. We can now sit down and eat and talk until it begins to thunder again and the rain bird begins to sing. Are some of you dissatisfied with this Feast?

ALL: None, Chief, none, Chief.

CHIEF: I am as happy as you are with today's Feast. But I am also happy for another reason. Shall I tell you why?

ALL: Tell us, Chief! Please tell us!

CHIEF: Very well. Today I have found a beautiful bride for myself. You all know her. I mean Tamara. May her father confirm that he will reserve her for me.

GWAZA (*Addressing them all*): Ladies here and my fellowmen here; truly have I promised, this very day, to reserve my daughter for the Great Chief. He has come openly, in broad daylight and declared his intentions for my daughter. Let no other man come in darkness and search for her—or woe unto him!

CHIEF (*Pleased*): That's well said. (*Looking up into the sky and then facing the people.*) Since the sun has sunk so low I don't want to keep you here any longer. I had better depart now. Stay well, all of you. (*He gets up to go.*)

ALL: Go well, Chief. (*They follow the* CHIEF *and sing the same processional song as they sang at the time of his arrival.* KHETIWE *and* TAMARA *remain behind.*)

KHETIWE: What a lucky girl you are, Tamara! To be chosen by the Chief is not an ordinary thing. One day your friends will approach you on their knees.

TAMARA: Why kneel on the ground when approaching a friend?

KHETIWE: That's the way a chief's wife ought to be approached even if she is one's personal friend. It is a mark of respect. Now see how lucky you are, Tamara.

TAMARA: I don't see anything unusual in marrying a chief. I think husbands are the same whether they are chiefs or not. Does your fiancé write you?

KHETIWE: He hasn't written to me for at least six months.

(*Enter* YAMANYA.)

YAMANYA (*Crossly*): Khetiwe, what are you doing here, you lazy girl? You know how to eat but not how to work. Born lazy, growing up lazy—what sort of a girl are you?

KHETIWE: Mother, if you want to give me some work, can't you just do so without flying into a rage?

YAMANYA: Don't contradict me when I speak. I have told you that before. Once more—do you understand?

KHETIWE (*Trembling*): I do, Mother.

YAMANYA: Now go along and stop giggling. Go to the bush and bring some firewood. Then go to the well and get some water. Take the biggest calabash and be quick, you lazy girl. (*She gives her a push.*)

KHETIWE: I shall leave home. No more of this for me.

(LANGA *comes in to see what the fuss is about.*)

LANGA: Leave home! My wife and my daughter, what is all this?

YAMANYA: Get away, don't take notice. (*Approaches* LANGA *threateningly and he retreats.*)

KHETIWE: Goodbye, Tamara. (*Exit.*)

TAMARA (*To* YAMANYA): Why did you push my friend like that? See, she has gone.

YAMANYA: You shut up. I am not your mother to speak to as you wish. Dare you to ask me again and I'll twist those insolent lips of yours.

(TAMARA *ducks and hurries toward her house.*)

SCENE 2

It is some months later by a stream on the outskirts of the village. TAMARA *has just undergone ritual ablutions and dressed in new clothes to indicate her entry into adult life. A number of women are seated around her. It is a private and secluded place. The time is late afternoon.*

NYEMBEZI: Now that you have washed your body and put on new clothes, I am going to explain to you the significance of the ceremony. Are you listening?

TAMARA (*Meekly*): Yes, Aunt.

NYEMBEZI: You are now no longer a little girl but a grown-up, so talk like one. Do you understand?

TAMARA (*Sitting down awkwardly*): Yes, Aunt, I think so.

NYEMBEZI: You haven't sat down correctly. Do so at once.

TAMARA (*Adjusting her posture*): How do they sit that sit correctly?

NYEMBEZI (*Facing* ZINYANGA): Do you hear what our daughter says? She doesn't yet know how to sit correctly. My sister-in-law, you must be ashamed of yourself. Haven't you found time to teach her even the simplest things?

ZINYANGA: She seems to have grown up all of a sudden. Tamara to me is just a child of thirteen.

NYEMBEZI (*Sarcastically*): Hear her and what she says. Months ago at the Feast of the Harvest you said she was thirteen, and now you still say she is thirteen. Is it possible for the moon to remain a crescent once it has risen?

ZINYANGA (*Helplessly*): No, it is not possible.

NYEMBEZI: How, then, do you expect a child to remain a child once it is born?

ZINYANGA: I just lost count of time.

NYEMBEZI: Be exact.

SMALL BOY (*Standing behind* AUNT NYEMBEZI): Be exact. (*Dodges away.*)

NYEMBEZI: Who is that imitating me? (*Sees the boy running away and laughing.*) Chase that boy, Zinyanga and the rest of you. He is a cheeky intruder. This is not the sort of ceremony for boys to see.

ZINYANGA: The boy has run away, but I see a man heading this way.

NYEMBEZI: Go and warn him to keep away. This is women's business and nothing to do with men.

ZINYANGA: I will go and tell him. (*Directs the man away politely by signs.*)

NYEMBEZI (*Back to her instructions*): Tamara, put your legs together and sideways. Always sit down like that. It is the correct way for a woman. Do you understand?

TAMARA: Yes, Aunt, but I feel pain in my knees when I sit down like this.

NYEMBEZI (*Impatiently*): Shut up and stop telling lies. All decent women sit like that and never complain. Are your legs any different from other people's?

TAMARA (*Aside scowling*): No, I suppose not. (*Aside.*) But it still hurts.

NYEMBEZI: Then don't complain. Now I have another rule for you. Are you listening?

TAMARA (*Fed up*): I am listening all the time.

NYEMBEZI: Don't answer me like that. I will not stand impoliteness. Just say, "Yes, my aunt."

TAMARA (*Grinning*): Yes, my aunt.

NYEMBEZI: You must not keep the company of grown-up boys. It is no longer proper for you. You are reserved for the Chief and we don't want to hear stories about you. You must go to the Chief as a pure and innocent bride. Do my words enter your ears?

TAMARA (*Not very impressed*): They do.

NYEMBEZI: Now here is a pounding stick. Show me how you would pound maize.

TAMARA (*Demonstrating*): I would do it like this.

NYEMBEZI (*Disgusted*): You would disgrace us all if you held the pounding stick like that. (*Turning toward* ZINYANGA.) My dear sister-in-law, you don't seem to have taught Tamara even a simple task like pounding. Just look at the way she handles the stick. You would think she was going to kill a snake.

ZINYANGA (*Defensively*): You want me to kill my only child with work.

NYEMBEZI: Your only child, indeed! Haven't you got three sons?

ZINYANGA: My only daughter, then.

NYEMBEZI (*Pouting*): Be exact always—ooogh!

SMALL BOY (*Coming back with a bow and a hat of leaves on his head*): Be exact always, ooogh!

NYEMBEZI: Is that boy back?

ALL: Ho, ho, ho. Tut, tut, tut. (BOY *runs away.*)

NYEMBEZI: And there, look, I see another man plodding toward us. Go and warn him to keep away. Tell him if he comes here we will pull his beard off.

ZINYANGA: That is old man Chindele Kubwa. Though he has eyes he doesn't see clearly. His ears, too, are full of wax.

NYEMBEZI: Then leave the poor man alone. (*Turning again toward* TAMARA.) That is not the way to hold the pounding stick. Let me show you how to do it. (*Demonstrating.*) Now do likewise.

TAMARA (*Trying hard*): Like this.

NYEMBEZI: Don't hold your neck like that. Keep it straight.

TAMARA: Like this?

NYEMBEZI: Yes, like that. Always like that.

TAMARA (*Quizzing her face*): But it hurts my neck.

NYEMBEZI: Learn to do what I tell you without complaining. By answering me back, you are trying to show off before the grown-ups? Tell me, do you think you are clever?

TAMARA: No, Aunt.

NYEMBEZI: Then don't keep answering back, or I'll slap you. (TAMARA *scowls.*) Here is an axe. Go to that side of the bush and collect firewood. I want to see how much stamina you have. The ceremony can continue later. You are ignorant of the many rules that make a capable woman. It is my duty to make good your ignorance before you join your future husband. Then your in-laws and everybody else will say, "Truly, Tamara was well brought up." Go at once and get the wood. We will wait here for you.

TAMARA (*Writhing*): Whew! (*Takes the axe.*)

NYEMBEZI: Already you feel tired, I can see.

TAMARA: I have never done such exercise before.

NYEMBEZI: It is your mother's fault. She has just allowed you to grow up without teaching you any rules of behavior. Today, however, you are facing another woman. I will not leave you half taught just because you complain of exhaustion. It is my duty to see that you are properly trained to be the Chief's bride. (*To the village women.*) We must deliver to the Chief the sort of bride that he expects of us. Come, let us walk about while we wait for Tamara to return. (*They stroll off.*)

SCENE 3

The roadside near the village. TAMARA *is plodding home with a load of firewood. The sun is blood-red in the west. It is twilight.* TAMARA *enters.*

TAMARA (*Speaking aloud to herself*): How tiresome this ceremony is. I hate my aunt and everything she teaches me.

(KHETIWE *enters from the other direction, pushing her scooter.*)

KHETIWE: Hello! Tamara. With whom are you talking, heavily-laden girl?

TAMARA (*Not recognizing her*): Hello! madam.

KHETIWE: Do you like cutting all that firewood and then bringing it home on your head?

TAMARA: I don't like it at all.

KHETIWE: I thought you did, otherwise you would have bothered to reply to my letters.

TAMARA: Letters?

KHETIWE: Since I have been away I have written you three letters. Have you not received them?

TAMARA: But I don't know you, madam.

KHETIWE: Really, Tamara. Perhaps you don't recognize me in this hat and with these sunglasses. Let me take them off. (*She removes her hat and sunglasses.*) Now—do you remember me?

TAMARA (*Amazed*): It's Khetiwe! Well—

KHETIWE (*Pleased*): Come nearer and have a good look.

TAMARA (*Putting down her firewood, she walks all round* KHETIWE): Yes, it really is you. But you have changed so much.

KHETIWE: Have I? How?

TAMARA (*Excited*): Everything about you has changed. Your clothes are immaculate and expensive-looking. Your voice and manner seem to have changed too, Khetiwe.

KHETIWE: Don't call me Khetiwe. It is no longer my name.

TAMARA (*Incredulously*): You've even changed your name!

KHETIWE: These days I am called Doris Day.

TAMARA: That's a strange name. Who gave it to you?

KHETIWE: I chose it myself when I saw a picture at the New Theatre called *The Pajama Game*. The leading star was a girl called Doris Day. I enjoyed her acting so much that I wished it were me. I hope to become a film star myself one day.

TAMARA: What is a film star?

KHETIWE: You will know what a film star is when you have been to town and have seen a picture.

TAMARA: And so you expect to be like Doris Day?

KHETIWE: Yes, I want to act as she does and sing like her. I want to look like her in every way. Have you noticed how I've done my hair?

TAMARA: Is that the way Doris Day does her hair?

KHETIWE: Just like it. Why don't you come nearer and smell my perfume?

TAMARA: I dare not, Khetiwe.

KHETIWE: Doris Day.

TAMARA: I dare not, Doris Day. You smell so sweet—even from where I stand—but I stink of sweat. If I come nearer, you'll feel sick.

KHETIWE: Of course not! It is to see you I've driven here on my scooter.

TAMARA (*Embracing* KHETIWE): You must be doing very well. Our old teacher, Mr. Chama, has been teaching for many years but he has never managed to buy a bicycle for himself or nice clothes for his dear wife, while you've already managed to buy a scooter and lovely clothes.

KHETIWE (*Smiling*): I didn't earn much money in my first job as a nursemaid. I found out this at once.

TAMARA: How then did you get all these nice things?

KHETIWE: This skirt I got from my first husband. The scooter belongs to my present husband.

TAMARA (*Exclaiming*): So you have been married twice already!

KHETIWE: I had to.

TAMARA (*Innocently*): Who received the bride price on you since your parents were not there?

KHETIWE: I received it myself. (*She laughs briefly.*) Do you think marriages in the town are like those here in the village?

TAMARA: I have no idea what they are like.

KHETIWE: They are quite different, most of them are. Since the girl lives there without her father and the boy is also there without his father, the question of arranging for a go-between and paying the bride price does not arise. Those who are in love just go straight ahead and become husband and wife.

TAMARA: Really! What happened to your first husband?

KHETIWE: I left him because he couldn't afford anything else but a secondhand bicycle, whereas my friends' husbands were providing them with motorcycles and plenty of clothes.

TAMARA: How happy you must be, now that you can ride a scooter.

KHETIWE: This is nothing nowadays. A friend of mine, Sophia, has married a man with a car. I may soon give up my present husband for someone with a decent car.

TAMARA: Can real marriage end just like that?

KHETIWE: Whoever is used to town life would not be surprised.

TAMARA: The way you look now, no wonder any man with a car would be attracted. You are so beautiful.

KHETIWE: Am I beautiful?

TAMARA: You are very beautiful.

KHETIWE (*Pleased*): Many men tell me so. Yes, I know a senior civil servant who looks at me as if I were a beautiful queen.

TAMARA: Aha! So there is a senior civil servant somewhere!

KHETIWE: Ah, yes, why should I not tell you? This man, I know, is tired of his wife. He often tells me that she is old, dull and fat. Whenever he goes anywhere important he feels ashamed to take her with him because she is so dowdy. He takes me with him whenever my husband is away.

TAMARA: Do you dance as well as other town people?

KHETIWE: Certainly I do.

TAMARA: You are wonderful!

KHETIWE: That is why the civil servant is after me.

TAMARA: How can he be when you are already married to someone else?

KHETIWE: You are too much of a village girl. You don't seem to understand what we mean by marriage in the town.

TAMARA: You are right. Town marriages I don't understand. (*She stares at* KHETIWE's *skirt.*)

KHETIWE: You are fascinated by my clothes?

TAMARA (*Admiringly*): They are wonderful.

KHETIWE: You will never have anything like them if you choose to remain in the village all your life.

TAMARA: Not even if I marry the Chief?

KHETIWE: What is a chief these days compared with a senior civil servant? Many common people with a good education earn more money than any chief, including the one who has proposed to you. Come along with me, and see the wonders of town life.

TAMARA: I'd love to, but how can I follow you just now?

KHETIWE: Why not?

TAMARA: I have just matured and I am still undergoing the initiation ceremony. My aunt and other women are waiting for me at this very moment.

KHETIWE: What is an initiation ceremony but a barbaric custom? Forget about it, and come with me.

TAMARA: How can you say that? What about the Evil Spirits?

KHETIWE: Now, now, Tamara, that is just a lot of superstitious nonsense. The things our parents say will happen to us if we break their rules, don't really happen. Be modern-minded, girl, and come along with me to the town where life is gay. There is no fetching of firewood or maize to pound. Oh, Tamara, come and see for yourself the nightclubs and theatres and learn to dance. The village is not for you.

TAMARA: But—I—I—daren't. My aunt—

KHETIWE: Never mind her. The young ones must live in the town and enjoy themselves.

TAMARA (*Impulsively*): All right, I'll come. Let me sit on the back. (*She climbs on the scooter and off they go.*)

ACT II

SCENE 1

It is exactly a year ago since the CHIEF *came to the village. Again the harvest has been gathered and it is the time of festival. But something has gone wrong. Somehow the preparations are only being made halfheartedly. It is morning and the scene is similar to that at the beginning of the play. Preparations are being made for some event by the villagers.* ZINYANGA *and Aunt* NYEMBEZI *are much in evidence. So is* LANGA, *but there is no sign of Gwaza or Tamara. All is centered round the big chair covered with a skin.*

NYEMBEZI (*To a villager*): Put those flowers down there. (*And to another.*) And the fruit beside his chair.

ZINYANGA (*Carrying a jar*): And I have made a special brew of beer to please him. (*Puts it near, ready.*)

NYEMBEZI: It'll take more than that to please him. When the Chief arrives to claim Tamara and finds she's not here, he'll not be appeased with beer—even yours, dear sister.

(ZINYANGA *weeps quietly.*)

YAMANYA (*Comfortingly*): Try not to worry, Zinyanga. It's not your fault. We'll just have to explain.

LANGA (*Thoughtfully*): It'll take a lot of explaining.

ZINYANGA: Why ever did she do it? What made her go off like that, without a word?

NYEMBEZI: She was a sullen, stupid and disobedient daughter who refused to cooperate when we tried to teach her to behave like a woman.

ZINYANGA (*Tearfully to* NYEMBEZI): You frightened her away. It's all your fault—and I shall tell the Chief so.

NYEMBEZI: Nonsense! The girl was a good-for-nothing. The Chief is well rid of her.

LANGA (*Soothingly*): Now, nothing is to be gained by quarreling. It's all most unfortunate. Tamara's been gone for months and we can only hope our friend, Gwaza, will be fortunate enough to find her in the town.

YAMANYA: Yes, it's over a week since Nyirenda's letter came, telling us about Khetiwe.

NYEMBEZI (*Interrupting*): She's another good-for-nothing. If you ask me, she secretly tempted Tamara away and I'm quite sure they are both living in the town.

LANGA: I think there's a good chance you are right. I'm only hoping that Gwaza will find her and bring her back for all our sakes.

ZINYANGA (*Interrupting*): And particularly the Chief's—

LANGA (*Heavily and sadly*): And I would be very happy if he had persuaded Khetiwe to come, too.

NYEMBEZI (*Briskly*): Well, he hasn't found either of them yet—much less brought them back. (*To* ZINYANGA, *nastily.*) Have you thought how you're going to break the news to the Chief?

(ZINYANGA *wails again and they all comfort her, except* NYEMBEZI.)

YAMANYA: We'll all tell him together and accept village responsibility.

LANGA (*Gently*): Since I am the headman in Gwaza's absence, perhaps I should tell him.

ZINYANGA: Oh, Langa! Our good friend. We shall be always in your debt. How will you say it?

LANGA (*Practicing*): Gama—our Chief! (*Bows low to the empty chair.*)

I and my friends have some sad news for you. (*Hesitates.* ALL *say* "Go on. Go on," *etc.*) A year ago you fell in love with Tamara, the beautiful daughter of my old friend and headman, Gwaza, and his wife, Zinyanga, who makes the beer that pleases you. (*He has run out of breath. Tries again.*) Tamara sang for you and you asked her in marriage. Her aunt and her parents agreed if you would wait a year until she had matured. (*He falters.*) Er—unfortunately—Tamara ran away recently to the town and—and—her father has gone to bring her back.

NYEMBEZI (*In a thunderous voice as if she were the Chief*): Oh! And where *is* she? *Why* is she not here?

LANGA (*Lost in the drama*): I—I don't know, sir, I—oh! Chief, we don't know.

(*All bow to the empty chair and make apologetic noises. While they are all bent over, a* MESSENGER *appears behind them, looking perplexed.*)

MESSENGER: Is there one Langa here?

(*All jump up startled.*)

LANGA (*Recovering*): Yes. I am Langa. Who are you?
MESSENGER: I have hurried from the town with a message.

(*All crowd round and listen.*)

ZINYANGA: Speak! Tell us quickly. Is it news of Tamara?
YAMANYA: And Khetiwe?
NYEMBEZI (*Impatiently*): Never mind her. Your news, young man.
MESSENGER: Gwaza sends greetings to Zinyanga, his wife, and Langa, his friend. He has found Tamara and they are on their way home. Gwaza says he hopes to arrive before the Chief gets here.

(VILLAGERS *all cheer.*)

LANGA: Thank you, thank you, good man. I hope you will accept our hospitality and join in our feast.

(*The* VILLAGERS *lead him away and make a fuss over him.*)

NYEMBEZI (*Snapping into the attack*): There's not a moment to lose. The moment Tamara arrives she must be bathed and prepared for the ceremony. Come, Zinyanga. Let us get everything ready. (*Issuing orders right, left and center.*) And bring more flowers. And more fruit. And more beer. (*She has everybody running about.*)

(*Suddenly, in the midst of the melée,* TAMARA *walks in with her father.* GWAZA *looks old and tired, but* TAMARA *is fresh and transformed. Instead of her village clothes, in which we last saw her, she is all dressed up like* KHETIWE *in town clothes, with high heels, jewelry, a hat and a hairdo. There is a noticeable silence.*)

NYEMBEZI (*Roars*): Tamara!

ZINYANGA (*Crying out*): Tamara! My daughter! (*And they rush and embrace lovingly.* GWAZA *looks on sadly.*) But look at you, all dressed up! What will the Chief say?

TAMARA (*Quite grown up*): Oh! I don't much care. He can take me the way I am—or not at all.

ZINYANGA: But, Tamara—he'll—he'll expect you to look like you did last year when you sang for him.

TAMARA (*Shrugging*): That was last year.

GWAZA: Now, Tamara. Remember our long talk on the way home and what you promised.

NYEMBEZI (*To* GWAZA): What's she been up to?

GWAZA (*Ignoring* NYEMBEZI): Tamara, you agreed to come home and keep your promise to marry the Chief.

(TAMARA *looks glum.*)

ZINYANGA: Tamara, our dear daughter. If you love us, and for the honor of our village, you must keep your promise.

TAMARA (*Resignedly*): All right, I will. I'll keep my promise, but I'm not going back to wearing village clothes.

LANGA (*Gently and persuasively*): Tamara, you have been to the town and learned strange customs and new ways. Nevertheless, by coming back here you show your respect to us *and* your promise. Part of that promise means not only marrying the Chief, but pleasing him. Whatever you choose to wear when you are his wife is his affair and yours. But today you should—you must—go to him as a simple village maiden, just as he knew you.

(All clap and murmur agreement with these sentiments and TAMARA *is persuaded.)*

TAMARA: Oh, well! For today I will—but he needn't think he's going to make me do just what he wants.

ZINYANGA: Tush, girl, and come on.

(There is the sound of drums and cheering in the distance. All listen, thunderstruck.)

NYEMBEZI *(Springing into action)*: It's the Chief! he's coming! He's almost here! *(With one massive swipe she propels* TAMARA *into the hut.)* Into the hut, girl. Off with those clothes!

*(*NYEMBEZI, TAMARA *and* ZINYANGA *disappear into the hut.* GWAZA, LANGA *and the remaining* VILLAGERS *prepare to greet the* CHIEF. *The sounds of his arrival grow louder.* BIZINGO, *the Drummer, enters as before, followed by his retinue—and last—*CHIEF GAMA, *and his* SENIOR COUNSELLOR. *The procession opens up in front of the throne.* BIZINGO *takes up his position on one side,* SENIOR COUNSELLOR *on the other. The* CHIEF *steps forward in stately fashion, stands in front of his throne and bows to the crowd. They all bow in return and he sits down.)*

GWAZA *(Bowing low)*: Welcome, O Chief, on this anniversary.

ALL: Welcome, Chief Gama. Welcome! *(They all bow.)*

CHIEF: Greetings, Gwaza, my headman. You are well, I trust?

GWAZA: Yes, Chief, indeed I am well—but tired.

CHIEF: Ho! Tired—why tired?

LANGA *(Tactfully interrupting)*: Gwaza has been very busy with preparations for the Chief's visit. *(Significantly.)* Naturally, it has been an anxious time.

CHIEF: Ha. Yes. No doubt. And you, too, are well, Langa?

LANGA *(Gravely and bowing low)*: I thank the Chief for his question. I am well enough and all the better for this happy occasion.

CHIEF: It is well said. Now for the purpose of my visit. How is Tamara—and *where* is she? Why is she not here to greet me?

GWAZA: In just one moment, Chief Gama, she will appear as a bride. You know what women are with preparations.

CHIEF: Even with a year to get ready!

LANGA: Even with a year to get ready, O Chief! Such are women.

GWAZA: Gama, Chief, you will remember my wife as a perfectionist. Everything must be right. Even now she must be putting the finishing touches to Tamara.

CHIEF (*Eagerly*): Is she matured? Is she beautiful?

GWAZA (*Soberly*): She has certainly matured. As for her beauty, the Chief must judge.

(*Suddenly* TAMARA *arrives, escorted by village maidens, her mother and her aunt. She is dressed beautifully, but simply, in village style. All her town sophistication has gone.* ZINYANGA, *too, is all dressed up for the occasion and* NYEMBEZI *is strikingly overdressed. She is wearing everything she possesses, determined to dominate the proceedings. The* CHIEF *has eyes only for* TAMARA. *He is spellbound.* TAMARA *is led forward by her aunt and the* SENIOR COUNSELLOR, *standing beside the* CHIEF, *does the talking.*)

SENIOR COUNSELLOR (*To* NYEMBEZI): Have you brought with you a healthy bride?

NYEMBEZI: The bride is fit and well. If she falls ill tomorrow, that illness will be from here.

SENIOR COUNSELLOR: Know ye and your daughter that the bridegroom's mother is an old woman. She has no more strength to pound or cook.

NYEMBEZI: Our daughter has already been instructed to help her mother-in-law with domestic duties.

SENIOR COUNSELLOR: Let your daughter know that at this village there are children of many types. Some are clean but others have dirty noses. When they feel thirsty and come to her for water, she must give it to all without discrimination.

NYEMBEZI: Tamara comes from a family noted for generosity. We never say, "This child is mine, that one is not mine." We regard all children as our children.

SENIOR COUNSELLOR: Bear with us. This is the day when everything worth saying should be said so that your daughter may know what sort of people she has come to live with.

NYEMBEZI: Speak what you have in mind. We are listening.

SENIOR COUNSELLOR: The Chief has many people under him. Some are rich, some are poor. They will come to see him about their problems as they have always done. Your daughter must treat all that come without discrimination.

NYEMBEZI: I have taught our daughter to respect all grown-ups and those that deserve it. (*Pause.*) Will you also allow us to have our say?

SENIOR COUNSELLER: You are free people. Speak, we will listen to you.

NYEMBEZI: Tamara has now left her parents behind. We expect you to treat her as one of your daughters and not like a slave. If she does anything that displeases you, send her back to us. Though she may appear foolish in your eyes, yet to us she is more precious than the cattle you have paid for her.

SENIOR COUNSELLOR: The way any young wife is treated by those with whom she lives depends on her behavior. If she speaks well with other people, they will speak well with her. If she speaks ill of other people, then they will also speak ill of her. That is our reply.

NYEMBEZI (*Bows gravely*): We have nothing else to say.

SENIOR COUNSELLOR: Now we claim our daughter-in-law. (*He takes a spear and places it gently on* TAMARA's *shoulders and speaks to her.*) You are now ours. We will defend you with this spear against any attempt to take you from us.

(NYEMBEZI *leads* TAMARA *forward and hands her to the* SENIOR COUNSELLOR. *There is rejoicing, clapping of hands, blowing of trumpets on the side of the bridegroom. The* SENIOR COUNSELLOR *takes her hand and leads her to the* CHIEF, *who leads her away to a house which has been prepared for them.*)

SCENE 2

Inside the bridegroom's house, which is simply furnished. TAMARA *is seated on a carpet while the* CHIEF *is seated on a chair on which is spread a leopard skin. It is midnight.*

CHIEF (*Looking at* TAMARA, *smiling lovingly*): So tonight you are my wife, and how do you feel about it?

TAMARA: I don't know.

CHIEF: You should be able to say. Aren't you the most fortunate of girls? See now, all my people are your people. You are the first lady of the tribe. Is that not wonderful?

TAMARA: I don't know.

CHIEF: Never mind. I know you must be feeling shy. (*He clears his throat.*) Now go to the bed and spread the bedsheets.

TAMARA: Were the bedsheets left unspread just to wait for me?

CHIEF: It is your duty as a wife.

TAMARA: Tonight please perform the duty for me. Tomorrow I will do it myself.

CHIEF (*Spreads the bedsheets but looks annoyed*): Take off my shoes.

TAMARA: Tonight take them off yourself. Tomorrow I may take them off for you.

CHIEF (*Aside*): Is this girl refusing to carry out my orders tonight because she is tired or because she takes me for an ordinary husband? (*He takes off his shoes, very upset.*) Now, my wife, come to bed. It is time to sleep.

TAMARA: I have never taken my clothes off in front of a man.

CHIEF: But we are married.

TAMARA: Congratulations, you are married! I am not yet married myself.

CHIEF: You speak in words I do not understand.

TAMARA: It is plain language I use.

CHIEF: How can I be married to you without you being married to me?

TAMARA: There is no riddle in that you are married but I am not yet married. It is simple.

CHIEF: It is getting late. You must be feeling tired. Come to bed and lie down. Let us stop arguing. (*He moves nearer her.*)

TAMARA (*Stubbornly*): I will sleep where I am.

CHIEF: But we are married. Once a man and woman are married they don't sleep separately. What are you afraid of?

TAMARA: I am not afraid. I merely choose to sleep by myself.

CHIEF (*Walking toward* TAMARA): Now, now, wife of the Chief, come with me to our bed. This is not the time for you to talk like this. If talking is a good thing, then we can do that in bed as well. (*He holds out his hand to her.*)

TAMARA: Don't touch me. Keep away. Do you see this? (*She stands up, pointing a knife in his face.*)

CHIEF: What are you doing?

TAMARA: If you dare touch me, I'll use this knife.

CHIEF: You'd stab me?

TAMARA: Yes, if you touch me.

CHIEF (*Looking pathetic and pleading*): Come along, my wife. When a man and a woman are married they don't threaten each other with knives.

TAMARA: I have already told you I am not your wife. (*She stoops down.*) Here is a line which now divides us. (*She draws it with the knife.*) If you cross it, I will shed your blood, I warn you.

CHIEF (*Getting angry at last*): You, girl, who do you think you are? Must I kneel before you in order to get you to my bed? By paying your father with head of cattle and money, haven't I secured the right to lead you to my bed without being questioned by anybody, even by yourself?

TAMARA (*Imperiously*): Go to my father and claim back your cattle. Then come back and give me my freedom.

CHIEF (*Persuasively*): Tamara, don't treat me as if I were any ordinary man. The whole tribe falls on its face when I appear. Sub-chiefs, like your own father, are appointed and dismissed by me. Who are you, then, not to submit to my commands?

TAMARA (*Unyielding*): Say what you like. You may even kill me, but you will not get me into your bed. (*The* CHIEF *goes and sits on the bed, silent and furious.* TAMARA *lies down on the carpet and falls asleep. After a little while the* CHIEF *gets up and tries to grab her. Suddenly sitting up.*) Get out. Go back or else you lose some of your blood.

(*The* CHIEF *retreats, and lies on his bed and finally drops off to sleep.* TAMARA *wakes, sees that the* CHIEF *is asleep, and quietly leaves the room. There is a long pause and then the cock crows. He wakes up and looks round the room. He is alone.* TAMARA *has left him.*)

CHIEF (*Frantically*): Tamara, Tamara! Where are you? My wife, where are you? (*He runs round the hut shouting.*) Tamara! Tamara!

(*Enter* DRUMMER, *wrapped in a blanket.*)

DRUMMER (*Inquiringly*): I heard you call, Chief.
CHIEF: Where is she?
DRUMMER: Who, Chief?
CHIEF: My wife! Where is she?

DRUMMER (*Aghast*): Did she not sleep here?

CHIEF: When I ask a question I expect an answer, not another question. Do you understand?

DRUMMER (*Apologetically*): Yes, Chief.

CHIEF: Where is she, then?

DRUMMER: How do I know, Chief? I was away in my house. I thought she was here with you.

CHIEF: No, she has slipped out. Go and call the Senior Counsellor immediately.

DRUMMER: Should I beat the drum as usual?

CHIEF: No! Just go to his house quietly and quickly and tell him to come here at once.

(*The* SENIOR COUNSELLOR *bustles in, unceremoniously.*)

SENIOR COUNSELLOR: Chief, what has happened? I heard you shouting.

(DRUMMER *goes outside and sits waiting.*)

CHIEF (*Off his head*): Where is she?

SENIOR COUNSELLOR: Who?

CHIEF: My wife, whom I married only last night.

SENIOR COUNSELLOR: Is she gone? (*The* CHIEF *stares at him dourly.*) Did she not sleep here?

CHIEF: Why don't you people answer questions briefly? She is not here. Can't you see? (*Loudly*) SHE IS NOT HERE!

SENIOR COUNSELLOR: Didn't she say where she was going?

CHIEF: Are you mad? Where is my wife? Tell me at once, I command you!

SENIOR COUNSELLOR (*Reprovingly*): My son, your position as Chief truly gives you authority to command me. But I have been counsellor here since you were born. Your late father used to seek my advice in a gentle manner. He had respect for my age.

CHIEF (*Rudely*): Do you want me to kneel before you? That makes you a chief and me a commoner.

SENIOR COUNSELLOR: I see you are the type of chief who has no respect for those who are older than he is. Let me take my staff and go. (*He starts to walk away.*)

CHIEF (*Relenting*): Hey! Come back. Don't be so angry. When a person is worried he says anything. (SENIOR COUNSELLOR *returns*.) My bride slept here but she refused to come to my bed. When I woke she had gone.

SENIOR COUNSELLOR (*Gravely*): I am sorry to hear that. It is possible she went back home. Did she look unhappy?

CHIEF: I cannot say whether she was unhappy. But I can say she was disobedient.

SENIOR COUNSELLOR: I think you may have frightened her. It is certainly very strange, but there is only one thing to do.

CHIEF (*Pathetically*): Tell me, what should be done?

SENIOR COUNSELLOR: We must send the Drummer to the girl's father and find out if she has gone back to her family.

CHIEF: Do as you think fit. My heart is aching with grief.

(COUNSELLOR *goes out and talks to* DRUMMER.)

SENIOR COUNSELLOR: Hey, Drummer! Go to Emoneni village and see subchief Gwaza——

DRUMMER: I am ready to do that.

SENIOR COUNSELLOR: —and tell him his daughter has disappeared and—

DRUMMER: Your instructions will be carried out to the letter.

SENIOR COUNSELLOR: —and ask him if she is there. If so, tell him she must return at once or Gwaza himself will have a case to answer.

DRUMMER: Should I take the drum and beat it all the way?

SENIOR COUNSELLOR: No! This is not the time to beat the drum.

DRUMMER: How then do people know the Chief's bride has run away from him?

SENIOR COUNSELLOR: They are not supposed to know, and you keep it to yourself. Just go at once and see Gwaza.

DRUMMER: Running without my drum does not please me. How will people know I am the Drummer?

SENIOR COUNSELLOR: I have told you, this is not an occasion for the drum. Be sensible, boy. The drum is used for spreading ordinary messages throughout the land. A marriage problem is not for all and sundry to know about, particularly this one.

DRUMMER: Are not the Chief's subjects entitled to know his family problems?

SENIOR COUNSELLOR (*His patience exhausted*): Enough. Do as I bid
—at once!
DRUMMER: Sorry, old man. I will go immediately and without my
drum.

> (*The old man watches him disappear and then returns inside
> the* CHIEF's *hut. He has hardly got inside when somebody outside
> knocks.*)

CHIEF: Who is that? See who it is. Perhaps it is Tamara.
SENIOR COUNSELLOR: I don't think so. Let me go and see. (*Trudges
to the opening.*) Who is there?

> (*A* MAN *and his* WIFE *appear looking hatefully at each other.*)

VILLAGE HUSBAND (*Bowing low*): We have just been quarreling, Chief.
Perhaps you could help settle our problems.
CHIEF (*Feelingly*): So you too have a problem with your wife. Let
me hear the problem.
HUSBAND: My wife threatens to leave me and go back to her parents.
She has become very insolent of late. Will you please forbid her
to run away?
CHIEF (*Aside*): I wish I had the power to prevent my own. (*To* VIL-
LAGE WIFE.) Woman, why are you so troublesome to your husband?
VILLAGE WIFE: Chief, before you call me troublesome, please ask why
there is no peace in our house. Then you will know who is destroy-
ing our marriage.
CHIEF: Man, speak! What is the cause of the quarrel?
HUSBAND: Oh, Chief, my wife has become very disobedient of late.
She used to be polite, soft-spoken and obedient when we were
first married. Now, since she has become a member of the
Women's Freedom League, she does nothing willingly, if at all.
CHIEF: For example?
HUSBAND: Last night, I told her to boil water for me to wash. She
refused, saying she was tired.
CHIEF: I condemn you, woman, for disobedience to your husband.
If he needs you to do something for him, you must always do it.
WIFE: He—

CHIEF (*Abruptly*): Woman, wait your turn. (*Turning to her* HUS-BAND.) Go on. I don't think you finished.

HUSBAND: She no longer treats me with respect.

CHIEF (*To the* WOMAN): You should always respect your husband. It is your duty as a wife. In the house the husband comes first, the wife second; the husband commands and the wife obeys.

HUSBAND: I often buy her new clothes and send money to her parents. Yet she goes about grumbling to her fellow women that I don't care for her.

CHIEF (*Furiously, facing the* WOMAN): Thankless woman! You should always be grateful when your husband gives you something or sends gifts to your parents. For your disobedience and ingratitude to your husband I find you guilty of trying to wreck the marriage. Now go back to—

WIFE: Chief, where is your sense of justice? How can you declare me guilty before giving me an opportunity to defend myself? Have I no mouth to speak with?

CHIEF: For woman the mouth is meant for eating, not talking. Domestic quarrels are too frequent these days because women talk too much. I—

WIFE: I don't agree. . . .

SENIOR COUNSELLOR: Listen, talkative one. The Chief hasn't finished yet.

CHIEF: I command you to go back to your husband. I don't like women who argue with their husbands. They have no right to do so. Again, I say, go back to your husband and see to his needs.

WIFE: Chief, will you not listen to my side of the question? I pray you, O Chief, listen to me before you force me back.

HUSBAND: Do you even disobey the Chief, my wife? Have you no fear?

WIFE: Shut up! You have already told him your lies. Now let me tell him the truth.

SENIOR COUNSELLOR: Woman, you are the most troublesome I have ever come across in my long life. You must know that everybody else, man or woman, obeys the Chief without question. You are only a girl. What makes you so impertinent?

WIFE (*Knowingly*): A chief deserves complete obedience from his subjects provided that he listens to complaints impartially, but not if he settles cases as if he had his own quarrels with women.

CHIEF: The witch!

SENIOR COUNSELLOR: Indecent language! Who do you think you are?

WIFE (*Haughtily*): A citizen with rights.

SENIOR COUNSELLOR: You are nothing more than a girl. What girl has sense enough to advise a chief? I have never heard of such a thing in all my eighty years. Go back to your husband and continue with your duties as a cook and begetter of children.

WIFE: I won't go back unless I am allowed to give evidence of the way he treats me.

CHIEF (*Interested*): How does he treat you? Come, speak briefly and quickly.

HUSBAND: Chief, anything she tells you will only be a lie. I treat her very well. See those clothes on her body. I bought them for her only last week. She didn't even thank me.

CHIEF: Woman, now there is no need for you to speak. I can see that your husband speaks the truth.

HUSBAND: Great is the Chief! (*To his* WIFE.) He agrees I deserve thanks for the clothes and other things I give you.

WIFE: Do you mean that because I wear your clothes I must not complain if you treat me like a slave?

HUSBAND: Do I treat you as a slave if I buy you nice clothes?

WIFE: Clothes! Clothes! Oh, I see. It is through my clothes that you want to keep me chained to you like a dog. (*Clearing her throat.*) Did you buy me this turban? Tell me, did you?

HUSBAND: Of course I did. You didn't bring it with you.

WIFE: Answer my question. Was it you or my parents who bought me this turban?

HUSBAND: It was I, of course.

WIFE (*Taking the turban off her head*): Here is your thing. Take it back! (*Throws it down.*) And did you buy me this blouse?

HUSBAND: Who else would do so?

WIFE: The truth! The truth!

HUSBAND: You know I bought it for you, impudent woman.

WIFE: Here you are then. Take back your thing. (*She pulls off her blouse and throws it down in front of him.*) And this skirt, did I get it from you?

HUSBAND: I bought you everything you have except your sharp tongue.

WIFE (*Undressing; the men are embarrassed and move away*): Don't

run away. Come and pick up your things. You married me naked.
Naked am I prepared to return to my parents.

(*The men all dash from the hut, pursued by the* VILLAGE WIFE
pulling off her garments as they all disappear.)

SCENE 3

The same, three days later. The CHIEF *is lying on his bed in great
distress. It is afternoon.*

CHIEF: Three days since the Drummer went to the village of Gwaza
and no news yet. When will he return? With his foolish tongue
he is probably blabbing about my problems and people are laughing behind my back at my predicament. O Almighty! Have pity
on me. I can't stand much more humiliation. To think that I, the
mighty Gama, am a descendant of Magalela the powerful, who
could order the parents of any beautiful daughter to surrender
her—and they would instantly obey. And here am I, after paying
Gwaza half my fortune for Tamara, though married I have no
wife. All my people will be laughing. And the humiliation of it.
Never before has a bride refused to sleep with her husband—especially when he is a chief. Oh! Magalela! Breathe into my nostrils
the authority you once wielded. Give me the voice of a lion—your
voice—so that when I speak, my people tremble and fall upon their
faces. I am sick at heart. My body aches. I shall die before they
find Tamara. (*Rolls about in agony upon the bed.*) Help! I need
help! Ho! Senior Counsellor!

(SENIOR COUNSELLOR *comes running in.*)

SENIOR COUNSELLOR: My Chief? You called. Are you ill?
CHIEF: I have a lump in my throat and a pain in my stomach.
SENIOR COUNSELLOR (*Anxiously*): Then you must be ill.
CHIEF: The pain is spreading all over my body. I can now feel it in
my chest. Call my doctors. I can't die before I see Tamara again.
Be quick! Call them in.
SENIOR COUNSELLOR: That will I do, my Chief. (*A knock at the door.
Goes to the door and looks out. The* DRUMMER *is standing outside.*)
It is you, Drummer, what news?

DRUMMER: I am accompanied by many important people now waiting outside.

SENIOR COUNSELLOR: Nobody is important except the Chief and his advisers. Who are they?

DRUMMER (*Pleased with himself*): Subchief Gwaza, some other men and women and a pretty young woman.

SENIOR COUNSELLOR: What business have they here?

CHIEF (*Raising his head off the pillow*): Did the Drummer say Gwaza was accompanied by his daughter?

DRUMMER (*To* CHIEF): I said he was accompanied by men, women and a pretty young woman, O Chief.

CHIEF (*Hardly daring to hope*): Young woman? What young woman?

DRUMMER: The same young woman you wedded and who ran away.

(SENIOR COUNSELLOR *eyes him, embarrassed.*)

CHIEF: Tell them to come in. (*Sits up on the bed, watching the entrance anxiously. The* DRUMMER *beckons them in. Enter* GWAZA, *accompanied by* ZINYANGA, NYEMBEZI, YAMANYA, LANGA, *the* VILLAGE HUSBAND *and the* VILLAGE WIFE.)

GWAZA (*Looking terrified*): We kneel before you, Chief. Long may you live.

CHIEF: Drummer, fetch a stool for the subchief. Then bring in some beer so that they may quench their thirst. (*Searches anxiously for* TAMARA *among the group. Sadly.*) I was expecting you to bring back my wife.

GWAZA: Long may you live, Chief, and may this illness depart from your body. I have come to apologize for the sudden disappearance of my daughter. It is not because she does not want the marriage. Neither is it because she is without respect for the Chief, her husband. No, Chief, these are not the reasons. Tamara, as you know yourself, is still quite a young girl. You married her very soon after she matured. Not being old enough, she was somewhat frightened of her new life. But at heart she loves you.

CHIEF: I am indeed happy and relieved to hear that, but where is Tamara herself?

GWAZA: Some people in this land are terribly jealous. They have been spreading lies about Tamara. They go about spreading rumors just to destroy other people's happiness.

CHIEF: No rumors about Tamara have ever reached my ears and, in any case, I don't care what anybody else says about her. My only question is—where is she?

GWAZA: She is outside. I told her to wait outside so that I could explain the position first.

CHIEF (*Excitedly*): Then bring her in. No woman should be kept outside the house of a husband who adores her. (GWAZA *goes out and comes back with* TAMARA, *looking expressionless.*) Oh, Tamara! Tamara! Have you truly come back to me? (*He holds out his hands, welcoming her, but she sulkily sits on a mat several feet away.*) Why did you desert me on our wedding night? (*Gently.*) Tamara, come and sit by me.

NYEMBEZI: We brought Tamara back and are here to plead on her behalf. She is a nice girl. I myself have taught her the customary rules of behavior, but she has no experience. (*Turning to her niece.*) Now listen to me, Tamara. Disagreements between newly-married couples are not unusual, but it is not good to run away from your husband. Remember what I have taught you, and stay well with your husband, the Chief.

GWAZA: Promise, my daughter, that you will not run away again. Promise this.

TAMARA: I promise to run away to any place I like in search of freedom. If I cannot find it here, I must try elsewhere.

GWAZA: You talk always of freedom. What sort of freedom is this? We are not slaves.

TAMARA: How can a woman be free when she is dominated by her man?

GWAZA: I don't understand.

CHIEF: Neither do I.

TAMARA: Unless I am promised equality, I am not staying. I am going to look for it elsewhere.

GWAZA: My daughter, what is your real fear? From the beginning of time the husband has been the head of the house, the wife his handmaid. Things work out quite naturally this way. What then is your worry if you are a wife to your husband?

TAMARA: Slavery is not a good thing because it has been going on for centuries. I will only stay here if I am promised a democratic marriage.

GWAZA
SENIOR COUNSELLOR } A democratic marriage!

GWAZA (*To* TAMARA): What is a democratic marriage? Explain, for I don't understand.

SENIOR COUNSELLOR: I have lived on earth long enough to see all members of my generation disappear into the next world. But I have never seen a democratic marriage or even heard of one.

TAMARA: The first day of our marriage my husband commanded me to do all sorts of things for him, even to take off shoes from his feet. Perhaps you think this is marriage, but I call it servitude.

GWAZA: Forget it. It is finished.

ZINYANGA: No, it is not finished. The Chief must not treat my daughter like a slave.

NYEMBEZI: You keep quiet, Zinyanga. We are not at a maize-pounding place where you may sing anything.

TAMARA: I am glad my mother is with me on this occasion. This is the one time we must all speak frankly. I have come back here for reasons you, my parents, know full well. It is because I want to save you from dishonor and debt that I agreed to return. But I reserve the right to go away again if ever I am treated like a servant.

LANGA: Does that mean that, when I talk, my wife should also listen to me instead of always forcing me to listen to her?

TAMARA: I mean just that.

LANGA (*Facing his wife jubilantly*): Hear her, my wife? She speaks great sense. Let us treat each other as equals.

YAMANYA: Those who take ideas from children will be treated like children.

TAMARA: My husband has heard for himself my views about marriage. I don't want to call him Chief, because he is a chief only outside the house, in politics, not in marriage. What, then, are his views on what I have said? I should like to know before I commit myself to staying here.

CHIEF (*Standing up and walking toward* TAMARA): Welcome home, where you will be treated as a beloved wife and never as a servant. I will pay full attention to your views about anything concerning us. (*They embrace.*) We will go to the town and have a civil marriage and you will have equal rights with me. All my things are your things and all my people are your people. We will order councils to be elected in every village and they shall send a repre-

sentative to sit on my council. Does that please you, my beloved
Tamara?

TAMARA: Yes, beloved husband. You make me very happy. Let us
start to make this little corner of Africa a place where the rights
of all men—and women as well—(*She smiles meaningly and the*
CHIEF *takes the point*)—are equally respected. Let us work together
for this ideal. (*They embrace each other and Tamara's family em-*
brace each other and the DRUMMER *and the* SENIOR COUNSELLOR *and*
the CHIEF *embraces* NYEMBEZI *as the play ends.*)

The Tingalary Bird

BY

MARY MELWOOD

THE TINGALARY BIRD has been described as a *Who's Afraid of Virginia Woolf?* for young people. One of the many appealing aspects of the play is that the comparison is warranted. The childless couple Mary Melwood has created spend three acts quarreling, taunting and playing games singed with cruelty before they realize that in spite of past mistakes, secrets and lies they still have each other. As they do, sunlight spills into the room bringing to a close a harrowing yet comic night of self-revelation, just as it does for George and Martha in the Albee play. But no one should be afraid of Mary Melwood for this reason. Here *is* a play for young people, and an excellent one at that, being the first children's drama to win a British Arts Council Award. Audiences in England have greeted it enthusiastically, and productions in Canada and the United States, where it only recently was introduced, also have proved enormously popular.

This theatre piece is best defined as "theatre of the absurd." It depicts a world out of order inhabited by characters who live out of harmony with each other, and often with themselves, who speak a language also out of the ordinary. (The fact that the dramatist with only two speaking characters holds hundreds of children "enthralled," as one director put it, testifies in itself to the sprightly and varied excellence of the dialogue.) Everything about the Old Man and the Old Woman is cockeyed, off-balance, somewhat insane if you will: he makes a bird cage out of string; she irons with a cold iron; they lock guests out of their inn; they dine on an old bone. Theirs is a topsy-turvy cottage filled with "assorted jumble," existing in a windy, dark, chaotic universe that blows through the door and into the room threatening to extinguish them as it does their candle from time to time. Anything can happen here, from the unexplained arrival of a fantastic bird who resembles a god to the unexplained departure of the same bird who then resembles a piece of black cloth. They dwell in a forest of uncertainty (the Old Woman, no longer able to trust or see good in people, is always threatening someone); of selfishness (the Old Woman has made their lives miserable by saving for a rainy day she cannot recognize when it arrives); and of love lost and forgotten (the old couple who once welcomed everyone now find it difficult to face each other). Some might say, without being too wrong, that it is a picture of the modern world, a world in need of a Tingalary Bird to set it straight.

At one point the Old Woman says to the Old Man, ". . . I want the truth, remember . . . and see that *your* idea of the truth is *my* idea of the truth, which isn't always the case." What is the truth? the play asks again and again, in many different ways, about many different things. The bird is beautiful to one, ugly to the other. Who is right? Did the Old Woman fly? She says no. The Old Man says yes. We know the answer, or do we? Just because we see her does not mean that it is true; it is *our* truth, but that is not necessarily *the* truth.

Rather than being esoteric and philosophic, the play overflows with comedy, suspense and theatricality. Good absurdist that she is, Miss Melwood exploits her medium with audience participation and a panoply of stage magic, including special effects, flying, dancing, singing and the playing of several games. Everywhere the action is drenched in theatre, much of which exists as effectively on the page as it does on the stage.

The playwright, a mother of two sons currently studying at the University of Sussex, lives in Nottingham, England, where in the summer of 1970 she wrote the successful presentation of an outdoor entertainment entitled *Masquerade in the Park,* seen by as many as 1,200 people at a time who crowded around the action on all sides. Her first play (she says she "always" wrote plays) was produced in her native Midland village, Carlton-in-Lindrick, when she was twelve. For years her mother had supplied the concerts and plays for this community, mostly performed by the countryside children. Although her rural life passed long ago, she still treasures memories of a village background which she believes distills itself into everything she writes whether or not she knows it or intends it.

Miss Melwood's second play for children, *Five Minutes to Morning,* also won a British Arts Council Award. Her ambition is to bring "children's theatre out into the streets, especially to the poor districts and find the sort of children who are never taken anywhere. The love for theatre is there as it is elsewhere."

The Tingalary Bird

CHARACTERS

THE OLD MAN
THE OLD WOMAN
THE SAILOR
THE TINGALARY BIRD

"The Tingalary Bird" was first presented with the Unicorn Theatre for Young People at the Arts Theatre in London on December 21st, 1964.

SCENE

The interior of an old inn, fallen into disuse.

ACT I

*A poor room in a small inn at the edge of a forest. It is a winter eve-
ning and growing dark, but the shapes of twisted old trees can be seen
crowding the dwelling.*

*Above the door of the inn is a battered sign upon which is written
"The-Come-and-Sit-Down-Inn." Some of the words have been crossed
out and others written above them so that the message of the sign is
now "Stop-Outside-and-Go-Away." Just outside the door is a small
clearing amidst the trees where stands a signpost. One of its arms is
pointing backstage and saying "To the Village." The other points
forward and says "To the Sea."*

*The room, which occupies the left part of the stage, has been the
bar-parlor of the inn. In the middle of the left-hand wall is an old-
fashioned fireplace choked with pieces of wood. Over it is a chimneypiece crowded with things. At the end nearest the audience from a
rail in the wall hangs a much larger than life-size pair of spectacles.
At the far end is a large hairbrush and comb like a rake. The side
nearest the audience belongs to the POOR OLD MAN and there his
rickety three-legged stool is placed. The side farthest from the audience belongs to the MEAN OLD WOMAN and there is her wooden rocking
chair with a yellow cushion in it, and a bright woolen shawl folded
over the back. On the wall by the fire and near her chair hangs a
copper warming pan, and near to this, her broomstick is propped up.
Behind her chair, to the left, is a hidden door through which she
makes her entrance. On the center wall backstage is a cupboard and
above it a wall clock with only one finger. At certain times during
this play the tick of the clock is preternaturally loud.*

*To the left of the cupboard is the window, which looks out into
the trees. A small empty birdcage made of string hangs limply from
a hook. There are shutters instead of curtains.*

To the right of the cupboard a half-opened door allows a glimpse into a crowded little lean-to room which is bursting with washday paraphernalia—an old-type washtub, for instance, and dolly-legs, mangle and scrubbing board. There is an iron pump with a curly handle.

The door into the forest is in the center of the wall which makes a right-angle with the back wall of the room. To the right of this door, nearer the audience, is a shelf over which is printed in shaky, childish writing "For a Rainy Day." It is full of assorted jumble amongst which can be seen a rusty, dusty watering can and a dented old tin marked "Buns." In the middle of the stage is a bare wooden table with a chair at either end. Various small signs that this cottage has once been an inn can be imagined.

When the play begins the left side of the stage is in darkness, the room and its objects being only vaguely seen. Along the path through the trees, at the right side of the stage, comes the SAILOR *from the village. He seems to know the inn, and notices the sign over the door with a wry smile. He comes front stage to sing his song to the audience.*

SAILOR (*singing*):

> I'm a wandering sailor,
> With a story to tell,
> And if you believe it,
> P'r'aps I've told it too well.
>
> This poor little dwelling
> Is cold and unkind,
> And over its threshold,
> No welcome I'll find.
>
> So out in the forest
> I'll go on my way,
> And see you no more till
> The end of the play!

(When the SAILOR *has finished his song he walks over to the left and makes his exit. As he does so, he is seen to carry on his back a small wicker birdcage covered by a black cloth. Now the forest darkens and the light increases on the left side of the stage to*

show the room of the inn. The POOR OLD MAN *is struggling, with the help of a pair of wheezy bellows, to make the fire burn. The wind grows stronger, rattling the doors and windows, and puffing smoke and soot down the chimney into the room.)*

POOR OLD MAN (*Recoiling*): Smoke! Smoke! Nothing but smoke—except soot. What a mess! She'll be furious. (*He takes the broom and tries to clear up the hearth.*) No wonder we never get a decent fire with all this soot in the chimney. (*He puts the broom aside and cranes his neck up the chimney. Another gust of wind blows a puff of smoke into his face. He coughs and chokes. Doors and windows rattle violently.*) Go away! Go away, Wind! Can't you read the sign, "Stop-Outside-and-Go-Away"? Go and blow somewhere else before we're smothered with soot. (*He picks up the broomstick again and tries to tidy around the hearth, muttering to himself.*) I don't know *what* she'll say . . . all this mess. . . . 'Tisn't my fault, I'm sure. . . . And it's *SO* cold. . . . (*For a moment, forgetting what he is doing, he sits on the rocking chair and folds the shawl over his shoulders for a minute's repose, leaning over the dead fire and rubbing his hands together. Then he quickly jumps up, guiltily shakes out the yellow cushion with sooty hands, then blows the soot from it. He rearranges the shawl on the back of the chair and props up the broomstick close by, always treating these properties with a mixture of sly respect and envy. He bends down, blowing soot from the chair and cushion, with much tut-tutting to himself.*) Oh dear, oh dear! I shouldn't have sat in it. I've got my own nice comfortable stool, haven't I? I can draw it right up to the fire . . . close (*draws up stool and huddles over fire*), so close that I'd burn—if there was any fire. . . . Why, I remember . . . (*He breaks off as a tremendous gust of wind rattles the door and blows in his wife, the* MEAN OLD WOMAN, *from the hidden door at the back. This entrance must come as a dramatic shock. The* MEAN OLD WOMAN *is wrapped up in a red blanket, entwined by a clothesline which is dangling from a huge basket of washing which she is carrying. An enormous iron, perched on top of the piled-up clothes in the basket, trails a long flex, which of course is not destined to connect with anything but is there just for the absurdity of it and to trip her up. Her hair is blown-about and she has pinned clothes pegs in it, like hairpins. As she bursts in, a huge scrubbing brush falls from underneath the blanket and is followed by a shower of pieces of soap and lumps of washing soda.*)

MEAN OLD WOMAN: Whew! What a wind! It's nearly blown my hair right off! (*She puts down her basket, etc., in the doorway of the lean-to shed, removes her red blanket and puts it on top of the washing. Picking up objects she has dropped and at the same time scattering clothes pegs all about her, she moves toward the* OLD MAN.) I'm *so* glad to be safe indoors in my dear little home with my dear little—(*Her voice changes so abruptly that the* OLD MAN *jumps.*) What have you been doing up that chimney again, HEY?

OLD MAN: Ch-chimney? I . . . I haven't . . .

MEAN OLD WOMAN: Look at the soot! Look at *you.* Oh, what a mess!

OLD MAN: It's the wind. . . . It keeps blowing . . .

MEAN OLD WOMAN: Of course it keeps blowing. . . . That's what wind is *for.*

OLD MAN: . . . the soot down the chimney. You should have the sweep in, like I keep on saying.

OLD WOMAN (*To audience*): There he goes again. Nothing to do all day but think of ways of spending money. There's nothing like it for passing the time. (*To* OLD MAN.) The sweep indeed! I'll sweep the chimney myself . . . in the spring. You just leave things alone . . (*She is looking sharply around the hearth with darting glances.*) and don't go *touching* things. (*With a lightning gesture she seizes her broomstick and with a few swift sudden strokes she sweeps the soot into the hearth and the* OLD MAN *away from it up onto his stool. From one of her pockets—and her apron seems to have any amount of them—she takes a garment with which she proceeds to dust about the chimneypiece, grumbling all the time.*) Sooty fingerprints everywhere . . . *and* footprints. Here, dust yourself with this. *You're* as black as a boot. (*She throws her duster at the* OLD MAN *who begins to dust himself with it. She sees that it is a garment from her washing basket, seizes it from him crossly and holds it up.*) Now see what you've done! Who's going to wear that now, I'd like to know. (*Before the* OLD MAN *can get out an answer another puff of wind sends smoke down the chimney again, and his words change to a cough. The* OLD WOMAN *stuffs her duster into one pocket and feels through the others.*) About that cough of yours. I've been to the A-cough! the A-cough!—A-*COUGH*-e-pary (*She brings out the word like a sneeze.*) and he says—(*this must be gabbled at great speed.*)—What-sort-of-a-cough-is-it-and-I-says-the-sort-that-keeps-ME-awake-all-night-and-he-say-This-is-the-stuff-as'll-do-the-trick-Give-it-him-strong-he-says-and-here-it-is-Open   your mouth! (*She has taken a large greeny-black bottle from one pocket and a big spoon from another and with the last words of her speech she seizes the* OLD MAN's *nose, jerks his head back and rams a spoonful of medicine down his throat, all in movements as quick as possible. The* OLD MAN *chokes and nearly falls off his stool.*) There! That'll do you good. (*To audience.*) I don't know what he'd do if he hadn't ME to look after him. (*She puts spoon and medicine on chimneypiece. She then glances into the warming pan as into a mirror, takes her brush and comb for a quick scrape at her hair, puts herself to rights and sits down in her rocking chair, folding her shawl about her shoulders.*) Now! Aren't you glad to see me after being alone all day? I expect you're longing for a-nice-little-chat. (*The* POOR OLD MAN *has hardly recovered from the effects of drinking his medicine, but he manages to say, although with a tinge of apprehension—*)

OLD MAN: Ch-Chat! (*He becomes aware of her inquisitorial gaze and nervously gets up from his stool. She grabs him and puts him back.*)

OLD WOMAN: Yes. Chat. We'll have a little chat, shall we? (*Amiably.*) A little bit of talk is what makes these long winter evenings so cosy—(*snaps suddenly*)—and I want the truth, remember . . . and see that *your* idea of the truth is *my* idea of the truth, which isn't always the case. (*Pause.*) Has anybody been here today while I've been out earning our living?

OLD MAN: Who wants to come here anymore? What is there to make them welcome nowadays?

OLD WOMAN: Keep to the point . . . and answer the question. Has anybody been in this room?

OLD MAN: Yes. (*Pause.*) I've been in it.

OLD WOMAN: Any callers? Any travelers? Any of your disreputable friends, otherwise called customers?

OLD MAN: You know I haven't any friends . . . customers . . . since you sent them all away.

OLD WOMAN: We can't afford friends—or customers either. And don't think I haven't noticed that you've dodged the question. (*She picks up her broomstick.*) Remember, *I* like plain Yeses and Noes.

OLD MAN: No, then.

OLD WOMAN: No, what?

OLD MAN: No, your Majesty. (*He cannot help laughing. She gives him a poke with her stick. His laughter stops.*) I mean, no, nobody's been here.

OLD WOMAN (*Suspiciously*): No nobodies . . . no nobodies. . . . If two noes make a yes as some people seem to think.

OLD MAN: Nobody's been here but me—(*pause*)—except for—(*He breaks off.*)

OLD WOMAN: So there *was* somebody. I thought as much. Quick! Tell me! Who was it? You and—

OLD MAN: My little bird.

OLD WOMAN: Oh. The bird. (*She glances at the empty cage hanging in the window.*) Hullo! Where is it? (*The* OLD MAN *is silent.*) So it's gone. I told you it was a silly idea to make it a cage of string. Might as well not have put it in a cage at all.

OLD MAN: It needed somewhere of its own . . . and string doesn't hurt little wings as wires do.

OLD WOMAN: And you left the door open all the time. No wonder it flew away.

OLD MAN: It didn't fly away. (*Pause.*) It died.

OLD WOMAN: So it died, did it? Moody little thing. It died of sulks, I suppose.

OLD MAN: It died of No-fire-and-not-enough-crumbs. (*Pause.*) I don't know *what* I'll tell the Sailor if he comes back for it. He let me look after it as a favor.

OLD WOMAN: Favor! And not a penny toward its keep!

OLD MAN: He told me to take good care of it.

OLD WOMAN: I'll take good care of *him* if he dares to come here again. The Pirate! Coming here and cheating us of our hard-earned victuals.

OLD MAN: It wasn't his fault he'd lost all his money.

OLD WOMAN (*Mockingly*): Oh no!

OLD MAN: And he was *very* hungry.

OLD WOMAN: Oh yes!

OLD MAN: And he promised to bring the money the next time he came.

OLD WOMAN: Next time he'd come to rob us, simpleton. I saw him staring all around with his sharp black eyes! It was a good thing *I* came home when I did and made short work of him. (*She chuckles.*) Oho! He won't forget my trademark in a hurry. (*She brandishes her broomstick.*) So his bird died, did it? And a good thing, too!

OLD MAN: All the same . . . (*He breaks off.*)

OLD WOMAN: All the same? (*She gets up, walks over to the birdcage and takes it down. She stands, thoughtfully, turning it over in her hands.*)

OLD MAN (*Anxiously*): You're not going to throw it away, are you?

OLD WOMAN: Do I ever throw anything away? (*She walks front stage to face audience standing at the left side of the stage. The* OLD MAN *walks front stage, stands at the right.*) There *must* be something we could use it for.

OLD MAN: We could put another bird in it.

OLD WOMAN: What do we want with a bird, eating us out of house and home? Think of something that doesn't cost money. Quick. Any ideas? (*She invites the audience holding up the cage.*) What's that? A toast rack.

OLD MAN: A toast rack? But we never have any toast.

OLD WOMAN: We may have some day—when we can afford it. (*She leaves the front of the stage, goes to the table and picks up one of the chairs.*)

OLD MAN: Not while we have fires like this. (*He goes to the fireplace.*)

OLD WOMAN: That's a good fire. Look at all the wood in it.

OLD MAN: Yes, but it don't burn.

(*The* OLD WOMAN *carries the chair and puts it beneath the Rainy Day shelf. She climbs up to put the birdcage away with the other jumble. From her perch she looks down at the* OLD MAN *and says in an explanatory manner as if to a child:*)

OLD WOMAN: It's a wood fire . . . but if the wood burned there wouldn't be any wood on it, would there? So—it wouldn't *be* a wood fire . . . and it couldn't be a good fire . . . so you'd still have something to grumble about, wouldn't you? (*She gets down with the air of having triumphantly proved her point. While the* OLD MAN *is turning over her words in his mind, she puts back the chair, then goes to the lean-to room, takes the red blanket from her washing basket and drapes it over the table. Then she goes for her big iron, and comes back, trying to disentangle it from its flex.*)

OLD MAN (*To audience*): Hurrah! She's going to iron! Now we'll have to have a good fire. (*Begins to poke the wood on the fire.*)

OLD WOMAN: Stop poking the fire. The kind of ironing *I'm* going to do can be done with a cold iron, thank you very much. Anybody can iron with a *hot* iron.

(Disappointed, the OLD MAN *sits on his stool and watches the* OLD WOMAN *as she proceeds to do the ironing. She brings her clothes basket up to the table, then takes her stance with the iron. She twirls the loose flex round and round above her head, then throws it, like a lasso around the* OLD MAN. *She takes from the pile of washing an outlandish garment, which she holds up so that the audience can have a good look.)*

OLD MAN: What's that?

OLD WOMAN: Don't be impertinent. I don't ask my clients what they are wearing.

OLD MAN: That'll take a bit of straightening out with a cold iron.

(The OLD WOMAN *leans heavily on the iron for some time.)*

OLD WOMAN: It's all a question of weight . . . and waiting. . . . Haven't you ever heard of patience? *(She leans on the iron, and waits . . . and waits. . . . The* OLD MAN *watches her . . . and the clock's tick is heard . . . and then the wind blows . . . and blows. The* OLD WOMAN *at last removes the iron and hopefully holds up the garment. It is more creased than ever. The light in the room is gradually fading.)* There! You see!

OLD MAN: I can't see. Let's have a candle. *(Jumps up.)*

OLD WOMAN *(Picks up the lasso and jerks it)*: I'll get it. You make yourself useful and put all this away. *(The* OLD MAN *gets out of the lasso—and begins to gather up the ironing things while the* OLD WOMAN *goes to the cupboard. She takes a key from her pocket and with the air of gravest secrecy unlocks the cupboard door, taking care that the* OLD MAN, *who is watching every movement, cannot peep over her shoulder and see inside. She takes out a candle in a candlestick and locks up again. She carries the candle to the table and lights it with a match taken from her apron pocket. The* OLD MAN *claps his hands as if at a performance—and the candle goes out.)* Now see what you've done. *(The* OLD MAN *looks crestfallen. The* OLD WOMAN *goes to the cupboard and the whole procedure occurs again. At last the candle is lighted and burning steadily in the center of the table. Then the wind blows vehemently, and the doors and the windows rattle. Putting her hands round the flame.*) Drat the wind. Go and close the shutters—or the draft will put the candle out. Go on, silly, do you think I'm made of matches?

(*The* OLD MAN *goes to the window but before he fastens the shutters, he peers outside into the wood.*)

OLD MAN: What a noise the trees are making. I'm sorry for anybody who is out tonight. (*Hesitates, looks at the* OLD WOMAN.) It's nice to see a candle shining—if you're outside in the dark.

OLD WOMAN: I'm *not* outside but I might as well be in this draft. Close the shutters.

OLD MAN (*Still hesitating*): It's a pity we're out of business. It's just the night for customers.

OLD WOMAN: Customers! I've had enough of them, thank you very much. Shoo! to customers! Let them stay at home, say I . . . and if they're the sort of customers who came here before—we'll be all the better off. Now close the shutters. . . . (*The* OLD MAN *does so, at last.*) And bolt the door as well. Make sure nobody gets in.

(*The* OLD MAN *potters about locking up and the* OLD WOMAN *goes to her rocking chair. The* OLD MAN *comes back to her.*)

OLD MAN: All's bolted and barred. *We're* locked in and *they're* locked out.

OLD WOMAN (*Jumping*): Who! Who are you talking about?

OLD MAN: Why, nobody. Anybody.

OLD WOMAN: You just be careful . . . that's all. . . . With your nobodies and anybodies. Thank goodness there's only the two of us. (*The* OLD MAN *sits down on his stool at the other side of the fire.*) Just you and me in our cozy little home—

(*The wind blows harder than ever and she breaks off. Smoke puffs down the chimney. They both jump back.*)

OLD MAN: There's the soot again. That's the end of the fire.

OLD WOMAN: It's bedtime then. (*She jumps up as if ready to go.*)

OLD MAN: Bedtime? What about supper?

OLD WOMAN (*To audience*): There he goes again. I never knew such a man for extravagant ideas.

OLD MAN: I'll lay the table. (*He speedily gets tablecloth, knives, etc. from drawer in the table and sets the table in a rush.*)

OLD WOMAN (*Seeing table*): What makes you think it's knives and forks? It's not Christmas. (*She goes to the cupboard, which she unlocks, standing with her back to the audience.*)

OLD MAN (*Drooping*): Only spoons . . . again?

OLD WOMAN: Knives and forks if you like. (*She whips around to face the audience and is carrying a huge bone on a dish and a piece of bread. She comes to the table and puts them down on it.*) I don't care *how* you tackle it.

OLD MAN (*Dismayed*): The Bone! Again!

OLD WOMAN: Sit down—or you won't get any!

OLD MAN: What a meal it must have been for the lucky people who had it first. (*The* OLD WOMAN *takes a pair of carvers and sharpens the knife. The* OLD MAN *goes to the fireplace and takes down the pair of spectacles; returns to the table wearing them. He looks at the audience and says:*) The bigger the spectacles the more you see.

OLD WOMAN (*Carvers poised*): Ssh. Listen. I thought I heard something.

OLD MAN: You heard my stomach rumbling. It's so empty. Go on. Carve the Bone. (*He puts his elbows on the table and peers over his spectacles as the* OLD WOMAN *ceremoniously performs with the carving knife and fork. He almost believes that her flourishes are part of a magic ritual that might put meat on his plate. The* OLD WOMAN *listens again.*)

OLD WOMAN: There it is again. Ssh!

OLD MAN: It's the wind blowing through the keyhole.

OLD WOMAN (*Low voice*): It doesn't sound like the wind.

OLD MAN: What does it sound like?

OLD WOMAN (*Concentrating*): Like—like—singing.

OLD MAN: No harm in singing. (*He hums the* SAILOR's *tune.*)

OLD WOMAN (*Excitedly*): That's it. You! It was you!

OLD MAN: No, it wasn't.

OLD WOMAN: You've just sung it. That's what I heard.

OLD MAN: That was the song the Sailor taught me to play on my little harp before you took it away and sold it for fourpence.

OLD WOMAN: Well, I don't like it, so don't sing it.

OLD MAN: I tell you I wasn't singing—

OLD WOMAN: I tell you you were. Oh, eat your supper and be quiet. (*She puts the bone on his plate.*)

OLD MAN: Hey! You've got all the meat.

OLD WOMAN: Those that work the hardest must eat the most.

OLD MAN (*Pushing chair back*): I'm going to have one of my fainty fits.

OLD WOMAN: Then you're better off without any supper. Nobody should faint on a full stomach. (*As quick as lightning she whips the bone from his plate onto the dish and the dish in the cupboard and the door locked again. The* OLD MAN *gets up disconsolately and goes to the window. The* OLD WOMAN *goes back to the table and resumes her supper. But the wind roars terribly now, and the house rattles violently.*)

OLD MAN (*Peeping through the shutters*): It's raining now. Torrents of rain. It's just the sort of night . . . not to get lost in.

OLD WOMAN: It's just the sort of night to appreciate the difference between outside and in. (*More gusts of wind.*) When I hear all that noise outside I feel so snug and dry I could laugh. (*She begins to laugh, but her laughter ends in a cry as she drops her knife and fork with a clatter as the* SAILOR's *Song is heard loud and clear.*)

SAILOR'S VOICE (*Singing*):

> Oh, people with houses
> Are lucky and dry,
> They carelessly smile as
> The homeless go by.

(*She stares at the* OLD MAN, *who is dreamily looking through a chink in the shutters.*)

OLD MAN: It's a bad thing to be homeless on a night like this.

OLD WOMAN: So it wasn't you! That wasn't your old croak!

OLD MAN: What's the matter? Has something gone down the wrong way?

OLD WOMAN (*Hoarsely*): I heard it again. The same song—only closer —and if it wasn't you—*WHO WAS IT?*

OLD MAN: Noises in the ears! That's what you've got! You must ask that A-cough, A-cough, A-cough—that person who sells cough mixture if he's got any ear mixture. Or you can try a drop of *my* medicine if you like. (*He moves toward the chimneypiece, but the* OLD WOMAN *stops him.*)

OLD WOMAN (*Terrified*): Stop! Don't move! Keep quiet! Somebody's outside and going to rob us. That's what it is. (*Shrieks.*) Help! Help!

OLD MAN: Who could rob us? We haven't got anything.

OLD WOMAN: Help! Help!

OLD MAN: And who could help us, either, here in this wood?

OLD WOMAN: Don't—don't . . . make it worse.

OLD MAN: If only you hadn't sold my little harp for fourpence, I'd have played you a tune to calm your nerves. Fourpence was such a silly price.

OLD WOMAN: It paid for the food and drink that rascally Sailor had for nothing. (*The sound of the storm grows more and more violent. The light dims. There is a great crash at the door. The candlestick on the table falls over, the light goes out. The stage is dim. There is great commotion.*) Don't tell me *that's* nobody. Help! Help!

OLD MAN (*calmly*): It's somebody knocking to ask the way. After all, this *is* an inn . . . or used to be. (*He begins to walk toward the door, but the* OLD WOMAN *runs after him and stops him.*)

OLD WOMAN: Wait! Wait! What are you going to do?

OLD MAN: Open the door of course.

OLD WOMAN: You must be out of your senses. (*Calls.*) We're not open. . . . We're closed. . . . Go away. . . . We don't want any customers. . . . Nobody's welcome. (*There is another great crash at the door.*) Oh, bless and preserve us! Don't open the door.

(*Another great bang at the door.*)

OLD MAN: Whoever it is will knock it down, seemingly if I don't. (*He walks calmly toward the door.*) Wait a minute, whoever you are, I'm coming.

(*The stage now darkens so that the action cannot be seen. There is the sound of footsteps, then another crash, then the sound of the door being unbolted. There is a Whooosh of air rushing into the room, a gasp from the* OLD WOMAN, *then a pause, followed by the sound of the door being closed and bolted. All these actions are followed by the ear, in darkness.*)

OLD WOMAN (*Calling*): Who is it? For Mercy's sake, *tell* me who it is.

(Sound of footsteps. Then silence.) Where are you? Are you there? Have you gone and left me? *(Her voice rises in fright.)*

OLD MAN: Here I am. *(The stage goes a little lighter but is still dim. Now it can be seen that the* OLD WOMAN *is crouching under the table. She has lighted the candle and is holding it in a shaking hand, gradually finding the courage to put out her head and peer about. The* OLD MAN *is standing strangely still between her and the door in such a position that he is able to conceal something behind his back, a shape vague but large. It is still too dark for her, or the audience, to see what it is.)* What are you doing under there? Come out.

OLD WOMAN: Who was it?

OLD MAN: Nobody.

OLD WOMAN *(Crawling from under the table)*: Why didn't you say so straightaway? All that noise must have been a tree falling.

BIRD: CRAWK!

OLD WOMAN *(Frozen)*: What's that? *(Pause.)* Why—why—are you standing so still? . . . Move away. *(Her voice falters.)* What are you hiding? *(The* OLD MAN *partly moves. The light flashes, then grows dim. The candle drops from the* OLD WOMAN'S *hand and goes out. She gives a terrified cry. Noise of thunder and wind. Vivid flashes of lightning. Shrinking away.)* What is it? What's that—behind you?

(The OLD MAN *moves aside. Behind him, between the flashes of lightning, can be seen a big, black, covered object, absolutely still and dark. Lightning flashes again and again, then the stage grows completely dark. The* OLD WOMAN *cries again in fear, and the* BIRD, *through the blackness, speaks.)*

BIRD: CRAWK! CRAWK!

(Darkness.)

ACT II

As the light slowly fills the stage, the OLD WOMAN *is discovered at the left side of it, cringing behind her broomstick. The* OLD MAN, *holding a lighted candle, is standing near the birdcage, which is at the right side of the room and covered by a black cloth. The scene is held thus for a few minutes as if the characters are under a spell. Then the* OLD MAN, *like a statue struggling from its immobility, makes a movement toward the cage. The* OLD WOMAN *stops him with a hoarse cry when she sees that he is about to lift off the black cover.*

OLD WOMAN: Stop! Wait! You—you don't know what's underneath that.

OLD MAN (*Calmly*): I shan't know until I look, shall I? (*He makes another movement to lift up the cloth. This time the* OLD WOMAN *stops him with a fierce rap of her stick upon the floor.*)

OLD WOMAN: Stop a bit. (*He pauses.*) Think! Whenever you see anything new always stop and ask yourself—

Will it bounce?
Will it bang?
Will it *burst?*

OLD MAN (*Obediently*):

Will it bounce?
Will it bang?
Will it burst?

OLD WOMAN: Better poke it and see. Stand . . . away! (*With a sudden loud cry she darts across to the cage and gives it a poke with her stick. The* OLD MAN, *startled, nearly drops the candle. There is a great disturbance underneath the cloth. The* OLD WOMAN *hastily draws back.*) Sakes alive! What is it?

(*The* OLD MAN *holds the light and draws away the cloth from the cage.*)

OLD MAN: It's a bird in a cage. That's all.

(*Silence. They absorb the sight before them. The great* BIRD *droops in the cage.*)

OLD WOMAN: That's all? All bird . . . *all* of it? (*She tentatively walks around the cage, keeping her distance from it by making a wide circle. The* OLD MAN *puts the candle down on the table.*)

OLD MAN: Some of it's cage, of course. (*He touches the wicker bars.*) Good strong cage, too: no string here.

OLD WOMAN: Where did you find it? Where was it?

OLD MAN: On the doorstep.

OLD WOMAN: The doorstep? How did it get there?

OLD MAN: P'r'aps it flew.

OLD WOMAN: Cages can't fly. (*The* BIRD *is still silent. The* OLD WOMAN *looks at it dubiously.*) Somebody must have put it there.

OLD MAN: Hooray! Somebody's left us a present.

OLD WOMAN: Why should anybody do that, blockhead?

OLD MAN: P'r'aps somebody likes us. P'r'aps somebody's paying us back for a kindness we've forgotten about.

OLD WOMAN: Nonsense. If I'd ever done a kindness *I* wouldn't forget it.

BIRD: CRAWK!

OLD WOMAN: And it's not much of a kindness to leave *that!*

BIRD: CRAWK! CRAWK! CRAWK!

OLD WOMAN: It can't even sing! Quick! Open the door and put it outside again!

OLD MAN: Poor thing'll get soaked through.

OLD WOMAN: Don't stand there. Get rid of it. Whoever put it there can take it away again. Somebody's hanging about outside, you may be sure. (*She goes to the window, opens the shutters and peers outside, rubbing the glass to see better, and making threatening gestures with her fists.*)

OLD MAN: Can you see somebody?

OLD WOMAN: No. It's too dark . . . and too wet. But be sure they can see me! (*More gestures.*) Be off! You don't frighten me! Whoever you are! (*Comes from the window, leaving shutters open.*) Take it outside. Present indeed! That's not the sort of present I like. (*The* OLD MAN *steps nearer to the cage, half fearful, half fascinated. The* BIRD *stirs and flutters his wings. The* OLD MAN *steps back.*) Go on. Out with it. What are you afraid of? (*The* OLD MAN *makes a tentative gesture toward the* BIRD). Wait a bit, though, it's a good wicker cage. I could use it for a clothes basket. (*Pause.*) I'll keep the cage. Take it to the doorstep . . . then let the Bird out. It'll fly away.

(*Pause. They look at the motionless silent* BIRD *as it broods in its cage. An expression of sly mischief struggles through the look of fear on the* OLD MAN's *face.*)

OLD MAN (*slowly*): Supposing it doesn't.

OLD WOMAN: Doesn't what?

OLD MAN: Fly . . . away. . . .

OLD WOMAN: Of course it'll fly away. It's the nature of birds to fly away. (*Pause, while her confidence begins to trickle away.*) Isn't it?

OLD MAN: Suppose-this-isn't-a-natural-sort-of-Bird-somehow.

OLD WOMAN: What do you mean? (*The* OLD MAN *is silent. They both look at the quiet* BIRD. *The* OLD WOMAN *slowly and thoughtfully walks around the cage again, and comes back to where she started from. Crossly.*) Go on. Say what you mean—if you know what you mean . . . which I often doubt.

OLD MAN: I don't *know* what I mean.

OLD WOMAN: There you are!

OLD MAN: I just *feel* what I mean.

OLD WOMAN (*Impatiently*): Are *you* going to move it—or am I?

(*The* OLD MAN *walks close to the cage and nervously lays hands on it. Then he stretches both arms around it as far as he can, then drops them.*)

OLD MAN: It's no use. I can't.

OLD WOMAN: Nonsense. Try again.

(*The* OLD MAN *tries again but gives up.*)

OLD MAN: No good. I can't move it an inch.

OLD WOMAN: It can't be any heavier than it was before.

OLD MAN: It seems heavier.

OLD WOMAN (*Sarcastically*): Oh, very odd! You can't move it out though you did move it in.

OLD MAN (*With mystery*): Or—did *it* move *me?*

(*Another pause. They look at each other. Then the* OLD WOMAN *recovers herself.*)

OLD WOMAN: I've had enough of this. Either that Bird goes or *I* go. (*Pause. The* OLD MAN *does not move.*) Either that Bird goes—or YOU go.

(*The* OLD MAN *puts his arms around the cage again.*)

OLD MAN: Take it to the doorstep, you said.

OLD WOMAN: Yes.

OLD MAN: Open the cage, you said.

OLD WOMAN: Yes.

OLD MAN: And let it fly away.

OLD WOMAN: *Let* it? *Make* it! And if it won't, give it a good hard push—with your foot.

BIRD: CRAWK! CRAWK! CRAWK! (*The* BIRD *flaps his wings, greatly perturbed.*)

OLD MAN: Now see what you've done.

OLD WOMAN: All I can see is a greatly ugly thing that I didn't ask for and don't want—and WON'T HAVE. (*She stamps her feet and bangs her broomstick on the floor.*)

BIRD: CRAWK! CRAWK! CRAWK!

OLD MAN (*Upset*): You've gone and offended him now. (*Low voice.*) I believe he can understand every word we say.

OLD WOMAN: HE! HIM! I've never heard such rubbish in my life. If IT doesn't like what *I* say IT can put up with it . . . and take ITSELF off before I . . .

BIRD: CRAWK! CRAWK! CRAWK! (*The* BIRD *makes a huge flapping noise directed at the* OLD WOMAN, *who jumps back from the cage, rather frightened.*)

OLD MAN: What did I tell you? You'd better be careful of your tongue.

BIRD (*More gently*): CRAWK! CRAWK!

OLD MAN: Or it'll be getting you into trouble . . . not for the first time, either. (*The* OLD MAN *begins making advances to the* BIRD.) Hullo then! (*He puts out a careful finger and prepares to tickle the* BIRD. *The* OLD WOMAN *screams at the sight, and the* OLD MAN *jumps, pulling his finger back.*)

OLD WOMAN: Careful! It'll have your finger off.

(*The* OLD MAN *recovers from the fright she gave him and again puts his finger through the bars of the cage, the* OLD WOMAN *watching to say "I told you so." The* BIRD *sidles up to be caressed however, and the* OLD MAN *turns to the* OLD WOMAN *in triumph.*)

OLD MAN: 'Course he won't have my finger off. Look at him. He's quite affectionate. Did he want to have his nice feathers tickled, then, eh?

(*Out of the* BIRD'S *eyes now beam two great golden lights as he looks at the* OLD MAN. *The* OLD WOMAN *gasps—the* OLD MAN *goes on fondling the* BIRD. *Now the* OLD WOMAN, *jealous of the* OLD MAN'S *success, also approaches the cage, jostling the* OLD MAN *aside. She puts out, not her finger, she will not risk that, but the handle end of her broomstick, to give the* BIRD *a poke. She comes too near for the* BIRD'S *liking, and he rears up in the cage. His beautiful yellow eyes turn to a vivid green and send out a baleful stream of green light upon her. She screams, and retreats.*)

OLD WOMAN: Mercy on us! It's a monster!

(*But the* OLD MAN *coos and fondles the* BIRD.)

OLD MAN: Pretty Bird. Oh, he's a pretty fellow! Pretty Dickeybird.
OLD WOMAN (*From a safe distance*): Pretty he calls it . . . it's as ugly as sin.
OLD MAN (*Bending to the* BIRD): She says you're ugly, Dickeybird.
OLD WOMAN (*Shouting*): So it is . . . (*to audience*) isn't it?
OLD MAN: Ugly? With such beautiful golden eyes?
OLD WOMAN (*Mocking him*): Beautiful golden eyes (*to audience*) when they're green, as green as grass. Let me look . . . just in case I made a mistake. . . . (*The* BIRD *turns green eyes upon her. She jumps away from him, walks up front to face the audience and stands at the left side of the stage. To audience.*) That Bird has green eyes. If I'm wrong you can all . . . Yell!

(*Behind her back the* BIRD'S *eyes turn to yellow for the* OLD MAN, *who looks at them, then walks up front and stands at the right side of the stage, opposite the* OLD WOMAN.)

OLD MAN (*To audience*): My Bird has golden eyes. If I'm right you can all CLAP.

(*Pause.*)

OLD WOMAN: Rubbish! You're *all* wrong. Its eyes are as green as—as rhubarb. (*She dips into her pocket and produces a stick of vivid*

green rhubarb, which she swishes at the startled OLD MAN.) Here.
Chop this up for your new pet. (*Laughs.*) I'm sure that'll be good
for its gizzard. P'r'aps it'll make it sing. (*She runs up to the cage
and thrusts the rhubarb through the bars. The* BIRD *rises up in
anger, the* OLD MAN *follows her.*)

BIRD: CRAWK! CRAWK! CRAWK!

(*Its green eyes shoot light over her. She recoils from the cage,
her laughter cut short, trying in dumb show to tell the audience
that she was right about the eyes being green. The* OLD MAN
moves to the cage to quieten the BIRD. *It is silent now and its
eyes are normal. The* OLD MAN *and the* OLD WOMAN *stare at it.*)

OLD WOMAN: And another thing. . . . Look at the size of it. But perhaps *you're* going to say it's a *little* bird.

OLD MAN: Oh no! I'm not going to say it's a little bird. I'm going to
say it's Big . . . as Big as . . . as Big as a Boy.

OLD WOMAN (*Moving up front stage, left side*): As Big as a Boy?
(*Pause.*) Then I'll say—it's as Big as a Bear!

(*The* OLD MAN *moves up front stage right. They both face the
audience.*)

OLD MAN (*As if playing a game*): I'll say—it's as Big as a—Battleship.

OLD WOMAN: I'll say—it's as Big as—as Big as a Baboon.

OLD MAN: It's as Big as—a Barn.

OLD WOMAN: As Big as a—Bandit.

(*Their excitement mounts up.*)

OLD MAN (*Thinking hard*): As Big as . . . as Big as . . . as Big
as . . .

OLD WOMAN (*Bursting in and thinking she is winning*): —As a Ball-
room—as a Bank—as a Barge!

OLD MAN (*Getting a word out at last*): —As a Bantam.

(*The* OLD WOMAN *hoots with laughter.*)

OLD WOMAN (*To audience*): Bantam, he says. Bantams aren't big,
stupid.

OLD MAN (*Ideas nearly played out*): As Big as a Birdcage, then.

OLD WOMAN: No, it isn't. Or it couldn't have got inside it in the first place, could it? Now it's my turn. It's—it's—(*with an air of finality*) It's as—Big—as a Beast. I've won! I've won! (*She faces the audience triumphantly and claps her hands for herself. The* OLD MAN *slyly sidles away to the birdcage and puts his head down to whisper to the* BIRD.)

OLD MAN: She called you a Beast, Dickeybird.

BIRD: CRAWK! CRAWK!

OLD MAN: Yes . . . *and* a Barge . . . *and* a Baboon . . . and a . . . and a . . .

OLD WOMAN (*Seeing what he is up to*): BRUTE!

OLD MAN: Yes—*and* a Brute.

BIRD: CRAWK! CRAWK!

(*The* OLD MAN *strokes the* BIRD *appeasingly*.)

OLD MAN: But *I* say you're Big, Beautiful and—

OLD WOMAN (*Scornfully*): Go on.

OLD MAN: —and—Bituminous.

OLD WOMAN (*Incredulously*): Bitu—Bitu—

OLD MAN: Bituminous.

OLD WOMAN: You don't know what that means.

OLD MAN: Yes, I do. I know more than you think I know.

OLD WOMAN: What does—Bitu—bituminous mean, then?

OLD MAN: Find out for yourself. (*To audience.*) That's the best way. Look it up in the dictionary.

OLD WOMAN: I haven't one.

OLD MAN: Find one.

OLD WOMAN: There isn't such a thing as a dictionary in the house.

OLD MAN: Then there should be. Every house should have a dictionary in it. A dictionary's—most important—like the foundations of this desirable property—or the roof—or the chimneys.

OLD WOMAN (*Instantly suspicious at the word*): Chimneys? What's it got to do with chimneys? (*To herself.*) Looking things up in dictionaries, looking things up in chimneys. (*To* OLD MAN.) I keep telling you to keep away from my chimney. (*She walks over to the fireplace, very uneasy in her mind, and begins to look about.*) I believe you *do* know more than I think you know.

OLD MAN: Of course I do. But go on looking. You're getting warm. That's right. Just keep near the chimney.

(*The* OLD WOMAN *begins to examine the fireplace.*)

OLD WOMAN (*Speaking to herself*): Chimney! Chimney! Why so much about chimney? Eh?

OLD MAN (*Laughing*): That's a clue of course. I'm just giving you a clue.

OLD WOMAN: Clue? (*She is more uneasy than ever.*) I don't know what you're getting at. (*Pause.*) Has it anything to do with—soot? (*She brings out the word "soot" very carefully, trying him.*)

OLD MAN (*Considering*): It might have. Let me see. You get soot in the chimney . . .

OLD WOMAN: Soot in the chimney . . . !

OLD MAN: Soot in the chimney when you burn COAL . . . COAL . . . see? Oh, I'll give it away. Coal—is *Bituminous*. There now. You know what it means.

OLD WOMAN: Oh!

OLD MAN: And my Bird is Bituminous because it is coal-BLACK. (*He goes to the cage.*)

OLD WOMAN: Oh, Whew! (*Almost collapsing; fans herself.*) All that fuss about a word—and a bird. I shall have to sit down a bit! (*She goes to sit down.*)

BIRD: CRAWK! CRAWK! CRAWK! (*The* BIRD *shuffles and stretches inside the cage, as if pressed for room.*)

OLD MAN: He hasn't enough room inside that cage. (*Pause.*) Let's have him out.

(*The* OLD WOMAN *jumps up in horror.*)

OLD WOMAN: Out. That thing—loose! (*She looks at the* BIRD *in horror.*)

OLD MAN: I thought you said—let it out.

OLD WOMAN: I meant *outside*. Not in here. There isn't room.

OLD MAN (*To the* BIRD): It'd be a bit of fun though, wouldn't it?

(*The* BIRD *bridles under the* OLD MAN's *attentions, then squawks and flutters. The* OLD MAN *laughs with pleasure.*)

OLD WOMAN: Get it out of the house at once. Nobody's house should have a thing like that in it. (*She gives a sudden shriek.*) Its eyes! Look at its eyes. They've turned on again.

(*The* BIRD's *eyes are a baleful green again. They play on the* OLD WOMAN *like a green searchlight.*)

OLD MAN: You've got to go, Dickeybird. She don't like your eyes.

OLD WOMAN: Eyes like a crocodile . . . and I bet it eats like a crocodile, too.

OLD MAN (*whispering to* BIRD): You're a crocodile now, Dickeybird.

OLD WOMAN (*Grumbling*): It'd eat us out of house and home.

BIRD: CRAWK! CRAWK!

OLD MAN: He's hungry. Why didn't I think of it before? Here Dickeybird. (*Darts to the table and picks up a crust.*) Have a bit of bread.

OLD WOMAN: Bread!

OLD MAN: It's only the bit I didn't eat for supper. Goodness! All gone!

OLD WOMAN: What did I tell you? Eats like a crocodile. (*She wrings her hands in despair while the* BIRD *scuffles and squawks.*)

BIRD: CRAWK! CRAWK! CRAWK!

OLD MAN: He don't like the way you keep on about crocodiles.

BIRD: CRAWK! CRAWK!

OLD MAN: He'd like some more bread, though. Oh, he's clever.

OLD WOMAN: It'll eat everything we've got. There's nothing clever about that.

BIRD: CRAWK! CRAWK! CRAWK!

OLD WOMAN (*Shaking her fist at the* BIRD): And stop that silly noise!

OLD MAN: He's singing for his supper. That's his way of saying, "More Bread, Please." Say it again, Dickey.

BIRD (*Winsomely*): CRAWK! CRAWK! CRAWK!

(*The* OLD MAN *is charmed. He turns to the* OLD WOMAN.)

OLD MAN: Come on. Give me the key to the cupboard. I know there's more bread in there. (*The* OLD MAN *goes demandingly up to the* OLD WOMAN, *who backs away from him, clutching the pocket of her apron. She tries to fend him off with her stick, but he is not so frightened of it now.*)

OLD WOMAN: That's not for eating.

OLD MAN: What is it for, then?

OLD WOMAN: It's for keeping.

BIRD: CRAWK! CRAWK! CRAWK!

OLD MAN: Don't worry, Dickeybird. *That* loaf isn't going on the Rainy-Day shelf. (*To* OLD WOMAN.) Come on. The key, if you please. Quick. You can see he's getting impatient. (*The* BIRD *scratches at the bars of the cage, flaps his wings and makes rasping bird noises. The* OLD WOMAN *has been driven into a corner by the* OLD MAN *and though she tries to swipe at him with her broom, he nimbly jumps over it every time she lunges at his legs. He finally pushes it aside and holds out his hand.*) The key, please.

OLD WOMAN: You shan't have it. I *WON'T* be bamboozled by a bird.

BIRD (*Furiously*): CRAWK! CRAWK! CRAWK!

OLD MAN (*Calmly*): Better hand it over. Look . . . he's pecking through the bars. (*She quietly gives up the key.*) Thank you! (*The* OLD MAN *walks firmly to the cupboard, unlocks the door, has a good leisurely look inside, then takes out a loaf. He does not re-lock the cupboard when he shuts the door. When the* OLD WOMAN *holds out her hand for the key, he makes as if to give it to her, then thinks better of it, and puts it in his pocket. With a baffled look, she lets her hand fall to her side, while he walks to the cage and, standing with his back to the audience, so as to hide the* BIRD, *he thrusts the loaf through the bars.*) Here you are, Dickeybird.

BIRD: CRAWK! CRAWK! (*Muffled.*) CRAWK!

OLD WOMAN: A whole loaf. We're ruined.

OLD MAN: He's ever so grateful. (*He moves so that the audience can see the* BIRD, *who is rubbing against the bars of the cage, and affectionately nuzzling the* OLD MAN'S *hand.*)

OLD WOMAN: Grateful! So he should be. That's a week's breakfasts gone down its gizzard.

OLD MAN: Who cares about breakfasts!

OLD WOMAN (*To audience*): How noble he feels—giving away *my* breakfasts.

BIRD: CRAW-W-W-K!

OLD MAN: More bread? Sorry, Dickeybird. Cupboard's empty. (*Walks to the cupboard.*) See for yourself. (*Opens the cupboard door.*)

BIRD: CRAWK! CRAWK!

OLD MAN (*Turning to* OLD WOMAN): You see how reasonable he is. (*To* BIRD.) You understand we can't give you what we haven't got, don't you, my pretty? Good, Dickeybird.

OLD WOMAN (*Front stage to audience*): Did you ever hear such a fool? Good Bird—*kind* Bird—for eating our last crumb. (*She whirls on the* OLD MAN.) Out with the wretched thing before I take my broomstick to it.

OLD MAN: Ooh! The broomstick.

BIRD: CRAWK! CRAWK! CRAWK!

OLD WOMAN: And not so much of your Crawk! Crawk! Crawk! You don't frighten me.

(*The* BIRD *jumps about in his cage, as if he will tear it apart.*)

OLD MAN: You know how to get his feathers up, I will say that. He wouldn't half come for you, if he could.

OLD WOMAN: Make sure the cage is fastened then. Quick!

BIRD: CRAWK! CRAWK! CRAWK!

OLD MAN (*His ear to the cage*): He says he'd like a little stroll. (*Begins to unfasten the cage door.*)

OLD WOMAN (*To audience*): Was ever woman cursed with such a duffer? I said, Fasten it *in,* not let it *out.* (*She raps the* OLD MAN's *fingers with her stick.*) Out of my way. I'll see to it myself. Who's frightened of a Bird, especially a Beastly, Bad, Bi—Bituminous Bird like this. (*She elbows the* OLD MAN *out of her way and, standing with her back to the audience, bends toward the cage.*)

BIRD: CRAWK! CRAWK! CRAWK! CRAWK!

(*Sound of much scratching and flapping. The* OLD WOMAN *screams and hops about in pain, one finger in her mouth.*)

OLD MAN (*Mildly*): You went a bit too close, my dear.

OLD WOMAN: Oh, my finger! my finger! (*The* BIRD *cackles. The* OLD MAN *turns away to hide a smile, the* OLD WOMAN *sucks her finger . . . and thinks. The* OLD MAN *stands by the cage, gently stroking the* BIRD, *which caresses his hand. A sly look comes onto the face of the* OLD WOMAN. *She tiptoes into the lean-to room where all the washing things are stored, and disappears. Soon there is the sound of things being moved about, then of pots clattering and breaking. Eventually she struggles out of the room, heated and disheveled, her arms clasped around an enormous brown stewpot, which she tries to hide from the* BIRD *by walking sideways with her back turned to the cage. She staggers front stage, left side, and dumps the pot, looking with great significance from it to the* BIRD, *from the* BIRD *to the pot, with a measuring eye. She tries to attract the*

OLD MAN's *attention, but he is engrossed with the* BIRD *and takes no notice of her. At last she calls to him in a loud, impatient whisper.*) Husband!

OLD MAN (*At last*): Yes, my dear.

OLD WOMAN (*Gestures to him to come over*): I want to tell you something—in private . . . so that—IT—can't hear me. Psst. Are you deaf?

OLD MAN: What d'you say?

OLD WOMAN: Come over here—it's a secret. (*She is seething with impatience but tries to be pleasant.*)

OLD MAN: Call him a pretty Bird, then.

OLD WOMAN (*Small voice*): Pretty Bird.

OLD MAN: So that he can hear.

OLD WOMAN (*Savagely*): PRETTY BIRD—(*To audience.*) DRAT IT. (*The* BIRD *preens in his cage and the* OLD MAN *smiles.*) Come on then. Don't take all night. (*Curiosity gets the better of the* OLD MAN *and he tiptoes over to the* OLD WOMAN *and stands front stage, opposite to her, facing audience. In a whisper.*) How would you fancy a nice fowl pie?

OLD MAN (*In loud voice*): A FOUL Pie? Of course, I wouldn't fancy a foul pie. Who likes foul food? Oh, a FOWL pie. That's different.

(*The* OLD WOMAN *dances about with exasperation.*)

OLD WOMAN: Keep your voice down, stupid. I bet it's a scraggy thing for all it's so big, more feather than flesh, you may be sure. But— (*She breaks off. There is a significant pause. Her meaning slowly dawns on the* OLD MAN *as she gestures toward the* BIRD *and points to the big stewpot.*)

OLD MAN (*Looking first at the* BIRD, *then at the pot*): You mean?

OLD WOMAN: I dare say there's a good picking on it . . . and I think it'd just go in . . . with a bit of maneuvering.

OLD MAN (*Dazed*): Maneuvering?

OLD WOMAN: Of course . . . it might taste a bit strong . . . but I'd make a nice gravy.

OLD MAN: Gravy?

OLD WOMAN: So . . . go on. (*She pushes him toward the* BIRD.) You just wring its neck and I'll stew it in . . . (*She points to the pot.*) It may stew quite tender if I put a lump of soda with it.

OLD MAN: Wring its neck . . . stew it . . . sssoda?

OLD WOMAN: Sssh! (BIRD *squawks*.) Now see what you've done, you good-for-nothing old duffer. Now it knows what we're going to do.

OLD MAN: We! I like that! *I'm* not going to do anything. I'm not going to wring his neck . . . *I'm* not going to stew him and . . . THAT—for your big brown pot. (*He gives the pot a kick and sends it skidding off stage.*) Eh, Birdie? (*He walks over to the* BIRD.)

BIRD: CRAWK! CRAWK! CRAWK! CRAWK!

> (*The* OLD MAN *puts a protective arm about the cage and turns to the* OLD WOMAN.)

OLD MAN: You've unsettled him now and no mistake. (*To the* BIRD.) It's all right, my precious, nobody's going to eat you. As for me . . . I wouldn't pull one little feather from your beautiful tail.

OLD WOMAN (*Shouting*): Well, I would. I'll pull its tail right off if I get the chance. I'll—I'll stuff cushions with it. (*She rushes to find her broomstick and seizes it, her confidence flooding up again.*)

BIRD: CRAWK! CRAWK! CRAWK!

> (*The* OLD WOMAN *advances upon the birdcage with her broomstick.*)

OLD WOMAN: I'll give you CRAWK! CRAWK. CRAWK. (*The* OLD MAN *intervenes.*) And you as well if you don't get out of my way. (*Threatening him with broom.*)

OLD MAN: Watch out, Dickeybird. (*He tries to stop the* OLD WOMAN's *attack. They fall into fencing positions. She has her stick and he has only his right arm to use as a foil, but he parries her blows with it.*)

OLD WOMAN (*Mimicking the* OLD MAN's *voice*): Watch out, Dickeybird . . . because I'm going to give you a wallop right on your ugly head. (*The* OLD MAN *is weakening now and losing his position. She is almost at the point of victory, ready to trample down the* OLD MAN *and attack the cage when the lights go out, there is a strange long-drawn-out call from the* BIRD *and an anguished yell from the* OLD WOMAN. *Then a clap of thunder reverberates around the stage and the auditorium. Silence and darkness follow. A Pause. The lights come on to reveal the* BIRD *in all his glory. His big beautiful tail is spread out to show iridescent colors, his eyes are blazing green and golden lights. He is out of his cage and in command of the stage, calm, magnificent, possessive, like a Bird-god. The* OLD MAN *seems to have dwindled. He stands humbly, almost blinded by the beauty of the sight. The* OLD WOMAN *is cowering upon the table, her face hidden by her apron, a picture of abject terror. The scene is held thus for a few seconds, then the* OLD WOMAN, *peeping from under her apron, raises her head to give a trembling cry.*) Help me, husband. Help me!

OLD MAN: Oh, wonderful Sir!

OLD WOMAN: Husband, husband . . . help me!

(*The* OLD MAN *behaves as if he is awakening from a dream. He slowly turns and looks at the* OLD WOMAN.)

OLD MAN (*Bewildered*): Why . . . what are you doing up there?

OLD WOMAN (*Whispering*): I'm keeping away from the Monster.

BIRD: CRAWK! CRAWK! CRAWK! (*The* BIRD *moves forward. The* OLD WOMAN *thinks that he is coming for her. She screams and hides under her apron, but he is merely stretching his legs, trying out his wings first separately, then together, bending and stretching, with a noble dignity.*)

OLD MAN (*Tremulously*): Beautiful, wonderful Sir!

(*The* OLD WOMAN *now lifts up her head. The* BIRD'*s tail closes up so that its colors are hidden.*)

OLD WOMAN (*Whimpering*): I want to get off this table.

OLD MAN (*Making obeisance*): What country do you come from, beautiful Sir? What marvelous place can be your home?

OLD WOMAN (*To audience*): Bowing now! What next? (*To* OLD MAN.) Give me my broomstick.

OLD MAN: Never mention that dreadful word! (*The* OLD WOMAN *bends all ways trying to see where her broomstick is. It is only just out of reach. She does not see when the* BIRD *again spreads out its tail for the* OLD MAN.) Have you ever seen the like? A peacock is a dull bird compared to this. All the colors of the rainbow.

OLD WOMAN (*To audience*): A plain black bird and he sees all the colors of the rainbow in it.

(*The* BIRD *comes out front stage and standing so that the* OLD

WOMAN *still cannot see, he shows the audience the full extent of his colored tail feathers.*)

OLD MAN (*Coming front stage*): You see.

OLD WOMAN: *You* see what *you* want to see and *I'll* see what *I* want to see . . . and I see a black bird . . . and I'm not going to see any different if I stay here till Doomsday. (*The* BIRD *closes his tail and strolls toward the* OLD WOMAN, *who nervously crouches away from him on the extreme edge of the table. With a last vestige of bravado she picks up her apron and flaps it.*) Shoo! Husband, save me!

(*The* OLD MAN *makes a wheedling noise to the* BIRD, *who turns away from the* OLD WOMAN. *Behind his back she makes a sly move to put one leg off the table. The* BIRD *immediately turns round on her. She draws her leg up. The* BIRD *moves away again. She creeps forward on the table as if going to spring off. The* BIRD *spins round to her—she draws back. They repeat this several times in a sort of rhythm. The* OLD MAN *begins to clap his hands in time.*)

OLD MAN: If only we had some music! . . . You see, you shouldn't have sold my little harp for fourpence. But wait a minute, Birdie, noble Sir. (*The* OLD MAN *takes a chair from the table, puts it beneath the Rainy-Day shelf, climbs up and rummages about until he finds the string birdcage. The* OLD WOMAN *looks from him to the audience as if saying, "Whatever is the silly fellow going to do next?" The* OLD MAN *sits on the chair back, a pleased smile on his face as he fingers the strings of the birdcage.*)

OLD WOMAN (*As if making a good joke*): What are you going to do now—play that?

OLD MAN: Why not? There are plenty of chords on it. (*He strikes a magnificent chord, as if it is a harp. When it responds, a look of delight spreads over his face.*) Whyever didn't I think of this before? (*He sits on the back of the chair and draws his fingers across the strings as he must have done many a time on his little harp. At first he plays hesitantly, wonderingly. The* OLD WOMAN, *unbelievingly, and the* BIRD, *approvingly, look on. Soon he begins to play more confidently. He smiles to the audience.*) And I've never had a birdcage lesson in me life. (*He plays on. Music seems to come from all around him, tumbling from the rafters, coming from all corners of the stage and auditorium, rising, falling, echoing. He stops, overcome.*) All that music in this little cage! (*He plays again. The* BIRD *listens in high appreciation, gravely nodding his head, twitching a wing in time, moving his feet as if longing to dance; the* OLD WOMAN *puts her hands over her ears and rocks in agony.*)

OLD WOMAN: Oh my nerves, my nerves! Ten thousand screaming cats, my poor nerves!

OLD MAN (*Calling out in excitement*): Now, Birdie, dance. (*And so, to the* OLD MAN'S *music, the* BIRD *dances, a beautiful, stately, magical dance. His tail spreads out and closes again. Sometimes it is all black, sometimes shining in rainbow colors, and all the time the* BIRD *goes round and round the table in such a way that the* OLD WOMAN, *though waiting for the opportunity, dare not try to climb down. The lights on the stage change then change again. At last the* BIRD *shows the* OLD MAN *that he wishes to have him for a partner. The* OLD MAN *bashfully demurs at first as if overcome by the honor, then he takes the floor, holding delicately onto a wing tip of the* BIRD.) What about the music, though? I know. Here. *You* can play it. (*He throws the birdcage he has been playing to the* OLD WOMAN.)

OLD WOMAN: Me? *I* can't play.

OLD MAN: Yes you can. You'll pick it up. Just think of a tune, it'll come by itself tonight. (*The* BIRD *gives a warning flap of his wing toward the* OLD WOMAN, *who hastily strikes a chord; not a very good one. They all grimace.*) Try again. You'll improve with effort. (*She tries again, pulling faces at the audience at the discords.*) You're not thinking of what you're playing. You're thinking how you can get off the table. (*She tries again.*) Practice makes Perfect. (*She plays again.*) You've got quite a nice touch, I do declare.

OLD WOMAN (*Flattered*): Have I really? (*She continues to play.*) If this is all there is to it, it's quite easy. All that fuss people make about practice. (*She strums away and the music improves. The* OLD MAN *and the* BIRD *bow to each other. Then they try the dance —not without mistakes.*)

OLD MAN:

> You hop.
> *I* hop—

Then we'll hop together.
You hop—
And never lose a feather.

(*The* BIRD *and the* OLD MAN *go into a dance to the* OLD WOMAN'S *music. She is sitting quite engrossed in her playing, in the middle of the table. The lights flash, and grow dim, and change color. A big silver moon appears in the window and its rays stream into the room. Suddenly the* OLD WOMAN'S *mood alters. A strange chord, a dissonance, changes the tone of the music and the happy, magical mood of the dance. Now the* OLD WOMAN, *still playing, stands up on the table and cavorts about. There is irony in her music, there is bad temper in it, there is the iron-hand-in-the-velvet-glove in it . . . and more iron than velvet the longer she plays. Faster and faster beats her music until it seems the* OLD MAN *and the* BIRD *are in its power, they are so captivated by its fantastic spirit. At last, as they whirl about her, in wider and wider circles around the table, she slyly puts her leg down to the floor, her toe nearly touches the floor—then there is a clap of thunder, the lights flash, the* BIRD *gives a cry and rushes toward her. As quick as possible she is up on the table again, and throws the birdcage at the* BIRD. *It bounces on the floor with a tuneless twang. The music is all gone. The magic has fled. The stage is full of ordinary light.*)

OLD MAN: Now you've spoiled everything.

OLD WOMAN: You don't think I'm going to stand on this table forever do you?

OLD MAN: Why did you have to spoil the dance?

OLD WOMAN: Dance? I never saw such a shimble-shamble in all my life. (*She turns to the* BIRD *and begins to flap her apron.*) Go back into your cage, you . . . creature, whatever you are. Shoo! Do something useful . . . lay an egg, or better still, fly away. We don't want things like you around here. We're *respectable*.

BIRD: CRAWK! CRAWK! NAUGHTY. NAUGHTY.

OLD MAN: What! What did he say?

OLD WOMAN: Shoo! Shoo!

OLD MAN: He talked! He talked!

OLD WOMAN (*To audience*): Right off his head, even worse than usual. Just wait till I get off this table. I'll teach him a lesson. (*She marches up and down the table. The* BIRD *approaches her.*) Get away, Fowl!

BIRD: Naughty girl! Naughty girl! Tell him! Tell him!

OLD WOMAN: Go away! Shoo!

OLD MAN: He talked again!

OLD WOMAN: Oh, shove it into its cage—for goodness' sake.

OLD MAN: He talked; or, marvels and wonders! Oh, now I can believe in anything I like—in miracles and mermaids—and happy endings—

OLD WOMAN: I'll end you when I get off this table.

BIRD: CRAWK! CRAWK! CRAWK!

OLD WOMAN: *And* you. Crawk, crawk, crawk! D'you call *that* talking?

BIRD: Tell him where you put it. Tell him where you put it.

OLD WOMAN: Trying to sing now, are you?

BIRD: Naughty girl! Naughty girl! Tell him where you put it, CRAWK CRAWK CRAWK.

OLD WOMAN: If you don't shut that beak of yours, I'll—

BIRD: CRAWK! CRAWK! TELL HIM! TELL HIM!

OLD WOMAN: I'll smother you with my apron.

OLD MAN (*Thoughtfully*): Tell *him*. Tell who? Does he mean—me?

BIRD: CRAWK! CRAWK! CRAWK! CRAWK!

OLD MAN: Yes, he does.

BIRD: CRAWK! CRAWK! TELL. TELL. TELL. TELL.

OLD MAN: Tell what, Dickeybird?

BIRD: CRAWK! CRAWK! Naughty girl. Tell him where you put it.

OLD MAN (*To* OLD WOMAN): Go on, then. Tell me where you put it.

OLD WOMAN (*Astonished*): What?

OLD MAN: I don't know what. It's just what he keeps on saying—so tell me where you put it.

OLD WOMAN: So you *have* been peeping and prying.

BIRD: Tell him ⎫
OLD MAN: Tell him ⎭ where you put it (*together*).

(*The* OLD WOMAN *shrieks and stamps her feet on the table.*)

OLD WOMAN: I won't! I won't! I won't! (*The* BIRD *and the* OLD MAN *look at each other and hesitate. The* OLD WOMAN *leans over and manages to grab her broomstick, which has been kicked nearer to her during the dance. Then she gives a wild red Indian yell and points behind them. They both involuntarily turn their heads. During this moment, holding on to her broomstick, she gives a great leap into the air, almost up to the ceiling, then with a whoossh and a scream she flies right over their heads and stands opposite to them, behind the stick, all her strength and confidence recovered. Again she is at the left side of the stage and they are at the right. To audience.)* Now I'll show 'em. I'll have 'em both out of the house, I will. *(She rushes at the* BIRD, *but he spreads his wings and rises up to the ceiling. She hesitates, then, not to be outdone, she gives one, two, three leaps in the air and at the third leap achieves flight. Mad with joy and excitement at being aloft—she is not used to flying as she is not really a witch—she goes for the* BIRD *with a lot of hasty, excited little blows which never really amount to much. The* BIRD *is never vicious or excited. He merely parries her ridiculous frenzy with calm and powerful wings, almost benevolently as one fends off an excited puppy. As she withdraws for another attack he suddenly seems to weary of her nonsense and drops down to the hearth, leaving her aloft. For a second or two she loses him and cries in triumph.)* I've won! I've won!

(Down below the OLD MAN, *who has been gazing upwards in wonder at the battle, now recovers himself to speak to the* BIRD, *who is investigating the chimney.)*

OLD MAN: Mind the chimney, Dickeybird. Your pretty feathers'll be all over soot.

OLD WOMAN *(Still aloft)*: Soot! Chimney! *(Now she sees what the* BIRD *is doing and struggles to get down to floor level, waving her arms and legs about like a poor swimmer.)* Get away from there! Get away from that fireplace! You fiend! *(She is down at last and, quite demented, rushes at the* BIRD.*)* Oh, the soot! Look at the soot! I'll kill it! I'll kill it! *(Commotion. The* OLD MAN *gets in the way, but she pushes him aside and hangs on to the* BIRD, *who seems intent upon going up the chimney. Beside herself.)* Now I'm going to wring your wicked neck!

OLD MAN: No! No! No!

OLD WOMAN: Yes! Yes! Yes!

BIRD: CRAWK! CRAWK! CRAWK! (*There is a crash and a flash
. . . and a tinkling shower of coins spills all over the floor.*)
CRAWK! CRAWK! CRAWK!

OLD WOMAN: Oh, the soot, the soot! I'm choking! I'm dying!

(*Silence.*)

OLD MAN (*Wonderingly*): It's all come down. So *that* was the soot in
the chimney. (*He takes up a handful of coins and lets them trickle
through his fingers.*)

BIRD (*Very gently, as if he knows his work is done*): CRAWK!
CRAWK! CRAWK!

(*Darkness.*)

ACT III

When the scene opens the OLD WOMAN *is crawling about the floor
feverishly picking up the spilled money. The* OLD MAN *is sitting on
the table, center stage, dreamily trickling coins from one hand into a
leather bag which he holds in the other. The* BIRD *has withdrawn to
the back of the stage, where he stands with benevolently inclined
head and folded wings, watching the couple.*

OLD MAN: Well, I never!

BIRD (*Mildly*): CRAWK! CRAWK!

OLD MAN: All this money! Whose is it?

(*The* OLD WOMAN *lifts up her face. It is all over soot.*)

OLD WOMAN (*From the floor*): Mine.

BIRD (*Disturbed*): CRAWK! CRAWK! CRAWK!

OLD WOMAN: Ours, then, though, begging *its* pardon. (*Gestures toward* BIRD.) I'll venture to remind you that *I* was the one who saved
it.

OLD MAN: Is it real?

OLD WOMAN: Of course it's real, stupid. Don't you know real money when you see it?

OLD MAN: It's such a long time since I saw any. When I was in business my customers never seemed to have any.

OLD WOMAN (*Very cynically*): Hmmph!

OLD MAN: Then, you see, Dickeybird, the strength went out of my arms—*and* legs—and my poor wife had to earn the living for both of us.

OLD WOMAN: Scrubbing and cleaning—

OLD MAN: Yes.

OLD WOMAN: Washing and ironing—

OLD MAN: Yes, yes!

OLD WOMAN: Baking and aching—

OLD MAN: Tut-tut. You don't have to go over all *that*.

OLD WOMAN: Trying to save a bit here and there for a rainy day.

OLD MAN: Oh, that rainy day! It's all up there, you know. (*Points impatiently to the Rainy-Day shelf.*)

OLD WOMAN: There'll be plenty of rainy days now we're old.

OLD MAN: What about all those fine days we could have enjoyed so much more than we did? (*Trickles money from hand to hand.*) Oh, the fun we could have had!

OLD WOMAN: All the same . . . you'll admit you've got a thrifty little wife . . . to save such a nice little nest egg. (*Crawling about the floor the* OLD WOMAN *has come to rest beneath the* OLD MAN's *feet as he sits on the table. She squats on her knees and looks up at him now.*)

OLD MAN: All the same we could have enjoyed a bit more company . . . and we could certainly have spared a meal for a hungry traveler without bothering about the bill.

OLD WOMAN: All the same, you won't say "No" to *this*, I'm sure. (*She gets up from the floor and goes to put the coins which she has collected into the bag the* OLD MAN *is playing with. She tries to take the bag, but to her surprise the* OLD MAN *retains a firm hold on it.*)

OLD MAN: All the same—you needn't have sold my little harp for fourpence . . . and you needn't have thrown out the Sailor for not having any money. And you needn't have hit him over the head with your broomstick. He told the best tales I've ever heard in my life. . . .

OLD WOMAN (*Interrupting*): I'm sure he did! (*She pulls at the bag.*)

OLD MAN (*Also pulling the bag*): It was worth a lot of suppers just to sit and listen to him. All the same—

OLD WOMAN (*Tugging the bag*): All the same—

OLD MAN (*He has pulled the bag away from her*): All the same—(*He makes a stream of coins from bag to hand and vice-versa*). All the same. I can buy another harp, a bigger one, and my friends will soon be around when they hear about this.

OLD WOMAN: *That* you may be sure of.

OLD MAN (*Jumping up and retaining the bag*): And now there's no soot in the chimney, we can have a roaring fire before we go to bed. Let's have the matches. (*Hesitating slightly, she at last produces a box of matches from her apron, which is all sooty now. He lights the fire.*) Burn fire, burn! (*A flame shoots up in the fireplace. The* OLD MAN *rubs his hands and dances about with glee, the money bag jingling.*) Don't look so glum. There'll be plenty of firewood lying about outside after the storm. You can be out nice and early a-picking it up. (*He sings.*)

A-picking-it-up.
A-picking-it-up.

(*Money drops out of the bag. The* OLD WOMAN *bends to pick it up. The* OLD MAN *ignores her and pokes the wood on the fire.*)

OLD WOMAN: I knew it. Throwing the money around already. We're ruined. Drat you, Bird, if it hadn't been for you—(*She breaks off; looks round in surprise.*) Why, where is it?

OLD MAN: Where's what? (*Looks around.*) What d'you mean?

OLD WOMAN: The Bird. It's gone.

OLD MAN: Gone? (*He is bewildered.*) Gone? Gone where? (*Runs to her.*) What have you done with him?

OLD WOMAN: Me? I haven't done anything. It's gone, that's all.

OLD MAN: Gone? I don't believe it. He can't have gone. He wouldn't go—like that—without so much as a cry . . . (*The* OLD MAN *rushes around the room, trying window and door, looking up the chimney. He forgets to bother about the money bag, which falls to the floor. He finds that the door into the forest is unlocked. He looks accusingly at the* OLD WOMAN.) You've done it! It's your fault! You opened the door.

OLD WOMAN: I swear I never! (*Her eye is on the money bag. The* OLD MAN *runs through the door into the forest.*)

OLD MAN (*Crying*): Come back, beautiful Bird.

OLD WOMAN: He's gone. Cage and all. (*She cannot disguise her satisfaction.*)

OLD MAN: Cages can't fly.

OLD WOMAN: Find it, then.

(*The* OLD MAN *comes back into the room and starts looking for the cage.*)

OLD MAN: Not even a goodbye. I can't believe it. Gone! Gone! Gone!

OLD WOMAN: Shut the door quick in case it comes back. (*She darts to the door and bolts it, then turns around to face the* OLD MAN, *looking much more like her old self. The* OLD MAN *is a picture of grief.*)

OLD MAN (*Wringing his hands*): If only I'd taken more care of him!

(*The* OLD WOMAN *calmly goes and picks up the money bag.*)

OLD WOMAN: Never mind about the bird. Let's count the money.

OLD MAN (*Bitterly*): The money! If it hadn't been for the money I'd still have *him.* Oh, I always wanted a talking bird.

OLD WOMAN (*Busy with the money*): You've got me, haven't you? *I* talk, don't I?

OLD MAN: Anyone can have a talking wife.

OLD WOMAN: Not one like me. (*Her voice has now such a grim note in it that he is startled. He realizes that the atmosphere has changed. He looks around, as if seeking help.*) No use staring around in the air. Look on the floor and make sure we haven't lost any money. (*She empties the money bag onto the middle of the table and begins to count up, very much in possession of the situation.*)

OLD MAN (*Bewildered*): What's happening? (*To audience, front stage.*) Everything's going wrong. If only the Bird had stayed!

OLD WOMAN (*Deliberately*): What bird? (*The* OLD MAN *stares at her, dumbfounded. Then he stares at the audience.*) I said . . . What bird are you talking about? If you mean the miserable little thing that died . . . here's his cage. (*She finds the discarded string birdcage which she threw at the* BIRD *earlier on. She throws it now, contemptuously, at the* OLD MAN. *She is feeling more and more like her old self. The* OLD MAN *picks up the cage. He holds it like a harp, and tries to play it. The* OLD WOMAN *goes up front stage left.*)

OLD MAN (*Trying the strings*): I can't play it.

OLD WOMAN: He's trying to play a birdcage! (*Doubles up with laughter.*) Did you ever? (*She begins mockingly to copy his gestures.*) You look like the Old Tingalary Man. (*She begins to play an imaginary violin.*) Only *he* had a fiddle! (*She begins to sing, fiddling vigorously.*)

> Tingalary, O me Sary!
> Ting-a-lary Man!

(*Now she has caught the* OLD MAN'S *attention. She changes her fiddle-playing gestures to harp-playing ones like his, and he quickly changes to playing the fiddle, sawing with one arm over the other, and dropping the birdcage. Singing rapidly.*) Join in—"I'll do all that ever I can!"

(*They both sing together.*)

> I'll do all that ever I can
> To follow the Tingalary Man.

(*They go dancing round the room, each playing the imaginary harp and fiddle, changing and rechanging instruments and singing together.*)

> Ting-a-lary! O me Sary!
> Ting-a-lary Man!
> I'll do all that ever I can
> To follow the Tingalary Man!

(*It is possible for the audience to join in this game, which goes in this way. The one who is Tingalary [the* OLD MAN] *pretends to play the fiddle. Different instruments are chosen by other people. [The audience could be divided into sections, each section with one instrument.] When Tingalary changes from his fiddle to one of the other instruments, the players of that all quickly change over to the fiddle. When Tingalary changes back to the fiddle, the other players quickly resume their own instrument. The point of the game is to make the changeover quickly, or take the place of Tingalary. The traditional tune is simple and quickly picked up. A word sheet could be lowered.)*

(At last the OLD MAN *and the* OLD WOMAN *finish the game. The* OLD WOMAN *flops down, fanning herself, but the* OLD MAN *goes back to the birdcage and picks it up.)*

OLD WOMAN: Whew! That's done me a lot of good, I'm sure! Why, it's I don't know how many years since I played that.

OLD MAN (*Shaking the cage*): It's not long since *I* played it, though! Why can't I play it now, I wonder?

OLD WOMAN: If you can't understand why you can't play a birdcage, you'll never understand anything in this world! Whatever next!

OLD MAN: Next, I suppose you'll be saying *you* didn't fly.

OLD WOMAN: I? Fly? (*She jumps up and shrieks with laughter.*)

OLD MAN: Yes. Up there! Right up to the ceiling!

OLD WOMAN: Up there? Me? Curi-oss-ities and Fabul-oss-ities—I! Fly! The only flying I ever do is in my dreams. (*She goes away on a flounce around the room. The* OLD MAN *steps up front stage.*)

OLD MAN (*To audience*): Oh dear—and I was *so* hoping A.B. was going to be nicer than B.B.

OLD WOMAN (*Also stepping front stage*): A.B.? B.B.?

OLD MAN (*Still speaking to audience*): Everything seemed to be getting so much more pleasant—A.B.

OLD WOMAN (*To audience*): A.B.? B.B.? He means A.M. and P.M.

OLD MAN: What *is* A.M.?

OLD WOMAN: What *is* A.M.? Oh, you ignoramus! (*Pause.*) A.M.'s ALL MORNING, of course. And P.M. is—

OLD MAN (*Quickly*): Past Morning.

OLD WOMAN: Naturally.

OLD MAN: Then I *don't* mean A.M. and P.M. I mean A.B. and B.B. (*To audience.*) You know what I mean, don't you? (*Pause.*) B.B. means Before the Bird. A.B. means After the Bird. And I've got a feeling that A.B. is going to be worse than B.B.

OLD WOMAN: A.B. B.B. How he goes on. (*Yawns.*) It's A.M. now. (*Looks at clock.*) Five minutes to something. We'd know what if you'd only put a new finger on the clock instead of dreaming so much.

OLD MAN: Dreaming? It's not true.

OLD WOMAN: That's what I'm telling you. Of course it's not true. Magic Bird my eye! It's not more true than—than Tingalary!

OLD MAN: That's only a game . . . only pretending.

OLD WOMAN: So is your Magic Bird . . . it's just a—Tingalary Bird. . . . It doesn't exist.

OLD MAN: But . . . (*groping*) what about the money then?

OLD WOMAN: The money?

OLD MAN (*Excitedly*): It was the Magic Bird who told me about it.

OLD WOMAN: Pooh. Nothing magic about that! Little birds are always telling me things . . . especially things other people don't want me to know about. (*Pause.*) You must be sensible, you know.

OLD MAN: Must I?

OLD WOMAN: You don't want to be *in*sensible do you? 'Cos if you do it won't take a minute. (*She picks up her stick as if to hit him.*)

OLD MAN (*Quickly*): I'll be sensible, I suppose.

OLD WOMAN: That's better. Now let's reason it out. *I* put the money in the chimney myself. . . . The only miracle about *that* is that *you* didn't find it before with all your poking and prying about. There's no magic about it.

OLD MAN: No magic?

OLD WOMAN: There's no magic at all.

OLD MAN: I don't believe it. . . . (*Indicates audience.*) And they don't believe it either. (*To audience.*) Do you? There, you see.

OLD WOMAN: See? See what? See whom? (*She peers outwards to the auditorium, hand shading eyes.*) I don't see anything . . . at least I only see what I want to see. That's far the best way, you know. (*The* OLD MAN *looks flabbergasted. The* OLD WOMAN *goes demandingly up to him and holds out her hand. He looks uncomprehending.*) Come on. Give it to me. (*Pause.*) The key to *my* cupboard. (*Pause.*) Don't think I've forgotten where it is. . . . (*The* OLD MAN *fumbles through pockets.*) It's in *that* pocket . . . there. (*She points to the pocket where he put it. He takes out the key and, thoroughly intimidated, gives it to her.*) That's more like it. I feel better now. Better and better. And I'll feel better still when I've got the money safely locked up. (*Up to now the money bag is still on the table where she put it. She now goes up to it, but before she puts her hand on it she says to the* OLD MAN: Still being reasonable, *I'm* the one who can look after it properly and if money doesn't belong to those who can look after it—it ought to. (*She puts out her hand to pick up the money but before she can do so, the stage darkens, claps of thunder are heard again, and the wind howls.)* Mercy! I thought that was all over!

(*Lightning flashes. There is the sound as of great wings rushing overhead, then scratching at the window. The* OLD MAN *rushes to the window in great joy.*)

OLD MAN: He's come back! He's here.

BIRD (*Off*): CRAWK! CRAWK!

OLD WOMAN: The money! It's yours, husband. Take it—take it for mercy's sake, but DON'T—DON'T—DON'T LET THAT— THAT TINGALARY THING in again.

(*The* OLD MAN *is not listening. He is trying with frantic haste to open the window. Lightning flashes and thunder rumbles all the time.*)

OLD MAN: Don't go away! Wait! Wait for me! Come back! Come back! (*He has opened the window at last—and crying, "Come back," he is halfway out himself, stretching out his arms—straining outwards as if in response to some invisible power. The* OLD WOMAN *grabs his coat tails and she echoes his cry of "Come back!"*)

OLD WOMAN: Come back! Come back!

OLD MAN (*Calling*): Wait for me! Take me with you! Take me with you—(*His voice echoes strangely. The* OLD WOMAN *hangs grimly on to his coat tails. The thunder and lightning intensify—then subside. The* OLD MAN *sags back into the room. The* OLD WOMAN *falls onto the floor. SILENCE. Then:*)

OLD WOMAN (*To audience*): I should have missed him if he'd got away! (*Anxiously, after a pause.*) Has it gone?

(*The* OLD MAN *has his head in his hands.*)

OLD MAN: I was too slow, too slow! It's too late! He's gone.

OLD WOMAN (*Sotto voce*): Thank goodness. *You* can have the money, husband dear. It's all yours.

OLD MAN: *Now* you won't say he wasn't here? You won't ever again disbelieve in my beautiful talking Bird?

OLD WOMAN: Well . . . it's true that *I'm* here. And it's true that *you're* here. (*She has hold of his coat.*)

OLD MAN: He is truer than true! My beautiful, talking Bird is truer than true. (*The* OLD MAN *pulls away from the* OLD WOMAN, *muttering to himself as he goes around the room.*) Truer than true! Truer than me! Truer than you! And look at this—(*He has spotted the black cloth that covered the wicker birdcage, and holds it up.*) I *knew* there was something to prove it. Now you won't be able to say the Magic Bird wasn't here. This proves everything. . . . The Bird *was* here. . . . I *did* play the little birdcage and you *did* fly—right up there with your broomstick!

OLD WOMAN: I'm not quite sure that I like what *that* remark might imply.

(*The* OLD MAN *tosses the black cloth to her; she drapes it around herself like a cloak. The* OLD MAN *goes to the wide-open window and looks out.*)

OLD MAN: Goodbye, Beautiful Bird, Goodbye!

OLD WOMAN: That air's too fresh. It'll make you sneeze. Close the window. (*She preens and fancies herself in the black cloak.*)

OLD MAN: Adieu! and Farewell!

OLD WOMAN: And close it tight! Dear me, this is just the thing for these dark nights.

(*The* OLD MAN *shuts the window and comes into the room.*)

OLD MAN: Vanished!

OLD WOMAN: Have I really? I thought you meant me. Never mind, it'll come in useful for a rainy day. (*Folding up the cloth, she takes a chair and puts it beneath the Rainy-Day shelf. As she reaches up to put the cloth away with the other things, the shelf falls down and the piled-up rubbish scatters about all over the floor. The tin of buns bursts open and scatters stale buns that burst like splashes of plaster over the floor. Agonized.*) Oh, my shelf! My treasures! My rainy-day things! My darlings! My beauties! (*She runs this way and that, quite distracted. The* OLD MAN *begins to pick up things. He tries a bun with his teeth, then throws it outside in disgust. He picks up a wooden cradle and brings it forward.*)

OLD MAN: What's this?

OLD WOMAN (*Passionately*): Leave it alone! Give it to me! (*She grabs it from him, blowing off the dust.*)

OLD MAN (*Bewildered*): But we haven't any children.

OLD WOMAN: We might have had. (*She puts the cradle on the table and rocks it.*)

OLD MAN: How many . . . might we have had?

OLD WOMAN (*Promptly*): Three. Tom. Harry. And Elsie-May.

OLD MAN: That's four.

OLD WOMAN: Elsie-May is all one-and-the-same . . . might have been. This was hers . . . would have been. (*She puts her hand into the table and takes out a dusty rag doll. She holds this in her arms, then abruptly turns her back to the audience. The* OLD MAN *examines the cradle. The* OLD WOMAN *turns around and sings these words to the traditional tune of "Rock-a-bye-Baby," standing front stage with doll.*)

> Rock-a-bye-Baby, dear Elsie-May,
> Stay in the treetop all through the day,
> No use to whimper up there at the top
> Hardworking Mother's too busy to stop!

That's what I used to sing . . . or would have sung! (*She throws the doll to the* OLD MAN, *who takes up the song.*)

OLD MAN (*sings*):
> Rock-a-bye Baby, dear Elsie-May,
> Mother is busy, but Father can play.
> Up in the treetop, no need to yell,
> Father will climb up and rock there as well.

OLD WOMAN: Spoiling things as usual! (*She snatches the doll, begins to rock it in her arms, and waltzes around the room as she sings.*)

> Rock-a-bye Baby, dear Elsie-May,
> Mother won't spoil you, whatever folks say.
> When evening comes, from tree at the top,
> Right to the bottom, dear Baby can drop!

(*She joins the* OLD MAN *front stage.*)

OLD MAN: What a nice little family. I'm glad I've joined in!

OLD WOMAN: Too late! Too late. They've gone. (*She puts the doll away in the cradle.*)

OLD MAN: Why? What's happened to 'em?

(*They stand together front stage, each with a hold on the cradle.*)

OLD WOMAN (*Giving a tug*): Same as happens to other people's families. They've all grown up and flown away. It's the nature of families to fly! (*The* OLD MAN *gives a tug. The cradle breaks in two and falls to the floor, with the doll.*) So that's that! (*She picks up the doll and puts it on the table. She goes for her broomstick to sweep up the bits. As she begins to sweep she cannot resist a few surreptitious attempts to make it fly, but it does not respond. She shrugs her shoulders and begins to sweep the room. The* OLD MAN, *who is also tidying things, stops.*)

OLD MAN: There's something yellow on the floor.

OLD WOMAN (*Pouncing*): Gold! You must have dropped it! Quick! Put it in the bag! (*She searches the floor.*) I can't see anything! Where is it?

OLD MAN: Here . . . and here . . . and here. It's everywhere. The room's filling up with it.

(*The room is slowly filling with warm, yellow light.*)

OLD WOMAN: Daylight! That's all it is! It's morning—and we haven't been to bed.

(*The* OLD MAN *goes to the open door, into the forest.*)

OLD MAN: How beautiful the forest looks after the storm.

(*The* OLD WOMAN *follows him to the door with her broom, but she sees a drift of dead leaves around the doorstep and crossly begins to sweep them away.*)

OLD WOMAN: The trouble with forests is—trees, and the trouble with trees is—leaves, and the trouble with leaves is—they fall off—and *I'm* the one who has to sweep them up. It isn't fair! It isn't fair! It isn't fair! (*She throws her broomstick away. Perhaps it is a gesture of abdication.*) I'm sick of trying to keep this forest tidy. I'm going to bed. Goodnight! (*She marches inside—and goes to the door at the left.*)

OLD MAN: Good *DAY!*

OLD WOMAN: How do you know it's going to be a good day? If it's anything like the night we've had, *I* don't want it! (*Yawns.*) Don't forget to wind the clock up. (*The* OLD MAN *picks up her broom and props it outside the door. The* OLD WOMAN *hesitates, sees that the* OLD MAN *is still outside looking out toward the sunrise. She looks at the money bag, which is still on the table. She walks up to it. Her fingers itch to be on it. She stretches out her hand, looking stealthily about as she does so. Her hand descends. There is an almost inaudible note of thunder. She draws back her hand, not quite sure if she really heard anything. She tries again. This time her hand is actually upon the bag when there is a real crash of thunder which makes her leap in the air.*) Whew! I'm going. (*She exits left. The* OLD MAN *is still outside. The* OLD WOMAN *puts her head into the room and calls to him.*) Don't forget to put the money away! (*She disappears for an instant, then comes back. When she sees that the* OLD MAN *is still outside and unaware of her, she steals up to the table, reaches out her hand, picks up the rag doll and goes out with it, left. Silence. The clock's tick is heard again. The* OLD MAN *sits on the doorstep and idly picks up a handful of dead leaves. He begins to send them away one by one.*)

OLD MAN:

    This day, next day, sometime—never!
    This day, next day, someday—

(*He comes to the last leaf.*)

    Someday you'll come back, Beautiful, glorious Bird.
    Someday you'll come back.

(*He comes into the house, goes into the lean-to room and disappears. There is the sound of things being moved about, then the* OLD MAN *comes out, carrying a newly painted inn sign. This says, "The Come-Inn-and Welcome." He props it up and looks at it very proudly. He carries it outside, climbs up, takes down the unfriendly sign and puts up the new one. With great satisfaction.*) Come in and welcome! Don't know what sort of a day you're going to be. . . . (*Turns out toward sun.*) But whatever you're going to be—come in and welcome, Day! (*The* OLD MAN *comes into the room, setting the door open for the sun to shine in. He stands center stage, caught in a ray of sunlight and still looking through the open door into the distance. At last he moves out of the stream of light. The clock's tick reminds him he must wind it up. Now he stands scratching his head and trying to remember what else he is supposed to do. The children in the audience really end this play. All through the performance they have repeatedly taken part in it. The* OLD WOMAN *has left the money bag on the table and has told the* OLD MAN *to take care of it. But his mind is on the* BIRD, *not on the money. Yawning sleepily he begins to go on his way to bed. He remembers that he has to remember something. But what? He begins to play a game with the children in the audience, HOT or COLD, touching first this object, then another. If the children mean him to do so, he will pick up the money bag and go to bed. If not, he will go quite happily without it. There is a pause. The whole stage is bathed in light. Birds sing. Along the path from the village the* SAILOR *comes on his way to the sea. He passes the inn door, noticing the new sign with a smile. He comes up to the front of the stage and sings his farewell song to the audience.*)

SAILOR:

> I'm a wandering Sailor,
> My story is told,
> Old Man and Old Woman
> I'll leave with their gold.
>
> This dear little dwelling
> Has door opened wide,
> The weary and hungry,
> May rest there inside.
>
> Let Friendship and Laughter,
> Create from today,
> A new way of living,
> In work and in play.
>
> I'm a wandering Sailor,
> With no more to tell,
> So I'll love you—and leave you—
> And bid you—Farewell!

(When the SAILOR'S *song is over and he has made his bow to the audience, he turns to make his exit. It is seen that the small wicker birdcage which he carries on his back is now uncovered— and that it contains a replica in miniature—of the Tingalary Bird.)*

Your Own Thing

BY

DONALD DRIVER,
HAL HESTER

AND

DANNY APOLINAR

*I*N THE MID-1960s Hal Hester and Danny Apolinar collaborated on a musical adaptation of a work for which they had not secured the legal rights. When they found themselves unable to do so, they could not produce the play and returned to Puerto Rico, where they lived, to write a new musical. This time it was to be based on a novel or play in the public domain, that is, one which would be free of entanglements such as copyrights, percentages and literary agents. They began reading Shakespeare, who already had been responsible for the plots and characters of several musical-comedy hits. (*The Boys from Syracuse* was based on *The Comedy of Errors; Kiss Me, Kate* was drawn from *The Taming of the Shrew;* and *West Side Story* was adapted from *Romeo and Juliet.*) The moment they came upon *Twelfth Night* they knew they had the material for their next venture, because Shakespeare here offered them a situation of concern to audiences on both sides of the generation gap. After all, what could be more modern than boys who looked like girls and girls who looked like boys, celebrating themselves and each other in songs of unalloyed joy and abandon? Shakespeare said prophetically, "If music be the food of love, play on—" even if he did not know of the electric guitars, electric organs, electric fender bass and percussion that Hester and Apolinar had in mind.

Shakespeare's timeliness, although in part attributable to his sense of universal comedy, also resulted from a custom of the Elizabethan theatre which allowed no actress on stage but substituted teenage boys to play the women's roles. In several of his comedies Shakespeare shows young ladies disguising themselves as young men, which meant that the audience saw a young man dressing himself as a young woman who was disguising herself as a young man! Confusing, perhaps, but very contemporary, too, in a day when hair, beads, jewelry, sandals and psychedelic colors have revolutionized identities among the young into one "now" generation.

A New York performer and director named Donald Driver became excited by the idea of a rock version of *Twelfth Night,* and joined the team to write the book, the nonmusical sections of the script. Driver could not employ all of Shakespeare's play but took the main plot, which concentrates upon the romantic involvement of two young couples whose "spirit of love" dominates all else. Surprisingly enough for a musical comedy, he altogether discarded Shakespeare's clowns, Sir Toby Belch, Sir Andrew Aguecheek, Feste, Maria, even Malvolio. Yet Driver's book still is comic, for in their place he created a montage of familiar faces (contemporary clowns, maybe?) who surround the action and comment upon it from the projected screens that frame the stage. Shakespeare himself inspired the new title from his original subtitle, *What You Will,* as much an Elizabethan glorification of individuality then as *Your Own Thing* is now. The theme is further exemplified in the lyrics "I just want to be a free man, to be me, man," and "Tell it like it is, if it makes you happy."

The concept of an up-to-date *Twelfth Night* did not end in the title or in the rock score with its songs of the moment, "Baby, Baby," "The Now Generation," and "Hunca Munca," but was carried throughout the entire production. For the first time in a hit musical comedy, *Your Own Thing* mixed media by employing 12 slide projectors, two movie projectors and two tape recorders as well as live sound effects. Pop art, comic strips and collages flashed before the audience, along with actual photographs and traffic noises of New York City, which, believe it or not, represented Shakespeare's Illyria! The chorus of faces—those of New York City's Mayor Lindsay, Shirley Temple, John Wayne, and the rest—was superimposed upon the action. The Apocalypse rock group blasted forth. And the musical, alive and mechanical, took off with such a salvo that it could not pause for an intermission.

It may come as a surprise to those who saw performances of this rambuctious musical, so vivacious and visual on stage, that it is also enjoyable to read. Driver's book speeds forward with the same vitality, the lyrics still flaunt their impudence, and the comic commentary continues to spout its own thing as freely as it did in the theatre. So even without the music (which can be heard readily on the RCA original-cast recording), *Your Own Thing,* as a reading experience, comes rocking to life and, to borrow one of its own expressions, finds its groove.

The New York production opened on January 13, 1968, and ran through the spring of 1970 for a total of 933 performances. It became the first off-Broadway show to win the New York Drama Critics Circle Award and the Outer Critics Circle Award. Touring companies criss-crossed the United States and a London production followed. Here, then, is a rock musical, based on a play more than 300 years old, written in Puerto Rico but set largely in New York City, which has charmed international audiences, old and young alike. Impossible, we might have thought, but, as Gertrude Stein once said, "If it can be done, why do it?" That question alone should keep theatre alive for generations to come.

Your Own Thing

CHARACTERS

OLIVIA, *a very charming, witty and deliciously droll woman of thirty who owns and operates a discotheque. She loves to be surrounded by the young and is dressed in very chic versions of the latest fashion fad.*

ORSON, *a graduate of the beat generation who has become a theatrical agent and whose biggest client is the Apocalypse rock-and-roll group. His love affair with Olivia has been long and literary; his attempts to emulate the* now *generation are heartfelt and hopeless. He is a square.*

VIOLA *and* SEBASTIAN, *two members of the* now *generation who previous to their separation in the shipwreck had been a rock duo. They are completely uninhibited and adventuresome. Their identical dress and hairstyle cause them to be mistaken for one another.*

APOCALYPSE: DANNY, JOHN *and* MICHAEL, *members of a four-man rock and roll group. They wear far-out clothes, long hair, and say and do anything that pleases them.*

NURSE, *a nurse.*

PURSER, *a sailor who befriends Viola after the shipwreck.*

STAGE MANAGER, *runs Olivia's discotheque for her and is constantly frustrated by the behavior and language of the* now *generation.*

MUSICAL NUMBERS

NO ONE'S PERFECT, DEAR	SEBASTIAN *and* VIOLA
THE FLOWERS	VIOLA
I'M ME! (I'M NOT AFRAID)	APOCALYPSE
BABY! BABY!	APOCALYPSE *and* VIOLA
COME AWAY, DEATH	SEBASTIAN
I'M ON MY WAY TO THE TOP	SEBASTIAN
LET IT BE	OLIVIA
SHE NEVER TOLD HER LOVE	VIOLA
BE GENTLE	VIOLA *and* ORSON
WHAT DO I KNOW?	VIOLA
BABY! BABY! (*reprise*)	APOCALYPSE, SEBASTIAN *and* VIOLA
THE NOW GENERATION	APOCALYPSE *and* VIOLA
THE MIDDLE YEARS	SEBASTIAN
THE MIDDLE YEARS (*reprise*)	OLIVIA
WHEN YOU'RE YOUNG AND IN LOVE	ORSON
HUNCA MUNCA	APOCALYPSE *and* COMPANY
DON'T LEAVE ME	OLIVIA, SEBASTIAN *and* ORSON
DO YOUR OWN THING	APOCALYPSE

PREFACE

When reading the following script, one must keep in mind the fact that film and slide projections, taped and live sound effects accompany the written word to form a mixed-media collage which is the final effect of the script.

Nine actors portray the ten characters: Viola, Sebastian, Olivia, Orson, The Apocalypse (Danny, John, and Michael), the Nurse, the Purser, and the Stage Manager. The following characters are projected on slides and their voices are recorded on tape: Everett Dirksen, Mayor Lindsay, Queen Elizabeth, Buddha, the Sistine God, W. C. Fields, John Wayne, Shirley Temple, Shakespeare, the Pope, Jesus Christ, and Louis XIV. Other slide projections are either scenic environments, comic-strip balloon writing (projected over the head of the actor thinking those thoughts), or projections which are extensions of what an actor is thinking; for example, slides of Viola appear when Orson is singing of his love for her. And further, when Orson is fantasizing his fears of homosexuality, the characters he imagines are projected around him.

Motion picture is used in conjunction with slide effects to provide a more total environment such as a shipwreck, or to depict the size of New York City, or to produce a psychedelic effect—as in the "Hunca Munca" dance.

SETTING

The all-white setting suggests a Shakespearean stage. Upstage there are two platform ramps, one higher than the other, running from one wing to the other. Behind them is a cyclorama or rear projection

*screen. There are five entrances from the wings on either side: R1
and L1 are sliding doors and on both sides of each door there is a
bench; R2 and L2 are wing entrances; R3 and L3 are the first platform ramp; R4 and L4 are the second platform ramp; R5 and L5 are
upstage of the platform ramps and have a set of stairs leading up to
the top platform ramp. There is no act curtain used.*

LIGHTING

*Normal stage lighting is used except when there are projections.
When projections are used, backlighting is used on the set, and the
actors are lit by follow spots.*

MUSIC

*The orchestra consists of an electric organ, an electric guitar, an
electric fender bass and percussion.*

Overture: "Baby"

Music cut off.

DIRKSEN (*Slide*): If music be the food of love, play on! I can't remember if that's Marlowe or Bacon.

> (*The shipwreck: The film begins with an explosion aboard ship
> and continues throughout the scene showing a shipwreck at sea
> and the ship finally sinking. Accompanying slide projections are
> stills taken from that movie and projected on the set surround-
> ing the surface upstage on which the film is projected to com-
> plete the environmental picture.*)

VOICE OVER: Passengers, please don't be alarmed. Please don't panic.
The lifeboats are being lowered. We'll take on women and children
as soon as the ship's Xerox and IBM machines are loaded.

(*During the shipwreck scene the entire company appear as passengers running about, trying to put on life preservers, jump overboard, and generally escape the disaster.* VIOLA *and* SEBASTIAN *are finally the last passengers left on board.*)

SEBASTIAN: Viola, where are you going?

VIOLA: I'm going back to the cabin.

SEBASTIAN: Vi, you can't go back to the cabin!

VIOLA: I've got to save our orchestrations.

SEBASTIAN: Stupid sister, we're sinking.

VIOLA: Then you get them.

SEBASTIAN: The hell you say. What do they matter if I drown getting them?

VIOLA: OK, Phi Bate, how'll we get work?

SEBASTIAN: We get new orchestrations.

VIOLA: Wonderful! They cost a fortune!

SEBASTIAN: Then God dammit, I'll hum.

VIOLA (*Laughing*): You're always off pitch.

SEBASTIAN: All right, you go get them!

VIOLA (*Sudden anger*): You'd let me, wouldn't you?

SEBASTIAN (*Sings*):

> Why can't you ever be nice?
> Why can't you ever be nice?
> Why can't you ever be nice,
> Be nice once or twice?

VIOLA (*Sings*):

> Look who's talkin',
> Look who's squawkin',
> Look who's callin' the pot black.

SEBASTIAN (*Sings*):

> Look who's talkin',
> Look who's squawkin',

VIOLA (*Sings*):

> Get off my back.

BOTH (*Sing*):

> No one's perfect, dear.

SEBASTIAN (*Sings*):

> Why can't you be kind to me?

VIOLA (*Laughing*): See, you're off pitch!

SEBASTIAN: Vi-o-la, listen to me . . .

VIOLA: Some brother you are. You don't give a damn if we end up back in Akron, Ohio.

SEBASTIAN: You want a singing job in the bottom of the ocean?

VIOLA: It's no farther under than Akron!

SEBASTIAN: Why do you always have to argue? God damn you, Vi, we're sinking!

VIOLA (*Sings*):

> Why can't you ever be nice?
> Why can't you ever be nice?
> Why can't you be nice to me,
> Nice and brotherly?

SEBASTIAN (*Sings*):

> Look who's talkin',
> Look who's squawkin',
> Look who's callin' the pot black.
> Look who's talkin',
> Look who's squawkin',

VIOLA (*Sings*):

> Get off my back.
> No one's perfect.

SEBASTIAN (*Sings*):

> No one's perfect.

VIOLA (*Sings*):

> No one's perfect.

SEBASTIAN (*Sings*):

> No one's perfect.

BOTH (*sing*):

> No one is perfect, dear.

SEBASTIAN: One of these days, Vi . . .

VIOLA: Oh, I hate you so much!

PURSER (*Enters, addressing Viola*): For Christ sakes! Don't just stand there, fella, get your sister to the lifeboat! (*Exits.* SEBASTIAN, *in anger, starts to follow* PURSER *off.*)

VIOLA: Oh no! You're not going anywhere without those orchestrations!

SEBASTIAN: All right then! I'll go get them! (*Exits.*)

VIOLA (*Starts to follow, bending over at orchestra pit*): I should think you would!

SEBASTIAN (*Mimic*): I should think you would.

PURSER (*Enters*): Come on! Move your ass, mister, we're going fast! (*Slaps* VIOLA'S *ass.*) Move your ass, lady, we're going fast.

> (*Blackout.* PURSER *and* VIOLA *exit. Film out. Slides out. Projections: Slides of waterfront buildings in semiabstract. Lights. Enter* PURSER *and* VIOLA.)

VIOLA: What country, friend, is this?

PURSER: This is Illyria, lady.

VIOLA:

> And what should I do in Illyria?
> My brother, he is in Elysium.
> Perchance he is not drowned;
> What think you sailor?

PURSER:

> It is perchance that you yourself were saved.

VIOLA:

> And so perchance may he be.

PURSER:

> True, madam; and, to comfort you with chance,
> Assure yourself, after our ship did split,
> When you, and those poor number saved with you
> Hung on your driving boat, I saw your brother
> Most provident in peril, bind himself
> (Courage and hope both teaching him the practice)
> To a strong mast that lived upon the sea:
> Where, like Orion on the dolphin's back,
> I saw him hold acquaintance with the waves.
> So long as I could see.

VIOLA:

> Know'st thou this country?

PURSER:

> Ay, madam, well, for I was bred and born
> Not three hours travel from this place. (*Exits.*)

VIOLA (*calling after* PURSER): Who governs here?

> (*Lights down.*)

MAYOR LINDSAY (*Slide*): Illyria is a fun city. Cough, cough.

VIOLA: And what should I do in Illyria?

(During this song the motion-picture film shows varying shots of New York City skyline and skyscrapers. The film is at the same time beautiful and impersonal; and in a nutshell, capsulizes the exterior shapes of twentieth-century urban life. The slide projections which accompany this film are stills of steel and glass structures and change constantly during the song.)

VIOLA *(Sings)*:

> So much glass, so much steel,
> What's there to care? What's there to feel?
> All that glass, all that chrome,
> Can I ever call this place home?

> Here the air is gray and smoggy.
> My eyes burn and my head seems groggy.
> How do the flowers grow
> In their sweet little box
> In their neat little row?

> Here come the men to plant new flowers.
> The beautiful people must see beautiful flowers
> From their beautiful ivory towers.

> So much glass, so much steel,
> What's there to care? What's there to feel?
> All that glass, all that chrome,
> Can I ever call this place home?

> Time to change another season.
> If I watch I may find the reason
> Why flowers never die
> In their glass-covered box
> 'Neath their gas-covered sky.

> Here come the men to plant new flowers.
> The beautiful people must see beautiful flowers
> From their beautiful ivory towers.

So much glass, so much steel,
What's there to care? What's there to feel?
All that glass, all that chrome,
Can I ever call this place home?
Can I ever call this place home?

BALLOON (*Slide, over* VIOLA's *head*): "Oh dear God. I fear Sebastian lost in the shipwreck."

SISTINE GOD (*Slide*): She's talking to me. Shipwrecks, you know, are my specialty.

BALLOON (*Slide, over* VIOLA's *head*): "I've never been without him. How will I ever get a singing job?"

BUDDHA (*Slide*): Disaster may be your specialty; but next to harmony, mine is rock.

(*Buddha bell rings and Buddha hand appears with card.*)

VIOLA (*Reading Buddha card*): "Boy wanted." (VIOLA *inspects herself; collapses her chest.*) Why not? (VIOLA *does choreographed dance, exits.*)

(*Projection: Telephone environment.* ORSON *enters;* OLIVIA *enters separately. Both close doors; lights up. This scene is played like a normal scene without pantomiming use of telephones.*)

ORSON (*Speaking front*): Hello, Olivia.

OLIVIA (*Speaking front*): Orson, old charmer, that's got to be you.

ORSON: It is, Olivia, I love you.

OLIVIA: Orson, is this a business call?

ORSON: Olivia, I love you.

OLIVIA: No, you're just stimulated by rejection.

ORSON (*Turning to* OLIVIA): I am not.

OLIVIA (*Turning to* ORSON): All right, then you're too old for me.

ORSON: I am not; we're the same age.

OLIVIA: That proves it; I like younger men. Orson, is this a business call? Are you calling me about your rock group?

ORSON: Will you have dinner with me?

OLIVIA: Soon, Orson, soon.

ORSON: Olivia—

OLIVIA: Orson, did you call me up for another emotional setback?

ORSON: No! It *is* about my singing group, The Four Apocalypse.

OLIVIA: Well, finally! What about them? Don't tell me the boys dropped you for a new agent?

ORSON: Ha! Ha! Only one.

OLIVIA: What?

ORSON: I lost one of the Apocalypse.

OLIVIA: Oh no! You didn't lose Death? Or Famine?

ORSON: No, Disease. He's been drafted.

OLIVIA (*Going center to* ORSON): Oh! That's terrible. I've advertised all four.

ORSON (*Going center to* OLIVIA): Now look, Olivia—

OLIVIA: How would you like to go to a discotheque to hear a quartet and get a trio? Business is business, Orson. I want all four or none.

ORSON: Surely you wouldn't cancel out?

OLIVIA: Orson, what good are Death, War, and Famine without Disease?

ORSON: With all those postpubic, long-haired, beriberi types hanging around, can't you recommend one?

OLIVIA: They're all matched sets, I wouldn't want to break up any.

ORSON: Olivia . . .

OLIVIA: There goes that tone again.

ORSON: But I do love you.

OLIVIA: Orson, believe me, what you have is just an unresolved umbilical sense memory. (*Opens door.*)

ORSON: Oh, Olivia.

OLIVIA: I want all four or none. (*Exits, closing door.*)

ORSON: I'll get a new Disease. . . . Olivia, are you listening to me? She's mean.

(*Projection: Interior,* ORSON's *office. Lights build.* APOCALYPSE *enter.*)

DANNY: What did Olivia say this time, Orson, baby?

MICHAEL: How's the romance going?

JOHN: Going to be a June wedding?

(*All grab* ORSON *and hum various wedding marches.*)

ORSON: She says she'll cancel if we don't come up with a fourth Apocalypse for her discotheque.

JOHN: Four? We're only three.

MICHAEL: Yeh. Three was always bad news.

DANNY (*Stirring cauldron*): Like the three witches in *Macbeth*.

MICHAEL (*Stabbing himself*): The Triumvirate!

JOHN: Don't forget the waltz!

(DANNY *grabs* ORSON *and begins waltzing.*)

ORSON: God damn you guys. I need help!

MICHAEL: God damn you guys. He needs help!

JOHN: I think you can safely say that.

DANNY (*Overlapping above line*): There's a sense of desperation there.

ORSON: We'll discuss finding a replacement for your drafted leader if you clowns all will come down a minute.

MICHAEL: Down, everybody.

ORSON: We've got thirty-two . . . (APOCALYPSE *fall to their knees imitating the three monkeys, "Hear no evil, see no evil, speak no evil."* JOHN *blows high toot on kazoo for "Speak no evil."*) We've got thirty-two weeks of bookings. The contract reads a rock group of four. We've now got three. As I see it, we need one more. (APOCALYPSE *follow* ORSON *on their knees.*)

DANNY: Now we're getting somewhere.

JOHN: Orson, I have a split personality. Will that help?

MICHAEL: I know his other half. He can't do anything.

JOHN: He can, too. He can lie, cheat, and steal.

DANNY: I'll verify that.

ORSON: Miserable children!

JOHN, MICHAEL, DANNY: *Orson!*

ORSON: Can't you creeps ever be serious?

MICHAEL: OK, creeps, get serious. Let's give it a little Corelli fugue here.

(APOCALYPSE *play a perfect three-part Corelli fugue on kazoos, and dance a minuet.*)

ORSON: They should have drafted all four of you!

DANNY: Hey, look. There's sadness in the room.

MICHAEL: Don't cry, boys, it's bad for your nasal passages.

ORSON: Go on. Keep it up. Keep it up. When you're all starving, let's see you come up with the funnies.

MICHAEL: He needs help. OK, brain pool, give it the Auguste Rodin.

(APOCALYPSE *imitate pose of Rodin's* The Thinker.)

JOHN: I've got it. Nobody would know if there were only three of us, if we just kept shifting position all night. (APOCALYPSE *get in close line, all facing same direction,* JOHN *in the middle.*) We could call ourselves the Lucky Pierres.
MICHAEL (*Falsetto*): I love it.
DANNY: It's an "In" joke.
ORSON: Get out! . . . Get out!
APOCALYPSE (*Barbershop harmony*): The roses are blooming in Picardy . . .

(*As* APOCALYPSE *exit, lights down.*)

QUEEN ELIZABETH (*Slide*): Why do they need a fourth musician? In my day troubadours sang alone.
BOGART (*Slide*): We call that folk singing. The government frowns on it.
SISTINE GOD (*Slide*): The old queen's right. Four's not a Biblical number.
QUEEN ELIZABETH (*Slide*): Did I hear that Vatican Manifestation on the ceiling refer to me as the "old queen"?
JOHN WAYNE (*Slide*): It don't matter who they put in the group. I can't tell the boys from the girls anyway.
BOGART (*Slide*): You do have a problem.

(*Lights up.*)

ORSON: I can't get through to these guys. God knows I've tried. There's no generation gap with me. I read *Ramparts* and *The East Village Other*. I've been to the Electric Circus. I've studied their language. I read that article in *McCall's* by Lynda Bird. I've studied their music, and everything teen, their every scene. I try every way I can to get through to them with God knows what-not. Even pot. Blahh. It makes you hungry. I gained four pounds on the candy bars alone. To them I'm Orson Uptight. Big Square. Nowhere. But I'm not! I'm the personification of all the accumulated knowledge of the beat generation and I try to be it. Why can't they see it? What do I have to do to show I know . . . how to be one of them? (*Exits.* APOCALYPSE *enter during end of* ORSON'S *speech.*)

DANNY (*Sings*):

> I don't have to show anyone
> I want to be one of them;
> 'Cause deep inside is the feeling of pride,
> The me from which the mighty oaks stem.

MICHAEL (*Sings*):

> This is a man, look at his hair,
> Not your idea of a he-man.

DANNY (*Sings*):

> Think what you will, what do I care?
> I just want to be a free man,
> To be me, man.

JOHN (*Sings*):

> This is a man, look at his clothes,
> Not your idea of a tough man.

DANNY (*Sings*):

> Think what you will, this is no pose.
> Don't have to pretend I'm a rough man,
> I'm enough, man.

MICHAEL (*Sings*):

> This is a man, look at his eyes,
> They're expressive.

DANNY (*Sings*):

> I can feel.

JOHN (*Sings*):

> This is a man, look at his heart,
> It's impressive.

DANNY (*Sings*):

> I am real.

ALL (*Sing*):

> Why does everybody have to be afraid to be a human being?
> Why does everybody have to be afraid of other people seeing?

DANNY (*Sings*):

> Everybody has emotion buried deep inside.
> When they feel one truthful emotion,
> They feel that's what they've got to hide.

JOHN (*Sings*):

> Me—I'm not afraid to cry,
> Me—I'm not afraid to die,
> I'm not afraid to weep when I'm sad,
> I'm not afraid to laugh when I'm glad,
> I'm not afraid to know when I'm bad,
> I'm not afraid to love.

MICHAEL (*Sings*):

> Me—I'm not afraid to live,
> Me—I'm not afraid to give,
> I'm not afraid when the nights are too long,
> I'm not afraid to admit when I'm wrong,
> I'm not afraid to sing a new song,
> I'm not afraid to love.

DANNY (*Sings*):

> Me—I'm not afraid to be,
> Me—I'm not afraid to see,
> I'm not afraid to give all my love,
> I'm not afraid of heaven above,
> I am the new man, a true man, more human and free,
> But most of all, I'm not afraid of me.

ALL (*Sing*):

> Our generation can't live in the past.
> I know that tomorrow won't last.
> That's the reason our hearts beat much faster.

DANNY (*Sings*):

> I'm not the starry-eyed boy next door,
> I'm not the life of the party,
> I've got to be what I've got to be.
> I'm me!
> I'm not the prince in a fairy tale,
> I'm not as strong as an oak tree,
> I like the feeling of feeling free.
> I'm me!
>
> My generation can't live in the past.
> I know that tomorrow won't last.
> That's the reason my heart beats much faster.

ALL (*Sing*):

> I can do anything I want to do.

I can make every dream I dream come true.
There may be things that I'll never
Completely see.
But look at me! Look! You can see that I'm real!
I'm alive! I'm me.

(*Blackout.* APOCALYPSE *exit.*)

SHIRLEY TEMPLE (*Slide*): Death, War, Disease and Famine. That's not very nice.
BUDDHA (*Slide*): Best you go with it. It makes your stocks rise.
JOHN WAYNE (*Slide*): Why don't they call themselves "The He-Men" or something?
LOUIS IV (*Slide*): What were those magical items on the boys' costumes, that run up and down?
BOGART (*Slide*): They're called zippers, Louis.

(*Lights up. Projection: Interior,* ORSON'S *office.* VIOLA *enters, with short dance. Stops.*)

VIOLA (*Reading Buddha card*): Buddha says: "Boy Wanted." Out of sight. (VIOLA *continues dance cross to door.* ORSON *enters through door.* APOCALYPSE *enter during the end of* VIOLA'S *dance.*)
ORSON (*Taking Buddha card from* VIOLA): Buddha. That your agent? (APOCALYPSE *cross down to* VIOLA *and* ORSON. *Music vamp starts and continues under dialogue to song.*) What's your instrument?
VIOLA: I'm a boy. (*Realizing . . .*) Oops! (*Takes tambourine from* MICHAEL.) Yes! (*Plays tambourine.*)
ORSON: Can you sing?
VIOLA (*In high soprano voice*): "AAHHH!" . . . I'm a tenor.
ORSON: Name?
VIOLA: Uh . . . Charlie! Uh . . . Charlie . . . uh . . .
ORSON: Disease! Let's see your work.

(*While* APOCALYPSE *sing* "Baby, Baby," VIOLA, *making mistakes, tries to sing along with them, play the tambourine, dance and give a good audition. The impression is more frantic than anything as she tries to copy each of their styles. She wins them over as they end up copying hers.*)

VIOLA *and* APOCALYPSE (*Sing*):

> Somethin's happenin' makes me want to fly,
> Baby! Baby! Baby! Baby!
> Somethin's happenin', some new kind of high,
> Baby! Baby! Baby! Baby!
> Over and over and over and over and over
> And over and over and over
> Over and over and over and over and over
> And over and Oh!
>
> Somethin's happenin' makes me want to pop,
> Baby! Baby! Baby! Baby!
> Somethin's happenin' goin' to the top,
> Baby! Baby! Baby! Baby!
> Over and over and over and over and over
> And over and over and over
> Over and over and over and over and over
> And over and Oh!
> Somethin's happenin' makin' me feel good,
> Baby! Baby! Baby! Baby!
>
> Somethin's happenin', gonna knock on wood,
> Baby! Baby! Baby! Baby!
> Over and over and over and over and over
> And over and over and over,
> Baby! Baby!
> Over and over and over and over and over
> And over and
> Rockabye, bye bye, baby!

(*All ad-lib.*)

ORSON: You're real groovy. You're . . . you know . . . ah . . .

DANNY: Solid?

ORSON: Yeh, solid.

JOHN: Jackson!

ORSON: Jack . . . Bug out!

JOHN: You'll learn to cope with the parochial entrenchment of the Victorians.

ORSON: Get out!

APOCALYPSE (*Barbershop harmony as they exit, backing out*):
> Daddy, dear old daddy,
> You've been more like a mother to me.

VIOLA: They're very unusual. Thanks, thanks for the audition!

ORSON: I'm Orson. Your new agent.

VIOLA: Really! Then I can join the group?

ORSON (*Starting to kneel*): Want me to get down on my knees and beg you?

VIOLA (*Stopping him*): No! You don't have to do that!

ORSON: I was about to grow long hair and plug myself in. (VIOLA *laughs but switches to "bad joke" take.*) But I don't sing that well. I have trouble staying on pitch. You know, Charlie, that never struck me before. Could a little thing like that make me square?

VIOLA: Oh no. Just the right square can be awfully groovy.

ORSON: I wish someone would tell that to Olivia.

VIOLA: Olivia?

ORSON: She's the woman I love.

VIOLA: Oh. And she thinks you're square?

ORSON: Like Bert Parks! Look! Olivia listens to young kids like you. If I gave you a letter, you could deliver it to her in person, and then maybe you could put in a good word for me . . . like what you just said.

VIOLA: What'd I just say?

ORSON: That I'm not square.

VIOLA: You're not? Oh no. You're not!

ORSON:
> She will attend it better in thy youth
> Than in a nuncio's of more grave aspect.

VIOLA: Hmm?

ORSON:

Dear lad, believe it;
For they shall yet belie thy happy years
That say thou art a man. Diana's lip
Is not more smooth and rubious; (VIOLA *sneaks a look at her upper lip.*)
> thy small pipe
Is as the maiden's organ, shrill of sound, (VIOLA *feels her throat.*)
And all is semblative a woman's part. (VIOLA *covers her breasts;* ORSON *opens door.*)

I know thy constellation is right apt
For this affair. (ORSON *pulls* VIOLA *off*.)
VIOLA: This scene's getting freaky!

(*Blackout. As* ORSON *pulls* VIOLA *off, closing door, music*.)

SHAKESPEARE (*Slide*): Why do they always quote my commercial
   crappe!

(*Music. Projection: Exterior environment of trees and foliage.*
SEBASTIAN *enters, in wheelchair, and hospital robe, covered with
blanket*.)

SEBASTIAN:
          My stars shine darkly over me; my sister
          Vi, though it was said she much resembled me,
          Was yet of many accounted beautiful;
          She bore a mind that envy could not but call fair.
          Drowned in salt water. I'll drown her remembrance
          In more stinging brine of despair. (*Sings*.)

          Come away, come away, death,
          And in sad cypress let me be laid.
          Fly away, fly away, breath:
          I am slain by a lost lovely maid.

          My shroud of white, stuck all with yew,
          O, prepare it!
          My part of death, no one so true
          Did share it.

          Not a flower, not a flower sweet
          On my black coffin let there be strown.
          Not a friend, not a friend greet
          My poor corpse, where my bones shall be thrown.

          A thousand, thousand sighs to save.
          Lay me, O, where
          Sad brother never find my grave
          To weep there!

Come away, come away, death
And in sad cypress let me be laid.
Fly away, fly away, breath:
I am slain by a lost lovely,
Lost lovely maid.

(*Lights up; slide environment out.* NURSE *enters with basin, thermometer, and washcloth, closes door.*)

NURSE (*Seeing only the back of* SEBASTIAN *in wheelchair*): Good morning, miss. I'm the relief nurse; all right, miss . . . (*She shakes down thermometer.*)

SEBASTIAN: Now, look . . .

NURSE (*Putting thermometer in Sebastian's mouth*): Keep this under your tongue, miss, while I give you your sponge bath.

SEBASTIAN: Ub blub . . .

NURSE: You do want me to bathe you, don't you?

SEBASTIAN (*Lighting up; high voice*): Uh huh!

NURSE (*Puts chair in bed position*): Well then, just relax, honey. Relax! Take your arm out of your sleeve. Well, you got quite a little crack on the head there, didn't you? What happened?

SEBASTIAN (*Still sitting up; takes arm out of its sleeve*): Uhh . . .

NURSE (*Going to basin*): Ah, ah, ah, that's a rhetorical question, girl. (SEBASTIAN *lies down. Crossing back to* SEBASTIAN, NURSE *lifting his left arm up to wash it.*) Give me your arm. (*Pause.*) Do we always wear our armpits Italian style?

SEBASTIAN (*Falsetto*): Uh . . . mn . . .

NURSE (*Continuing to wash arm*): Chacun à son goo, as the French say. Like I say, I'm just here until Thursday. I'm relieving the regular nurse so she can have her varicose veins removed. (*Puts arm down, having finished washing it.*) Boy, if the cement floors don't break them down, the patients snapping your girdle will. (*Slaps* SEBASTIAN *with washcloth.*) I just passed my Army nurse's exam. I'm on my way to Vietnam next Thursday. (NURSE *slaps* SEBASTIAN *with cloth again, crosses to basin, wrings out cloth.*) I figure it's a lot safer to face a spread of Vietcong mortars than one convalescent with a well-aimed finger. (*Crossing back to* SEBASTIAN, *continuing to bathe him, this time starting with the back.*) We girls must stick together, right?

SEBASTIAN (*High voice*): Right!

NURSE (*Washing him and getting progressively lower on his body*):
You know, being a nurse is no Florence Nightingale movie. The
patients couldn't care less how much work you put in. They're
just interested in . . . (*She reaches* SEBASTIAN's *crotch. She does
take front, looks under robe, screams! and throws down rag.*) You
ought to be ashamed of yourself!

SEBASTIAN (*He takes out thermometer as he sits up*): Oh dear. I'm
sorry to hear that. You really think so? (*Opens robe, ducks his head
inside to inspect himself.*)

NURSE (*Taking thermometer and reading it*): We'll have to take this
over.

SEBASTIAN (*Lighting up*): The bath, too?

NURSE: You should be in the army with a haircut.

SEBASTIAN: I don't quite see the connection.

NURSE: It would straighten you out.

SEBASTIAN: Well, you've already done that. Zabadabadoo! (*He falls
back down.*)

NURSE (*Putting chair into upright position again*): You see! That's
what I mean. OK, that's enough. In the army with a haircut!

SEBASTIAN: I'll probably get there soon enough without you wishing
it on me. Who said, "A coward, a most devout coward, religious
in it"?

NURSE (*Starting to push wheelchair off. Lights start down*): You're
not afraid of going to war, are you?

SEBASTIAN: Oh no, just of being shot.

(SEBASTIAN *and* NURSE *exit.*)

DIRKSEN (*Slide*): That sort of thing gives aid and comfort to the
enemy.

JOHN WAYNE (*Slide*): My country right or wrong!

BOGART (*Slide*): I think Hitler said the same thing.

POPE (*Slide*): But God is on our side.

BUDDHA (*Slide*): Which one?

(*Projection: Return to slides of trees and foliage used in previous
scene.* SEBASTIAN *and* NURSE *enter.* SEBASTIAN *on foot, dressed.
Lights restore.*)

NURSE: I won't be seeing you again. Will you write to me and let me know whither you are bound?

SEBASTIAN (*He kisses* NURSE *on the cheek*): My determinate voyage is mere extravagancy. Fare you well at once.

NURSE: The gentleness of all the gods go with thee. (*Exits.*)

SEBASTIAN: And what should I do in Illyria? (*Music introduction into song: "I'm on My Way to the Top." During the introduction, the environment changes from trees to city skyscrapers and skyline. The slides are of the same type used in the song "The Flowers." The last slide to appear is the Buddha. Buddha bell rings and Buddha hand appears with card. Reading Buddha card.*) "Boy Wanted." Groovy. (*Buddha hand exits. First verse of song is sung to Buddha.*)

> I'm a guy going places, and I'm leaving today.
> I've got plenty to do and I'd do it with you,
> But I've no time to stop.

(*Buddha hand appears. During next line of song,* SEBASTIAN *and Buddha shake hands.*)

> I'm on my way to the top.

(*Buddha hand exits. Buddha slide goes out and is replaced with a skyscraper slide to go with the rest of the environment.*)

> I've got all of the aces, hear me holler hooray!
> Don't you wait up for me, I've got places to see
> That would make your eyes pop.
> I'm on my way to the top.

(SEBASTIAN *crosses to* ORSON'S *door, knocks on door.* ORSON *enters.*)

ORSON (*Taking Buddha card from* SEBASTIAN): This Buddha must be a poor loser. *I'm* your new agent.

SEBASTIAN: You are?

ORSON: Look, Charlie, the first thing you've got to learn to do is trust me.

SEBASTIAN: Right, right, I will.

ORSON: I've been thinking about that letter to Olivia.

SEBASTIAN: What letter?

ORSON: You got the letter?

SEBASTIAN: No, sir.

ORSON: Charlie, didn't my secretary give you a letter?

SEBASTIAN: No, sir.

ORSON: Well, it doesn't matter. I wrote a stronger one. One I know will really get through to her. Here.

SEBASTIAN: What do I do with it?

ORSON (*Pushing* SEBASTIAN *on his way*):

> Good youth, address thy gait unto her;
> Be not denied access; stand at her doors
> And tell them there thy fixed foot shall grow
> Till thou have audience! (ORSON *exits, closing door.*)

SEBASTIAN: He's freaked out! (*He sings.*)

> This is the life I was made for!
> I'm giving all that I've got!
> This is the time that I've prayed for!
> Here I come ready or not!
>
> I don't care if time races, I'm determined to stay.
> Don't say anything more, hang a sign on my door,
> 'Cause I'm closing up shop!
> I'm on my way to the top!
> I'm on my way to the top!
> I'm on my way to the top!

(*Lights out.* SEBASTIAN *exits. Projection: Interior.* OLIVIA'S *wallpaper. Bright colored flowers.* APOCALYPSE *and* VIOLA *enter.* MICHAEL *first. He enters in a follow spot, then lights up. Door is closed by last person.*)

MICHAEL (*High, Southern accent*): Fifth floor, ladies lingerie, everybody out. (OLIVIA *enters, closing door behind her. To* OLIVIA.) Olivia, Charlie.

OLIVIA (*To* VIOLA): Hi! Well, I'm certainly glad Orson got a fourth.

MICHAEL (*To* VIOLA): Charlie, Olivia.

VIOLA: I'm the new Disease.

OLIVIA (*To* VIOLA): You're kinda young, aren't you? (*To* MICHAEL.) He doesn't even have a beard.

JOHN: The fault is not in his stars, dear Olivia, but in his genes.

(*Lights down.*)

BALLOON (*Slide, over* VIOLA's head): "My God! Do you think they've guessed?"

(*Lights restore.*)

OLIVIA: How did you meet up with the Dead-End Kids?
MICHAEL: Dead-End Kids?
DANNY: Miss Olivia's frame of reference is late thirties.
JOHN: It makes for mischievously medieval witticisms.
MICHAEL: It's like joking in a foreign language.
VIOLA: Come on, you guys, you'll embarrass her.
OLIVIA: Naw! If I can turn 'em on, I can turn 'em off.
DANNY (*Whacking tambourine on his knee*): Score one!
VIOLA: Are you guys always such a bunch of fools?

(*The following section takes on the quality of Shakespeare low comedy. The* APOCALYPSE *become the clowns,* OLIVIA *and* VIOLA, *the straight men. The staging is Elizabethan burlesque, with the lines accented with a series of "freezes" (or poses). Additional accent comes from the drums. Projection: A line drawing of Shakespeare's Globe Theatre, in black and white.*)

JOHN (*Big move*): Good sir, I'll bet I can prove you're a fool.
VIOLA (*Move*): You can?
JOHN (*Big move, sitting on floor in front of* VIOLA): Dexteriously, good sir.
VIOLA: Good fool, make your proof.
MICHAEL (*Big move*): Good sir, why mourn'st thou?
VIOLA (*Move*): Good fool, for my brother's death.
DANNY (*Big move rolling over* MICHAEL's *back*): I think his soul is in hell, sir, and black.
VIOLA: I know his soul is in heaven, fool, and white.
JOHN: The more fool, sir, to mourn for your brother's soul, being in heaven and *white*. Think if he were on earth and *black*.

(APOCALYPSE, *with music accompaniment, do back roll up stage to first step of platform. They sit and remain motionless. Lights down to pin spots on* OLIVIA *and* VIOLA. VIOLA *stands center stage in a "freeze," tambourine hanging on one arm.*)

OLIVIA:

No beard! That really does it.
How now?
Methinks I feel this youth's perfections
With an invisible and subtle stealth
To creep in at mine eyes.
Even so quickly may one catch the plague?
Well, let it be.

(*During the following song, the stage continues to remain motionless, except for* OLIVIA, *who uses the tambourine during song.*)

You can catch cold very fast, well, let it be.
It can take hold very fast, well, let it be.
If this happens to me, well, let it be.
Well, let it be.

If I've found love very fast, well, let it be.
And if this love doesn't last, well, let it be.
If this happens, at least it happens to me,
So let it be.

Have I really found my groove? Well, let it be.
Or is this a stupid move? Well, let it be.
Whatever happens, I'll have to wait and see,
Just let it be.

You can call it what you will, but let it be.
If I have to pay the bill, then let it be.
If this happens, I'll take what's coming to me.
Just let it be, well, let it be.
Well, let it be.

(OLIVIA *flips tambourine back on* VIOLA's *arm. Lights change.*
APOCALYPSE *and* VIOLA *come out of their freezes.*)

> Now Jove in his next commodity of hair
> Send thee a beard.

VIOLA: By my troth, I'll tell thee, I am sick for one, 'though I would not have it grow on my chin. (*Led by* VIOLA, *who does not actually leave the stage,* APOCALYPSE *exit in single file, still playing the clowns. Their exit is with music.* OLIVIA *pantomimes paying them, as they pass by her. Projection: On music cut off, environment restores to* OLIVIA's *wallpaper.*) Orson wanted me to wait until the guys weren't around. He asked me to deliver this letter. He wanted it delivered in person. (*Hands* OLIVIA *the letter.*)

OLIVIA: Oh! Here, you read it.

VIOLA: Oh, I couldn't do that.

OLIVIA (*Nonchalantly tossing letter on the floor*): Then let's just forget it; and in the meantime, why don't you sit down and we can get acquainted?

VIOLA (*Picking up letter*): . . . I'll read it! Orson's really very nice, you know.

> "You couldn't really mean it.
> You're only kidding.
> You couldn't really mean it."

OLIVIA: Here we go.

VIOLA:

> "Anyone can see, you prefer me
> To those kids you've been hanging around."

OLIVIA: Stop. That line again.

VIOLA:

> "To those kids you've been hanging around."

OLIVIA: The line before that.

VIOLA:

> "Anyone can see you prefer me."

OLIVIA (*Seductively*): You read very well.

VIOLA (*Giving* OLIVIA *the letter*): Orson's really not as square as you'd think. Anyway, he's really very nice, and he loves you.

OLIVIA (*Smiling*): Yes, well, tell him it's hopeless . . . but, have him send another letter by . . .

VIOLA: By tomorrow?

OLIVIA: No, by boy. (OLIVIA *exits, closing door.*)

VIOLA:

> Fortune forbid my outside have not charmed her,

Poor lady, she were better love a dream. (VIOLA *does dance cross to* ORSON'S *door.*)

ORSON (*Enters L1*): Did she get it? Did she send an answer?

VIOLA: Hopeless. But she said send another letter.

ORSON: I knew it! She's hooked! (ORSON *exits L1 closing door.* VIOLA *takes letter and does dance exit R4, with letter in her teeth.* SEBAS-TIAN *enters R3 with letter in his teeth and does dance cross to* OLIVIA'S *door R1.*)

OLIVIA (*Enters R1 door.* SEBASTIAN *gives her the letter.* OLIVIA *gives it back to him*): You read it.

SEBASTIAN (*Reading*):
> "You can't deny you love me.
> You're only faking.
> You can't deny you love me."

OLIVIA: No, I can't.

SEBASTIAN (*Reading*):
> "Anyone can see how happy you'd be
> With me always hanging around."

OLIVIA: Repeat the last line.

SEBASTIAN (*Reading*):
> "With me always hanging around."

OLIVIA: I like it!

SEBASTIAN (*Folding up the letter and giving it to* OLIVIA): Right, shall I take an answer?

OLIVIA: No, but bring another letter. (*Exits R1 closing door.*)

SEBASTIAN:
> She made good view of me; indeed, so much
> That methought her eyes had lost her tongue.

(SEBASTIAN *does dance cross to* ORSON'S *door L1.* ORSON *enters L1 before* SEBASTIAN *gets there and* SEBASTIAN *knocks on* ORSON'S *forehead.*) Another letter ought to land her.

ORSON (*Staggering from the clubbing* SEBASTIAN *has accidentally given him, takes out a letter and gives it to* SEBASTIAN *and exits L1, closing door*): Right!

(SEBASTIAN *does dance cross and exits R4, with letter in his teeth.* VIOLA *enters R3, with letter in her teeth, and does dance cross to*

OLIVIA's *door R1.* OLIVIA *enters R1;* VIOLA *gives her the letter.*
OLIVIA *gives the letter back and sits, waiting to be read to.*)

VIOLA (*Reading*):
   "I can't believe you mean it. I think you're kidding.
   I know I really love you."
OLIVIA: Hold it! That line again.
VIOLA (*Catching* OLIVIA; *reading*):
     "I think you're kidding."
OLIVIA (*Laughing*): Wrong! The last one.
VIOLA (*Reading*):
     "I know I really love you."
OLIVIA: Well, you said it. (OLIVIA *ogles* VIOLA. VIOLA *gives the letter
 to* OLIVIA.)
VIOLA: These are Orson's words. They're not very persuasive, are
 they?
OLIVIA: Doggerel.
VIOLA:
   If I did love you with dear Orson's flame . . .
OLIVIA (*Anxious*): What would you do?
VIOLA:
   Make me a willow cabin at your gate
   And call upon my soul within the house,
   Write loyal cantons of contemned love
   And sing them loud, even in the dead of night.
OLIVIA (*Rising*): I'll bring my Ovaltine and meet you about two.
 (OLIVIA *unzips* VIOLA's *zipper.*)
VIOLA: Whoa! (VIOLA *turns quickly upstage and zips her zipper up.*) I
 meant if I were Orson.
OLIVIA: Oh, yes. Well, tell him the answer's the same, it's nowhere.
 But . . . uh . . . let's sleet and snow it with another letter. Shall
 we? (*Exits R1 closing door.* VIOLA *does dance cross to* ORSON's *door
 L1.*)
VIOLA: Soft, now follows prose.

  (ORSON *enters.*)

ORSON: She flipped.
VIOLA: Nowhere.
ORSON: Is the Post Road still open?

VIOLA: Right.

(ORSON *puts letter in* VIOLA's *hand and exits L1, closing door on his own arm.* VIOLA *does dance cross C.; she attaches letter to string and exits R4 dragging letter behind her.* SEBASTIAN *struts on R3 with letter on a twig; crosses to bench up of R1 door, stands on it with branch hidden behind his back and knocks.* OLIVIA *enters R1 door.* SEBASTIAN *offers her the letter and* OLIVIA *takes it.*)

OLIVIA: How thoughtful. (OLIVIA *takes the letter off the twig and gives it back to* SEBASTIAN. *She then turns with the twig, giving it a confused look.*)
SEBASTIAN (*Reading*):
        "Let's make a date for dinner.
        Let's go this evening.
        Let's make a date for dinner."
OLIVIA: What time?
SEBASTIAN: It says eight o'clock. Shall I tell him? (SEBASTIAN *folds letter and gives it to* OLIVIA.)
OLIVIA: Why? And spoil his dinner. (OLIVIA *exits R1 closing door.*)
SEBASTIAN: Right. (SEBASTIAN *starts dance cross to* ORSON's *door R1 but gives up, finishes it walking, and opens R1 door.*)
ORSON (*Revealed L1 in doorway*): How's the Post Road?
SEBASTIAN: Fast, man, fast.
ORSON: Dinner?
SEBASTIAN: I think you could safely say that. But she wants another letter around eight.
ORSON (*Giving* SEBASTIAN *another letter*): Charlie, you're a real friend to take care of this for me. (ORSON *exits L1 closing door.* SEBASTIAN *winks at audience and exits R4.* VIOLA *enters R3 dragging letter on string, and does short dance which ends with her jumping on the letter. She takes out a lock from her pants and locks her zipper. Then does dance cross to* OLIVIA's *door R1.* OLIVIA *enters R1, takes the letter on the string, flicks* VIOLA's *lock with it.*)
OLIVIA (*Referring to lock*): How long ya in fer? (OLIVIA *gives raucous laugh at her own bad joke.* VIOLA *ignores her.* OLIVIA *notices a padlock key on the other end of the string, and delightedly shows it to* VIOLA.)
VIOLA (*Panicked*): My key!!!

OLIVIA: Ah! (*Triumphant.*) I'll spring you about eight! (OLIVIA *exits R1 closing door.*)

VIOLA:

> How will this fadge? My master loves her dearly,
> And I (poor monster) fond as much on him;
> As she (mistaken) seems to dote on me.
> What will become of this?

(VIOLA *does dance cross to* ORSON's *door L1. As she passes Center: Environment: change to warm yellow stripped background on full set.* ORSON *enters L1 and closes door.* VIOLA, *not noticing him, does wild frug in her frustration. She finally sees him and embarrassedly recovers her composure.* ORSON *enters L1. Opens and closes door.*)

ORSON: Success!

VIOLA: Failure.

ORSON: She loves me.

VIOLA: Forget it!

(*Pause.*)

ORSON: You can tell me straight out. I can take it.

VIOLA: Orson, face it.

ORSON: Not even dinner?

VIOLA: Never.

ORSON: But you said one more letter would do it.

VIOLA: She's never going to love you.

ORSON: I don't believe it. You got the wrong girl, the wrong house.

VIOLA: You're going to have to accept it sooner or later.

ORSON: Later. Why later?

VIOLA: Say there's a girl, and there could be, who loves you as much as you love Olivia. Now, if you couldn't love her, you would tell her; and she'd have to accept it, right?

ORSON (*Sullen*): No woman's heart could hold such passion. Besides, they lack retention.

VIOLA: But I know . . .

ORSON: What do you know?

VIOLA:

> Too well what love women to men may owe.

In faith, they are as true of heart as we.
My father had a daughter lov'd a man,
As it might perhaps, were I a woman,
I should love your lordship.

ORSON:

And what's her history?

VIOLA:

She never told her love,
She never told her love,
But let concealment like a worm in the bud
Feed on her damask cheek.

She sat like patience, like patience on a monument,
Smiling, smiling, smiling at grief.

ORSON: What happened to your sister?

VIOLA: I don't know yet.

ORSON: Is she anything like you?

VIOLA: Spittin' image.

ORSON: She must be very attractive. . . . (*They stare at each other for long pause; then realizing.*) . . . Charlie! I'll send another letter. No! I don't want to send another letter. Oh, hell! I don't seem to be able to do anything right. How about you? I mean, I'll bet you do it right, everything. Have you ever been in love, Charlie?

VIOLA: Once.

ORSON: What was she like?

VIOLA: About your complexion.

ORSON: Oh. Uh huh . . .

VIOLA: About your age.

ORSON: It's a nice age.

VIOLA: And a lot of your wonderful qualities.

ORSON: Come to think of it, nobody ever sends me any letters. How'd it turn out? I mean you and the girl?

VIOLA: I don't know yet.

ORSON: Still hanging on, huh? Sorry. I mean for you. No, that's not nice. I guess I don't go about it right. If you want to know the truth, I don't do well with girls. I don't understand it. There's a lot of things about girls I don't understand. (ORSON *crosses and sits on bench.*)

VIOLA (*Crossing to* ORSON *and kneeling in front of him; sings*):

> When you love a girl, be very gentle.
> Write her pretty sonnets, give her pretty things.
> When you love a girl, be very gentle.
> Whisper in her ear the words she likes to hear.

ORSON (*Sings*):

> When I love a girl, I'll be very gentle.
> I'll write her sonnets, I'll give her things.
> When I love a girl, I'll be very gentle.
> And if I can, I'll be her gentleman.

VIOLA (*Sings*):

> When you love a girl, be very gentle.
> Give her pretty presents tied with pretty strings.
> When you love a girl, be very gentle.
> Tell her that she's lovely, tell her she's your love.

ORSON (*Sings*):

> When I love a girl, I'll be very gentle.
> I'll give her presents tied with pretty strings.
> When I love a girl, I'll be very gentle.

BOTH (*Sing*):

> And all through life, she'll be my (your) gentle wife.

(ORSON *rises, pauses, looks back at* VIOLA *confused. Exits. Blackout, except for follow spot on* VIOLA.)

JOHN WAYNE (*Slide*): That man's falling for that boy!
BOGART (*Slide*): That's your old problem. It's a girl.
JOHN WAYNE: Yeh, but he don't know that.
BOGART: Would it change anything if he did?
JOHN WAYNE: Sure! It'd be decent.
BOGART: No, just legal.
QUEEN ELIZABETH (*Slide*): I say, "Pair anybody off with anything."
The only crime I know is loneliness.

(*Music underscoring starts.*)

SHAKESPEARE (*Slide*):

> What is love? 'Tis not hereafter;
> Present mirth hath present laughter;
> What's to come is still unsure.
> In delay there lies no plenty;

> Then come kiss me, sweet and twenty:
> Youth's a stuff will not endure.

VIOLA (*Sings*):

> What do I know of me?
> What do I know of you?
> What do I know of rainbows after rain?
> Where does the wind go after the storm?
> Where does the sky meet the sea?
> Where is that feeling friendly and warm
> And when will it happen to me?
>
> What do I know of life?
> What do I know of love?
> What are the signs that I'm supposed to see?
>
> How will I tell them?
> How will I feel?
> How will I ever know?
> When will there come one?
> Where will my someone be?

(APOCALYPSE *choral background off stage.*)

> What do I know of life?
> What do I know of love?
> How come I'm not the me I used to be?
> Where is it happ'ning?
> Where is it at?
> When will I ever know?
> What is the sum of?
> What's to become of me?

(*Blackout.* VIOLA *exits. Music introduction.* SEBASTIAN *discovered center of top platform. Projection: Abstract slides of bright reds, yellows, and green. Environment for interior of* OLIVIA'S *discotheque.*)

SEBASTIAN (*Sings*):

> Somethin's happ'nin', makes me want to fly.
> Somethin's happ'nin', some new kind of high.

(SEBASTIAN *crosses to* OLIVIA'S *door, jumps on bench up from door.*)

> Over and over and over and over
> I'm goin' where I've never been.
> Over and over and over and over
> I've waited for this to begin.

(SEBASTIAN *knocks on* OLIVIA'S *door.* APOCALYPSE *enter on platform.*)

APOCALYPSE: Make tracks, man! We've been lookin' for you!
SEBASTIAN (*Joining* APOCALYPSE *on platform*): Go with it! Baby, I'm here!

SEBASTIAN *and* APOCALYPSE:
> Somethin's happ'nin', makin' me feel good
> Baby! Baby! Baby! Baby!

(OLIVIA *enters, leaving door open. She has* VIOLA'S *padlock key.*)

APOCALYPSE:
> Somethin's happ'nin', gonna knock on wood
SEBASTIAN (*To* OLIVIA):
> 8:00 o'clock and here's your mail.
APOCALYPSE:
> Over and over and over and over and over
> And over and over and over and over and
> Over and over and over and over and over
> And oh!

(*As the* APOCALYPSE *sing the above,* OLIVIA *takes letter and with key unlocks padlock on* SEBASTIAN'S *shirt, pulls zipper part way down, then turns to go back through door. She is stopped by whistle from* SEBASTIAN. SEBASTIAN *pulls zipper the rest of the way down.* OLIVIA *drops key on stage and exits.*)

SEBASTIAN:
> Somethin's happ'nin', happ'nin', happ'nin'

(SEBASTIAN *exits R1.*)

APOCALYPSE (*Crossing downstage to door.* MICHAEL *picks up key*):
    Happ'nin', happ'nin', happ'nin', happ'nin',

(APOCALYPSE *cross upstage again to stage right on platform, with backs to audience as if to leave. R1 door closes.*)

        Somethin's happ'nin', baby! Baby!
        Somethin's happ'nin'! Baby!

(*Music vamp continues.* VIOLA *enters, unseen by* APOCALYPSE, *in a rush to center stage from door L1. Straightens out her shirt. Door is left open.*)

VIOLA: Sorry I took so long, fellas!

(APOCALYPSE, *in time with music tag, do a double take toward* VIOLA, *thinking that she just left with* OLIVIA. *Lights build.* APOCALYPSE *cross downstage to* VIOLA.)

MICHAEL (*holding up key*): Hey.
VIOLA: My key! Where'd you get it?
MICHAEL: Olivia dropped it. Here, this will get you back into Yale.
VIOLA: Thanks. (*All ad-lib boos at* MICHAEL's *joke.*) Boy, am I tired!
JOHN: Why?
VIOLA: I've been doing all of Orson's work for him.
MICHAEL (*Indicating* OLIVIA's *door*): You couldn't have gotten much done.
JOHN: Does he give you ten percent for that?
VIOLA (*Referring to the letters to* OLIVIA): For playing post office?
MICHAEL: Post office??
JOHN: That's like spin the bottle.
MICHAEL: Oh, that's quick.

(JOHN *gives quick kiss to* DANNY, *who resents it.*)

VIOLA: Come on, you guys. Tell me about old Orson. I mean, you've known him for a long time. What's his bag?
DANNY: Would you believe brown paper?

VIOLA: How long has this scene been going on with Olivia?

MICHAEL: For Orson, about five years.

JOHN: For Olivia, never.

VIOLA: Poor Orson.

JOHN: Poor Orson! He's an agent.

VIOLA: You guys are kinda hard on him.

DANNY: He hates us.

MICHAEL: Yeah, because he thinks we take ninety percent of his salary.

VIOLA: Well, I don't think he's such a bad guy.

MICHAEL: Charlie, we know your story.

VIOLA: You do?

MICHAEL: You got no problem. You can move in on Orson whenever you like.

DANNY: Sure, he needs a little shakin' up.

JOHN: He can't find his bag, because it's always over his head.

DANNY: Orson's so busy trying to groove, he'll never know you're making the big move.

VIOLA: Have you finks known about me all the time?

MICHAEL: Sure, you think we're stupid?

VIOLA: Will I lose my job?

DANNY: Man, what do you think we are?

JOHN: We'll keep your secret.

VIOLA: You will?

JOHN: Sure.

MICHAEL: We know you're Olivia's mailman.

DANNY: We know *Olivia!*

JOHN: Olivia's yours, Charlie. Orson's in Limboville.

VIOLA: Ahhh! (*Switching octaves, from high to low.*) Ah! Olivia's all mine?! Wonderful!

STAGE MANAGER (*Enters L1, leaving door open. He is carrying five "Hunca Munca" costumes and one pair of moccasins*): Here are your freak suits for tonight, guys. You better try them on before they go out of style. (*He puts costumes on top of platform.*)

DANNY: Establishment!

MICHAEL: Barf earner!

VIOLA: Flower cruncher!

STAGE MANAGER: Jerks!

MICHAEL: Jerks! Oh! Delirious! (MICHAEL *faints into* JOHN's *arms.*)

DANNY: Midforties, Freudian implication . . .

MICHAEL: Derivation—thirties!—from pud puller.

JOHN: Biblically rooted . . . Old Testament . . . onanism!

MICHAEL: Oh! Jerk! Jerk! Ooo! A collector's item.

DANNY: Write it down.

STAGE MANAGER: Your studs, links, and curlers are in the pockets.

JOHN: Sartorial paranoid!

MICHAEL: Hey! That's what I was going to call him. You've got E.S.P. Hey, John's got E.S.P.

STAGE MANAGER: E.S.P. I'm warning you guys. Don't bring that stuff in here. (*He exits.*)

JOHN: He ought to try I.B.M. He's punchy.

DANNY: Your studs, links and curlers are in the pockets.

(*This number is staged and choreographed in the style of modern rock dances.*)

VIOLA (*Sings*):
> We're revolting from the age when lines were drawn
> To separate the sexes.

ALL (*Sing, crossing to L1 door*):
> We're revolting from the age when all the men
> Came from the state of Texas.

DANNY (*Sings*):
> Men and women used to be so far apart in every way
> That it's a mother wonder that there's still a mother
> Human race today.

(VIOLA *and* APOCALYPSE *give the* STAGE MANAGER *the raspberries, through the door.*)

MICHAEL (*Sings*):
> What's it all about

DANNY (*Sings*):
> Makes me stomp and shout,

VIOLA (*Sings*):
> Makes me want to move,

JOHN (*Sings*):
> Makes me want to groove.

DANNY (*Sings*):

I'm so tightly trussed,

MICHAEL (*Sings*):

All this shakin' just

JOHN (*Sings*):

Makes me want to bust

VIOLA (*Sings*):

Right out of my body.

ALL (*Sing*):

Got a feel and the feel is feeling right.
Everybody is gonna fly tonight,
Do the things they don't allow.
We are the now generation.

Gotta move on in, make the band begin.
Waitin' for tonight, gotta look just right.

DANNY (*Sings*):

Got the latest gear,

MICHAEL (*Sings*):

Buttons up to here,

JOHN (*Sings*):

Ready to appear,

ALL (*Sing*):

We can't look shoddy.

VIOLA (*Sings*):

Let your hair down and shake out all your curls.
What's the difference, the boys all look like girls.

ALL (*Sing*):

Baby, you can take a bow, we are the now generation.

Many miniskirts, polka-dotted shirts,
What's the harm to be dressed from Carnaby?

DANNY (*Sings*):

How we love to dance

MICHAEL (*Sings*):

In bell-bottomed pants.

JOHN (*Sings*):

We can take a chance,

ALL (*Sing*):

We might get tangled.

VIOLA (*Sings*):
>With our clothes on you can't tell us apart.
>Just be careful you look before you start.

ALL (*Sing*):
>You could get surprised and how!
>We are the now generation.
>
>Let me fill your cup, let me rev you up,
>Baby, turn me on, au-go-go 'til dawn.
>Lots of L.S.D., pot for you and me.
>If you don't agree, you're too star-spangled.
>
>Stuff your crewcuts and prim morality
>Up your stone-age conventionality.
>Stay at home and milk a cow.
>We are the now generation,
>Our generation is now,
>Our generation is now,
>Our generation is here

(STAGE MANAGER *appears in door L1.*)

>And now.

(*Music cut off.* APOCALYPSE *and* VIOLA *give* STAGE MANAGER *"the finger."* STAGE MANAGER *slams door shut!*)

VIOLA (*Crossing up right to platform, with* MICHAEL): Hey, there are five freak suits. How come?

MICHAEL (*Handing* VIOLA *her costume*): Here, this one's yours. The extra one was for Fred before the poor bastard got drafted.

JOHN: I told him, "Fred," I said, "go north!" I told him, "You can see Niagara Falls on a box of Shredded Wheat, just get the hell across that border."

VIOLA: Wheeee!

MICHAEL (*Feigning cowardice*): I don't want to go to war!

JOHN (*Imitating World War I posters, pointing finger at* DANNY, *who is facing upstage*): Uncle Sam wants you!!!

DANNY (*Turning around and squinting eyes*): Me, a Vietcong??? (*Pan-

tomimes throwing grenade; pulling ring with teeth and throwing at audience.)

(*Lights start down. Music underscoring starts.* APOCALYPSE *start changing into their costumes.* VIOLA *sees this; with costume in hand, she lets out small shriek and dashes out through door L1, closing door behind her. As* VIOLA *leaves,* SEBASTIAN *enters R1 door dressed in white undershorts, shirt, shoes and socks. His pants are over his arm.* SEBASTIAN *closes door as he enters.*)

MICHAEL (*seeing* SEBASTIAN): Come on, man, you're not getting into your freak suit.

(SEBASTIAN *looks puzzled, does take to audience, then willingly joins* APOCALYPSE *and begins changing into the costume they hand him. During the following slide sequence,* MICHAEL *takes off shirt and shoes, exits L3, carrying his freak suit and* SEBASTIAN'S *boots.* JOHN *undresses down to his socks and undershorts, exits L4 carrying clothes and freak suit.* DANNY *puts on red beret and exits L2 carrying his freak suit and* SEBASTIAN'S *clothes.* SEBASTIAN *changes completely into freak suit and moccasins.*)

QUEEN ELIZABETH (*Slide*): Will, they're taking their clothes off on stage.
SHAKESPEARE (*Slide*): So it would seem, madam.
SHIRLEY TEMPLE (*Slide*): We must return to the old standards of public morality.
POPE (*Slide*): This can never be given a good rating.
BOGART (*Slide*): What about the Old Testament? There's some stuff in there I never saw in burlesque.
JOHN WAYNE (*Slide*): Look at the red beret that guy's got on. Fruity.

(*During the above line,* DANNY *is seen in red beret leaving the stage L2. Lights should be enough to see* APOCALYPSE *undress.*)

BOGART (*Slide*): O, yeah? What if the color was green?
JOHN WAYNE: That's different! What's the theatre comin' to anyway? You know, now they're even using four-letter words right in public, on the stage.
QUEEN ELIZABETH (*Slide*): Let's hear them!

(*Lights restore. Projection: Soft, abstract pink and blue design.
Environment for interior of* OLIVIA's *apartment.*)

SEBASTIAN (*Sitting on lower platform*):
          What relish is in this? How runs the stream?
          Or am I mad, or else this is a dream.
          Let fancy still my sense in Lethe steep;
          If it be thus to dream, still let me sleep.

(OLIVIA *enters R1, closing the door behind her.*)

Did you like my audition? (*Suddenly realizing what he's said from*
OLIVIA's *amused look.*) I meant my singing.

OLIVIA: Take it easy, Charlie, you've already got the job. You're the
best thing that ever happened to their group. My group, too.

(SEBASTIAN *crosses to* OLIVIA.)

SEBASTIAN: I can't believe all this is happening. You're not going to
change your mind, are you? Look, I need this job. Really! And I'm
clean, courteous, loyal . . .

OLIVIA: Easy! I'm not going to change my mind.

SEBASTIAN: Good! You know, when you get to know me *inside* (OLIVIA
smiles at this), you'll find I'm quite a fellow. I'm very serious. I
want to be a geologist.

OLIVIA: A geologist!

SEBASTIAN: I knew you'd think that was too square.

OLIVIA: No, that's not true at all. Geology's close to "rock."

SEBASTIAN (*Sinks to floor*): Blaahh!

OLIVIA: Well, Shakespeare did it.

SEBASTIAN: And with no less shame. (*Pause.*) You're an out-of-sight
lady.

OLIVIA: Thanks, Charlie.

SEBASTIAN: My name is Sebastian.

OLIVIA: Oh . . . it's not Charlie? Strange. Oh, well. So you want to
be a geologist! What are you doing about it? I mean, school and
everything?

SEBASTIAN (*Rising*): I read every book I get a hold of. Collect samples.
You see, Vi and I had been saving money . . .

(*Music underscoring: "Come Away, Death."*)

OLIVIA (*Thinking there's another woman*): Vi?
SEBASTIAN: Vi was my sister.
OLIVIA (*Relieved, then realizing he said "was"*): Was?
SEBASTIAN: Yes.
OLIVIA (*Diplomatically*): You don't want to talk about it?

(*Music out.*)

SEBASTIAN: I'd rather not.
OLIVIA: You started to say you were saving money.
SEBASTIAN: Yes, for school. That's why I took up singing rock. So I could stash away the bread to be a geologist.
OLIVIA: You know, you're not going to believe this, but I wanted to be an archeologist once.
SEBASTIAN: You're putting me on.
OLIVIA: I swear. One summer I went on a college expedition to diggings outside Cyrene, in Libya. You know where that is.
SEBASTIAN: No.
OLIVIA: Oh, well, it's not important. I was given four square yards to excavate for my project. I dug all summer. I think I got the only four square yards in history where man has never set foot. One nice thing though, I was given a young Libyan boy to assist me. I spent most of the summer digging him. (*Realizing what she has just said,* OLIVIA *turns.*)
SEBASTIAN (*Tactfully changing the subject to hide his disappointment*): Archeology. Man, that's groovy. How'd you ever get into the discotheque racket?
OLIVIA: Life always seems to give us another four square yards (*realizing she's doing it again*) to dig somewhere.
SEBASTIAN (*Crossing to* OLIVIA): You and me'd make a good team. You could dig up the rocks and I could, like, identify them. What do you think?
OLIVIA: Sounds heaven. (SEBASTIAN *gives her a short kiss.*) Ah, that line again.

(*They kiss again—longer.*)

SEBASTIAN: You still haven't told me how you got from your four square yards in Libya to your discotheque off Third Avenue.

OLIVIA: Well, after that summer I went *back* to Sarah Lawrence. . . . Did I tell you I had a minor in music? Well, I did. Anyway, Mother wanted me to be a cellist but old Daddy was an account executive at B.B.D. & O. and figured if the cello image wasn't too risky, the position I had to play it in was.

(*Lights down. Both follow spots on* SEBASTIAN. OLIVIA, *miming conversation, sits and she continues silent monologue.*)

SEBASTIAN:

This is the air; that is the glorious sun,
This pearl she gave me, I do feel 't and see 't;
And though 'tis wonder that enwraps me thus,
Yet 'tis not madness. What a groovy lady.
I'll bet she thinks, "He's a pleasant interlude—for a kid.
Nice sense of humor, ambitious—for a kid." God damnit,
I'm nearly twenty. That's old—for a kid.

I finally made it! I shook myself free.
No more wondering what became of me.
I know where I'm going, no crocodile tears
Solved the riddle, I'm in my middle years.
The nights now are shorter tho' somewhat less gay.
No more time to waste, I live each day
And I happen to like it, so give a few cheers,
Tune my fiddle, I'm in my middle years.
It's sublime to live and love in my security.
Old man time can't blame it on my immaturity.
Look and see!
I've got a few wrinkles. I wear them with pride.
I've worked hard for them, I've nothing to hide.
No more nights on the town.
No more playing around.
I've won my medal an' done all my pedalin',
Ready for settlin' down.
Hey diddle diddle! Here's to the middle years.

(*Lights restore.*)

OLIVIA: Sebastian, are you listening to me?

SEBASTIAN (*Caught daydreaming*): Yeah, every word.

OLIVIA: I asked you how old you were.

SEBASTIAN (*Wary*): You mean for a kid?

OLIVIA: No, I mean for you.

SEBASTIAN: In years?

OLIVIA: If you make it looks, you've got to give me a handicap.

SEBASTIAN: Do you have to poke it with a stick and give it a name? (*Starts to exit.*)

STAGE MANAGER (*Enter L2 with handful of forms*): Hey, Disease. I've been looking for you. Fill these out, W4, Blue Cross, HIP. And don't play it cute like your freak friends. I don't want to know what war your name is, how many Famines you got for dependents or the city morgue for your address. Just your right Goddamn name. (*Exits R2.*)

(SEBASTIAN *sits upstage of R. door and begins reading forms.*)

BALLOON (*Slide over* OLIVIA's *head*): "I asked you how old you were."

BALLOON (*Slide*): "Big mouth."

BALLOON (*Slide*): "Why did you have to ask that? Things were going great."

SEBASTIAN (*Reading forms with self-amusement*): Name, age, this number, that number, how many unions, how many diseases, how many years, first war, second war, Korea, present police action? It's a grand old flag. . . . Instead of your age, why don't they ask, "the number of people you love?"

BALLOON (*Slide, over* OLIVIA's *head*): "Why did you have to mention that Libyan boy?"

BALLOON (*Slide*): "Olivia is a dirty old man."

BALLOON (*Slide, superimposed over "Man"*): "Lady."

OLIVIA: Right! (*She and* SEBASTIAN *look at each other at the sound of her voice.*)

BALLOON (*Slide*): "I asked you how old you were."

BALLOON (*Slide*): "I asked you how old you were?"

BALLOON (*Slide*): "I asked you how old you were?"

OLIVIA: What you really meant was not, "How old are you, you marvelous, beautiful youth?", but, "Olivia, are you too old?" That's the horrible, terrible truth.

SEBASTIAN (*Handing her the forms*): Here. This'll tell you how "young" I am. (*Exits R1. Leaves door open.* OLIVIA *looks at card. It is the cue for her song.*)

OLIVIA:

> He's twenty, I'm thirty. Does it matter?
> When I'm forty, he'll be thirty. Does it matter?
> Rules, labels, slots, categories
> Lead the way to lonely purgatories.
> What does it matter?

(*She sets the forms down beside her on the bench.*)

> I finally made it! I shook myself free!
> No more wondering what became of me.
> I know where I'm going, no crocodile tears
> Solved the riddle, I'm in my middle years.
> The nights now are shorter tho' somewhat less gay.
> No more time to waste, I live each day.
> And I happen to like it, so give a few cheers,
> Tune my fiddle, I'm in my middle years.
> It's sublime to live and love in my security.
> Old man time can't blame it on my immaturity.
> Look and see!

(SEBASTIAN *enters R1, stands in doorway overhearing her.*)

> I've got a few wrinkles. I wear them with pride.
> I've worked hard for them, I've nothing to hide.
> No more nights on the town.
> No more playing around.
> I've won my medal an' done all my pedalin',
> Ready for settlin' down.
> Hi diddle diddle! Here's to my middle years.

SEBASTIAN: I'm sorry. I got up-tight about my age. I thought you were putting me down for being young or something. If you let me see you after work tonight, I'll age a little for you, I promise.

OLIVIA: OK. You age a little and I'll grow up.

(SEBASTIAN *exits R2.* VIOLA *disgustedly enters L3 with letter.* STAGE MANAGER *enters R1.*)

STAGE MANAGER: Hey, Disease. Have you got those forms filled out yet?

VIOLA: What forms?

STAGE MANAGER: Come on, Goddammit! Do you guys always have to be such smart asses!

OLIVIA (*Giving him the forms* SEBASTIAN *had given her*): Here.

STAGE MANAGER (*To* VIOLA): You couldn't just give them to me. You had to make a whole Goddamn production out of it. (*Starts to exit; reading forms.*) What's this? "Number of dependents?" "The world"?! What is that? "The world"! You couldn't just say one, two or three?

VIOLA: I don't have *any*.

STAGE MANAGER: You couldn't say that?! The government isn't interested in your Goddamn love movement! They want numbers, like one, two, three, four, five . . . (*Exits R1, closing door behind him.*)

VIOLA: What's his high?

OLIVIA: Do I know?

VIOLA: Here's another letter from Orson.

OLIVIA (*Mock excitement*): How very exciting.

VIOLA: Shall I open it?

OLIVIA: Please, my hands will shake.

VIOLA (*Not amused*):
> "I give you back your freedom
> I cannot love you."

OLIVIA: My Orson?

VIOLA (*Lighting up*):
> "Try to be resigned.
> Make up your mind
> That you'll have to find
> Some other beau . . ."

OLIVIA (*Taking letter from* VIOLA): Let me see that?!

VIOLA: He doesn't love you any more!

OLIVIA: Well, it's nothing to cheer about. It's like a big drop in A.T.&T. (VIOLA *starts to exit* L2.) Hey, where're you off to?

VIOLA (*Crossing back to* OLIVIA): I'll be back in time for work.

OLIVIA (*Taking* VIOLA's *hand*): OK. I'll see you up in my place afterward.

VIOLA (*Pulling hand away*): Look, Olivia. I'm not what you think I am. I mean, with me this job is going to be strictly business. And if you don't want to play it that way, then I'll quit. (*Exits L3 at a run.*)

(OLIVIA *looks after her, does confused take toward audience and exits R1, closing door behind her. Lights down.*)

ORSON (*Enters L1 and leaves door open, carrying books under arm and reading one*): . . . "It is not uncommon that these latent desires appear, previously suppressed by fear of society's hostility . . . (*Looks around suspiciously and closes door*) and because the afflicted individual cannot include them in his own concepts of masculine behavior . . ." That's uncool! ". . . behavior which the same society has strictly regulated for him. The sudden appearance of these desires can cause great personality upheaval and mental anguish." (*One chord of crash from orchestra.* ORSON *switches books under his arm. Interrupts his own reading of second book.*) I'm glad mother's dead! (*Continuing.*) "Throughout history, civilizations have arisen in which the love of one man for another has been an accepted part of the society in which it arose." (*Looks up with eyes.*) "So much so that legend has grown up over the devotion of such lovers." (*Eyes look right and left.*) "Every school child has read of Damon and Pythias, King David and . . ." King David?! ". . . and his friend Jonathan." (*Pause.*) Yes, I read about them in Sunday school. (*Pause, then quietly.*) Is that what they were doing?

(*During this song, slides are projected over the entire set showing* VIOLA *in beguiling poses. He sings.*)

When you're young and in love,
When you're young and in love,
It's a beautiful thing.
You're a kid on a swing.
You feel higher than high.

When you're young and in love,
When you're young and in love,
Everybody's a king.
All the world starts to sing.
You can float in the sky.

You feel young though you're old.
You have powers untold.
You can make every commonplace thing
That you do seem a real work of art.

Every hour goes so fast,
Every breath seems your last.
This is merely the magical, mystical,
Musical song in your heart.

When you're young and in love,
When you're young and in love,
Every bell starts to ring, every season is spring,
Every bird is a dove,
When you're young and you're really in love.

(ORSON *fantasy sequence: During the following sequence, slide projections in silhouette of Romans, Greeks, Old Testament Hebrews, the American Western character are accompanied by tableaux freezes in silhouette up center involving the* APOCALYPSE, VIOLA *and* SEBASTIAN. ORSON *reads from book.*) "In the Greek and Roman legions, lovers were known to be inseparable—living and dying together." (*Projection: Slides with blue tint, the color of which is matched on the cyclorama upstage, show Greek and Roman warriors in battle. Freeze:* MICHAEL, JOHN, VIOLA, *in Hunca Munca costumes on platforms in matching warrior tableau.* ORSON *walks excitedly upstage into that tableau.*) Charlie! This is it! (DANNY *enters L3 on ramp and runs sword through* ORSON'S *back.*) Ahh! (*Blackout.* ORSON, *in follow spot, reads from a book.*) "However, the Senate did not encourage or sympathize with this practice." The Establishment again. (*Projection: Roman Senate with red-orange tint, the color of which is matched on the cyclorama upstage. Freeze:* MICHAEL, JOHN, DANNY *in matching tableau.* ORSON *puts book down, takes bench, and moves it away from wall, stands on it. He sings.*)

Amo, amas, amat.
Amo, amas, amat.

Distinguished citizens of Rome! Love is a gas! It's where it's at! And if your own thing is against Establishment's barf concepts, you can drop out and groove with it. Right? Cato *père!* (JOHN *turns thumbs down.*) Cato *fils!* (MICHAEL *turns thumbs down.*) Cicero! (DANNY, *after pause, gives him the "up yours" third finger.*) Hmmn?? (*Blackout. Projection: Greek students lamenting the death of their teacher in blue tint, the color of which is matched on the cyclorama upstage.* ORSON *staggers upstage, sits on lower platform, pantomimes cup of hemlock. To audience with "Old Fraternity" bravura.*) Hi, gang! The Senate's throwing the bash. It's a new kind of high called hemlock. (*Singing.*)
When you're young and in . . .

(ORSON *collapses in one beat and dies. Projection: Old Testament Hebrews in profile in green tint, the color of which is matched on the cyclorama upstage. Music under.*)

VOICE OVER (VIOLA): King David? King David?

(ORSON *sits up bewildered.*)

ORSON: Charlie?
This is merely the magical, mystical,
Musical song in your heart.

(ORSON *pantomimes playing harp. Blackout. Shadow of giant is cast on cyclorama.*)

GOLIATH (*Offstage*): Hey, you!
ORSON: Who? Me?
GOLIATH (*Offstage*): Yeah! Come on out and fight, you big fag!

(ORSON *takes out his handkerchief, pulls a button off his vest, makes a sling, and lets fly at upstage shadow. Shadow, hit in forehead, collapses out of sight. Blackout.*)

JOHN WAYNE (*Slide*): Get him on location in a Western and we'd straighten him out.

(ORSON *staggers as if being slapped by invisible hand.*)

ORSON: Pow! Pow! What the hell're you mad at me for, Wyatt? Come on, Marshall, you heard what he called me. What's one dead Philistine more or less?

(*Projection: Western hanging scene in sunset colors, which are matched on upstage cyclorama. Freeze:* APOCALYPSE, SEBASTIAN, *and* STAGE MANAGER *in matching tableau. Rope noose flies in.* ORSON *backs up to lower platform with his hands behind back as follow spot pins on his head.*)

COWBOY (*Tape*): We don't want no sissy-type, dude-type, lady-type fellers in these parts. Stand by to slap the team!

VIOLA (*Sings, enters L1, closing door behind her*):

I never told my love,
I never told my love,
But let

ORSON (*Opening eyes slowly*): Charlie!

VIOLA (*Sings*):

Concealment

ORSON: Charlie! You, too?

VIOLA (*She nods, sings*):

Like a worm

ORSON: I was afraid to say anything.

VIOLA (*Sings*):

In the bud

ORSON: But it's okay.

VIOLA (*Sings*):

Feed on my damask cheek.

ORSON: There was King David and Jonathan, and a *whole lot* of Greeks.

VIOLA (*Sings*):

I sat

ORSON (*Suddenly aware of cowboys*): Charlie, there's still time for you to get away.

VIOLA (*Sings*):

Like patience

ORSON: They don't know it's you yet.

VIOLA (*Sings*):

Like patience

ORSON: Please, Charlie, listen!

VIOLA (*Sings*):

On a monument,

ORSON: You gotta run!

VIOLA (*Sings*):

Smiling,

ORSON (*Out the side of his mouth*): Charlie! Listen to me!

VIOLA (*Sings*):

Smiling,

ORSON (*Side of his mouth and high squeak*): Run!

VIOLA: Smi-i-i-i . . .

ORSON: Charlie! They're from *Marlboro* country!

(*Blackout.* ORSON *leaps off lower platform, falling on his behind. Lights restore.* VIOLA *rushes to him center and falls on her knees.*)

VIOLA: Orson! Orson! Are you all right?

ORSON: Where am I?

VIOLA: You fell off a step.

ORSON: Is my neck broken?

VIOLA: That's not what you fell on.

ORSON: What about the rope burns!

VIOLA: Orson, love, there aren't any.

ORSON: You called me "love." Charlie, we've got to play this thing cool!

VIOLA: Orson, I've got something to tell you. I didn't tell you the truth about myself.

ORSON: I'll tell you. I didn't *know* the truth about myself. But it's okay, Charlie. If that's where it's at, we'll make it work.

VIOLA: I would have told you sooner but at first I was afraid you'd fire me. And then back and forth, back and forth with all those love letters to Olivia . . .

ORSON (*Referring to* OLIVIA): *That's* when I was *confused.* Charlie, I'm glad you feel the same way.

VIOLA (*Putting her face to his hand*): Call me Viola.

ORSON (*Rising*): Charlie, that's not playing this thing very cool.

VIOLA (*Rising, amused*): Well, you can't call me Charlie.

ORSON: Give me time, I'm new at this!

VIOLA: New at what?

ORSON: Well, you don't have to believe this if you don't want to, but it's the truth. (VIOLA *moves in smiling.* ORSON *turns front to speak.*) You're the first boy I ever loved.

VIOLA (*Small voice*): What?!!

ORSON: It's the truth. The first boy. I swear on my mother's . . .

VIOLA (*Holding up her hand and saying with delight*): But I'm a girl.

ORSON (*Embarrassed*): Charlie, it's too soon to talk about role-playing.

VIOLA: You mean you love me because I'm a boy?

ORSON: It was that or nothing. Charlie, you're . . . you're my . . . Him.

VIOLA: Why, you . . . You're a . . .

ORSON: Don't say it! For God's sake; I know what you're gonna say!

VIOLA: You don't love me. You don't even know who I am. You're in love with a boy.

ORSON (*Now being afraid Charlie has changed his mind*): I'm in love with you! The rest is somebody else's mistake.

VIOLA: Yeah, mine!

ORSON: But you said you felt the same way!

VIOLA: I do; but for different reasons!

ORSON: But if that's your thing, what the hell's the problem?

VIOLA (*Big anger*): I'd be a big disappointment in bed!

ORSON (*Afraid of the lynch mob*): For God's sake, Charlie! We could get arrested!

VIOLA: You're the one who's "arrested"! (VIOLA, *in tears, picks up* ORSON's *books and whams him in the gut and on the head.* ORSON *goes down. She exits in tears.*)

ORSON (*Rises, picks up books*): Charlie! I mean, Viola! I mean . . . Oh my God! (*Exits after* VIOLA.)

(APOCALYPSE *enter with* SEBASTIAN *onto platforms upstage. During this number the following visual effects are used together: a completely mad-hatter motion-picture film of bands marching, science-fiction characters, and assorted funny, totally unrelated scenes. The slide projections are polarized geometric shapes which seem to move in and out with the beat. An overhead slide projector covers the entire set with a moving liquid projection of colored, free-form shapes. The lighting is a kaleidoscope of colors. The total effect is one of a dimly lighted psychedelic happening. It takes place in* OLIVIA's *discotheque, where the* APOCALYPSE *are performing.*)

APOCALYPSE *and* SEBASTIAN (*Sing*):
> Something new in cabarets,
> Flashing floors with lights ablaze,
> Crashing bores with eyes aglaze.
> Join the craze.
> Do the hunca munca.
>
> Lights go white to red to blue,
> Every color, ev'ry hue.
> Silver birds come into view.
> Me and you
> Do the hunca munca.

DANNY (*Sings*):
> Here's one dance that can't be angelic.
> Here's one dance that can't end up a relic.
> Furthermore, you'll find the floor
> Hypo, mycro, psychedelic.

APOCALYPSE *and* SEBASTIAN (*Sing*):
> Soon you'll get the feeling of
> Crazy ceilings up above.
> Just the dance to turtle dove,
> Fall in love.
> Do the hunca munca.

(*The dance section: This is a three-minute series of cross-overs involving the entire company in mimic situations and entanglements, including mistaken identity, unrequited love, and old-fashioned silent-movie antics. Throughout the number* OLIVIA *and* ORSON *chase* VIOLA *and* SEBASTIAN *about the stage in an attempt to corner them. At one point, after a full-company dance,* OLIVIA *manages to trap* VIOLA, *tweak her cheeks and* VIOLA *says:*)

VIOLA: I'm really quitting now! You're all a bunch of sex maniacs! (*Exits R1.*)

(SEBASTIAN *enters R2, crosses to* OLIVIA.)

SEBASTIAN (*To* OLIVIA): Are we still on for tonight?
OLIVIA (*To* SEBASTIAN): Sex maniac! (*She slaps* SEBASTIAN *and exits L1.*

SEBASTIAN *follows her off, trying to placate her. The number con-tinues to its end with much door slamming, door opening, appear-ing and disappearing which culminates in a final full-company dance and reprise of number.*)

ALL (*Sing*):

Do the hunca munca.
Do the hunca munca.
Do the hunca munca.
Do the hunca munca.
Do the hunca munca.

(*End film, projections; light change; company freeze on knees.*)

DIRKSEN (*Slide*):

"Oh Time, thou must untangle this, not I;
It is too hard a knot for me t'untie."
I remember that from a Christmas sticker.

(*Full-company exit to music except* OLIVIA, *who sits on bench stage right, and* SEBASTIAN, *who sits on bench stage left, both in dim follow spot.*)

SHIRLEY TEMPLE (*Slide*): I think it's time for the moms and pops of America to take big brother to the woodshed and remind him who is running things.

W. C. FIELDS (*Slide*): And a little child shall lead them.

POPE (*Slide*): Penitence is demandatory. Illicit coitus is being flaunted.

QUEEN ELIZABETH (*Slide*): It certainly pays to head your own church.

SISTINE GOD (*Slide*): How's she ever going to get by with disregard for a higher power?

BUDDHA (*Slide*): She'll get by with a little help from her friends.

(*Another Buddha appears near* SEBASTIAN. *During the song, Buddha arms appear giving both* OLIVIA *and* SEBASTIAN *cards, which they read. When they have read the cards, projections ap-pear over their heads.*)

COPY (*Slide*): Pride and twenty cents get you a ride on the subway.

OLIVIA (*Sings*):
>Don't leave me, don't go away.
>Please don't leave me, say that you'll stay.

SEBASTIAN *and* OLIVIA (*Sing*):
>Believe me, you know it's true.

OLIVIA (*Sings*):
>You need me.

SEBASTIAN (*Sings*):
>And I need you.

BOTH (*Sing*):
>Fill, please fill my heart
>Until, until my heart is still.
>We'll be together.

(*Environment change to warm, richly colored abstract.*)

>Don't leave me, don't go away.
>I love you, what more can I say?
>Take (please take my heart) my heart
>Or break (or break my heart) my heart
>But don't leave me.

(*They cross center toward each other but they never meet. The moment is interrupted by:*)

ORSON (*Off stage R1, sings*):
>Don't leave me, don't go away

(*Enters R1 leaving door open, lights build.*)

>Please don't leave me, say that you'll stay.

(*To* SEBASTIAN.) Charlie!

SEBASTIAN: My name is Sebastian.

ORSON: I'll call you whatever you want, Charlie; Sebastian! Brunehilde! . . . (ORSON *falls to his knees, grabbing* SEBASTIAN'S *legs. He sings.*)
>I need you and you need me.
>Fill my heart until my heart is still.
>We'll be together . . .

(SEBASTIAN *frees himself of* ORSON, *pushing* ORSON *to the floor.*)

SEBASTIAN: He's really freaked out!! Get him out of here!! (*Exits.*)

OLIVIA: Orson! Have you lost your mind?!

ORSON: Isn't it obvious?

OLIVIA: Orson, it isn't acid!

ORSON: No, it's bitter gall.

VIOLA (*Enters L2 and crosses between* OLIVIA *and* ORSON. *To* OLIVIA): I've come to give you back your clothes.

ORSON: Charlie!

OLIVIA: Cool it, Charlie. Orson's on a bum trip. He needs help.

VIOLA: Help! He needs treatment!

ORSON (*Grabbing* VIOLA *by the wrist and caressing her*): Don't leave me.

VIOLA (*To* OLIVIA): See what I mean?

ORSON (*Sings*): Don't go away.

OLIVIA (*Slapping* ORSON's *hands and freeing* VIOLA): Orson! You cut that out! (OLIVIA *puts hand on* VIOLA's *shoulder, pulling her protectively toward her.*)

VIOLA (*Slapping* OLIVIA's *hands and freeing herself*): *You* cut that out!

ORSON (*To* OLIVIA): I told you he loved me! Charlie! (*Grabs* VIOLA's *leg.* VIOLA *pushes him over backwards.*)

VIOLA: I'm not Charlie! (*She takes off her vest-jacket and shirt and throws them at* ORSON. *She wears only a feminine bra. Sings.*)
     But look at me, look! You can see that I'm real.
     I'm alive.

     (*Shouted.*) I'm me!

ORSON (*Slow smile at* VIOLA's *breasts*): Charlie?!

OLIVIA: Sebastian?!

SEBASTIAN (*Enters R1, leaves door open*): What's the ma . . . Vi!! Boy, am I glad to see you! (SEBASTIAN *and* VIOLA *embrace.*)

ORSON: One face, one voice, one habit, and two persons?

SEBASTIAN:
     I had a sister
     Whom the blind waves and surges have devour'd.
     I should my tears let fall upon your cheek
     And say "thrice welcome, drowned Viola!"

OLIVIA (*Trying to stay calm*): Wait a minute. Wait a minute. Who delivered the notes from Orson?

VIOLA: I did.

SEBASTIAN: I did.

OLIVIA (*Starting over again*): Well, which one . . . with me . . . ah
. . . (OLIVIA *gestures through the door where she and* SEBASTIAN
disappeared earlier. SEBASTIAN *raises his hand.* OLIVIA *collapses
against door with relief. Then recovering—*) I hoped it would turn
out that way. (*To* ORSON.) Alas, poor fool, how have they baffl'd
thee!

ORSON: Who's baffled? The fourth boy I hired and fell in love with
wasn't a boy; he's a girl. But he's not a girl, he's twins. (SEBASTIAN
and VIOLA *look at each other with affection.*) And do I get my
pick? (SEBASTIAN *and* VIOLA *look at each other with anger.*) No, I
don't get my pick! Because the boy doesn't like boys, and the girl
doesn't like boys who like boys, and I never did like boys until
she came along . . . Oh God! (*Turning to* VIOLA.) Charlie, honest, I love you! Can't you see it's good? My love hasn't changed
just because you have.

VIOLA: But you really thought I was a boy!

ORSON: I also really thought you were to be loved no matter what
you were.

VIOLA: You mean you love me just for me? No matter what I appear
to be?

ORSON: If you were a cricket, I'd snap your hind leg.

VIOLA (*Embracing* ORSON, *who is on his knees*): Oh, Orson, I love
you!

OLIVIA (*To* SEBASTIAN): You don't mind me being older?

SEBASTIAN: It's where I'm at. You don't mind me being younger?

OLIVIA: Listen, it's my bag.

VIOLA (*To* ORSON): You don't mind me being a girl?

ORSON: I'll just go with it, you're my thing.

OLIVIA: Sebastian!

SEBASTIAN: Olivia!

VIOLA (*Who is embracing the kneeling* ORSON): Orson!

ORSON: Charlie! (*He does take as he recognizes what he said, as lights
go down.*)

SHAKESPEARE (*Slide*): I had the same trouble with the ending.

(OLIVIA *and* SEBASTIAN *exit in character* R1 *and close door.*
ORSON *and* VIOLA *exit* L1 *in character and close door.* APOCALYPSE
enter and climb steps, cross over ramp and down center during:)

APOCALYPSE (*Sing*):

> Do your own thing,
> Pay no attention to people who look down on you.
> Do your own thing.
> It makes no difference who turns away and frowns at you.
> There'll come a day when the world will need you.
> There'll come a day when the world will need you.
> Tell it like it is, if it makes you happy.
> Why should you have to hide upon a shelf,
> Why shouldn't you be truthful to yourself?
>
> You may change someday,
> You may find another way
> But for now, just for now:
> Do your own thing,
> Find your own dream,
> Dig your own soul,
> Or dig your own hole
> And die.

(*After the solo bows are completed and music ends, a full-company Shakespearean tableau is formed as the lights go down, and:*)

SISTINE GOD *and* COPY (*Slide*): "Hey, boy."
CHRIST *and* COPY (*Slide*): "Yes, Father?"
SISTINE GOD *and* COPY (*Slide*): "When are you going to get a haircut?"

(*Blackout.*)

Recommended Readings

BOOKS OF PLAYS FOR YOUNG PEOPLE

BIRNER, WILLIAM B., editor. *Twenty Plays for Young People*. The Anchorage Press, 1967.

HOLBROOK, DAVID, editor. *Thieves and Angels: Dramatic Pieces for Use in Schools*. Cambridge University Press, 1962.

MOSES, MONTROSE, editor. *A Treasury of Plays for Children*. Little, Brown and Company, 1921.

——, editor. *Another Treasury of Plays for Children*. Little, Brown and Company, 1926.

——, editor. *Ring Up the Curtain!* Little, Brown and Company, 1932.

WALKER, STUART. *Portmanteau Plays*. Stuart and Kidd Company, 1917.

——. *Portmanteau Adaptations*. Stuart and Kidd Company, 1921.

WAY, BRIAN. *Three Plays for the Open Stage*. Sir Isaac Pitman, 1966.

BOOKS ABOUT CHILDREN'S THEATRE AND DRAMA
FOR YOUNG PEOPLE

BYERS, RUTH. *Creating Theatre*. Trinity University Press, 1968.

CHILVER, PETER. *Staging a School Play*. Harper and Row, 1967.

COGGIN, PHILIP A. *The Uses of Drama*. George Braziller, 1956.

COURTNEY, RICHARD. *Play, Drama and Thought*. Cassell and Company, 1968.

CROSSCUP, RICHARD. *Children and Dramatics*. Scribners, 1966.

DAVIS, JED H., and MARY JANE WATKINS. *Children's Theatre: Play Production for the Child Audience*. Harper and Row, 1960.

SIKS, GERALDINE BRAIN, and HAZEL BRAIN DUNNINGTON, editors. *Children's Theatre and Creative Dramatics*. University of Washington Press, 1961.

SWORTZELL, LOWELL. "Children's Drama," *The Reader's Encyclopedia of World Drama*, edited by John Gassner and Edward Quinn. Thomas Y. Crowell Company, 1969.

WAGNER, JEARINE, and KITTY BAKER. *A Place for Ideas—Our Theater*. Trinity University Press, 1965.

WARD, WINIFRED. *Playmaking with Children*. Appleton-Century-Crofts, 1957.

——. *Theatre for Children*. The Children's Theatre Press, 1958.

BOOKS ABOUT GENERAL THEATRE AND DRAMA

BENTLEY, ERIC. *The Life of the Drama*. Atheneum, 1967.

BROCKETT, OSCAR G. *History of the Theatre*. Allyn and Bacon, 1968.

————. *The Theatre: An Introduction* (second edition). Holt, Rinehart and Winston, 1969.

ESSLIN, MARTIN. *The Theatre of the Absurd*. Doubleday, Anchor Books, 1969.

GASSNER, JOHN. *Masters of the Drama*. Dover Publications, 1954.

————. *Directions in Modern Theatre and Drama*. Holt, Rinehart and Winston, 1965.

————. *Dramatic Soundings: Evaluations and Retractions*. Crown Publishers, 1968.

HARTNOLL, PHYLLIS, editor. *The Oxford Companion to the Theatre*. Oxford University Press, 1967.

ROBERTS, VERA. *On Stage: A History of Theatre*. Harper and Row, 1962.

TWENTY-ONE of the world's great modern plays have been brought together in a long-needed anthology for the young by a Professor of Educational Theatre at New York University. Lowell Swortzell rescues these masterworks of the modern repertory from the outside trappings of sets, lights, and costumes in an effort to help the reader "discover that there is a theater not only in the head, but also in the heart."

The collection ranges from Thornton Wilder's *Childhood* and Bertolt Brecht's *He Who Says Yes* and *He Who Says No* to the theater miniatures of Ruth Krauss, Langston Hughes' *Soul Gone Home*, and William Saroyan's *The Man with the Heart in the Highlands*. Other contributors include Rabindranath Tagore, Luigi Pirandello, Sean O'Casey, Federico García Lorca, Gertrude Stein, and August Strindberg. Professor Swortzell also provides an introduction, an important statement on the reading of dramatic literature, and notes for each play.

All Ages